# Record of Indentures

of

## Individuals Bound Out as Apprentices, Servants, Etc.

and of

## German and Other Redemptioners in the Office of the Mayor of the City of Philadelphia

October 3, 1771, to October 5, 1773

Copied Under the Direction of the Publication Committee
of the Pennsylvania-German Society from the
Original Volume in Possession of

### The American Philosophical Society

Held at Philadelphia for Promoting Useful Knowledge

LANCASTER, PA.
1907

## Notice

In many older books, foxing (or discoloration) occurs and, in some instances, print lightens with wear and age. Reprinted books, such as this, often duplicate these flaws, notwithstanding efforts to reduce or eliminate them. The pages of this reprint have been digitally enhanced and, where possible, the flaws eliminated in order to provide clarity of content and a pleasant reading experience.

*Copyright © 1907, Pennsylvania-German Society*

Originally published
Lancaster, Pennsylvania
1907

Reprinted by:

Janaway Publishing, Inc.
732 Kelsey Ct.
Santa Maria, California 93454
(805) 925-1038
www.janawaygenealogy.com

2011

ISBN: 978-1-59641-241-5

*Made in the United States of America*

# Record of Indentures

of

Individuals Bound Out as Apprentices,

Servants, Etc.

in Philadelphia, Penna.
by
Mayor John Gibson, 1771-72,
and
Mayor William Fisher, 1773

## RECORD OF INDENTURES OF INDIVIDUALS

| Date. | Name. | From the Port of | To Whom Indentured. |
|---|---|---|---|
| 1771. October 3rd | Kayer, Johannes Erkhard[1] | Rotterdam | David Deshler and his assigns |
| | Tubb, Michael[1] | Rotterdam | Michael Mumper and his assigns |
| | Boury, James[1] | Rotterdam | Philip Wager and his assigns |
| | Bush, Dionisus[1] | Rotterdam | Philip Wager and his assigns |
| | Schnyder, Matthias[1] | | John Frank and his assigns |
| | Bernardin, Mary Christiana[1] | Rotterdam | Jacob Wister and his assigns |
| | Trube, Barbara[1] | Rotterdam | John Waggoner and his assigns |
| October 4th | Pruet, Mary | | Richard Footman and his assigns |
| | Baker, Henry[1] | | Gerardus Clarkson and his assigns |
| | Baker, William[1] | | Adam Goose and his assigns |
| | Bernard, James[2] | | James Stuart, merchant |
| | Fleming, John[1] | | Joseph Baker and his assigns |
| | Allison, William | | John Sheerman |
| | Bell, James | | Frazier Kinsley |
| October 5th | Catherine Staagnerin | Rotterdam | Phineas Paxson and his assigns |
| | Meyer, Frederick[3] | Rotterdam | Phineas Paxson and his assigns |
| | Stanton, James | | William Slater and his assigns |
| | Reely, James | | |
| | Williams, Ann[3] | | William Holderafft and his assigns |

[1] To be found all necessaries and at the expiration have freedom dues.
[2] To be found all necessaries and at the expiration have one new suit of apparel.
[3] To be found all necessaries and at the expiration have two complete suits of apparel, one whereof to be new.

## BOUND OUT AS APPRENTICES, SERVANTS, ETC.

| RESIDENCE. | OCCUPATION. | TERM. | AMOUNT. |
|---|---|---|---|
| Saltzberg twp., Northampton co.. | Servant | 2 yrs., 6 mo. | £ 9. 16. 6. |
| Monockin twp., York co. | Servant | 5 yrs., 6 mo. | £ 30. |
| Philadelphia | Servant | 2 yrs. | £ 7. |
| Philadelphia | Servant | 3 yrs., 6 mo. | £ 20. |
| Philadelphia | Servant, to be taught the baker's trade, to read and write. | 6 yrs. | £ 11. 18. |
| Manor twp., Lancaster co. | Servant | 4 yrs. | £ 23. 13. 9. |
| West Kerlin twp., Lancaster co.. | Servant | 5 yrs. | £ 10. |
| Philadelphia | Servant | The remaining part of a term of 4 years commencing 22 May last.. | £ —. |
| Philadelphia | Servant | 6 yrs. | £ 20. |
| Philadelphia | Servant | 8 yrs. | £ 20. |
| Philadelphia | Servant, to be taught the art and mystery of a mariner and navigation. | 4 yrs. | |
| Philadelphia | Servant | 4 yrs. from 23d Aug... | £ 14. |
| | Servant, to be taught the art, trade and mystery of a spinning wheel maker, and have three quarters schooling and be taught to keep his books. | 4 yrs., 8 mo. | |
| Philadelphia | House carpenter, to be taught the art, trade and mystery of a house carpenter, have two winters schooling and be taught the first five rules in common arithmetic. | 5 yrs. | |
| Northampton twp., Bucks co. | Servant | 6 yrs. | £ 21. 5. 6. |
| Northampton twp., Bucks co. | Servant | 7 yrs. | £ 20. |
| New London twp., Chester co. | | 4 yrs each from 30th Sept. last, the time of arrival). | £ 14. each. |
| Evesham twp., Burlington co., West New Jersey. | Servant | 3 yrs., 6 mo. | 9s. |

[4] To be found all necessaries and at the expiration have two complete suits of apparel, one whereof to be new, and 40s. in money.

[5] At expiration have two complete suits of apparel, one whereof to be new.

| Date. | Name. | From the Port of | To Whom Indentured. |
|---|---|---|---|
| | Harley, Catherine [4] | | John Haltzell Taylor and his assigns. |
| | Deshler, Charles | | Abraham Hasselberry and his assigns. |
| | Yerkyes, Andrew [3] | Rotterdam | John Room and his assigns |
| October 7th | Kempf, Jacob Fredk [3] | | Philip Knor and his assigns |
| | Flower, Margaret [3] | | Henry Lentz and his assigns |
| | Sinkler, Robert [3] | | William Bower and his assigns |
| | Mackendon, Hannah [2] | | Edward Wager Russell and his wife |
| | Stamper, Mary [3] | | Elias Lewis Freichel and his assigns |
| | Hughes, John,[5] cancelled with consent of parties, Nov. 21, 1771. | | Peter Biggs |
| | Barrett, Mary | | Thomas Badge and his assigns |
| | Murphy, Edmond | Rotterdam | Joshua Jones and his assigns |
| October 8th | Grubb, Jacob | | Thomas Dickinson, cordwainer, and his assigns. |
| | Leichtin, Maria Barbara [3] | Rotterdam | John Fromberg and his assigns |
| | Thomton, Benamin [1] | | William Powell and his assigns |
| | Kremewald, Jacob [3] | | |
| | Kremewald, Jacob [3] | Rotterdam | Jacob Barge and his assigns |

## List of Indentures.

| Residence. | Occupation. | Term. | Amount. |
|---|---|---|---|
| Philadelphia | To be taught the mantua maker's business, have six months' day schooling. | 8 yrs. | |
| Philadelphia | To be taught the art, trade and mystery of a tin plate worker, and be found meat, drink, washing and lodging only. | 3 yrs., 6 mo. | |
| Mantua Creek, Gloucester co., N. J. | Servant to have two quarters schooling.[3] | 7 yrs. | £13. |
| Philadelphia | To be taught the tailor's trade, have six months' day schooling at Dutch school, and six months' evening schooling at English school.[8] | 6 yrs. | |
| Passyunk twp., Philadelphia co. | Servant, to be taught housewifery, to sew, knit and spin, have three months' schooling,[3] 40/ in money and a new spinning wheel. | 4 yrs., 6 mo. | |
| Philadelphia | To be taught the house-carpenter's trade, house carpenter.[3] | 6 yrs., 5 mo. | |
| Philadelphia | To be taught the art, trade and mystery of staymaker, to read in the Bible, write a legible hand and cypher as far as the rule of three. | 6 yrs., 9 mo. 23 days. | |
| Northern Liberties | To be taught housewifery, to sew plain work, read in the Bible, write a legible hand and cypher. | 7 yrs., 21 d. | |
| Philadelphia | Marble mason and stone cutter, to be taught the art, trade and mystery of a marble mason and stone cutter. | 2 yrs. | |
| Southwark | Servant, to have necessaries except clothing, and at the expiration of her time to have fifty shillings Irish sterling. | 1 yr., commencing the 7 Aug. last, the day of her arrival in America as stipulated by an indenture under the hand of the Mayor of Cork in Ireland. | |
| Lower Dublin twp., Phila. co. | | 4 yrs. from the 30th Sept. last, consideration at the time of arrival. | |
| Philadelphia | Cordwainer's trade, have three quarters' day schooling.[1] | Remaining part of term of 12 yrs., 11 mo. | £10 |
| Philadelphia | Servant, to be found all necessaries[3] | 5 yrs. | £21.9 |
| Philadelphia | Apprentice, to be taught the plane making business, have five quarters' schooling. | 4 yrs., 6 mo. and 12 d. | |
| Philadelphia. | | | |
| Philadelphia | Servant | 3 yrs., 6 mo. | £22.8.7. |

| Date. | Name. | From the Port of | To Whom Indentured. |
|---|---|---|---|
| 1771. Oct. 8th | Kremewald, Jacob, assigned by Jacob Barge. | | William Harry and his assigns |
| | Creus, Benjamin | London | John Wood and his assigns |
| | Snuke, John[3] | | John Harken and his assigns |
| | Kirby, Charles | | Michael Dawson |
| | Harding, Thomas,[1] assigned by Capt. James Garregues. | | Charles Pemberton and his assigns |
| | Pontin, Elizabeth[3] | | Mary Murgatroyd and her assigns |
| | Jordan, George[3] | Rotterdam | Adam Kochard and his assigns |
| | Senftin, Barbara[1] | Rotterdam | Philip Oldwilder and his assigns |
| October 9th | Cain Barnard | Ireland | George Davis and his assigns |
| | Schrödter, Johan Daniel | Rotterdam | Ludwick Kuhn and his assigns |
| | Schrödter, Johan Daniel | | Jacob Shoemaker and his assigns |
| | Trube, Juliana[3] | Rotterdam | George Heald and his assigns |
| | Stohes, Robert | | William Proctor and his assigns |
| | McCarthy, John | | Ephraim Blain and his assigns |
| | Young, John George[1] | | John Eshelman and his assigns |
| | Young, John George | | John Hawry and his assigns |
| | Young, Maria Elizabeth[1] | | Jacob Eshelman and his assigns |
| | Moyer, John | | Peter Wolfe and his assigns |
| | Cauffman, Jacob | | Thomas Atmore and his assigns |
| | Young, Jacob, and Maria Barbara, his wife. | Rotterdam | Jacob Stahly and his assigns |
| | Kurtz, John | Rotterdam | John Cramer and his assigns |
| | Miller, George, and Anna Barbara, his wife. | Rotterdam | John Bishop and his assigns |
| October 10th | Miller, David[3] | Rotterdam | John Bishop and his assigns |
| | Schnyder, Conrad[3] | Rotterdam | John Bishop and his assigns |
| | Schnyder, Anna[3] | Rotterdam | John Bishop and his assigns |
| October 11th | Hamill, John | Ireland | Robert Gray and his assigns |
| | Hamill, John | | Samuel Woods and his assigns |
| | Duff, James[3] | Ireland | Samuel Wilson and his assigns |
| | Troan, Thomas | | Andrew Scott and his assigns |
| | Schell, Alexander | London | Michael Gitts and his assigns |

## List of Indentures.

| Residence. | Occupation. | Term. | Amount. |
|---|---|---|---|
| Hagars twp., Conecocheig, Md. | | 3 yrs., 6 mo. | £ 22. 8. 7. |
| Philadelphia | Servant, to be employed at the watchmaker's business only.[5] | 2 yrs. | £ 15. |
| Philadelphia | | 4 yrs., 7 mo. and 6 d. | £ 14. |
| Philadelphia | Apprentice, pilot, to be taught the art and mystery of a pilot in the river and bay of Delaware, be found all necessaries and have one Spanish dollar for each and every vessel he may be pilot of during the term, and also the whole pilotage of the last vessel he may be pilot of in his said apprenticeship. | 4 yrs. | |
| Philadelphia | | 7 yrs. | £ 18. |
| Philadelphia | Servant | 4 yrs., 6 mo. | £ 20. |
| Lower Locken twp., Northampton co. | Servant | 8 yrs. | £ 28. |
| Manor twp., Lancaster co. | Servant (note 1, to the value of £ 5 lawful money of Pa. or £ 5 in money aforesaid which said servant may choose). | 4 yrs. | £ 18. 14 |
| Philadelphia | Servant[5] | 2 yrs. | £ 12. |
| Philadelphia | Servant (note 1, to the value of £ 10 current money of Pa. or £ 10 in money which said servant may choose). | 4 yrs. | £ 25. 6. |
| Reading, Berks co. | | 4 yrs. | £ 25. 6. |
| Christiana Hundred, New Castle co. | Servant, to be taught to read in the Bible, write a legible hand. | 9 yrs. | £ 9. |
| Mt. Pleasant twp., Bedford co. | | 4 yrs. | £ 15. |
| East Pennsborough, Cumberland co. | | 4 yrs. | £ 15. |
| Strasburg twp., Lancaster co. | Servant | 7 yrs. | £ 26. |
| Strasburg twp., Lancaster co. | | 11 yrs. | £ 26. |
| Strasburg twp., Lancaster co. | Servant | 8 yrs. | £ 16. |
| Manchester twp., York co. | Servant | 6 yrs. | £ 21. 3. 6. |
| Philadelphia | Apprentice, to be taught the art, trade and mystery of a hatmaker and found in hats, to find him meat, drink and lodging the last six years and six months of the term. | 7 yrs., 6 mo. | |
| Chansford twp., York co. | Servants (note 2, besides the old). | 6 yrs. each. | £ 44. 3. |
| Derry twp., Lancaster co. | Servant, taught to read and write English.[1] | 6 yrs. | £ 28. |
| Exeter twp., Berks co. | Servants (note 2, besides the old). | 6 yrs. each. | £ 20. |
| Exeter twp., Berks co. | Servant, to be taught to read in the Bible, write a legible hand. | 15 yrs. | £ 20. |
| Exeter twp., Berks co. | Servant | | £ 20. |
| Exeter twp., Berks co. | Servant | 6 yrs. | £ 20. |
| Philadelphia | Servant[5] | 2 yrs., 9 mo. | Passage. |
| Donegal twp., Lancaster co. | | 2 yrs., 9 mo. | £ 17. 10. |
| Donegal twp., Lancaster co. | Servant | 5 yrs. | £ 17. |
| Augusta co., Va. | | 3 yrs., 6 mo. | £ 16. |
| Philadelphia | Servant, staymaker (note 1, to the value of £ 10 lawful money of Pa. | 4 yrs. | £ 15. |

| Date. | Name. | From the Port of | To Whom Indentured. |
|---|---|---|---|
| 1771.<br>October 12th | Kane, James | | Samuel Wilson and his assigns |
| | Pocock, James[1] | Ireland | Charles Risk and his assigns |
| | Pocock, James[1] | | Benjamin Wallace and his assigns |
| | Schielle, Pierre[3] | Rotterdam | Jacob Graaf and his assigns |
| | Drummond, Michael | | Andrew Scott and his assigns |
| | King, Elizabeth | | John Price and his assigns |
| | Spöght, Magdalen | | Lewis Stanner and his assigns |
| | Jordi, Michael[3] | Rotterdam | George Landsgrove and his assigns |
| | Smith, Johan Michael, and Maria Elizabeth, his wife (note 1, or £11 in money which they choose). | Rotterdam | Samuel Miles and his assigns |
| | Smith, Johan Michael and wife. | Rotterdam | Geo. Burkhart and his assigns |
| | Trubb, Rosina[3] | | Samuel Miles and his assigns |
| | Trubb, Rosina[3] | | George Burkhart and his assigns |
| | Jordi, George Frederick[3] | | George Landsgrove and his assigns |
| | Borsch, Erasmus,[1] and Regina, his wife. | Rotterdam | Samuel Wallis and his assigns |
| October 14th | Brehmner, Joseph (note 1, or £10 in money). | | Bonaventure D'artöis and his assigns. |
| | Aitkins, John[5] | Rotterdam | William Taylor and his assigns |
| | Morgan, Samuel | | Enoch Morgan and his assigns |
| | Sugg, Dorothy | | Elizabeth Test and her assigns |
| | Onoust, Elizabeth, Jr. (note 3, and £4 in money). | | George Heyl and his assigns |
| | McElvenan, Daniel | | Andrew Reed and his assigns |
| | Hunt, Richard | | Andrew Bankson, Jr., and his assigns. |
| | Meyer, Peter[3] | Rotterdam | John McClanachan and his assigns |
| | Staagnerin, Susanna[3] | Rotterdam | John Weaver and his assigns |
| | Morgan, Samuel | | Joseph Gilbert and his assigns |
| October 15th | Thomas, Ruth[3] | | Alexander Mills and his assigns |
| | Monday, John[1] | | William Key and his assigns |
| | Mentor, Mary[3] | | William Key and his assigns |
| | Diver, Anthony | | Josiah Robert Lockhart and his assigns. |
| | Crossen, Edward[3] | | Charles Risk and his assigns |
| | Spadin, Mary[3] | Rotterdam | Philip Truckinmiller and his assigns. |
| October 16th | Flin, Daniel | | John Montgomery and his assigns |
| | McCormick, Thomas (note 2, besides his old). | Ireland | Mordecai Evans and his assigns |
| | Wimer, Philip[3] | Rotterdam | Ulrick Conrad and his assigns |

## List of Indentures.

| Residence. | Occupation. | Term. | Amount. |
|---|---|---|---|
| Donegal twp., Lancaster co. | | 8 yrs. | £ 19. 10. |
| Philadelphia | Servant | 4 yrs. | £ 16. |
| Hanover twp., Lancaster co. | | 4 yrs. | £ 16. |
| Rowan twp., Cumberland co. | Servant | 4 yrs. | £ 18. 14. |
| Augusta co., Va. | An apprentice | 3 yrs. | £ 18. |
| Lower Chichester, Chester co. | | 3 yrs., 6 mo. | £ 15. |
| Upper Dublin, Philadelphia co. | | 6 yrs. | £ 20. |
| Williamsborough twp., Burlington co., W. Jersey. | Servant, to be taught to read in the Bible, write a legible hand. | 12 yrs. | £ 15. |
| Philadelphia | Servants | 3 yrs., 9 mo. | £ 39. 9. 1. |
| Frederick, in the co. of Frederick, Md. | | 3 yrs., 9 mo. | £ 39. 9. 1. |
| Philadelphia | Servant | 4 yrs., 6 mo. | £ 19. 10. 7. |
| Frederick Town, Frederick co., Md. | | 4 yrs., 6 mo. | £ 19. 10. 7. |
| Williamsborough twp., Burlington co., W. Jersey. | Servant, to be taught to read in the Bible, write a legible hand. | 8 yrs. | £ 15. |
| Philadelphia | Servants | 5 yrs. each. | £ 42. 1. |
| Northern Liberties | Apprentice, to be taught the coppersmith's trade, to read, write and cypher as far as the rule of three. | 16 yrs., 10 mo. | |
| Philadelphia | Servant, to be employed at the business of goldsmith. | 1 yr., 6 mo. | £ 14. 14. 6. |
| Philadelphia | Apprentice | 7 yrs. | £ 5. |
| Philadelphia | Servant | 4 yrs., 3 mo. 21 days. | £ 5. |
| Philadelphia | Apprentice, to be taught housewifery, sew plain work and knit, have six months schooling. | 4 yrs., 11 mo., 7 d. | |
| Antrim twp., Cumberland co., in this province. | Servant | 4 yrs. | £ 17. |
| Philadelphia | Apprentice | 7 yrs. | £ 3. |
| Antrim twp., Cumberland co., in this province. | Servant | 4 yrs. | £ 17. |
| Philadelphia | Servant | | £ 21. 5. 6. |
| Philadelphia | Apprentice, to be taught the art, trade and mystery of a hatter, have three months' night schooling in each year, at the father's expense, the master to find meat, drink, washing and lodging and during the last three years working apparel and at the expiration have £ 5 in money. | 7 yrs. | £ 5. |
| Philadelphia | Apprentice, taught housewifery, read in the bible. | 3 yrs. | |
| Woolwich twp., Gloucester co., West Jersey. | | 1 yr. | £ 10. |
| Woolwich twp., Gloucester co., West Jersey. | Servant | 3 yrs. | £ 10. |
| Lancaster, Lancaster co. | | 4 yrs. | £ 16. |
| Philadelphia | Servant | 3 yrs. | £ 17. |
| Philadelphia | Servant | 7 yrs. | £ 27. |
| East Marlborough twp., Chester co. | Servant | 4 yrs. | £ 15. |
| Limerick twp., Phila. co. | Servant | 2 yrs. | £ 9. 1. |
| S. Branch, Augusta co., Va. | Servant | 7 yrs. | £ 26. |

| DATE. | NAME. | FROM THE PORT OF | TO WHOM INDENTURED. |
|---|---|---|---|
| 1771. October 16th | Dougherty, Lettice | | John Atkinson and his assigns |
| | Armstrong, John[3] | | Joseph Cruse and his assigns |
| | Stienert, Eve[3] | | Christian Kniver and his assigns |
| | Drislaan, Peter, and Elizabeth Barbara, his wife. | Rotterdam | Baltzer Gole |
| | Kast, Johannes, and Rachel Barbara, his wife. | | Nicholas Houer and his assigns |
| | Wimer, George[3] | Rotterdam | John Martin Fritz and his assigns |
| | Barnicle, John Adam[3] | | Henry Miller and his assigns |
| October 17th | Lock, Philip[3] | | Thomas Francis and his assigns |
| | Lock, Esther[3] | | Thomas Francis and his assigns |
| | Stuber, Anna[3] | Rotterdam | Jacob Carpenter and his assigns |
| | Stuber, Maria[3] | Rotterdam | John Stanbaugh and his assigns |
| | Young, Henry[3] | London | Samuel Howell and his assigns |
| | Rutberger, John Michael[3] | | Wm. Cowperthwait and his assigns |
| | Hays, William | | John Cole and his assigns |
| October 18th | Park, Nelly | | John Jones and his assigns |
| | Collins, John | | Thomas Kinney and Peter Mackie and their assigns. |
| | Hull, Hugh[3] | Ireland | James Irwin and his assigns |
| | Teisser, Stephen | | David Davis and his assigns |
| October 19th | Haley, John | | Alexander Brown and his assigns |
| | McDonnald, Charles | | Robert Plenck and his assigns |
| | Metzin, Margaret[3] | Rotterdam | Berndh Idle and his assigns |
| | Maxwell, Ann | Ireland | Robert Carson and his assigns |
| | Brownin, Anna Maria | Rotterdam | George Thumb and his assigns |
| October 21st | Outerbridge, Rumsey White | | Joseph Dean |
| | Raboteau, Elias | | Israel Pemberton and his assigns |
| | Lynch, Mary[3] | | William Faris and wife |
| | Cain, Richard, and Bell, his wife. | Ireland | Robert Cleuch and his assigns |
| | McKenzie, William | | John Ross |
| October 22nd | Barker, William[3] | | Robert Gill |
| | Brown, William | | John Duche and his assigns |
| | Kiser, Adam[3] | Rotterdam | George Hincle and his assigns |

## List of Indentures.

| Residence. | Occupation. | Term. | Amount. |
|---|---|---|---|
| Newtown, Bucks co. | Servant | 3 yrs., 3 mo. | £ 15. |
| Philadelphia | Taught the cordwainer's trade, read in the Bible, write a legible hand and cypher as far as the rule of three. | 13 yrs. | |
| Philadelphia | Taught to read in the Bible. | 5 yrs. | |
| Hagar's Town, Frederick co., Md. | Servants (note 2, beside their old). | 5 yrs. each. | £ 43. 4. 6. |
| Frederick Town, Frederick co., Md. | Servants, at expiration each to have one complete suit of apparel besides the old. | 5 yrs. each. | £ 42. 0. 6. |
| Robertson twp., Berks co. | Servant | 6 yrs. | £ 30. |
| Mt. Bethel twp., Northampton co. | Servant | 4 yrs., 6 mo. | £ 27. 9. |
| Philadelphia | Taught the art, trade and mystery of a skinner. | 5 yrs. | |
| Philadelphia | Taught housewifery, sew plain work. | 5 yrs., 6 mo. | |
| Lampeter twp., Lancaster co. | Servant | 6 yrs. | £ 30. |
| Strasburg twp., Lancaster co. | Servant | 7 yrs. | £ 30. |
| Philadelphia | Servant | 3 yrs. | £ 16. |
| Burlington co. | Servant[5] | 5 yrs., 3 mo. | £ 30. |
| Philadelphia | Taught art, trade and mystery of a boat builder, found meat, drink, washing, lodging and working apparel. | 5 yrs., 3 mo. 8 days. | |
| Southwark | Servant | 4 yrs., 6 mo. | £ 15. 10. |
| Morris twp., Morris co., E. Jersey. | Servant | 3 yrs. | £ 7. |
| Middletown twp., Cumberland co. | | 3 yrs., 11 mo. | £ 19. |
| Amity twp., Bucks co. | Servant | 4 yrs. | £ 15. |
| Middleton twp., Cumberland co. | | 4 yrs. | £ 14. |
| Schenectady, Albany co., N. Y. | Servant | 3 yrs., 6 mo. | £ 17. |
| Frederick Town, Frederick twp. | Servant | 4 yrs. | £ 18. |
| Philadelphia | Servant[1] | 3 yrs., 5 mo. 21 d. | £ 12. 10. |
| Southwark | Servant, taught to read in the Bible, found in meat, drink, washing, lodging and apparel.[6] | | £ 12. |
| Philadelphia | Taught the art and mystery of a merchant and bookkeeping, found meat, drink, washing and lodging, apprentice free, the mother to provide sufficient apparel. | 3 yrs., 6 mo. | £ 27. |
| Philadelphia | Taught to read, write and cypher[5] | 2 yrs., 2 mo. 6 d. | |
| Philadelphia | Taught housewifery, sew plain work, read in the Bible, write a legible hand. | 9 yrs., 3 mo. | |
| Schenectady, Albany co., N. Y. | Servants, found meat drink, washing and lodging only. | 1 yr., 7 mo. each. | £ 15. |
| Philadelphia | Taught the art and mystery of a merchant and bookkeeping. | 5 yrs. | |
| Philadelphia | Taught the art and mystery of a mariner and navigator. | 7 yrs. | |
| Southwark | Taught the boat builder's trade, have three quarters' evening schooling, found meat, drink, washing, lodging and working apparel, and at expiration have the tools he works with. | 3 yrs., 11 mo., 23 d. | |
| Earl twp., Lancaster co. | | 3 yrs., 6 mo. | £ 19. 18. |

| Date. | Name. | From the Port of | To Whom Indentured. |
|---|---|---|---|
| 1771. October 22rd | Row, Jacob[3] | | Philip Clumperg and his assigns |
| | Rickertin, Leina[3] | Rotterdam | John Scull and his assigns |
| | Doak, John[1] | | Isaac Maris and his assigns |
| | Doak, John[1] | | James Eddy |
| | Shippey, Sarah[3] | | Daniel Barnes and his assigns |
| October 23rd | Reitberger, Regina[3] | Rotterdam | John Haine and his assigns |
| | Reitberger, Hans George[3] | Rotterdam | John Haine and his assigns |
| | Atkinson, John[3] | | Abraham Bonsall and his assigns |
| | Kessell, Michael | | John Stromb and his assigns |
| | Crumbach, Conrad, Jr.[3] | | Henry Schleesman and his assigns |
| | Hoedmacher, Jacob[3] | Rotterdam | Peter Conrad and his assigns |
| | Early, James | | Joseph Pemberton, Jr., and his assigns. |
| | Reitberger, Michael[1] | Rotterdam | John Miller and his assigns |
| October 24th | William (a negro slave) | | Benjamin Betterton and his assigns |
| | Correy, Ann (note 2, besides her old). | Ireland | Patrick Scott and his assigns |
| | Metzler, Susanna Elizabeth[3] | Rotterdam | William Will and his assigns |
| | Stuart, Joseph[3] | | Jeremiah Lynch and his assigns |
| | McGear, Jane[3] | | Capt. George Stevenson and his assigns. |
| October 25th | Rowan, John | | Presley Blackiston and his assigns |
| | Heynold, Johannes, and Anna Barbara, his wife. | | Thomas May and his assigns |
| | Kennedy, William | | Alexander McKeehan and his assigns. |
| | Jordan, Francis | Ireland | Humphrey Fullerton and his assigns. |
| | Warh, William | Ireland | Anthony Pritchard and his assigns |
| | McElduff, Daniel | | Humphrey Fullerton and his assigns. |
| | Garret, Jane | Ireland | Benjamin Poultney and his assigns |
| October 26th | Montgomery, Mary | | Benjamin Wallace and his assigns |
| | Husbands, Richard | | Joseph Luken and his assigns |
| | Ferguson, James | | Isaac Anderson and his assigns |
| | Shields, Judith | | Joshua Ash, Jr., and his assigns |
| October 28th | Aldridge, Robert[3] | | Ezekiel Miriam |
| | Pancake, Maria Elizabeth[3] | Rotterdam | Frederick Deitz and his assigns |
| | Darby, Abraham[2] | | Godfrey Keplar and his assigns |
| | Barlow, Richard | | William Littleton and his assigns |
| | Deatz, Martin[3] | | Henry Swaldbeck and his assigns |

## List of Indentures.

| Residence. | Occupation. | Amount. | Term. |
|---|---|---|---|
| Philadelphia | Taught the business of a surgeon barber, read in the Bible, write a legible hand and cypher. | 6 yrs. | |
| Reading, Berks co. | Servant | 7 yrs. | £ 21. |
| Marple twp., Chester co. | To have two winters' night schooling. | 5 yrs. | £ 7. 10. |
| | | 6 yrs. | |
| Philadelphia | Taught housewifery, sew and knit, read in the Bible, write a legible hand. | 12 yrs., 7 mo., 24 d. | |
| Heidelberg twp., Berks co. | Servant, taught to read in the Bible. | 9 yrs. | £ 10. |
| Heidelberg twp., Berks co. | Servant, taught to read in the Bible. | 8 yrs. | £ 11. |
| Derby twp., Chester co. | Taught art, trade and mystery of farming or husbandry, to read, write and cypher as far as rule of three. | 15 yrs., 4 mo., 12 d. | |
| Northern Liberties | | 3 yrs., 9 mo. 10 d. | £ 21. |
| Philadelphia | Taught the tailor's trade, have one quarter evening schooling. | 3 yrs., 2 mo. | |
| Hamilton twp., Northampton co. | Servant | 4 yrs. | £ 20. 4. |
| Philadelphia | Servant | 4 yrs. | £ 15. |
| Manor twp., Lancaster co. | Servant, taught to read in the Bible, write a legible hand. | 13 yrs. | £ 8. |
| Philadelphia | Taught the trade of a cooper, allowed time to go to evening school two quarters. | 9 yrs. | |
| Philadelphia | Servant | 2 yrs., 3 mo. | £ 7. 10. |
| Philadelphia | Servant, taught to read in the Bible, write a legible hand. | 6 yrs. | £ 20. |
| Philadelphia | Taught the cordwainer's trade, read, write and cypher as far as rule of three. | 11 yrs., 4 mo., 15 d. | |
| Philadelphia | Taught housewifery and to sew, have one year schooling.[3] | 10 yrs., 5 mo., 6 d. | |
| Philadelphia | Taught the trade of cordwainer, and have one quarter night schooling.[5] | 4 yrs., 6 d. | |
| Milfred hundred, Cecil co., Md. | | 3 yrs., 6 mo. | £ 39. 10. each. |
| W. Pennsborough, Cumberland co. | Servant, to be found common necessaries and apparel during the term. | 2 yrs., 2 mo. | £ 7. 10. |
| Antrim twp., Cumberland co. | Servant[5] | 2 yrs. | £ 7. 10. |
| Charles Town, Chester co. | Servant[5] | 2 yrs. | £ 11. 10. |
| Antrim twp., Cumberland co. | | 3 yrs., 6 mo. | £ 18. |
| Philadelphia | Servant[6] | 2 yrs., 6 mo. | £ 7. 10. |
| Paxton twp., Lancaster co. | | 4 yrs. | £ 15. |
| Upper Dublin twp., Phila co. | | 4 yrs. | £ 20. |
| Chester twp., Burlington co., W. Jersey. | | 3 yrs., 3 mo. | £ 15. |
| Derby, Chester co. | | 4 yrs. | £ 16. |
| Philadelphia | Taught cordwainer's trade, have six months' schooling. | 6 yrs., 8 mo. 2 w. | |
| Philadelphia | Servant | 3 yrs., 10 mo., 21 d. | £ 18. |
| Philadelphia | Taught the blacksmith's trade, to read in the Bible, write a legible hand. | 5 yrs., 6 mo. | |
| Marshfield, York co. | | 4 yrs., 6 mo. | £ 15. |
| Philadelphia | Taught the cedar cooper's trade, have three quarters' night schooling. | 9 yrs., 2 mo. 28 d. | |

| Date. | Name. | From the Port of | To Whom Indentured. |
|---|---|---|---|
| 1771. October 28th | Seibold, George[3] | London | Michael Seibert and his assigns |
|  | Patterson, John | Ireland | James Andrew and his assigns |
|  | Casey, Richard | Ireland | James Andrew and his assigns |
| October 29th | McConnaughy, Mary |  | Thos. Poultney and his assigns |
|  | Rush, James[3] |  | John Galloway and his assigns |
|  | Rhoads, Mary[3] |  | Samuel Lyons and his assigns |
| 1771. October 29th | Fightenberger, John George[3] | London | Reuben Haines and his assigns |
|  | Tucker, George[3] | Bristol | Jonathan Meredith and his assigns |
|  | McKerragher, David |  | John Harken and his assigns |
|  | Strickenberger, John Adam[3] | London | George Helichner and his assigns |
|  | Dunwoodies, John |  | John Harken and his assigns |
|  | Hand, Dominick | Ireland | David Chambers and his assigns |
|  | Adair, James, Jr.[3] |  | James Roney and his assigns |
|  | Feorch, Michael (note 1, and £6 in money). |  | Israel Pemberton and his assigns |
|  | Meyer, Felix[3] | London | Samuel Miles and his assigns |
|  | Meyer, Felix[3] |  | Michael Fockler and his assigns |
|  | Feorch, Martin[3] |  | Charles Pemberton and his assigns |
|  | Grabenstine, John[3] | London | William Ripple and his assigns |
|  | Grabenstine, John[3] |  | Matthew Keyer and his assigns |
|  | Hirkerin, Christiana[3] | Rotterdam | John Wood and his assigns |
|  | Kirker, Johan Jacob[3] | Rotterdam | John Wood and his assigns |
| October 30th | Lomehart, Jacob | London | John Knage and his assigns |
|  | Paxton, William |  | David Pancoast |
|  | Higgins, Ann[3] |  | John Brickell and his wife |
|  | Hector, Caspar[3] | London | Jacob Freeze and his assigns |
|  | Rogers, James[3] |  | John Bringhurst and his heirs |
|  | Cave, Thomas (note 3, and £4 of sterling money of Great Britain). |  | John Moore and his assigns |
| October 31st | McKerragher, David |  | William Moore and his assigns |
|  | Dunwoodie, John |  | William Moore and his assigns |
|  | Bickerton, John |  | Jonathan Meredith and his assigns |
|  | Fobmer, John Gotleib | London | Michael Schreiber and his assigns |
|  | Brown, George | London | George Douglas and his assigns |
|  | Brown, George |  | Robert Pearson and his assigns |
|  | Wilson, Mary[3] |  | John Brown and his assigns |
|  | Hardie, Robert, Jr. |  | Capt. Thomas Edward Wallace |

## List of Indentures.

| Residence. | Occupation. | Term. | Amount. |
|---|---|---|---|
| Greenwich twp., Sussex co., East Jersey. | | 2 yrs., 3 mo. | £ 14. 19. 6. |
| Hanover twp., Lancaster co. | (Note 1) | 2 yrs. | £ 10. |
| Hanover twp., Lancaster co. | (Note 1) | 2 yrs., 3 mo. | £ 13. |
| Borough of Lancaster. | | 3 yrs. | £ 7. |
| Philadelphia | Taught the tailor's trade, have four quarters' evening schooling. | 7 yrs., 11 mo., 25 d. | |
| Southwark | Servant | 2 yrs., 3 mo. 11 d. | £ 2. 10. |
| Philadelphia | | 3 yrs. | £ 17. 18. |
| Philadelphia | Taught the currier's trade. | 6 yrs. | £ 20. |
| Philadelphia | | 2 yrs. | £ 12. |
| Richmond twp., Berks co. | | 5 yrs. | £ 15. 7. 6. |
| Philadelphia | | 3 yrs. | £ 15. |
| Philadelphia | Servant[5] | 9 yrs. | £ 9. |
| Philadelphia | Taught the cordwainer's trade, read in the Bible and write a legible hand, cypher as far as the rule of three. | 6 yrs. | |
| Philadelphia | Servant | 4 yrs. | £ 15. |
| Philadelphia | | 3 yrs. | £ 16. 11. 6. |
| Fredericks Town, Fredk. co., Md. | | 3 yrs. | £ 16. 11. 6. |
| Philadelphia | Servant | 7 yrs., 21 d. | £ 18. |
| Philadelphia | Servant | 3 yrs. | £ 15. 17. 10. |
| New York | | 3 yrs. | £ 15. 17. 10. |
| Deptford twp., Gloucester co., West New Jersey. | Servant | 4 yrs. | £ 16. |
| Deptford twp., Gloucester co., West New Jersey. | Servant | 16 yrs. | £ 11. 5. |
| Bethel twp., Lancaster co. | Servant, to have £ 10 lawful money of Pa.[5] | 2 yrs., 6 mo. | £ 15. |
| Philadelphia | Taught the house carpenter's trade[5] | 5 yrs., 10 mo., 7 d. | |
| Philadelphia | Taught to read, write and cypher[5] work, have two quarters' schooling. | 9 yrs., 6 mo. | |
| Upper Alves Creek, Salem co., W. Jersey. | Servant | 2 yrs., 9 mo. | £ 15. 17. 10. |
| Germantown | Taught art, trade and mystery of a coach and chair maker, have six months' evening schooling. | 5 yrs., 6 mo. | |
| W. Pennsborough, Cumberland co., Pa. | Taught the art trade and mystery of a miller. | 3 yrs., 8 mo. 23 d. | |
| Middletown, Cumberland co. | | 2 yrs. | £ 11. 10. |
| Middletown, Cumberland co. | | | £ 15. |
| Philadelphia | | 9 yrs., 1 mo. 3 w. | £ 7. 10. |
| Philadelphia | Servant, to the value of £ 6 lawful money of Pa. or £ 6 in money assd., which said servant may choose.[1] | 3 yrs. | £ 15. 14. 6 |
| Philadelphia | Servant, have £ 10 lawful money of Pa. in lieu of freedom dues.[5] | 3 yrs. | £ 15. 14. 6. |
| Nottingham, Burlington co., West Jersey. | | 3 yrs. | £ 15. 14. 6. |
| Northern Liberties | Taught housewifery, sew plain work, have one year schooling. | 10 yrs., 5 mo. | |
| Philadelphia | Taught the art, trade and mystery of a mariner and navigator, found meat, drink, washing and lodging, his uncle to provide ap- | 5 yrs., 6 mo. | |

| Date. | Name. | From the Port of | To Whom Indentured. |
|---|---|---|---|
| 1771. October 31ˢᵗ | | | |
| | Collins, James (note 2, besides his old). | | Thos. and Andrew Kennedy and their assigns. |
| Nov. 1ˢᵗ | Odenkirken, John Peter[3] | Rotterdam | Daniel Clymer and his assigns |
| | Girau'd, William | | Mary May and her assigns |
| | Kellon, John[3] | | John M. Dowell and his assigns |
| | Oerter, John Jost[3] | Rotterdam | Dr. Wm. Shippen, Jr., and his assigns. |
| | Knie, John Nicholas[3] | Rotterdam | Gotleib Hartman and his assigns |
| | Kelly, Edward | | William Bell and his assigns |
| | Burback, Philip | Rotterdam | John Leech and his assigns |
| | Stebir, Anna Maria | Rotterdam | John Riely and his assigns |
| | Wissard, David | London | Wendle Lerban and his assigns |
| | Sheefer, Frederick | Rotterdam | Caleb Foulk and his assigns |
| | Outerman, John Henry[1] | | Rudolph Bunner and his assigns |
| | Outerman, John Henry[1] | | George Dorsch and his assigns |
| | Ellen, Anna Gertrude[1] | Rotterdam | Rudolph Bunner and his assigns |
| | Ellen, Anna Gertrude[1] | | Emanuel Carpenter and his assigns |
| | Neiterhouse, Daniel[3] | Rotterdam | John Warner and his assigns |
| | Shoemaker, Alexander[3] | Rotterdam | Conrad Weaver and his assigns |
| | Shoemaker, Alexander[3] | | Stephen Bernard and his assigns |
| Nov. 2ʳᵈ | Rhoads, Mary | | Caleb Piles and his assigns |
| | Cain, Bernard | | Richard Robinson and his assigns |
| | Hapape, George | Rotterdam | Wm. Englefreid and his assigns |
| | Nolt, Christiana[3] | Rotterdam | Henry Keppell and his assigns |
| | Formanin, Elizabeth[3] | Rotterdam | Henry Keppell and his assigns |
| | Formanin, Elizabeth[3] | | Martin Lauman and his assigns |
| | Bombergherin, Margaret | | Michael Rapp and his assigns |
| | McDevit, William (note 1, and £10 in money). | | John Kelly and his assigns |
| | Stevir, John[3] | Rotterdam | Richard Smith, Jr., and his assigns |
| | Schup, Jacob (note 3, and three English Guineas). | Rotterdam | Henry Drinker and his assigns |
| | Ortman, Johannes[3] | Rotterdam | William Rippy and his assigns |
| | Griffiths, Mary | | Matthew Potter and his assigns |
| | McCarthy, Michael (note 3, and tools he works with). | | John Rice and his assigns |
| | Shafer, Jacob[1] | Rotterdam | Martin Reese and his assigns |
| | Schnyder, Peter (note 3 and £5 lawful money of this province). | Rotterdam | John Sellers and his assigns |
| Nov. 4ᵗʰ | Acramon, Paulus[3] | Rotterdam | Jacob Rupley and his assigns |
| | Baker, Honackel[3] | Rotterdam | Christopher Raighart and his assigns. |
| | O'Brien, Samuel | | Samuel Rhoads and his assigns |
| | Gibbons, Margaret[1] | | George Miller and his assigns |
| | Gregor, John Bernard | | Joshua Lamberger and his assigns |
| | Havel, John[3] | | Joseph Bosler and his assigns |
| | Rone, Mary, Jr.[3] | | Thomas Pugh and his wife |

## List of Indentures.

| Residence. | Occupation. | Term. | Amount. |
|---|---|---|---|
| | parel the first two years and the remaining three years and six months to be found in apparel by the master.[5] | | |
| Philadelphia | Servant | 2 yrs., 6 mo. | £12. |
| Philadelphia | Servant | 6 yrs., 10 mo., 7 d. | £25. |
| Philadelphia | Apprentice | 3 yrs., 19 d. | £5. |
| N. London twp., Chester co. | | 4 yrs. | £6. |
| Philadelphia | Servant | 8 yrs., 6 mo. | £25. |
| Bart twp., Lancaster co. | Servant | 2 yrs. | £14.6.9. |
| Philadelphia | | 2 yrs. | £12. |
| Blockley twp., Phila. co. | Servant[5] | 3 yrs. | £18.18.11. |
| Philadelphia | Servant, and at expiration have the legal freedom dues. | 6 yrs. | £20. |
| Philadelphia | Servant, have £10 lawful money of this province.[5] | 2 yrs., 6 mo. | £14.19.6. |
| Philadelphia | Servant, taught to read and write English and have freedom dues. | 9 yrs. | £25. |
| Philadelphia | Servant | 3 yrs. | £21.16.8¼. |
| Hempfield twp., Lancaster co. | | 3 yrs. | £21.16.8¼. |
| Philadelphia | Servant | 4 yrs. | £24.11.1½. |
| Lancaster co. | | 4 yrs. | |
| Philadelphia | Servant | 3 yrs., 6 mo. | £20.2.10. |
| Bristol twp., Phila. co. | Servant | 4 yrs. | £22.18.1. |
| Berks co. | | 4 yrs. | £22.18.1. |
| E. Marlborough, Chester co. | | 2 yrs., 3 mo. 11 d. | £16. |
| Philadelphia | | | £10. |
| Philadelphia | Servant (note 5, have £8 current money of this province). | 3 yrs. | £17.18.6. |
| Philadelphia | Servant | 4 yrs. | £23.6. |
| Philadelphia | Servant | 4 yrs. | £21.18.8. |
| Lancaster | | 4 yrs. | £21.18.8. |
| Upper Dublin twp., Phila. co. | | 4 yrs. | £16. |
| Philadelphia | Taught the cordwainer's trade, read, write and cypher as far as rule of three. | 7 yrs. | £20. |
| Burlington, W. Jersey | Servant, taught to read in the Bible, write a legible hand. | 8 yrs. | £21.16.2. |
| Philadelphia | Servant | 4 yrs. | £21.0.7. |
| Lurgan twp., Cumberland co. | Servant | 3 yrs. | £21.16.8. |
| Southwark. Northern Liberties | Taught the shipwright's trade, have one quarter evening schooling each winter of the term. | 5 yrs. | |
| Philadelphia | Servant, taught to read and write English. | 6 yrs. | £30. |
| Derby twp., Chester co. | Servant | 8 yrs. | £30. |
| Manor twp., Lancaster co. | Servant | 3 yrs., 6 mo. | £21.13. |
| Lancaster | Servant | 3 yrs., 6 mo. | £14.14.9. |
| Philadelphia | | 4 yrs. | £11.18. |
| Berks co. | Taught housewifery and to read. | 10 yrs., 3 mo., 12 d. | £13.15. |
| Philadelphia | Servant, taught to read and write and have freedom dues. | 9 yrs. | £16. |
| Vincent twp., Chester co. | Servant, have two months schooling. | 5 yrs., 2 mo. | £25.10.6. |
| Philadelphia | Apprentice, taught housewifery, sew plain work, have one year schooling | 8 yrs., 10 mo. | |

| Date. | Name. | From the Port of | To Whom Indentured. |
|---|---|---|---|
| 1771. Nov. 4th | Etter, Peter[3] | Rotterdam.. | John Groch and his assigns |
| | Swaine, Leah[3] | | Joseph Sermon and his assigns |
| | Evey, Adam[1] | | Capt. Samuel Wright |
| | Smith, Godfrey | Rotterdam.. | Christopher Sower and his assigns |
| | Hickman, Selby,[1] | | William Hussey |
| | Garret, Jane | | William Rippey and his assigns |
| | Batersby, Bell | | William Rippey and his assigns |
| | Sheaffer, Michael (note 3, and £5 lawful money of this province). | Rotterdam.. | Peter Dickey and his assigns |
| | Schnell, John George[1] | | James Wharton and his assigns |
| | Schnyder, Hannah Margaret[1] | | Christopher Marshall, Jr., and his assigns. |
| | Fisher, Nicholas (note 1, freedom dues to the value of £5 or £5 in money). | | John Moody and his assigns |
| | Swain, Ann[3] | Bristol | George Napper and his assigns |
| | Carruth, Margaret[5] | Ireland | Capt. Thos. Powell and his assigns |
| | Mallenbach, Mary Elizabeth[3] | Rotterdam.. | Rudolph Brunner and his assigns |
| | Mallenbach, Mary Elizabeth[3] | | Peter Spyker and his assigns |
| | Lindsay, Elizabeth | | Peter Dickey and his assigns |
| | Hehlman, Sophia | Rotterdam.. | Henry Haines and his assigns |
| | Diethoff, Godfrey Henry (note 3, or £10 in money in lieu of the new suit). | Rotterdam.. | John Graff and his assigns |
| | Rice, Henry[3] | Rotterdam.. | Nicholas Weaver and his assigns |
| | Patton, Margaret | | James Steel and his assigns |
| | Harding, Thomas | | John Wiggins and his assigns |
| | Lindsay, William, Jr.[3] | | Peter Dickey and his assigns |
| | Cockran, Blaney | | John Davis |
| | Vaugh, Patrick | | John Davis and his assigns |
| | Hymanin, Catherina[3] | | John Bockius and his assigns |
| | Felbach, Elizabeth Margaret[3] | Rotterdam.. | Andrew Hodge and his assigns |
| | Senfft, George (note 1, or £8 in money). | Rotterdam.. | Godfrey Twells and his assigns |
| | Shneall, Catherine[3] | Rotterdam.. | Peter Care and his assigns |
| Nov. 5th | Shneall, Mary[3] | Rotterdam.. | Conrad Weaver and his assigns |
| | Teace, Jacob | England | Christopher Hausman and his assigns. |
| | Miller, Ann | | Middleton Hablethwait and his assigns. |
| | Merrit, James[3] | | William Smith and his assigns |
| 1771. Nov. 5th | Silvey, Jean | | William Hunter and his assigns |
| | Hehlman, Elizabeth Catherine[3] | Rotterdam.. | Jacob Rote and his assigns |
| | Huthman, Charles Frederick[3] | | Frederick Earnest and his assigns |

[1] To be found all necessaries and at the expiration have freedom dues.
[2] To be found all necessaries and at the expiration have one new suit of apparel.
[3] To be found all necessaries and at the expiration have two complete suits of apparel, one whereof to be new.

## List of Indentures.

| Residence. | Occupation. | Term. | Amount. |
|---|---|---|---|
| Salisbury, Lancaster co.......... | Servant ........................ | 2 yrs., 3 mo. | £ 11. 8. 4. |
| Philadelphia ................... | Servant ........................ | 7 yrs....... | £ 15. |
| Philadelphia ................... | Taught the art and mystery of a mariner and navigator. | 7 yrs., 4 mo. | |
| Germantown ................ | Servant, found meat, drink, washing and lodging. | 1 yr., 6 mo. | £ 25. 12. |
| Philadelphia ................... | Taught the art, trade and mystery of a tailor, have four quarters' winter night schooling at reading and arithmetic. | 5 yrs., 10 mo. | |
| Lurgan twp., Cumberland co... | Servant ........................ | 2 yrs., 6 mo. | £ 7. 10. |
| Lurgan twp., Cumberland co... | ................................ | 3 yrs., 6 mo. | £ 16. |
| Lurgan twp., Cumberland co... | Servant ........................ | 6 yrs....... | £ 30. |
| Philadelphia ................... | Servant ........................ | 6 yrs....... | £ 18. |
| Philadelphia ................... | Servant, taught to read and write English. | | £ 18. 14. |
| Philadelphia ................... | Servant ........................ | 3 yrs....... | £ 15. |
| Philadelphia ................... | Taught the mantua maker's business. | 3 yrs....... | £ 15. |
| Philadelphia ................... | Servant ........................ | 2 yrs., 1 mo. | £ 8. |
| Philadelphia ................... | Servant, taught to read in the Bible. | 7 yrs....... | £ 30. |
| Tulpehocken twp., Berks co..... | ................................ | 7 yrs....... | £ 30. |
| Lurgan twp., Cumberland co... | Servant, to have two complete suits of apparel, one whereof to be new. | 4 yrs....... | £ 12. |
| Philadelphia ................... | Servant (note 5, have £ 5 lawful money of this province). | 3 yrs., 6 mo. | £ 25. |
| Philadelphia ................... | Servant ........................ | 3 yrs., 9 mo. | £ 25. |
| Philadelphia ................... | Servant ........................ | 3 yrs., 3 mo. | £ 21. 16. 10. |
| Philadelphia ................... | ................................ | 4 yrs....... | £ 16. |
| Paxton twp., Lancaster co...... | Servant ........................ | 7 yrs....... | £ 19. |
| Lurgan twp., Cumberland co... | Taught art, trade and mystery of a weaver, read in the Bible, write a legible hand. | 19 yrs. | |
| Middleton twp., Cumberland co.. | ................................ | 7 yrs....... | £ 3. |
| Middleton twp., Cumberland co.. | ................................ | | £ 11. |
| Germantown, Phila. co......... | Servant ........................ | 4 yrs....... | £ 21. 7. 6. |
| Philadelphia ................... | Servant ........................ | 4 yrs....... | £ 20. |
| Philadelphia ................... | Servant ........................ | 2 yrs., 9 mo. | £ 14. 19. 6. |
| Bristol twp., Phila. co.......... | Servant ........................ | 4 yrs....... | £ 20. |
| Bristol twp., Phila. co.......... | Servant ........................ | 4 yrs....... | £ 20. |
| Philadelphia ................... | Servant, to have apparel during the time only. | 2 yrs., 6 mo. | £ 14. 19. 6. |
| Philadelphia ................... | Apprentice ..................... | 13 yrs., 7 mo. | £ 15. |
| Philadelphia ................... | Apprentice, taught art, trade and mystery of a white smith and bellows maker, read, write and cypher as far as rule of three. | 15 yrs., 2 mo. | |
| W. Caln, Chester co............ | Servant ........................ | 4 yrs....... | £ 13. |
| Philadelphia ................... | Servant ........................ | 3 yrs., 6 mo. | £ 22. 3. |
| Philadelphia ................... | Apprentice, taught art, trade and mystery of a tailor, have one | 9 yrs. | |

⁴ To be found all necessaries and at the expiration have two complete suits of apparel, one whereof to be new, and 40s. in money.

⁵ At expiration have two complete suits of apparel, one whereof to be new.

| Date. | Name. | From the Port of | To Whom Indentured. |
|---|---|---|---|
| 1771. | | | |
| Nov. 5th | McGuire, John³ | Jamaica | Henry Lisle and his assigns |
| Nov. 6th | Graatz, Michael, and Clara Maria,³ his wife. | Rotterdam | Michael Haberstick and his assigns |
| | Furman, Christopher¹ | Rotterdam | George Miller and his assigns |
| | Farnsworth, James³ | | James Roney and his assigns |
| Nov. 7th | Felbach, Johannes Peter³ | Rotterdam | Robert and Ellis Lewis and their assigns. |
| | Nicholson, George | | Capt. Robert White and his assigns |
| | Schnell, Johannes³ | Rotterdam | Daniel Heister and his assigns |
| | Hessius, Martin (note 2, besides his old, or £6 in money). | Rotterdam | Jacob Stanbaugh and his assigns |
| | Hessius, Martin (note 2, besides his old, or £6 in money). | | John Carpenter and his assigns |
| | Schus, George³ | Rotterdam | Lawrence Shine and his assigns |
| | Norris, Aaron | | Benjamin Horner and his assigns |
| Nov. 8th | Balitz, Henry | | John Venn and his assigns |
| Nov. 9th | Cooney, John | | George Mifflin and his assigns |
| | Tungst, Ludwig Her¹ | Rotterdam | James Tilghman and his assigns |
| | Thomas Valentine (note 2, besides his old). | Rotterdam | Richard Wistar and his assigns |
| | Hepener, John (note 2, besides his old). | Rotterdam | Richard Wistar and his assigns |
| | Kelly, Edward (note 2, or £8 in cash). | | Thomas Middleton |
| Nov. 11th | Schnyderin, Mary Barbara³ | Rotterdam | John Cornman and his assigns |
| | Plumb, Johannes³ | Gottenberg | George Bryan and his assigns |
| | Sapporin, Christiana³ | Rotterdam | Joseph Neide and his assigns |
| | Sappor, Johannes³ | Rotterdam | Joseph Neide and his assigns |
| | Shields, Judith | | John Vanderen |
| Nov. 12th | Moffatt, Joseph² | | Davenport Marott and his heirs |
| | Burbach, Philip³ | | William Young and his assigns |
| | Metzler, Elizabeth³ | Rotterdam | Philip Flick and his assigns |
| | Bickerton, John | | Matthew Grimes and his assigns |
| | Feehan, William³ | | Jonathan Meredith and his assigns |
| | Adams, Isaac | | Joseph Drinker and his assigns |
| | Inglis, Sarah¹ | | John Kelly and his assigns |
| | Ta Chester, Martha³ | Ireland | James Huston and his assigns |

| Residence. | Occupation. | Term. | Amount. |
|---|---|---|---|
| | year night schooling to read and write English and German, and cypher as far as rule of three. | | |
| Philadelphia | Servant | 3 yrs. | £ 7. |
| Conestoga twp., Lancaster co. | Servant | 3 yrs., 6 mo. each. | £ 26. 3. |
| Upper Allowaysle twp., Salem co., W. Jersey. | Servant | 3 yrs. | £ 21. 17. 8½. |
| Philadelphia | Taught the art, trade and mystery of a cordwainer, have one quarter night schooling. | 5 yrs. | |
| Philadelphia | Servant | 7 yrs. | £ 30. |
| Philadelphia | Taught the art and mystery of a mariner and navigator, found meat, drink, washing and lodging, find him in apparel during the last three years of term and at expiration have one complete new suit of apparel besides his old. | 4 yrs. | |
| Upper Salford, Phila. co. | Servant | 4 yrs. | £ 30. |
| Strasburg twp., Lancaster co. | Servant | 2 yrs. | £ 10. 9. 5. |
| Strasburg twp., Lancaster co. | | 2 yrs. | £ 10. 9. 3. |
| Philadelphia | Servant | 3 yrs., 5 mo. | £ 21. 2. |
| Philadelphia | Taught art, trade and mystery of a hatter, found meat, drink, washing, lodging and mending, also shoes and hats. | 7 yrs. | |
| Philadelphia | | 5 yrs., 8 mo. | £ 6. |
| Philadelphia | | 3 yrs., 1 mo. | £ 20. |
| Philadelphia | Servant, taught to read and write the English language. | 7 yrs., 4 mo. | |
| Philadelphia | Servant | 5 yrs. | £ 21. 10. 8. |
| Philadelphia | Servant | 3 yrs., 6 mo. | £ 19. 3. |
| Philadelphia | Taught the trade of baker | 2 yrs., 9 mo. | |
| Philadelphia | Servant | 8 yrs. | £ 30. |
| Philadelphia | Servant, taught to read, write and cypher as far as rule of three. | 7 yrs. | |
| Bohemia, Cecil co., Md. | Servant | 5 yrs. | £ 22. |
| Bohemia, Cecil co., Md. | Servant, taught to read in the Bible, write a legible hand. | 14 yrs., 1 mo., 21 d. | £ 23. 10. 10. |
| Roxborough twp., Phila. co. | | 4 yrs. | £ 16. |
| Philadelphia | Taught the trade of a spinning wheel and chair maker, to read in the Bible, write a legible hand. | 5 yrs., 4 mo. 19 d. | |
| Kingsessing, Phila. co. | Servant | 3 yrs., 6 mo. | £ 18. 18. 11. |
| Philadelphia | Servant | 5 yrs. | £ 20. |
| Philadelphia | | 9 yrs., 1 mo. 3 w. | £ 15. |
| Philadelphia | Taught the currier's trade have three quarters' evening schooling. | 6 yrs., 8 mo. | |
| Philadelphia | | 4 yrs. | £ 10. |
| Philadelphia | Taught to read, write and cypher, housewifery and to sew. | 10 yrs., 11 mo. | £ 5. |
| Philadelphia | Servant | 3 yrs. | £ 13. |

| Date. | Name. | From the Port of | To Whom Indentured. |
|---|---|---|---|
|  | Giffin, Hannah[3] |  | Hudson Burr and his assigns |
| Nov. 13th | Welch, Nicholas[3] | Rotterdam | John Fretter and his assigns |
|  | Daily, Henry |  | Robert Pennel and his assigns |
|  | Naglee, James (note 2, or £10 in money). |  | Rudolph Lehr |
| Nov. 14th | Reading, Francis[3] |  | Daniel King and his assigns |
|  | Magere, Lydia[3] |  | Ann Paice and her heirs |
|  | Gilmore, David |  | John Moody and his assigns |
| Nov. 15th | Hoffman, Catherina[3] | Rotterdam | John Manderfield and his assigns |
|  | Cherry, Catherine[3] | Ireland | Capt. James Cockran and his assigns |
|  | Jenks, Henry William[3] | Rotterdam | Edward Midleton and his assigns |
|  | Wolffin, Maria Cath. |  | Edmund Beach and his assigns |
| Nov. 16th | Brooks, Philip[3] | Liverpool | Robert Aitkin and his assigns |
|  | Ungerin, Elizabeth[3] |  | Jacob Falconstine and his assigns |
|  | Donaldson, John |  | John McCalla and his assigns |
|  | Openkircher, John George[3] | Rotterdam | George Titman and his assigns |
| Nov. 18th | Hanible, Godfrey[3] |  | Samuel Wheeler and his assigns |
|  | Schnell, Henry[3] | Rotterdam | John Care and his assigns |
|  | Burton, Jonathan |  | Esther Lennill and her assigns |
|  | Hantz, Magdalene |  | Christopher Wegman and his assigns |
|  | Else, Johan |  | Samuel Potts and his assigns |
|  | Mengle, Paul |  | Samuel Potts and his assigns |
|  | Freeston, John |  | Joshua Moore and his assigns |
| Nov. 19th | Sturgis, Stokely |  | Presley Blackiston and his assigns |
|  | Ordts, Mary[3] |  | John Rohr and his assigns |
| Nov. 20th | Catterrer, Eve Catherine |  | Henry Catterrer and his assigns |
|  | Steiner, Elizabeth[3] | Rotterdam | Joshua Cresson and his assigns |
|  | Panslerine, Anna Maria[3] | Rotterdam | George Young and his assigns |
|  | Flick, William (note 1, to value of £10 or £10 in money). | Rotterdam | Wm. Eckhart and his assigns |
|  | Klien, Anthony[3] | Rotterdam | Henry Slaymaker and his assigns |
|  | Miller, Katheriana Barbara[3] |  | Jacob Ehrenzaller and his wife |
|  | Tyson, Agnes[1] |  | Allen Moore and his assigns |
|  | Emorsher, Mary Elizabeth[1] |  | Joseph Russell and his assigns |

# List of Indentures.

| Residence. | Occupation. | Term. | Amount. |
|---|---|---|---|
| Philadelphia | Apprentice, taught housewifery, sew plain work, read in the Bible, write a legible hand and cypher as far as rule of three. | | |
| Macungee, Northampton co. | Servant | 5 yrs., 6 mo. | £ 30. |
| Middletown, Chester co. | | 7 yrs. | £ 19. |
| Philadelphia | Taught the loaf bread baker's business, have two quarters' afternoon schooling. | 2 yrs., 10 mo., 23 d. | |
| Philadelphia | Taught the art, trade and mystery of a brass founder, have four quarters' evening schooling. | 7 mo. | |
| Philadelphia | Taught housewifery, quilting, to sew and knit, have nine months day schooling. | 9 yrs., 4 mo. 11 d. | |
| Philadelphia | | 2 yrs. | £ 6. 5 |
| Northern Liberties | Servant | 4 yrs., 6 mo. | £ 12. |
| Philadelphia | Servant | 4 yrs., 10 mo. | £ 12. |
| Philadelphia | Servant | 5 yrs. | £ 20. |
| Southwark | | 4 yrs. | £ 21. |
| Philadelphia | Servant, taught the book binder's business. | 3 yrs. | £ 10. 4 |
| Passyunk, Phila. co. | Apprentice, taught housewifery, sew, knit and spin, read in the Bible. | 3 yrs. | |
| Philadelphia | Apprentice, taught the tailor's trade, found meat, drink, washing and lodging. | 8 yrs., 10 mo., 7 d. | |
| Exford twp., Sussex co., W. Jersey. | Servant, taught to read and write English. | 9 yrs. | £ 20. |
| Philadelphia | Taught the art, trade and mystery of the white smith and cutler's trade, have seven months' evening schooling. | 1 yr., 7 mo. 24 d. | |
| Bristol twp., Phila. co. | Servant | 6 yrs. | £ 18. |
| | Apprentice | | £ 0. 5. 0. |
| Lebanon twp., Lancaster co. | | 6 yrs., 1 mo. | £ 10. |
| Potts Grove, Phila. co. | | 3 yrs., 9 mo. 13 d. | £ 15. |
| Potts Grove, Phila. co. | | 3 yrs., 8 mo. 14 d. | £ 10. |
| Philadelphia | Taught the art trade and mystery of a cabinet maker, found all necessaries, have two winters' evening schooling, one whereof to be at expense of the father, the other at expense of the master. | 5 yrs., 10 mo., 8 d. | |
| Philadelphia | Taught to read in the Bible. | 9 yrs., 11 mo. | |
| Philadelphia | Servant, taught to read in the Bible. | 9 yrs. | £ 8. 10. |
| Bernard twp., Berks co. | Servant | 5 yrs., 6 mo. | £ 0. 5. 0. |
| Philadelphia | Servant | 8 yrs. | £ 25. |
| Moyamensing | Servant | 5 yrs., 3 mo. | £ 25. 5 |
| Philadelphia | Servant | 4 yrs., 6 mo. | £ 22. 9. |
| Strasburg twp., Lancaster co. | Servant | 4 yrs. | £ 20. 19. 5. |
| Philadelphia | Apprentice, taught housewifery, sew, knit and spin. | 8 yrs., 4 mo. 19 d. | |
| Philadelphia | Servant | 5 yrs. | £ 25. |
| Philadelphia | Servant | 7 yrs. | £ 30. |

| Date. | Name. | From the Port of | To Whom Indentured. |
|---|---|---|---|
| 1771.<br>Nov. 20th | Emorsher, Mary Elizabeth[1]<br>Edelsin, Barbara[1] | <br>Rotterdam | Adam Grubb and his assigns<br>Daniel Gross and his assigns |
| | Hertzin, Ann Elizabeth[1] | | Joseph Warner and his assigns |
| | Mark, Peter[1] | | William Crispin and his assigns |
| | Mum, Katherine[1] | Rotterdam | George Schlosser and his assigns |
| | Deiderick, John[1] | Rotterdam | George Graff and his assigns |
| | Schnyder, John Peter, and Anna Catherina, his wife (note 2, besides their old). | Rotterdam | Arthur St. Clair and his assigns |
| | Schnyder, John Yoest,[1] and Catherine Elizabeth, his wife).[1] | Rotterdam | Arthur St. Clair and his assigns |
| | Sheffer, Jacob | Rotterdam | Arthur St. Clair and his assigns |
| | Foltz, Frederick[1] | Rotterdam | Lewis Farmer and his assigns |
| | Foltz, Frederick[1] | | Andrew Kickline and his assigns |
| | Schweitzer, John, and Barbara, his wife.[1] | Rotterdam | William Pennel and his assigns |
| | Lorenz, John Casper | Rotterdam | William Pennel and his assigns |
| | Scheleburgh, Elizabeth[3] | Rotterdam | John Staddleman and his assigns |
| | Sharick, John Jacob[1] | Rotterdam | William Forrest and his assigns |
| | Franger, Adam (note 3, also 4 Spanish dollars). | | John Slaymaker and his assigns |
| | Doehr, Frederick (note 3, and 4 Spanish dollars). | Rotterdam | Daniel Slaymaker and his assigns |
| | Boyer, John Gabriel[3] | Rotterdam | Henry Lisle and his assigns |
| | Affling, Margaret[3] | Rotterdam | Richard Wister and his assigns |
| | Schmeeterin, Elizabeth[3] | Rotterdam | Cathe. Wistar and her assigns |
| | Borgen, Elizabeth[3] | | Isaac Greenleaffe and his assigns |
| | Bremin, Elizabeth Catherine[3] | Rotterdam | Caleb Attmore and his assigns |
| | Bremin, Elizabeth Catherine[3] | | Arney Lippencott and his assigns |
| | Borgen, Mary Elizabeth[1] | | Jacob Comerad and his assigns |
| | Raddman, Conrad[3] | | Martin Kreider and his assigns |
| | Raddman, Conrad[3] | | Jacob Guyger and his assigns |
| | Smith, William[3] | | William Jenkins and his assigns |
| | Smith, William[3] | | Gabriel Davis and his assigns |
| | Harington, John[3] | | Thomas Johnston and his assigns |
| | Sadleigh, Margaret[1] | | Anthony Groff and his assigns |
| | Hoffman, Johan Nicholas[3] | | Martin Kreider and his assigns |
| | Hoffman, Johan Nicholas[3] | | Michael Whiteler and his assigns |
| | Plesh, John[3] | Rotterdam | Philip Moses and his assigns |
| | Mingen, Mary Elizabeth[3] | | Martin Kreider and his assigns |
| | Mingen, Mary Elizabeth[3] | | John Bender and his assigns |
| | Hatmanin, Christiana[3] | | Martin Kreider and his assigns |
| | Hatmanin, Christiana[3] | | Curtz and his assigns |
| | Nolt, Christiana | | Andrew Possette and his assigns |
| | Redley, Henry, (note 3, £8 in money in lieu of said new suits). | Rotterdam | Abraham Hirtant and his assigns |
| | Drexler, Peter, and Barbara, his wife (note 2, besides their old). | Rotterdam | Cornelius Williamson and his assigns. |
| | Garret, Catherine | | George Goodwin and his assigns |
| | Waggoner, John Jacob (note 3, and £3 in money). | | John Greybill and his assigns |
| | Fuller, Elizabeth[3] | Rotterdam | Frederick White and his assigns |
| | Knibell, John[1] | | Peter Dick and his assigns |
| | Sceiler, John, Jost[3] | | Henry Wax and his assigns |

## List of Indentures.

| RESIDENCE. | OCCUPATION. | TERM. | AMOUNT. |
|---|---|---|---|
| Borough of Chester............. | | 7 yrs....... | £ 30. |
| Lower Lawken twp., Northampton co. | Servant ................................ | | £ 22. 11. |
| Philadelphia ................. | Servant ................................ | 4 yrs....... | £ 23. 14. |
| Philadelphia ................. | Servant ................................ | 7 yrs....... | £ 30. |
| Philadelphia ................. | Servant ................................ | 4 yrs., 6 mo. | £ 24. 19. |
| Philadelphia ................. | Servant ................................ | 10 yrs...... | £ 25. |
| Bedford twp., Bedford co........ | Servant ................................ | 2 yrs. each. | £ 17. |
| Bedford twp., Bedford co........ | Servant ................................ | 5 yrs. each. | £ 45. 14. |
| Bedford twp., Bedford co........ | Servant, found all necessaries and at expiration have two complete suits of apparel besides the old. | 3 yrs....... | £ 16. |
| Philadelphia ................. | Servant ................................ | 4 yrs....... | £ 24. 9. 3. |
| Rockhill twp., Bucks co......... | | 4 yrs....... | £ 24. 9. 3. |
| Middletown, Chester co......... | Servants ............................... | 5 yrs., 3 mo. each. | £ 50. |
| Middletown, Chester co......... | Servant (note 5, have £ 10 in lieu of freedom dues). | 2 yrs., 10 mo. | £ 23. 2. |
| Lower Merion twp., Phila. co... | Servant ................................ | 4 yrs., 3 mo. | £ 23. 15. 10. |
| Springfield, Chester co......... | Servant ................................ | 8 yrs....... | £ 30. |
| Strasburg twp., Lancaster co..... | Servant ................................ | 3 yrs....... | £ 23. 6. 3. |
| Strasburg twp., Lancaster co..... | Servant ................................ | 3 yrs....... | £ 23. 15. 5. |
| Philadelphia ................. | Servant ................................ | 6 yrs....... | £ 30. |
| Philadelphia ................. | Servant ................................ | 4 yrs....... | £ 25. 18. |
| Philadelphia ................. | Servant ................................ | 4 yrs....... | £ 23. 14. 9. |
| Philadelphia ................. | Servant ................................ | 4 yrs....... | £ 24. 16. |
| Philadelphia ................. | Servant ................................ | 6 yrs., 6 mo. | £ 30. |
| Springfield twp., Burlington co., W. Jersey. | ................................ | 6 yrs., 6 mo. | £ 30. |
| Philadelphia ................. | Servant ................................ | 4 yrs....... | £ 24. 14. 3. |
| Philadelphia ................. | Servant ................................ | 3 yrs., 6 mo. | £ 26. 6. |
| Within three miles of Lancaster.. | | 3 yrs., 6 mo. | £ 26. 6. |
| Philadelphia ................. | Servant ................................ | 3 yrs., 3 mo. | £ 26. 9. 1. |
| Carnarvan twp., Lancaster co.... | | 3 yrs., 3 mo. | £ 26. 9. 1. |
| Antrim twp., Lancaster co....... | Servant ................................ | 4 yrs....... | £ 14. |
| Philadelphia ................. | Servant ................................ | 5 yrs....... | £ 25. 7. 6. |
| Philadelphia ................. | Servant ................................ | 3 yrs., 9 mo. | £ 25. 6. 5. |
| Lancaster co., near Dunkers Town. | ................................ | 3 yrs., 9 mo. | £ 26. 5. |
| Philadelphia ................. | Servant, to the value of £ 12, or £ 12 in money. | 5 yrs....... | £ 25. 15. |
| Philadelphia ................. | ................................ | 3 yrs., 6 mo. | £ 23. 14. |
| Near Lancaster, Lancaster co..... | ................................ | 3 yrs., 6 mo. | £ 23. 14. |
| Philadelphia ................. | Servant ................................ | 4 yrs....... | £ 24. 6. 5. |
| Earl twp., Lancaster co......... | ................................ | 3 yrs....... | £ 24. 6. 5. |
| Philadelphia ................. | ................................ | 4 yrs....... | £ 23. 12. 6. |
| Hempfield twp., Lancaster co.... | Servant ................................ | 3 yrs....... | £ 26. |
| Amwell twp., Hunterdon co..... West Jersey................... | Servant ................................ | 4 yrs. each. | £ 46. 13. 5. |
| Philadelphia ................. | Servant ................................ | 4 yrs....... | £ 11. 10. |
| Earl twp., Lancaster co......... | Servant ................................ | 3 yrs....... | £ 18. 14. |
| Strasburg twp., Lancaster co..... | Servant ................................ | 4 yrs., 6 mo. | £ 22. 10. 6. |
| Philadelphia ................. | Servant ................................ | 5 yrs., 6 mo. | £ 24. 14. 10. |
| Ealsuss twp., Berks co.......... | Servant ................................ | 3 yrs., 6 mo. | £ 19. 14. |

| DATE. | NAME. | FROM THE PORT OF | TO WHOM INDENTURED. |
|---|---|---|---|
| 1771. | Shafer, Magdalene[3] | Rotterdam.. | Jacob Barge and his assigns........ |
| Nov. 20th... | Shafer, Magdalene[3] | | John Miller and his assigns........ |
| Nov. 21st... | Lapport, John[3] | Rotterdam.. | Francis Sinner and his assigns....... |
| | Loudenslager, Henry[3] | Rotterdam.. | Jacob Barge and his assigns........ |
| | Loudenslager, Henry[3] | | John Burkholder and his assigns.... |
| | Everhart, Anthony | Rotterdam.. | Jacob Morgan and his assigns........ |
| | Eagle, Philip[1] | Rotterdam.. | Jacob Barge and his assigns........ |
| | Eagle, Philip[1] | | Sebastian Whitman and his assigns.. |
| | Loudenslager, John Leonard[3]. | Rotterdam.. | Jacob Barge and his assigns........ |
| | Loudenslager, John Leonard[3]. | | Wendel Gilbert and his assigns...... |
| | Starck, Ludwig[3] | | Wendel Lerban and his assigns...... |
| | Berriarin, Anna Barbara[3] | | Christopher Waggoner and his assigns. |
| | Berriarin, Anna Barbara[3] | | George Hibener and his assigns..... |
| | Weberin, Regina[1] | | James Reynolds and his assigns..... |
| | Carter, Rachel[3] | | James Dickinson and his assigns..... |
| | Retchin, Anna Margaret[3] | | Simon Glass and his assigns........ |
| | Hoffman, Jacob (note 3, and of the value of £10). | | William Young and his assigns..... |
| | Hoaff, John Peter[3] | | Jacob Whitman and his assigns..... |
| | Schnyderin, Mary[1] | | William Cooper and his assigns..... |
| | Leiben, Ann Elizabeth[1] | | Henry Keppele, Jr., and his assigns.. |
| | Leiben, Ann Elizabeth[1] | | Matthias Slough and his assigns..... |
| | Fritzin, Elizabeth[3] | | Henry Keppele, Jr., and his assigns.. |
| | Fritzin, Elizabeth[3] | | Matthias Slough and his assigns..... |
| | Boyerin, Susanna[3] | | James Wharton and his assigns...... |
| | Melichor, Adam | | George Schlosser and his assigns.... |
| | Dorety, Charlotte[3] | Rotterdam.. | Philip Moses and his assigns........ |
| | Benderin, Elizabeth[1] | Rotterdam.. | Thomas Cuthbert and his assigns.... |
| | Crousam, Michael,[3] and Elizabeth, his wife.[3] | Rotterdam.. | William Duncan and his assigns.... |
| | Folmer, John Gotleib | | Amos Harvey and his assigns....... |
| | Benner, Martin[3] | Rotterdam.. | Peter Souder and his assigns........ |
| | Eysingring, Hans George[3]... | Rotterdam.. | Johannes Bunner and his assigns.... |
| | Carter, Elizabeth | | John Harrison and his assigns....... |
| | Wilhelm, Johan[3] | Rotterdam.. | Mensucan Hughes and his assigns... |
| | Werner, William | | Richard Redman and his assigns.... |
| | Vanhold, Conrad (note 3, and have $1.00 next May). | Rotterdam.. | John Ogden and his assigns......... |
| Nov. 22nd... | Louks, Jacob | | Caleb Branton and his assigns....... |
| | Cairum, Dominicus[1] | Rotterdam.. | Philip Mouse and his assigns........ |
| | Haun, George[3] | Rotterdam.. | John Rupp and his assigns.......... |
| | Ungerin, Anna Catherina[1]... | Rotterdam.. | Anthony Lippencott and his assigns.. |
| | Bremer, Hans George[3] | Rotterdam.. | Elizabeth Sailor and her assigns..... |
| | Walbron, Francis[3] | | Philip Flick and his assigns......... |
| | McSwiney, Timothy | | Joseph White and his assigns........ |

## List of Indentures.

| Residence. | Occupation. | Term. | Amount. |
|---|---|---|---|
| Philadelphia | Servant | 3 yrs., 1 mo. | £25. 15. |
| Strasburg twp., Lancaster co. | | 3 yrs., 1 mo. | £25. 15. |
| Philadelphia | Servant | 5 yrs. | £25. 12. 10. |
| Philadelphia | Servant | 3 yrs. | £25. 3. 1. |
| Lancaster twp., Lancaster co. | | 3 yrs. | £25. 3. 1. |
| Philadelphia | Servant | 3 yrs. | £19. 14. 6. |
| Philadelphia | Servant | 5 yrs. | £26. 14. 6. |
| Manheim twp., Lancaster co. | | 5 yrs. | £26. 14. 6. |
| Philadelphia | Servant | 3 yrs. | £26. 6. 1. |
| Manheim twp., Lancaster co. | | 3 yrs. | £26. 6. 1. |
| Philadelphia | Servant | 2 yrs., 6 mo. | £20. 14. |
| Worcester twp., Phila. co. | Servant | 6 yrs. | £36. 3. 6. |
| Worcester twp., Phila. co. | | 6 yrs. | £36. 3. 6. |
| Philadelphia | Servant | 4 yrs. | £26. |
| Philadelphia | Apprentice, taught housewifery, sew and read in the Bible. | 3 yrs., 3 mo. 26 d. | |
| Lower Merion, Phila. co. | Servant | 3 yrs., 6 mo. | £22. 10. |
| Kingsessing twp., Phila. co. | Servant | 3 yrs., 6 mo. | £25. |
| Moyamensing twp., Phila. co. | Servant, to have one year and si months' night schooling. | 15 yrs., 6 mo. | £12. |
| Newtown twp., Gloucester co., W. New Jersey. | Servant | 5 yrs. | £30. |
| Philadelphia | Servant | 6 yrs. | £26. 3. |
| Lancaster | | 6 yrs. | £26. 3. |
| | Servant | 3 yrs., 6 mo. | £25.18. |
| Lancaster | | 3 yrs., 6 mo. | £25.18. |
| Philadelphia | Servant | 7 yrs. | £25. |
| Philadelphia | Apprentice, taught tanner and currier's business, found meat, drink, washing and lodging. | 5 yrs. | |
| Philadelphia | Servant, taught to read and sew | 10 yrs. | £5. |
| Philadelphia | Servant | 7 yrs., 8 mo. 2 d. | £20. |
| Hopewell twp., Cumberland co. | Servants, found all necessaries and at expiration one spinning wheel, one falling axe and a maul and wedges. | 4 yrs., 6 mo. each. | £45. |
| Pennsbury twp., Chester co. | | 1 yr. | £20. |
| Hopewell twp., Cumberland co. | Servant | 3 yrs., 6 mo. | £27. |
| Worcester twp., Phila. co. | Servant | 4 yrs. | £20. 2. 10. |
| Philadelphia | | 7 yrs. | £1. |
| Cape May twp., Cape May co., West N. Jersey. | Servant, taught to read in the Bible, write a legible hand and cypher. | 13 yrs. | £11. |
| Philadelphia | Apprentice, taught the tin plate worker's business, found meat, drink, washing and lodging only. | 3 yrs. | |
| Springfield twp., Chester co. | Servant | 3 yrs., 3 mo. | £23. 2. |
| Birmingham, Chester co. | | 5 yrs., 6 mo. | £21. |
| Philadelphia | Servant, employed at the stocking weaver's business only. | 4 yrs., 6 mo. | £24. 10. 7. |
| Philadelphia | Servant, employed at cordwainer's business. | 3 yrs., 6 mo. | £26. 5. |
| Springfield twp., Burlington co., W. N. Jersey. | Servant | 8 yrs. | £30. |
| Perkioming, Phila. co. | | 3 yrs. | £30. |
| Philadelphia | Taught the biscuit baker's business, have six quarters' evening schooling. | 12 yrs., 6 mo. | |
| Bristol twp., Bucks co. | Apprentice | 4 yrs. | £12. |

| Date. | Name. | From the Port of | To Whom Indentured. |
|---|---|---|---|
| 1771. Nov. 22nd... | Davis, Susanna[3] | | John Vance and his assigns |
| | Henin, Maria Catharine[3] | Rotterdam | Thomas Meyer and his assigns |
| | Shinckle, Anna Rosina[3] | Rotterdam | Isaac Whitelock and his assigns |
| | Yonkle, Yost Henry[3] | Rotterdam | Arney Lippencott and his assigns |
| | Swaine, John[3] | | Richard Trueman and his heirs |
| | Leib, John Nicholas[3] | Rotterdam | John Rhea and his assigns |
| | Hainor, Christian[3] | Rotterdam | Christian Reiff and his assigns |
| | Weil, John Peter[3] | Rotterdam | Christian Fiss and his assigns |
| | Gran, Martin (note 1, to value of £7 in money. | Rotterdam | Peter Crompaucher and his assigns |
| | Morteny, John Nicholas[3] | Rotterdam | Richard Wister and his assigns |
| | Sharick, Henry[3] | | William Jenkins and his assigns |
| | Boyerin, Anna Maria[3] | Rotterdam | Mary Eddy and her assigns |
| | Loudenslager, Henry (note 3, or £10 in money). | Rotterdam | Anthony Loick and his assigns |
| | Apple, Henry (note 5, have £10 current money of Pa.). | Rotterdam | John Reedle and his assigns |
| | Fick, David, Jr. | | George Miller and his assigns |
| | Lear, John Bernard[3] | Rotterdam | Jacob Bright and his assigns |
| | Lear, John Bernard[3] | | Michael Bright and his assigns |
| | Boeltz, John Michael[3] | Rotterdam | John Cline and his assigns |
| Nov. 23rd... | Stiver, Frederick[3] | Rotterdam | John Froxell and his assigns |
| | Coxe, Amarias (note 2, and usual consideration). | | William Wilmore and his assigns |
| | Loudenslager, Hans George, and Maria Catherina, his wife (note 2, besides their old). | Rotterdam | Peter Miller and his assigns |
| | Loudenslager, Anna Barbara[3] | Rotterdam | Ulrick Storefert and his assigns |
| | Salsbury, John[3] | | Samuel Harker and his assigns |
| | Lawrence, Henry | | Henry Ridgeway and his assigns |
| | Lynn, Valentine (note 1, or £10 in money). | Rotterdam | Henry Meyer and his assigns |
| | McKee, John[3] | Ireland | Jonathan Paschall and his assigns |
| | Violante, Anna Catherine (note 1, and 6 sheep or £10 in money). | Rotterdam | William Rogers and his assigns |
| | Berryman, William | | Dr. James Luper |
| | Kessler, John George[3] | Rotterdam | Richard Hall and his assigns |
| | Kessler, John George[3] | | Charles Pettit and his assigns |
| | Wolff, John Nicholas (note 3, and £6 lawful money of this province). | | George Strein and his assigns |
| | Grocehart, John William (note 1, and £4 in money). | Rotterdam | David Schnyder and his assigns |
| | Haws, Conrad,[1] and Anna Barbara,[1] his wife. | Rotterdam | Jacob Carpenter and his assigns |

## List of Indentures.

| RESIDENCE. | OCCUPATION. | TERM. | AMOUNT. |
|---|---|---|---|
| District of Southwark | Taught housewifery, sew plain work, read in the Bible, write a legible hand. | 14 yrs., 5 mo., 18 d. | |
| Philadelphia | Servant | 4 yrs. | £ 24. 12. 8. |
| Borough of Lancaster | Servant | 4 yrs., 6 mo. | £ 29. |
| Springfield twp., Burlington co., West Jersey. | Servant, to have one quarter's schooling. | 10 yrs. | £ 26. 17. 6. |
| Philadelphia | Apprentice, taught the cabinet and frame maker's business, have two quarters' evening schooling. | 6 yrs., 2 mo. 20 d. | |
| Philadelphia | Servant, have one quarter schooling. | 6 yrs. | £ 30. |
| Coventry twp., Chester co. | Servant | 4 yrs. | £ 21. |
| Philadelphia | Servant | 3 yrs., 6 mo. | £ 23. 18. 2. |
| Coventry twp., Chester co. | Servant | 3 yrs., 3 mo. | £ 23. |
| Philadelphia | Servant | 7 yrs. | £ 24. 13. 8. |
| Philadelphia | Servant | 10 yrs. | £ 25. 12. 6. |
| Philadelphia | Servant | 7 yrs. | £ 30. |
| Lower Socken, Northampton co. | Servant | 3 yrs. | £ 24. 18. 10. |
| Philadelphia | Servant | 3 yrs. | £ 26. |
| Germantown, Phila. co. | Apprentice, taught the clock and watch maker's business, found meat, drink, washing and lodging only, and at expiration have one complete new suit of apparel. | 2 yrs., 11 mo. | |
| Philadelphia | Servant | 3 yrs., 6 mo. | £ 26. 1. 5. |
| Reading, Berks co. | | 3 yrs., 6 mo. | £ 26. 1. 5. |
| Upper Salford twp., Phila. co. | Servant, taught to read and write a legible hand. | 11 yrs. | £ 21. 13. |
| Gwinnet twp., Phila. co. | Servant | 8 yrs. | £ 30. |
| Philadelphia | Apprentice, taught baker's business, read, write and cypher as far as rule of three. | 13 yrs., 3 mo. | |
| Upper Milford, Northampton co. | Servant | 4 yrs. each. | £ 45. 15. 7. |
| Upper Salford, Phila. co. | Servant | 3 yrs., 4 mo. | £ 23. 12. 2. |
| Woolwich twp., Gloucester co., W. Jersey. | Servant | 2 yrs., 7 mo. 2 d. | £ 10. |
| Springfield twp., Burlington co., W. Jersey. | | 6 yrs. | £ 17. |
| Concord twp., Chester co. | Servant | 4 yrs. | £ 26. |
| Kingsessing, Phila. co. | Servant, have six months' schooling. | 7 yrs., 6 mo. 24 d. | £ 8. |
| Evesham twp., Burlington co., W. N. Jersey. | Servant | 4 yrs., 6 mo. | £ 18. |
| Prince George co., Md. | Apprentice, taught to read, write and cypher as far as rule of three and the art of navigation [5]. | 4 yrs., 6 mo. 7 d. | |
| Philadelphia | Servant | 8 yrs. | £ 30. |
| Burlington, W. N. Jersey | | 8 yrs. | £ 30. |
| Northern Liberties | Servant, taught the art and mystery of a weaver, have four winters' Dutch schooling. | 15 yrs. | £ 6. to be paid him at expiration. |
| Lower Dublin twp., Phila. co. | Servant, taught the miller's business. | 4 yrs. | £ 22. 14. |
| Lampeter twp., Lancaster co. | Servant | 4 yrs. | £ 40. |

| Date. | Name. | From the Port of | To Whom Indentured. |
|---|---|---|---|
| 1771. Nov. 25th... | Tauhawer, Conrad (note 5, and have £5 lawful money of this province). | | Daniel Burkhard and wife.......... |
| | McGlauchlin³ ....................... | | Catherine Batson ................ |
| | Carter, Rachel........................ | | John Pinkerton and his assigns...... |
| | Fierly, Jacob³............... | Rotterdam.. | Detrick Rees and his assigns........ |
| | Stahl, Godfreid³........... | Rotterdam.. | Nathan Levering and his assigns.... |
| | Stahl, Godfreid³........... | | William Levering and his assigns... |
| | Grimes, Moses............... | | Francis Gwiney and his assigns..... |
| | Courtenay, Francis......... | | Anthony Fortune and his assigns..... |
| Nov. 26th... | Sheirmanin, Eve Cathe.³..... | Rotterdam.. | Christian Brown and his assigns..... |
| | Dorcy, John (note 5, receive according to the custom of the country). | Ireland .... | John Inglis and his assigns......... |
| | Schaanfelder, John Daniel.... | Rotterdam.. | William Taylor and his assigns..... |
| | Schnyderin, Catherine Elizabeth.³ | Rotterdam.. | Charles Marshall and his assigns.... |
| | Turner, Neil................. | | Jacob Van Sciver and his assigns.... |
| | Shields, Lilly³............... | Ireland .... | William Reece and his assigns...... |
| | Grouss, Matthias (note 5, have £10 current money of Pa.). | Rotterdam.. | Jacob Barge and his assigns........ |
| | Grouss, Matthias (note 5, have £10 current money of Pa.). | | John Shartz and his assigns......... |
| | Keaffan, Elizabeth³.......... | Rotterdam.. | George Cooper and his assigns...... |
| | Dewald, Daniel³............. | | James Craig and his assigns......... |
| Nov. 27th... | Hand, Ovid.................. | | James Glenn and his assigns........ |
| | Burg, Philip Jacob³......... | Rotterdam.. | Andrew Burkhard and his assigns... |
| | Taylor, John George (note 1, to value of £10 lawful money of this province or £10 in money aforesaid). | | Henry Sherer and his assigns........ |
| | Wilson, Mark................ | | Samuel Cooper and his assigns...... |
| | Fravell, John, and Anna Eliza. his wife (note 2, besides their old). | Rotterdam.. | John Frees and his assigns.......... |
| 1771. Nov. 27th... | Fravell, John, and Anna Eliza., his wife). | | Jacob Frees and his assigns......... |
| | Maxwell, Ann................ | | Thomas Jones and his assigns....... |
| | Smith, William............... | | William Lawrence ................ |
| | Neitsel, John³............... | Rotterdam.. | Peter Keir and his assigns.......... |

## List of Indentures.

| Residence. | Occupation. | Term. | Amount. |
|---|---|---|---|
| Passyunk twp., Phila. co. | Apprentice, taught to read in Bible, write a legible hand and cypher as far as rule of three. | 11 yrs., 11 mo., 2 w. | |
| Philadelphia | Apprentice, taught housewifery, sew plain work, have nine months' schooling. | 6 yrs., 4 mo. | |
| Philadelphia | | 3 yrs., 3 mo. 26 d. | £ 5. 5. |
| Philadelphia | Servant | 3 yrs., 3 mo. | £ 24. 16. |
| Roxbury twp., Phila. co. | Servant | 3 yrs. | £ 20. 14. |
| Roxbury twp., Phila. co. | | 3 yrs. | £ 20. 14. |
| Philadelphia | | 10 yrs. | £ 40. |
| Philadelphia | | 3 yrs. | £ 16. |
| Bethlehem twp., Northampton co. | Servant | 4 yrs., 6 mo. | £ 18. 14. |
| Philadelphia | Servant | 3 yrs. | £ 16. |
| Philadelphia | Servant, employed in the goldsmith and jeweller's business only, found meat, drink, washing and lodging, to wear the clothes he now has and whatever necessary clothing he may want during the term, the master to provide and at expiration have one complete new suit of apparel. | 2 yrs., 6 mo. | £ 18. 14. |
| Philadelphia | Servant, taught to read in the Bible, write a legible hand. | 6 yrs. | £ 20. |
| Northern Liberties | Apprentice, taught the cordwainer's trade, found meat, drink, washing, lodging and working apparel only. | 3 yrs. | |
| New Town, Chester co. | Servant | 3 yrs., 9 mo. | £ 16. |
| Philadelphia | Servant | 3 yrs. | £ 22. 15. 4. |
| Strasburg twp., Lancaster co. | | 3 yrs. | £ 22. 15. 4. |
| Philadelphia | Servant | 5 yrs. | £ 27. |
| Philadelphia | Servant | 12 yrs., 6 mo. | £ 23. 15. |
| Philadelphia | Apprentice | 4 yrs., 8 mo. | £ 0. 5. 0. |
| Philadelphia | Servant | 3 yrs. | £ 24. 17. 4. |
| Allen twp., Northampton co. | Apprentice, taught the cordwainer's and farmer's business. | 4 yrs., 6 mo. 19 d. | |
| Newton twp., Gloucester co., W. Jersey. | | 6 yrs. | £ 18. |
| Philadelphia | Servant | 4 yrs., 6 mo. | £ 41. 16. each. |
| Alloways Cr., Salem co., West Jersey. | | 4 yrs., 6 mo. | £ 41. 16. each. |
| Hill Town twp., Bucks co. | Servant | 3 yrs. | £ 10. |
| Philadelphia | Apprentice, taught art and mystery of a mariner and navigator, found meat, drink, washing, lodging and working apparel only. | 5 yrs., 5 mo. | |
| Woolwich twp., Gloucester co., W. Jersey. | Servant | 3 yrs. | £ 23. 10. 7. |

| Date. | Name. | From the Port of | To Whom Indentured. |
|---|---|---|---|
| 1771. Nov. 26th | Goldy, Nicholas Samuel (note 1, or £7 current money of Pa.). | Rotterdam.. | Isaac Clark and his assigns......... |
| | Marksin, Anna Magdalene[3].. | ............ | Robert Whyte and his assigns....... |
| | Shively, George (note 3, or £5 lawful money of Pa.). | Rotterdam.. | Matthias Shively and his assigns.... |
| Nov. 28th | Harding William............ | Ireland .... | Joseph Fox and his assigns.......... |
| | Eyrick, Jacob[3]............. | Rotterdam.. | John Strom and his assigns......... |
| | Kuch, John Peter (note 1, to value of £10 lawful money of this province or £10 in money aforesaid). | Rotterdam.. | George Cline and his assigns........ |
| | Nie, John, and Anna Eliza., his wife (note 2, besides their old). | Rotterdam.. | William Steer and his assigns....... |
| Nov. 29th | Raubenheimer, Jacob, (note 5, have £10 lawful money of Pa. in lieu of freedom dues) | Rotterdam.. | Frederick Shinkle and his assigns.... |
| | Raubenheimer, Jacob (note 5, have £10 lawful money of Pa. in lieu of freedom dues. | ............ | Isaac Perkins and his assigns........ |
| | Long Elinor[1]................ | ............ | Joseph McCoy and his assigns....... |
| | Cathill, Cornelius............ | ............ | Benjamin Flower and his assigns.... |
| | Neitser, Sophia[3]............. | Rotterdam.. | Samuel Rhoads, Jr., and his assigns.. |
| | Cooper, Francis[3]............ | ............ | Ephraim Falkner and his assigns.... |
| | Belford, James (note 2, besides his old). | ............ | Joseph Burr, Jr., and his assigns.... |
| Nov. 30th | McCray, James................ | ............ | William Reynolds and his assigns... |
| | Griffiths, William............ | ............ | Thomas Hale and his assigns........ |
| | Sullivan, Honor[3]............ | ............ | Alexander Fraser and his assigns.... |
| | Hopper, William[3].......... | ............ | Leonard Kroesen and his assigns.... |
| Dec. 2nd | Penton, Aaron[3]............. | ............ | Jacob Graff and his assigns......... |
| | Yotz, Ann Margaret[3]........ | Rotterdam.. | William Jenkins and his assigns...... |
| | Were, Elizabeth ............ | ............ | John Raybon and his wife........... |
| | Trompeler, John Peter,[3] and Anna Sabina, his wife.[2] | Rotterdam.. Rotterdam.. | William Bausman and his assigns... |
| | Trompeler, Eva Margaret[3].. | Rotterdam.. | William Bausman and his assigns... |
| | Vucherer, Jacob (note 5, have £8 lawful money of Pa.). | Rotterdam.. | Jacob Brown and his assigns........ |
| | Hossey, Peter[3] ............. | ............ | Robert Fitzgerald and his assigns.... |

## List of Indentures.

| Residence. | Occupation. | Term. | Amount. |
|---|---|---|---|
| Stoney Brook, Middlesex co., New Jersey. | Servant | 4 yrs., 6 w. | £ 24. 18. |
| Philadelphia | Servant | 6 yrs., 6 mo. | £ 30. |
| Marlborough twp., Phila. co. | Servant | 6 yrs. | £ 42. 12. 6. |
| Philadelphia | Servant⁵ | 2 yrs. | £ 11. 18. |
| Northern Liberties | Servant | 4 yrs. | £ 26. 15. |
| Philadelphia | Servant | 6 yrs. | £ 23. 13. |
| Lebanon twp., Lancaster co. | Servant | 4 yrs., 9 mo. each. | £ 46. 8. |
| Philadelphia | Servant | 3 yrs. | £ 21. 6. |
| Duck Creek Hundred, Kent co., on Delaware. | | 3 yrs. | £ 21. 6. |
| Letterkenny twp., Cumberland co. | Servant, taught to sew, knit and read. | 10 yrs., 5 mo. | £ 14. 10. |
| Philadelphia | Apprentice, taught art, trade and mystery of a hatmaker, found meat, drink, washing and lodging and have £ 18 lawful money of Pa. every year of the term and at expiration one complete new suit of apparel. | 4 yrs., 11 mo. | |
| Philadelphia | Servant | 5 yrs. | £ 19. 3. 10½. |
| Southwark | Apprentice, taught the ship joiner's trade, read, write and cypher as far as rule of three. | 8 yrs., 1 mo. 3 d. | |
| Northampton twp., Burlington co., W. New Jersey. | Servant | 3 yrs. | £ 8. |
| Southwark | Apprentice, taught the art, trade and mystery of a hatmaker, have one year evening schooling and have all necessaries. | 7 yrs. | |
| Philadelphia | Servant | 5 yrs., 11 mo., 3 d. | £ 5. |
| Philadelphia | Servant | 3 yrs., 8 mo. 5 d. | £ 1. |
| Southampton twp., Bucks co. | Apprentice, taught the art and mystery of farming or husbandry, have one year schooling after the age of 12 years. | 10 yrs., 5 mo. | |
| Philadelphia | Apprentice, taught the tailor's trade, have six months' night schooling. | 5 yrs., 5 mo. 23 d. | |
| Philadelphia | Servant | 8 yrs. | £ 30. 7. 6. |
| Philadelphia | Apprentice, taught the leather breeches maker's trade.⁵ | 1 yr., 11 mo. | |
| Lancaster, Lancaster co. | Servant | 4 yrs., 6 mo. | £ 31. 12. 4 |
| | Servant | | £ 10. |
| Lancaster, Lancaster co. | Servant, taught to read in the Bible, write a legible hand. | 16 yrs., 3 mo., 1 w. | |
| Philadelphia | Servant | 2 yrs., 9 mo. | £ 25. |
| Philadelphia | Apprentice, taught the block and pump maker's business, have nine months' evening schooling. | 7 yrs., 6 mo. | |

| Date. | Name. | From the Port of | To Whom Indentured. |
|---|---|---|---|
| 1771. Dec. 2nd | Miller, Gustavus[3] | | John Stille and his assigns |
| | Kenner, Godfreid[3] | Rotterdam | Jacob Graff and his assigns |
| | Kessler, George Peter[1] | Rotterdam | Daniel Carty and his assigns |
| Dec. 3rd | Murray, Eneas | | Caleb Hewes and his assigns |
| | Grubb, Jacob | | Christian Rudolph and his assigns |
| | Minnies, Hans Michael[3] | | Isaac Paschall and his assigns |
| | Smallwood Martha[3] | | John Morton and his assigns |
| Dec. 4th | Bodall, John | | Thomas Robinson and his assigns |
| | Kates, Philip[5] | | John Moody and his assigns |
| | Himblehaver, Jacob[3] | Rotterdam | William Englefreid and his assigns |
| | Michelin, Maria Catherina[3] | Rotterdam | Adam Foulk and his assigns |
| | Piltz, Michael, and Barbara, his wife (note 2, besides their old). | Rotterdam | Michael Waggoner and his assigns |
| | Piltz, Casper[3] | Rotterdam | Michael Waggoner and his assigns |
| | Piltz, Rosina Barbara[3] | Rotterdam | Michael Waggoner and his assigns |
| | Solcher, Stephen (note 5, have £10 lawful money of Pa. in lieu of freedom dues). | Rotterdam | George Shepherd and his assigns |
| | Welsh Ludwig[3] | | Jacob Meckling and his assigns |
| Dec. 5th | Harvie, John (note 3, and tools he works with). | | Samuel Brasstar and his assigns |
| | Forrest, William (note 5, £12 lawful money of Pa.). | | John Williams and his assigns |
| | Valentine, Margaret | | Edward Brooks, Jr., and his assigns |
| | Hockstettler, Henry | | William Carson and his assigns |
| | Eyrichin, Sophia[3] | Rotterdam | Adam Fleck and his assigns |
| | Spencer, Jane[3] | | Jacob Holliday and his assigns |
| | Herr, Jacob[3] | London | Thomas Needrow and his assigns |
| | Miller, John (note 5, £10 lawful money of Pa. in lieu of freedom dues). | Rotterdam | Henry Funk and his assigns |
| | Miller John | | John Hise and his assigns |
| | Snuke, John | | Charles Sexton and his assigns |
| Dec. 6th | Dougherty, John | | William Brisben and his assigns |
| | Green, George[3] | Rotterdam | Rev. Wm. Stringer and his assigns |
| | Wanamaker, Jacob[3] | Rotterdam | James Hutton and his assigns |

[1] To be found all necessaries and at the expiration have freedom dues.
[2] To be found all necessaries and at the expiration have one new suit of apparel.
[3] To be found all necessaries and at the expiration have two complete suits of apparel, one whereof to be new.

## List of Indentures.

| Residence. | Occupation. | Term. | Amount. |
|---|---|---|---|
| Philadelphia | Servant, to be employed at the tailor's trade only. | 2 yrs., 6 mo. | £25. |
| Philadelphia | Servant | 3 yrs., 6 mo. | £25.10. |
| Chester twp., Burlington co., W. Jersey. | Servant | 9 yrs., 6 mo. | £25. |
| Philadelphia | | 3 yrs., 6 mo. | £12.5. |
| Philadelphia | | 12 yrs., 11 mo. | £10. |
| Philadelphia | Servant, taught to read in the Bible and write a legible hand. | 10 yrs., 6 mo. | £25. |
| District of Southwark | Apprentice, taught housewifery, sew plain work, read in the Bible and write a legible hand. | 7 yrs., 11 mo., 26 d. | |
| Southwark | Servant, taught art, trade and mystery of a house carpenter and found meat, drink, washing, lodging and mending. | 1 yr., 10 mo. 28 d. | |
| Philadelphia | Servant | 1 yr. | £40. |
| Philadelphia | Servant | 5 yrs. | £23.17. |
| Philadelphia | Servant | 4 yrs., 6 mo. | £22.18.6. |
| Pipe Creek hundred, Frederick co., Md. | Servant | 3 yrs. | £25. |
| Pipe Creek hundred, Frederick co., Md. | Servant, taught to read in the Bible, write a legible hand. | 13 yrs. | £10. |
| Pipe Creek hundred, Frederick co., Md. | Servant, taught to read in the Bible and write a legible hand. | 7 yrs. | £18. |
| Philadelphia | Servant, employed at the baker's business. | 4 yrs., 6 mo. | £22. |
| Lower Locken twp., Northampton co. | Servant, taught to read in the Bible, write a legible hand. | 7 yrs. | £20. |
| Northern Liberties | Apprentice, taught the art, trade and mystery of a shipwright. | 4 yrs., 4 mo. | |
| Northern Liberties | Apprentice, taught the art, trade and mystery of a boat builder, time to go to evening school one quarter in each and every winter of the term, the mother paying the expense. | 6 yrs., 5 mo. 26 d. | |
| Borden Town, Burlington co., W. Jersey. | | 6 yrs. | £10. |
| Philadelphia | Apprentice | 13 yrs., 6 mo. | £20. |
| N. Wales, Phila. co. | Servant, taught to read in Bible | 7 yrs. | £20. |
| Londongrove, Chester co. | Apprentice, taught housewifery, sew, knit and spin, read in Bible, write a legible hand, cypher as far as rule of three. | 11 yrs., 2 mo. | |
| Bristol twp., Phila. co. | Servant | 2 yrs., 6 mo. | £16.13. |
| Philadelphia | Servant | 2 yrs., 9 mo. | £22.14. |
| Heidelbergh twp., Lancaster co. | | 2 yrs., 9 mo | £22.14. |
| Burlington co., W. Jersey | | 4 yrs., 7 mo. 6 d. | £18. |
| Salisbury twp., Lancaster co. | | 2 yrs. | £11. |
| Philadelphia | Servant | 4 yrs., 3 mo. | £25.9. |
| Maiden Cr. twp., Berks co. | Servant | 6 yrs. | £30. |

[4] To be found all necessaries and at the expiration have two complete suits of apparel, one whereof to be new, and 40s. in money.
[5] At expiration have two complete suits of apparel, one whereof to be new.

| DATE. | NAME. | FROM THE PORT OF | TO WHOM INDENTURED. |
|---|---|---|---|
| 1771. Dec. 6th | Bacher, Anna Catherine[3] | Rotterdam | John Wister and his assigns |
| | Halterman, Hannis[3] | | Samuel Bachman |
| | Hearst, Sebastian[3] | London | Reuben Haines |
| | Hearst, Sebastian[3] | | David Cooper and his assigns |
| | Mareah, Mary[1] | London | Adam Ehart |
| | Hausler, Henry[3] | London | John Ellick and his assigns |
| | Lullerin, Margaret[3] | London | Adam Foulke and his assigns |
| | Schestermiller, Conrad[3] | London | Adam Foulke |
| | Schestermiller, Conrad[3] | | William Lively |
| | Lullerin, Margaret | | Adam Reikard and his assigns |
| | Fisher, George Frederick | | Henry Sheaff and his assigns |
| Dec. 7th | Fry, Michael | London | Abraham Hier and his assigns |
| | Green, George | Rotterdam | Rev. William Stringer and his assigns. |
| | Hertz, John Henry | Rotterdam | Jacob Rees and his assigns |
| | Braubert, Anna Maria | London | Salomia Chanceller and her assigns |
| | Fry, Martin | London | Casper Gier and his assigns |
| | Horster, John Christian, and Maria Margaret his wife. | Rotterdam | Michael Haberstick and his assigns |
| | Marksin, Mary Elizabeth | Rotterdam | Michael Haberstick and his assigns |
| | Marksin, Mary Elizabeth | | Benedict Brechbill and his assigns |
| | Horster, John Dice | Rotterdam | Michael Haberstick and his assigns |
| | Horster, John Lawrence | Rotterdam | Michael Haberstick and his assigns |
| | Horster, Maria Magdn | Rotterdam | Michael Haberstick and his assigns |
| | Schnyder, John Christopher | Rotterdam | John Cannon and his assigns |
| Dec. 9th | Braubert, John William | London | Wiliam Jenkins and his assigns |
| | Braubert, John William | | Thomas Green and his assigns |
| | Coggins, Michael | | Christopher White and his assigns |
| | Meyer, Christopher | Rotterdam | Michael Kinsler and his assigns |
| | Stroub, John | London | Frederick Hagner and his assigns |
| | Trauslebach, John William | Rotterdam | Martin Kreider and his assigns |
| Dec. 10th | Meyer, Barbara | London | John Wister and his assigns |
| | Meyer, Barbara | | John Carpenter and his assigns |
| | Schnyderin, Elizabeth | Rotterdam | Peter Eaby and his assigns |
| | Grimes, John | London | Christian Ritz and his assigns |
| | Schnyderin, Anna Catherine | Rotterdam | John Russell and his assigns |
| 1771. Dec. 10th | Elberson, John | | Daniel Gorton and his assigns |
| | LeBlanc, Joseph | | Joseph LeBlanc and his assigns |
| | Waggonerin, Anna Margt | Rotterdam | Michael Haberstick and his assigns |
| Dec. 11th | Russell Thomas | | William Bellamy and his assigns |

## List of Indentures.

| Residence. | Occupation. | Term. | Amount. |
|---|---|---|---|
| Philadelphia | Servant | 6 yrs. | £26.10.3. |
| Upper Sacken twp., Bucks co. | Servant | 2 yrs., 3 mo. | £13.2.9. |
| Philadelphia | Servant | 3 yrs. | £19.7. |
| Near Woodbury, Gloucester co. | | 3 yrs. | £19.7. |
| Philadelphia | Servant | 4 yrs. | £17.8. |
| Philadelphia | Servant | 4 yrs., 6 mo. | £23.19.6. |
| Philadelphia | Servant | 3 yrs. | £17. |
| Philadelphia | Servant | 3 yrs., 6 mo. | £16.19. |
| Baltimore, Md. | | 3 yrs., 6 mo. | £16.19. |
| Lancaster | | 3 yrs. | £17.0.6. |
| Philadelphia | Apprentice, have three quarters' schooling, taught the grocer's business. (Note 3, and £10 lawful money of Pa.). | 7 yrs. | |
| Mt. Joy twp., Lancaster co. | Servant[3] | 2 yrs., 2 mo. | £19.11. |
| Philadelphia | Servant, taught to read and write English.[3] | 4 yrs., 6 mo. | £25. |
| Germantown, Phila. co. | Servant[3] | 4 yrs., 6 mo. | £20.17.6. |
| Philadelphia | Servant[3] | 9 yrs. | £26. |
| Philadelphia | Servant[1] | 4 yrs. | £19.11. |
| Conestoga twp., Lancaster co. | Servant (note 3, besides their old). | 4 yrs. each. | £30. |
| Conestoga twp., Lancaster co. | Servant[3] | 5 yrs., 6 mo. | £30. |
| Strasburg twp., Lancaster co. | | 5 yrs., 6 mo. | £30. |
| Conestoga twp., Lancaster co. | Servant, taught to read well in the Bible, write a legible hand.[3] | 14 yrs., 6 mo. | £8. |
| Conestoga twp., Lancaster co. | Servant, taught to read well in the Bible, write a legible hand.[3] | 14 yrs., 11 mo., 2 d. | £10. |
| Conestoga twp., Lancaster co. | Servant, taught to read well in the Bible, write a legible hand.[3] | 10 yrs., 1 mo. | £6. |
| Philadelphia | Servant, taught to read and write English well and cypher as far as rule of three.[3] | 10 yrs., 6 mo. | £20. |
| Philadelphia | Servant[3] | 8 yrs. | £27.9.3. |
| Sadsbury twp., Lancaster co. | | 8 yrs. | £27.9.3. |
| Philadelphia | Taught the cordwainer's trade (note 3, and have six months' evening schooling). | 6 yrs., 6 mo. 20 d. | |
| Movamensing twp., Phila. co. | Servant, taught to read in Bible, write a legible hand and cypher as far as rule of three.[3] | 10 yrs. | £40. |
| Philadelphia | Servant[3] | 2 yrs., 6 mo. | £16.13. |
| Philadelphia | Servant, have one year's schooling, allowed the customary time to prepare him to receive the sacrament. | 8 yrs. | £29. |
| Philadelphia | Servant (note 3, and £3 lawful money of Pa.). | 4 yrs. | £23. |
| Strasburg twp., Lancaster co. | | 4 yrs. | £23. |
| Leacock twp., Lancaster co. | Servant[3] | 4 yrs., 6 mo. | £23.18. |
| Southwark | Servant[3] | 5 yrs., 3 mo. | £15.7.4. |
| Philadelphia | Servant, taught to read in Bible, write a legible hand.[3] | 10 yrs. | £15. |
| Philadelphia | Taught the art and mystery of a pilot in the bay and river Delaware, have six months' schooling[3] | 4 yrs., 6 mo. | |
| Philadelphia | Apprentice, taught the wigmaker and hair dresser's business, have five winters' evening schooling[3]. | 7 yrs., 6 mo. | |
| Conestoga twp., Lancaster co. | Servant[3] | 6 yrs. | £36.11.6. |
| Philadelphia | Apprentice, taught the art, trade and mystery of a French bur | 3 yrs. | |

| Date. | Name. | From the Port of | To Whom Indentured. |
|---|---|---|---|
| 1771.<br>Dec. 11th.... | | | |
| | Richards Joseph | | Richard Tittermary and his assigns.. |
| | Moyer, George | | Philip Souder and his assigns........ |
| | Smith, John Henry | Rotterdam.. | Charles Wharton and his assigns..... |
| | Braubert, Catherine | London.... | Benjamin Fuller and his assigns..... |
| | Sniderin, Elizabeth | Rotterdam.. | John Wharton and his assigns....... |
| | Mallenbach, John George.... | Rotterdam.. | Joseph Cain and his assigns......... |
| | Shireman, John Nicholas, and Catherine Elizabeth, his wife. | Rotterdam.. | Philip Miller and his assigns........ |
| | Schleitz, Peter | London.... | Martin Rhorer and his assigns....... |
| | Volks, Daniel | London.... | Martin Rhorer and his assigns....... |
| | Strausin, Christiana | London.... | Martin Kreider and his assigns...... |
| | Kugler, Hans Adam | London.... | William Todd and his assigns....... |
| | Kuglerin, Margaret | London.... | William Todd and his assigns....... |
| | Metzler, Elizabeth | | Moses Coxe and his assigns.......... |
| | Eyrichin, Anne Christiana | Rotterdam.. | Thomas Penrose and his assigns...... |
| | Shoumacker, Elizabeth | London.... | Felix Bingly and his assigns........ |
| | Shoumacker, Jacob | London.... | Felix Bingly and his assigns........ |
| | Shumacker, Johannes | London.... | Felix Bingly and his assigns........ |
| Dec. 12th.... | Pompey | | John Jackson and his assigns........ |
| | Uhl Charles | | Jacob Shalluss and his assigns....... |
| | Hartshorne, Mary | | Capt. Alexander Dyar and wife...... |
| | Mehbin, Patrick | | John Galloway and his assigns...... |
| | Sheaffer, Martha | | Rudolph Lear and his assigns........ |
| | Leasch, Philip | | John Hill and his assigns........... |
| | Doneller, John | | William Shedaker and his assigns.... |
| | Smith, Charles | Lisbon..... | George Miller and his assigns....... |
| Dec. 13th.... | Sheaffer, Rebecca | | Jacob Brown and his assigns........ |
| | James, Catherine | | Samuel Fisher and wife............. |

## List of Indentures.

| Residence. | Occupation. | Term. | Amount. |
|---|---|---|---|
| | mill stone maker, have two shillings current money of Pa. each week during the first two years and six shillings money aforesaid each week for the last year (note 2, besides his old). | | |
| Philadelphia | Apprentice, taught the rope maker's trade, have one quarter evening schooling each winter of the term.[3] | 8 yrs., 3 mo. | |
| Hopewell twp., Cumberland co., W. Jersey. | Apprentice, have one years' schooling taught the farming business[3] | 4 yrs., 10 mo., 22 d. | |
| Philadelphia | Apprentice, taught to read in Bible, write a legible hand.[3] | 13 yrs. | £20. |
| Philadelphia | Apprentice[3] | 11 yrs., 1 mo., 17 d. | £18.3.4. |
| Philadelphia | Servant, taught to read[3] | 6 yrs. | £25. |
| New Town twp., Gloucester co., W. N. Jersey. | Servant, taught to read in Bible[3] | 10 yrs. | £20. |
| Springfield twp., Phila. co. | Servant (note 5, have £5 current money of this province and the best cow the master may then own). | 4 yrs. each. | £43.16.5 |
| Conecocheig, Frederick co., Md. | Servant (note 3, and one axe, one grubbing hoe, a maul and wedges, or 40 shillings in money). | 3 yrs. 6 mo. | £16.13. |
| Conecocheig, Frederick co., Md. | Servant (note 3, and one axe, grubbing hoe, maul and wedges, or 4 shillings in money. | 6 yrs. | £17.5.3. |
| Philadelphia | Servant[3] | 5 yrs. | £13. |
| Philadelphia | Apprentice, taught the coach harness making business, read in the Bible and write a legible hand in English.[3] | 14 yrs. | £12. |
| Philadelphia | Servant, taught to read in Bible, write a legible hand.[3] | 14 yrs. | £10. |
| Philadelphia | | 5 yrs. | £20. |
| Philadelphia | Servant[3] | 8 yrs., 4 mo | £24. |
| Lampeter twp., Lancaster co. | Servant[3] | 6 yrs. | £22. |
| Lampeter twp., Lancaster co. | Servant[3] | 4 yrs. | £22. |
| Lampeter twp., Lancaster co. | Servant[3] | 6 yrs. | £22. |
| Philadelphia | A free negro apprentice | 15 yrs., 2 mo. | £15. |
| Philadelphia | Servant, have one quarter's evening schooling each winter of the term.[3] | 10 yrs. | £10. |
| Philadelphia | Apprentice, taught to read in Bible, write a legible hand, housewifery and to sew.[3] | 5 yrs., 6 mo. 8 d. | |
| Philadelphia | | 3 yrs. | £10. |
| Philadelphia | Servant, taught to read Bible[3] | 4 yrs., 3 mo. | £4. |
| Philadelphia | Apprentice, taught art, trade and mystery of a cart and wheel wright, have two quarters' night schooling.[3] | 4 yrs. | |
| Philadelphia | Servant, taught art, trade and mystery of a biscuit maker, setting excepted.[3] | 2 yrs. | |
| Windsor twp., Berks co. | Servant (note 3, or £5 in money in lieu of the new suit). | 4 yrs. | £25. |
| Philadelphia | Servant, taught to read in Bible[3] | 3 yrs. | £5. |
| Philadelphia | Apprentice, taught housewifery, sew plain work.[3] | 3 yrs., 10 mo. | |

| Date. | Name. | From the Port of | To Whom Indentured. |
|---|---|---|---|
| 1771. Dec. 13th.... | Thomas, Heber | | George Pickering and his assigns.... |
| Dec. 14th.... | Sarah, a negro | | Richard Palmer and his assigns...... |
| | Balt, Anthony Walter | | William Ganet and his assigns...... |
| | Brown, John | | Moses Rankin and his assigns........ |
| | Wever, Magdalene | Rotterdam.. | Mark Bird and his assigns.......... |
| | Gale, Nicholas | | Charles Gough and his assigns....... |
| | Rausch, Johannes, Anna Cartraut, his wife, Angus, Anthony and Anna Curtie, their children. | Rotterdam.. | Mark Bird and his assigns.......... |
| | Schnyder, John Peter, Maria Catherine, his wife, Anna Catherine and Eliza Catherine their children. | Rotterdam.. | Mark Bird and his assigns.......... |
| | Weaver, Christian, Anna Timothea, his wife, and John Peter, their son. | Rotterdam.. | Mark Bird and his assigns.......... |
| | Emor, Andreas, and Elizabeth, his wife, Seneca and Anna Maria, their daughters. | Rotterdam.. | Mark Bird and his assigns.......... |
| | Rausch, Johannes Peter, and Anna Margaret, his wife. | Rotterdam.. | Mark Bird and his assigns.......... |
| | Hines, William | | Humphry Fullerton and his assigns... |

| RESIDENCE. | OCCUPATION. | TERM. | AMOUNT. |
|---|---|---|---|
| Philadelphia | Servant, taught the cabinet maker's trade, have two quarters' evening schooling, also time to go to evening school two other quarters, his guardian paying expense of schooling.[3] | 5 yrs., 6 mo. 17 d. | |
| Philadelphia | Servant[3] | 10 yrs. | |
| Willis twp., Chester co. | Servant, taught the farmer's business, have fifteen months' schooling.[3] | 14 yrs., 2 d. | |
| Philadelphia | Servant, taught art and mystery of a mariner (note 2, besides his old or £5 lawful money of Pa.). | 3 yrs. | |
| Union twp., Berks co. | Servant, taught to read[3] | 12 yrs. | £15. |
| Blockey twp., Phila. co. | Apprentice, taught art, trade and mystery of a farmer, to read in the Bible, write a legible hand and cypher as far as rule of three.[3] | 14 yrs. | |
| Union twp., Berks co. | Servants, to be found a log house to live in and a garden free of rent, to be employed in cutting cord wood, for which they are to be allowed 22d. per cord until they have earned the aforesaid £49.3, and if the master employ them about any other business he shall allow each of them 22d. and provisions each day, and when they shall have earned the £49.3 with the charge of their support this indenture to be void. | 7 yrs. each | £49.3. |
| Union twp., Berks co. | Servants, to be found a log house to dwell in and garden clear of rent, employed in cutting cord wood at 22d. per cord until they have earned said sum of £30.8, and provided the master shall at any time employ them about any other business, to allow them each 22d. per day, and when they shall have earned £30.8 then this indenture to be void. | 7 yrs. each. | £30.8. |
| Union twp., Berks co. | Servant, to be found a log house to dwell in and a garden rent free, employed at cutting cord wood at 22d. per cord until they have earned the said sum of £36.9, and provided the master shall at any time employ them about any other business, to allow each 22d. per day each day they are so employed, and when they shall have earned the £36.9 this indenture to be void. | 7 yrs. each. | £36.9. |
| Union twp., Berks co. | Servants, the condition of agreement as above. | 7 yrs. each. | £23.15. |
| Union twp., Berks co. | Servants, the condition of agreement as above. | 7 yrs. each. | £49.11.3. |
| Philadelphia | Aprentice, taught the joiner and chair maker's business, have | 5 yrs., 5 mo. 13 d. | |

| Date. | Name. | From the Port of | To Whom Indentured. |
|---|---|---|---|
| 1771.<br>Dec. 14th.... | | | |
| Dec. 16th.... | Smith, George | | Christian Percy and his assigns...... |
| | Drexell, David | Rotterdam.. | Joseph Wharton and his assigns...... |
| | Shouman, Hannapy | Rotterdam.. | Joseph Serman and his assigns....... |
| | Swanson, Nicholas | | Isaia Bell .......................... |
| | Schnyder, Andrew, and Anna Maria, his wife. | Rotterdam.. | Robert Morris and his assigns....... |
| | Milikin, Thomas | | William Scull ..................... |
| | McGuire, Rose (infant of six months). | | Jacob Hare and his assigns.......... |
| | Bellangee, John | | Henry Fisher and his assigns........ |
| | Burch, Mary | | James Berry and his assigns......... |
| Dec. 17th.... | Anderson, Archibald | | John Williamson and his assigns..... |
| | Leonard, Ruth | | Ann Bevan and her assigns.......... |
| | Koch, Johannes, and Maria Eliza, his wife. | Rotterdam... | John Innis and his assigns.......... |
| | Brown, Elizabeth | | Jonathan Hempster and his assigns... |
| Dec. 18th.... | Kennedy, Charles | | James Stuart and his assigns........ |
| 1771.<br>Dec. 18th.... | Albrecht, Frederick | | Valentine Haynes and his assigns.... |
| | Wigmore, John | | Capt. George May.................. |
| | McCormick, John | | Anthony Fortune and his assigns..... |
| | Warner, Hezekiah | | John Motchler and his assigns....... |

## List of Indentures.

| Residence. | Occupation. | Term. | Amount. |
|---|---|---|---|
| | three quarters' evening schooling (note 2, of value of £10 lawful money of Pa.). | | |
| Northern Liberties | Apprentice, taught the potter's trade, have four quarters' evening schooling.[3] | 6 yrs. | |
| Southwark | Servant[3] | 5 yrs., 6 mo. | £25. |
| Philadelphia | Servant (note 3, and one Spanish dollar). | 5 yrs., 6 mo. | £30. |
| Philadelphia | Apprentice, taught the cordwainer's trade (note 3, and the tools he works with). | 2 yrs., 11 mo. | |
| Philadelphia | Servants (note 5, each to have £10 lawful money of this province in lieu of freedom dues). | 3 yrs. each | £21.14. |
| Philadelphia | Apprentice, taught the art, trade and mystery of a chaise maker, read, write and cypher as far as through rule of three.[3] | 7 yrs., 2 mo. 2 w. | |
| | Apprentice, taught housewifery, sew plain work, knit, read in the Bible, write a legible hand. | 17 yrs., 6 mo. | |
| Lewis T., Sussex co., on Delaware | Apprentice, taught the art and mystery of a pilot in the river and bay of Delaware (note 2, besides his old, have 7s. 6d. for every vessel he shall pilot up said bay and river during the term). | 4 yrs., 8mo. 4 d. | |
| Radnor twp., Chester co. | Servant, have 21 months' schooling (note 5, have a young cow and calf and ewe and lamb, a pair of new sheets and freedom dues) | 12 yrs. | £0.10.0. |
| Southwark | Apprentice, taught the cooper's trade, have three quarters' evening schooling.[3] | 5 yrs., 7 mo. | |
| Philadelphia | Servant, taught housewifery, make plat hats, have three quarters' schooling.[3] | 5 yrs., 8 mo. 11 d. | |
| Near Conecocheig, Frederick Town, Frederick co., Md. | Servants (note 3, each) | 4 yrs. each. | £40.16.6. |
| Alloways Creek twp., Salem co., W. N. Jersey. | Servant[3] (in consideration of clothing her at this time and for the covenants following to be performed). | 1 yr., 6 mo. | |
| Philadelphia | Apprentice, serve on board the ship Polly and Peggy or any other vessel the master may choose belonging to this port, to be taught the art of a mariner and navigator (note 2 besides his old). | 3 yrs., 6 mo. | |
| Philadelphia | Apprentice, taught the cedar cooper's trade, taught to read and write Dutch perfectly, read in the English Bible (note 3, also a single set of tools). | 13 yrs. | |
| Philadelphia | Apprentice, taught the art and mystery of a mariner and navigation (note 2, besides his old, Davis's quadrant, a mariner's compass, scale and dividers). | 7 yrs. | |
| Philadelphia | | 7 yrs. | £11. |
| Philadelphia | Apprentice, taught to read in Bible, write a legible hand and cypher as far as through rule of three.[3] | 17 yrs., 1 mo. | |

| Date. | Name. | From the Port of | To Whom Indentured. |
|---|---|---|---|
| 1771. Dec. 18th... | Steynbecker, Johan Gotleib, and Margaret Catherine, his wife. | Rotterdam.. | Adam Holt and his assigns.......... |
| Dec. 19th.... | Steynbecker, Anna Mary .... | Rotterdam.. | Adam Holt and his assigns.......... |
| | Steynbecker, Anna Elizabeth. | Rotterdam.. | Adam Holt and his assigns.......... |
| Dec. 20th.... | Wolffe, Daniel ............. | Rotterdam.. | Michael Lapp and his assigns........ |
| Dec. 21st.... | Waltman, John Frederick ... | Rotterdam.. | William Craig and his assigns....... |
| | McCormick, William ............... | | Henry Ridgway and his assigns...... |
| | Roche, John ........................... | | Michael Swarts and his assigns...... |
| | Mitchell, Margaret ...................... | | Francis Fearis and his assigns........ |
| Dec. 23rd.... | McCulloch, Margaret .................. | | Emanuel Josiah and his assigns...... |
| | Andrews, John, Jr.................... | | James Nevill and his assigns........ |
| | Roach, Mary Dixon ..................... | | John Harken and his assigns......... |
| | Roach, Mary Dixon ..................... | | Capt. Francis Fearis and his assigns.. |
| | Gilbert, Samuel ........................ | | Jacob Vansciver and his assigns..... |
| | Benckler, John ........................ | | Jacob Doubedissell and his assigns... |
| | Reisdorf, Peter ............. | Rotterdam.. | William Cox and his assigns........ |
| Dec. 24th.... | Hearsch, Leonard ........... ........... | | Michael App and his assigns........ |
| | Baker, John William ....... | London .... | Owen Biddle and his assigns.......... |
| | Roch, Mary Dixon..................... | | James Hume and his assigns........ |
| | Self, John ................. | | Cornelius Cooper and his assigns..... |
| Dec. 26th.... | Ecksteen, Anna Margt....... | Rotterdam.. | Capt. James Miller and his assigns... |
| | Lout, Jacob ............................ | | Peter Mahrling and his assigns..... |
| Dec. 27th.... | Thomas, Hezekiah ..................... | | Lambert Wilmore and wife.......... |
| | Reily, John, Jr..................... | | Stephen Paschall and his assigns..... |
| | Yertz, Ann Elizabeth........ | Rotterdam.. | David Thomson and his assigns..... |
| | Smith, John ........................... | | William West, Jr., and his assigns... |
| | Carlos, Joseph and Rozenberger, George. | | William West, Jr., and his assigns... |
| | Baptisto, John ........................ | | William West, Jr., and his assigns... |
| Dec. 28th.... | Stuart, Elinor ....................... | | John Power and his assigns.......... |
| | Stuart, Elinor ....................... | | John Cary and his assigns.......... |
| | Landes, Henry ........................ | | William Richards ................... |

| Residence. | Occupation. | Term. | Amount. |
|---|---|---|---|
| Oxford twp., Phila. co. | Servants (note 2, besides their old). | 6 yrs. each. | £ 40. 11. |
| Oxford twp., Phila. co. | Servant, taught to read and write perfectly and allowed time to go to the minister to receive the sacrament.[3] | 12 yrs. | £ 10. |
| Oxford twp., Phila. co. | Servant, taught to read and write perfectly and allowed time to go to the minister to receive sacrament.[3] | 10 yrs. | £ 10. |
| East Whitland, Chester co. | Servant[3] | 4 yrs. | £ 23. 10. 2. |
| Philadelphia | Servant, have one quarter evening schooling.[3] | 8 yrs., 7mo. | £ 23. |
| Springfield twp., Burlington co., West Jersey. | Servant[3] | 4 yrs. | £ 15. 6. 3. |
| Plumsted twp., Bucks co. | Servant, found all necessaries. | 1 yr., 2 mo. | £ 3. 10. |
| Philadelphia | | 4 yrs. | £ 15. 10. |
| Philadelphia | | 3 yrs. | £ 10. |
| Northern Liberties | | 7 yrs. | £ 16. |
| Philadelphia | | 4 yrs. | £ 15. |
| Philadelphia | | 4 yrs. | £ 15. |
| Northern Liberties | Apprentice, taught the cordwainer's trade, have one quarter evening schooling.[3] | 5 yrs., 28 d. | |
| Philadelphia | Apprentice, taught the butcher's trade (note 1, or £ 5 in money). | 2 yrs., 3 mo. | |
| Bristol twp., Bucks co. | Servant (note 2, besides his old) | 2 yrs., 6 mo. | £ 18. |
| Northern Liberties | Apprentice, taught house carpenter's trade. found meat, drink, washing, lodging and working apparel, and at expiration have one jack plane, one smoothing plane, fore plane and handsaw. | 2 yrs., 6 mo. | |
| Philadelphia | Servant[3] | 12 yrs. | £ 17. 5. 5. |
| Philadelphia | | 4 yrs. | £ 15. |
| Philadelphia | | 6 yrs. | £ 10. |
| Philadelphia | Servant[3] | 7 yrs. | £ 30. |
| Philadelphia | Apprentice, taught the tailor's trade, have three quarters' schooling.[3] | 7 yrs., 4 mo. | |
| Philadelphia | Apprentice, taught the mantua maker's trade, read in Bible, write a legible hand, time to go to school two quarters, her guardian paying expense of schooling.[3] | 5 yrs., 1 mo. 11 d. | |
| Philadelphia | Apprentice, taught the cutler's trade, found meat, drink, washing and lodging. | 4 yrs., 10 mo. | |
| Southwark | Servant[3] | 8 yrs. | £ 25. |
| Philadelphia | Servant[1] | 4 yrs. each. | £ 20 each |
| Philadelphia | Servants[1] | | |
| Philadelphia | Servant[1] | 4 yrs. | £ 18. |
| Philadelphia | Apprentice, taught housewifery, sew plain work, read in Bible, write a legible hand.[3] | 7 yrs., 8 mo. | |
| Southwark | | 7 yrs., 8 mo. | £ 0. 5. |
| Philadelphia | Apprentice, taught to read, write and cypher, to understand the rule of three and the business of an apothecary and as much Latin as will qualify him for | 5 yrs., 10 mo., 19 d. | |

| Date. | Name. | From the Port of | To Whom Indentured. |
|---|---|---|---|
| 1771. Dec. 28th.... | | | |
| | Ernst, Antonio | | Hugh Means and his assigns........ |
| | Ernst, Antonio | | Samuel Lyons and his assigns........ |
| | Fullerton, Mary | | Thomas Craig and wife............ |
| Dec. 30th.... | Hess, Eve | | John Christian Lesher and his assigns. |
| | Teet, Benjamin | | James Pickering and his assigns...... |
| | Nowlan, John | | John Little and his assigns.......... |
| | Keeler, Nicholas, and Maria Clara, his wife. | Rotterdam.. | John Cudenheimer and his assigns.... |
| | Keeler, Nicholas, Jr.......... | Rotterdam.. | John Cudenheimer ................ |
| | Keeler, Susanna Margaret ... | Rotterdam.. | John Cudenheimer and his assigns.... |
| | Wilcocks, Peter | | James Whitcall and his assigns....... |
| Dec. 31st.... | Lemonin, Anna Cathe....... | | Michl. Taylor and his assigns........ |
| | Shourer, John, Jr............ | | Peter Shourer and his assigns........ |
| | Shefferin, Ann Mary......... | | Joseph Johnson and his assigns....... |
| | King, George, Jr............. | | Jacob Cline and his assigns.......... |
| | Winey, Juliana | | Catherine Carpenter and her assigns. |
| 1772. Jan. 1st..... | Wilkins, Joshua | | John Norris and his assigns.......... |
| | Shireman, John George...... | Rotterdam.. | Bentick Kneiderling and his assigns.. |
| | Shireman, Derval | | Bentick Kneiderling and his assigns.. |
| | Shireman, Elizabeth ......... | Rotterdam.. | Joseph Russell and his assigns....... |
| | Weberin, Mary Elizabeth ... | | Isaac Taylor and his assigns........ |
| Jan. 2nd..... | Mulloney Eleanor ......... | | Benjamin Poultney and his assigns... |
| | Koch, Johannes, and Mary Eliza., his wife. | | John Wister and his assigns......... |
| | McDaniel, George | | Patrick Hogan and his assigns....... |

## List of Indentures.

| Residence. | Occupation. | Term. | Amount. |
|---|---|---|---|
| | that business, at expiration have two complete suits of apparel, one whereof to be new. | | |
| Philadelphia | Servant[3] | 4 yrs. | £ 20. |
| Firmanner twp., Cumberland co. | | 4 yrs. | £ 10. |
| Philadelphia | Apprentice, taught housewifery, sew and knit, read in the Bible, write a legible hand.[3] | 8 yrs., 8 mo. 22 d. | |
| Upper Dublin twp., Phila. co. | Servant, taught housewifery, sew, knit and spin, read in Bible.[3] | 9 yrs., 6 mo. | 5/. |
| Philadelphia | Apprentice, taught the tailor's trade, have six months' evening schooling and found all necessaries. | 4 yrs., 9 mo. 12 d. | |
| Philadelphia | Servant, found all necessaries. | 1 yr., 1 mo. | £ 4. 3. |
| Philadelphia | Servants (note 3, each). | 6 yrs. each. | £ 49. |
| Philadelphia | Servant, taught to read and write[3]. | 17 yrs. | £ 15. |
| Philadelphia | Servant, taught to read, write and spin.[3] | 16 yrs., 6 mo. | £ 5. |
| Philadelphia | Apprentice, taught the cordwainer's trade found sufficient meat, drink, washing and lodging and apparel, shirts and stockings excepted, which the father is to find, and pay expense of making his outside apparel and at expiration have one complete new suit of apparel. | 5 yrs., 9 mo. 10 d. | |
| Northern Liberties | | 4 yrs. | £ 4. |
| Bristol twp., Phila. co. | Servant | 8 yrs., 8 mo. | £ 30. |
| Southwark | Servant | 6 yrs. | £ 13. |
| Philadelphia | Apprentice, taught the tailor's trade, read and write the German language perfectly.[3] | 13 yrs. | |
| Philadelphia | Apprentice, have two quarters' night schooling, taught housewifery.[1] | 11 yrs., 6 mo. | |
| Northern Liberties | Aprentice, taught the shipwright's trade, have three quarters' evening schooling (note 5, and have £ 6 lawful money of Pa. and the tools he works with). | 5 yrs., 10 mo., 11 d. | |
| Maxatawney twp., Berks co. | Servant[3] | 5 yrs., 6 mo. | £ 40. |
| Maxatawney twp., Berks co. | Servant, taught to read in Bible, write a legible hand, found all necessaries, shall not have freedom dues at expiration neither be subject to the penalty inflicted by act of assembly on servants for absenting themselves from their master's service. | 5 yrs., 6 mo. | |
| Philadelphia | Servant[3] | 7 yrs. | £ 27. 10. |
| Pennsborough twp., Chester co. | Servant[3] | 12 yrs., 6 mo., 17 d. | £ 17. |
| Philadelphia | | 4 yrs. | £ 14. |
| Philadelphia | Servants (note 3, each). | 4 yrs. | £ 42. 0. 6. |
| Philadelphia | Apprentice, taught the tallow-chandler and soap boiler's trade, read in Bible, write a legible hand and cypher as far as through rule of three.[3] | 12 yrs., 3 mo., 18 d. | |

| Date. | Name. | From the Port of | To Whom Indentured. |
|---|---|---|---|
| 1772.<br>Jan. 2nd..... | Koch, Johannes, and Mary Eliza., his wife. | .......... | John Templer and his assigns........ |
| Jan. 3rd..... | Sullivan, Joan .................. | .......... | William Norton and his assigns...... |
| | Archdeacon, John .......... | .......... | Brent Spencer and his assigns........ |
| Jan. 4th..... | Michelin, Maria Catherine... | .......... | Henry Leisey and his assigns......... |
| | Green, William ............ | .......... | John Leaby and his assigns.......... |
| Jan. 6th..... | Suterin, Barbara ............ | .......... | Mary Weavan and her assigns...... |
| | Hyte, Valentine ............ | .......... | Jacob Paul and his assigns.......... |
| | Wall, Martin ............... | .......... | Adam Stricker .................... |
| | O'Scullion, Hannah ......... | .......... | Hannah Christie and her assigns..... |
| | Sartoriusin, Christiana ...... | Rotterdam.. | Hugh Roberts and his assigns........ |
| | Bruner, John Adam ......... | .......... | George Heyl and his assigns........ |
| | Finley, Mary ............... | .......... | John Adam Schwaab and his assigns. |
| | Graafin, Maria Catherine ... | .......... | Peter Lowr and his assigns.......... |
| | McAllister, Alexander ....... | .......... | Joseph McCarrol and his assigns..... |
| | Enders, Paulus and Maria Eliza., his wife. | .......... | Azariah Dunham and his assigns..... |
| Jan. 7th..... | Enders, John Peter ............ | .......... | Azariah Dunham and his assigns..... |
| | Archdeacon, John .............. | .......... | John Cottringer and his assigns...... |
| | Dressler, Michael ............ | .......... | Joseph Stainsbury and his assigns.... |
| | Tripley, Casper ............... | .......... | James Webb, Jr., and his assigns.... |
| Jan. 8th..... | West, John .................... | .......... | William Lane and his assigns....... |
| | Minheer, Anna Elizabeth ...... | .......... | Michael Bower and his assigns...... |
| | Minheer, George .............. | .......... | Michael Bower and his assigns...... |
| | Fleck, John ................... | .......... | Andrew Alster and his assigns....... |
| | Williams, Hannah ............. | .......... | Robert Levess and his assigns........ |
| | Joost, Johan Nicholas, and Anna Eve, his wife. | Rotterdam.. | John Leshert and his assigns........ |
| | Efert, Martin, and Anna, his wife. | Rotterdam.. | John Leshert and his assigns........ |
| | Effert, Martin ............. | Rotterdam.. | John Leshert and his assigns........ |

## List of Indentures.

| Residence. | Occupation. | Term. | Amount. |
|---|---|---|---|
| Earl twp., Lancaster co. | | 4 yrs. | £42.0.6. |
| Philadelphia | Servant | 4 yrs. | £12. |
| Philadelphia | Servant, taught the tailor and harness maker's business.[3] | 4 yrs. | £20. |
| Hill twp., Bucks co. | | 4 yrs., 6 mo. | £24. |
| Moyamensing twp., Phila. co. | Apprentice, taught the art and mystery of husbandry and farming, read in Bible, write a legible hand and cypher as far as rule of three.[3] | 19 yrs., 9 mo., 18 d. | |
| Philadelphia | Apprentice | 7 yrs., 4 mo. 10 d. | £5. |
| Northern Liberties | Servant | 4 yrs. | £7.10. |
| Northern Liberties | Apprentice, taught the art, trade and mystery of a blacksmith, have three quarters' night schooling.[1] | 4 yrs., 10 mo., 23 d. | |
| Philadelphia | Apprentice | 3 yrs. | 5/. |
| Philadelphia | Servant[3] | 4 yrs. | £24.15. |
| Philadelphia | Apprentice, taught the leather breeches maker and skinner's trade, have six months' evening schooling.[3] | 5 yrs., 11 mo., 24 d. | |
| Northern Liberties | Apprentice, taught housewifery and spinning, read in Bible correctly (note 2, besides the old, or £5 lawful money). | 5 yrs., 9 mo. | |
| Hanover twp., Phila. co. | Servant[3] | 5 yrs., 6 mo. | £25.6.6. |
| Sadsbury twp., Lancaster co. | Apprentice, taught the business of a farmer (note 2, besides his old) | 2 yrs., 6 mo. | |
| New Brunswick, Middlesex co., E. Jersey. | Servants (note 3, each) | 5 yrs. each. | £35.11. |
| New Brunswick, Middlesex co., E. Jersey. | Servant, taught to read in Bible, write a legible hand in English[3]. | 12 yrs. | £16. |
| Philadelphia | Servant, taught the tailor's trade[3]. | 3 yrs., 11 mo., 26 d. | £15. |
| Philadelphia | Apprentice, taught to read in Bible, write a legible hand and cypher as far as and through rule of three, and at expiration have two complete suits of apparel, one whereof to be new. | 4 yrs. | |
| Lancaster | Servant[3] | 3 yrs., 11 mo., 3 d. | £20. |
| Woolwich twp., Gloucester co., W. Jersey. | Servant | 7 yrs. | £10. |
| Philadelphia | Servant[3] | 3 yrs. | £12. |
| Philadelphia | Servant, have two years' Dutch schooling.[3] | 13 yrs. | £8.6.5. |
| Philadelphia | Apprentice, taught the cordwainer's trade, have three quarters' evening schooling (note 3, also a kit of tools). | 7 yrs. | |
| Hamilton twp., Northampton co. | Servant | 5 yrs. | £14.10. |
| Oley, Berks co. | Servant (note 2, besides their old). | 5 yrs. each. | £49.17.2. |
| Oley, Berks co. | Servant (note 3, each and a pot and frying pan). | 5 yrs. each. | £40.17.6. |
| Oley, Berks co. | Servant, taught to read in Bible and write a legible hand, and at expiration have legal freedom dues. | 13 yrs. | £6. |

| Date. | Name. | From the Port of | To Whom Indentured. |
|---|---|---|---|
| 1772. Jan. 8th | Prost, Francisco, and Nicholas Bizo. | | James Potter and his assigns |
| | Thompson, Cornelius | | Paul Fooks and his assigns |
| Jan. 9th | Prost, Francisco | | George Lattimore and his assigns |
| | Jones, Thomas | | James Ewing and his assigns |
| | Saunders, Jacob | Rotterdam | Joseph Frazer and his assigns |
| | Rook Margaret | | William Smith and his assigns |
| Jan. 10th | Hoffman, Francis | Rotterdam | Thomas Roberts and his assigns |
| | Black, James, Jr. | | Gunning Bedford and his assigns |
| | Scheaffer, Catherine | | Francis Lesher and his assigns |
| | Kuch, John Peter | | Henry Kurtz and his assigns |
| | Wilbert, Henry, and Maria, his wife. | Rotterdam | Samuel Wallace and his assigns |
| | Schnyder, Johannes, and Anna Catherine, his wife. | Rotterdam | Samuel Wallace and his assigns |
| | Schnyder, Johannes, and Anna Catherine, his wife. | | John Loudon and his assigns |
| | Schnyder, John Ludwig | | Samuel Wallace and his assigns |
| Jan. 11th | Schnyder, John Ludwig | | John Loudon and his assigns |
| | Long, Jacob | | Joseph Job and his assigns |
| | Butcher, Benjamin | | Abraham Kentzing and his assigns |
| | Erigh Zachariah, and Ann Catherine, his wife. | Rotterdam | Samuel Wallace and his assigns |
| | Erigh, Christopher | Rotterdam | Samuel Wallace and his assigns |
| | Erighin, Sophia | Rotterdam | Samuel Wallace and his assigns |
| Jan. 13th | Streiff, David | | George Knor and his assigns |
| | Mommaton, William | | Thomas Renard and his assigns |
| | Ring, Benjamin | | Christian Rudolph and his assigns |
| | Coates, William | | William Inglefreid and his assigns |

---

[1] To be found all necessaries and at the expiration have freedom dues.
[2] To be found all necessaries and at the expiration have one new suit of apparel.
[3] To be found all necessaries and at the expiration have two complete suits of apparel, one whereof to be new.

## List of Indentures.

| Residence. | Occupation. | Term. | Amount. |
|---|---|---|---|
| Antrim twp., Cumberland co. | Servant[3] | 4 yrs. each. | £30. |
| Philadelphia | Apprentice, taught to read in Bible, write a legible hand, cypher as far as and through the rule of three.[3] | 8 yrs., 7 mo. | |
| Jacobs Swamp, Bedford co. | | 4 yrs. | £15. |
| Hallam twp., York co. | Servant[3] | 2 yrs., 9 mo. 13 d. | £28. |
| Philadelphia | Servant[3] | 6 yrs. | £30. |
| Philadelphia | Apprentice, taught housewifery, sew plain work and knit, read in Bible perfectly, write a legible hand.[3] | 7 yrs., 1 mo. 7 d. | |
| Charles Town twp., Chester co. | Servant, taught the farming business, read in Bible, write a legible hand.[3] | 13 yrs., 8 mo. | £10. |
| Philadelphia | Apprentice, taught the house carpenter trade, found meat, drink, washing, lodging and shoes. | 6 yrs., 2 mo. | |
| Philadelphia | Apprentice, taught to read in Bible, write a legible hand, sew, knit and spin, also housewifery.[3] | 6 yrs. | |
| Philadelphia | Servant | 6 yrs. | £23.13. |
| Philadelphia | Servant (note 2, besides their old). | 5 yrs. each. | £48. |
| Philadelphia | Servant (note 3, each). | 5 yrs., 6 mo. each. | £52. |
| Buffalo Valley, Berks co. | | 5 yrs., 6 mo. each. | £52. |
| Philadelphia | Servant, found all necessaries and by mutual agreement not to have freedom dues. | 5 yrs., 6 mo. | |
| Buffalo Valley, Berks co. | | 5 yrs., 6 mo. | £0.5.0. |
| Philadelphia | Apprentice, taught the stocking weaver's trade, have six months' evening schooling (note 3, of the value of £10). | 8 yrs., 11 mo., 14 d. | |
| Philadelphia | Servant[3] | 5 yrs. | £26. |
| Philadelphia | Servant (note 3, and £22 current money of this province, each). | 5 yrs. each. | £8.11.5. |
| | Servant[3] | 8 yrs., 4 mo. 27 d. | £25. |
| | Servant[3] | 10 yrs., 6 mo., 18 d. | £15. |
| Philadelphia | Apprentice, taught the loaf bread baker's business and found all necessaries. | 7 mo. | |
| Philadelphia | Servant | 2 yrs. | £10. |
| Philadelphia | Apprentice, taught the cordwainer's trade, read in Bible, write a legible hand and cypher as far as and through the rule of three (note 3, and of the value of £10 lawful money of Pa.). | 11 yrs., 5 mo. | |
| Philadelphia | Servant, have meat, drink, washing, lodging, one new coat, pair breeches and also 20/ each month during 12 months of said term. | 1 yr., 1 mo. | £4.10.9. |

[4] To be found all necessaries and at the expiration have two complete suits of apparel, one whereof to be new, and 40s. in money.

[5] At expiration have two complete suits of apparel, one whereof to be new.

| Date. | Name. | From the Port of | To Whom Indentured. |
|---|---|---|---|
| 1772. Jan. 14th | Powell, Ann | | John Bartram, Jr., and his assigns |
| | Maffet, Mary | | William Shippen |
| Jan. 15th | Williams, William | | Conrad Alster and his assigns |
| | Wheeler, John | | John Little and his assigns |
| | Mitchell, Margaret, alias Davenport. | | Thomas Brown and his assigns |
| | Booz, David | | William Cox and his assigns |
| | Ladbroke, David | Rotterdam | Jacob Dedrick and his assigns |
| | Ladbroke, Maria Elizabeth | Rotterdam | Jacob Dedrick and his assigns |
| Jan. 16th | Green, Thomas, Jr. | | Simon Fitzgerald and his assigns |
| Jan. 17th | Fortune, Thomas | | William Weston and his assigns |
| | Clammer, John | | Peter Banot and his assigns |
| | O'Scullion, Hannah | | Andrew Overturf and his assigns |
| Jan. 20th | Wicks, Samuel | | Anthony Fortune |
| | Roberts, Robert | | Samuel Baker and his assigns |
| | Templer, Margaret | | Joseph Falconer and his assigns |
| | Monjoy, John | | William Niles and his assigns |

## List of Indentures.

| Residence. | Occupation. | Term. | Amount. |
|---|---|---|---|
| Kingsessing twp., Phila. co. | Apprentice, taught housewifery, sew, knit and spin, read in Bible and write a legible hand (note 3 and a pair of stays). | 7 yrs., 2 mo. 20 d. | |
| Philadelphia | Apprentice, taught to sew and mark well and read and write well. | 5 yrs., 1 mo. 5 d. | |
| Philadelphia | Apprentice, taught the cordwainer's trade, have two quarters' winter evening schooling (note 3, and the necessary tools for a cordwainer). | 5 yrs., 3 mo. | |
| Philadelphia | | 2 yrs., 10 mo. | |
| Philadelphia | Servant[5] | 3 yrs., 3 mo. 13 d. | |
| Philadelphia | Apprentice, taught the rush bottom chair maker's business, read in Bible well, write a good legible hand and common arithmetic as far as rule of three and at expiration have legal freedom dues, said Cox to endeavor to instruct him in the Windsor chair making business. | 12 yrs., 1 mo., 13 d. | |
| Newtown twp., Gloucester co., W. Jersey. | Servant[3] | 2 yrs., 6 mo. | £ 10. |
| Newtown twp., Gloucester co., W. Jersey. | Servant, taught to read in Bible, write a legible hand (note 3, and a new spinning wheel). | 10 yrs., 1 mo., 24 d. | £ 10. |
| Philadelphia | Apprentice, taught the cordwainer's trade, read, write and cypher as far as and through the rule of three, allowed time to go to evening school six months, the father paying the expense of schooling and not to be assigned to any person without consent of his father.[3] | 9 yrs., 11 mo. | |
| Philadelphia | Servant[5] | 2 yrs., 3 mo. | £ 6.16.9. |
| Southwark | Apprentice, taught the potter's business (note 2, besides his old and of the value of £ 10 lawful money of Pa.). | 2 yrs. | |
| Philadelphia | Apprentice, taught the leather breeches maker's business (note 5, have clothes to the value of £ 3 money of Pa.). | 2 yrs., 2 mo. | |
| Philadelphia | Servant[5] | 3 yrs. | £ 22. 11. |
| Philadelphia | Apprentice | 7 yrs. | 5/. |
| Southwark | Apprentice, taught housewifery, sew plain work, allowed time to attend the minister to be prepared for the sacrament, if the parties disagree and the father pay said Falconer £ 5.10 within six months from this date he agrees to deliver her to her father (note 2, besides her old). | 3 yrs., 2 mo. | |
| Philadelphia | Apprentice, to have broad cloth outside apparel of 18/ per yard for his freedom dues. | 3 yrs., 6 mo. | £ 5. |

| Date. | Name. | From the | To Whom Indentured |
|---|---|---|---|
| 1772. Jan. 20th.... | Reardon, Ann | | Lawrence Upman and his assigns..... |
| Jan. 21st.... | Brown, Mary | | George Leib and his assigns......... |
| Jan. 22nd.... | Valentine, Henry | | James Hartley and his assigns....... |
| | Smith, John | | John Elton and his assigns.......... |
| Jan. 23rd.... | Simmerman, Henry | Rotterdam.. | George Epley and his assigns........ |
| | Spell, George Henry | Rotterdam.. | Philip Moses and his assigns......... |
| | Pearson, John | | George Goodwin ................... |
| | Keffer, John | | Benjamin Kendall and his assigns.... |
| | Stetzer, William | | Joseph Master and his assigns........ |
| | Allison, Margaret | | Thomas Boyd and his assigns........ |
| | Davis Sarah | | William Logan and his assigns....... |
| | Shot, John | Rotterdam.. | John Reinhart and his assigns........ |
| | Katz, Jonas | | James Barnes and his assigns........ |
| 1772. Jan. 24th.... | Davenport, Enoch | | Capt. Peter Osborne................ |
| | Gapen, Robert Bonell | | John Dunlap and his assigns......... |
| | Mingers, Jacob | Rotterdam.. | Christian Caufman and his assigns... |
| | McGlaughlan, Peter | | David McCollough and his assigns... |
| | Scheibly, Hans Jacob, and Anna Maria, his wife. | Rotterdam.. | Thomas Gilpin and his assigns...... |
| | Scheibly, Hans Jacob, and Anna Maria, his wife. | Rotterdam.. | Geo. Gilpin and his assigns......... |
| | Scheibly, Jacob | | Thomas Gilpin and his assigns....... |
| | Scheibly, Jacob | | George Gilpin and his assigns....... |

## List of Indentures.

| Residence. | Occupation. | Term. | Amount. |
|---|---|---|---|
| Northern Liberties | Apprentice, taught housewifery and to sew, read and write and have legal freedom dues. | 9 yrs., 6 mo. | £ 8. |
| Northern Liberties | Apprentice, taught housewifery, sew, knit and spin, read well in Bible.[5] | 4 yrs., 8 mo. 20 d. | |
| Philadelphia | Apprentice, taught the art and mystery of merchandize.[5] | 7 yrs. | £ 0. 5. 0. |
| Philadelphia | Apprentice, taught the art, trade and mystery of a joiner, found meat, drink, washing and lodging, have three quarters' night schooling and found apparel the four last years, and at expiration have freedom dues. | 7 yrs. | 5/. |
| Philadelphia | Servant[3] | 4 yrs. | £ 23. |
| Philadelphia | Servant, have three quarters' evening schooling.[3] | 11 yrs. | £ 10. 14. |
| Philadelphia | Apprentice, taught the ropemaker's business.[3] | 4 yrs. | |
| Philadelphia | Apprentice, taught the cordwainer's business (note 2, besides his old). | 10 yrs., 5 mo., 17 d. | |
| Philadelphia | Apprentice, taught the cooper's trade, have three quarters' night schooling.[3] | 3 yrs., 6 mo. 4 d. | |
| Allens twp., Northampton co. | Apprentice, taught housewifery, sew, knit, spin, read in Bible, write a legible hand, cypher as far as and through rule of three (note 3, and £ 8 lawful money of Pa.). | 7 yrs. | |
| W. Nantmeal twp., Chester co. | Apprentice, taught housewifery, sew, knit, spin, read in Bible, write a legible hand.[3] | 11 yrs., 6 mo. | |
| Philadelphia | Servant, have one shilling each week during the term (note 3, or £ 10 in money of this province). | 4 yrs. | £ 30. |
| Philadelphia | Apprentice, taught the painter's and glazier's business, have one quarter schooling each year (note 5, have £ 10 lawful money of Pa.). | 5 yrs., 6 mo. 6 d. | |
| Philadelphia | Apprentice, taught the art and mystery of a mariner and navigation, found meat, drink, washing and lodging. | 6 yrs. | |
| Philadelphia | Servant | 4 yrs. 2 mo. 3 w. | £ 25. |
| Carnarvan twp., Lancaster co. | Servant (note 3, the breeches to be of buck skin, worth 30 shillings money of Pa., also one heifer with a calf). | 5 yrs. | £ 43. 11. 10. |
| Philadelphia | Apprentice, taught the art and mystery of a mariner and navigation.[3] | 3 yrs. | |
| Philadelphia | Servants (note 2, besides their old). | 6 yrs. each. | £ 39. 1. 1. |
| Alexandria, Va. | | 6 yrs. each. | £ 39. 1. 1. |
| Philadelphia | Servant, taught to read in Bible[3]. | 14 yrs. | £ 10. |
| Alexandria, Va. | | 14 yrs. | £ 10. |

| Date. | Name. | From the Port of | To Whom Indentured. |
|---|---|---|---|
| 1772. Jan. 24th | Willis, Rebecca | | George Aston and his assigns |
| | Willis, Rebecca | | Morris Philips and his assigns |
| | Mercer, William | | Robert Parish and his assigns |
| Jan. 25th | Vint, Joshua | | Peter January |
| | Johnston, John | | Renier Lukens |
| | Wilhelm, Catherine | Rotterdam | Henry Lisle and his assigns |
| | Wilhelm, John Henry | Rotterdam | Henry Lisle and his assigns |
| | McGwirin, Daniel | Ireland | John Montgomery and his assigns |
| Jan. 27th | Myers, John Philip | | Henry Schwalbeck and his assigns |
| Jan. 28th | Mahull, Sarah | Newry | William McDowell and his assigns |
| | Dobbins, Hugh | | Joseph Bolton and his assigns |
| Jan. 29th | Thomas, Ruth | | William McClay |
| | Welch, Mary | | Charles Lyon, Jr., and wife |
| | Ryan, Grace | | Joseph Brown and his assigns |
| | Steel, Mary | | Richard Mason, his heirs and assigns. |
| | Smith, Mary | | Major Walbron and his assigns |
| | Smith, Mary | | Matthew Pratt and his assigns |
| | Yeoman, Seth | | Hugh King and his assigns |
| Jan. 31st | Duff, William | | James Huston and his assigns |
| Feb. 1st | Snowhill, John George | | Henry Bushart and his assigns |
| Feb. 3rd | Duff, John | | Samuel Duffield and Sharpe Delaney. |
| | Clemer, Henry | | Jacob Bristol and his assigns |
| Feb. 4th | Esteue, Michael, alias Stephen | | Thomas Harrison and his assigns |
| Feb. 5th | Vint, John | Ireland | Joseph Ogden and his assigns |

| Residence. | Occupation. | Term. | Amount. |
|---|---|---|---|
| Philadelphia | Apprentice, taught housewifery, sew, knit and spin, read in Bible, write a legible hand.[3] | 12 yrs. 7 mo. | |
| Radnor twp., Chester co. | | 12 yrs. 7 mo. | 5/. |
| Philadelphia | Apprentice, taught the art and mystery of a wheat fan maker, have three quarters' evening schooling.[3] | 4 yrs. | |
| Philadelphia | Servant (note 5, have £5 in lieu of freedom dues). | 2 yrs., 6 mo. | £11. |
| Upper Dublin twp., Phila. co. | Servant (note 5, but no freedom dues). | 2 yrs. | £7.14. |
| Philadelphia | Servant[3] | 6 yrs. | £19. |
| Philadelphia | Servant, taught to read in Bible, write a legible hand.[3] | 17 yrs. | £1. |
| | Servant[5] | 3 yrs. | £14. |
| Philadelphia | Apprentice, taught the cedar cooper's trade, have one quarter's evening schooling.[3] | 3 yrs., 6 mo. | |
| Haddonfield, Gloucester co., W. Jersey. | Servant[3] | 3 yrs. | £9. |
| Philadelphia | Apprentice, found all necessaries except apparel, permitted to go to night school at the father or his friend's expense. | 4 yrs., 6 mo. 5 d. | |
| Whiteclay Creek Hundred, New-Castle co., and his assigns. | Apprentice, taught housewifery and spin.[3] | 2 yrs., 1 mo. 15 d. | |
| Philadelphia | Apprentice, taught housewifery and spin, read in Bible, write a legible hand.[3] | 5 yrs., 10 mo., 9 d. | |
| Philadelphia | Servant | 4 yrs. | £15. |
| Northern Liberties | Apprentice, taught housewifery, sew plain work, read in Bible, write a legible hand (note 3, and £7 current money of this province). | 6 yrs., 2 mo. | |
| Philadelphia | Apprentice, taught housewifery, sew plain work, have six months' schooling.[3] | 3 yrs. | |
| Philadelphia | | 3 yrs. | 5/. |
| Southwark | Apprentice, found meat, drink, washing and lodging, and make up to his master any loss of time occasioned by his sickness or indisposition. | 8 mo. | |
| Philadelphia | | 4 yrs. | £15.15 |
| Philadelphia | Apprentice, taught the cordwainer's trade, have four quarters' day schooling and four quarters' evening schooling.[3] | 9 yrs. | |
| Philadelphia | Apprentice, taught the art and mystery of an apothecary and druggist, found meat, drink, washing and lodging and have one year's schooling. | 4 yrs. 6 mo. 10 mo., 10 d. | |
| Philadelphia | Apprentice, taught the loaf bread baker's business, have three quarters' schooling (note 2, or £8 in cash). | 4 yrs. | |
| Philadelphia | | 4 yrs. | £25. |
| Philadelphia | Servant (note 5, have £5 current money of this province in lieu of freedom dues). | 2 yrs., 6 mo. | £10. |

| Date. | Name. | From the Port of | To Whom Indentured. |
|---|---|---|---|
| 1772. | McQuaters, Hugh | Ireland | Capt. David Kennedy and his assigns. |
| Feb. 5th | McQuaters, Hugh | | Capt. David McCullough and his assigns. |
| | Lupprian, John | | John Evans and his assigns. |
| | Lupprian, John | | John Evans. |
| | Kribbs, John Henry | | Christian Purcy and wife. |
| Feb. 6th | Tomlinson, William | | Andrew Carson and his assigns. |
| | Henrickson, Peter | | John Hyde and his assigns. |
| | Ryan, Grace | | George Casner and his assigns. |
| | Shubert, Daniel | | Philip Heyl and his assigns. |
| Feb. 7th | Bender, Mary | | John Beck and his assigns. |
| | Sullivan Timothy | | Lamb Torbert and his assigns. |
| | Self, John | | John Facey and his assigns. |
| | Miller, John, and Mary, his wife, and Ursula, their daughter. | Rotterdam | Jacob Hahn and his assigns. |
| Feb. 8th | Power, Nicholas | | William Fustin and his assigns. |
| Feb. 10th | Potts, John | | Henry Potts and his assigns. |
| | Forrest, Thomas | | Alexander Kidd. |
| | Gyler, John | | Christian Yost and his assigns. |
| | Darcy, Mary Ann | | John Moore and his assigns. |
| | Overstake, Jacob | | John Barnhill. |
| | Nail, Henry | | Henry Cress and his assigns. |
| Feb. 11th | Cornish, Robert, Jr. | | John Hood and his assigns. |

## List of Indentures.

| Residence. | Occupation. | Term. | Amount. |
|---|---|---|---|
| Philadelphia | | 2 yrs., 6 mo. | £ 7. 10. |
| Philadelphia | Apprentice taught art and mystery of navigation and a mariner.³ | 2 yrs., 6 mo. | £ 7. 10. |
| Philadelphia. | | | |
| Philadelphia | Apprentice, taught pulling and cutting fur, dyeing and finishing hats, to read, write and cypher as far as rule of three.³ | 9 yrs., 8 d. | |
| Northern Liberties | Apprentice, taught the potter's trade, have four quarters' night schooling and at expiration £ 10 in lieu of freedom dues. | 6 yrs., 11 mo. | |
| Philadelphia | Apprentice, taught the leather breeches maker's business, found meat, drink, washing and lodging, have four new shirts, two pair new shoes and one shilling and six pence each week during the term. | 2 yrs. | |
| Philadelphia | Servant, employed at the shallop business (note 5, have £ 3 current money of Pa.). | 1 yr., 9 mo. | £ 6. 16. 8. |
| Whitpain twp., Phila. co. | Servant | 4 yrs. | £ 11. 10. |
| Philadelphia | Apprentice, taught loaf bread baker's business, have four quarters' schooling at English school (note 3, and £ 5 current money of Pa.). | 6 yrs., 11 mo., 25 d. | |
| Philadelphia | Apprentice, taught housewifery and sew (note 3, and £ 3 current money of Pa.). | 2 yrs., 11 mo. | |
| N. Town twp., Bucks co. | Servant³ | 2 yrs., 8 mo. 20 d. | £ 12. |
| Philadelphia | Servant | 6 yrs. | £ 10. |
| Upper Milford, Northampton | Servant (note 2, besides the old). Servant, not to have freedom dues. | 4 yrs., 3 mo. each. | £ 61. 2. |
| Germantown, Phila. co. | Servant | 3 yrs., 6 mo. | £ 14. 10. |
| Philadelphia | Apprentice | 9 yrs., 2 mo. 23 d. | 5/. |
| Philadelphia | Apprentice, taught to read, write and cypher as far as and through rule of three, merchants' accounts of bookkeeping (note 1, or £ 10 lawful money of Pa.). | 4 yrs., 8 mo. | |
| Philadelphia | Apprentice, taught the trade of a leather breeches maker, read in Bible, write a legible hand.³ | 9 yrs., 10 mo. | |
| Philadelphia | Apprentice, taught housewifery and sew, read in Bible, write a legible hand.³ | 9 yrs., 15 d. | |
| Philadelphia | Apprentice, taught the art and mystery of a grocer, read and write well, and common arithmetic so as to understand the rule of three (note 2, to value of £ 10, or £ 10 in money and also £ 20 in money). | 5 yrs., 9 mo. | |
| Philadelphia | Apprentice, taught the cordwainer's trade, have two quarters' evening schooling.³ | 4 yrs., 10 mo. | |
| Philadelphia | Apprentice, taught the art trade and mystery of a woman's stuff shoemaker, have four quarters' | 9 yrs., 7 mo. 28 d. | |

| Date. | Name. | From the Port of | To Whom Indentured. |
|---|---|---|---|
| 1772. | | | |
| Feb. 11th | Yertz, John, Maria Clara, his wife, and Maria Cathe., their daughter. | Rotterdam | John Ettress and his assigns |
| | Yertz, John Peter | Rotterdam | John Ettress and his assigns |
| | Yertz, Christian | Rotterdam | John Ettress and his assigns |
| | Yertz, Arnold | Rotterdam | Robert Morris and his assigns |
| | Shreckgast, Elizabeth Margaret. | | George Godfreid Felter and his assigns. |
| | Weinnheimer, Henry, Jr. | | Harman Johnston and his assigns |
| Feb. 12th | Williams, George | | John Duele and his assigns |
| | Navil, Edward | Ireland | William Mitchell and his assigns |
| | Hensler, Philip Conrad | | Samuel Neave and his assigns |
| | Campbell, James | | Joseph Lippencott and his assigns |
| Feb. 13th | Fojon, Jean | Lisbon | Robert Wallace and his assigns |
| | Shouman, John Henry | | Arnold Creamer and his assigns |
| | Shouman, Eve Maria | | Michael App and his assigns |
| | Albright, Michael | | John Helm and his assigns |
| Feb. 13th | Hartley, John | | William Shippen and wife |
| Feb. 14th | Ward, John | | William Weston and his assigns |
| | Harper, Robert | | William Hartshorne |
| | Muck, Jacob | | Thomas Search |
| Feb. 15th | Fojon, Jean | | Christopher Bigamy and his assigns |
| Feb. 17th | Cramer, Andrew | | David Solomon |
| | Crispin, William | | Jesse Rose and his assigns |
| | West, James | | Hezekiah Hebberd and his assigns |
| | Gray, John | | George Campbell and his assigns |
| Feb. 18th | Jordan, Rachel | | Joseph Hunt and his assigns |
| Feb. 19th | Sourman, Philip, Jr. | | Andrew Bossett and his assigns |

## List of Indentures.

| Residence. | Occupation. | Term. | Amount. |
|---|---|---|---|
| | evening schooling (note 5, have £10 lawful money of Pa.). | | |
| White Marsh twp., Phila. co. | Servant (note 2, besides the old), the children shall not have freedom dues. | 4 yrs. each. | £30. |
| White Marsh twp., Phila. co. | Servant, taught to read in Bible, write a legible hand.[1] | 9 yrs. | £10. |
| White Marsh twp., Phila. co. | Servant, taught to read in Bible write a legible hand.[1] | 11 yrs. | £10. |
| Philadelphia | Servant[1] | 10 yrs. | £10. |
| Smithfield, Northampton co. | Servant | 3 yrs., 6 mo. | £11.10. |
| Philadelphia | Apprentice, taught the art and mystery of a merchant and bookkeeping (note 3, and £10 lawful money of Pa.). | 6 yrs. | |
| Piles Grove, Salem co., W. N. Jersey. | Servant[3] | 5 yrs. | £27. |
| Philadelphia | Servant[3] | 3 yrs., 6 mo. 14 d. | £15. |
| Philadelphia | Servant | 3 yrs. | £10. |
| Hadonfield, Gloucester co., W. N. Jersey. | Apprentice, taught the art, trade and mystery of a goldsmith, read in Bible, write a legible hand, cypher as far as and through rule of three.[3] | 13 yrs. | |
| Earl twp., Lancaster co. | Servant[1] | 4 yrs. | £18. |
| Northern Liberties | Servant, taught husbandry, read in Bible, write a legible hand, cypher as far as and through rule of three.[3] | 18 yrs. | 5/. |
| Northern Liberties | Servant, taught housewifery, sew, plain work, read in Bible, write a legible hand.[3] | 14 yrs. | 5/. |
| Philadelphia | Apprentice, taught the oak and cedar cooper's trade (note 1, to value of £10 or £10 in money). | 2 yrs. | |
| Philadelphia | Apprentice, taught the cooper's trade, have two quarters' schooling.[3] | 5 yrs., 6 mo. | |
| Philadelphia | Servant[8] | 1 yr. | £1.10. |
| Philadelphia | Apprentice, taught merchants' accounts or bookkeeping and found meat and drink only. | 5 yrs., 6 mo. | |
| Philadelphia | Apprentice, taught the wheelwright's trade, have three quarters' evening schooling (note 5, have £10 in lieu of freedom dues). | 6 yrs., 6 mo. | |
| Roxbury twp., Phila. co. | Servant | 4 yrs. | £16. |
| Philadelphia | Apprentice, taught the trade of a cedar cooper (note 3, and £10 current money of Pa.). | | |
| Philadelphia | Apprentice, taught the trade of a house carpenter.[5] | 4 yrs., 10 mo., 11 d. | |
| Philadelphia | Apprentice, taught the house carpenter's trade, found meat, drink, washing, lodging, stockings and working shirts. | 3 yrs., 8 mo. 7 d. | |
| Philadelphia | | 5 yrs. | £14. |
| Goshen, Chester co. | Servant | 2 yrs., 6 mo. | £6. |
| Philadelphia | Apprentice, taught the cordwainer's trade, have two quarters' night schooling.[3] | 8 yrs. | |

| Date. | Name. | From the Port of | To Whom Indentured. |
|---|---|---|---|
| 1772. Feb. 19th | Fisher, John | | John Dickinson and his assigns |
| | Herrington, Thomas | Ireland | John Cothringer and his assigns |
| | Butler, Thomas | | Phineas Buckly and his assigns |
| Feb. 21st | Hall, William | | Henry Wellfling and his assigns |
| | Henry, William | | Samuel Henry and his assigns |
| Feb. 22nd | Connelly, Mary | | James Cooper and his assigns |
| | Verner, Philip | | Jacob Lewis and his assigns |
| | Sayes, William | | William Hick and his assigns |
| | Waltman, Maria Magdalene | | Thomas Willing and his assigns |
| | Hisel, Elizabeth | | Francis Senner and his assigns |
| Feb. 24th | Sadleigh, Margaret | | Thomas Masterman and his assigns |
| | Jacobs, Andreas | Rotterdam | James Jacks and his assigns |
| | Paisley, Ann | | George Easterly and wife |
| | Kindernear, Catherine | | Major Walbron and his assigns |
| | Kindernear, Catherine | | Capt. John Eve and his assigns |
| Feb. 26th | Boyer, John | | Jacob Jones and his assigns |
| | Lyon, Lambert | London | Joseph Abraham |
| | Drineiser, George | | James Beorn and his assigns |
| | Bayer, John Ulrick | London | Israel Pemberton and his assigns |
| | May, Enoch | | John Buckingham and his assigns |
| | Rathburn, Mary | | John Buckingham and his assigns |
| | Hector, Frederick | London | Philip Eadenburn and his assigns |
| | Monsias, Deitrick | London | David Shaffer and his assigns |
| | Johnson, Susanna | | Thomas Robinson and his assigns |
| Feb. 27th | Cline, Theobald | London | Casper Graff and his assigns |
| | Goddard, George | | Matthew Potter, Jr |
| | Henrice, Hyronimus | London | Deitrick Metzner and his assigns |
| | Hartman, Jacob | London | Thomas Nedrow and his assigns |
| | White, Mary | | William Kirkpatrick and his assigns |
| | Gallacher, Michael | | Patrick Loughan and his assigns |
| Feb. 28th | Focht, John Henry | London | Lewis Brahm and his assigns |
| | Harris, Margaret | | John Atkinson, and Margaret, his |

## List of Indentures.

| Residence. | Occupation. | Term. | Amount. |
|---|---|---|---|
| Philadelphia | Servant | 1 yr., 6 mo. | £20. |
| Philadelphia | Servant[3] | 4 yrs. | £12. |
| Bristol twp., Bucks co. | Apprentice, taught the biscuit baking business, have two quarters' night schooling.[3] | 3 yrs., 8 mo. 25 d. | |
| Philadelphia | Apprentice, taught the cordwainer's trade, have six months' schooling (note 5, have £7 in money). | 8 yrs. | |
| Philadelphia | Apprentice, taught the hatmaker's trade, have three months' evening schooling each winter day during the term.[5] | 7 yrs., 6 mo. | |
| Philadelphia | Servant[3] | 3 yrs., 1 mo. | £10. |
| Philadelphia | Servant, taught to read in Bible, write a legible hand, cypher far as rule of three.[3] | 8 yrs. | £15. |
| Prince Town N. J. | | 3 yrs. | £14. |
| Philadelphia | Servant[1] | 6 yrs. | £31. |
| Philadelphia | Apprentice, taught housewifery, sew, knit and spin, read in the Bible, write a legible hand.[3] | 5 yrs. | |
| Northern Liberties | Servant | 5 yrs. | £25. 7. 6. |
| Manor twp., Lancaster co. | Servant[3] | 4 yrs. | £18. |
| Philadelphia | Apprentice, taught housewifery, sew, knit and spin, read perfectly, and write a good legible hand, both Dutch and English[3] | 11 yrs. | |
| Philadelphia | Apprentice, taught housewifery, sew, knit and spin, read in Bible.[3] | 6 yrs., 10 mo., 7 d. | |
| Philadelphia | | 6 yrs., 10 mo., 7 d. | £0. 5. 0. |
| Philadelphia | Apprentice, taught trade of an oak cooper, have four quarters' night schooling (note 3, and tools fitting for a journeyman cooper). | 9 yrs. | |
| Philadelphia | Servant, to have legal freedom dues. | 4 yrs. | £14. 6. 3. |
| Philadelphia | Servant, to have legal freedom dues. | 4 yrs. | £14. 19. 7. |
| Philadelphia | Servant[3] | 4 yrs. | £18. |
| Northern Liberties | Apprentice | 5 yrs., 9 mo. | £10. |
| Northern Liberties | Servant, taught to read in Bible, write a legible hand.[3] | 2 yrs., 8 mo. | 20/. |
| Bristol twp., Phila. co. | Servant[3] | 3 yrs., 7 mo. | £17. |
| Philadelphia | Servant[3] | 3 yrs., 6 mo. | £18. 15. |
| Charles twp., Chester co. | Apprentice, taught housewifery, sew, knit and spin, read in Bible, write a legible hand and cypher as far as rule of three.[3] | 11 yrs., 5 mo., 23 d. | |
| Philadelphia | Servant[3] | 3 yrs., 6 mo. | £20. 6. |
| Southwark | Apprentice, taught the blacksmith's trade, read, write and cypher.[1] | 1 yr., 8 mo. 14 d. | |
| Philadelphia | Servant[3] | 3 yrs., 6 mo. | £20. |
| Bristol twp., Bucks co. | Servant (note 3, and four Spanish dollars). | 2 yrs., 9 mo. | £16. 6. 3. |
| Philadelphia | | 9 yrs., 1 mo. 3 w. | 5/. |
| Philadelphia | Servant | 2 yrs., 6 mo. | £10. |
| Philadelphia | Servant[3] | 3 yrs. | £17. 18. 2 |
| Philadelphia | Apprentice, taught housewifery, sew plain work, read in Bible, | 15 yrs. | |

| Date. | Name. | From the Port of | To Whom Indentured. |
|---|---|---|---|
| 1772. | | | |
| Feb. 28th | Fritz, John Andreas | London | wife, and their or either of their assigns.<br>John Boyle and Robert Glen and their assigns. |
| Feb. 29th | Schnyder, Eve Maria | Rotterdam | Paul Isaac Voto and his assigns |
| | Haninger, John Frederick | London | John Solter and his assigns |
| | Thomson, William | | James Bayly |
| | Wood, Joseph | | Samuel Wheeler and his assigns |
| March 3rd | Hendrickstitz, John | | Dr. William Smith and his assigns |
| | Early, James | | Capt. Isaac All and his assigns |
| | Cullynane, Daniel | Ireland | Samuel Fitzgerald and his assigns |
| | Younger, Ann | | George Younger and his assigns |
| | Cullynane, Jeremiah | Ireland | Robert Slater and his assigns |
| March 4th | Biays, Joseph | | William McMullan and his assigns |
| | Balitz, Henry | | Andrew Hertzog and his assigns |
| March 5th | Barnicle, John Adam | | Deitrick Rees and his assigns |
| | Woller, Christopher, and Johanna, his wife. | London | Levi Hollingsworth and his assigns |
| | Woller, Christopher, and Johanna, his wife. | | Henry Hollingsworth and his assigns. |
| | Moisner, Henry | London | Christopher Kurfess and his assigns |
| March 6th | Robinson, James | | Seth Mattack and his assigns |
| March 9th | Hatch, Eleanor | | Joseph Ong and his assigns |
| March 10th | Flick, John | | John Reedle |
| | Smith, Christian | London | Ludwig Kuhn and his assigns |
| | Laujay, Anthony | | David Jones and his assigns |
| March 11th | Henry, Elizabeth | | Thomas Whitlock and his assigns |
| March 12th | Jenkins, Thomas | | John Boon and his assigns |
| | Boores, James | | William Milnor and his assigns |
| March 14th | Drafts, John | | Moore Furman and his assigns |
| March 14th | Nelson, William | | John Martin Taylor and his assigns |
| March 16th | Archer, Sarah | | Capt. William Hawkins and his assigns. |

## List of Indentures.

| Residence. | Occupation. | Term. | Amount. |
|---|---|---|---|
| | write a legible hand and cypher as far as rule of three.[3] | | |
| Philadelphia | Servant, taught to read and write perfectly.[3] | 9 yrs. | £5. |
| Philadelphia | Servant, taught to read and write[3]. | 7 yrs. | £16. |
| Philadelphia | Servant[3] | 2 yrs., 9 mo. | £19.10. |
| Alexander twp., Hunterdon co., W. N. Jersey. | Apprentice, taught the art of farming, read, write and cypher as far as rule of three.[3] | 10 yrs. | |
| Philadelphia | Apprentice, taught the art, trade and mystery of a cutler, allowed time to go to school in winter evenings.[3] | 3 yrs., 4 mo. | |
| Philadelphia | Servant[3] | 3 yrs. | £15.5.?. |
| Philadelphia | Servant | 4 yrs. | £13.5. |
| Philadelphia | Servant, the said servant to pay £3 to his said master at expiration of his servitude.[3] | 2 yrs. | £11. |
| Philadelphia | Servant | 10 yrs., 6 mo. | £2.10. |
| New Port. N. Castle co., on Delaware. | Servant (note 2, of value of £5, or £5 in money). | 2 yrs., 6 mo. | £11. |
| Southwark | Apprentice, taught the ship joiner's trade.[3] | 2 yrs., 3 mo. 26 d. | |
| Philadelphia | Apprentice | 5 yrs., 8 mo. | £4. |
| Philadelphia | Servant[1] | 5 yrs., 7 mo. | £27.9. |
| Philadelphia | Servants, at expiration have legal freedom dues and £10 in cash, and in case they have children to serve six months longer, the master providing necessaries for the children. | 4 yrs. each.. | £35.10. |
| Cecil co., Md. | | 4 yrs. each.. | £35.10. |
| Philadelphia | Servant[3] | 3 yrs. | £15.19.9. |
| Philadelphia | Apprentice taught cooper's trade, have one quarter's night schooling, the apprentice to serve time out either in the city or the Liberties.[3] | 2 yrs., 4 mo. | |
| Newtown twp., Gloucester co., W. Jersey. | Servant[3] | 4 yrs., 8 mo. 17 d. | 20/. |
| Philadelphia | Apprentice, taught the tailor's trade, have one quarter's night schooling.[3] | 5 yrs., 9 mo. | |
| Philadelphia | Servant[3] | 4 yrs. | £17. |
| Philadelphia | Apprentice, taught the cordwainer's trade, have nine months' day, and six months' night schooling.[3] | 10 yrs. | |
| Philadelphia | Apprentice, taught the mantua maker's trade, read in Bible, write a legible hand.[3] | 6 yrs. | |
| Alsace twp., Berks co. | Servant | 5 yrs. | £25. |
| Philadelphia | Apprentice, taught the cooper's trade. | 6 yrs. | £10. |
| Philadelphia | Apprentice, taught to read and write and the art of a seaman and navigation, and at expiration have two complete suits of apparel, one whereof to be new. | 3 yrs. | |
| Philadelphia | Servant | 2 yrs., 6 mo. | £13. |
| Philadelphia | Apprentice, taught housewifery and sew (note 2, besides her old) | 1 yr. | |

| Date. | Name. | From the Port of | To Whom Indentured. |
|---|---|---|---|
| 1772. | Reily, Mary | | Edward Reily and his assigns....... |
| March 16th. | Worril, Robert | | John Weaver and his assigns........ |
| March 17th. | Craaflin, Hannah | | Zacharias Endres and his assigns.... |
| | McDonnald, William | | Martin Pitch and his assigns........ |
| | Fitzgerald, Mary | | Thomas Thomson and his assigns.... |
| | McCullough, Eleanor | Ireland | John Tolbert and his assigns........ |
| | Winkler, Frederick | | Benjamin Harbeson and his assigns.. |
| | Fitzgerald, Eleanor | | John Morton and his assigns........ |
| | Shitzing, Eva | | John Shutz and his assigns......... |
| | Burton, Jonathan | | Daniel Meredith and his assigns..... |
| | Shea, Michael | | John Tolby and his assigns......... |
| March 18th. | Jacob Slummer | | Peter Helme ...................... |
| | Kraft, Adam | | Martin Weis and his assigns........ |
| | Dodd, Thomas | | Dr. Daniel Aldenbruck and his assigns. |
| | Stayner, William | | Mark Freeman and his assigns...... |
| | McGra, Biddy | | Allen Brown and his assigns........ |
| | Sullivan, Honor | | Allen Brown and his assigns........ |
| | Doyle, William | | Andrew Tybout and his assigns..... |
| | Kentner, Mary | | John Barnhill ..................... |
| March 19th. | Miller, Jacob | | Peter Mier and his assigns.......... |
| | Haselton, John | | Isaac Jones and his assigns......... |
| | Fuller, Matthias | | Christian Percy and his assigns...... |
| March 19th. | Gilbert, John, Jr. | | Thomas Sachewil Walker and his assigns. |
| | Wisdom, Catherine | Ireland | Francis Grice and his assigns....... |
| March 21st. | Cassard, Daniel | | Michael Cook and his assigns........ |

---

[1] To be found all necessaries and at the expiration have freedom dues.
[2] To be found all necessaries and at the expiration have one new suit of apparel.
[3] To be found all necessaries and at the expiration have two complete suits of apparel, one whereof to be new.

## List of Indentures.

| Residence. | Occupation. | Term. | Amount. |
|---|---|---|---|
| Philadelphia | Apprentice | 8 yrs., 4 mo. | £4. |
| Oxford twp., Phila. co. | Apprentice | 5 yrs., 4 mo. | £10. |
| Northern Liberties | Apprentice, taught the mantua maker's business.[3] | 5 yrs., 2 mo. | |
| Philadelphia | Apprentice, taught the cordwainer's trade, read, write and cypher as far as rule of three (note 2, and his tools). | 2 yrs., 9 mo. 22 d. | |
| Southwark | Servant | 4 yrs. | £10. |
| Philadelphia | Servant[5] | 3 yrs. | £12.10. |
| Philadelphia | Apprentice, taught the coppersmith's trade, have four quarters' evening schooling.[3] | 8 yrs., 11 mo. | |
| Philadelphia | Servant | 4 yrs. | 5/. |
| Philadelphia | Servant | 9 yrs. | £3. |
| Philadelphia | Apprentice, taught the brass founder's trade. | 3 yrs., 9 mo. 22 d. | |
| Philadelphia | Servant | 7 yrs. | £8. |
| Northern Liberties | Apprentice, taught trade of a cedar cooper, have one year schooling, and at expiration have freedom dues. | 8 yrs., 1 mo. 16 d. | |
| Philadelphia | Servant, found meat, drink, washing and lodging. | 6 mo. | £6. |
| Philadelphia | Servant[3] | 3 yrs. | £15. |
| Philadelphia | Apprentice, found all necessaries and taught to read and write. | 3 yrs. | |
| Fannet twp., Cumberland co., this Province. | Servant | 5 yrs. 6 mo. | £7. |
| Fannet twp., Cumberland co., this Province. | Servant | 3 yrs., 8 mo. 5 d. | £13. |
| Philadelphia | Apprentice, taught the hat maker's business, found meat, drink, washing and lodging, allowed time to go three quarters to night school, his parents paying the expense. | 7 yrs. | |
| Philadelphia | Apprentice taught housewifery, read well in English.[3] | 5 yrs. | £3. |
| William twp., Northampton co. | Servant | 9 yrs. | £30. |
| Northern Liberties | Apprentice, taught the shipwright's trade, have one quarter's evening schooling every winter during the term (note 3, and the tools he works with). | 11 yrs. | |
| Northern Liberties | Apprentice, taught potter's trade read and write perfectly, cypher as far as and through the rule of three.[3] | 14 yrs., 3 mo. | |
| Philadelphia | Apprentice, taught the tailor's trade, have one quarter's evening schooling every winter during the term.[3] | 5 yrs., 2 w. | |
| Southwark | Servant (note 5, have the usual allowance according to the custom of the country). | 2 yrs., 2 mo. | £13. |
| Hatfield twp., Phila. co. | Apprentice, taught husbandry, read and write perfectly and | 17 yrs., 10 mo. | |

[4] To be found all necessaries and at the expiration have two complete suits of apparel, one whereof to be new, and 40s. in money.

[5] At expiration have two complete suits of apparel, one whereof to be new.

| Date. | Name. | From the Port of | To Whom Indentured. |
|---|---|---|---|
| 1772. | | | |
| March 21st. | Tanner, John | | Jacob Whitman and his assigns...... |
| March 23rd. | Dundass, John | | Francis Gurney and his assigns...... |
| | Dundass, John | | Thomas Dundass and his assigns.... |
| | Hokenterfer, Conrad | | Frederick Hagner and his assigns.... |
| | Myer, Henry | | Philip Nas and his assigns.......... |
| | Myer, Valentine | | Rudolph Sayer and his assigns....... |
| March 24th. | Fulton, William | | Andrew Carsen and his assigns...... |
| | Brock, Nicholas | | William Tenant and his assigns..... |
| | Bett (a mulatto) | | Samuel Moore and his assigns...... |
| | Helvenstein, John | | Henry and Peter Kurtz and his assigns. |
| | Moffatt, Margaret | | Manuel Eyre and his assigns........ |
| | Belt (a mulatto) | | Mary Campbell and her assigns..... |
| | Singeizer, Mary | | Lawrence Upman and his assigns.... |
| March 24th. | Fench, Thomas | | Henry Reynolds and his assigns...... |
| March 25th. | Brampton, Mansfield | | Benjamin Town .................... |
| | Brown, James | | Christian Rudolph and his assigns... |
| March 26th. | Lawrie, John | | George Rowan and his assigns....... |
| | Lawrie, Mary | | Dr. George Weed and his assigns.... |
| | Kenner, Godfreid | | Jacob Sceit and his assigns.......... |
| | Faulkner, Peter | | George Christini and his heirs...... |

## List of Indentures.

| Residence. | Occupation. | Term. | Amount. |
|---|---|---|---|
| | cypher as far as and through rule of three.[3] | | |
| Moyamensing twp., Phila. co. | Servant, found meat, drink, washing and lodging, at expiration pay him at the rate of fifteen shillings Pa. currency per month fore each month of the term. | 6 mo. | £2.5. |
| Philadelphia | Apprentice, taught the art and mystery of a shopkeeper and bookkeeping and found all necessaries. | 7 yrs., 11 mo., 8 d. | |
| Reading, Berks co. | | 7 yrs., 11 mo., 8 d. | £0.5. |
| Philadelphia | Apprentice, taught the tailor's trade, have nine months' evening schooling at an English school.[3] | 5 yrs., 11 mo., 24 d. | |
| Philadelphia | Apprentice, taught the tailor's trade, read and write Dutch and English (note 3, or £ ¢ money of Pa.). | 17 yrs. | |
| Philadelphia | Apprentice, taught the loaf bread baker's business, have three years schooling.[5] | 11 yrs. | |
| Philadelphia | Apprentice, taught the skinner and breeches maker's business, have two quarters' schooling.[3] | 4 yrs. | |
| | Servant, found meat, drink, washing and lodging and one shirt. | 5 mo. | £6.16.6. |
| Southwark | Apprentice, taught housewifery, knitting and sewing and to read[3] | 14 yrs. | |
| Philadelphia | Apprentice, taught the trade of a tobacconist, and in case the masters want to dispose of him, he shall choose for himself as master (note 3, or £10 money of Pa.) | 6 yrs. | £7. |
| Kensington, Phila. co. | Apprentice, taught housewifery, read and write a legible hand.[1] | 5 yrs., 10 mo., 12 d. | |
| Southwark | Apprentice, taught to read, spin and sew well.[3] | 14 yrs. | |
| Northern Liberties | Servant, taught to read and write perfectly.[3] | 11 yrs., 6 mo. | £2.15. |
| Wilmington, New Castle co., on Delaware. | Apprentice, taught cooper's trade, read well in Bible, write a legible hand, cypher as far as rule of three.[3] | 14 yrs., 7 mo., 13 d. | |
| Philadelphia | Apprentice, taught the tin plate worker's business, have one quarter's evening schooling.[3] | 6 yrs., 6 mo. | |
| Philadelphia | Apprentice | 9 yrs., 9 mo. 2 w. | £12. |
| Southwark | Apprentice, taught the cooper's trade, have four quarters' evening schooling.[3] | 10 yrs. | |
| Philadelphia | Apprentice, taught housewifery and to sew, read and write perfectly and cypher as far as the rule of three.[3] | 9 yrs. | |
| Philadelphia | | 3 yrs., 6 mo. | £10. |
| Philadelphia | Apprentice, taught the leather breeches maker's trade, have one quarter's evening schooling, allow time to go to evening school four other quarters within | 10 yrs., 3 mo. | |

| Date. | Name. | From the Port of | To Whom Indentured. |
|---|---|---|---|
| 1772. | | | |
| March 27th. | Davies, William | | Thomas Proctor and his assigns..... |
| | Onoust, Elizabeth, Jr........ | | Elizabeth Onoust ................. |
| March 28th. | Roberts, Abraham | | Samuel Hopkins and his assigns..... |
| | Hopkins, Richard | | Samuel Hopkins and his assigns..... |
| | Mauks, George | | Baltzer Cleymer and his assigns..... |
| March 30th. | Cook, Philip | | Peter Mahrling and his assigns...... |
| | Adams, Isaac | | Joseph Waggoner and his assigns.... |
| | Linch, Mary | | James Linch ...................... |
| | Chub, John | | Samuel Richards and his assigns.... |
| March 31st. | Wallace, Eliazer | | Presly Blackiston and his assigns.... |
| | Graff, Casper | | Peter Trais and his assigns.......... |
| | Carter, Rachel | | Jacob Wisart and his assigns........ |
| | Wilkinson, Hannah | | George Thimb and his wife......... |
| April 4th... | Higas, Jacob | | Jacob Hagner and his assigns....... |
| | Finley, John | | Robert Aitkin ..................... |
| | Holmes, Henry | | John Brown and his assigns......... |
| | Williams, Thomas | | John Hawerth and his assigns...... |
| | Williams, Thomas | | John McIlvain and his assigns...... |
| | Street, Benjamin | | John Duncan and his assigns........ |
| April 6th... | Strickland, John | | Robert Allison and his assigns....... |
| | Hupbecker, Margaret | | David Ubes and his assigns......... |

## List of Indentures.

| Residence. | Occupation. | Term. | Amount. |
|---|---|---|---|
| | the term, the mother paying the expense of the schooling.[3] | | |
| Philadelphia | Servant, taught the house carpenter's trade (note 2, besides his old). | 3 yrs. | £25. |
| | | 4 yrs., 11 mo., 7 d. | £0.15. |
| Philadelphia | Apprentice, taught the house carpenter's trade, have two quarters' evening schooling.[3] | 4 yrs., 6 mo. 18 d. | |
| Philadelphia | Apprentice, taught the house carpenter's trade, found meat, drink, washing and lodging, the parents to find apparel.[5] | 5 yrs., 5 mo. 5 d. | |
| | | 1 yr., 9 mo. | £1.7. |
| Philadelphia | Servant (note 3, and 19/6 in money) | 3 yrs., 6 mo. | £22. |
| Philadelphia | Servant to be employed at the tailor's business only (note 1, to the value of £10 lawful money of Pa.). | | |
| Philadelphia | Apprentice | 4 yrs. | £7. |
| | Apprentice | 9 yrs., 3 mo. | £0.5.0. |
| Philadelphia | Apprentice, taught the cordwainer's trade, have eight months' evening schooling.[3] | 2 yrs., 10 mo., 16 d. | |
| | Apprentice, taught the cordwainer's business and found all necessaries. | 3 yrs., 23 d. | |
| Philadelphia | Apprentice, taught the leather dresser or skinner's trade, found working apparel only (at expiration have £5 lawful money of Pa. in lieu of freedom dues). | 2 yrs. | |
| Philadelphia | Apprentice | 3 yrs., 3 mo. 26 d. | £5.10. |
| Southwark | Apprentice, taught house and needle work, read and write perfectly and cypher as far as rule of three.[3] | 2 yrs., 11 mo. | |
| Philadelphia | Apprentice, taught the trade of a cooper, have two quarters' schooling the beginning of the term and time to go two quarters to school the last of the term, his mother paying the last.[3] | 7 yrs. | |
| Philadelphia | Apprentice, taught the book binder's business, the master receiving £10 money of Pa. every year during the term.[5] | 6 yrs. | |
| Philadelphia | Servant | 3 yrs. | £9. |
| Philadelphia | Servant[3] | 4 yrs., 1 mo. 11 d. | £21. |
| Ridley twp., Chester co. | | 4 yrs., 1 mo. 11 d. | £21. |
| Philadelphia | Apprentice | 7 yrs. | £3. |
| Southwark | Apprentice, taught the house carpenter's trade, found meat, drink, washing and lodging and at expiration have £10 current money of Pa., the mother to find him in apparel during the term. | 6 yrs. | |
| Northern Liberties | Apprentice, taught housewifery, sew, knit and spin, have six months' day schooling at a | 2 yrs., 6 mo. | |

| Date. | Name. | From the Port of | To Whom Indentured. |
|---|---|---|---|
| | Askins, Samuel | Bristol | Isaac Hazlehurst and his assigns |
| | Christian, William | | Manuel Eyre and his assigns |
| | Derrick, David, Jr. | | Manuel Eyre and his assigns |
| | Slaughter, John | | David Paul and his heirs |
| | Grubb, Joseph | | William Lownes and his assigns |
| | Seifert, George | | Andrew Bachman and his assigns |
| April 7th | Tielman, Elizabeth | | William Harvey and his assigns |
| | Tielman, Elizabeth | | Francis Lambert and his assigns |
| | Weaver, Margaret | | Conrad Hess and his assigns |
| | Weber, Jacob | | Paul Jones |
| | Power, Robert | | Michael Macganon and his assigns |
| April 8th | Brockington, Martha | | Abigail Griffiths |
| | Wood, Henry | | George Westcott and his assigns |
| | Kemble, Hezekiah | | Benjamin Olden, his executors and administrators. |
| April 9th | Leib, William | | Christian Stahr and his assigns |
| | Hadley, John | | William Davey and his assigns |
| | Guillemaint, John Baptiste | | James Plunket and his assigns |
| April 11th | Ludwig, Martin | | George Fetter |
| | Risler, Michael | | Samuel Wallace and wife |

| Residence. | Occupation. | Term. | Amount. |
|---|---|---|---|
| Philadelphia | Dutch school (note 3, and a new spinning wheel). Servant, taught to read and write perfectly.[3] | 6 yrs., 7 mo. | £12. |
| Northern Liberties | Apprentice, taught the shipwright's trade, have one quarter's evening schooling each winter during the term (note 5, have £8 current money of Pa. in lieu of freedom dues). | 6 yrs. | |
| Northern Liberties | Apprentice, taught the shipwright's trade, have one quarter's evening schooling each winter (note 5, have £8 current money of Pa. in lieu of freedom dues). | 3 yrs., 6 mo. 15 d. | |
| Greenwich twp., Gloucester co., W. N. Jersey. | Apprentice, taught the farming business, read in Bible, write a legible hand and cypher as far as and through the rule of three.[3] | 10 yrs., 5 mo. | |
| Philadelphia | Apprentice, taught the house carpenter's trade, found meat, drink, washing and lodging and working apparel, shoes excepted (shoes and Sunday apparel found by his father-in-law, Valentine Weaver). | 5 yrs., 8 mo. | 5/. |
| Philadelphia | Apprentice, taught the tailor's trade, read well in Bible.[3] | 4 yrs., 11 mo. | |
| Pennsbury, Chester co. | Apprentice, taught housewifery, sew, knit and spin, read in Bible, write a legible hand.[3] | 9 yrs., 4 mo. | |
| London Grove twp., Chester co. | | 9 yrs., 4 mo. | 5/. |
| Northern Liberties | Apprentice, taught housewifery, sew, knit and spin, read in Bible, write a legible hand, agreed that if the master dispose of the said apprentice's time, the father is to have the preference of purchasing it.[3] | 8 yrs. | |
| Lower Merion, Phila. co. | | 10 yrs. | £16. |
| Philadelphia | Apprentice, taught the plasterer's trade, read, write and cypher through the rule of three.[1] | 5 yrs., 11 mo. | |
| Philadelphia | Apprentice, taught to read in Bible, write a legible hand and cypher as far as and through the rule of three, also housewifery and to sew.[3] | 8 yrs., 6 mo. | |
| Philadelphia | Servant[3] | 2 yrs. | £20. |
| Philadelphia | Apprentice, taught the cordwainer's trade, have six months' evening schooling and three months' day schooling.[3] | 7 yrs., 4 mo. 2 d. | |
| Whitemarsh twp., Phila. co. | Servant[5] | 2 yrs. | £1.5. |
| | Servant | 4 yrs. | £12. |
| Philadelphia | Servant[1] | 4 yrs., 6 mo. | £20. |
| Philadelphia | Apprentice, taught the butcher's trade, have six months' schooling, learn English (note 3, and a chopper, cleaver and knife). | 3 yrs., 7 mo. 2 w. | |
| Philadelphia | Apprentice, taught the farmer's business, read and write perfectly and cypher as far as and through the rule of three (note 1, | 7 yrs., 3 mo. | |

| Date. | Name. | From the Port of | To Whom Indentured. |
|---|---|---|---|
| 1772. | | | |
| April 11th.. | Grove Elizabeth | | Nicholas Rash and his assigns....... |
| | Hubley, Adam | | Henry Keppell, Jr................ |
| | Neise, Adam | | Jacob Whitman and his assigns...... |
| | Johnson, James | | Jacob Peters and his assigns........ |
| | Udt, Jacob | | Anthony Noble and his assigns...... |
| April 13th.. | Howell, William | | John Burchall and his assigns....... |
| | Murray, John | | John Snow and his assigns.......... |
| April 14th.. | Douglass, Thomas | Ireland .... | George Goodwin and his assigns.... |
| | Connollan, Mary | | John Hawkins and his assigns....... |
| | Harkeson, Margaret | Ireland .... | Lawrence Cooke and his assigns..... |
| | Howell, Mordecai | | Stephen Phipps and his assigns...... |
| | Hodges, Richard, Jr. | | William Coates and his assigns...... |
| April 15th.. | Helmbolt, George Christopher. | | Henry Cammerer ................. |
| | Jackson, Sarah | | Mark Bird and his assigns.......... |
| | Kennedy, Robert | | George Whitman and his assigns.... |
| | Hehlman, Sophia | | John Putt and his assigns.......... |
| | Levingston, William | | Dr. Samuel Kennedy and his assigns. |
| | Butler, William | | Thomas Hewit and his assigns...... |
| | Leister, Ann, and Manney, Rose. | | William Hamilton and his assigns... |
| | Goodacre, Hannah | Ireland .... | William Hamilton and his assigns... |
| | Conner, Elizabeth | | John Grant and his assigns.......... |
| April 16th.. | Stevens, Thomas | | John Ashburne and his assigns...... |
| | Maguire, John | | John Bean and his assigns.......... |
| | Minhere, Ann Elizabeth | | George Hisler and his assigns....... |
| | Street, Benjamin | | Holton Jones and his assigns........ |
| April 18th.. | Armitage, Elizabeth | | William Shedacre and his assigns.... |
| | Borgen, Maria Elizabeth | | Philip Moses and his assigns........ |
| | Kemble, Levi | | Jacob Graff and his heirs........... |
| | Hehlman, Sophia | | Joseph Brown and his assigns....... |

## List of Indentures.

| RESIDENCE. | OCCUPATION. | TERM. | AMOUNT. |
|---|---|---|---|
| | also 100 acres of land in Northumberland co.). | | |
| Philadelphia | Apprentice, taught housewifery, sew, read in Bible, write a legible hand.[3] | 4 yrs., 8 mo. | |
| Philadelphia | Apprentice, taught the art and mystery of a merchant and found all necessaries. | 2 yrs. | |
| Moyamensing | | 17 yrs. | £15. |
| Philadelphia | Apprentice, have seven quarters' winter evening schooling (note 1, to the value of £10 or £10 in cash). | 7 yrs. | |
| Southwark | Servant (note 3, and the value of £10). | 2 yrs., 6 mo. | £18. |
| Philadelphia | Apprentice, taught the cordwainer's trade, have six months' night schooling and three months' day schooling.[3] | 6 yrs., 11 mo., 2 w. | |
| Philadelphia | Apprentice, taught the cooper's trade, read in Bible, write a legible hand cypher as far as and through the rule of three.[3] | 13 yrs. | |
| Philadelphia | Servant[2] | 7 mo. | £8.10. |
| Wilmington, N. Castle co. | | 4 yrs. | £14. |
| Philadelphia | Servant[3] | 3 yrs., 11 mo., 20 d. | £9. |
| Philadelphia | Apprentice, taught the tailor's trade, have one quarter's evening schooling, found meat, drink, washing and lodging, sufficient apparel, shoes, stockings and shirts excepted, which the uncle is to provide, and at expiration have one complete new suit. | 5 yrs., 7 mo. | |
| Northern Liberties | Apprentice, taught the tanner and currier's business, have eight quarters' evening schooling.[3] | 8 yrs., 2 mo. 26 d. | |
| Philadelphia | | 2 yrs. | £14. |
| Union twp., Berks co. | Servant | 4 yrs. | £16. |
| Philadelphia | Apprentice, taught the tailor's trade, read and write English and Dutch perfectly, cypher as far as and through rule of three[3] | 11 yrs. | |
| Rockland twp., Berks co. | Servant | 3 yrs., 6 mo. | £18. |
| E. Whiteland, Chester co. | Servant[5] | 1 yr., 6 mo. | £5. |
| Greenwich twp., Gloucester co., W. Jersey. | Servant[3] | 2 yrs., 6 mo. | £6. |
| Philadelphia | | 4 yrs. each | £10. each. |
| Philadelphia | Servant[3] | 4 yrs. | £10. |
| Philadelphia | | 4 yrs. | £12. |
| Southwark | | 6 yrs., 11 mo. | 7/6. |
| Worcester, Phila. co. | | 3 yrs. | £12. |
| Oxford twp., Phila co. | Servant[3] | 2 yrs., 10 mo. | £13. |
| Germantown | | 7 yrs. | £3. |
| Philadelphia | | 8 yrs., 3 mo. | £3. |
| Philadelphia | | 4 yrs. | £21.7.6. |
| Philadelphia | Apprentice, taught the bricklayer's trade.[5] | 3 yrs., 11 mo., 22 d. | |
| Philadelphia | | 3 yrs., 6 mo. | £18. |

| Date. | Name. | From the Port of | To Whom Indentured. |
|---|---|---|---|
| 1772. April 21st.. | Batt, William | | James Harris and his assigns........ |
| | McNamara, Mary | | Aquilla Jones and his assigns........ |
| April 22nd.. | Quin, Patrick | | Michael Simpson and his assigns.... |
| | Hurley, Elizabeth | | Elizabeth Sawyer and her assigns.... |
| | Boyle, Caleb | | Thomas Barr and his assigns........ |
| | Grimes, Moses | | John Hales and his assigns.......... |
| | Gray, John | | Thomas Edward Wallace and his assigns. |
| | Snitzer, George | | George Cooper and his assigns...... |
| April 23rd.. | Seabright, John | | Enoch Morgan and his assigns...... |
| | Rowland, John | | Samuel Jackson and his assigns...... |
| April 24th.. | Leonard, Thomas | | Adam Clampfer and his assigns..... |
| April 25th.. | Hoffman, Maria Catherine | Rotterdam.. | George Young and his assigns....... |
| | Swiger, Jacob | | Daniel Barnes and his assigns....... |
| | Vant, John Frederick | | John Zeller ........................ |
| | Albright, John Frederick | London .... | John Zeller and his assigns.......... |
| April 27th.. | Evans, Joseph | | Daniel Dupuy and son............. |
| | | | Daniel Dupuy, Jr.................. |
| | Schnyder, Christian, Jr | | Peter Cooper and his assigns........ |
| | Kempf, Matthias | | Jacob Deigel and his assigns........ |

## List of Indentures.

| Residence. | Occupation. | Term. | Amount. |
|---|---|---|---|
| Philadelphia | Apprentice, taught cordwainer's trade, have six months' night schooling.[3] | 6 yrs., 9 mo. 10 d. | |
| Philadelphia | Apprentice, taught housewifery, sew plain work, read in Bible, write a legible hand.[3] | 9 yrs., 9 mo. 26 d. | |
| Paxton twp., Lancaster co. | Servant | 5 yrs. | £15. |
| Philadelphia | Apprentice | 11 yrs., 9 mo. | £10. |
| Philadelphia | Apprentice, taught the tailor's trade, have six months' winter night schooling or three months' day.[1] | 5 yrs., 1 mo. 9 d. | |
| Philadelphia | Servant | 10 yrs. | £40. |
| Southwark | Apprentice, taught the art and mystery of a mariner, read and write perfectly and cypher as far as and through the rule of three[3] | 4 yrs., 10 mo. | |
| Philadelphia | Apprentice, taught the skinner's trade, have three months' Dutch and three months' English schooling.[3] | 10 yrs. | |
| Philadelphia | Apprentice | 5 yrs. | £5.14. |
| Philadelphia | Apprentice, taught the art of a mariner and sent to school at such times as he may be in port of Phila., taught to read, write and cypher, and if qualified the art of navigation.[5] | 3 yrs. | |
| Philadelphia | Apprentice | 7 yrs. | £15. |
| Moyamensing twp., Phila. co. | Servant, taught to read perfectly in Bible, have liberty to go to the Dutch minister to receive the sacrament when she arrives at age of eighteen.[3] | 11 yrs., 10 mo., 23 d. | £8. |
| Northern Liberties | Apprentice | 14 yrs., 7 mo. | £10. |
| Philadelphia | Servant[1] | 3 yrs. | £16. |
| Philadelphia | Servant, found only shoes, stockings and trousers and one hat when demanded, no freedom dues. | 3 yrs. | £16. |
| Philadelphia | Apprentice, taught the silversmith's trade, large work excepted.[5] | 7 yrs., 7 mo. 22 d. | |
| Philadelphia | Apprentice, taught the cordwainer's trade, found meat, drink, washing and lodging, time to go two quarters to night school, the grandfather paying the expense, the grandfather to find apparel the first two years and the master the remaining part of the term (have two complete suits of apparel, one to be new). | 4 yrs., 1 mo. | |
| Philadelphia | Apprentice, taught the art and mystery of a painter and glazier, have one year and six months, nine months of which to be at an English, and nine months at Dutch school.[3] | 6 yrs. | |

| Date. | Name. | From the Port of | To Whom Indentured. |
|---|---|---|---|
| 1772. April 27th | Repson, John Jr | | Frederick Wilpper and his assigns |
| | Wiggmore, James | | William Marshall |
| April 28th | Hastings, John | | John Head and his assigns |
| | Gorton, Daniel, Jr | | Champless Allen and his assigns |
| | Campbell, Robert | | David Ware and his assigns |
| | Steward, John | | George Lohrman and his assigns |
| April 29th April 30th | Aptin, Maria Elizabeth | | Jacob Groff and his assigns |
| | Kenny, John | | Dr. James Graham and his assigns |
| | Moyer, Rosina | | John Leise and his assigns |
| | Wholohan, Thomas | | Robert Moody |
| | Smith, Sarah | | Ann Hard Castle |
| | Smith, Sarah | | Edith Caudell |
| | Patterson Mary | | Mary Alison |
| | Brian, Helian | | Jacob Frank |
| | Erenfeighter, David | | William Todd |
| | Mitchell, John | | Samuel Wharton and his assigns |
| | Lee, James | | James Coffee |
| | Scott, John | | Jacob Harman |
| | Callaghan, Cornelius | | Abel Rees |
| May 1st | Smith, Nicholas | | Joseph Cornelius |
| | Archer, Elizabeth | | George Bullock |
| | Barry, Mary | | Alexander Ross |
| | Hickey, Catherine | | Thomas Cullin and his assigns |
| | Bohilly, John | | Peter Haldiman and his assigns |
| | Bison, Charles | | Edward Oxley and his assigns |

## List of Indentures.

| Residence. | Occupation. | Term. | Amount. |
|---|---|---|---|
| Northern Liberties | Apprentice, taught the butcher's trade, have three quarters' schooling at an English school[3]. | 2 yrs., 5 mo. 19 d. | |
| Philadelphia | Apprentice, taught the art and mystery of a pilot in the bay and river Delaware, read and write perfectly, cypher as far as and through the rule of three (note 2, besides his old). | 6 yrs. | |
| Philadelphia | Apprentice, taught the art and mystery of a mariner and navigation, read, write and cypher as far as and through the rule of three.[3] | 2 yrs., 9 mo. 11 d. | |
| Philadelphia | Apprentice, taught the cooper's trade have three quarters' night schooling.[3] | 8 yrs., 1 mo. 25 d. | |
| Philadelphia | Apprentice, taught the cordwainer's trade, read and write perfectly and cypher as far as and through the rule of three (note 3, and a set of working tools). | 7 yrs. 3 mo. | |
| Philadelphia | Apprentice, taught the tailor's trade, have four quarters' day schooling.[3] | 7 yrs. | |
| Philadelphia | Servant | 5 yrs. | £ 8. |
| Philadelphia | | 4 yrs. | £ 20. |
| Hill twp., Bucks co. | Servant | 7 yrs. | £ 17. 15. |
| Turbot twp., Northumberland co. | | 4 yrs. | £ 20. |
| Philadelphia | Apprentice, taught housewifery, read and write well and arithmetic as far as rule of three (note 1, of value of £ 7, or that sum in cash). | 8 yrs., 11 mo. | |
| Philadelphia | | 8 yrs., 11 mo. | 1/. |
| Philadelphia | Apprentice, taught housewifery, sew and knit, read and write (note 2, and one old). | 2 yrs., 9 mo. | |
| Philadelphia | | 4 yrs. | £ 15. |
| Philadelphia | Apprentice, taught the coach making business, have three quarters' schooling.[1] | 6 yrs., 9 mo. | |
| Philadelphia | | 6 yrs. | £ 18. |
| Philadelphia | Have freedom dues | 6 yrs. | £ 20. |
| Philadelphia | Have freedom dues | 7 yrs. | £ 17. |
| Tradufflin twp., Chester co. | Have freedom dues | 4 yrs. (3½) See N. B., p. 146. | £ 14. 10. |
| Philadelphia | Apprentice, taught the trade of a chaise body and carriage maker, found meat, drink, washing and lodging and found in apparel, the apprentice paying the master for it after he is free. | 2 yrs., 1 mo. | |
| Philadelphia | | 4 yrs. | £ 15. |
| Philadelphia | | 4 yrs. | £ 15. |
| Potts Grove, Phila co. | | 4 yrs. | £ 15. |
| Philadelphia | | 8 yrs. | £ 10. |
| Philadelphia | Servant, taught the tailor's trade, found meat, drink, lodging and washing, have at expiration legal freedom dues or £ 5. | 1 yr., 6mo. | £ 9. 8. 6. |

| Date. | Name. | From the Port of | To Whom Indentured. |
|---|---|---|---|
| | Deal, Samuel | | Casper Singer and his assigns |
| May 2nd | Demler, Henry | | George Dowig |
| | Harding, Thomas | | Thomas Montgomery and his assigns. |
| | Humphrys, Thomas | | Robert Sewell |
| | Roche, Thomas | | Thomas May and his assigns |
| | Harlikey, Philip | | Thomas May and his assigns |
| May 4th | Fulton, Robert | | John McCullock and his assigns |
| May 4th | Perry, Richard, Jr. | | Reese Meredith and his assigns |
| | Connell, Jeffry and Mary Bryan. | | John Little and his assigns |
| | Huffty, Samuel | | James Armitage and his assigns |
| | Roche, Mary | | Robert Aikin and his assigns |
| | Sheedy, Margaret | | Jesse Maris and his assigns |
| | Roche, John | Ireland | Andrew Doz and his assigns |
| | Rawleigh, Elizabeth | | George Ashbridge and his assigns |
| May 5th | Melberger, Henry | | Andrew March and his executors |
| | Grogan, Nathaniel | | Daniel Montgomery and his assigns |
| | Warren, Thomas | | William Bellamy and his assigns |
| | Fry, Henry | | George Honey, Jr., and his assigns |
| | Wells, William | | David Thomson and his assigns |
| | England, John | | Henry Neill and his assigns |
| | Scanlan, Mary | | George Smedley and his assigns |
| | Lee, James | | Charles Read, Jr., and his assigns |
| | Pierce, Hannah | | Capt. George Stainforth and his assigns. |
| | Low, Elizabeth | | Edward Batchelor and his assigns |
| | Rue, Lewis | | Anthony Wright |
| | Fitzmeiry, Margaret | | William Aldimus and his assigns |
| | Davis, Thomas | | James Armitage and his heirs |

| Residence. | Occupation. | Term. | Amount. |
|---|---|---|---|
| Lancaster | Apprentice, taught the farmer's business, have five quarters' night schooling.[1] | 5 yrs., 11 mo., 7 d. | £20. |
| Philadelphia | Apprentice, taught the art and mystery of a jeweler and goldsmith, found all necessaries and mending, except clothing. | 5 yrs. | |
| Mill Cr. Hundred, New Castle co. | | 4 yrs. | £16. |
| Philadelphia | Apprentice, taught navigation[3] | 4 yrs. | |
| Cecil co., Md. | | 4 yrs. | £20. |
| Cecil co., Md. | | 3 yrs. | £16. 5. |
| Philadelphia | Apprentice, taught the house carpenter's trade, found meat, drink, washing, lodging and shoes only. | 2 yrs., 5 mo. 16 d. | |
| Philadelphia | Apprentice, taught the art of a mariner. | 4 yrs., 5 mo. 11 d. | |
| Philadelphia | | 4 yrs., each. | £17. £13. |
| | Apprentice | 6 yrs., 9 mo. 24 d. | |
| Philadelphia | The master to discharge the servant at expiration of three years provided he behaves well. | 4 yrs. | £14. 6. |
| Springfield twp., Chester co. | | 5 yrs. | £13. 10. |
| Philadelphia | Servant, taught to read and write perfectly and cypher as far as rule of three.[3] | 7 yrs. | £14. 16. |
| Goshen twp., Chester co. | | 4 yrs. | £13. 10. |
| Northern Liberties | Apprentice (note 5, have £15 lawful money of Pa.). | 3 yrs. | |
| Philadelphia | | 4 yrs. | £20. |
| Philadelphia | | 4 yrs. | £16. |
| Philadelphia | Apprentice, taught the art and mystery of a merchant and bookkeeping, read and write perfectly and cypher as far as and through the rule of three.[3] | 10 yrs., 11 mo., 15 d. | |
| Southwark | Apprentice, taught the art, trade and mystery of a shipwright, found meat, drink, washing, lodging and working apparel (note 3, and of the value of £8 current money of Pa.). | 5 yrs., 26 d. | |
| Philadelphia | Servant | 8 yrs. | £15. |
| Willis twp., Chester co. | | 4 yrs. | £14. |
| Evesham twp., Burlington co., W. Jersey. | Servant | 6 yrs. | £14. |
| Northern Liberties | | 4 yrs. | £15. |
| Philadelphia | | 4 yrs. | £15. |
| Philadelphia | Apprentice taught the cordwainer's trade, have two quarters' night schooling, one to be the ensuing winter and the other the last winter of term.[3] | 4 yrs. | |
| Northern Liberties | Apprentice taught housewifery, sew, knit and spin, read and write perfectly (note 3, a bed and bedding of value of £5). | 9 yrs., 11 mo., 21 d. | |
| Southwark | Apprentice, taught the house carpenter's trade, allowed time to go to school at nights every winter, the father to pay the expense note 5, have £4 in money). | 3 yrs., 6 mo. | |

| Date. | Name. | From the Port of | To Whom Indentured. |
|---|---|---|---|
| May 5th | Carruth, Margaret | | Nathan McClellan and his assigns |
| | Testin, Thomas | | James Wood and his assigns |
| | Harrison, Joseph | | John Cole and his assigns |
| May 6th | House, Joseph | | Alexander Ross |
| | Kennedy, Catharin | | Aaron Musgrove and his assigns |
| | Mahony, Daniel, and Elizabeth Herlity. | | George Ashbridge, Jr. |
| | Rogers, Alexander | | Lawrence, Ganet |
| | Rice, Ann | | Edward, Barret and his assigns |
| May 7th | McDonnell, John | | Samuel Henry and his assigns |
| | Sheffner, Francis | | Peter Waggoner and his assigns |
| | Bryan, Archibald (a free negro servant). | | Cuff Drabo (a free negro) and his assigns. |
| May 8th | Dougherty, Robert | | Robert McCalla and his assigns |
| | Kennedy, Daniel | | James Hendracks and his assigns |
| | Mahony, Mary | | John Ringo and his assigns |
| | Tillison, John | | John Brown and his assigns |
| | Murphy, Edmond, and Isabella, his wife. | | Thos. Mayberry |
| | | | Thos. Mayberry and his assigns |
| | Hays, Patrick | | Gunning and his assigns |
| May 9th | Founder, John | | Syriac Judah and his assigns |
| | Whitcomb, William | | William Hazelwood and his assigns |
| | Rogers, Bridget | | Joseph Johnson and his assigns |
| | Huffty, Sarah | | Jacob Liverey and his assigns |
| | Pierce, Hannah | | Capt. Robert Hardie and his assigns |
| | Pierce, Hannah | | Capt. Robert Hardie and his assigns |
| | Lynch, Michael | | Lawrence Howard and his assigns |
| May 11th | Galler, John | | John Douglass and his assigns |
| | Bradshaw, William | | Samuel Jackson and his assigns |

---

[1] To be found all necessaries and at the expiration have freedom dues.
[2] To be found all necessaries and at the expiration have one new suit of apparel.
[3] To be found all necessaries and at the expiration have two complete suits of apparel, one whereof to be new.

## List of Indentures.

| RESIDENCE. | OCCUPATION. | TERM. | AMOUNT. |
|---|---|---|---|
| Warren twp., Bucks co. | Servant | 2 yrs., 1 mo. | £ 8. |
| Merion twp. | Apprentice, taught husbandry or farming, read and write perfectly, cypher as far as and through the rule of three.[3] | 7 yrs., 7 mo. 25 d. | |
| Philadelphia | Apprentice, taught the boat builder's trade, found meat, drink, washing, lodging and working apparel, and at expiration have £ 3 current money of Pa. | 3 yrs., 8 d. | |
| Fort Pitt | Apprentice, taught the art and mystery of a merchant and bookkeeping and found all necessaries. | 7 yrs. | |
| Philadelphia | | 4 yrs. | £ 10. |
| Goshen, Chester co. | (Note 1) | 4 yrs. each. | £ 18. |
| | (Note 1) | | £ 14. |
| Blockley twp., Phila. co. | Have legal freedom dues, the indenture being for four years, one year being up by Robert Hardie. | 3 yrs. | £ 14. |
| Philadelphia | | 4 yrs. | £ 13. |
| Trenton, Hunterdon co., W. Jersey. | | 5 yrs. | £ 15. |
| Philadelphia | Apprentice, taught cordwainer's trade, have one year's day, and six months' night schooling.[3] | 8 yrs., 7 mo. 17 d. | |
| Philadelphia | | 4 yrs. | £ 9. |
| Salisbury twp., Lancaster co. | Have freedom dues | 3 yrs., 6 mo. (one half year being given up). | £ 14. 2. 8. |
| Alexandria, Va. | | 6 yrs. | £ 16. |
| Amwell, Hunterdon co., W. Jersey | | 4 yrs. | £ 14. |
| Lower Chichester, Chester co. | | 2 yrs., 6 mo. | £ 11. |
| | Servant[3] | 4 yrs. | £ 30. |
| Mt. Holly, Burlington co., W. Jersey. | Servant[3] | 4 yrs. | |
| N. Castle, Hundred in the Lower Counties. | | 8 yrs. | £ 13. |
| Oxford twp., Phila. co. | Apprentice, taught farming or husbandry, read and write perfectly.[3] | 15 yrs., 6 mo. | |
| Philadelphia | Servant, taught the comb maker's trade. | 5 yrs. | £ 16. |
| Blockley twp., Phila. co. | | 4 yrs. | £ 14. 6. |
| Bristol twp., Phila. co. | Apprentice, taught housewifery, sew, knit and spin, read and write perfectly, cypher as far as and through the rule of three.[3] | 13 yrs., 6 mo. | |
| Philadelphia | | 4 yrs. | £ 15. |
| Philadelphia | | 3 yrs., 11 mo., 19 d. | £ 15. |
| Marple twp., Chester co. | | 4 yrs. | £ 16. |
| Philadelphia | Apprentice | 7 yrs. | £ 10. |
| Philadelphia | Apprentice, taught art and mystery of a mariner and navigation, read and write perfectly, cypher as far as rule of three.[3] | 4 yrs. | |

[4] To be found all necessaries and at the expiration have two complete suits of apparel, one whereof to be new, and 40s. in money.

[5] At expiration have two complete suits of apparel, one whereof to be new.

| Date. | Name. | From the Port of | To Whom Indentured. |
|---|---|---|---|
| 1772.<br>May 11th | Murphy, Dennis<br>McCullough, Margaret<br>Cunningham, Thomas<br>Peters, George | | Benjamin Armitage and his assigns..<br>John Trapnell and his assigns......<br>Jacob Graff and his assigns.........<br>John Trapnell and his executors..... |
| May 12th | Hooley, Daniel<br>Miller, John<br>Lynch, Elizabeth | | Richard Hartshorn and his assigns...<br>Frederick Stonemetz and his assigns..<br>Joseph Talum and wife............ |
| May 13th | Sullivan, Patrick<br>Ferguson, Joseph<br>Driscoll, Jeremiah<br>Roche, Edward<br>Roche, Edward | Ireland | Samuel McClong and his assigns....<br>John Handlyn and his assigns.......<br>Abraham Shelly and his assigns.....<br>Francis Wade and his assigns.......<br>Col. Daniel Claues and his assigns.. |
| May 14th | Mills, David<br>Reardon, Darby<br>Cuningham, David<br>Hart, James<br>Collins, Maurice, and Connor, Timothy.<br>Ahir, Honor<br>Burkhard, Daniel | | Robert Wood and his assigns........<br>James Partridge and his assigns.....<br>Wm. McFee and his assigns.........<br>Charles McLean and his assigns.....<br>Abraham Holmes and his assigns....<br>Abraham Holmes and his assigns....<br>Valentine Stillwaggon and his assigns. |
| May 14th | Anquetin, John<br>Walter, George, and Walter, Philip.<br>Walter, Mary<br>Connell, John, and Eleanor, his wife.<br>Walter, Catherine<br>Walsh, Patrick<br>Walsh, Patrick<br>McCullough, James, and McCullough, Sarah.<br>Ahir, Mary | Cork | William Byrne and his assigns......<br>George Filter and his assigns........<br>John Jacob and wife..............<br>Duncan Leech and his assigns.......<br>Francis Grey .....................<br>Michael Graats ....................<br>David Franks and his assigns.......<br>Andrew Todd and his assigns......<br>Daniel Huston and his assigns....... |

## List of Indentures.

| Residence. | Occupation. | Term. | Amount. |
|---|---|---|---|
| Southwark | Servant | 4 yrs. | £20. |
| Derby twp., Chester co. | | 3 yrs. | £6. |
| Philadelphia | | 3 yrs., 6 mo. | £15. |
| Derby twp., Chester co. | Servant [5] (one half of the year being given up). | 3 yrs. | 12/. |
| Bensalem twp., Bucks co. | | 4 yrs. | £18. |
| Philadelphia | Apprentice | 9 yrs. | £10. |
| Philadelphia | Apprentice, taught housewifery and sew, read and write perfectly.[3] | 9 yrs., 10 mo. | |
| Upper Alloways Cr., Salem co., W. Jersey. | | 5 yrs. | £15. |
| Philadelphia | Apprentice, taught the turner's trade, have three months' night schooling.[5] | 5 yrs., 11 mo., 18 d. | |
| Philadelphia | (Note 1, and £5 in money) | 4 yrs. | £17. |
| Philadelphia | Servant [5] | 3 yrs. | £14.6. |
| Ft. Johnson, Albany co., N. Y. Govt. | | 3 yrs. | £14.6. |
| Philadelphia | | 4 yrs. | £1.10. |
| Christiana Bridge, New Castle co. | | 4 yrs. | £15. |
| Edgemont twp., Chester co. | | 4 yrs. | £14. |
| Philadelphia | Apprentice, taught tailor's trade, have six months night schooling [3]. | 6 yrs., 10 mo., 25 d. | |
| Donegal twp., Lancaster co. | | 2 yrs., 6 mo. each. | £10. each. |
| Donegal twp., Lancaster co. | | 4 yrs. | £12.10. |
| Northern Liberties | Apprentice, found meat, drink, washing, lodging, mending and hats, taught the hatmaker's trade, allowed time to go to evening school each winter, his father-in-law paying expense of the schooling, found apparel during the last three years of the term only (at expiration have two complete suits, one to be new). | 7 yrs. | |
| Philadelphia | Taught to read and write well [1]. | 4 yrs. | £12. |
| Philadelphia | Apprentice, each to be taught the art, trade and mystery of a cordwainer, have one year schooling (note 3, each). | 9 yrs., 6 mo. 25 d. 11 yrs., 7 mo., 25 d. | |
| Philadelphia | Apprentice, taught housewifery, sew, knit, spin, read and write perfectly (note 3, and £4 lawful money of Pa.). | 4 yrs., 8 mo. 9 d. | |
| Philadelphia | Servant, it is agreed for every child they have during the term, each to serve three months for its maintenance, and the master to maintain the present child, Daniel, and find all necessaries gratis (note 3, each). | 3 yrs., 11 mo., 14 d. | £22.10. |
| Philadelphia | Apprentice, taught housewifery, sew, knit and spin, read and write perfectly (note 3, and £4 lawful money of Pa.). | 9 yrs., 9 mo. 17 d. | |
| Philadelphia | Servant [3] | 3 yrs. | £16. |
| Philadelphia | To serve his master in the country of the Illinois or elsewhere. | 3 yrs. | £16. |
| East Whiteland twp., Chester co. | (Note 1) | 7 yrs. | £30. |
| | (Note 1) | 4 yrs. | |
| Strasburg twp., Lancaster co. | | 4 yrs. | £13. |

| Date. | Name. | From the Port of | To Whom Indentured. |
|---|---|---|---|
| 1772. May 14th... | Bayer, John Ulrich | | Charles Read, Jr., and his assigns.... |
| May 15th... | McCreary, Mary | | Thomas Nelson and his assigns...... |
| | Leech, Walter Moore | | Jeremiah Warder, Jr............... |
| | Bryan, Patrick | | Jonathan Coates and his assigns..... |
| | Miller, John | London | Henry Haines and his assigns........ |
| | McIlroy, Mary | | Andrew Porte and his assigns....... |
| | Beard, Edward | | Thomas Rutherford and his assigns.. |
| | Abbott, Thomas | | Thomas Cliffton and his assigns..... |
| | Riordan, Mary | Ireland | John Cox and Charles Thomson and their assigns. |
| May 16th... | Cook, Elizabeth | | Anthony Birkenbill and his assigns... |
| | Creeden, Catherine | | Christian Grover and his assigns.... |
| May 16th... | Gillispey, Alexander | | John Kinkaid and his assigns........ |
| | Wholohan, Martin; Lyons, Bartholomew; Pygott, Jno.; Keeffe, David; Whetston, Nathaniel; Connell, John; Rehilly, Daniel; Laughlin, Dennis; Vise, Michael; Ryan, Patrick. | | John Cox and Charles Thomson and their assigns. |
| | Collins, Stephen, and Moroney, Thomas. | | John Cox and Charles Thomson and their assigns. |
| | Riordan, Thomas........... | Ireland | John Cox and Charles Thomson and their assigns. |
| | Logan, Samuel, and Dixon, William. | | James Wilson and his assigns........ |
| | Dinwiddie, Ann, and Duff, Rachel. | | James Wilson and his assigns........ |
| | Maulsby, Barnabas | | Morris Maulsby and his assigns..... |
| May 18th... | Brenock, Robert | | Isaac Baker and his assigns......... |
| | Cockran, William | | George Bunner .................... |
| | Brenock, Robert | | Isaac Baker and his assigns......... |
| | McKeigh, George | | Thomas Robinson and wife......... |
| | Wren, John, and Riordan Margt. | | George Woods and his assigns...... |
| | Oquener, Ann | Island of Jersey | James Cresson and his assigns....... |
| | De St. Croix, Ann........... | Island of Jersey | Isaac Lobdell and his assigns........ |
| | Phister, Charlotte | | Peter Kurtz and his assigns......... |
| May 18th... | Ball, Israel | | Edward Bonsall and his assigns..... |

## List of Indentures.

| Residence. | Occupation. | Term. | Amount. |
|---|---|---|---|
| Evesham twp., Burlington co., W. Jersey. | .................. | 4 yrs. | £ 24. |
| Philadelphia | .................. | 6 yrs. | £ 14. |
| Philadelphia | Apprentice, taught the art and mystery of navigation (note 2, besides his old). | 3 yrs., 17 d. | |
| Charles Town twp., Chester co. | .................. | 4 yrs. | £ 14. |
| Philadelphia | Servant [3] | 3 yrs., 3 mo. | £ 15. 6. 3. |
| Philadelphia | .................. | 3 yrs. | £ 10. |
| Paxton twp., Lancaster co. | .................. | 4 yrs. | £ 17. |
| Philadelphia | Apprentice, taught the sadler's trade, have nine months' evening schooling and found all necessaries. | 7 yrs. | |
| Northampton twp., Burlington co., W. Jersey. | Servant, and for each child, she, the said Mary, shall have during term, she shall serve a further term of three months.[3] | 3 yrs., 11 mo., 13 d. | £ 8. 10. |
| Passyunk, Phila. co. | Apprentice, six months' day schooling and taught housewifery.[3] | 7 yrs., 10 mo., 25 d. | |
| Passyunk, Phila. co. | .................. | 4 yrs. | £ 14. |
| Carlisle, Cumberland co. | .................. | 4 yrs. | £ 17. 10. |
| Northampton twp., Burlington co., W. Jersey. | .................. | 4 yrs. each. | £ 13. each. |
| Northampton twp., Burlington co., W. Jersey. | .................. | 4 yrs. each. | £ 11. 10. each. |
| Northampton twp., Burlington co., W. Jersey. | Servant, to serve three months over the term for every child his wife may have within the term of three years, 11 mo., 13 d., as mentioned p. 159.[5] | 1 yr., 11 mo. 12 d. | £ 8. 10. |
| Leacock twp., Lancaster co. | .................. | 4 yrs. | £ 14. each. |
| Leacock twp., Lancaster co. | .................. | 4 yrs. each. | £ 13. each. |
| Whitemarsh, Phila. co. | Apprentice, taught art, trade and mystery of a millwright, have one quarter schooling each year[4] | 6 yrs., 11 mo., 23 d. | |
| Northern Liberties, Phila. co. | .................. | 4 yrs. | £ 15. |
| Northern Liberties, Phila. co. | .................. | 4 yrs. | £ 14. |
| Northern Liberties, Phila. co. | Apprentice, taught the bricklayer's trade.[1] | 5 yrs. | |
| Southwark | Apprentice, taught the house carpenter's trade, time to go to night school each winter, the father paying expense.[3] | 7 yrs., 3 mo. | |
| Bedford, Bedford co. | .................. | 4 yrs. each. | £ 15. £ 11. |
| Philadelphia | Servant [3] | 7 yrs. | £ 17. |
| Philadelphia | Servant [3] | 7 yrs. | £ 17. |
| Philadelphia | Apprentice, taught housewifery, allowed time to attend the minister to be prepared to receive the sacrament.[5] | 2 yrs., 6 mo. | |
| Philadelphia | Apprentice, taught trade of a house carpenter, found meat, drink, | 5 yrs., 10 mo., 12 d. | |

| Date. | Name. | From the Port of | To Whom Indentured. |
|---|---|---|---|
| 1772. | | | |
| June 18th | Innes, Robert | | Valentine Brown and his wife....... |
| | White Sarah | | William Kirkpatrick and his assigns. |
| | Rochenberger, George | | Adam Brockhauser ............... |
| | Pelan, Robert | | Samuel Brice and his assigns........ |
| | McFalls, James | Ireland | George Clymer and his assigns...... |
| | Dooley, David | | John Campbell and his assigns...... |
| | Brown, Mary | | John Aikin and his assigns.......... |
| | Stowas, John | Bristol | Amos Wickersham and his assigns... |
| | Morgan, Samuel | | Samuel Cooper and his assigns....... |
| | Gardner, John | Ireland | Samuel Correy and his assigns...... |
| May 19th | Wilcox, John | | William Austin and his assigns..... |
| | McKay, Daniel | | Joseph Potts and his assigns........ |
| | Peeling, Hershaw | | James Wilson and his assigns....... |
| | Peeling, Joshua | | James Wilson and his assigns....... |
| | Ramsey, Joseph, and Ramsey, Alexander. | Ireland | Adam Keer and his assigns.......... |
| | McDaniel, William | | William Hasleton, his executors and assigns. |
| | Heyder, John, Hendrick | London | Andrew Burkhard and his assigns... |
| | Linton, Mary | | John Raser and his assigns.......... |
| May 19th | Hanse, Conrad | | George Whey ...................... |
| | Young, Edward | | Thomas Penrose and his assigns..... |
| | Anderson, John | | Thomas Penrose and his assigns..... |
| | Runner, Martin | | George Kemble and his assigns...... |
| | Duke, John | | William Lownes and his assigns..... |

## List of Indentures.

| Residence. | Occupation. | Term. | Amount. |
|---|---|---|---|
| | washing, lodging and working apparel, and time to go to night school each winter, the mother paying the expense. | | |
| Northern Liberties | Apprentice, taught the lock and white smith's trade, have one year schooling (note 5, and £10 current lawful money of Pa.). | 13 yrs. | |
| Philadelphia | Apprentice, taught to read and write perfectly and cypher, also the trade of a mantua and stay maker.[3] | 3 yrs., 6 mo. | |
| Philadelphia | Apprentice, taught the tailor's trade, have one quarter's night schooling.[3] | 5 yrs., 6 mo. | |
| Pennsborough twp., Cumberland co. | | 4 yrs. | £14. |
| Philadelphia | Servant[3] | 4 yrs. | £20. |
| Bensalem twp., Bucks co. | | 4 yrs. | £11. |
| Welch Tracts, New Castle co. | | 4 yrs. | £16. |
| Philadelphia | Servant, taught to read and write perfectly, cypher as far as and through the rule of three.[3] | 6 yrs., 11 mo., 7 d. | £15. |
| Newtown twp., Gloucester co., W. Jersey. | | 4 yrs. | £18. |
| Philadelphia | Servant, taught the art and mystery of pulling and cutting fur and finishing hats, have two quarters' night schooling, four months of which to be in the ensuing winter.[3] | 5 yrs. | £10. |
| Philadelphia | | 5 yrs. | £18. |
| Pottsgrove, Phila co. | | 4 yrs. | £15. |
| Leacock twp., Lancaster co. | | 4 yrs. | £14. |
| Leacock twp., Lancaster co. | | 3 yrs. | £14. |
| Warwick twp., Bucks co. | Servant, found meat, drink, washing and lodging and at expiration paid according to the custom of the country. | 11 mo., 25 d. each. | £5.10. each. |
| Philadelphia | Apprentice, taught the farmer's business, have four quarters' schooling.[3] | 14 yrs., 18 d. | |
| Philadelphia | Servant, employed at shoemaker's trade.[3] | 4 yrs. | £18.9.2. |
| Philadelphia | | 3 yrs., 6 mo. | £10. |
| Philadelphia | Apprentice, taught trade of a chair maker, have two quarters' night schooling.[3] | 4 yrs. | |
| Southwark | Apprentice, taught the shipwright trade (note 5, have the tools he works with and £6 current lawful money of Pa.). | 4 yrs., 21 d. | |
| Southwark | Apprentice, taught the shipwright trade (note 5, have his working tools and £6 lawful money of Pa.). | 5 yrs., 4 d. | |
| Philadelphia | Apprentice, taught the trade of a barber, have twelve months' schooling and at expiration have legal freedom. | 6 yrs. | |
| Philadelphia | | 5 yrs., 8 mo. 19 d. | £15. |

| Date. | Name. | From the Port of | To Whom Indentured. |
|---|---|---|---|
| 1772. May 20th | McCurdy, Elizabeth | | Godfrey Twells and wife, Sarah |
| | Templeton, John | | John Montgomery and his assigns |
| | Shustren, Michael | | George White and his assigns |
| | Grantham, John | | John Stille and his assigns |
| | Standley, Peter, Jr. | | Robert Davis, his heirs and assigns |
| | Benjamin, Isaac | | Abraham Franks and his assigns |
| May 21st | Colbreath, William; Crowley, John; Bennet, Mary; Pearce, Hannah; Hannesley, Eleanor; Collins, Mary; Dehany, Thomas, and Doran, Bridget. | | James Ray and his assigns |
| | Buckley, Mary | | James Ray and his assigns |
| May 22nd | Roche, Thomas | | Henry Neile and his assigns |
| | Gamble, Robert (alias Campbell). | | Charles Allen and his assigns |
| | Campbell, Robert | | Charles Allen and his assigns |
| | Hurley, Mary | | William Goddard and his assigns |
| | Fitzgerald, Mary | | Mary Bartram and her assigns |
| | Lyon, William | | Stephen Shewell and his assigns |
| | Gray, Ann | | Joseph Shewell and his assigns |
| | Hoffman, Godfrey | London | John Webster and his assigns |
| May 23rd | Fisher, Maudline | | Abraham Freed and his assigns |
| | Garrett, John | | Caleb Ash and Joseph Leviss and their assigns. |
| | McDaniel, Maurice, and Eleanor, his wife. | | Isaac Wayne and his assigns |
| | Till, Nicholas | | William Eckhart and his assigns |
| | Gallagher, Patrick, and Margaret, his wife. | | William Stewart and his assigns |
| May 25th | Schriner, Adam | | Richard Tittermary and his assigns |
| | Miller, John | | Michael Shennick and executors |
| May 26th | Goodshins, John | | George Heitel (or Keitel) and his assigns. |
| | Glauwell, Lancelot | | William Lownes and his assigns |

## List of Indentures.

| Residence. | Occupation. | Term. | Amount. |
|---|---|---|---|
| Philadelphia | Apprentice, taught housewifery, to sew, knit and spin, read well and write a good legible hand. | 6 yrs., 10 mo., 25 d. | |
| Carlisle, Cumberland co. | | 5 yrs. | £ 13. |
| Philadelphia | | 8 yrs. | 5/. |
| Philadelphia | Apprentice, taught the tailor's trade, found all necessaries and have six months' night schooling. | 7 yrs., 4 mo. | |
| Southwark | Apprentice, taught the cooper's trade, read and write well, and common arithmetic as far as rule of three, and at expiration have legal freedom dues. | 11 yrs., 1 mo., 13 d. | |
| Philadelphia | Servant, taught the tobacconist's trade (note 1, and £ 5 in cash). | 5 yrs. | £ 5. for his use. |
| Little Britain twp., Lancaster co. | | 4 yrs. each. | £ 12. each. |
| Little Britain twp., Lancaster co. | | 5 yrs. | £ 12. |
| Philadelphia | Servant[3] | 3 yrs., 1 mo. 13 d. | £ 16. |
| Kent co., Md. | | 3 yrs. | £ 16. 10. |
| Kent co., Md. | Servant[3] | 2 yrs., 11 mo., 22 d. | £ 16. 10. |
| Philadelphia | | 4 yrs. | £ 12. |
| Philadelphia | | 4 yrs. | £ 12. |
| Philadelphia | | 1 yr. | £ 12. |
| Philadelphia | | 3 yrs. | £ 12. |
| Philadelphia | Servant[3] | 2 yrs., 6 mo. | £ 14. 12. 6. |
| N. Britain twp., Bucks co. | Servant[3] | 7 yrs. | £ 18. |
| Clennwell, Gloucester co. | | 3 yrs., 6 mo. | £ 10. |
| East Town, Chester co. | | 4 yrs. each. | £ 7. each. |
| Philadelphia | Apprentice, taught the biscuit maker's trade, sent to evening school each winter (note 1, or £ 10 current money of Pa.). | | £ 7. |
| Newtown twp., Cumberland co. | | 4 yrs. each. | £ 15. each. |
| Southwark | Apprentice, taught the ropemaker's trade, sent to evening school each winter.[3] | 5 yrs., 3 mo. 3 w., 3 d. | |
| Northern Liberties | Apprentice, taught the cordwainer's trade, have six months' night schooling and at expiration have two complete suits of apparel, one to be new. | 6 yrs., 6 mo. 8 d. | |
| Philadelphia | Apprentice, taught the trade of a leather dresser and breeches maker, have two quarters' night schooling and one quarter's night schooling.[1] | 5 yrs., 3 mo. 10 d. | £ 5. |
| Philadelphia | Apprentice, taught the trade and mystery of a house carpenter, allowed time to go to evening school three months each winter (note 2, besides his old). | 6 yrs. | |

| Date. | Name. | From the Port of | To Whom Indentured. |
|---|---|---|---|
| May 26th, 1772. | Birchin, Robert George | | John Chambers and his assigns |
| May 27th | Bert, Robert | | John Slemens and his assigns |
| May 28th | McIntire, Andrew | | John Ross and his assigns |
| | White, John | | Valentine Stillwaggon and his assigns. |
| | Merrit, James | | James Alexander and his assigns |
| May 29th | Simmons, Robert | | Richard Collier and his assigns |
| | Melarky, Bridget | | Philip Tanner and his assigns |
| | Lawrence, Benjamin | | Jacob Bunner and his assigns |
| | Kean, Charles | | George Brown |
| | Johnson, Elizabeth | | John Branson and wife, Sarah, and their executors. |
| May 30th | Minheer, Ann Elizabeth | | Leonard Shallcroft and his assigns |
| | Fitzgerald, Thomas | | Sebastian Muffler and wife, Mary |
| June 1st | Caldwell, Ann | | John Maxwell Nesbit and his assigns. |
| | Covert, Isaac, Jr. | | Joseph Henszey and his assigns |
| | Mulleahy, James | | William Lawrence and his assigns |
| | Bradshaw, Edward | Ireland | Michael Washington and his assigns. |
| | Magrath, John | Cork | John Thomson and his assigns |
| | Vanbooskirk, Jacob, Jr. | | Joseph Coleman and his assigns |
| June 2nd | Crawford, Mary | | William Adcock and his assigns |
| | Wisdom, Catherine | | John Marshall and his assigns |
| | Stewart, James | | John Little and his assigns |
| | Burnside, Robert | Ireland | David Patton and his assigns |
| | Riggen, Charles | | Matthew Grimes and his assigns |
| June 3rd | Flower, John Anthony | | James Cook and his assigns |
| | Jauch, Margaret | | Michael Taylor and his assigns |
| | Jauch, Elizabeth | | Michael Gitz and his assigns |
| | Church, Sylvanus | | Peter McKinley and his assigns |
| June 4th | Currell, Thomas | | James Maginnis |
| | McQuaid, Mary, Jr. | | Jonathan Gostelow and his assigns |

## List of Indentures.

| Residence. | Occupation. | Term. | Amount. |
|---|---|---|---|
| Philadelphia | Apprentice, taught the sail maker's trade, found meat, drink and lodging (note 2, besides his old). | 7 yrs., 2 mo. | |
| Cumberland twp., York co. | | 2 yrs. | £ 10. |
| Philadelphia | Apprentice | 7 yrs. | £ 10. |
| Philadelphia | Apprentice | 7 yrs. | 5/. |
| Philadelphia | Apprentice, taught trade of a blacksmith, taught to read and write perfectly, and cypher as far as and through rule of three[3] | 14 yrs., 7 mo., 7 d. | |
| Philadelphia | | 4 yrs. | £ 10. |
| E. Nottingham, Chester co. | Apprentice, taught housewifery, sew, knit, spin, read and write perfectly.[3] | 11 yrs., 8 mo., 18 d. | |
| Philadelphia | Apprentice, taught the hatter's trade.[3] | 8 yrs. | |
| W. Pennsbury twp., Cumberland co. | Servant, taught art and mystery of farming.[3] | 3 yrs., 20 d. | |
| Newtown twp., W. Jersey | Apprentice, taught housewifery, sew, knit and spin, read in Bible and write a good legible hand, and at expiration have two complete suits of apparel, one to be new. | 8 yrs., 4 mo. 17 d. | |
| Oxford twp., Phila. co. | | 2 yrs., 10 mo. | £ 13. |
| Philadelphia | Apprentice, taught the baker's trade.[3] | 5 yrs. | £ 10. |
| Philadelphia | Apprentice, taught housewifery[3] | 6 yrs. | |
| Philadelphia | Apprentice, taught trade of a Windsor chair maker, have four quarters' evening schooling.[3] | 6 yrs., 5 mo. | |
| Hickory Town, Phila. co. | | 4 yrs. | £ 15. |
| Philadelphia | Servant, if he pay or cause to be paid the sum of £ 8 within the space of two months next ensuing then this indenture to be void. | 1 yr., 8 mo. | £ 8. |
| Philadelphia | Servant[3] | 3 yrs., 5 mo. 18 d. | £ 12. 10. |
| Philadelphia | Apprentice, taught the cooper's trade have four quarters' night schooling (note 1, or £ 10 in money). | 7 yrs. | |
| Philadelphia | Servant | 4 yrs. | £ 10. |
| Movamensing, Phila. co. | Servant | 2 yrs. | £ 5. |
| Philadelphia | Servant[3] | 4 yrs., 6 mo. | £ 16. |
| Paxton twp., Lancaster co. | Servant[3] | 3 yrs., 6 mo. | £ 13. |
| Philadelphia | Apprentice | 6 yrs., 1 mo. | £ 2. |
| Philadelphia | Apprentice, taught the art of a mariner (note 2, besides his old) | 7 yrs. | |
| Northern Liberties | Apprentice, taught housewifery, sew, knit and spin, read and write the German language perfectly (note 3, and £ 4 in lawful money of Pa.). | 9 yrs., 11 mo., 2 w. | |
| Philadelphia | Apprentice, taught the mantua maker's trade, read and write the German language perfectly[3]. | 8 yrs., 3 mo. | |
| Philadelphia | Apprentice, taught the tailor's trade, read and write perfectly and cypher as far as and through rule of three.[3] | 6 yrs., 8 mo. 6 d. | |
| Philadelphia | | 6 yrs., 6 mo. | 5/. |
| Philadelphia | Apprentice | 5 yrs., 3 mo. | £ 1. 8. 9. |

| Date. | Name. | From the Port of | To Whom Indentured. |
|---|---|---|---|
| 1772. June 5th.... | Braizier, Anthony, Joseph | | Martin Fiss and his assigns |
| | Jackson, Archibald | | Henry William Stiegel and his assigns. |
| | Flanagan, Patrick | | Henry William Stiegel and his assigns. |
| | Williams, John | | Henry William Stiegel and his assigns. |
| June 5th.... | Mildenberger, Michael | | John Norris and his assigns |
| | Moore, Samuel | | Capt. George Gilbert and his assigns. |
| | Patterson, John | | Thomas Bamford and his executors.. |
| June 6th.... | Yocom, Charles | | John Whiteall |
| | Vandergrift, Abraham | | Jacob Weaver and his assigns |
| | Farrel, Patrick | | Conrad Johnson and his assigns |
| | Miller, John | | John Lampater and his assigns |
| | Biggart, James | | Isaac Hopkins and his assigns |
| 1772. June 8th.... | McClean, Ann | | Henry Ireland and wife Elizabeth |
| | McHerron, Daniel | | William Brown and his assigns |
| | Tyman, John | | John Lewis and his assigns |
| | Londve, John | | William Walker and his assigns |
| | Fletcher, Abraham | | James Walker and his assigns |
| | Cammel, Sarah | | Philip Cammel |
| June 9th.... | Prilkinton, Edward | | Menan Kenard |
| | Cline, Theobald | | Rudolph Bunner and his assigns |
| | Hodgekinson Anthony | | John Milnor and Thomas Hough and their assigns. |
| | Poulson, Zachariah, Jr. | | William Baker and his assigns |
| | Garret, Catherine | | Wickersham, Elijah, and his assigns.. |

| RESIDENCE. | OCCUPATION. | TERM. | AMOUNT. |
|---|---|---|---|
| Philadelphia | Apprentice, taught the baker's trade, read and write perfectly, cypher as far as and through rule of three.[3] | 5 yrs., 7 mo. | |
| Manheim twp., Lancaster co. | | 4 yrs. | £15. |
| Manheim twp., Lancaster co. | | 5 yrs. | £15. |
| Manheim twp., Lancaster co. | | 7 yrs. | £15. |
| Northern Liberties | Apprentice, taught the shipwright's trade, have three quarters' evening schooling (note 5, have £6 lawful money of Pa. and tools he works with). | 4 yrs. | |
| Philadelphia | Apprentice, taught art and mystery of a mariner and navigation, read and write perfectly and cypher (note 2, besides his old). | 8 yrs., 2 mo. | |
| Lancaster | Servant (note 2, besides his old of the value of £6 lawful money of Pa.). | 1 yr. | £5.5.3. |
| Philadelphia | Apprentice, taught the cordwainer's trade, have one quarter half days schooling.[1] | 6 yrs., 7 mo. 7 d. | |
| Northern Liberties | Apprentice, taught the art trade and mystery of a tanner and currier, have nine months' evening schooling.[3] | 3 yrs., 6 mo. 25 d. | |
| Lower Dublin, Phila co. | Servant | 4 yrs. | £14. |
| Northern Liberties | Apprentice, taught the art, trade and mystery of a butcher or victualler.[3] | 4 yrs., 6 mo. | |
| Philadelphia | Servant[3] | 3 yrs., 10 mo., 15 d. | £15. |
| Northern Liberties | Apprentice, taught housewifery and sew, have one year and six months' schooling and time to go one other year to school before she arrives at age of 17, the father paying the expense of said year's schooling.[3] | 13 yrs. | |
| Northern Liberties | Apprentice, taught the shipwright's trade, have one quarter's evening schooling each winter (note 3, and the tools he works with). | 6 yrs. | |
| Ewkland, Chester co. | | 4 yrs. | £17. |
| Terrone twp., York co. | | 4 yrs. | £16. |
| Terrone twp., Chester co. | | 4 yrs. | £17. |
| | Apprentice | 8 yrs., 4 mo. | 5/. |
| Philadelphia | Apprentice, taught sail maker's trade, have one quarter's evening schooling each winter (note 2 besides his old). | 5 yrs., 8 mo. | |
| Philadelphia | Servant | 3 yrs., 6 mo. | £16. |
| Philadelphia | Apprentice, taught the cooper's trade, have two quarters' winter evening schooling (note 2, besides his old). | 6 yrs., 6 mo. 15 d. | |
| Philadelphia | Apprentice, taught the baker's business, read in the Bible, write a legible hand, cypher as far as rule of three.[3] | 10 yrs. | |
| Middle Town, Lancaster co. | Servant | 4 yrs. | £18. |

| Date. | Name. | From the Port of | To Whom Indentured. |
|---|---|---|---|
| | Philips, Benjamin | | Richard Dennis and his heirs and his assigns. |
| | Connelly, Catherine | | Richard Ham and Elizabeth, his wife. |
| June 10th | Whelly, Clare | | Thomas Craig |
| | Kelly, William | | Robert Connolly and his assigns |
| | Johns, Hanibel | | Benjamin Levy and his assigns |
| | Nantz, Benjamin | | Benjamin Swett, Jr., and James Stuart and their assigns. |
| | Quirey, Thomas | | Benjamin Swett, Jr., and James Stuart and their assigns. |
| | Gilmore, John | | Charles Robeson and his assigns |
| | Preston, Thomas | | John Duncan and his assigns |
| | Boden, John, Jr. | | John Barker and his assigns |
| | Hanlan, Eleanor | | William Bellamy and his assigns |
| | Henry, John | | William Logan and his assigns |
| | Moseley, Richard | | Benjamin Worral and his assigns |
| | Griffin, Joanna | | George Wilson and his assigns |
| | Burns, Hugh | | Luke McCabe |
| June 12th | Highman, Jane, and Fagan, Judith. | | John Harken and his assigns |
| | Colclough, Ann | | John Harken and his assigns |
| | Rickertin, Lina | | Wm. Shoemaker and his assigns |
| | Nicholson, Elizabeth | Ireland | John Harken and his assigns |
| June 13th | Darby, Ann | | Jacob Testin and wife, Ann |
| | Donaldson, James | | Samuel Penrose and his assigns |
| | Bryan, Mary | | John Rice and his assigns |
| | Quin, Arthur | | John Kille and his assigns |
| June 15th | Kelly, Charles | | Daniel McMannemy |
| | Smith, Benjamin | | John Somerwell and his assigns |
| | Dick, James | | Thomas Kearny and his assigns |
| | Thomson, William | | William Carson and his assigns |
| | Pompey (a negro) | | Mary Bingham and her assigns |
| | Guigan, Adam | Ireland | Elias Adiddle and his assigns |
| | Donaldson, James | | Robert Davison and his assigns |
| June 16th | Graham, John | Ireland | John Lewis and his assigns |

## List of Indentures.

| Residence. | Occupation. | Term. | Amount. |
|---|---|---|---|
| Southwark | Apprentice, taught the shipwright's trade, have one quarter's night schooling each winter.[3] | 7 yrs., 3 mo. | |
| Philadelphia | Apprentice, taught housewifery and sew, have six months' schooling and in case of her death before the expiration of the term the indenture to be void.[3] | 5 yrs., 5 mo. | |
| Philadelphia | | 4 yrs. | £ 10. |
| Southwark | Servant[5] | 2 yrs. | £ 6. |
| Philadelphia | Servant[5] | 3 yrs. | 5/. |
| Philadelphia | Apprentice, taught the art and mystery of a mariner and navigation, read and write perfectly, cypher as far as and through rule of three.[3] | 7 yrs. | |
| Philadelphia | Apprentice, taught art and mystery of a mariner, found meat, drink, washing and lodging, have £ 15 lawful money of Pa. each year, and at expiration have one complete new suit of apparel. | 3 yrs. | |
| Philadelphia | Servant[3] | 5 yrs. | £ 20. |
| Philadelphia | Apprentice, taught art and mystery of pulling and cutting fur, dyeing and finishing hats, read and write (note 1, to the value of £ 12, or £ 12 in money). | 3 yrs., 9 mo. | |
| Philadelphia | Apprentice, taught the tailor's trade, read and write perfectly, cypher as far as and through rule of three.[3] | 10 yrs., 1 mo., 20 d. | |
| Philadelphia | | 4 yrs. | £ 12. |
| Philadelphia | | 4 yrs. | £ 16. |
| Philadelphia | Apprentice, taught trade of a house carpenter.[1] | 6 yrs. | £ 8. |
| Philadelphia | | 4 yrs. | £ 10. |
| Philadelphia | Servant, found all necessaries excepting clothing. | 4 mo. | £ 9. 5. 1. |
| Philadelphia | | 4 yrs. each. | £ 10. each. |
| Wilmington, N. Castle co. | | 4 yrs. | £ 14. |
| Manor of Moreland, Phila. co. | Servant | 7 yrs. | £ 21. |
| Philadelphia | Servant[3] | 3 yrs., 9 mo. 22 d. | £ 10. |
| Derby twp., Chester co. | Apprentice, taught housewifery, sew, knit and spin, read and write perfectly (note 3, and a cow and calf). | 7 yrs., 4 mo. 12 d. | |
| Kingsessing twp., Phila. co. | Apprentice | 13 yrs. | £ 8. |
| Kensington, Phila. co. | Apprentice, taught housewifery, sew, read and write perfectly.[3] | 4 yrs. | |
| Woolwich twp., Gloucester co., W. Jersey. | Servant[5] | 1 yr., 6 mo. | £ 6. 10. |
| Red Lion Hundred, N. Castle co. | Servant[3] | 2 yrs., 9 mo. | £ 16. 10. |
| Pennsueck, Salem co., W. Jersey | | 4 yrs. | £ 16. 10. |
| Pennsueck, Salem co., W. Jersey | | 4 yrs. | £ 16. 10. |
| Philadelphia | | 2 yrs., 9 mo. | £ 15. |
| Philadelphia | Apprentice | 15 yrs., 2 mo. | £ 17. |
| Springfield, Chester co. | Servant[5] | 2 yrs. | £ 7. 10. |
| Antrim twp., Cumberland co. | | 2 yrs., 3 mo. | £ 12. 3. 0. |
| Ewkland, Chester co. | Servant, found meat, drink, washing and lodging, only. | 1 yr., 2 mo. | £ 7. 10. |

| Date. | Name. | From the Port of | To Whom Indentured. |
|---|---|---|---|
| 1772.<br>May 16th | Miller, John | | George Stuart and his assigns |
| | Dowling, James, and Brown, John. | | James Wilson and his assigns |
| | Hulton, Matthew | | James Wilson and his assigns |
| | Donelly, William | Ireland | George Stuart and his assigns |
| | Middleton, Elizabeth | | Joseph Perk and his assigns |
| | Moore, John | | James Wilson and his assigns |
| | Tyman, John | | James Wilson and his assigns |
| | McCaulpin, Catherine | | Samuel Morris and his assigns |
| | Dell, Nicholas | | James Dalton and his assigns |
| | Alle, Jacob | | John Galloway and his assigns |
| | Stout, Samuel | | Thomas Shields and his assigns |
| June 17th | Haughton, Thomas | | Dennis Daugherty and his assigns |
| | Taggart, John | Ireland | Samuel Fairlamb and his assigns |
| | Connolly, Margaret | Ireland | Thomas Craig and his assigns |
| | Shimfessell, Maria Catherine | | Ludowick Shimfessell and his assigns |
| | McClosky, John | | Samuel Miller and his assigns |
| June 18th | Higgans, Thomas | | Thomas Middleton and his assigns |
| | Connolly, Mary | Londonderry | John Harkins and his assigns |
| | Orner, John | | Charles Chamberlain and his assigns |
| | White Samuel | | William Hiron and his assigns |
| | Dawson, Elizabeth | | Isaac Maris and his assigns |
| | Magalligal, Ann | | John Rhea and his assigns |
| | McDeed, Catherine | Londonderry | Elisha Worrell and his assigns |
| June 19th | McNeal, John | | Casper Graff and his assigns |
| | Neitser, Sophia | | John Milnor and his assigns |
| | Kokenterfer, Jacob | | Joy Castle |
| | Moser, John | | Christopher Zimmerman and his assigns. |
| | Osborne, John | | John Gensell |
| June 20th | Schmeeterin, Elizabeth | | William Neise and his assigns |
| | Moore, Francis | | William White and his assigns |

[1] To be found all necessaries and at the expiration have freedom dues.
[2] To be found all necessaries and at the expiration have one new suit of apparel.
[3] To be found all necessaries and at the expiration have two complete suits of apparel, one whereof to be new.

## List of Indentures.

| Residence. | Occupation. | Term. | Amount. |
|---|---|---|---|
| Buckingham twp., Bucks co. | Servant, found meat, drink, washing and lodging, only. | 1 yr. | £20. |
| Leacock twp., Lancaster co. | | 4 yrs. each. | £14. each. |
| Leacock twp., Lancaster co. | | 6 yrs. | £14. |
| Baltimore co., Md. | Servant (note 2, besides his old). | 3 yrs., 3 mo. | £14. 10. |
| N. Town twp., Cumberland co. | | 4 yrs. | £14. 10. |
| Leacock twp., Lancaster co. | Servant, employed in the clothier or fuller's business.[5] | 2 yrs. | £9. |
| Leacock twp., Lancaster co. | Servant[3] | 4 yrs. | £14. |
| Philadelphia | | 3 yrs., 6 mo. | £17. |
| Philadelphia | | 4 yrs. | £10. |
| Philadelphia | Apprentice, taught the tailor's trade, have two quarters' day schooling and time to go one other quarter to school, his uncle, Thomas Tilton, paying for said quarter, all to be given when he reaches age of 16 or 18 (note 2 besides his old). | 9 yrs., 11 mo., 23 d. | |
| Philadelphia | Apprentice, taught art, trade and mystery of a goldsmith, found meat, drink, washing and lodging, allowed time to go one winter to evening school, the father paying the expense. | 5 yrs., 3 mo. | |
| Philadelphia | Servant | 4 yrs. | £11. |
| Chester twp., Chester co. | Servant, found meat, drink, washing and lodging, shoes and stockings. | 6 mo. | £3. 9. 6. |
| Philadelphia | Servant[3] | 3 yrs. | £15. |
| | Servant | 8 yrs. | £0. 5. 0. |
| Elsenborough twp., Salem co., W. Jersey. | | 3 yrs. | £17. |
| Philadelphia | | 3 yrs. | £12. |
| Wilmington | Servant[3] | 4 yrs. | £10. |
| Philadelphia | Apprentice, taught the cordwainer's trade, have three quarters' night schooling, one at a Dutch, and other two at an English school.[3] | 5 yrs. | |
| Philadelphia | | 4 yrs. | £14. |
| Marple twp., Chester co. | | 4 yrs. | £14. 2. 6. |
| Philadelphia | | 4 yrs. | £15. |
| Haverford twp., Chester co. | Servant[3] | 4 yrs. | £14. 2. 6. |
| Philadelphia | | 4 yrs. | £12. |
| Philadelphia | | 5 yrs. | £18. |
| Philadelphia | Apprentice, taught the art and mystery of a mariner and navigation (note 2, besides his old, or £10 lawful money of Pa.). | 4 yrs. | |
| Northern Liberties | Apprentice, taught the cordwainer's trade, read and write the German and English language (note 3, and the tools he works with). | 10 yrs. | |
| Philadelphia | Apprentice, taught the art of mariner and navigation.[3] | 8 yrs., 1 mo. 22 d. | |
| Springfield Manor, Phila. co. | Servant | 4 yrs. | £24. 6. 9. |
| Philadelphia | Apprentice, taught the art and mys- | 6 yrs. | £15. |

[4] To be found all necessaries and at the expiration have two complete suits of apparel, one whereof to be new, and 40s. in money.

[5] At expiration have two complete suits of apparel, one whereof to be new.

| Date. | Name. | From the Port of | To Whom Indentured. |
|---|---|---|---|
| June 23rd... | Dougherty, Edward | | John McGonnagle |
| | Hunter, Margaret | | George Taylor and his assigns |
| | Pree, John (free negro) | | George Taylor and his assigns |
| | Atkinson, Charles | | George Taylor and his assigns |
| | Murray, Judith | | George Taylor and his assigns |
| | Conner, Bryan | | Joseph Wood and his assigns |
| | Thomson, Robert | | James Caldwell and his assigns |
| | Campbell, James | Ireland | Joseph Smith and his assigns |
| | Carlan, John | | William Johnson and his assigns |
| | Hughes, Jane | | William Snowden and Ann, his wife |
| | Burk, Margaret | Ireland | Jane Tennent and her assigns |
| 1772. June 23rd... | Grace, Mary | | Joseph Coleman and his assigns |
| June 24th... | Haninger, John Frederick | | Sebastian Muffler and his assigns |
| | Dunnaphan, James | | Thomas Leiper and his assigns |
| June 25th... | Carney, Michael | Ireland | George Taylor and his assigns |
| | Shere, Ann and Cannon, Bridget. | Ireland | George Taylor and his assigns |
| | Adams, Martha | Ireland | George Taylor and his assigns |
| | Woodward, Nice | | Joseph Johnson and his assigns |
| | Callwell, William | | William Green and his assigns |
| | Odle, Edward W. | | Joseph Pemberton and his assigns |
| | Porter, John | Ireland | Jacob Gerand and his assigns |
| June 26th... | Castle, John | | Benjamin Loxley and his assigns |
| | Roche, Margaret | | Benjamin Loxley and his assigns |
| June 27th... | Hamilton, Patrick | Ireland | Dr. Samuel Kennedy and his assigns |
| | Carter, Joseph | | Margaret Carter and her assigns |
| | Beckford, Elizabeth | | Michael Schwartz |

## List of Indentures.

| RESIDENCE. | OCCUPATION. | TERM. | AMOUNT. |
|---|---|---|---|
| | tery of a pilot, have six months' schooling, found meat, drink and lodging and have freedom dues. | | |
| Philadelphia | Servant [5] | 2 yrs. | £ 10. |
| Chambers Town, Cumberland co. | Servant [3] | 2 yrs. | 20/. |
| Chambers Town, Cumberland co. | Servant, taught to read perfectly [3] | 5 yrs. | 20/. |
| Chambers Town, Cumberland co. | Servant [3] | 3 yrs. | 20/. |
| Chambers Town, Cumberland co. | Servant [3] | 2 yrs. | 20/. |
| Philadelphia | Servant [5] | 3 yrs. | 5/. |
| Philadelphia | Apprentice, taught the art and mystery of a mariner and navigation and found meat and drink only. | 2 yrs., 10 mo., 23 d. | |
| Philadelphia | Servant [3] | 4 yrs., 11 mo., 21 d. | £ 10.4 |
| Philadelphia | | 3 yrs. | £ 15.12. |
| Philadelphia | Apprentice, taught mantua maker's trade, have three quarters' schooling, in case of her death, the indenture to be void (note 2, besides the old). | 3 yrs., 9 mo. 13 d. | |
| Springfield, Chester co. | Servant [3] | 3 yrs., 9 mo. 20 d. | £ 13.10. |
| Philadelphia | Apprentice, taught housewifery, to sew, knit and spin and read and write perfectly. [3] | 7 yrs. | |
| Philadelphia | | 2 yrs., 9 mo. | £ 18.10. |
| Philadelphia | Apprentice, taught the tobacconist's business, read and write perfectly, have two quarters' night schooling. [3] | 1 yr., 9 mo. 3 d. | |
| Chambers Town, Cumberland co. | Servant [3] | 2 yrs., 11 mo., 19 d. | £ 10. |
| Chambers Town, Cumberland co. | Servant [3] | 3 yrs., 11 mo., 19 d. each. | £ 20. each. |
| Chambers Town, Cumberland co. | Servant [3] | 3 yrs., 5 mo. 19 d. | £ 10. |
| Southwark | Apprentice, taught housewifery, sew, knit and spin, read and write perfectly. [3] | 11 yrs. | |
| Kent co. | Servant, to have two shirts, one frock, two pairs shoes and stockings, two pairs trousers, and found washing and lodging. | 6 mo. | £ 1.7.6. |
| Philadelphia | Servant, found meat, drink, washing and lodging, two pairs trousers, two pairs shoes, two shirts. | 6 mo. | £ 2.4.9. |
| Philadelphia | Servant, taught the art, trade and mystery of a tailor. [3] | 2 yrs., 6 mo. | £ 11. |
| Philadelphia | Apprentice, taught house carpenter's trade, found meat, drink, washing, lodging and working apparel, time to go to evening school one quarter each winter, Capt. Joy Castle paying the expense of the schooling. | 5 yrs. | |
| Philadelphia | | 7 yrs. | £ 12. |
| E. Whiteland twp., Chester co. | Apprentice, found all necessaries only. | 2 yrs., 9 mo. | £ 10.10. |
| Philadelphia | Apprentice | 5 yrs. | £ 3. |
| Plumstead twp., Bucks co. | Servant, provided with a new suit of clothes immediately (note 5, | 2 yrs. | 10/. |

| Date. | Name. | From the Port of | To Whom Indentured. |
|---|---|---|---|
| 1772. | | | |
| June 29th... | Crawford, Andrew | | Benjamin Moses Clava |
| | Evey, Adam | | Moore Furman |
| | Reardon, Ann | | Alexander Henderson and his assigns. |
| | Iden, Jacob | | Adam Fonarden and his assigns |
| | Martin, Elizabeth | | Dr. John Day and his heirs |
| | Wisdom, Catherine | | Wm. Weston and his assigns |
| | Howard, Mary | | John Marshall and his assigns |
| June 30th... | Wallington, Charles | | Samuel Griskham, heirs and assigns.. |
| | Raworth, John | | John Rice and his assigns |
| | Watson, Benjamin Johnson... | | David Cumming, Jr., and his assigns. |
| | Smith, John | | William Scull and his assigns |
| | Fisher, Nicholas | | John Perkins and his assigns |
| | Paradee, John, Jr. | | James Irvine, his heirs and assigns... |
| | Carey, Arthur | Ireland | James Wilson and his assigns |
| | Lynch, Teady | Ireland | James Wilson and his assigns |
| | Higgans Charles | | James Wilson and his assigns |
| July 1st.... | Matts, John | | George Leib and his assigns |
| | Carter, Williams, Jr. | | Menan Kenard and wife |
| | Smith, James | | Thomas Proctor and his assigns |
| | McCollum, James | | Thomas Lowe and his assigns |
| | Thomas, Jacob | | John Odenheimer and his assigns |
| | Govier, Joseph | | Garret Hulsekamp |
| July 2nd.... | Fling, William | | Edward McGigging, his heirs and assigns. |

## List of Indentures.

| RESIDENCE. | OCCUPATION. | TERM. | AMOUNT. |
|---|---|---|---|
| | to be well clothed, with one suit and 30 s. in money). | | |
| Woolwich twp., Gloucester co., W. Jersey. | Apprentice, taught art and mystery of a shopkeeper, have one year's schooling.[3] | 8 yrs., 4 mo. 15 d. | |
| Philadelphia | Apprentice, taught the art and mystery of a mariner and navigation.[1] | | |
| Philadelphia | Apprentice | 9 yrs., 6 mo. | £ 8. |
| Philadelphia | Apprentice, to have freedom dues to the value of £ 10 in money. | 7 yrs. | £ 5. |
| Philadelphia | Apprentice, taught housewifery, have two winters' schooling.[3] | 3 yrs., 8 mo. | £ 3. |
| Philadelphia | Servant | 2 yrs., 2 mo. | £ 6. |
| Moyamensing twp., Phila. co. | | 4 yrs. | £ 12. |
| Philadelphia | Apprentice, taught the house carpenter's trade, have one quarter's evening schooling each winter, the mother paying the expense.[3] | 5 yrs., 11 mo., 10 d. | |
| Northern Liberties | Apprentice, taught the shipwright's trade, have one quarter's evening schooling every winter.[3] | 2 yrs., 1 mo. 19 d. | |
| Philadelphia | Apprentice, taught art, trade and mystery of a tin plate worker, have 5 quarters' evening schooling.[3] | 9 yrs. | |
| Philadelphia | Apprentice, taught the trade of a chaise maker.[3] | 4 yrs. | |
| Philadelphia | Servant | 3 yrs. | £ 15. |
| | Apprentice, taught the hatter or pelt maker's business, found meat, drink, washing, lodging and hats, and liberty to go and see his parents two weeks of every year. | 7 yrs. | |
| Leacock twp., Lancaster co. | Servant[1] | 2 yrs., 8 mo. 14 d. | £ 12. |
| Leacock twp., Lancaster co. | Servant[1] | 2 yrs., 11 mo. | £ 12. |
| Leacock twp., Lancaster co. | | 1 yr., 3 mo. | £ 8. |
| Northern Liberties | Apprentice, taught trade of a tanner and currier, found all necessaries, and have two quarters' night schooling. | 2 yrs., 11 mo., 15 d. | |
| Philadelphia | Apprentice, taught the sail maker's trade.[3] | 5 yrs., 9 mo. 6 d. | |
| Philadelphia | Apprentice, taught the house carpenters trade, have one quarter's evening schooling each winter, found meat, drink, washing, lodging and mending.[3] | 6 yrs., 1 mo. 14 d. | |
| Philadelphia | | 3 yrs. | £ 14. |
| Philadelphia | Apprentice[3] | 4 yrs. | £ 13. 12. |
| Philadelphia | Apprentice, taught art and mystery of a pilot in the bay and river Delaware and for every vessel he shall pilot he shall have one Spanish dollar, when the river is stopped, have schooling (note 2, besides his old). | 1 yr., 9 mo. | |
| Philadelphia | Apprentice, taught the bricklayer's trade, read and write perfectly | 1 yr., 10 mo. 10 d. | |

| Date. | Name. | From the Port of | To Whom Indentured. |
|---|---|---|---|
| | Denham, Martha | | Peter Sutter and his assigns |
| | Denham, Martha | | Capt. Wm. Gamble and his assigns |
| | Linton, Leah | | Hugh Crawford and his assigns |
| | Gordon, James Samuel | | Edmond Milne and his assigns |
| July 3rd | Power, Mary | | Andrew Rogers and his assigns |
| | Howell, James | | Andrew Rogers and his assigns |
| July 4th | Young, Martha | | Susanna Dewar and her assigns |
| | Hare, George | | John Fagan and his assigns |
| July 6th | Butler, Patrick | | Isaac Vannost and his assigns |
| | Lindley, John | | John Phiz and his assigns |
| | Wallington, Timothy | | Henry Robinson |
| | McDonnell, Collin | | Thomas Harrison |
| July 7th | Gaskill, Elinor | | Thomas Gaskill and his assigns |
| | Dodd, Thomas | | John Righter and his assigns |
| | Hacket, Michael | | James Webb and his assigns |
| | Oulden, John | | Peter Cheeseman and his assigns |
| | Kearns, William | | Peter Cheeseman and his assigns |
| July 9th | Madden, Thomas | | William Smith and his assigns |
| | Mara, Richard | | William Smith and his assigns |
| | Duggan, James | | John Donald and his assigns |
| July 10th | Kent, Elizabeth | | George Taylor and his assigns |
| | Power, Charles | | David Jones and his assigns |
| | Hines, William | | Richard Mason and his assigns |
| | McNamara, Johanna | | James Wilson and his assigns |
| | Shea, Anslace, and Bell, Mary. | | James Wilson and his assigns |
| | Murphy, Mary, and Walsh Catherine. | | James Wilson and his assigns |
| | Witson, Ann | | James Wilson and his assigns |
| | Ryan, John | | James Wilson and his assigns |
| | Dunn, Lawrence; Sweeney, Edward; Cerby, John; McGee, Charles; Connor, James; Doyle, Patrick, and Ryan, John. | | James Wilson and his assigns |
| | Sheehm, Daniel | | James Wilson and his assigns |
| | Molony, Joseph; Ryan, Patrick; Fitzgerald, John, and Fitzgerald, Maurice. | | James Wilson and his assigns |
| | Hannahan, James | | James Wilson and his assigns |
| July 11th | King, Mary | | Anthony C. Morris |

## List of Indentures.

| Residence. | Occupation. | Term. | Amount. |
|---|---|---|---|
| | and cypher as far as and through rule of three.[1] | | |
| Philadelphia | Apprentice, taught housewifery, sew and knit, read and write perfectly.[2] | 9 yrs., 2 mo. | |
| Philadelphia | | 8 yrs., 10 mo. | £0.5.0. |
| Roxborough twp., Phila. | | 3 yrs., 6 mo. | £8. |
| Philadelphia | Servant[3] | 6 mo. | |
| Hanover twp., Lancaster co. | Servant | 3 yrs., 6 mo. | £4.15. |
| Hanover twp., Lancaster co. | Servant | 6 yrs. | £16. |
| Philadelphia | Apprentice, taught to read Bible, write a legible hand, housewifery and sew.[3] | 6 yrs., 10 mo. 20 d. | |
| Philadelphia | | 5 yrs. | £15. |
| Philadelphia | Apprentice, taught block maker's business.[3] | 4 yrs., 6 mo. | £9. |
| Philadelphia | Apprentice, taught the sail making business and found working apparel. | 5 yrs. | |
| Philadelphia | Apprentice, do every kind of work, found all necessaries and have one quarter's day schooling. | 2 yrs., 8 mo. 22 d. | |
| Philadelphia | Apprentice, taught the tailor's trade, have five quarters' night schooling.[1] | 6 yrs. 11 mo., 7 d. | |
| Philadelphia | Apprentice | 10 yrs., 7 mo. | 5/. |
| Merion twp., Phila. co. | Servant | 3 yrs. | £17. |
| Lancaster twp., Lancaster co. | | 7 yrs. | £18. |
| Gloucester twp., Gloucester co., W. Jersey. | | 5 yrs. | £18. |
| Gloucester twp., Gloucester co., W. Jersey. | | 5 yrs. | £18. |
| Brandywine, N. Castle | Servant[5] | 2 yrs., 3 mo. | £10.9.6. |
| Brandywine, N. Castle | Servant[5] | 2 yrs., 7 mo. | £11.2. |
| Southwark | Servant[5] | 3 yrs., 6 mo. | £10.2.5. |
| Conecocheague, Cumberland co. | Servant (note 2, besides his old) | 2 yrs. | £5. |
| Philadelphia | Apprentice | 11 yrs. | £7.10. |
| Philadelphia | Apprentice, taught the joiner and chair maker's business, have three quarters' evening schooling (note 2, of the value of £10 money of Pa.). | 4 yrs., 10 mo., 17 d. | |
| Leacock twp., Lancaster co. Leacock twp., Lancaster co. | | 4 yrs. each. | £12. each. |
| Leacock twp., Lancaster co. | | 5 yrs. each. | £12. each. |
| Leacock twp., Lancaster co. | | 6 yrs. | £12. |
| Leacock twp., Lancaster co. | Servant | 8 yrs. | £14. |
| Leacock twp., Lancaster co. | | 4 yrs. each. | £14. each |
| Leacock twp., Lancaster co. Leacock twp., Lancaster co. | | 6 yrs. each. | £14.0.0. |
| Leacock twp., Lancaster co. | | 5 yrs. | £14.0.0. |
| Philadelphia | Apprentice, taught housewifery, sew, read, write and cypher.[1] | 4 yrs., 1 mo. | |

| Date. | Name. | From the Port of | To Whom Indentured. |
|---|---|---|---|
| 1772.<br>July 11th... | Coleman, Mary<br>Higgins, Edward<br>Keefe, James | | Thomas Garret and his assigns<br>Abraham Higgins and his assigns<br>Daniel Cronog and his assigns |
| | Tower, John<br>Foster, David<br>Fitzgerald, Maurice<br>Meyer, Rachel | | Stephen Porter and his assigns<br>Andrew Moyhan and his assigns<br>Michael Wills and his assigns<br>George Wirt and his assigns |
| July 13th... | Cahill, Judith, and Fitzgerald, Joanna.<br>Gilmore, John<br>Davis, Israel | | James Wilson and his assigns<br>Peter Robeson and his assigns<br>Cadwalader Dickinson and his assigns. |
| July 13th... | Flyn, Samuel | Ireland | Edward Barret and his assigns |
| | Dunphy, Edward<br>Doran, Bridget<br>Coleman, Patrick<br>McNeil, Laughlin<br>Peters, George, and Stuart, Elizabeth.<br>Peters, George, and Stuart, Elizabeth.<br>Crowley, Mary | Ireland<br>Ireland | Samuel Morton<br>William Garret, Jr., and his assigns<br>Nathan Garret, Jr., and his assigns<br>John Hanna and his assigns<br>Jehu Jones and his assigns<br>George Taylor and his assigns<br>Enos Leeley and his assigns |
| | Sweeney, John | | John O'Bryan |
| July 14th... | Keho, William<br>Ford, Benjamin<br>Shute, Atwood | Ireland | Isaac Knight and his assigns<br>Thos. Shortall and his assigns<br>Robert Morris |
| | Owen, Abigail | Ireland | Andrew Gregg and his assigns |
| | Owen, Abigail | | Simon Shirlock and his assigns |
| | Seeger, Wm. Frederick<br>Ryan, John<br>Connell, Michael | Ireland | Peter Wiltberger and his assigns<br>Seth Pancoast and his assigns<br>Abraham Lewis and his assigns |
| | O'Bryan, John | Ireland | Griffith Jones and his assigns |
| | McGuire, Redmon, and Johnson, Elizabeth. | | George Taylor and his assigns |
| July 15th... | Power, Catherine<br>Dechan, Bridget<br>Lawrence, John<br>Cron, William<br>Power, John<br>Francis, Richard; Dunn, Patrick; Sweeny, Richard.<br>Ballard, John<br>Lyons, Catherine; Grainger, Mary; Ryan, Margt.; Downs, Catherine; Power, | Ireland<br>Ireland | John Pinkerton and his assigns<br>George Taylor and his assigns<br>George Taylor and his assigns<br>Joseph Ogden and his assigns<br>Patrick Burnes and his assigns<br>James Ray and his assigns<br>James Ray and his assigns<br>James Ray and his assigns |

| Residence. | Occupation. | Term. | Amount. |
| --- | --- | --- | --- |
| Willistown, Chester co. | Servant. | 3 yrs. | £11.10.0. |
| Rockhill twp., Bucks co. | | 1 yr., 9 mo. | £17.0.0. |
| Willistown, Chester co. | Servant, have one month's day schooling every year.[3] | 3 yrs., 6 mo. | £11.10.0. |
| Lancaster | Servant[5] | 3 yrs., 6 mo. | £11.17.0. |
| Philadelphia | Servant. | 1 yr., 8 mo. | £7.15.0. |
| Plymouth twp., Phila. co. | Servant. | 6 yrs. | £18.0.0. |
| Philadelphia | Apprentice, taught the tailor's trade, have six months' day schooling in the summer season.[3] | 7 yrs., 11 mo., 23 d. | |
| Leacock twp., Lancaster co. | | 4 yrs. each. | £12.0.0. each. |
| Philadelphia | | 5 yrs. | £20.0.0. |
| Philadelphia | Apprentice, taught the cordwainer's trade, have nine months' evening schooling.[3] | 5 yrs., 5 mo. 16 d. | |
| Southwark | Apprentice, taught the butcher's trade.[3] | 5 yrs. | £18.0.0. |
| Philadelphia | | 5 yrs. | £18.0.0. |
| Willis Town, Chester co. | | 4 yrs. | £14.0.0. |
| Derby twp., Chester co. | Servant[3] | 3 yrs. | £11.12.0. |
| Philadelphia | Servant[3] | 3 yrs. | £11.10.5. |
| Philadelphia | Servant[1] | 4 yrs. each. | £12.0.0. |
| Chambers Town, Cumberland co. | Servant[1] | 4 yrs. each. | £12.0.0. each. |
| Cohanney, Cumberland co., W. Jersey. | | 4 yrs. | £13.0.0. |
| | Apprentice, taught the tailor's trade (note 2, besides his old). | 5 yrs. | |
| Abbington, Phila. | Servant[5] | 2 yrs., 6 mo. | £10.14.2. |
| Philadelphia | | 6 yrs., 6 mo. | £0.5.0. |
| Philadelphia | Apprentice, taught the art and mystery of a mariner, found meat, drink, washing, lodging and apparel, the father to provide apparel and accommodation when in Phila. | 5 yrs., 9 mo. | |
| Philadelphia | Servant[3] | 3 yrs., 11 mo. | £14.0.0. |
| Southwark | | 3 yrs., 11 mo. | £14.0.0. |
| Philadelphia | | 3 yrs., 9 mo. | £23.7.6. |
| Marple twp., Chester co. | | 4 yrs. | £17.0.0. |
| Willis twp., Chester co. | Servant (note 3, and eight Spanish dollars). | 3 yrs., 6 mo. | £11.12.9. |
| Willis twp., Chester co. | Servant (note 5, have £6 lawful money of Pa. in lieu of freedom dues). | 3 yrs., 6 mo. | £13.8.0. |
| Chambers Town, Cumberland co. | Servant[1] | 4 yrs. each. | £12.0.0. pd. for each of their use. |
| Philadelphia | Servant (note 3, £5 in money) | 4 yrs. | £10.12.0. |
| Chambers Town, Cumberland co. | Servant[3] | 3 yrs. | £12.0.0. |
| Chambers Town, Cumberland co. | Servant[3] | 3 yrs. | £12.0.0. |
| Philadelphia | Servant[3] | 3 yrs, 3 mo. | £11.8.0. |
| Southwark | | 8 yrs. | £16.0.0. |
| Little Britain twp., Lancaster co. | | 4 yrs. each. | £14.0.0. each. |
| Little Britain twp., Lancaster co. | | 5 yrs. | £14.0.0. |
| Little Britain twp., Lancaster co. | | 4 yrs. each. | £12.0.0. each. |

| Date. | Name. | From the Port of | To Whom Indentured. |
|---|---|---|---|
| | Margaret; Mahar, Catherine; Barry, Ann. | | |
| | Connor, Francis, and Campbell, John. | | James Ray and his assigns.......... |
| | Connor, William ................... | | James Ray and his assigns.......... |
| | Traverse, Edmond ................. | | James Ray and his assigns.......... |
| | Bryan, Augustine .................. | | Thomas Felton and his assigns....... |
| | Young, Edward .................... | | John Young ....................... |
| | Whitsitt, Richard .......... | Ireland .... | Matthias Graff and his assigns....... |
| July 16th... | Wass, Edmond ..................... | | John Trapnell and his assigns....... |
| July 17th... | Hennesy, Patrick .................. | | Asher Woolman and his assigns..... |
| | Kennedy, Mary ............ | Ireland .... | James Boyd and his assigns.......... |
| July 18th... | Callan, Charles ............ | Ireland .... | James Little and his assigns......... |
| | Fagen, William ............ | Ireland .... | James Little and his assigns......... |
| | Davison, William .......... | Ireland .... | James Little and his assigns......... |
| | Barron, Patrick ............ | Ireland .... | James Little and his assigns......... |
| | Foster, Margaret .................. | | Joseph Miller and his assigns........ |
| | Davison, William .................. | | George Williamson and his assigns... |
| July 20th... | Rable, Christian ................... | | Samuel Prince and his heirs ........ |
| | Berry, William .................... | | John Logan and his assigns.......... |
| | Fitzgerald, Elinor ................. | | William Carlisle and his assigns..... |
| | Murphy, Mary ..................... | | Robert Bell and his assigns.......... |
| | Hudtman, John Matts.............. | | Lewis Truckenmiller and his assigns.. |
| | Weyen, Elizabeth .......... | Holland ... | Peter David Hansel ............... |
| | Campbell, Eleanor ................. | | Daniel Meredith and his heirs....... |
| | Kerr, Thomas ............. | Ireland .... | William Richards and his assigns.... |
| | Kreamer, John ..................... | | George Sternfeltz and his assigns..... |
| | McMeans, Robert, and McMeans, Thomas. | | John Logan and his assigns.......... |
| | Burn, Mary ....................... | | Joseph Price and his assigns........ |
| | Shan, John ........................ | | Ellis Lewis and his assigns.......... |
| | Graham, Sarah .................... | | Andrew Bower and his wife, Barbara. |

## List of Indentures.

| Residence. | Occupation. | Term. | Amount. |
|---|---|---|---|
| Little Britain twp., Lancaster co. | Connor to be employed at the cordwainer's business. | 4 yrs. each. | £ 14. 0. 0. each. |
| Little Britain twp., Lancaster co. | Cordwainer's business | 4 yrs. | £ 14. 10. 0. |
| Little Britain twp., Lancaster co. | Business of a tailor | 4 yrs. | £ 14. 10. 0. |
| Philadelphia | Apprentice, taught bricklayer's trade, sent to night school each winter.[3] | 4 yrs., 10 mo., 16 d. | |
| Philadelphia | Apprentice, taught the saddler's trade.[1] | 2 yrs., 8 mo. | |
| Lancaster | Servant, found meat, drink, washing, lodging. | 1 yr., 6 mo. | £ 8. 0. 0. |
| Derby | At expiration £ 5 lawful money of Pa. over and above his freedom dues. | 5 yrs. | £ 11. 7. 2. |
| Northampton twp., Burlington co., W. Jersey. | | 4 yrs. | £ 15. 0. 0. |
| Charlestown, S. C. | Servant[3] | 3 yrs., 10 mo. | £ 15. 0. 0. |
| Philadelphia | Servant, and if he pay or cause to be paid James Little £ 9. 4 in twenty days from this date, the indenture to be void.[5] | 2 yrs., 6 mo. | £ 9. 4. 0. |
| Philadelphia | Servant, and if he pay or cause to be paid to James Little the sum of £ 15 lawful money of this province in twenty days from this date, the indenture to be void.[5] | 2 yrs., 6 mo. | £ 15. 0. 0. |
| Philadelphia | Servant[3] | 4 yrs. | £ 15. 0. 0. |
| Philadelphia | Servant, and if said Barron pay or cause to be paid James Little or his attorney in thirty days from this date £ 7. 10 lawful money of Pa. the indenture to be void.[5] | 2 yrs., 6 mo. | £ 7. 10. 0. |
| Haverford twp., Chester co. | Servant | 3 yrs. | £ 12. 10. 0. |
| Philadelphia | Servant | 4 yrs. | £ 15. 10. 0. |
| Philadelphia | Apprentice, taught the cordwainer's trade, have six months' evening schooling.[3] | 4 yrs. | |
| Mendham twp., Morris co., E. Jersey. | | 3 yrs., 6 mo. | £ 14. 0. 0. |
| Philadelphia | | 5 yrs. | £ 2. 0. 0. |
| Philadelphia | Servant[3] | 4 yrs. | £ 12. 0. 0. |
| Philadelphia | Apprentice, taught tailor's trade, have one year and six months' schooling.[3] | 11 yrs. | |
| Blockley twp., Phila. co. | Servant, have freedom dues | 4 yrs., 3 mo. | £ 15. 0. 0. |
| Philadelphia | Apprentice, taught housewifery and sew, have one quarter's schooling in the sixth and seventh year of her apprenticeship.[3] | 11 yrs. | |
| Philadelphia | Servant[5] | 3 yrs. | £ 6. 0. 0. |
| Northern Liberties | Apprentice, taught baker's trade, have one year's schooling.[3] | 12 yrs. | £ 3. 0. 0. |
| Mendham twp., Morris co., E. Jersey. | | 3 yrs. each. | £ 14. 10. each. |
| Southwark | | 4 yrs. | £ 11. 12. 0. |
| Philadelphia | | 4 yrs. | £ 12. 0. 0. |
| Northern Liberties | Apprentice, taught housewifery, sew, knit, spin, read in Bible.[3] | 8 yrs., 4 mo. 21 d. | |

| Date. | Name. | From the Port of | To Whom Indentured. |
|---|---|---|---|
| July 21st | Humphrys, John, Jr. | | Thomas Williams and his assigns |
| | Collins, Patrick | | Samuel Paul and his assigns |
| | Thompson, Margaret | | David Cowen and his assigns |
| | Bayas, Jane | | Ann Williams |
| | Hair, George | | Bryan O'Hara and his assigns |
| | Walsh, Richard | | Samuel Howell, Jr., and his assigns |
| | Mannin, Elizabeth | | John Hilson |
| | McMunon, Patrick | | David Kayle and his assigns |
| | Matthews, Mary | | Jacob Kimberlin, Jr., and his assigns |
| July 22nd | Correy, Martha | Ireland | William Musgrove and his assigns |
| | Russell, Patrick | | Martin Pendergast and his assigns |
| | Padget, John | For Jamaica | Jacob Hanse and his assigns |
| | Jordan, John | | John Hannah and his assigns |
| | Gilmore, John | | John Potts and his assigns |
| | Owen, Abigail | | Robert Dougherty and his assigns |
| | Farron, Margery | Ireland | Robert Dougherty and his assigns |
| | Magrath, John | | Christopher Curfiss and his assigns |
| July 23rd | Yotz, Anna Margaret | | Curtis Grubb and his assigns |
| | Griffith, John; Phelan, Michael; Bolon, John; Connor, Thomas; Ford, Dennis; Roberts, Patrick; Feenaghty, James; Fowler, Thomas; Egan, Patrick; Murray, Thomas, and Price, Thomas. | | David and Thomas Fulton and their assigns. |
| | Reade, Elinor; Beach, Rebecca; McNamara, Elinor, and Murphy, Mary. | | David and Thomas Fulton and their assigns. |
| | Linch, Mary | | John Marshall and his assigns |
| | Cullen, Patrick | Ireland | Joseph Porter and his assigns |
| | Cullen, Patrick | | Charles Read and his assigns |
| | Barnacle, John Adam | | Adam Kuhn and his assigns |
| | Amerson, William | Ireland | Joseph Johnson and his assigns |
| July 24th | Hutton, William | | Robert Boyes |
| | McNeal, Charles | | Paul McKnight and his assigns |
| | Meyer, Catherine | | Samuel Smith and his assigns |
| | Meyer, Catherine | | James Penny and his assigns |

## List of Indentures.

| Residence. | Occupation. | Term. | Amount. |
|---|---|---|---|
| | Apprentice, taught the cordwainer's trade, have two quarters' schooling, one to be in the last year of apprenticeship.[3] | 7 yrs. | |
| Greenwich twp., Gloucester co., W. Jersey. | | 4 yrs. | £ 16. 0. 0. |
| Salisbury twp., Lancaster co. | | 5 yrs. | £ 13. 10. 0 |
| Philadelphia | Apprentice, taught mantua maker's business.[5] | 2 yrs., 5 mo. | |
| Philadelphia | Apprentice, taught the peruke maker's trade, have two quarters' night schooling.[1] | 5 yrs., 10 mo., 9 d. | £ 15. 0. 0. |
| Philadelphia | Servant[3] | 3 yrs., 6 mo. | £ 14. 7. 9. |
| Philadelphia | Apprentice, taught housewifery and mantua maker's trade, and make bonnets and cloaks, have one year schooling.[1] | 7 yrs., 6 mo. 14 d. | |
| Philadelphia | | 2 yrs., 6 mo. | £ 6. 0. 0. |
| Elizabeth twp., Frederick co., Md. | Servant[5] | 2 yrs. | £ 10. 0. 0. |
| Philadelphia | Servant[2] | 2 yrs., 6 mo. | £ 6. |
| Southwark | | 3 yrs. | £ 9. 5. 0. |
| Philadelphia | Servant, if he pay or cause to be paid £ 16 in ten days after his arrival in Jamaica the indenture to be void.[5] | 1 yr. | £ 16. 0. 0. Jamaica currency. |
| Philadelphia | Apprentice, taught the brush maker's business, read, write and cypher befitting to keep a tradesman's books.[3] | 13 yrs. | |
| Pottsgrove, Phila. co. | | 5 yrs. | £ 20. 0. 0. |
| Philadelphia | | 3 yrs., 11 mo. | £ 14. 0. 0. |
| Philadelphia | Servant[3] | 3 yrs., 4 mo. 24 d. | £ 12. 0. 0. |
| Philadelphia | | 3 yrs., 5 mo. 18 d. | £ 6. 0. 0. |
| Cornwell Furnace, Lancaster co. | Servant | 8 yrs. | £ 30. 12. 0. |
| Nottingham twp., Chester co. | | 4 yrs. each. | £ 14. 0. 0. each. |
| Nottingham twp., Chester co. | | 4 yrs. each. | £ 12. 0. 0. each. |
| Moyamensing twp., Phila. co. | Apprentice, taught housewifery, sew plain work, read and write perfectly.[3] | 7 yrs., 9 mo. 24 d. | |
| Philadelphia | Servant (note 5, have £ 5 in money) | 2 yrs., 8 mo. | £ 13. 0. 0. |
| Burlington, W. N. Jersey | | 2 yrs., 8 mo. | £ 13. 0. 0. |
| Lancaster, Lancaster co. | | 5 yrs., 7 mo. | £ 25. 0. 0. |
| Southwark | Apprentice, taught rope maker's business.[3] | 5 yrs. | £ 3. 0. 0. |
| Philadelphia | | 7 yrs., 11 mo. | £ 14. 0. 0. |
| West Nantmill twp., Chester co. | | 10 yrs. | £ 10. 0. 0. |
| Philadelphia | Apprentice, taught to read in Bible, write a legible hand, sew, knit, spin, also housewifery.[8] | 13 yrs., 6 mo. | |
| Wilmington, N. Castle co. | | 13 yrs., 6 mo. | £ 0. 5. 0. |

| Date. | Name. | From the Port of | To Whom Indentured. |
|---|---|---|---|
| 1772. July 25th | Evans, Jacob | | Henry Cary and his assigns |
| July 25th | Hall, Levi | | John Kinner and his assigns |
| | Harrison, Joseph | | William Stretch |
| | Davis, William | | William Davis |
| | Hall, Martha | | Robert Morris and his assigns |
| July 27th | Gray, Martha | | Barny Cane and his assigns |
| | Dexter, Richard Backhouse | | James Starr and his assigns |
| | Cosman, Thomas | | John Johnson and his assigns |
| | McColter, George | Ireland | Joseph Johnson and his assigns |
| | Barns, Robert | | Joshua Cresson and his assigns |
| | Norris, William | | Joseph Johnson and his assigns |
| | Bickerton, George, Jr. | | James Rickey and his assigns |
| | Nicholson, Elizabeth | | Ann Stricker and her assigns |
| | Kain, John | | David Ware and his assigns |
| | Shields, Alexander, and Ferguson, Margaret. | Ireland | John Purden and his assigns |
| | Burk, Margaret | | Robert Gray and his assigns |
| | French, Richard | | William Connell and his assigns |
| July 28th | Chapman, Mary | | Septimus Levering and wife |
| | Shrader, John | | Cornelius Sylvin and his assigns |
| | McDonald, Susanna | | William Logan and his assigns |
| July 29th | Nixon, Margaret | | James Mercer and his assigns |
| | Leahy, Catherine | Ireland | Azariah Dunham and his assigns |

## List of Indentures.

| Residence. | Occupation. | Term. | Amount. |
|---|---|---|---|
| Philadelphia | Apprentice, taught art, trade and mystery of a baker of loaf bread and biscuit, have two quarters' evening schooling (note 5, have £10 lawful money of Pa. or lawful freedom dues). | | |
| Springfield, Phila. co | Apprentice, taught art, trade and mystery of a surgeon barber, read and write perfectly and cypher as far as and through rule of three.[3] | 16 yrs. 2 mo. | |
| Philadelphia | Apprentice, taught to pull and cut, also finishing and dyeing hats.[1] | 4 yrs., 6 mo. | |
| Philadelphia | | 4 yrs. | £ 5. 0. 0. |
| Bristol twp., Phila co | Apprentice, taught housewifery, sew, knit and spin, read and write a good legible hand, cypher as far as rule of three.[3] | 10 yrs., 1 mo., 4 d. | |
| Passyunk | Servant, found meat, drink, washing and lodging and one new shift, petticoat, apron, pair of shoes and a short gown. | 1 yr., 6 mo. | £ 3. 0. 0. |
| Philadelphia | Apprentice, taught the cordwainer's trade, have three quarters' evening schooling.[3] | 6 yrs., 10 mo., 14 d. | |
| Philadelphia | | 7 yrs. | £ 10. 10. 7. |
| Southwark | Servant, taught the cordwainer's trade.[8] | 5 yrs. | £ 15. 0. 0. |
| Philadelphia | Apprentice, taught the grocer's trade (note 2, besides his old). | 4 yrs., 3 mo. 11 d. | |
| Southwark | Servant | 4 yrs. | £ 16. 0. 0. |
| Philadelphia | Apprentice, taught the cordwainer's trade, have one quarter's evening schooling each winter of the last four years (note 2, besides his old and of the value of £10 lawful money of Pa.). | 7 yrs., 2 mo. | |
| Northern Liberties, Phila. co | Servant | 3 yrs., 9 mo. 22 d. | £ 16. 0. 0. |
| Philadelphia | Apprentice, taught the cordwainer's business, taught to read in Bible and write a legible hand (note 3, and a set of tools). | 9 yrs., 3 mo. 3 d. | |
| Philadelphia | Servant[1] | 2 yrs., 11 mo., 20 d. each. | £ 11. 10. 0. each. |
| Philadelphia | Servant[3] | 3 yrs., 10 mo., 18 d. | £ 13. 10. 0. |
| Philadelphia | Apprentice, taught art, trade and mystery of a cabinet and chair maker, have two quarters' evening schooling, one of which to be in the last years of apprenticeship.[3] | 8 yrs., 2 mo. 4 d. | |
| Northern Liberties | Apprentice, taught housewifery and sew, have two quarters' schooling.[3] | 10 yrs., 5 mo. | |
| Southwark | Apprentice, taught art, trade and mystery of a bricklayer and stone mason.[5] | 2 yrs. | |
| Philadelphia | | 4 yrs. | £ 14. 0. 0. |
| Leacock twp., Lancaster co | Servant[3] | 2 yrs., 6 mo. | £ 5. 0. 0. |
| N. Brunswick, Middlesex co., E. Jersey. | Servant[3] | 2 yrs., 11 mo., 7 d. | £ 14. 0. 0. |

| Date. | Name. | From the Port of | To Whom Indentured. |
|---|---|---|---|
| | Denham, Elizabeth, Jr. | | John Strub and his wife |
| | Adams, John | | Thomas Proctor and his assigns |
| | Rawle, Elizabeth | | Aquilla Jones and his assigns |
| | Williams, William | | James Mercer and his assigns |
| | Nicholson, Christian | | James Mercer and his assigns |
| | Harrison, Rebecca | | Kerr Patrick and his assigns |
| July 30th | Arthur, William | | Allen Congleton and his assigns |
| | Britt, Daniel | | Lazarus Pine, Jr., and his assigns |
| | Shoemaker, Chloe | | Christian Galley |
| July 31st | Creinor, Frederick, and Anna Eve, his wife. | | John Lashert and his assigns |
| | Brossius, Elizabeth | | Paul Kober and his wife |
| August 1st | Dunlap, Sarah | | Elizabeth McNeil and her assigns |
| | Biesman, Catherine | | James Smith |
| | Riggin, Charles | | Robert Cooper and his assigns |
| | Saunders, Esther | | John Brooks and his assigns |
| | Higgins, Thomas | Ireland | William Semple and his assigns |
| August 3rd | Eyrick, Jacob | | George Holstine and his assigns |
| | Mullcahy, James | | John Raser and his assigns |
| | Turner, James | Ireland | John Martin and his assigns |
| | McMichael, Robert | | John Webster and his assigns |
| | Pender, John | | Jacob Pender and his assigns |
| | Kuhn, John | | William Englefreid and his wife |
| | McGear, Jane | | Ann McGear and her assigns |
| August 4th | Waggner, Frederick, Jr. | | William Baker and his assigns |
| | Washby, Francis | | Thomas Nevell and his wife |

[1] To be found all necessaries and at the expiration have freedom dues.
[2] To be found all necessaries and at the expiration have one new suit of apparel.
[3] To be found all necessaries and at the expiration have two complete suits of apparel, one whereof to be new.

## List of Indentures.

| Residence. | Occupation. | Term. | Amount. |
|---|---|---|---|
| Philadelphia | Apprentice, taught housewifery and sew, have one year's schooling.³ | 13 yrs. | |
| Philadelphia | Apprentice, taught house carpenter's trade, found meat, drink, washing and lodging, time to go to evening school two quarters each winter, the father paying the expense of the schooling. | 3 yrs., 9 mo., 3 d. | |
| Newtown twp., Gloucester co., W. Jersey. | Apprentice, taught housewifery, sew, knit and spin, have six months' schooling.³ | 7 yrs., 3 mo. | |
| Leacock, Lancaster co | Servant, found meat, drink, washing and lodging, one pair shoes, and one pair stockings. | 6 mo. | £ 1.0.0. |
| Leacock, Lancaster co | Servant⁵ | 2 yrs. | 20/. |
| Southwark | Servant⁵ | 3 yrs. | 35/. |
| Pennsneck, Salem co., W. Jersey | Servant⁵ | 3 yrs. | £ 10.0.0. |
| | Apprentice, taught to read, write and cypher as far as said master is capable of instructing him which the apprentice is to be kept at during the term and taught merchant's accounts.³ | 12 yrs. | |
| Philadelphia | | 7 yrs. | 5/. |
| Oley, Berks co | | 4 yrs. | £ 18.7.10. |
| Philadelphia | Apprentice, taught housewifery, sew, spin and knit, read and write perfectly.³ | 12 yrs., 4 mo., 10 d. | |
| Southwark | Apprentice, taught housewifery and sew, read in Bible, write a legible hand.³ | 5 yrs., 10 mo. | |
| Germantown | | 26 yrs. | 20/. |
| Philadelphia | Apprentice | 6 yrs., 4 mo. | £ 4.0.0. |
| Derby twp., Chester co | Apprentice | 5 yrs. | 5/. |
| Philadelphia | Servant⁵ | 3 yrs., 11 mo., 14 d. | £ 14.0.0. |
| Heidelberg twp., Lancaster co | | 4 yrs. | £ 25.10.0. |
| Philadelphia | Servant⁵ | 2 yrs., 11 mo. | £ 15.0.0. |
| Philadelphia | Servant⁵ | 1 yr., 6 mo. | £ 8.0.0. |
| Philadelphia | Apprentice, taught the cabinet and chair maker's trade, found meat, drink, washing and lodging, mother to provide apparel the first two years and the master the remaining time.³ | 5 yrs., 5 mo. | |
| Northern Liberties | Apprentice | 6 yrs. | £ 3.0.0. |
| Philadelphia | Apprentice, taught the cordwainer's trade, have six months' schooling.³ | 6 yrs., 1 mo. | |
| Kent co. on Delaware | Servant | 10 yrs., 5 mo., 6 d. | £ 2.0.0. |
| Philadelphia | Apprentice, taught the loaf bread baker's trade, read, write and cypher as far as and through the rule of three.³ | 5 yrs. | |
| Philadelphia | Apprentice, taught housewifery and sew, read in Bible, write a | 8 yrs., 1 mo., 10 d. | |

⁴ To be found all necessaries and at the expiration have two complete suits of apparel, one whereof to be new, and 40s. in money.

⁵ At expiration have two complete suits of apparel, one whereof to be new.

| Date. | Name. | From the Port of | To Whom Indentured. |
|---|---|---|---|
| 1772. | | | |
| August 4th.. | Lewis, Edward | | Thomas Tufft and his assigns........ |
| | Neil, Ann | | Nathaniel Donnell and his assigns.... |
| | Levers, James | | Joseph Pemberton and his assigns.... |
| | Byrne, John | | William Thomson and his assigns.... |
| August 5th.. | Swaine, Edward | | John Facey and his assigns.......... |
| | Davis, Edward | | Joseph Bolton ...................... |
| | Cray, Jacob Simon | | Andrew Craig and wife ............ |
| | Holliday, William | | Thomas McKean and his assigns.... |
| August 6th.. | Alexander, William | | Christopher Hausman and his assigns. |
| August 7th.. | Potts, William | | Hugh Roberts, Jr., and his assigns.... |
| August 8th.. | Engle, John, Jr. | | David Dominick and his assigns..... |
| | Founds, John | | Henry Ewald and his assigns........ |
| | Affler, Godfrey | London .... | George Knor and his assigns........ |
| | Prince, Jane | | John Thornton and his assigns....... |
| August 10th. | Taylor, Mazza | | Henry Leppy, his heirs and assigns... |
| | Christie, Martin, Jr. | | Mark Connor and wife............. |
| | Johnson, Samuel | | John Harrison and his assigns....... |
| | Sugg, Dorothea | | James Taylor and his assigns........ |
| August 10th. | Weaver, John, Jr. | | Charles Shnyder and his assigns...... |

## List of Indentures.

| Residence. | Occupation. | Term. | Amount. |
|---|---|---|---|
| | legible hand (note 3, and £3 lawful money of Pa.). | | |
| Philadelphia | Apprentice, taught the cabinet maker's trade, have three quarters' winter's night schooling.³ | 7 yrs., 7 mo. 19 d. | |
| Philadelphia | | 4 yrs. | £ 15. 0. 0. |
| Philadelphia | Apprentice | 11 yrs., 6 mo. | £ 14. 0. 0. |
| Wrights twp., Bucks co. | | 4 yrs. | £ 14. 0. 0. |
| Philadelphia | Servant | 5 yrs. | £ 14. 0. 0. |
| Philadelphia | Apprentice, taught house carpenter's trade, found meat, drink and lodging, while employed in any part of the country outside the city and in case the master dies during the apprenticeship, the executors shall assign him to another master of the same trade and he shall have the liberty to go about his own or mother's business, so that such time be made up again to his said master | 2 yrs. | |
| Philadelphia | Apprentice, taught the white smith's trade.³ | 4 yrs., 5 mo. 9 d. | |
| Willis twp., Chester co. | Servant, found meat, drink, washing and lodging, two pairs shoes, two pair trousers and two shirts only. | 2 yrs. | £ 8. 7. 7. |
| Philadelphia | Apprentice, taught the tailor's trade.⁵ | 4 yrs., 3 mo. | |
| Philadelphia | Apprentice, taught house carpenter's trade, found meat, drink, washing and lodging, time to go to evening school one quarter each winter, he or his friends paying expense of schooling. | 6 yrs., 8 mo. 20 d. | |
| Philadelphia | Apprentice, taught the painter and glazier's business, read in Bible, write a legible hand, cypher as far as and through rule of three³. | 8 yrs. | |
| N. Providence twp., Phila. co. | Servant⁵ | 2 yrs. | £ 8. 0. 0. |
| Philadelphia | Servant (note 3, and £ 3 in money) | 2 yrs. | £ 24. 0. 0. |
| Fallstownship, Bucks co. | Servant⁵ | 1 yr. | £ 1. 0. 0. |
| Moyamensing, Phila. co. | Apprentice, taught housewifery and sew, have one year's schooling at an English school and six months schooling to learn to sew³ | 9 yrs. | |
| Roxbury twp., Phila. co. | Apprentice, taught tailor's trade, read and write perfectly, cypher as far as and through the rule of three. In case of death of Mark and his wife, he shall serve the remaining part of his apprenticeship with their son, John Connor, of Roxbury, aforesaid tailor.³ | 13 yrs., 2 mo., 4 d. | |
| Philadelphia | Apprentice, taught the house carpenter's trade, and found meat, drink, washing and lodging. | 4 yrs. | |
| Philadelphia | Servant | 2 yrs., 3 mo. 21 d. | 20/. |
| Philadelphia | Apprentice, taught the painter and glazier's business, have two quarters' winter evening school- | 10 yrs., 4 mo. | |

| Date. | Name. | From the Port of | To Whom Indentured. |
|---|---|---|---|
| 1772. | | | |
| August 11th. | Hautsin, Maria Christian | | Daniel Elliott and his assigns |
| | Prittyman, William | | Magnus Miller and George Emlen, Jr., and their assigns. |
| | Shreiner, Henry | | Jacob Cline and his assigns |
| August 12th. | Archibold, Mary | | Daniel Jones and his wife |
| | Ryan, John | | Caleb Parry and his assigns |
| | Knappin, Christian | | Jacob Frees and his assigns |
| August 13th. | Moloney, Joseph | | William Standley and his assigns |
| | Morgan, Joseph | | Philip Mitman and his assigns |
| | Barron, Patrick | | John Roberts and his assigns |
| August 15th. | Dowdle, James | | Silas Jones and his assigns |
| August 17th. | Keen, Rebecca | | Mary Bingham and her assigns |
| | Johnson, James | | William Holderaff and his assigns |
| August 18th. | Tom (a free negro) | | William Holderaff and his assigns |
| | Connell, Jeffry | | William Plunket and his assigns |
| | Stirewald, George | | Samuel Watts and his heirs |
| August 19th. | White, Margaret | | Conrad Baker and his assigns |
| | Jones, Rose | | James Davis and his assigns |
| | Reeve, Damarus | | Thomas Coomb and wife |
| | Johnson, James | | Samuel Lippencott and his assigns |
| | Erwin, Joseph | | James Budden and Wm. Straker or either of them. |
| | Hall, William | | Isaac Vannost and wife |

## List of Indentures.

| Residence. | Occupation. | Term. | Amount. |
|---|---|---|---|
| | ing (note 3, and a diamond for cutting glass). | | |
| Donegal, Lancaster co. | Servant | 6 yrs. | £9.0.0. |
| Philadelphia | Apprentice, taught the art and mystery of navigation.[3] | 3 yrs. | |
| Philadelphia | Apprentice, taught tailor's trade, have three months' schooling at an English school, and he shall serve his apprenticeship in Phila.[3] | 5 yrs., 4 mo. 10 w. | |
| Montgomery twp., Phila. co. | Apprentice, taught housewifery, sew, knit and spin, read in Bible, write a legible hand.[3] | 5 yrs. | |
| Blockley twp., Phila. co. | | 8 yrs. | £18.0.0. |
| Upper Alloways Cr., Salem co., W. N. Jersey. | | 3 yrs., 8 mo. | £12.0.0. |
| Philadelphia | Apprentice, taught the potter's trade.[3] | 7 yrs., 4 mo. 26 d. | £18.0.0. |
| Philadelphia | Apprentice, taught the tailor's trade, read, write and cypher as far as and through rule of three.[3] | 6 yrs. | |
| Montgomery twp., Phila. co. | Servant, found meat, drink, washing and lodging, two pairs trousers, two shirts, two pairs stockings, two pairs shoes, one jacket, one hat, all to be new. | 1 yr., 1 mo. 2 w. | £16.12.0. |
| Derby, Chester co. | Servant[5] | 2 yrs. | £12.0.0. |
| Philadelphia | Apprentice, taught housewifery, sew, have one quarter's schooling, taught to write.[3] | 8 yrs., 8 mo. 17 d. | |
| Evesham twp., Burlington co., W. Jersey. | Servant[3] | 2 yrs., 9 mo. 19 d. | £10.0.0. |
| Evesham twp., Burlington co., W. Jersey. | Servant (note 3, of the value of £10, or £10 in money). | 1 yr. | 10/. |
| Turbot twp., Northumberland co. | Servant | | £17.0.0. |
| Philadelphia | Apprentice, taught tailor's trade, allowed time to go to night school two quarters, the father paying the expense of schooling[2]. | 4 yrs., 10 mo. | |
| Northern Liberties | Apprentice, taught housewifery, sew, knit and spin, have one year and six months' schooling.[3] | 11 yrs. | |
| Carlisle, Cumberland co. | Servant[5] | 1 yr., 6 mo. | £1.0.0. |
| Philadelphia | Apprentice, taught housewifery, read and write.[1] | 6 yrs. | |
| Evesham, Burlington co., W. Jersey. | | 2 yrs., 9 mo. 19 d. | £10.6.6. |
| Philadelphia | Apprentice, taught the art and mystery of a merchant and bookkeeping, the father to find and provide for him meat, drink, washing and lodging, the first two years, and apparel the whole term, and the said Budden and Straker, or either of them, provide meat, drink, washing and lodging the two last years and at expiration one complete new suit of apparel. | 4 yrs. | |
| Philadelphia | Apprentice, taught the block and pump maker's trade, have five winters' evening schooling.[3] | 8 yrs. | |

| Date. | Name. | From the Port of | To Whom Indentured. |
|---|---|---|---|
| 1772.<br>August 19th. | Brown, Joseph | | Joseph Lippencott and his assigns.... |
| August 22nd. | Craig, John | | Samuel Caldwell and his assigns..... |
| | Ent, Theobald | | John Webster and his assigns........ |
| August 24th. | Maginnis, Mary | | Thomas Craig and his assigns....... |
| | Clay, Margaret | | John Shaffer and his assigns......... |
| | Clay, Margaret | | Frederick Star and his assigns....... |
| | Dorety, Charlotte | | Rev. Casper Weyndbergh and his assigns. |
| | Clemer, Henry | | Catherine Clemer and her assigns.... |
| | Graham, James | | James McMachan and his assigns.... |
| August 25th. | Burk, Margaret | | Joseph McMichael and his assigns.... |
| | Hervey, Martha | | Peter Howard and his assigns....... |
| | Dickinson, William | | James Giffin ....................... |
| | McBride, Archibald | | Alexander Fulton and his assigns.... |
| August 26th. | O'Donnell, Mary | Ireland | Eliza. White and her assigns........ |
| | Dart, Ann | | John McKenny and his assigns....... |
| | Power, Charles | | Wm. Niles and his assigns........... |
| | Simson, Elizabeth | | George Kennedy and his assigns..... |
| | Quin, Alice | | James McCord and his assigns...... |
| August 27th. | Walker, David | Ireland | John Spencer and his assigns........ |
| | Gallacher, Charles | | John Jervis., Jr., and his assigns..... |
| | McDonnell, John | | Godfrey Haga and his assigns....... |
| August 28th. | Boch, Adam | | George Seitz and his assigns......... |
| | McArdel, Lawrence | | Seth Matlack and his assigns........ |
| | Herbeson, Jennet | Ireland | Isaac Massey and his assigns....... |
| August 29th. | Dunn, Elizabeth | Ireland | John James and his assigns.......... |
| | Atherson, Thomas | | Williamson Talbot and his assigns... |
| | O'Neil, Ann | | Jane Tenant and her assigns........ |
| | Ford, Esther | Ireland | James McCutcheon ................ |
| | McMullan, John | Ireland | Andrew McClelland and his assigns.. |
| | Christie, Robert | Ireland | Herman Vansant and his assigns..... |
| | Matthews, Mary | | Peter Merkin and his assigns........ |
| August 31st. | Hess, George | | Nicholas and Lewis Hess and their assigns or either of them. |
| | Piers, Thomas | Ireland | Benjamin Harbeson and his assigns.. |
| | McClean, Margaret | | Samuel Shaw and his assigns........ |

## List of Indentures.

| Residence. | Occupation. | Term. | Amount. |
|---|---|---|---|
| Haddonfield, Gloucester co., W. Jersey. | Apprentice, taught art, trade and mystery of a silversmith, read and write perfectly, cypher as far as and through the rule of three.[3] | 14 yrs. | |
| Philadelphia | | 4 yrs., 6 mo. | £ 14. 0. 0. |
| Philadelphia | Apprentice | 6 yrs., 1 mo. | £ 20. 0. 0. |
| Philadelphia | Servant[3] | 3 yrs., 23 d. | £ 9. 0. 0. |
| Philadelphia | Apprentice, taught housewifery, sew, knit and spin, read in Bible.[3] | 9 yrs., 6 mo. | |
| Northern Liberties | | 9 yrs., 6 mo. | 5/. |
| Philadelphia | Servant | 10 yrs. | £ 5. 0. 0. |
| Philadelphia | Apprentice | 4 yrs. | 5/. |
| Talbot, Northumberland co. | | 4 yrs. | £ 16. 0. 0. |
| Domore twp., Lancaster co. | Servant | 3 yrs., 10 mo., 18 d. | £ 12. 0. 0. |
| Philadelphia | Servant | 4 yrs. | £ 14. 10. |
| Forseham twp., Phila. co. | Apprentice, taught the weaver's trade, read in the Bible, write a legible hand and cypher as far as and through rule of three (note 1, to value of £ 10 lawful money of Pa. or £ 10 money aforesaid). | 12 yrs. | |
| N. London twp., Chester co. | Servant | 3 yrs. | £ 15. 0. 0. |
| Philadelphia | Servant[3] | 6 yrs., 10 mo. | £ 10. 0. 0. |
| Buckingham twp., Bucks co. | Servant | 5 yrs. | 5/. |
| Philadelphia | Apprentice | 11 yrs. | £ 7. 10. 0. |
| Philadelphia | | 4 yrs. | £ 17. 0. 0. |
| Sadsbury twp., Lancaster co. | Servant | 3 yrs., 6 mo. | £ 12. 0. 0. |
| Philadelphia | Servant[1] | 3 yrs., 3 mo. | £ 6. 0. 0. |
| Philadelphia | | 4 yrs. | £ 13. 0. 0. |
| Philadelphia | | 2 yrs. | £ 12. 0. 0. |
| Philadelphia | Apprentice, have six months' evening schooling, taught the tailor's trade.[3] | 4 yrs., 2 mo. | |
| Philadelphia | Apprentice, taught the cooper's trade (note 3, and of value of £ 10 lawful money of Pa. or £ 10 in money aforesaid). | 3 yrs. | £ 5. 0. 0. |
| Willis twp., Chester co. | Servant[2] | 3 yrs. | £ 10. 10. 0. |
| Philadelphia | Servant[1] | 3 yrs. | £ 12. 5. 0. |
| Northern Liberties | Servant, taught the tailor's trade, have six months' schooling and at expiration have two complete suits of apparel, one whereof to be new. | 5 yrs., 8 mo. 19 d. | |
| Springfield, Chester co. | | 3 yrs., 5 mo. 28 d. | £ 13. 5. 0. |
| Southwark | Servant[1] | 4 yrs. | £ 10. 0. 0. |
| Newton twp., Chester co. | Servant, found meat, drink, washing, lodging. | 1 yr. | £ 7. 10. 0. |
| Bensalem twp., Bucks co. | Servant[1] | 4 yrs. | £ 19. 0. 0. |
| Southwark | Servant[1] | 2 yrs., 8 mo. 3 d. | £ 6. 0. 0. |
| Philadelphia | Apprentice, taught the blacksmith's trade, have six months' evening schooling at an English school.[3] | 6 yrs., 2 mo. | |
| Philadelphia | Servant, taught the copper smith's trade.[3] | 6 yrs. | £ 18. 0. 0. |
| Chester, Chester co. | | 4 yrs. | £ 16. 0. 0. |

| Date. | Name. | From the Port of | To Whom Indentured. |
|---|---|---|---|
| 1772. | Hughes, Patrick | Ireland | Samuel Shaw and his assigns |
| | McAteer, William | | William Carson and his assigns |
| | Martin, Robert | Ireland | John Thompson and his assigns |
| | Chesney, Jane | Ireland | John Hambill and his assigns |
| | Chesney, Jane | | Abel Rees and his assigns |
| | McGowen, Mary | | William Wood and his assigns |
| | McVicker, Patrick | Ireland | Isaac Morton and his assigns |
| | Bamford, Ralph | | Barnard Vandegraft and his assigns |
| | Sherod, John | | John Hadley and his assigns |
| | Beach, Edmond, Jr. | | Benjamin Jones and his assigns |
| | McVicker, Archibald | | Hugh Crawford and his assigns |
| Sept. 1st | O'Donnell, Bell | | Robert McKim and his assigns |
| | McAteer, William | | Stephen Duncan and his assigns |
| | Creag, Isabella | | William Carson and his assigns |
| | Murphy, James | | David Potter and his assigns |
| | Reynolds, James | Ireland | Joseph Tanner and his assigns |
| | Donte, Samuel | | John Helm and his assigns |
| | Burton, John, Jr. | | Joseph Henderson and his assigns |
| | Stricklin, Elizabeth | Ireland | James Duncan and his assigns |
| | Russell, James | Ireland | Isaac Morton and his assigns |
| Sept. 2nd | Cotteral, Edward | | James Russell and his assigns |
| | Mason, John, and Mary, his wife. | Ireland | Matthew Robinson |
| | Mason, John, and Mary, his wife. | | David Robinson |
| Sept. 2nd | McCleaster, James | | George Allison and his assigns |
| | Dermoth, James | | Simon Fitzgerald and his assigns |
| | Clamene, John | | David McCullough and his assigns |
| | Clamene, John | | William McMonigall and his assigns |
| | Spiddey, William | | Robert Kennedy and his assigns |

## List of Indentures.

| Residence. | Occupation. | Term. | Amount. |
|---|---|---|---|
| Chester, Chester co............. | Servant, taught art and mystery of a miller.[3] | 4 yrs....... | £ 20. 0. 0. |
| Philadelphia .................... | ................................................ | 3 yrs., 6 mo. | £ 17. 0. 0. |
| Philadelphia .................... | Servant, found meat, drink, washing and lodging. | 2 yrs., 6 mo. | £ 7. 10. 0. |
| Philadelphia .................... | Servant (note 5, have one new gown. | 2 yrs., 6 mo. | £ 7. 10. 0. |
| Tredyffrin twp., Chester co...... | Servant ......................... | 2 yrs., 6 mo. | £ 7. 10. 0. |
| Philadelphia .................... | ................................................ | 3 yrs....... | £ 14. 0. 0. |
| Philadelphia .................... | Apprentice, taught biscuit baker's trade, have three quarters' night schooling.[1] | 4 yrs., 11 mo. | £ 14. 0. 0. |
| Lower Dublin twp., Phila co..... | ................................................ | 2 yrs....... | £ 10. 0. 0. |
| Southwark ...................... | Apprentice, taught the blacksmith's trade, have three winters' night schooling.[3] | 5 yrs., 4 mo. | |
| Philadelphia .................... | Apprentice, taught the hatter's or felt maker's business, found in apparel, and at expiration have two complete suits of apparel, one whereof to be new, and time to go to evening school eac' winter, the father paying the expense of schooling and find him meat, drink, washing and lodging. | 7 yrs. | |
| Roxbury twp., Phila. co......... | ................................................ | 3 yrs....... | £ 16. 0. 0. |
| Brandywine Hundred, N. Castle co. | ................................................ | 4 yrs....... | £ 14. 0. 0. |
| Carlisle, Cumberland co......... | ................................................ | 3 yrs., 6 mo. | £ 17. 0. 0. |
| Philadelphia .................... | ................................................ | 4 yrs....... | £ 16. 0. 0. |
| Cohansey, Cumberland co., W. Jersey. | ................................................ | 4 yrs....... | £ 17. 0. 0. |
| E. Nottingham, Chester co....... | Servant[1] ....................... | 3 yrs....... | £ 16. 0. 0. |
| Philadelphia .................... | Apprentice ...................... | 5 yrs., 8 mo. | £ 12. 0. 0. |
| Sadsbury twp., Chester co....... | Apprentice, taught husbandry or farming, read in Bible, write a legible hand, cypher as far as and through the rule of three (note 3, and £ 6 in money). | 14 yrs. | |
| W. Nantmill, Chester co........ | Servant, found meat, drink, washing, lodging and apparel. | 2 yrs., 6 mo. | £ 9. 0. 0. |
| Philadelphia .................... | Apprentice, taught the biscuit baker's business, have one quarter's night schooling.[3] | 4 yrs....... | £ 11. 0. 0. |
| Philadelphia .................... | Apprentice, taught the art of a mariner.[3] | 3 yrs....... | £ 15. 0. 0. |
| W. Nantmill twp., Chester co.... | Servant[5] ....................... | 3 yrs....... | £ 22. 10. 0. |
| W. Nantmill twp., Chester co.... | ................................................ | 3 yrs....... | £ 22. 10. 0. |
| Philadelphia .................... | Servant, found meat, drink, washing, lodging, one pair shoes and a jacket. | 15 mo...... | £ 8. 0. 0. |
| Philadelphia .................... | Servant, if he shall pay or cause to be paid £ 7. 10 in twelve months after this date, this indenture to be void.[3] | 2 yrs., 6 mo. | £ 7. 10. 0. |
| Philadelphia .................... | Servant[1] ....................... | 3 yrs. | |
| Pitsgrove, Salem co., W. N. Jersey | ................................................ | 3 yrs....... | £ 16. 0. 0. |
| Philadelphia .................... | Servant, taught the copper plate printing and picture framing business, have two quarters' night schooling.[1] | 6 yrs....... | £ 7. 10. 0. |

| Date. | Name. | From the Port of | To Whom Indentured. |
|---|---|---|---|
| Sept. 3rd | Leacock, Thomas | His and his wife's passage | Jos. McClintock and his assigns |
| | Byrns, Roger | | Jos. McClintock and his assigns |
| | Klein, John Philip | | Philip Deck and his assigns |
| | Carter, William | | David English and his assigns |
| Sept. 4th | Hamilton, Patrick | | David English and his assigns |
| | White, Jane | Ireland | James Roney and his assigns |
| | McCollum, James | | Thomas Lowe. July 1, 1772, and this day discharged from his indenture of servitude by his master, Thomas Lowe, under hand and seal. |
| | Quig, Dennis | Ireland | James Guest and his assigns |
| | McCann, Patrick | | Andrew Rogers and his assigns |
| | Mahon, Arthur | Ireland | Andrew Rogers and his assigns |
| | Martin, Thomas | Ireland | Christopher Little and his assigns |
| | Frickland, Robert | | Andrew Rogers and his assigns |
| | Welch, Neil | Ireland | John Smith and his assigns |
| | Crowley, Mary | | James Stuart and his assigns |
| | Ray, Isabella | Ireland | George Aston and his assigns |
| | Ray, Isabella | | Robert Boynes and his assigns |
| Sept. 5th | McDaniel, Maurice, and Elinor, his wife. | | Col. Daniel Claus |
| | Power, Mary | | John Stall and his assigns |
| | Fitzgerald, Mary | | Thomas Lyel and his assigns |
| | Bolton, John | | Henry Harper and his assigns |
| | Irwin, William | | Arthur Erwin and his assigns |
| | Irwin, Sarah | | William Erwin and his assigns |
| | Ramsey, Benjamin | | Allen McLeane and his assigns |
| | Gordon, Alexander | Ireland | Andrew Rogers and his assigns |
| Sept. 7th | Spain, Edward, Jr. | | James Budden and Wm. Straker or either of them. |
| | McCarthy, Michael | | James Budden and Wm. Straker and their assigns or either of them. |
| | Hines, William | | George Pickering and his assigns |
| | Peel, John | | Magnus Miller and Geo. Emlen, Jr., and their assigns. |
| | Grime, Eleanor | Ireland | William French and his assigns |
| Sept. 8th | McDonald, Hugh | | Thomas Harrison and his assigns |
| | McGowen, Mary | | John Hannah and his assigns |
| | Walker, John | | Leeson Simmons and his assigns |

## List of Indentures.

| Residence. | Occupation. | Term. | Amount. |
|---|---|---|---|
| Teboyn twp., Cumberland co. | Servant [2] | 6 yrs., 1 mo. 28 d. | £ 22. 10. 0. |
| Teboyn twp., Cumberland co. | | 3 yrs. | £ 15. 0. 0. |
| Philadelphia | Apprentice, taught tailor's trade, read in bible, write a legible hand, cypher as far as and through rule of three.[3] | 15 yrs., 6 mo., 12 d. | |
| Juniata, Rye twp., Cumberland co. | | 3 yrs. | £ 16. 0. 0. |
| Juniata, Rye twp., Cumberland co. | Apprentice, taught the lawyer's trade.[3] | 4 yrs. | £ 16. 10. 0. |
| Philadelphia | Servant (note 5, only) | 3 yrs., 3 mo. | £ 12. 0. 0. |
| | Servant. | | 5/. |
| Philadelphia | Apprentice, taught tailor's trade [3] | 4 yrs. | £ 10. 10. 0. |
| Hanover twp., Lancaster co. | | 3 yrs., 6 mo. | £ 17. 0. 0. |
| Hanover twp., Lancaster co. | Apprentice, taught the trade of a tanner and currier.[3] | 5 yrs. | £ 15. 10. 0. |
| Hanover twp., Lancaster co. | Servant [5] | 2 yrs. | £ 7. 0. 0. |
| Hanover twp., Lancaster co. | | 4 yrs. | £ 11. 0. 0. |
| Philadelphia | Servant, found meat, drink, washing, lodging, shoes and stockings. | | £ 7. 10. 0. |
| Philadelphia | Servant | 4 yrs. | £ 13. 0. 0. |
| Philadelphia | Servant [5] | 2 yrs. | £ 7. 16. |
| Christiana Hundred, N. Castle co. | | 2 yrs. | £ 7. 16. |
| Albany co., New York Province. | | 4 yrs. each. | £ 11. 10. 0. £ 10. 0. 0. |
| Philadelphia | | 3 yrs., 6 mo. | £ 4. 15. 0. |
| Wallonborough twp., Burlington co., W. N. J. | Servant | 4 yrs. | £ 13. 0. 0. |
| Philadelphia | | 6 yrs. | £ 14. 0. 0. |
| Bucks co. | | 3 yrs. | £ 7. 13. 9. |
| Plumstead twp., Bucks co. | | 3 yrs. | £ 7. 13. 9. |
| Philadelphia | Apprentice, taught the leather breeches maker's trade, found meat, drink, washing, lodging, one pair leather breeches and two pair of trousers, and at expiration have £ 5 lawful money of Pa. | 2 yrs. | |
| Hanover twp., Lancaster co. | Servant, the said servant to pay or cause to be paid to said master £ 11. 10 within one month from this date, then the indenture to be void.[5] | 2 yrs. | £ 7. 10. 0. |
| Philadelphia | Apprentice, taught the art of a mariner and navigation (note 2, besides his old). | 3 yrs., 10 mo. | |
| Philadelphia | Apprentice, taught the art of a mariner and navigation (note 2, besides his old). | 4 yrs., 1 mo. 25 d. | |
| Philadelphia | | 4 yrs., 1 mo. 17 d. | £ 0. 5. 0. |
| Philadelphia | Apprentice, taught the art and mystery of a mariner and navigation.[1] | 6 yrs., 5 mo. | |
| Abington twp., Phila. co. | Servant [1] | 4 yrs. | £ 13. 10. 0. |
| Philadelphia | Servant [5] | 3 yrs. | £ 15. 0. 0. |
| Philadelphia | Servant | 3 yrs. | £ 11. 00. |
| Philadelphia | Apprentice, taught the art of a mariner and navigation (note 2, besides his old). | 6 yrs., 2 mo. 21 d. | |

| Date. | Name. | From the Port of | To Whom Indentured. |
|---|---|---|---|
| 1772.<br>Sept. 9th.... | Campbell, James<br>Owen, John<br>Pote, William | | Edward Mitchell and his assigns.....<br>Henry Court and his assigns.........<br>Daniel Dawson and his assigns....... |
| Sept. 10th... | Wilcocks, John | | Joseph Rhoads and his assigns........ |
| | Baker, Jacob | | Jacob Bunner ....................... |
| Sept. 11th... | Campbell, Collin<br>Bloom, Peter | Ireland .... | William Graham and his assigns....<br>Philip Cline ........................ |
| | Boyer, John | | John Stromb and his assigns......... |
| Sept. 12th... | Small, John | | Benjamin Eyre and his heirs........ |
| Sept. 14th... | Day, Thomas<br>Henry, Elizabeth | Ireland .... | John Hunt and his assigns...........<br>Jacob Pumm and his assigns......... |
| Sept. 12th... | Gillen, James<br>Bacher, Ann. Cath.<br>McNeil, Locklin | | Jacob Peters and his assigns........<br>Michael Shubert and his assigns......<br>William Cliffton and his assigns..... |
| | Radney James | | Joshua Loring, Jr., and his assigns... |
| | McCullough, James | Ireland .... | Arney Lippencott and his assigns..... |
| | McAuly, Neil | Ireland .... | Arney Lippencott and his assigns..... |
| | Young, William, Jr........ | | Benjamin Eyre and his assigns....... |
| | O'Donnell, Mary | | Arney Lippencott and his assigns..... |
| Sept. 14th... | Babington, Richard<br>McConomy, James | | Simon Fitzgerald .................<br>James Bringhurst and his assigns.... |
| Sept. 15th... | Jacobs, John Peter | | Conrad Fisher and his assigns....... |
| Sept. 16th... | Farrel, Michael<br>Calahan, Patrick | Ireland .... | Sharpe Delany and his assigns.......<br>Amy Preston ....................... |
| Sept. 17th... | Osborne, Robert<br>Cushing, James | Ireland ....<br>Ireland .... | John Smith and his assigns..........<br>William Todd and his assigns....... |

| Residence. | Occupation. | Term. | Amount. |
|---|---|---|---|
| W. Marlborough twp., Chester co. | Servant | 4 yrs., 11 mo., 21 d. | £ 16.0.0. |
| Philadelphia | Apprentice | 8 yrs., 8 mo. | £ 3.0.0. |
| Philadelphia | Apprentice, taught the white smith's trade, read in Bible, write a legible hand, cypher as far as and through rule of three.[3] | 12 yrs. | |
| Philadelphia | Apprentice, taught the house carpenter's trade have three quarters' evening schooling, found meat, drink, washing, lodging and working apparel. | 3 yrs. | |
| Philadelphia | Apprentice, taught the hatter or feltmaker's trade, found meat, drink, washing and lodging only. | 3 yrs. | |
| Philadelphia | Servant[5] | 4 yrs. | £ 10.0.0. |
| Philadelphia | Apprentice, taught the tailor's trade, read in Bible, write a legible hand and cypher as far as and through rule of three.[3] | 7 yrs. | |
| Northern Liberties | Apprentice, taught husbandry or farming, have four quarters' evening schooling.[3] | 8 yrs., 6 mo. | |
| Northern Liberties | Apprentice, taught art, trade and mystery of shipwright and draughting a vessel, have one quarter's evening schooling each winter (note 1, and a set of tools) | 4 yrs., 9 mo. 12 d. | |
| Philadelphia | Servant[5] | 2 yrs. | £ 10.0.0. |
| Northern Liberties | Apprentice, taught housewifery, to read in Bible, write a legible hand (note 3, and one spinning wheel). | 9 yrs. | |
| Philadelphia | Servant | 2 yrs., 3 mo. | £ 11.0.0. |
| Philadelphia | | 6 yrs. | £ 24.0.0. |
| Philadelphia | Apprentice, taught the trade of a nailer.[3] | 3 yrs., 11 mo., 18 d. | £ 12.0.0. |
| Philadelphia | Servant, taught to read in Bible, write a legible hand, cypher as far as rule of three.[3] | 8 yrs., 1 mo. 15 d. | 5/. |
| Springfield twp., Burlington co., N. Jersey. | Servant[3] | 1 yr., 6 mo. | £ 7.10.0. |
| Springfield twp., Burlington co., N. Jersey. | Servant[3] | 1 yr., 6 mo. | £ 7.10.0. |
| Northern Liberties | Apprentice, taught shipwright's trade, have one quarter's evening schooling each winter (note 3, and the tools he works with). | 5 yrs., 5 mo. 3 d. | |
| Springfield twp., Burlington co., W. Jersey. | | 6 yrs., 10 mo. | £ 15.0.0. |
| | Servant | 5 yrs. | £ 0.7.6. |
| Philadelphia | | 2 yrs., 6 mo. | £ 15.0.0. |
| Douglas twp., Phila. co. | | 13 yrs., 6 mo. | £ 22.0.0. |
| Philadelphia | Servant[3] | 3 yrs. | £ 9.14.6. |
| Bristol twp., Phila. co. | Servant[3] | 3 yrs., 9 mo. 22 d. | £ 15.0.0. |
| Philadelphia | Servant[1] | 4 yrs. | £ 14.0.0. |
| Philadelphia | Apprentice, taught the wheelwright and carriage making business, have two quarter's night schooling (note 3, and £ 10 in money). | 5 yrs. | £ 8.15.0. |

| Date. | Name. | From the Port of | To Whom Indentured. |
|---|---|---|---|
| 1772. Sept. 17th | O'Harra, Thomas | | Andrew Carson |
| | Hamilton, John | Ireland | Alex. Allison and his assigns |
| | Gelwert, Frederick, Jr. | | Richard Footman |
| | Gelwert, Margaret | | Richard Footman and his assigns |
| | Cross, Daniel, Jr. | | Christopher Miller |
| | Wood, Robert | Ireland | John Patterson and his assigns |
| Sept. 18th | Craig, Matthew | | John Agnew and his assigns |
| | Kinkaid, John | | Thomas Afflick and his assigns |
| | Cloninger, Elizabeth | | Wm. Dean and his assigns |
| Sept. 19th | Standley, Peter, Jr. | | Samuel Wheeler and his assigns |
| | Martin, Joseph | | David Gibson and his heirs |
| | Cobron, Nancy | | James Wilson and his assigns |
| | Freil, Philip | | Ludwig Karcher |
| | Her, Mary | | James Wilson and his assigns |
| | Freil, Philip | | Ludwig Karcher and his assigns |
| Sept. 19th | Lynn, Philip | | Allen McLean, Jr., and his assigns |
| Sept. 21st | Ravenscroft, Richard | | Jacob Mayer and his assigns |
| | McGuigan, Catherine | | James Byrns and his assigns |
| | Thompson, David | | Robert Ferguson and his assigns |
| | Alekeiser, John | | Anna Maria Alekeiser and her assigns |
| | Fisher, George | | Wm. Drewry and his assigns |
| | Morgan, James | | Wm. Hurvey and his wife |
| | Howard, Mary | | John White and his assigns |
| | Her, Mary | | Wm. Standley and his assigns |
| Sept. 22nd | Wright, John | | Peter McKinley and his assigns |
| | Taylor, Anthony, Jr. | | Philip Kline and his assigns |
| | Docherty, Mark | | Richard Tittermary and his assigns |
| | Swaank, Margt. Elizabeth | | Lawrence Lapp and his assigns |
| Sept. 23rd | Parker, Hannah | | Sarah and Elizabeth Bazela or either of them. |
| | Hervey, Martha | | Thomas Evans and his assigns |
| Sept. 24th | Matthews, Mary | | Charles Roberts and his assigns |
| | Linton, John | Ireland | Adam Foulke and his assigns |

## List of Indentures.

| Residence. | Occupation. | Term. | Amount. |
|---|---|---|---|
| Philadelphia | Apprentice, taught the leather breeches maker and skinner's trade.[1] | 5 yrs. | |
| Baltimore co., Nods Forest, Md. | Servant, at expiration have two complete suits of apparel, one whereof to be new. | 3 yrs. | £8.0.0. |
| Philadelphia | Servant, the indenture cancelled | 10 yrs. | £10.0.0. |
| Philadelphia | Servant[1] | 2 yrs., 2 mo. 27 d. | £10.0.0. |
| Northern Liberties | Apprentice, taught the brush maker's trade, have two years' schooling at reading and writing and one year at cyphering, when he becomes perfect in reading and writing.[3] | 12 yrs. | |
| Philadelphia | Apprentice, taught the trade of a white smith.[5] | 3 yrs. | £7.10.0. |
| N. Town twp., Cumberland co. | | 2 yrs., 3 mo. | £9.0.0. |
| Philadelphia | Apprentice | 6 yrs., 2 mo. 2 w. | £13.0.0. |
| Harford, Phila. co. | Servant | 6 yrs. | £11.0.0. |
| Philadelphia | Apprentice, taught the cutter's trade, read and write well, and arithmetic so as to understand rule of three.[3] | 10 yrs., 9 mo., 13 d. | |
| Kingsessing twp., Phila. co. | Apprentice, taught the farmer and glazier's business, have eighteen months' schooling, six months wherof to be in the last four years of his apprenticeship. | 15 yrs., 11 mo. | |
| Leacock twp., Lancaster co. | | 4 yrs. | £10.0.0. |
| Philadelphia | Discharged and set free under the hand and seal of said Ludwig Karchel. | 3 yrs. | |
| Leacock twp., Lancaster co. | | 5 yrs. | £12.0.0. |
| Philadelphia | Servant[3] | 4 yrs. | £16.15.0. |
| Duck Creek Hundred, Kent co. | Servant, found all necessaries except clothing. | 1 yr., 6 mo. | £11.13.0. |
| Philadelphia | Servant | 3 yrs. | £8.0.0. |
| Philadelphia | | 4 yrs. | £13.0.0. |
| Philadelphia | Apprentice, taught art and mystery of shop and bookkeeping.[3] | 6 yrs., 9 mo. | |
| | Apprentice | 6 yrs., 6 mo. | £0.5.0. |
| Southwark | Servant | 6 yrs. | £15.0.0. |
| Southwark | Apprentice, taught the cooper's trade, read, write and cypher as far as and through rule of three[3] | 4 yrs., 9 mo. 16 d. | |
| Philadelphia | Servant | 4 yrs. | £11.0.0. |
| Philadelphia | Servant | 5 yrs. | £15.0.0. |
| Philadelphia | Servant | 4 yrs. | £11.0.0. |
| Philadelphia | Apprentice, taught the loaf bread baker's business, have three quarters' day schooling.[3] | 4 yrs., 8 mo. 6 d. | |
| Southwark | Apprentice | 4 yrs. | £5.0.0. |
| Philadelphia | Servant | 7 yrs. | £10.0.0. |
| Philadelphia | Apprentice, taught housewifery, sew and knit, have three quarters' schooling in the afternoon[1]. | 5 yrs. | |
| Edgemont twp., Chester co. | Servant | 4 yrs. | £10.10.0. |
| Ravaton twp., Somerset co., E. Jersey. | Servant | 2 yrs., 8 mo. 3 d. | £6.0.0. |
| Philadelphia | Servant, to be employed in attending shop, have two quarters' schooling.[3] | 4 yrs. | £12.0.0. |

| Date. | Name. | From the Port of | To Whom Indentured. |
|---|---|---|---|
| 1772. | Steiner, Roger | | Benjamin Betterton and his assigns... |
| Sept. 24th... | Sadler, Matthias | | Joseph Ogilby and his assigns........ |
| | McKee, William | | Humphry Fullerton and his assigns.. |
| Sept. 25th... | Owen, Robert | | William Blyth ...................... |
| Sept. 26th... | Widman, Elizabeth | | John Widman and his assigns........ |
| Sept. 28th... | Callan, Charles | | Robert Starrel and his assigns........ |
| | Sink, Abraham | | Theobald Sheible and his assigns.... |
| | Metzler, Elizabeth | | Henry Miller and his assigns........ |
| | Cross, Mary | | Jacob Comley and wife............. |
| | Salter, Thomas | | William Roberts, Jr., and his assigns.. |
| Sept. 29th... | Lennon, Mary | | Margaret Watson ................... |
| | Boyle, Mary | | Jonathan Fell and wife ............. |
| | Campbell, Collin | | Matthew Campbell and assigns...... |
| | Stayner, Roger | | Benjamin Betterton and his assigns... |
| | Walker, Lewis | | Richard Jones and his assigns........ |
| | Smith, Thomas | Ireland .... | John Sharpe and his assigns......... |
| | Smith, John | Ireland .... | John Sharpe and his assigns......... |
| | Smith, Isabella | Ireland .... | John Sharpe and his assigns......... |
| Sept. 30th... | Boltz, Johannes | | Isaac Sharpe and his assigns........ |
| | Meredith, Thomas, and Eleanor, his wife. | | James Pearson and John Tyler, their assigns or either of them. |
| | Brown, Ann | | Robert Wallace and his assigns...... |
| | Clarke, Ann | | Robert Wallace and his assigns...... |
| | Brown, Alexander | | Robert Wallace and his assigns...... |
| | Naglee, Joseph | | Henry Felton and his assigns........ |
| Oct. 1st..... | Griffith, Abel | | Peter Witmer (tailor).............. |

¹ To be found all necessaries and at the expiration have freedom dues.
² To be found all necessaries and at the expiration have one new suit of apparel.
³ To be found all necessaries and at the expiration have two complete suits of apparel, one whereof to be new.

## List of Indentures.

| Residence. | Occupation. | Term. | Amount. |
|---|---|---|---|
| Philadelphia | Apprentice | 7 yrs. | £ 0. 5. 0. |
| Philadelphia | Servant | 11 yrs. | £ 16. 0. 0. |
| Philadelphia | Servant¹ | 3 yrs. | £ 20. 0. 0. |
| Philadelphia | Apprentice | 13 yrs. | 5/. |
| Philadelphia | Servant | 5 yrs., 6 mo. | 5/. |
| Mill Cr. Hundred, New Castle co. | Servant | 2 yrs., 6 mo. | £ 14. 5. 0. |
| Philadelphia | Apprentice, taught the peruke maker and hair dresser's business, read in Bible and write a legible hand.³ | 7 yrs., 11 mo., 5 d. | |
| Cocalico twp., Lancaster co. | Servant | 5 yrs. | £ 19. 0. 0. |
| Northern Liberties | Apprentice, taught to read in Bible, write a legible hand and cypher as far as and through rule of multiplication, housewifery, sew and knit.³ | 6 yrs. | |
| Manor of Moreland, Phila. co. | Servant⁵ | 1 yr. | £ 5. 8. 1. |
| Philadelphia | Apprentice, taught the milliner's business.⁵ | 2 yrs., 2 mo. 26 d. | |
| Warwick twp., Bucks co. | Apprentice, taught housewifery, sew, knit and spin, read in Bible, write a legible hand and when she arrives at the age of twelve, give her one ewe (note 3, and a new spinning wheel). | 9 yrs., 10 mo., 19 d. | |
| Conecocheague, Cumberland co. | Servant | 4 yrs. | £ 18. 0. 0. |
| Philadelphia | Apprentice, taught the cooper's trade, have two quarters' evening schooling.³ | 1 yr., 7 mo. 2 w. | |
| Philadelphia | Apprentice, taught the house carpenter's trade, found meat, drink, washing, lodging and working apparel, shoes excepted, and in case of the master's death the apprentice shall not be assigned to any person without the approbation of his mother or guardian. | 5 yrs., 6 mo. | |
| Middletown twp., Cumberland co. | Servant, taught to read in Bible, write a legible hand, cypher as far as and through rule of three³. | 9 yrs., 9 mo. | £ 10. 0. 0. |
| Middletown twp., Cumberland co. | Servant, taught to read and write perfectly, cypher as far as and through rule of three.³ | 13 yrs., 2 mo., 26 d. | £ 10. 0. 0. |
| Middletown twp., Cumberland co. | Servant, taught to read and write well.¹ | 6 yrs. | £ 10. 0. 0. |
| Hopewell twp., Cumberland co., W. N. Jersey. | Servant | 10 yrs., 6 mo. | £ 15. 0. 0. |
| Philadelphia | | 4 yrs. each. | £ 24. 0. 0. £ 12. 0. 0. |
| Conestoga twp., Lancaster co. | Servant | 3 yrs. | £ 9. 0. 0. |
| Conestoga twp., Lancaster co. | Servant | 4 yrs. | £ 14. 0. 0. |
| Conestoga twp., Lancaster co. | | 5 yrs. | £ 8. 10. 0. |
| Philadelphia | Apprentice, taught house carpenter's trade, have six quarters' night schooling.³ | 10 yrs., 4 mo., 14 d. | |
| Philadelphia | Apprentice, learn his trade, have one quarter's night schooling and another quarter at expense of the | 5 yrs., 7 mo. 25 d. | |

⁴ To be found all necessaries and at the expiration have two complete suits of apparel, one whereof to be new, and 40s. in money.
⁵ At expiration have two complete suits of apparel, one whereof to be new.

| Date. | Name. | From the Port of | To Whom Indentured. |
|---|---|---|---|
| 1772. Oct. 1st | Swadley, John | Rotterdam | Abraham Kratz and his assigns |
| | Swadley, Jacob | Rotterdam | Henry Kephart and his assigns |
| | Johnson, Christiana | Rotterdam | Henry Stoufer and his assigns |
| | Felthisen, Ann Christiana | Rotterdam | Henry Stoufer and his assigns |
| | Griffiths, Mary | | Samuel Renich and his assigns |
| Oct. 2nd | Mayers, John | Rotterdam | Henry Conrad and his assigns |
| | Bauserin, Catherine | Rotterdam | Frederick Medenpell |
| | Perky, Hans Balsar | Rotterdam | Constantine Wilkins and his assigns |
| | Hofacher, Jacob | Rotterdam | Christian Schneider |
| | Hofacher, Jacob | | Michael Eberhart |
| | Willis, Joseph | | Jonathn. Dillworth |
| | Mouler, Franey | Rotterdam | John Ferree |
| | Bostion, Joseph | Rotterdam | Richard Wall |
| | Upstraw, Elizabeth | Rotterdam | Godfrey Schisler and his assigns |
| | Brown, Elizabeth | | James Kelly |
| | Judah, Martin | Rotterdam | William Lowman |
| | Niesees, William | Rotterdam | Lewis Davis and his assigns |
| | Schweetser, Ann | Rotterdam | Martin Reese |
| | Schweetser, Ann | | Mary Yunt |
| | Upfell, Christian | Rotterdam | Deterick Reese and his assigns |
| | Upfell, Christian | | William Bausman and his assigns |
| | Kaysler, John George | Rotterdam | Deterick Reese and his assigns |
| | Kaysler, John George | | Jacob Ringwald and his assigns |
| | Kilpart, Christian | Rotterdam | David Waggoner and his assigns |
| Oct. 3rd | Meyers, Jacob | Rotterdam | David Hall and his assigns |
| | Beck, Frantz | Rotterdam | John Ross |
| | Helberger, George | Rotterdam | Lewis Brail |
| | Stompf, Philip | | John Fisher and his assigns |
| | Houk, John | Rotterdam | Richard Edwards and his assigns |
| | Henrickson, Peter | | Christon. Sinklair and his assigns |
| | Kaysler, John George | Rotterdam | John Wise and his assigns |
| Oct. 5th | Parrott, Henry | Rotterdam | William Shute and his assigns |
| | Brockington, Mary | | Capt. Thomas Powell and wife |
| | Raimerin, Mary | Rotterdam | George Withers and his assigns |
| | Maybury, Jolly | | Wm. Raworth and his assigns |
| | Denn, George Hendric | Rotterdam | Wm. P. Smith and his assigns |
| | Bollard, Wilhelmina | Rotterdam | Wm. P. Smith and his assigns |

## List of Indentures.

| Residence. | Occupation. | Term. | Amount. |
|---|---|---|---|
| | guardian, a good new suit of clothes a year before he is free[5]. | | |
| N. Britain twp., Bucks co. | Servant (note 3, or £8 lawful money of Pa.). | 3 yrs. | £22.0.0 |
| Bedminster twp., Bucks co. | Servant (note 3, or £10 Pa. currency). | 3 yrs. | £22.10.0 |
| Bedminster twp., Bucks co. | Servant[3] | 4 yrs., 6 mo. | £18.0.0 |
| Bedminster twp., Bucks co. | Servant, taught to read in Bible[3]. | 8 yrs. | £18.0.0 |
| Guilford twp., Cumberland co. | Servant[3] | 2 yrs., 6 mo. 26 d. | £9.0.0 |
| Worcester twp., Phila co. | Servant (note 3, or £8 lawful money of Pa.). | 4 yrs. | £27.10.0 |
| Passyunk twp., Phila. co. | Servant have freedom dues. | 4 yrs. | £21.18.8 |
| Woolwich twp., Gloucester co., W. N. Jersey. | Servant[3] | 3 yrs., 6 mo. | £18.19.0 |
| Philadelphia | Servant[1] | | £23.3.7 |
| Bucks co | | 3 yrs. | £23.3.7 |
| Philadelphia | | 5 yrs., 6 mo. | £2.0.0 |
| Strasburg twp., Lancaster co. | Servant[1] | 10 yrs. | £30.0.0 |
| Philadelphia | Servant, taught to read and write and have freedom dues at the end. | 6 yrs. | £28.0.0 |
| Passyunk twp., Phila. co. | Servant[1] | 6 yrs. | £28.8.0 |
| W. Caln twp., Chester co. | Servant, to be dismissed with a suit of good clothes in her person. | 2 yrs. | £1.14.0 |
| Passyunk twp., Phila. co. | Servant[1] | 4 yrs. | £20.11.0 |
| Springfield twp., Chester co. | Servant[3] | 4 yrs., 3 mo. | £27.0.0 |
| Philadelphia | Servant[1] | 7 yrs. | £30.0.0 |
| Lancaster co. near Dunker Town. | For the above term and consideration. | | |
| Philadelphia | Servant (note 3, or £10 lawful money of Pa.). | 4 yrs. | £24.0.0 |
| Lancaster Borough. | | 4 yrs. | £24.0.0 |
| Philadelphia | Servant (note 3, or £8 lawful money of Pa.). | 2 yrs., 6 mo. | £18.19.0 |
| Earl twp., Lancaster co. | Servant[5] | 2 yrs., 6 mo. | £18.19 |
| N. Britain twp., Bucks co. | Servant[1] | 3 yrs., 6 mo. | £24.0.0 |
| Marple twp., Chester co. | Servant[3] | 6 yrs., 6 mo. | £27.14 |
| Philadelphia | Servant (note 3, and £5 in money) | 5 yrs. | £21.3.0 |
| Philadelphia | Servant (note 1, or £10 in cash). | 3 yrs. | £18.19.0 |
| Northern Liberties | Apprentice, taught the brushmaker's trade, read and write perfectly and cypher (note 1, to the value of £10). | 6 yrs. | £10.0.0 |
| Philadelphia | Servant[3] | 3 yrs. | £18.19.0 |
| Philadelphia | Servant | 1 yr., 9 mo. | £9.0.0 |
| Roxbury twp., Phila. co. | Servant (note 3, and two dollars). | 3 yrs., 6 mo. | £18.19.0 |
| Philadelphia | Servant[3] | 5 yrs. | £28.0.0 |
| Philadelphia | Apprentice, taught housewifery and sew, time to go to school two years, the grandfather paying expense of schooling and the master to give such further schooling as will perfect him in reading and writing.[1] | 12 yrs., 9 mo. | |
| Earl twp., Lancaster co. | Servant[3] | 6 yrs., 6 mo. | £20.0.0 |
| Philadelphia | Apprentice, taught art, trade and mystery of a hatmaker, found meat, drink, washing, lodging and hats, allowed liberty of night schooling, at his parents' expense. | 7 yrs. | |
| Elizabeth Town, E. New Jersey. | Servant[3] | 5 yrs. | £23.9.0 |
| Elizabeth Town, E. New Jersey. | Servant[3] | 6 yrs. | £22.8.0 |

| Date. | Name. | From the Port of | To Whom Indentured. |
|---|---|---|---|
| | Hersch, Elizabeth | Rotterdam | John Wilhelm Sternkorn and his assigns. |
| | Fagan, Samuel Bristil | | Joseph Baker and his assigns |
| Oct. 6th | Myardie, Barbara | Rotterdam | John Lawrence and his assigns |
| | Fintz, Casper | Rotterdam | Abraham Kentzing and his assigns |
| | Leverit, Samuel | Rotterdam | George Eckard and his assigns |
| | Owen, Abigail | Ireland | Andrew Gregg and his assigns |
| | Laudenslager, Jacob | | John Shute and his assigns |
| | Miller, Ludwig | Rotterdam | Michael Shriner and his assigns |
| | Hempel, John Gotleib | Rotterdam | George Bear and his assigns |
| 1772. Oct. 6th | Cash, Jacob | | Peter Couver and his assigns |
| | Smith Christian | | William Peters and his assigns |
| Oct. 8th | Hempell, Chas, Gotleib | Rotterdam | John Ellwood and his assigns |
| | Kretsor, John Henry | | Christian Gally and his assigns |
| | Rockenberger, George | | John Ink |
| | Smallwood, Jacob | | William Smallwood and his assigns |
| | McKay, William; McKay, Sandie; McKay, Donald. | Glasgow | Patrick Ewing and his assigns |
| | McKay, Angus; McKay, James. | Glasgow | Patrick Ewing and his assigns |
| | McKay, Jean | Glasgow | Patrick Ewing and his assigns |
| | Plash, John Christian, and Rosina Dorothea, his wife. | Rotterdam | James Whiteall and his assigns |
| | Meyer, Ann | Rotterdam | Joshua Lippencott and his assigns |
| | Owen, Abigail | | Patrick Ewing and his assigns |
| | Rainer, Peter | Rotterdam | Jacob Graff and his assigns |
| | Rainer, Philip | Rotterdam | Jacob Graff and his assigns |
| Oct. 8th | Rose, Abraham | | Samuel Boyd and his assigns |

## List of Indentures.

| Residence. | Occupation. | Term. | Amount. |
|---|---|---|---|
| Northern Liberties | Servant[3] | 5 yrs. | £ 23. 19. 0. |
| Philadelphia | Apprentice, taught to read in Bible, writ a legible hand and cypher through rule of three, in the last seven years of the term to be taught the hatter or felt maker's trade.[3] | 11 yrs., 2 mo., 21 d. | |
| Philadelphia | Servant[3] | 7 yrs. | £ 30. 0. 0. |
| Philadelphia | Servant (note 5, have £ 14 lawful money of Pa. in lieu of freedom dues). | 7 yrs. | £ 30. 0. 0. |
| Leacock twp., Lancaster co. | Servant (note 3, and a grubbing hoe, axe, maul and wedges). | 8 yrs. | £ 30. 0. 0. |
| Philadelphia | Servant[3] | 3 yrs., 8 mo. 7 d. | £ 14. 0. 0. |
| Southwark | Apprentice, taught the loaf bread baker's trade, read and write the English and German language perfectly, and cypher through rule of three.[3] | 12 yrs. | |
| Manheim twp., Lancaster co. | Servant, taught the art of a blacksmith, and at expiration have two complete suits of apparel, one whereof to be new. | 6 yrs., 6 mo. | £ 24. 9. 0. |
| Leacock twp., Lancaster co. | Servant, and at expiration have two complete suits of apparel, one whereof to be new. | 7 yrs. | £ 30. 0. 0. |
| Philadelphia | Apprentice, taught the tobacconist's trade, have one year's night schooling.[3] | 13 yrs., 6 mo. | |
| Ash Town, Chester co. | Servant | 4 yrs. | £ 29. 0. 0. |
| Bristol twp., Bucks co. | Servant[3] | 5 yrs., 6 mo. | £ 30. 0. 0. |
| Philadelphia | Apprentice, taught the tobacconist's trade, read, write and cypher as far as and through rule of three (note 1, to the value of £ 10, or £ 10 in money). | 8 yrs. | |
| Philadelphia | Apprentice, taught the tailor's trade, have one quarter's night schooling.[3] | 5 yrs., 10 d. | |
| | Apprentice | 5 yrs., 3 mo. 2 w. | 5/. |
| Little Britain twp., Lancaster co. | Servant[1] | 3 yrs. each. | £ 13. 0. 0. each. |
| Little Britain twp., Lancaster co. | Servant, at expiration each to have freedom dues. | 8 yrs. each. | £ 13. 0. 0. each. |
| Little Britain twp., Lancaster co. | Servant[3] | 4 yrs. | £ 13. 0. 0. |
| Deptford twp., Gloucester co., W. Jersey. | Servants (note 1, and have £ 10 in money (each), the woman to have a spinning wheel and chest). | 5 yrs. each. | £ 49. 19. 6. |
| Woolwich twp., Gloucester co. | Servant[3] | 6 yrs., 6 mo. | £ 25. 0. 0. |
| Little Britain twp., Lancaster co. | Servant | 3 yrs., 8 mo. 7 d. | £ 14. 0. 0. |
| Tyrone twp., Cumberland co. | Servant[5] | 2 yrs. | £ 17. 0. 0. |
| Tyrone twp., Cumberland co. | Servant, to teach, or cause him to be taught to read in Bible, write a legible hand, and at expiration have two complete suits of apparel, one whereof to be new. | 9 yrs. | £ 20. 0. 0. |
| Lancaster Borough | Apprentice | 5 yrs. | £ 10. 0. 0. |

| Date. | Name. | From the Port of | To Whom Indentured. |
|---|---|---|---|
| 1772. | Fagan, Joseph | | Hannah Caster and her assigns |
| | Fagan, Harman Enochs | | Samuel Painter and his assigns |
| | Adams, Abigail | | James Painter and his assigns |
| Oct. 9th | Matthew, Charles | | Detrick Reese and his assigns |
| | McDonald, John | Glasgow | Alexr. Bartram and his assigns |
| | Plantrick, Mary | | Richard Shewell and his assigns |
| | McClure, Catherine | | Robert McClure and his assigns |
| | McDonald, Catherine | Glasgow | Francis Lee and his assigns |
| | Tearny, Eleanor | | John Matthews and his assigns |
| | Shrader, John | | Robert Conn and his assigns |
| | Kelly, William | | Robert Conn and his assigns |
| | McKay, Alexander | Glasgow | William Richards and his assigns |
| | Burke, Margaret | | Robert Gray and his assigns |
| | Overer, Jacob | Rotterdam | David Whitehill and his assigns |
| | Murray, Robert | Glasgow | Benjamin Swett, Jr., and his assigns |
| | Murray, Helen | Glasgow | Benjamin Swett, Jr., and his assigns |
| | McKay, John | Glasgow | John Grant and his assigns |
| | McKay, Agness | Glasgow | David Evans and his assigns |
| | Sutherland, Christian | Glasgow | James Ingles and his assigns |
| | McKay, Margaret | Glasgow | John Elmsley and his assigns |
| | Hyer, John Casper | Rotterdam | Henry Lisle and his assigns |
| | Matthewson, Neil | Glasgow | Francis Gurney and his assigns |
| | Sutherland, Christian | Glasgow | Peter Howard and his assigns |
| | Engle, Mary | | David Dominick and his assigns |
| Oct. 10th | McKay, Catherine | Glasgow | Isaac Eyre and his assigns |
| | Sornin, Hannah Dorothea | Rotterdam | John Boyd Rigar and his assigns |
| | Reid, Elizabeth | | Thomas Lawrence and wife |
| | McKay, Catherine | Glasgow | John Murray and his assigns |
| | Anderson, Mary | | Benjamin Dismant and his assigns |
| | McKay, Neil | | Lewis Grant and his assigns |
| | Hitner, Frederick | | Samuel Morris |

| Residence. | Occupation. | Term. | Amount. |
|---|---|---|---|
| E. Bradford, Chester co. | Apprentice, taught to read in Bible, write a legible hand and cypher as far as and through rule of three (note 5, have good clothing, to go an apprentice to some trade). | 11 yrs., 6 mo., 25 d. | |
| E. Bradford, Chester co. | Apprentice, taught the blacksmith's trade, read in Bible, write a legible hand, cypher as far as and through rule of three.[3] | 14 yrs., 11 mo., 6 d. | |
| E. Bradford, Chester co. | Apprentice, taught to read in Bible, write a legible hand, cypher as far as and through the rule of multiplication, sew, knit and spin, also housewifery.[3] | 14 yrs., 1 mo., 25 d. | |
| Philadelphia | Servant[5] | 3 yrs. | £ 16. 10. |
| Philadelphia | Servant, taught to read in Bible, write a legible hand.[3] | 6 yrs. | £ 8. 1. 6. |
| Philadelphia | Servant, taught housewifery, sew, read in Bible.[3] | 4 yrs., 6 mo. 15 d. | £ 4. 0. 0. |
| Philadelphia | Servant | 2 yrs., 4 mo. 12 d. | £ 0. 5. 0. |
| Philadelphia | Servant, taught housewifery, read in Bible and sew.[3] | 7 yrs. | £ 5. 2. 0. |
| N. Brunswick, E. Jersey | Servant[3] | 2 yrs., 9 mo. 3 w. | £ 10. 0. 0. |
| Philadelphia | Apprentice | 2 yrs. | £ 4. 10. 0. |
| Philadelphia | Servant | 2 yrs. | £ 16. 0. 0. |
| Philadelphia | Servant, taught to read in Bible, write a legible hand.[3] | 9 yrs., 6 mo. | £ 5. 0. 0. |
| Philadelphia | | 3 yrs., 10 mo., 18 d. | £ 12. 0. 0. |
| Sadsbury twp., Lancaster co. | Servant[3] | 6 yrs. | £ 30. 0. 0. |
| Burlington, W. Jersey | Servant | 7 yrs. | £ 5. 0. 0. |
| Burlington, W. Jersey | Servant[3] | 4 yrs. | £ 5. 0. 0. |
| Philadelphia | Apprentice[3] | 4 yrs. | £ 8. 1. 6. |
| Philadelphia | Servant[3] | 3 yrs. | £ 8. 1. 6. |
| Philadelphia | Servant, taught to read in Bible[3]. | 6 yrs. | £ 8. 1. 6. |
| | Servant[3] | 3 yrs. | £ 8. 1. 6. |
| Philadelphia | Servant, have one quarter's evening schooling.[3] | 7 yrs. | £ 30. 0. 0. |
| Philadelphia | Servant[3] | 4 yrs. | £ 8. 0. 0. |
| Philadelphia | Servant[3] | 3 yrs., 6 mo. | £ 8. 1. 6. |
| Philadelphia | Apprentice, taught housewifery, sew, read in Bible, write a legible hand.[3] | 4 yrs. | |
| Chester, Chester co. | Servant[3] | 3 yrs. | £ 8. 1. 6. |
| Philadelphia | Servant, taught to read in Bible, privilege to go to take the sacrament at the age of 14 years.[3] | 6 yrs. | £ 30. 0. 0. |
| Philadelphia | Apprentice, taught housewifery and sew.[3] | 4 yrs. | |
| Philadelphia | Servant[3] | 3 yrs. | £ 8. 1. 6. |
| N. Providence, Phila. co. | Apprentice, taught to read in Bible, write a legible hand, sew, knit, spin and housewifery (note 3, a new spinning wheel, a cow, or £ 5 in money in lieu of the cow). | 14 yrs. | |
| Philadelphia | Apprentice, taught the trade of copper smith, read in Bible, write a legible hand and cypher[3] | 7 yrs., 6 mo. 3 w. | |
| Whitemarsh | Apprentice, taught the tanner and currier's trade, found meat, drink, washing and lodging and shoes, | 5 yrs. | |

| Date. | Name. | From the Port of | To Whom Indentured. |
|---|---|---|---|
| 1772. | | | |
| Oct. 12th | Bostian, Anna Catherine | Rotterdam | Philip Moses and his assigns |
| | McKay, George | | David Thomson and his assigns |
| | McDonald, William, Jr. | | William Ross and his assigns |
| | Grogin, James | | John Brown and his assigns |
| | Fielding, Hugh | | Michael Kainer and his assigns |
| | McKenzey, Charles | | John Galloway |
| | McKay, Anna | Glasgow | Wm. Falconer and his assigns |
| | Manning, Catherine | | Richard Richardson and his assigns |
| | Dobbs, John | | Wm. Logan |
| Oct. 13th | Wasserling, Johannes | Rotterdam | David Jones and his assigns |
| | Switzer, Henry | Rotterdam | James Jones and his assigns |
| | Shibely, Henry | Rotterdam | Andrew Kessler and his assigns |
| | Miller, Hans Jacob | Rotterdam | John Carmichael and his assigns |
| | McKay, Hector | | James Sutter and his assigns |
| Oct. 14th | Fortner, Robert | | John Fortner and his assigns |
| | Myardie, John | Rotterdam | Michael Clarke and his assigns |
| | Hersch, Elizabeth | | George Schlosser and his assigns |
| | McKay, Agness | | John Spence and his assigns |
| | Watt, John | | David Richardson and his assigns |
| | Deady, Abigail | | Edmond Miln and his assigns |
| Oct. 15th | Howard, Mary | | John Williams and his assigns |
| | Palmer, Jacob | Rotterdam | Adam Hersberger and his assigns |
| | Arnholt, Johannes | Rotterdam | Josiah Haines and his assigns |
| Oct. 16th | Bryan, William | | James Martin and his assigns |
| | Alexander, John | | Rev. John Elder and his assigns |
| | Ellison, Martha | | Robert Parke and his assigns |
| | Myer, Maria | Rotterdam | Joseph Horstetter and his assigns |

## List of Indentures.

| Residence. | Occupation. | Term. | Amount. |
|---|---|---|---|
| | and liberty to go to night school, the father paying the expense of schooling. | | |
| Philadelphia | Servant[3] | 8 yrs. | £29.7.6. |
| Southwark | Apprentice, taught the shipwright's trade, have one quarter's evening schooling each winter (note 1, or £7 in money and his working tools). | 8 yrs. | |
| Philadelphia | Apprentice, taught the cordwainer's trade, have four quarters' night schooling.[3] | 12 yrs., 10 mo. | |
| Philadelphia | Apprentice, taught the joiner's trade, have four quarters' night schooling.[3] | 6 yrs., 10 mo., 1 w. | |
| Philadelphia | Apprentice, taught the chairmaker's trade (note 5, have £16 in money in lieu of freedom dues). | 3 yrs., 6 mo. | |
| Philadelphia | Apprentice, to learn the art of tailoring.[3] | | £8.1.6. |
| Philadelphia | Servant, taught to read in the Bible.[3] | 7 yrs. | £8.1.6. |
| N. Providence, Phila. co. | Apprentice, taught to read in Bible, write a legible hand, sew, knit, spin and housewifery (note 3, a new spinning wheel and £3 in money). | 13 yrs., 10 mo., 20 d. | |
| St. Eustatia | Apprentice, taught the house carpenter and joiner's trade, and at expiration a set of bench tools, new, and one complete new suit of apparel besides his old or £5 in lieu of his clothes. | 4 yrs. | |
| Blockley twp., Phila. co. | Servant[3] | 7 yrs. | £24.19.0. |
| Blockley twp., Phila. co. | Servant (note 3, and 50 shilling in money). | 6 yrs., 6 mo. | £30.0.0. |
| Gloucester co., W. Jersey | Servant[3] | 7 yrs., 6 mo. | £30.0.0. |
| Derry twp., Cumberland co. | Servant[3] | 6 yrs., 6 mo. | £30.0.0. |
| Philadelphia | Servant, have two years schooling[3]. | 9 yrs. | £20.0.0. |
| Pottsgrove, Phila. co. | Apprentice | 7 yrs., 11 mo., 1 w., 5 d. | £17.0.0. |
| Philadelphia | Servant, taught to read in Bible, write a legible hand.[3] | 9 yrs. | £22.10.0. |
| Philadelphia | Servant | 5 yrs. | £23.19. |
| Philadelphia | Servant | 3 yrs. | £8.6.6. |
| Philadelphia | Apprentice, taught the hatter's trade.[1] | 6 yrs., 8 mo. | |
| Philadelphia | Servant, taught to read and write, sew, knit and spin and housewifery, to have at end of term freedom dues. | 6 yrs., 3 mo. | |
| Philadelphia | Servant | 4 yrs. | £11.0.0. |
| Lancaster | Servant[3] | 4 yrs. | £21.10.4. |
| Burlington twp., Burlington co., W. Jersey. | Servant[3] | 4 yrs. | £25.0.0. |
| Moyamensing twp., Phila. co. | Apprentice, taught the farmer's business, read in Bible, write a legible hand.[3] | 18 yrs., 10 mo. | |
| Paxton twp., Lancaster co. | | 3 yrs., 6 mo. | £17.0.0. |
| E. Caln. twp., Chester co. | | 4 yrs. | £15.0.0. |
| Heidleberg twp., Berks co. | Servant, taught to read in Bible, write a legible hand[3]. | 8 yrs. | £25.0.0. |

| Date. | Name. | From the Port of | To Whom Indentured. |
|---|---|---|---|
| 1772. Oct. 15th | Gawn, Mary | | James Webb and his assigns |
| | McClelland, Agnes | | James Webb, Jr., and his assigns |
| | O'Mullen, Catherine | Ireland | John Smith and his assigns |
| | Hanes, Thomas | | Patrick Bready and his assigns |
| | Oberer, Martin | Rotterdam | Thomas Smith and his assigns |
| | Sharp, Jacob | Rotterdam | Jacob Pritchett and his assigns |
| | Bamford, George | | John Jervis and his assigns |
| | Yeaunus, George | Rotterdam | Jacob Kemle and his assigns |
| Oct. 16th | Fullerton, John | | William Graham and his assigns |
| | McFall, Dennis | | John Bartholomew and his assigns |
| | Proctor, Jane | | Thomas Proctor and his assigns |
| | Hessin, Elizabeth | Rotterdam | Henry, Keppelee and his assigns |
| Oct. 17th | Bryan, Catherine | | Robert Clinch and his assigns |
| | Sinerin, Maudlina | Rotterdam | Martin Rees and his assigns |
| | Sinerin, Maudlina | Rotterdam | Mary Yuntin and her assigns |
| | Satorie, Jacob | Rotterdam | Benedick Essleman and his assigns |
| | Craff, Joseph | Rotterdam | Uriah Woolman and his assigns |
| | Craff, Joseph | | Abraham Woolman and his assigns |
| | Murray, John | Glasgow | Jacob Lewis and his assigns |
| | Pancake, John | | Wm. Rigby and his assigns |
| | Hagnorin, Elizabeth | Rotterdam | Miles Hillborn and his assigns |
| | Hess, Frederick William | Rotterdam | Richard Peters, Jr., and his assigns |
| | Smith, Jacob | Rotterdam | Robert Parke and his assigns |
| | Parrot, Alexander Daniel | Rotterdam | Joseph Rhoads and his assigns |
| | Bouchmiller, Joseph | Rotterdam | Peter Spycker and his assigns |
| | Knotestine, Jonas | Rotterdam | Mordecai Piersol and his assigns |
| | Wertman, Yerick | Rotterdam | Isaac Clarke and his assigns |
| | Myers, Verney | Rotterdam | Joseph Ferree and his assigns |
| | Hytz, John Jacob | Rotterdam | Joseph Hillborn and his assigns |
| | Tumberlin, Maria Catherina | Rotterdam | Wm. West and his assigns |
| | Rambo, William | | Jonathan Dungan and his assigns |
| | Frankford, Madelina | Rotterdam | Jacob Morgan and his assigns |
| | Frankford, Madelina | | John Price and his assigns |
| | Moore, Christopher | Rotterdam | Jacob Whitman and his assigns |
| | Miller, Michael | Rotterdam | Moses Cox and his assigns |
| | Frankford, Philip | | Philip Cole and his assigns |
| | Figley, Gotlip | Rotterdam | Thomas Robbins and his assigns |
| | Baum, John George | Rotterdam | Edward Darnall and his assigns |
| | McClelland, John, Jr. | Rotterdam | Fergus Purdon and his assigns |

## List of Indentures.

| Residence. | Occupation. | Term. | Amount. |
|---|---|---|---|
| Lancaster twp., Lancaster co..... | .................................. | 4 yrs....... | £15.0.0. |
| Lancaster twp., Lancaster co..... | .................................. | 3 yrs....... | £12.0.0. |
| Philadelphia .................. | Servant, found meat, drink, washing, lodging, shoes and stocking, one gown and two shifts. | 1 yr., 10 mo. 12 d. | £7.10.0. |
| Waterford twp., Gloucester co., W. Jersey. | Servant, found meat, drink, washing and lodging only, and if he pays the above money within the the term the indenture to be void. | 3 mo. ...... | £2.2.6. |
| Evesham twp., Burlington co., W. Jersey. | Servant[3] ...................... | 10 yrs...... | £30.0.0. |
| Northampton twp., Burlington co., W. Jersey. | Servant[3] ...................... | 5 yrs....... | £30.0.0. |
| Philadelphia .................. | .................................. | 2 yrs....... | £10.0.0. |
| Philadelphia .................. | Servant (note 1, or £8 lawful money of Pa.). | 3 yrs....... | £10.14.0. |
| Philadelphia .................. | .................................. | 4 yrs....... | £17.0.0. |
| E. Whiteland twp., Chester co... | .................................. | 4 yrs....... | £15.0.0. |
| Philadelphia .................. | Apprentice, taught housewifery, sew, read in Bible, write a legible hand.[3] | 14 yrs., 5 mo., 3 w. | |
| Philadelphia .................. | Servant (note 3, and two Spanish dollars). | 5 yrs....... | £24.5.0. |
| Schenectady, Albany co., N. Y... | Servant (note 5, have £5 Pa. currency). | 2 yrs....... | £2.0.0. |
| Philadelphia .................. | Servant[3] ...................... | 5 yrs....... | £27.0.0. |
| Hinckle Town, Lancaster co..... | .................................. | 5 yrs....... | £27.0.0. |
| Conestoga twp., Lancaster co.... | Servant, and at expiration have two complete suits of apparel, one whereof to be new. | 3 yrs....... | £20.5.0. |
| Philadelphia .................. | Servant[3] ...................... | 6 yrs....... | £21.10.6. |
| Northampton twp., Burlington co., W. Jersey. | .................................. | 6 yrs....... | £21.10.6. |
| Philadelphia .................. | Servant, taught to read in Bible[3].. | 4 yrs....... | £5.0.0. |
| Philadelphia .................. | Apprentice, taught the joiner's trade, have three quarters' night schooling, the mother paying the expense.[3] | 6 yrs., 4 mo. 17 d. | |
| Philadelphia .................. | Servant[1] ...................... | 4 yrs....... | £21.10.6. |
| Philadelphia .................. | Servant[3] ...................... | 6 yrs....... | £24.0.0. |
| E. Caln twp., Chester co........ | Servant[3] ...................... | 3 yrs., 3 mo. | £21.9.0. |
| Marple twp., Chester co......... | Servant[3] ...................... | 6 yrs., 3 mo. | £28.0.0. |
| Tulpehockin twp., Berks co...... | Servant[3] ...................... | 3 yrs., 6 mo. | £25.0.0. |
| W. Nantmill twp., Chester co.... | Servant[3] ...................... | 2 yrs., 3 mo. | £21.2.6. |
| Windsor twp., Middlesex co., W. Jersey. | Servant, and at expiration have freedom dues or £9 in cash. | 4 yrs....... | £24.0.0. |
| Strasburgh twp., Lancaster co.... | Servant[3] ...................... | 10 yrs...... | £18.0.0. |
| Philadelphia .................. | Servant[3] ...................... | 9 yrs....... | £25.0.0. |
| Philadelphia .................. | Servant[3] ...................... | 4 yrs....... | £21.0.0. |
| Cheltenham twp., Phila. co...... | Apprentice[3] .................... | 6 yrs., 10 26 d. | |
| Philadelphia .................. | Servant[1] ...................... | 8 yrs....... | £28.0.0. |
| Reading, Berks co............... | .................................. | 8 yrs....... | £28.0.0. |
| Phila. co., Moyamensing twp..... | Servant (note 5, have £9 in lieu of freedom dues). | 3 yrs....... | £19.4.6. |
| Philadelphia .................. | Servant[3] ...................... | 3 yrs., 4 mo. | £22.0.0. |
| Amity, Berks co................. | Servant[1] ...................... | 6 yrs., 6 mo. | £37.8.0. |
| Philadelphia .................. | Servant (note 3, or £7 Pa. currency). | 3 yrs....... | £25.19.9. |
| Evesham twp., Burlington co., W. Jersey. | Servant[3] ...................... | 4 yrs....... | £22.17.3. |
| Philadelphia .................. | Apprentice, taught the trade of a pitcher or paver, have two quarters' night schooling.[3] | 7 yrs....... | £12.0.0. |

| Date. | Name. | From the Port of | To Whom Indentured. |
|---|---|---|---|
| 1772.<br>Oct. 17th.... | Sheney, Ann Mary | Rotterdam.. | James Whiteall and his assigns. |
| | Hytz, Charlotta | Rotterdam.. | Adam Foulke and his assigns. |
| | Fisher, John | Rotterdam.. | John Grove and his assigns. |
| | Fust, Stephen | Rotterdam.. | Michael Rederback and his assigns. |
| | Smith, Peter | Rotterdam.. | Andrew McGlone and his assigns. |
| | Rengalsbacker, John Henry | Rotterdam.. | Robert Bass and his assigns. |
| | Pricein, Barbara | Rotterdam.. | John Hill and his assigns. |
| | Merkell, Theobald | Rotterdam.. | Matthias Slough and his assigns. |
| | Redick, Christian | Rotterdam.. | Joseph Stamper and his assigns. |
| | Mourer, George Henry | Rotterdam.. | George Emerick and his assigns. |
| | Souder, Johannes | | Thomas Batten and his assigns. |
| | Wortman, Michael | Rotterdam.. | Jacob Morgan and his assigns. |
| | Rup, Jacob | Rotterdam.. | John Whitmore, Jr., and his assigns. |
| | Disher, Conrad | Rotterdam.. | Andrew Groff and his assigns. |
| | Stump, Joseph | Rotterdam.. | Andrew Groff and his assigns. |
| | Gowasht, John | Rotterdam.. | Christopher Reigert and his assigns. |
| | Houk, Martin | Rotterdam.. | Richard Wistar and his assigns. |
| | Abale, John Jacob | Rotterdam.. | Richard Wistar and his assigns. |
| Oct. 19th.... | Link, Frederick | Rotterdam.. | John Heflein and his assigns. |
| | Freiklerin, Maria Elizabeth.. | Rotterdam.. | Conrad Graff and his assigns. |
| | Pricein, Appalonia | Rotterdam.. | Robert Bridges and his assigns. |
| | Bastian, Anthony | Rotterdam.. | Matthias Aspden and his assigns. |
| | Waggonhouse, Ludwick, and Waggonhouse, Elizabeth, his sister. | Rotterdam.. | Mordecai Lewis and his assigns. |
| | Waggonhousein, Elizabeth | | Phœbe Dubery and her assigns. |
| | Waggonhousein, Susanna | Rotterdam.. | Joseph Hillborn and his assigns. |
| | Zigler, David | Rotterdam.. | Matthias Slough and his assigns. |
| | Niver, Christian | Rotterdam.. | Valentine Sherer and his assigns. |
| | Wasom, Mary Cathn. | Rotterdam.. | Michael Ferdine and his assigns. |
| | Opleiter, Jacob | Rotterdam.. | Michael Rap and his assigns. |
| | Koch, Casper | London .... | John Hartman and his assigns. |
| | Torwart, Anna Barbara | Rotterdam.. | Jacob Witmore and his assigns. |
| | Whitman, Godfreid | Rotterdam.. | Jacob Winey and his assigns. |
| | Lampert, Andrew | Rotterdam.. | Peter Shriver and his assigns. |
| | Lindamire, Matthias | Rotterdam.. | Thomas Hollingshead and his assigns. |
| | Best, Abraham | | Daniel Murphy and his assigns. |
| | Hanrahan, Margaret | | Moses Coxe and his assigns. |
| | Greenan, Thomas | Ireland .... | Samuel Paul and his assigns. |
| | Ross, Andrew | Glasgow ... | James McCutcheon and his assigns. |
| | Lambert, Peter | Rotterdam.. | Christopher Reigart and his assigns. |

## List of Indentures.

| Residence. | Occupation. | Term. | Amount. |
|---|---|---|---|
| Deptford twp., Gloucester co., W. Jersey | Servant (note 3, and forty shillings Pa. currency). | 4 yrs, | £ 21. 10. 0. |
| Philadelphia | Servant[3] | 9 yrs. | £ 25. 0. 0. |
| Plymouth twp., Phila. co. | Servant[3] | 4 yrs., 2 mo. 8 d. | £ 29. 11. 3. |
| Mooreland twp., Phila. co. | Servant (note 3, and 40/ lawful money of Pa.). | 4 yrs. | £ 24. 12. 0. |
| Philadelphia | Servant (note 1, and provided he behaves himself faithfully £ 10 in money, with lawful interest, the interest to be paid annually). | 5 yrs. | £ 19. 0. 0. |
| Philadelphia | Servant, taught to read in Bible, write a legible hand.[3] | 8 yrs. | £ 13. 3. 0. |
| Middletown twp., Chester co. | Servant, taught to read in Bible[3]. | 10 yrs., 6 mo. | £ 25. 0. 0. |
| Philadelphia | Servant[3] | 4 yrs. | £ 27. 0. 0. |
| Philadelphia | Servant[3] | 4 yrs. | £ 24. 3. 3. |
| Pikeland twp., Chester co. | Servant[3] | 3 yrs., 6 mo. | £ 22. 3. 9. |
| Woolwich twp., Gloucester co., W. Jersey | Servant (note 1, or £ 10) | 3 yrs., 9 mo. | £ 22. 5. 5. |
| Philadelphia | Servant (note 3, or £ 9 Pa. currency and $8.00). | 3 yrs., 6 mo. | £ 26. 10. 0. |
| Lampeter twp., Lancaster co. | Servant[5] | 2 yrs., 6 mo. | £ 18. 13. 0. |
| Lancaster twp., Lancaster co. | Servant (note 3, and £ 3 Pa. currency). | 2 yrs., 6 mo. | £ 22. 13. 4. |
| Lancaster twp., Lancaster co. | Servant[3] | 3 yrs. | £ 23. 13. 0. |
| Lancaster twp., Lancaster co. | Servant[3] | 3 yrs., 3 mo. | £ 23. 48. 0. |
| Philadelphia | Servant[3] | 3 yrs. | £ 19. 13. 6. |
| Philadelphia | Servant (note 3, and $1.00) | 4 yrs., 9 mo. | £ 24. 7. 0. |
| Philadelphia | Servant (note 1, to the value of £ 10, or £ 10 in money). | 4 yrs. | £ 22. 10. 9. |
| Lancaster, Lancaster co. | Servant (note 1, of the value of £ 8, or £ 8 in money). | 4 yrs. | £ 20. 17. 9. |
| Philadelphia | Servant, taught to read in Bible[3]. | 11 yrs. | £ 30. 0. 0. |
| Philadelphia | Servant[1] | 9 yrs. | £ 28. 0. 0. |
| Philadelphia | Servant, the boy to be taught to read in Bible.[3] | 9 yrs. each. | £ 28. 1. 0. each. |
| | Servant.[1] | | |
| Philadelphia | | 9 yrs. | £ 28. 1. 0. |
| Philadelphia | Servant, and at expiration have freedom dues and one guinea. | 5 yrs. | £ 28. 1. 0. |
| Lancaster, Lancaster co. | Servant[3] | 3 yrs. | £ 24. 0. 0. |
| Whitpain twp., Phila. co. | Servant (note 3, and one pair boots whenever the servant chooses to have them). | 3 yrs. | £ 23. 9. 0. |
| Lancaster | Servant[3] | 6 yrs. | £ 30. 0. 0. |
| Upper Dublin twp., Phila co. | Servant, and at expiration have two complete suits of apparel, one whereof to be new. | 3 yrs., 6 mo. | £ 22. 11. 6. |
| Reading, Berks co. | Servant[5] | 2 yrs. | £ 16. 5. 3. |
| Lampeter twp., Lancaster co. | Servant, taught to read in Bible and write.[3] | 8 yrs., 6 mo. | £ 12. 11. 0. |
| Philadelphia | Servant[3] | 4 yrs., 6 mo. | £ 27. 0. 0. |
| Philadelphia | Servant (note 1, or £ 10 in money). | 3 yrs., 6 mo. | £ 24. 0. 0. |
| Evesham, Burlington co. | Servant[3] | 3 yrs., 6 mo. | £ 22. 3. 5. |
| Appoquinomy Hundred, N. Castle co. on Delaware | Apprentice | 8 yrs., 1 mo. 17 d. | £ 9. 0. 0. |
| Philadelphia | Servant | 5 yrs. | £ 3. 0. 0. |
| Greenwich twp., Gloucester co., N. Jersey | Servant, have three months evening schooling.[3] | 2 yrs. | £ 10. 0. 0. |
| Philadelphia | Apprentice, taught to read in Bible.[3] | 5 yrs. | £ 8. 1. 6. |
| Lancaster, Lancaster co. | Servant[3] | 3 yrs. | £ 22. 0. 0. |

| Date. | Name. | From the Port of | To Whom Indentured. |
|---|---|---|---|
| 1772. Oct. 19th.... | Uximer, Peter, and Barbara, his wife. | Holland | Samuel Pleasants and his assigns.... |
| | Dodd, Michael | Ireland | Abraham Borlen and his assigns..... |
| | Souder, Michael | Rotterdam.. | Sebastian Graff and his assigns...... |
| | Irwin, Jane | | Joshua Ash and his assigns.......... |
| | Bush, Hosewalt | Rotterdam.. | John Eastaugh Hopkins and his assigns............................. |
| | Porter, John Burger | Rotterdam.. | James Cooper and his assigns......... |
| | Yost, John | Rotterdam.. | John Mickel and his assigns......... |
| Oct. 20th.... | Schudi, Martin | London | John Young and his assigns........... |
| | Swartz, John Peter | Rotterdam.. | George Delp and his assigns......... |
| | Swartz, Catherine | Rotterdam.. | George Delp and his assigns......... |
| | Scanlan, Ann | Ireland | Robert Henry and his assigns........ |
| | Scanlan, Ann | | William Ledlie and his assigns...... |
| | Drexler, Francis Peter | Rotterdam.. | Daniel Burkhart and his assigns..... |
| | Frick, Francis | London | Martin Kryder and his assigns....... |
| | Frick, Francis | | Frederick Bertless and his assigns.... |
| | Richardson, John | | Andrew Butler and his assigns...... |
| | Swartz, Lawrence | Rotterdam.. | Jacob Ordt and his assigns.......... |
| | Bowry, Johanna Augusta | Rotterdam.. | Isaac Evans and his assigns......... |
| | Herer, John, and Regina Cath., his wife. | Rotterdam.. | Abraham Levan and his assigns...... |
| | Herer, Regina Cath. | | Isaac Levan and his assigns......... |
| | Fulson, Catherine Esther | | John Carpenter and his assigns...... |
| | Bardeck, George | London | Richard Humphrys and his assigns... |
| | Jahraus, George Adam | Rotterdam.. | John Bissell and his assigns.......... |
| | Lendiman, Christian | London | Thomas Bean and his assigns........ |
| | Meyer, Ann | | Joseph Saunders and his assigns...... |
| | Swicker, Phœnix | Rotterdam.. | Joseph Saunders and his assigns...... |
| | Shebela, John Reinhard | London | Christopher Zeller and his assigns.... |
| | Miller, Michael | Rotterdam. | Jacob Detrick and his assigns........ |
| | Miller, Michael | | Jacob Cuckert and his assigns........ |
| | Link, Frederick | Rotterdam.. | Andrew Burkhard and his assigns.... |
| | Cristel, James | Ireland | James Wilson and his assigns........ |
| | Morris, Hugh, Jr. | | James Longhead and his heirs........ |

## List of Indentures.

| Residence. | Occupation. | Term. | Amount. |
|---|---|---|---|
| Philadelphia | Servant, to have two complete suits of apparel, one whereof to be new, or else the husband to receive £7, and his wife £5 in cash, in lieu of freedom dues. | 3 yrs., 6 mo. each. | £40.0.0. |
| Evesham twp., Burlington co., W. Jersey. | Servant[3] | 4 yrs. | £18.0.0. |
| Manheim twp., Lancaster co. | Servant[3] | 3 yrs. | £23.0.0. |
| Derby twp., Chester co. | | 3 yrs. | £12.0.0. |
| Deptford twp., Gloucester co., W. Jersey. | Servant[3] | 4 yrs. | £22.11.5. |
| Deptford twp., Gloucester co., W. Jersey | Servant (note 3, and 8 Spanish dollars). | 5 yrs. | £27.17.6. |
| Gloucester, Gloucester co., W. Jersey. | Servant[1] | 4 yrs. | £22.0.0. |
| Vincent twp., Chester co. | Servant (note 3, or £10 lawful money of Penna.). | 3 yrs., 6 mo. | £13.7.0. |
| Hill Town twp., Bucks co. | Servant, taught to read in Bible, with a legible hand.[3] | 14 yrs. | £10.0.0. |
| Hill Town twp., Bucks co. | Servant, taught to read in Bible, write a legible hand.[3] | 9 yrs. | £10.0.0. |
| | Servant[3] | 4 yrs. | |
| Philadelphia | | 4 yrs. | £12.0.0. |
| Passyunk twp., Phila co. | Servant[3] | 3 yrs. | £19.10.0. |
| Philadelphia | Servant, to be employed at the skinner and breeches maker's trade during the term.[3] | 2 yrs. | £18.15.0. |
| New Germantown, Somerset co., W. Jersey. | | 2 yrs. | £18.15. |
| Dover, Kent co. on Delaware | Apprentice | 5 yrs., 9 mo. | £5.0.0. |
| Forks twp., Northampton co. | Servant[3] | 5 yrs., 9 mo. | £30.0.0. |
| Lampeter, Lancaster co. | Servant[1] | 4 yrs. | £22.0.0. |
| Exeter twp., Berks co. | Servant (note 5, the man to have freedom dues, or £8 in money). | 4 yrs. each. | £44.2.3. |
| | Servant (note 5, the woman freedom of £5). | | |
| Reading, Berks co. | | 4 yrs. | £22.1.1½. |
| Strasburg, Lancaster co. | | 4 yrs. | £26. |
| Philadelphia | Servant, to be employed at the goldsmith's trade during the term.[3] | 2 yrs. | £16.18.0. |
| Philadelphia | Servant (note 3, and of the value of £10, or £10 in money in lieu of the new suit). | 3 yrs. | £24.2.3. |
| Worcester twp., Phila co. | Servant (note 1, to the value of £10, or £10 in money). | 2 yrs. | £14.5.0. |
| Philadelphia | Servant, taught to read and write English.[1] | 9 yrs. | £18.14.0. |
| Philadelphia | Servant, taught to read and write English.[1] | 14 yrs. | £14.0.0. |
| Philadelphia | Servant, found meat, drink, washing and lodging and employed at the tailor's trade during the term. | 2 yrs. | £13.12.0. |
| Philadelphia | Servant[3] | 3 yrs. | £18.13.9. |
| Near East Town, Northampton co. | | 3 yrs. | £18.13.9. |
| Philadelphia | Servant[3] | 4 yrs. | £22.5.6. |
| Leacock twp., Lancaster co. | Servant[5] | 1 yr., 10 mo. | £9.0.0. |
| Philadelphia | Apprentice, taught the art and mystery of a shopkeeper and found meat, drink, washing, lodging, shoes and hats and at expiration have one complete new suit of apparel. | 6 yrs., 7 mo. | |

| Date. | Name. | From the Port of | To Whom Indentured. |
|---|---|---|---|
| 1772. | Brayfield, John | | William Salesbury and his assigns... |
| Oct. 19th.... | Tanner, John | | William Cooper and his assigns...... |
| | Love, David | | Samuel Cooper and his assigns....... |
| Oct. 20th.... | Whatley, David | | John Hyder and his assigns.......... |
| | Harlin, Thomas | | William Austin and his assigns...... |
| | Tachner, Fredrick | | John Hartman and his assigns........ |
| | Tachner, Fredrick | | David LeVan and his assigns......... |
| | Keeler, Abraham | Rotterdam.. | John Hartman and his assigns........ |
| | Girt, Conrad | Rotterdam.. | Wm. Sheafe and his assigns.......... |
| | Girt, Conrad | | Abraham Risk and his assigns........ |
| | Miller, Leonard | London .... | Henry Deits and his assigns.......... |
| | Miller, Leonard | | Michael Leaffe and his assigns....... |
| | Ryan, John | | Robert Fulton and his assigns........ |
| | Legrange, Thomas | | David and Thomas Fulton and their assigns. |
| | Rogers, John; Gibney, Lawrence; Myler, Richard; Dorsey, Anthony; Brenan, William; Smith, John; Ford, John; Morran, John; McLaughlin, John; Smith, John; Munay, John; Kelly, Daniel; Ryan, John; Ward, John; Badi, Robert; Coleman, William; Jackson, James; Ryan, James; Conolly, Timothy; Rowe, James; Caffery, Michael, and Smith, John. | | David and Thomas Fulton and their assigns. |
| | Quigly, Michael | | David and Thomas Fulton and their assigns. |
| | Cook, George; Byrne, Philip, and Conner, Thomas. | | David and Thomas Fulton and their assigns. |
| Oct. 21st.... | Campbell, Alexander | | Thomas Jenny ...................... |
| | Barrie, Peter | Ireland .... | David and Thomas Fulton and their assigns. |
| | Nevin, John | To St. Croix | Francis Merkoe and his assigns....... |
| | Fortune, William | | Daniel Huston ...................... |
| | Bough, Thomas | | Judah Foulke........................ |
| | Laudermilk, Jacob | Rotterdam.. | Henry Shack and his assigns......... |
| | Knery, Charles Frederick | London .... | Nicholas Weaver and his assigns..... |
| | Frankforder, Henry | Rotterdam.. | Benjamin Morgan and his assigns.... |
| | Hargan, Dennis | | Thomas Leiper and his assigns...... |
| | Paxton, William | Ireland .... | William Hurrie and his assigns...... |
| | Klet, Frederick | London .... | Thomas Palmer and his assigns....... |
| | McKay, Isabella | Glasgow ... | Elizabeth Sharpe and her heirs...... |

[1] To be found all necessaries and at the expiration have freedom dues.
[2] To be found all necessaries and at the expiration have one new suit of apparel.
[3] To be found all necessaries and at the expiration have two complete suits of apparel, one whereof to be new.

## List of Indentures.

| Residence. | Occupation. | Term. | Amount. |
|---|---|---|---|
| Philadelphia | | 5 yrs. | £ 20. 0. 0. |
| Newtown twp., Gloucester co., W. Jersey. | | 6 yrs. | £ 20. 0. 0. |
| Newtown twp., Gloucester co., W. Jersey. | | 7 yrs. | £ 20. 0. 0. |
| Philadelphia | | 5 yrs. | £ 20. 0. 0. |
| Philadelphia | | 5 yrs. | £ 20. 0. 0. |
| Exeter twp., Berks co. | Servant [1] | 4 yrs., 4 mo. | £ 31. 0. 4. |
| Berks co., Exeter twp. | | 4 yrs., 4 mo. | £ 31. 0. 4. |
| Berks co., Exeter twp. | Servant [5] | 3 yrs., 6 mo. | £ 24. 7. 11. |
| Philadelphia | Servant (note 5, have £ 9 in money in lieu of freedom dues). | 3 yrs. | £ 22. 0. 0. |
| Manheim twp., Lancaster co. | | 3 yrs. | £ 24. 1. 1. |
| Philadelphia | Servant [3] | 2 yrs. | £ 14. 2. 2. |
| Greenwich twp., Berks co. | | 2 yrs. | £ 14. 2. 0. |
| Philadelphia | Servant [5] | 4 yrs. | £ 16. 0. 0. |
| W. Nottingham, Chester co. | | 6 yrs. | £ 16. 0. 0. |
| W. Nottingham, Chester co. | | 4 yrs. each. | £ 16. 0. 0. each. |
| W. Nottingham, Chester co. | | 7 yrs. | £ 16. 0. 0. |
| W. Nottingham, Chester co. | | 5 yrs. each. | £ 16. 0. 0. each. |
| So. Susquehanna Hundred, Cecil co., Md. | Servant [5] | 2 yrs., 6 mo. | £ 12. 0. 0. |
| W. Nottingham, Chester co. | Servant [1] | 4 yrs. | £ 16. 0. 0. |
| St. Croix | Servant, found meat, drink, washing and lodging and £ 30 the first year, £ 40 the second year, and £ 50 the third year, St. Croix currency. | 3 yrs. | |
| Strasurg twp., Lancaster co. | Servant [1] | 4 yrs. | £ 15. 10. 0. |
| Philadelphia | Servant [1] | 6 yrs. | £ 20. 0. 0. |
| Heidelberg twp., Lancaster co. | Servant [3] | 3 yrs., 6 mo. | £ 24. 4. 6. |
| Philadelphia | Servant [3] | 3 yrs. | £ 20. 3. 10. |
| Philadelphia | Servant [3] | 8 yrs. | £ 30. 0. 0. |
| Philadelphia | Apprentice | 13 yrs., 3 mo., 3 w. | 5/. |
| Southwark | Servant, found meat, drink, washing and lodging, one pair buckskin breeches, one pair new shoes, two check shirts and one hat. | 1 yr., 1 mo. | £ 8. 0. 0. |
| Philadelphia | Servant [3] | 3 yrs. | £ 15. 15. 0. |
| Pittsgrove, Salem co., W. Jersey. | Servant (note 5, have £ 4 money of Penna., and if she has any | 3 yrs. | £ 4. 0. 0. |

[4] To be found all necessaries and at the expiration have two complete suits of apparel, one whereof to be new, and 40s. in money.

[5] At expiration have two complete suits of apparel, one whereof to be new.

| Date. | Name. | From the Port of | To Whom Indentured. |
|---|---|---|---|
| 1771.<br>Oct. 20th | McKay, Philip | | Elizabeth Sharpe and her executors |
| | Frankforderin, Eve Margt | Rotterdam | John Mertz and his assigns |
| | Shoeman, Peter | Rotterdam | Isaac Hoover and his assigns |
| | Founder, Barbara | | Isaac Hoover and his assigns |
| | Refeldt, George David | London | Benjamin Harbeson and his assigns |
| | Hoffman, Jacob | Rotterdam | John Eckhart and his assigns |
| | Wortman, Michael | | John Lesher and his assigns |
| | McCool, Patrick | Ireland | James Ray and his assigns |
| | Miller, William | Ireland | Thomas Rogers and his assigns |
| | Hann, John Casper | Rotterdam | Philip Shaeffe and his assigns |
| | Einwacter, John George | Rotterdam | Richard Wister and his assigns |
| | Frankforderin, Anna Maria | Rotterdam | William Bishop and his assigns |
| | Vaughan, John | Ireland | Robert Currey and his assigns |
| Oct. 22nd | Smith, William | London | Robert Loosley |
| | Martin, Maria Christiana | Rotterdam | John Brown and his assigns |
| | Bastian, Catherine | Rotterdam | Peter Dishong and his assigns |
| | Meyer, Maria Agness | Rotterdam | Abm. Ferree and his assigns |
| | Claus, Jacob | London | John Mifflin and his assigns |
| | Magill, James | | Thomas Proctor and his assigns |
| | Meyer, Mary | Rotterdam | Jacob Hoover and his assigns |
| | Legrange, Thomas | | Martin Juger and his assigns |
| | Ryan, James | | William Martin and his assigns |
| | Moran, John | | Daniel McBride and his assigns |
| | McCleland | | Francis Gottier and wife |
| | Dunbar, John | Glasgow | Alexander Ewens and his assigns |
| | Wirtzbackin, Rebecca | Rotterdam | Martin Bear and his assigns |
| | Whitely, Johan Wintle | Rotterdam | Matthias Hollepeter and his assigns |
| Oct. 23rd | Nowland, John | Dublin | David and Thomas Fulton and his assigns |
| | Sutherland, Robert | Glasgow | David Reese and his assigns |
| | McKay, Ann | Scotland | Saml. Preston Moore and his assigns |
| | Miller, Margaret | | James Wilson and his assigns |
| | Runey, Bartley | | Aaron Phipps and his assigns |
| Oct. 24th | Hanning, William | Ireland | Robert Smith and his assigns |
| | Johnson, David | | Peter January and his assigns |
| | Robeson, Margaret | | Valentine Brown and his assigns |
| | O'Hara, Mary | Ireland | William Graham and his assigns |
| | Wimer, Peter | Rotterdam | George Seits and his assigns |
| | Hemmell, John | Rotterdam | Dennis Habback and his assigns |
| | Ringlesbacher, Christian | Rotterdam | Samuel Bear and his assigns |
| | Pindle, George Frederick | Rotterdam | Samuel Bear and his assigns |
| | Pindle, George Frederick | | Jacob Bear and his assigns |
| | O'Hara, Mary | | Wm. Duffield and his assigns |

## List of Indentures.

| Residence. | Occupation. | Term. | Amount. |
|---|---|---|---|
| | children after the first year of her servitude, the husband be at the charge of supporting them.. | | |
| Pittsgrove. Salem co., W. Jersey. | Servant[5] | 1 yr. | 5/. |
| Pikes twp., Chester co. | Servant, taught to read in Bible, allowed time to take the sacrament at the age of 14 years[3] | 12 yrs. | £ 10.0.0. |
| Mastick twp., Lancaster co. | Servant[3] | 3 yrs. | £ 22.0.0. |
| Philadelphia | Apprentice | 11 yrs. | £ 7.0.0. |
| Philadelphia | Servant[3] | 2 yrs. | £ 14.1.0. |
| Heidleberg twp., Berks co. | Servant[3] | 4 yrs. | £ 30.0.0. |
| Oley, Berks co. | | 3 yrs., 6 mo. | £ 26.10.0. |
| Little Britain twp., Lancaster co. | Servant[5] | 1 yr., 6 mo. | £ 3.15.0 |
| W. Caln twp., Chester co. | Servant[3] | 4 yrs. | £ 14.0.0. |
| Newtown twp., Chester co. | Servant[3] | 3 yrs., 6 mo. | £ 26.0.0. |
| Philadelphia | Servant (note 1, and £ 20 in cash) | 5 yrs. | £ 28.0.0. |
| Mt. Joy twp., Lancaster co. | Servant, taught to read and write[3]. | 8 yrs. | £ 20.0.0. |
| Greenwich twp., Gloucester co. | Servant (note 1, and £ 5 in money) | 4 yrs. | £ 15.0.0. |
| Philadelphia | Servant[5] | 3 yrs. | £ 20.0.0. |
| Philadelphia | Servant[3] | 5 yrs. | £ 22.6.0. |
| Blockley twp., Phila. co. | Servant[3] | 6 yrs. | £ 8.0.0. |
| Strasburg, Lancaster co. | Servant[3] | 3 yrs., 9 mo. | £ 19.14.0. |
| Philadelphia | Servant[3] | 3 yrs. | £ 16.0.0. |
| Philadelphia | Apprentice, found meat, drink, washing, lodging and working apparel, have one quarter's evening schooling, and at expiration have £ 5 in money. | 1 yr., 3 mo. | |
| Mastick twp., Lancaster co. | Servant[3] | 5 yrs. | £ 18.14.0. |
| Philadelphia | Servant | 6 yrs. | £ 16.10.0. |
| Philadelphia | Servant | 4 yrs. | £ 16.10.0. |
| Brandywine Hundred, N. Castle co. | Servant | 4 yrs. | £ 17.0.0. |
| Philadelphia | Apprentice, taught housewifery and sew, read in Bible.[3] | 9 yrs. | |
| Virginia | Servant (note 3, and £ 10 sterling money of Great Britain). | 2 yrs., 9 mo. | £ 7.10.0. |
| Conestoga twp., Lancaster co. | Servant[3] | 3 yrs., 6 mo. | £ 21.15.9. |
| Warren twp., York co. | Servant[3] | 3 yrs., 6 mo. | £ 25.14.0. |
| W. Nottingham, Chester co. | Servant[3] | 4 yrs. | £ 16.0.0. |
| New Town twp., Chester co. | Servant, taught to read in Bible, write a legible hand (note 3, and £ 3 in money). | 12 yrs. | £ 10.1.6. |
| Philadelphia | Servant, taught to read in Bible, write a legible hand.[3] | 5 yrs. | £ 8.0.0. |
| Leacock twp., Lancaster co. | Servant | 4 yrs., 6 mo. | £ 14.0.0. |
| Uwchlan twp., Chester co. | Servant[1] | 2 yrs., 6 mo. | £ 11.7.6. |
| Uwchlan twp., Chester co. | Servant (note 2 besides his old) | 2 yrs., 9 mo. | £ 11.10.0. |
| Philadelphia | Apprentice, taught the cordwainer's trade, have two quarters' night schooling.[6] | 5 yrs. | |
| Northern Liberties, Phila. co. | Servant | 10 yrs., 7 mo. | £ 6.0.0. |
| Philadelphia | Servant[3] | 4 yrs. | £ 12.0.0. |
| Philadelphia | Servant[3] | 3 yrs. | £ 21.0.0. |
| Amwell, Hunterdon co. | Servant[3] | 4 yrs. | £ 25.3.6. |
| Near Lancaster | Servant, taught to read in Bible, write a legible hand.[3] | 9 yrs. | £ 15.0.0. |
| Near Lancaster | Servant, taught to read in Bible, write a legible hand, to cypher through rule of three.[3] | 11 yrs. | £ 14.0.0. |
| Conecocheague, Frederick co., Md. | | 11 yrs. | £ 14.0.0. |
| Peters twp., Cumberland co. | | 4 yrs. | £ 12.0.0. |

| Date. | Name. | From the Port of | To Whom Indentured. |
|---|---|---|---|
| 1772. Oct. 24th | Ringlesbachin, Salomia | Rotterdam | Samuel Bear and his assigns |
| | Adams, Charles | | Benjamin Canby |
| | Criner, Johannes | Rotterdam | Stephen Phipps and his assigns |
| | Stonemetz, John | Rotterdam | Allen Moore and his assigns |
| | Swigerin, Agnus Mary | Rotterdam | Anthony Williams and his assigns |
| | Whitman, Francis Charles | Rotterdam | Adam Fleck |
| | Conner, John | Ireland | Robert Fulton and assigns |
| | Fenrick, David Christopher | Rotterdam | John Room and his assigns |
| Oct. 26th | Smith, Charles | | Samuel Hughes |
| | Scott, John | | Robert Fulton and his assigns |
| | Whistler, William | Ireland | John Fox and his assigns |
| | Shaw, John | | Wm. Crain and his assigns |
| | Troy, Daniel | | Anthony Fortune and his assigns |
| | Drexler, Francis Peter | | Joseph Smith and his assigns |
| | Winder, Samuel, Fredk. | Rotterdam | Charles Linn and his assigns |
| | Coler, Margaret | Rotterdam | John Wilson and his assigns |
| | Vanderhoven, Neel Jacobse | Rotterdam | Mahlon Kirkbride and his assigns |
| Oct. 27th | McKay, John | | Charles Mease and his assigns |
| | Newton, Jonathan | | Isaac Forsyth and wife |
| | Joyce, Patrick | | Isaac Wayne and assigns |
| | Fickner, Martin | Rotterdam | Frederick Baker and his assigns |
| Oct. 28th | Balsdorf, Johan Frederick | London | Henry Debarrier and his assigns |
| | Back, Catherine | | Richard Robinson and his assigns |
| | Horeback, Peter | Rotterdam | Christian Schnyder and his assigns |
| | Horeback, Peter | | Peter Keichline and his assigns |
| | Burns, John | | Wm. Carr and his assigns |
| | Shreider, Frederick | London | Wm. Todd and his assigns |
| | Winstandly, Valentine | | David Blide and his assigns |
| | Reinhart, George | Rotterdam | Adam Deffebock and his assigns |
| Oct. 29th | McKay, Christiana | Scotland | Benjamin Poultney and his assigns |
| | Torewart, John | Rotterdam | Frederick Sager and his assigns |
| | Link, Jonathan | Rotterdam | Alexander Crawford and Alexander Carmichael and their assigns. |
| | Moroney, Thomas | | Robert Callender and his assigns |
| | Riordan, Thomas | | Robert Callender and his assigns |
| 1772. Oct. 29th | Riordan, Mary | | Robert Callender and his assigns |
| | Hogan, William | | Robert Huston and his assigns |
| Oct. 30th | Wilkin, Robert, Jr. | | John Mease |
| | Hanlon, Peter | | John Jones and his assigns |
| | Byrn, Dennis | | John Little and his assigns |

## List of Indentures.

| Residence. | Occupation. | Term. | Amount. |
|---|---|---|---|
| Near Lancaster | Servant, taught to read in Bible, write a legible hand.[3] | 8 yrs., 5 mo. | £ 15. 0. 0. |
| Philadelphia | Apprentice, taught the art of navigation; the guardian paying expense of schooling.[3] | 6 yrs. | |
| Philadelphia | Servant[3] | 7 yrs., 6 mo. | £ 23. 0. 0. |
| Philadelphia | Servant, have eighteen months' schooling.[1] | 13 yrs., 6 mo. | £ 12. 0. 0. |
| Bristol twp., Phila. co. | Servant, taught to read in Bible[3] | 7 yrs. | £ 18. 19. 0. |
| Gwinneth twp., Phila. co. | Servant (note 1, or £ 7 in cash) | 4 yrs. | £ 23. 8. 10. |
| Philadelphia | Servant[5] | 3 yrs., 6 mo. | £ 15. 0. 0. |
| Deptford twp., Gloucester co., W. Jersey. | Servant[3] | 4 yrs. | £ 20. 6. 9. |
| Woolwich twp., Gloucester co., W. Jersey. | | 4 yrs. | £ 21. 10. |
| Philadelphia | | 5 yrs. | £ 14. 0. 0. |
| Philadelphia | Servant[5] | 2 yrs. | £ 15. 0. 0. |
| Hanover twp., Lancaster co. | | 4 yrs. | £ 17. 0. 0. |
| Philadelphia | | 4 yrs. | £ 15. 0. 0. |
| Yorktown, York co. | Servant | 3 yrs. | £ 20. 0. 0. |
| Upper Providence twp., Chester co. | Servant[3] | 6 yrs., 3 mo. | £ 23. 0. 0. |
| Southwark | Servant[3] | 4 yrs. | £ 19. 13. 0. |
| Lower Makefield twp., Bucks co. | Servant[3] | 5 yrs. | £ 24. 16. 6. |
| Philadelphia | Apprentice, taught the mustard and chocolate maker's trade, read in Bible, write a legible hand and cypher through rule of three.[1] | 14 yrs., 6 mo. | |
| Philadelphia | Apprentice, taught the blacksmith's trade, have two quarters' night schooling.[3] | 7 yrs., 7 mo. 13 d. | |
| East Town, Chester co. | | 4 yrs. | £ 18. 0. 0. |
| Salisbury twp., Lancaster co. | Servant[3] | 3 yrs., 9 mo. | £ 23. 5. 0. |
| Philadelphia | Servant[3] | 2 yrs., 6 mo. | £ 14. 1. 0. |
| Philadelphia | Servant, taught to read and write, sew, knit and spin.[3] | 7 yrs., 1 mo. | £ 6. 0. 0. |
| Philadelphia | Servant (note 3, or £ 10 lawful money of Phila.). | 3 yrs. | £ 24. 0. 0. |
| Easton, Northampton co. | | 3 yrs. | £ 24. 0. 0. |
| Colerain, Lancaster co. | | 4 yrs. | £ 10. 0. 0. |
| Philadelphia | Servant (note 5, have £ 15 in lieu of freedom dues). | 3 yrs. | £ 15. 0. 0. |
| Northern Liberties | | 4 yrs. | £ 18. 0. 0. |
| Lampeter twp., Lancaster co. | Servant[3] | 3 yrs. | £ 21. 0. 0. |
| Philadelphia | Servant, taught to read and write[3]. | 11 yrs., 1 mo. | £ 3. 4. 0. |
| Lampeter twp., Lancaster co. | Servant[3] | 4 yrs., 6 mo. | £ 26. 0. 0. |
| Philadelphia | Servant, to be employed at the stone cutter's trade (note 1, to, the value of £ 10, or £ 10 in money). | 5 yrs. | £ 22. 10. 0. |
| Middletown twp., Cumberland co. | | 4 yrs. | £ 15. 0. 0. |
| Middletown twp., Cumberland co. | | 1 yr., 11 mo. 12 d. | £ 7. 10. 0. |
| Middletown twp., Cumberland co. | | 3 yrs., 11 mo., 13 d. | £ 7. 10. 0. |
| Middletown twp., Cumberland co. | | 4 yrs. | £ 17. 0. 0. |
| Philadelphia | Apprentice, taught the art and mystery of a merchant, found meat, drink, lodging only. | 3 yrs., 6 mo. | |
| Southwark | | 4 yrs. | £ 16. 0. 0. |
| Philadelphia | | 4 yrs. | £ 16. 0. 0. |

| DATE. | NAME. | FROM THE PORT OF | TO WHOM INDENTURED. |
|---|---|---|---|
| 1772. | Isaac, Wilson, and Isabella, his wife. | Ireland | Richard Malone and his assigns |
| | Croft, Catherine | | Abraham Peter and his assigns |
| | Bronwell, Casper | Rotterdam | Ludwig Kerckir and his assigns |
| | Deshler, Charles | | Benjamin Towne and his assigns |
| Oct. 31st | Maxilwin, George | Rotterdam | Daniel Beery and his assigns |
| | Pinkerd, Jonathan | London | Samuel Jeffreys and his assigns |
| | Blackham, Richard, and Wade, Christian. | | Thomas Gilpin and his assigns |
| | Logan, Bernard | | Robert Knox and his assigns |
| | Sullivan, James | Ireland | Wm. Clifton and his assigns |
| | Patton, Margaret | | James Logan and his assigns |
| | Duvenberger, Jacob | Rotterdam | Richd. Dutton and his assigns |
| | Clarke, Sarah, and Joy, Mary. | | William Montgomery and his assigns. |
| | Breadbacher, George | | William Montgomery and his assigns. |
| | Fell, Martha | | David Roberts and his assigns |
| | McNeal, Laughlin | | Benjamin Chew and his assigns |
| | Cummins, John | | Samuel Fisher and his assigns, Joseph Donaldson and his assigns, John Pringle and his assigns. |
| Nov. 2nd | Hinckle (or Kinckle), Rachel. | Rotterdam | Henry Young and his assigns |
| | Ackley, David | | Banjamin Paschall and his assigns |
| Nov. 2nd | Leacock, John, and Margaret, his wife. | | William Pollard and his assigns |
| | Lowrey, Samuel | | George Griffiths and his assigns |
| | Hease, Daniel | Ireland | Joseph Fox and his assigns |
| | Bowen, William | | William Montgomery and his assigns. |
| | Livingston, William | | William Montgomery and his assigns. |
| | Johnson, William, and Carr, Henry. | | William Montgomery and his assigns. |
| | Edwards, John | | William Montgomery and his assigns. |
| | McKeever, John | Ireland | Isaac Bushy and his assigns |
| | Neiles, William | Ireland | Thomas Bond and his assigns |
| | Mahagan, John | Ireland | George Shoemaker and his assigns |
| Nov. 3rd | Dawes, William, Jr. | | Thomas Marle and his assigns |

## List of Indentures.

| Residence. | Occupation. | Term. | Amount. |
|---|---|---|---|
| Turbot twp., Northumberland co. | Servant[1] | 2 yrs., 10 mo. each.. | £19.0.0. |
| | Servant[1] | | for their passage. |
| Philadelphia | | 6 yrs. | £6.0.0. |
| Philadelphia | Servant (note 5, have £10 in money). | 3 yrs. | £22.0.0. |
| Philadelphia | Apprentice | 3 yrs., 6 mo. | £11.0.0. |
| Coventry co., Chester co. | Servant[3] | 5 yrs. | £29.2.11. |
| Philadelphia | Servant, to be employed at the watchmaker's trade only.[3] | 3 yrs. | £15.0.0. |
| Philadelphia | | 8 yrs. | £14.0.0. |
| | | 4 yrs. | each. |
| Philadelphia | | 4 yrs. | £17.0.0. |
| Philadelphia | Servant[3] | 2 yrs., 6 mo. | £10.0.0. |
| Philadelphia | Apprentice | | |
| Upper Chichester twp., Chester co. | Servant[3] | 10 yrs. | £22.10.0. |
| Augusta co., Va. | Servant[3] | 2 yrs. each. | £5.0.0. for their use (each). |
| Augusta co., Va. | Servant[3] | 2 yrs. | £8.0.0. |
| Richland twp., Bucks co. | Apprentice, four months' day schooling, taught to sew, knit and spin, and at expiration two complete suits of apparel, one whereof to be new. | 2 yrs., 4 mo. 14 d. | |
| Philadelphia | Servant[3] | 3 yrs. | £15.0.0. |
| Philadelphia | Apprentice, to be taught the art of a mariner and navigation.[3] | 3 yrs., 9 mo. 10 d. | |
| Passyunk twp., Phila. | Servant[3] | 3 yrs., 6 mo. | £26.0.0. |
| Philadelphia | Apprentice, taught the cordwainer's trade, one quarter's night schooling in the second year, and two other quarters in the two last years.[1] | 8 yrs., 5 mo. 11 d. | |
| Philadelphia | | 4 yrs. each. | £20.0.0. £15.0.0. |
| Philadelphia | Apprentice, taught the tailor's trade, read in Bible, write a legible hand and cypher.[3] | 13 yrs. 7 mo. | |
| Philadelphia | Servant, found meat, drink, washing, lodging and working apparel. | 1 yr., 5 mo. 20 d. | £10.0.0. |
| Augusta co. | Servant[1] | 4 yrs. | £10.0.0. |
| Augusta co., Va., near Stentown | Servant, to have freedom dues, one old and one new suit. | 4 yrs. | £9.0.0. |
| Near Stenton, Augusta co., Va. | Servant[1] | 4 yrs. each. | £12.0.0. for their use. |
| Near Stenton, Augusta co., Va. | Servant[1] | 4 yrs. | £12.0.0. |
| Evesham, Burlington co., N. Jersey. | Servant[1] | 3 yrs. | £20.0.0. |
| Northampton twp., Burlington co., N. Jersey. | Servant[1] | 2 yrs. | £14.0.0. |
| Philadelphia | Servant, found meat, drink, washing and lodging, shirts, shoes and stockings. | 1 yr., 3 mo. | £10.0.0. |
| Philadelphia | Apprentice, taught the cooper's trade, allowed time to go to evening school every winter, the father paying the expense of schooling.[1] | 3 yrs., 5 mo. 12 d. | |

| Date. | Name. | From the Port of | To Whom Indentured. |
|---|---|---|---|
| 1772. | Tanner, John | | John Hallding and his assigns |
| | Burton, Thomas | Ireland | James Starr and his assigns |
| | McKay, George | London Derry | George Dunlap |
| | Crump, Margaret | | John Fisher and his assigns |
| | Wiest, Philip | Rotterdam | Samuel ——— and his assigns |
| | Moore, Jane | Ireland | Robert Clarke and his assigns |
| | McGuire, John | | John Jones and his assigns |
| | Mortimore, James | Ireland | Robert Little |
| Nov. 4th | Brotherson, John | | Evan Peters |
| | Ferguson, Margaret | | Peter January and his assigns |
| | Waggoner, Charles | Rotterdam | Jacob Viney and his assigns |
| | Becherin, Catherina | | Baltzar Spenglar and his assigns |
| | Kain, Michael | Ireland | Henry Kaudick and his assigns |
| | Fritz, Jacob | | Henry Katz and his assigns |
| | Painter, John George | Rotterdam | Jacob Deidrick and his assigns |
| | Craig, John | | Robert Johnson and his assigns |
| | Coulter, John | Ireland | James Wilson and his assigns |
| | Coulter, John | | William Ferguson and his assigns |
| | Itle, Adam | Rotterdam | William Haus and his assigns |
| | Hutton, William | Ireland | James Chamberlain and his assigns |
| Nov. 5th | Thompson, John | | William Williams and his assigns |
| | Neil, Judge | Ireland | Robert Harvey and his assigns |
| | Power, Thomas | | Anthony Moore and his assigns |
| | Mahagan, Michael | Ireland | William Crawford and his assigns |
| Nov. 6th | Davids, Hugh | | Benjamin Horner and his assigns |
| | Tracey, Eleazer | | James Alexander and his assigns |
| | Looney, Margaret | | James Read and his assigns |
| | Doyle, John | | Elizabeth Hoops and her assigns |
| | Simmons, Robert | | David Pleasentine and his assigns |
| | Zolt, William | Rotterdam | George Thomb and his assigns |
| | Kear, John George | Rotterdam | George Shepherd and his assigns |
| | Martin, Effew | | Robert Turner |
| Nov. 6th | McCoomb, Daniel | | Daniel Gorton and his assigns |

## List of Indentures.

| Residence. | Occupation. | Term. | Amount. |
|---|---|---|---|
| Philadelphia | Apprentice, taught the cordwainer's trade, found meat, drink, washing, lodging and working apparel, to have one hat, value 20/,[1] swanskin jacket, 1 pair leather breeches and one dollar. | 2 yrs. | |
| Philadelphia | Servant[3] | 3 yrs. | £ 15. 0. 0. |
| Philadelphia | Servant[5] | 2 yrs. | £ 14. 0. 0. |
| Passyunk, Phila. co. | Servant | 10 yrs. | £ 8. 0. 0. |
| Fannet twp., Cumberland co. | Servant[3] | 6 yrs. | £ 26. 9. 11 |
| Trenton twp., Hunterdon co., N. Jersey. | Servant[5] | 3 yrs. | £ 3. 0. 0. sterling. |
| Germantown, Phila. co. | | 3 yrs. | £ 9. 0. 0. |
| Fannet twp., Cumberland co. | Servant[5] | 2 yrs., 6 mo. | £ 12. 17. 6. |
| Philadelphia | Apprentice, taught pump making business, and the rough parts of the business of a house carpenter[3] | 2 yrs., 6 mo. | |
| Philadelphia | | 2 yrs., 11 mo., 20 d. | £ 11. 0. 0. |
| Philadelphia | Servant[3] | 7 yrs. | £ 30. 0. 0. |
| York Town, York co. | | 5 yrs., 6 mo. | £ 24. 0. 0. |
| Strasburg twp., Lancaster co. | Servant[1] | 3 yrs. | £ 16. 0. 0. |
| Whitemarsh twp., Phila. co. | Servant | 10 yrs., 5 mo. | |
| Waterford twp., Gloucester co., W. Jersey. | Servant[3] | 3 yrs., 8 mo. | £ 24. 0. 0. |
| New London twp., Chester co. | Servant[3] | 4 yrs., 2 mo. 17 d. | £ 16. 0. 0. |
| Leacock twp., Lancaster co. | Servant[1] | 3 yrs. | £ 15. 0. 0. |
| E. Nantmill, Chester co. | | 3 yrs. | £ 15. 0. 0. |
| Mackungee, Northampton co. | Servant[3] | 3 yrs., 6 mo. | £ 21. 15. 0. |
| Reading twp., York co. | Servant, found meat, drink, washing and lodging only. | 1 yr., 2 mo. 2 w. | £ 8. 0. 0. |
| Northern Liberties | Apprentice, taught the boat builder's trade.[6] | 4 yrs., 6 mo. | |
| Fannet twp., Cumberland co. | Servant (note 2, besides his old) | 3 yrs. | £ 18. 0. 0. |
| Mt. Bethel twp., Northampton co. | Servant | 6 yrs. | £ 16. 0. 0. |
| Letterkenny twp., Cumberland co. | Servant[3] | 4 yrs. | £ 16. 10. 0 |
| Philadelphia | Apprentice, taught the trade of a hatter or felt maker, found meat, drink, washing, lodging and hatts, time to go to evening school one quarter each winter, the father paying expense of schooling. | 7 yrs. | |
| Philadelphia | Apprentice | 11 yrs., 9 mo., 23 d. | £ 1. 10. 0. |
| Philadelphia | | 4 yrs. | £ 16. 0. 0. |
| Philadelphia | | 7 yrs. | £ 16. 0. 0. |
| Jones' Hundred, Kent co. | Servant | 4 yrs. | £ 20. 0. 0. |
| Southwark | Servant[3] | 4 yrs. | £ 24. 0. 0. |
| Philadelphia | Servant[3] | 5 yrs., 2 mo. | £ 22. 13. 0. |
| Philadelphia | Apprentice, taught housewifery, to sew and read, and when free to have two complete suits of apparel, one whereof to be new. | 2 yrs., 9 mo. | |
| Philadelphia | Apprentice, taught art and mystery of a pilot in the bay and river Delaware, read, write and cypher through rule of 3, master to give £ 3 in money towards being taught art of navigation, | 5 yrs., 5 mo. 23 d. | |

| Date. | Name. | From the Port of | To Whom Indentured. |
|---|---|---|---|
| 1772. | | | |
| Nov. 6th | Cullinan, Sarah | Ireland | Simon Fitzgerald and his assigns |
| | O'Neil, John | | John Leech |
| | O'Neil, Elizabeth | London Derry | John Leech and his assigns |
| | Davis, Samuel | | Aaron Levering |
| | Davis, Levi | | Jacob Levering |
| Nov. 7th | Yeager, John | Rotterdam | Vandel Butterswamp and his assigns |
| | Bradley, Madgey | | William Cockran and his assigns |
| | Dermoth, James | | Luke McKabe and his assigns |
| | McGuire, Philip | | James Ray and his assigns |
| Nov. 9th | Campbell, Archibald | | William Salsbury and his assigns |
| | Frame, William | | Jacob Rabsom and his assigns |
| Nov. 9th | Gaskin, Elizabeth | | Michael Kinger |
| | Lawser, Jacob Frederick | Rotterdam | Patrick Gordon and his assigns |
| | Funcks, Mary | | Joseph Hunter and his executors |
| Nov. 10th | Timmons, John | | Elizabeth Berry |
| | Dow, John | | Elijah Dow and his assigns |
| | Asson, Alkadi | | Robert Dove and wife |
| | Cummins, Timothy | | Joseph Johns |
| | Spanmen, Christiana Magdalena | Rotterdam | Jacob Kern and his assigns |
| Nov. 11th | Row, Martin | | Christopher Hansman and his heirs |

## List of Indentures.

| Residence. | Occupation. | Term. | Amount. |
|---|---|---|---|
| | in the last three years of his apprenticeship and at such times only as the navigation of Delaware shall be stopped. | | |
| Philadelphia | Servant[5] | 14 mo., 28 d. | £10.0.0. |
| Little Egg Harbour, N. J. | Servant, found all necessaries, excepting clothing, in lieu of which he is to receive 20/ during the term, and if more than that will purchase in clothing should be necessary, he is after the term to serve one month for every 20/ expended in clothes during his servitude. | 2 yrs., 7 mo. | £12.0.0. |
| | Servant, found all necessaries, excepting clothing. | yr. | £16.17.0. |
| Roxborough twp., Phila. co. | Apprentice, taught the tanner's and currier's business, have six months' night schooling, two complete suits of apparel, one whereof to be new and £15 in cash. | 5 yrs., 11 mo., 7 d. | |
| Roxborough twp., Phila. co. | Apprentice, to learn the art of a house carpenter and joiner, have three months' night schooling every winter.[3] | 3 yrs., 10 mo., 6 d. | |
| Providence twp., Phila. co. | Servant[3] | 8 yrs. | £25.0.0. |
| Philadelphia | | 4 yrs. | £7.0.0. |
| Philadelphia | | 2 yrs., 6 mo. | £12.0.0. |
| Little Britain twp., Lancaster co. | Servant[5] | 2 yrs., 3 mo. | £10.10.0. |
| Philadelphia | Apprentice, taught the block maker's trade.[3] | 1 yr., 1 mo. 12 d. | |
| Philadelphia | Apprentice, taught the tailor's trade, have six quarters' day schooling.[3] | 9 yrs., 2 mo. 26 d. | |
| Philadelphia | Apprentice | 12 yrs. | £5.0.0. |
| New Providence, Phila. co. | Servant[3] | 6 yrs. | £21.17.0. |
| Philadelphia co. | Apprentice, taught housewifery, sew, knit and spin, read in Bible, write a legible hand.[3] | 7 yrs., 5 mo. 21 d. | |
| Philadelphia | | 6 yrs. | 5/. |
| Southwark | Apprentice, taught blacksmith's trade, read write and cypher through rule of 3 (note 3, and £4 in money). | 6 yrs., 5 mo. | |
| Philadelphia | Apprentice, taught housewifery, sew, read in Bible, write a legible hand.[3] | 8 yrs., 5 mo. | |
| Philadelphia | Apprentice, taught house carpenter's trade, found meat, drink, washing, lodging and shoes, time to go and see his parent three weeks each year, in December, and time to go to night school every winter, the father paying expense of schooling, to serve his time either in Philadelphia, Northern Liberties or Southwark. | 4 yrs., 8 mo. | |
| Cumru twp., Berks co. | Servant[3] | 6 yrs. | £30.0.0. |
| Philadelphia | Apprentice, taught the tailor's trade, have one quarter's night | 2 yrs., 6 mo. | |

| Date. | Name. | From the Port of | To Whom Indentured. |
|---|---|---|---|
| 1772. | Colclough, James | | Francis Wade and his assigns |
| Nov. 11th | Moore, John | Ireland | John Hider, Jr., and his assigns |
| | Andrew, John, Jr. | | Edmond Kearney and his assigns |
| | Callaghan, James | Ireland | Benjamin Mason and his assigns |
| | Fagan, Peter | | Jacob Freebourne and his assigns |
| Nov. 12th | O'Conner, Charles | | James Whiteall and his assigns |
| | Harrison, Rebecca | | John Henry and his assigns |
| | Stephony, Francis | London | Peter Kester and his assigns |
| Nov. 12th | Wistar, Bartholomew | | Reuben Haines |
| | Sutherland, Cather | | Mary Carr and her heirs |
| | Brooker, John | | John Jones and his assigns |
| | Funks, Hannah | | William Morris and his heirs |
| | Mouder, John Jacob | | Robert Callender and his assigns |
| | McGuigan, Michael | | Richard Crayford and his assigns |
| | McGuigan, Michael | | Silas Parvin and his assigns |
| | Ellison, Martha | | Capt. William McCulloch and his assigns. |
| | Miller, George | | Isaac Webb and his assigns |
| Nov. 14th | McKay, Samuel | | John Walters and his assigns |
| | Mouder, John Jacob | | Alex. Wilcocks and his assigns |
| | Mum, Catherine | | George Leib and his assigns |
| | Otto, Ulrick | Rotterdam | Dr. Adam Kuhn, Jr., and his assigns. |
| | Otto, Ulrick | | Adam Simon Kuhn and his assigns |
| Nov. 16th | Hughes, Noah | | Joseph Rudulph and his assigns |
| | Aitkin, Thomas | | John Appowen and his assigns |
| | Wicks, Samuel | | Joseph Jennings and his assigns |
| | David, Charles | | Bryan O'Hara and his assigns |
| | Cross, Francis | | Thomas Yorke and his assigns |
| | Blanchard, William | | Benjamin Spring and his assigns |
| | Seymour, Henry | | Thomas Fisher and his assigns |
| | Marks, Thomas, and Eve, his wife. | Rotterdam | Jacob Beergz and his assigns |

| RESIDENCE. | OCCUPATION. | TERM. | AMOUNT. |
|---|---|---|---|
| | schooling at an English school the last winter, found meat, drink, washing and lodging and at expiration have a new coat. | | |
| Philadelphia | | 4 yrs. | £ 15. 0. 0. |
| Gloucester twp | Servant[3] | 3 yrs., 9 mo. 17 d. | £ 16. 0. 0. |
| Philadelphia | Servant | 7 yrs. | £ 13. 10. 0. |
| Northern Liberties, Phila. co | Servant[3] | 3 yrs. | £ 14. 0. 0. |
| Northern Liberties, Phila. co | | 7 yrs., 1 mo. | £ 15. 0. 0. |
| Philadelphia | Servant | 2 yrs., 4 mo. | £ 9. 10. 0. |
| Philadelphia | Servant | 3 yrs. | £ 9. 0. 0. |
| Heidleberg twp., Berks co | Servant, and if faithful the said master or assigns shall give him three months' of the above term.[3] | 4 yrs. | £ 17. 10. 0 |
| Philadelphia | Apprentice, taught the maltster and brewer's business and be supplied with meat, drink and lodging. | 2 yrs., 9 mo. 13 d. | |
| Southwark | Apprentice, housewifery, to sew and read in Bible.[3] | 11 yrs. | |
| Germantown, Phila. co | Apprentice, the said John Brooker was landed in Maryland from Europe and there bound (note 5, only). | 4 yrs. | |
| Philadelphia | Apprentice, taught housewifery, sew, read in Bible, write a legible hand.[3] | 5 yrs., 14 d. | |
| Middle Town twp., Cumberland co. | Servant | 6 yrs., 6 mo. | £ 30. 0. 0. |
| Hopewell twp., Cumberland co., W. Jersey. | Servant (note 5, only) | 2 yrs. | £ 5. 0. 0. |
| Hopewell twp., Cumberland co., W. Jersey. | | 2 yrs. | £ 5. 0. 0. |
| Philadelphia | Servant | 4 yrs. | £ 15. 0. 0. |
| E. Whiteland twp., Chester co | Servant | 7 yrs. | £ 15. 0. 0. |
| Kingsessing twp., Phila. co | Apprentice, taught farmer's business, have six quarters' schooling (note 3, and £ 8 in money). | 8 yrs., 11 mo., 8 d. | |
| Philadelphia | | 6 yrs., 6 mo. | £ 30. 0. 0. |
| Philadelphia | Servant[3] | 2 yrs., 6 mo. | £ 14. 0. 0. |
| Philadelphia | Servant, to have privilege of one month from this date, if in that time his friends can pay the consideration money and expenses the indenture to be void[5]. | 2 yrs., 6 mo. | £ 21. 0. 0. |
| Lancaster | Servant[6] | 2 yrs., 6 mo. | £ 21. 0. 0. |
| Moyamensing | Servant or apprentice, have six months' schooling three months whereof to be after he arrives at the age of sixteen years.[3] | 18 yrs., 2 mo. | £ 10. 0. 0. |
| Philadelphia | Apprentice | 7 yrs. | £ 15. 0. 0. |
| Philadelphia | | 3 yrs. | £ 10. 0. 0. |
| Philadelphia | Apprentice, taught the trade of a peruke maker, have four quarters' evening schooling.[3] | 7 yrs., 6 mo. | |
| Philadelphia | | 7 yrs. | £ 22. 10. 0. |
| Northern Liberties | | 5 yrs. | £ 22. 10. 0. |
| Philadelphia | | 5 yrs. | £ 25. 0. 0. |
| Richland twp., Bucks co | Servant[1] | 7 yrs. each. | £ 49. 18. 0. |

| Date. | Name. | From the Port of | To Whom Indentured. |
|---|---|---|---|
| 1772.<br>Nov. 16th... | Powell, William | | William Foster |
| | Miller, Margaret | | David Howell and his assigns |
| Nov. 17th... | Harford, Charles | | Joseph Engle and his assigns |
| | Seeger, Wm. Frederick | | Samuel Miles and his assigns |
| | James, John | | William Harris and his assigns |
| Nov. 18th... | Ulmer, Johan Frederick | Rotterdam.. | William Hembill and his assigns |
| | Boies, William | | Robert Montgomery and his assigns.. |
| | Conn, John | | John Hall Cooper and his heirs |
| | Mills, Joseph | Ireland.... | Philip McGuire and his assigns |
| | McNeiley, Alexander | | Peter Henderson and his assigns |
| | Dwire, Cornelius | Ireland.... | Archibald McIllroy and his assigns.. |
| | Brian, Helian | | Jacob Riderman |
| Nov. 19th... | Osborne, Robert | | Ellis Lewis and his assigns |
| | Sohns, Johan Jacob | Rotterdam.. | Charles Chamberlain and his assigns. |
| | Crawford, Jacob | | Jonathan Gortelow his heirs and assigns. |
| | Mibrin, Ann Mary | | Andrew Kirchner and his assigns |
| Nov. 20th... | Verner, Philip | | Henry Keppelegim[2] and his assigns |
| | Kemberlin, Juliana | Rotterdam.. | Jacob Barge and his assigns |
| Nov. 21st... | Shouk, Samuel, and Johan, Weinkeimer Sheller. | Rotterdam.. | William Eckhart and his assigns |
| | Regan, Lott | Ireland.... | Samuel Caldwell and his assigns |
| | Kelly, Thomas | | John Webb |
| Nov. 23rd... | Hays, John | | William Tolbert and his assigns |
| | Kenny, John | | Lewis Percy and his assigns |
| | Swatz, Mary | | Frederick Mans and his assigns |
| Nov. 24th... | Carens, John | Glasgow... | William Moore and his assigns |
| | Cramer, John | | William Dishong and his assigns |
| | Tresur, Richard | | Abraham Wayne and his assigns |
| | Mohler, Hans Jacob | Rotterdam... | Robert Ritchie and his assigns |
| Nov. 25th... | Gladwell, Peter | | Thomas Dean |
| | Marlins, Samuel | Ireland.... | James Wilson and his assigns |

## List of Indentures.

| Residence. | Occupation. | Term. | Amount. |
|---|---|---|---|
| Philadelphia | Servant, have two quarters' winter night schooling.[a] | 2 yrs., 10 mo., 9 d. | |
| Tredyffrin twp., Chester co. | | 4 yrs., 6 mo. | £ 14. 0. 0. |
| Evesham twp., Burlingham co., W. Jersey. | | 4 yrs. | £ 25. 0. 0. |
| Philadelphia | Servant, employed in attending his master's stores.[3] | 3 yrs., 4 mo. | £ 23. 10. 0. |
| W. Nottingham, Chester co. | | 6 yrs. | £ 22. 10. 0. |
| Philadelphia | Servant, employed at tailor's trade[3] | 4 yrs. | £ 30. 0. 0. |
| New London twp., Chester co. | Servant (note 3, and 30 shillings in money). | 2 yrs. | £ 30. 0. 0. |
| Concord twp., Chester co. | Apprentice, taught the cooper's trade, have two years' schooling[3] | 11 yrs., 8 mo., 27 d. | |
| Fannet twp., Cumberland co. | Servant[3] | 3 yrs., 11 mo., 13 d. | £ 13. 10. 0. |
| Philadelphia | Apprentice, taught art, trade and mystery of a turner, spinning wheel and windsor chair maker, read in Bible, write a legible hand and cypher through rule of 3.[3] | 6 yrs., 6 mo. 14 d. | |
| Philadelphia | Servant[5] | 2 yrs. | £ 15. 0. 0. |
| Northern Liberties, Phila. co. | | 4 yrs. | £ 7. 10. 0. |
| Philadelphia | Servant, taught the miller's business.[3] | 5 yrs. | £ 14. 0. 0. |
| Philadelphia | Servant[3] | 4 yrs. | £ 19. 2. 9. |
| Philadelphia | Apprentice, taught the joiner's trade, read in Bible, write a legible hand, cypher through rule of 3.[3] | 11 yrs., 11 mo., 11 d. | |
| Northern Liberties | Servant | 6 yrs. | £ 0. 5. 0. |
| Philadelphia | | 8 yrs. | £ 20. 0. 0. |
| Philadelphia | Servant (note 1, or £ 8 in money). | 4 yrs. | £ 22. 12. 6. |
| Philadelphia | Servant[3] | 4 yrs., 6 mo. each | £ 28. 0. 0. each. |
| Philadelphia | Servant[5] | 3 yrs. | £ 15. 0. 0. |
| Southwark | Servant[6] | 1 yr. | £ 3. 0. 0. |
| Northern Liberties | Apprentice, taught the tailor's trade, found meat, drink, washing and lodging and one suit of clothes and at expiration £ 20 in money. | 2 yrs., 3 mo. | |
| Augusta co., Va. | Servant | 4 yrs. | £ 14. 0. 0. |
| Philadelphia | Apprentice, taught housewifery and to sew, read in Bible, write legible hand.[3] | 9 yrs., 10 mo., 14 d. | |
| Southwark | Servant, if said servant pay or cause to be paid to the said Moore, his executors, administrators or assigns the above sum within three months next ensuing then the indenture to be void.[6] | 1 yr., 6 mo. | £ 8. 18. 5. |
| Philadelphia | Apprentice, taught the trade of a hosier or stocking weaver (note 3, and £ 10 in money). | 4 yrs., 6 mo. | |
| Philadelphia | | 6 yrs. | £ 20. 0. 0. |
| Philadelphia | Servant[3] | 8 yrs. | £ 27. 0. 0. |
| Bright Elm Stone, Sussex co., Eng. | Apprentice, taught the art of a mariner (note 5, have one good Hadley's quadrant and books for keeping a journal). | 3 yrs. | |
| Leacock twp., Lancaster co. | Servant[3] | 5 yrs., 11 mo., 5 d. | £ 12. 0. 0. |

| DATE. | NAME. | FROM THE PORT OF | TO WHOM INDENTURED. |
|---|---|---|---|
| | Marlins, John, Jr. | Ireland | James Wilson and his assigns |
| | Marlins, Margaret | Ireland | James Wilson and his assigns |
| | Dougherty, James | Ireland | James Wilson and his assigns |
| | Gilbert, Reynear | | Francis Nelson and his assigns |
| Nov. 26th | Gordon, Sarah | | Richard Briton and his assigns |
| | Bombarger, Michael | | Thomas Meyer and his assigns |
| | Robinson, William | | John Willis and his assigns |
| | Fair, Joseph | | Richard Palmer and his heirs |
| | Tanner, John | | William Griffiths and his assigns |
| Nov. 27th | Mullin, Neil | | James Hunter and his assigns |
| | Judah, Frederick | Rotterdam | Elizabeth Fuller and her assigns |
| Nov. 27th | Will, Sarah | | Matthias Sandham and his assigns |
| | Stackhouse, David | | Joseph Henszey and his assigns |
| | Nicholson, Makhum | Ireland | John Hoover and his assigns |
| Nov. 28th | Dehaven, Edward | | Jacob Bender and his assigns |
| | Ribble, Christopher, and Sibella Magdalen, his wife. | Rotterdam | George Syphers and his assigns |
| | Piers, William | | Levi Hollingsworth and his assigns |
| | Piers, William | | Samuel Ewing |
| Nov. 30th | Holsward, Andrew | Rotterdam | John Wister and his assigns |
| | Mullin, William | Ireland | John Davidson and his assigns |
| | Mullin, William | | Peter Shields and his assigns |

[1] To be found all necessaries and at the expiration have freedom dues.
[2] To be found all necessaries and at the expiration have one new suit of apparel.
[3] To be found all necessaries and at the expiration have two complete suits of apparel, one whereof to be new.

## List of Indentures.

| Residence. | Occupation. | Term. | Amount. |
|---|---|---|---|
| Leacock twp., Lancaster co. | Servant[3] | 7 yrs., 11 mo., 5 d. | £12.0.0. |
| Leacock twp., Lancaster co. | Servant[3] | 7 yrs., 11 mo., 5 d. | £12.0.0. |
| Leacock twp., Lancaster co. | Servant[3] | 11 yrs., 11 mo., 5 d. | £12.0.0. |
| Philadelphia | Apprentice, taught tailor's trade, have one quarter's day schooling, liberty to go see his friends two weeks in every year.[3] | 5 yrs., 7 mo. 29 d. | |
| Upper Freehold twp., Monmouth co., E. Jersey. | | 4 yrs. | £8.0.0. |
| Philadelphia | Apprentice taught the potter's trade, have two quarters' schooling, not to be assigned to any person without his or his mother's consent (note 1, to value of £10 or £10 in money) | 6 yrs. | |
| Philadelphia | Apprentice, taught the joiner's trade, have six quarters' night schooling, four of which to be at the master's expense and two at the expense of his mother.[3] | 7 yrs., 6 mo. | |
| Philadelphia | Apprentice, taught the joiner and chair maker's trade, have four winters' night schooling.[3] | 8 yrs., 6 mo. 4 d. | |
| Aston twp., Chester co. | Servant, to be employed at the farmer's business only (note 2, besides his old). | 3 yrs. | £12.0.0. |
| Newtown twp., Chester co. | | 4 yrs. | £12.0.0. |
| Southwark | Servant, taught the baker's business, read in Bible, write a legible hand.[6] | 9 yrs. | £20.0.0. |
| Philadelphia | Apprentice, taught housewifery, sew, knit and spin, have six months' day schooling.[3] | 8 yrs. | |
| Philadelphia | Apprentice, taught the turner and windsor chair maker's business, read in Bible, write a legible hand, cypher through rule of 3. In case of master's death he shall have a choice of one out of three persons whom he will serve.[3] | 11 yrs., 5 mo. | |
| Philadelphia | Servant, taught the baker's business, have six months' night schooling.[3] | 3 yrs., 9 mo. | £16.0.0. |
| Philadelphia | Apprentice, taught comb maker's business, have six years' schooling, allowed one week every harvest to go and see his father (note 2, besides his old). | 11 yrs. | |
| Evesham twp., Burlington co., W. Jersey. | Servant[3] | 4 yrs. each. | £48.14.11 |
| Philadelphia | Servant[3] | 4 yrs. | £20.0.0. |
| Cecil co., Md. | Servant[3] | | £20.0.0. |
| Philadelphia | Servant, have three months' evening schooling.[3] | 4 yrs., 11 mo., 18 d. | £22.18.0. |
| Philadelphia | Servant[3] | 5 yrs. | £14.0.0. |
| W. Nantmill, Chester co. | | 5 yrs. | £14.0.0. |

[4] To be found all necessaries and at the expiration have two complete suits of apparel, one whereof to be new, and 40s. in money.

[5] At expiration have two complete suits of apparel, one whereof to be new.

| Date. | Name. | From the Port of | To Whom Indentured. |
|---|---|---|---|
| 1772. Nov. 28th | Figely, Gotlip | | Henry Funk |
| | Leech, Edward | | Peter Sutter and his assigns |
| Nov. 30th | Duncan, Thomas | Ireland | Joseph Graisbury and his assigns |
| | Bryan, Elizabeth | | Henry Hale Graham and his assigns. |
| | Lynch, Thomas | | John Wall and his assigns |
| | Bryan, Eleanor | | John Wall and his assigns |
| | Lynch, Eleanor | | Andrew Carson and his assigns |
| | White, Jane | | John Harken and his assigns |
| | Brannon, Charles | | Philip Marot and his assigns |
| | Mohler, Maria | Rotterdam | James Allinby and his assigns |
| Dec. 1st | Baron, Silvester | | David Cummins and his assigns |
| | Sulivan, Roger | | Alexander Mahan and his assigns |
| | Roche, Catherine | | Robert Hardie and his assigns |
| | Smith, Robert | | Capt. Wm. Adamson and his assigns. |
| | Harding, Rebecca | | Charles Alexander and his assigns |
| | Fullerton, John | | Charles Pollock and his assigns |
| | Bush, Samuel | | Adam Clampffer and his assigns |
| Dec. 2nd | Blayer, Malkum | | Robert Cooper and his assigns |
| | Condect, Robert | | Joseph Fox and his assigns |
| | Donahow, Margaret | | Jonathan Hunter and his assigns |
| | Porter, Charles | Ireland | William Moody and his assigns |
| | Thomson, John | | William Gattes and his assigns |
| Dec. 3rd | Panslerin, Anna Maria | | Samuel Noble and his assigns |
| | Sugg, Dorothea | | Hannah Dunbar and her assigns |
| | Hill, George | | Henry Test and his assigns |
| Dec. 3rd | Beck, Paul, Jr. | | Wm. Sheaff and his assigns |
| | Forbenter, Catherine Elizabeth. | Rotterdam | Richard Wistar and his assigns |

## List of Indentures.

| Residence. | Occupation. | Term. | Amount. |
|---|---|---|---|
| Philadelphia | Servant (note 3, or £7 in cash) | 4 yrs., 3 mo. | £25.19.9. |
| Philadelphia | Apprentice, taught the hat maker's trade, found meat, drink, washing and lodging, shoes and hats, and at expiration have one complete new suit of apparel, allowed time to go to night school three quarters, the father paying the expense of schooling. | 7 yrs. | |
| Philadelphia | Apprentice, taught the tailor's trade.[3] | 4 yrs. | £13.0.0. |
| Chester | Servant | 4 yrs. | £15.0.0. |
| Philadelphia | Servant | 7 yrs. | £15.10.0. |
| Philadelphia | | 4 yrs. | £15.10.0. |
| Philadelphia | Servant | 4 yrs. | £13.0.0. |
| Philadelphia | Servant | 3 yrs., 3 mo. | £12.0.0. |
| Philadelphia | | 5 yrs. | £20.0.0. |
| Philadelphia | Servant, taught to read in Bible, write a legible hand.[3] | 7 yrs. | £15.0.0. |
| Philadelphia | | 4 yrs. | £16.0.0. |
| Lurgan twp., Cumberland co. | | 4 yrs. | £18.0.0. |
| Philadelphia | | 7 yrs. | £11.0.0. |
| Philadelphia | Apprentice, taught to read and write perfectly and cypher, also the art and mystery of a mariner and navigation (note 2, besides his old). | 10 yrs., 1 mo., 7 d. | |
| Southwark | Apprentice, taught housewifery and sew, have one year's schooling.[3] | 7 yrs., 3 mo. | |
| Millford twp., Cumberland co. | | 3 yrs. | £18.0.0. |
| Philadelphia | Apprentice, taught the hatter's trade, have liberty to go to night school at the father's expense and observe the Jewish Sabbath and holidays. | 7 yrs. | £20.0.0. |
| Philadelphia | | 2 yrs. | £9.0.0. |
| Philadelphia | Apprentice, taught trade of a blacksmith and farrier, have six months' evening schooling in the two last years of his apprenticeship.[3] | 7 yrs., 7 mo. 9 d. | |
| Edgmont twp., Chester co. | Servant | 4 yrs. | £16.0.0. |
| King George's Hundred, N. Castle co. | Servant[3] | 4 yrs. | £17.0.0. |
| Christiana Hundred, N. Castle co. | Apprentice, taught the cooper's trade, read in Bible, write a legible hand and cypher through rule of 3.[3] | 14 yrs., 7 mo. | |
| Northern Liberties | Servant | 5 yrs., 3 mo. | £18.0.0 |
| Philadelphia | Servant | 2 yrs., 3 mo. 21 d. | £1.2.3. |
| Philadelphia | Apprentice, taught the trade of hat maker, have liberty to go to evening school every winter, his mother and friends paying the expense (note 2, the coat and breeches and jacket to be of broadcloth). | 7 yrs. | |
| Philadelphia | Apprentice, taught the grocer's business, have one year schooling (note 2, besides his old). | 7 yrs., 10 mo. | |
| Philadelphia | Servant[3] | 4 yrs. | £23.17.10. |

| Date. | Name. | From the Port of | To Whom Indentured. |
|---|---|---|---|
| 1772. | Bettering, Juliana | Rotterdam | Catherine Wistar and her assigns |
| Dec. 3rd | Ritter, Conrad | Rotterdam | Sebastian Keely and his assigns |
| | Betts, John Yost | Rotterdam | Joseph Hillborn and his assigns |
| | Betts, John Yost | | Joseph Watson and his assigns |
| | Schuberstein, John | Rotterdam | Christian Snyder and his assigns |
| | Schuberstein, John | | John Hartman and his assigns |
| | Pieferin, Anna Eva | Rotterdam | Reuben Haines and his assigns |
| | Pieferin, Anna Eva | | Samuel Morris, Jr., and his assigns |
| | Louber, John Adam | Rotterdam | William Lawrence and his assigns |
| | Smith, Christian | Rotterdam | William Lawrence and his assigns |
| | Baur, Johan Philip | Rotterdam | Valentine Brobst and his assigns |
| | Hickman, Anna Catherine | Rotterdam | James Whitall and his assigns |
| | Hendricks, Sophia Elizabeth | Rotterdam | Abraham Mason and his assigns |
| | Roche, Catherine | Ireland | Francis Wade and his assigns |
| | Roche, Catherine | | Colo. Daniel Claws and his assigns |
| | Langenbach, Johan Yoest | Rotterdam | Killen White and his assigns |
| | Meyer, Charles | Rotterdam | Peter Care and his assigns |
| | Böttner, Johan Matthias | Rotterdam | James Boon and his assigns |
| | Riese, Samuel Peter | Rotterdam | George Mercker and his assigns |
| | Deitrick, Henry | Rotterdam | Edward Ripley and his assigns |
| | Dwire, Margaret; Kenny, Mary; Sweny, Catherine; Page, Elizabeth; Bell, Margeret. | | James Ray and his assigns |
| | Sullivan, Dennis | | James Ray and his assigns |
| | Harris, John; Reagon, James. | | James Ray and his assigns |
| | Dermot, Thomas; Collins, Timothy; Galley, Daniel; How, William; Sulivan, Philip. | | James Ray and his assigns |
| Dec. 4th | Neil, Robert | Ireland | Benjamin Sharpeless and his assigns |
| Dec. 4th | Bohn, Elizabeth | Rotterdam | Robert Kennedy and his assigns |
| | Bohn, Elizabeth | | Abraham Wayne and his assigns |
| | Donovan, Mary; Croneen, Margaret; Bryan, Mary; Kelly, Ann. | | James Wilson and his assigns |
| | Sulivan, Mary | | James Wilson and his assigns |
| | Keenan, Catherine | | James Wilson and his assigns |
| | Rogers, Eleanor | | Joseph Carson and his assigns |
| | Friday, Mary | | Edward Crawford and his assigns |
| | Ready, Thomas; Coody, William; Buchill, William. | | James Wilson and his assigns |
| | Corbert, William; Kane, Michael; Sulivan, Florence; Wright, James. | | James Wilson and his assigns |
| | Murriarty, Dennis | | Joseph Pemberton and his assigns |
| | Snyder, Philip Peter | Rotterdam | George Shade and his assigns |
| | Rose, John | Ireland | John Fatum and his assigns |
| | Linch, Eleanor | | Andrew Carson and his assigns |
| | Ohelvon, Lawrence | Rotterdam | George Thomson and his assigns |
| | Ohelvon, Lawrence | | John Philip Dehaus and his assigns |

| Residence. | Occupation. | Term. | Amount. |
|---|---|---|---|
| Philadelphia | Servant³ | 4 yrs. | £ 23. 19. 1. |
| Vincent twp., Chester co. | Servant, (note 1, to the value of £ 10). | 3 yrs. | £ 17. 3. 0. |
| Philadelphia | Servant³ | 3 yrs., 9 mo. | £ 18. 7. 0 |
| Buckingham twp., Bucks co. | | 3 yrs., 9 mo. | £ 18. 7. 0 |
| Philadelphia | Servant (note 1, or £ 10 in money in lieu thereof). | 3 yrs. | £ 18. 12. 0. |
| Lowhill twp., Northampton co. | | 3 yrs. | £ 18. 12. 0. |
| Philadelphia | Servant³ | 3 yrs., 6 mo. | £ 18. 5. 0. |
| Philadelphia | | 3 yrs., 6 mo. | £ 18. 5. 0. |
| Deptford twp., Gloucester co., W. Jersey | Servant³ | 6 yrs. | £ 21. 5. 0. |
| Deptford twp., Gloucester co., W. Jersey | Servant³ | 3 yrs., 6 mo. | £ 17. 2. 0. |
| Albany twp., Berks co. | Servant³ | 3 yrs., 11 mo. | £ 27. 14. 6. |
| Deptford twp., Gloucester co., W. Jersey | Servant³ | 3 yrs., 6 mo. | £ 18. 18. 6. |
| Philadelphia | Servant³ | 4 yrs., 6 mo. | £ 21. 14. 0. |
| Philadelphia | Servant³ | 3 yrs. | £ 17. 10. 0. |
| Albany co., N. Y. province | | 3 yrs. | £ 7. 10. 0. |
| Germantown, Phila. co. | Servant¹ | 4 yrs. | £ 27. 0. 0. |
| Bristol twp., Phila. co. | Servant (note 1, or £ 10 in money, in lieu thereof). | 3 yrs., 9 mo. | £ 13. 8. 5. |
| Exeter twp., Berks co. | Servant (note 1, and 10 shillings in money). | 4 yrs., 6 mo. | £ 28. 7. 0. |
| Northern Liberties | Servant³ | 3 yrs., 3 mo. | £ 19. 5. 0. |
| Manor twp., Lancaster co. | Servant (note 2, besides his old, worth £ 5, or £ 5 lawful money of Pa.). | 2 yrs. | £ 10. 0. 0. |
| Little Britain twp., Lancaster co. | Servant | 4 yrs. each. | £ 14. 0. 0. each. |
| Little Britain twp., Lancaster co. | Servant | 3 yrs. | £ 15. 0. 0. |
| Little Britain twp., Lancaster co. | Servant | 5 yrs. each. | £ 15. 0. 0. each. |
| Little Britain twp., Lancaster co. | Servant | 4 yrs. each. | £ 15. 0. 0. each. |
| Philadelphia | Servant, taught the tanner and currier's trade.³ | 5 yrs. | £ 7. 10. 0. |
| Philadelphia | Servant³ | 3 yrs., 9 mo. | £ 21. 9. 6. |
| Philadelphia | | 3 yrs., 9 mo. | £ 21. 9. 6. |
| Leacock twp., Lancaster co. | | 4 yrs. each. | £ 14. 0. 0. each. |
| Leacock twp., Lancaster co. | | 4 yrs. | £ 14. 14. 0. |
| Leacock twp., Lancaster co. | | 4 yrs. | £ 15. 0. 0. |
| Philadelphia | | 4 yrs. | £ 15. 10. 0. |
| Philadelphia | | 4 yrs. | £ 13. 0. 0. |
| Leacock twp., Lancaster co. | | 5 yrs. each. | £ 15. 0. 0. |
| Leacock twp., Lancaster co. | | 4 yrs. each. | £ 15. 0. 0. |
| Philadelphia | | 6 yrs. | £ 17. 0. 0. |
| Bristol twp., Phila. co. | Servant³ | 5 yrs. | £ 18. 14. 0. |
| Deptford twp., Gloucester co., W. Jersey | Servant³ | 4 yrs. | £ 17. 10. 0. |
| Philadelphia | | 4 yrs. | £ 13. 0. 0. |
| Philadelphia | Servant³ | 6 yrs. | £ 30. 0. 0. |
| Lebanon twp., Lancaster co. | | 6 yrs. | £ 30. 0. 0. |

| Date. | Name. | From the Port of | To Whom Indentured. |
|---|---|---|---|
| 1772.<br>Dec. 4th | Haas, Gerlack | Rotterdam | George Lohrman and his assigns |
| | Schull, Simon | Rotterdam | Joseph Shippen and his assigns |
| | Schull, Simon | | Edward Shippen, Jr., and his assigns. |
| | Freichefer, John Yost | Rotterdam | Joseph Shippen and his assigns |
| | Freichefer, John Yost | | James Burd and his assigns |
| | Freichefer, Christian | Rotterdam | Joseph Shippen and his assigns |
| | Freichefer, Christian | | Edward Shippen and his assigns |
| | Meyerin, Antonetto | Rotterdam | John Soltar and his assigns |
| | Mulcahee, Julian | | Anthony Fortune and his assigns |
| | Hyer, Anna Maria | Rotterdam | John Neily and his assigns |
| | Haus, John Martin | Rotterdam | James Whitall and his assigns |
| | Freichefer, John | Rotterdam | John Vanreed and his assigns |
| | Freichefer, John | | Henry Vanreed and his assigns |
| | Lear, Henry | Rotterdam | Philip Moses and his assigns |
| | Roland, Henry | Rotterdam | Henry Funk and his assigns |
| | Roland, Henry | | Christel Snyder and his assigns |
| Dec. 4th | Raspin, Maudlena | Rotterdam | Henry Funk and his assigns |
| | Raspin, Maudlena | | Benedict Esselmannear and his assigns. |
| | Albright, Jacob | Rotterdam | George Grouscoup and his assigns |
| | Musick, Peter | Rotterdam | Reinhard Kamer and his assigns |
| | Lattimore, John | London | Robert Torrens and his assigns |
| | Poul, Matthias | Rotterdam | Christopher Sower and his assigns |
| | Schleichter, Gotleib | Rotterdam | George Ward and his assigns |
| | Lehman, William | Rotterdam | James Whitall, Jr., and his assigns |
| | Ohelvon, Charles | Rotterdam | George Honey, Jr., and his assigns |
| | Ohelvon, Charles | | Henry Kintzer and his assigns |
| | Snyderin, Juliana Margaret | Rotterdam | Nicholas Schreiner and his assigns |
| | Appawlinson, Dorothea | Rotterdam | Samuel Massey and his assigns |
| | Rompin, Maria Elizabeth | Rotterdam | Charles Massey and his assigns |
| | Gheiseler, Charles | Rotterdam | Joseph Wharton, Jr., and his assigns |
| | Keller, Lawrence | Rotterdam | Peter Reeve and his assigns |
| Dec. 5th | George, Robert | | James Dickenson and his assigns |
| | Breadhaur, Johan Casper | | Michael Swoope and his assigns |
| | Hehlman, Sophia | | John Synder and his assigns |
| | Dickey, John | | James Cooper, his heirs and assigns |
| | Schoulgas, Catherine | Rotterdam | Amos Wickersham and his assigns |
| | Fink, John Adam | Rotterdam | Philip Flick and his assigns |
| | Rock, John | | Amos Strettell and his assigns |
| | Kemp, Johannes | Rotterdam | Luke Morris and his assigns |
| | Prugelin, Elizabeth | Rotterdam | Christopher Sower, Jr., and his assigns |
| | Scoup, Henry | | Aquilla Jones and his assigns |
| Dec. 5th | Baker, George Wm | Rotterdam | Benjamin Shoemaker and his assigns |

## List of Indentures.

| Residence. | Occupation. | Term. | Amount. |
|---|---|---|---|
| Philadelphia | Servant[3] | 5 yrs. | £25.0.0. |
| Philadelphia | Servant[1] | 6 yrs., 6 mo. | £19.15.0. |
| Philadelphia | | 6 yrs., 6 mo. | £19.15.0. |
| Philadelphia | Servant[3] | 3 yrs., 6 mo. | £21.0.0. |
| Paxton twp., Lancaster co. | | 3 yrs., 6 mo. | £21.0.0. |
| Philadelphia | Servant[3] | 6 yrs., 6 mo. | £20.14.10. |
| Lancaster, Lancaster co. | | 6 yrs., 6 mo. | £20.14.10. |
| Philadelphia | Servant[1] | 5 yrs. | £27.0.0. |
| Philadelphia | | 4 yrs. | £16.0.0. |
| Conestoga twp., Lancaster co. | Servant (note 1, or £5 in cash) | 6 yrs. | £25.0.0. |
| Deptford twp., Gloucester co., W. Jersey. | Servant[3] | 7 yrs. | £20.0.0. |
| Philadelphia | Servant (note 3, and £5 in money) | 3 yrs., 3 mo. | £20.14.6. |
| Amity twp., Berks co. | | 3 yrs., 3 mo. | £20.14.6. |
| Philadelphia | Servant[3] | 4 yrs. | £27.17.6. |
| Philadelphia | Servant[3] | 3 yrs., 2 mo. | £20.9.0. |
| Derby twp., Lancaster co. | | 3 yrs., 2 mo. | £20.9.0. |
| Philadelphia | Servant[3] | 4 yrs., 6 mo. | £20.4.0. |
| Lancaster, Lancaster co. | | 4 yrs., 6 mo. | £20.4.0. |
| Kensington, Phila. co. | Servant (note 1, or £10) | 3 yrs. | £19.11.0. |
| Philadelphia | Servant[3] | 5 yrs. | £20.16.10. |
| Philadelphia | Servant, to be employed at trade of a house carpenter and joiner[1] | 4 yrs. | £8.10.0. |
| Germantown, Phila. co. | Servant[3] | 3 yrs. | £22.8.4. |
| Deptford twp., Gloucester co. | Servant[3] | 5 yrs. | £28.7.0. |
| Deptford twp., Gloucester co., W. Jersey. | Servant[3] | 3 yrs. | £16.11.0. |
| Philadelphia | Servant[3] | 7 yrs. | £31.0.0. |
| Earl twp., Lancaster co. | | 7 yrs. | £31.0.0. |
| Northern Liberties | Servant[3] | 4 yrs., 6 mo. | £17.1.8. |
| Philadelphia | Servant[1] | 6 yrs. | £30.0.0. |
| Philadelphia | Servant[3] | 5 yrs. | £25.0.0. |
| Philadelphia | Servant[3] | 3 yrs., 6 mo. | £20.5.0. |
| Philadelphia | Servant[3] | 6 yrs. | £24.15.0. |
| Philadelphia | Apprentice, taught the cordwainer's trade, have six months' day, and three months' night schooling, and have three days every harvest for himself.[3] | 4 yrs., 6 mo. | |
| York Town, York co. | Servant | 6 yrs., 7 mo. | £20.8.0. |
| Northern Liberties | | 3 yrs., 6 mo. | £18.0.0. |
| Philadelphia | Apprentice, taught the business of felt making, have three quarters' night schooling, to serve his time in this province or N. Jersey if required.[5] | 7 yrs., 6 mo. | |
| Philadelphia | Servant[3] | 7 yrs. | £27.0.0. |
| Philadelphia | Servant (note 3, or £8 in money) | 4 yrs. | £28.8.0. |
| Philadelphia | Servant | 4 yrs. | £20.0.0. |
| Southwark | Servant, at expiration have legal freedom dues. | 9 yrs., 1 mo. | £20.0.0. |
| Germantown, Phila. co. | Servant[3] | 3 yrs., 6 mo. | £19.12.6. |
| New Town twp., Gloucester co., W. Jersey. | Servant | 6 yrs., 6 mo. and also 1 yr., 6 mo., adjudged by an order of Court of Quarter Sessions. | £20.0.0. |
| Philadelphia | Servant (note 1, and 2 dollars) | 4 yrs. | £30.0.0. |

| Date. | Name. | From the Port of | To Whom Indentured. |
|---|---|---|---|
| 1772. Dec. 5th..... | Benner, Johannes | Rotterdam.. | Henry Tancey and his assigns....... |
| | Lattes, Mariah | Rotterdam.. | John Test and his assigns.......... |
| | Cooper, John Herlack | Rotterdam.. | Peter Purkus and his assigns........ |
| | Remp, Jacob Henry | Rotterdam.. | Charles Prion and his assigns....... |
| | Ellerin, Barbara | Rotterdam.. | Joseph Lunen and his assigns....... |
| | Kallwasser, Johan Philip | Rotterdam.. | Patrick Gordon and his assigns..... |
| | De Pool, Carolina | Rotterdam.. | Joseph Kaighan and his assigns..... |
| | Longebin, John Zacherias | Rotterdam.. | Jacob Hinkle and his assigns....... |
| | Trautwine, Nicholas | Rotterdam.. | Charles Syng and his assigns....... |
| | Trautwine, Nicholas | | George Hinkle and his assigns...... |
| | Rouy, Weynance | Rotterdam.. | John Blackledge and his assigns.... |
| | Burke, Levi | | William Niles and his assigns...... |
| | Kerchner, George | Rotterdam.. | Thomas Moore and his assigns...... |
| | Kerchner, George | | John Price and his assigns.......... |
| | Yeaton, James | | Ichabod Wilkinson and his assigns... |
| | Shoulgas, Peter | Rotterdam.. | Jacob Snyder and his assigns....... |
| | Scyferin, Maria Elizabeth | Rotterdam.. | Rachael Graydon and her assigns.... |
| | Scyferin, Maria Elizabeth | | Jennet Marks and her assigns....... |
| | Pepfher, Catherina | Rotterdam.. | Rachael Graydon and her assigns.... |
| | Sexin, Barbara | Rotterdam.. | Theodore Meminger and his assigns.. |
| | Miller, John Phillip | Rotterdam.. | John Peirce and his assigns......... |
| | Patterson, Murdock | Rotterdam.. | Cunningham Sample and his assigns. |
| | McManis, Michael | Ireland .... | Cunningham Sample and his assigns. |
| Dec. 7th.... | Schuber, Henry | Rotterdam.. | George Clymer and his assigns...... |
| | Elgertin, Anna Catherine | Rotterdam.. | George Clymer and his assigns...... |
| | McDaniel, Edmond | Liverpool .. | John Cottringer and his assigns..... |
| | Knobloch, John George | Rotterdam.. | Richard Wister and his assigns..... |
| | Hall, Thomas | | John Hall (?)...................... |
| | Cooper, Daniel | Rotterdam.. | Martin Crider and his assigns...... |
| | Cooper, Daniel | | Milchor Shultz and his assigns...... |
| | Micklin, Mary | | John Druckenmiller and wife........ |
| | Osterdaugh, Yost Willhelm | Rotterdam.. | Adam Trisebach and his assigns..... |
| Dec. 7th.... | Birch, William | | John Patterson and his assigns...... |
| | Tamer, Maria | Rotterdam.. | Robert Bass and his assigns........ |
| | Stautz, John | | Jesse Row and his assigns.......... |
| | Habachin, Anna Elizabeth | Rotterdam.. | Lawrence Bast and his assigns....... |
| | Tomerin, Christiana | Rotterdam.. | Joseph Moulder and his assigns..... |
| | Freymuhts, John | Rotterdam.. | Christopher Myrtelus and his assigns. |
| | Peters, Arnold | Rotterdam.. | John Dehuff and his assigns........ |
| | Hortman, Philip | Rotterdam.. | John Hickisuiller and his assigns.... |
| Dec. 8th.... | Helman, Elizabeth Catherine | | John Pault ....................... |
| | McDonald, Coll | | Jacob Binder and his assigns........ |
| | Schoulgas, Andrew | Rotterdam.. | Michael Bishop and his assigns...... |
| | Schoulgas, Conrad | Rotterdam.. | Michael Bishop and his assigns...... |
| | Schoulgas, Henry | Rotterdam.. | Michael Bishop and his assigns...... |

## List of Indentures.

| Residence. | Occupation. | Term. | Amount. |
|---|---|---|---|
| Providence twp., Phila. co. | Servant, taught to read in Bible and write a legible hand.[3] | 10 yrs. | £ 20. 19. 0. |
| Woolwich twp., Gloucester co., W. Jersey. | Servant[3] | 6 yrs. | £ 23. 0. 0. |
| Germantown, Phila. co. | Servant[3] | 2 yrs., 6 mo. | £ 19. 13. 0. |
| Philadelphia | Servant[1] | 5 yrs., 6 mo. | £ 20. 15. 2. |
| Whitemarsh twp., Phila. co. | Servant[1] | 5 yrs. | £ 25. 0. 0. |
| New Providence twp., Phila. co. | Servant[3] | 6 yrs. | £ 25. 1. 4. |
| New Town twp., Gloster co., W. Jersey. | Servant[3] | 5 yrs. | £ 21. 14. 6. |
| Radnor twp., Chester co. | Servant[3] | 2 yrs., 6 mo. | £ 18. 7. 6. |
| Philadelphia | Servant[3] | 2 yrs., 9 mo. | £ 17. 0. 0. |
| Earl twp., Lancaster co. | Servant | 2 yrs., 9 mo. | £ 17. 0. 0. |
| Moreland, Phila. co. | Servant (note 2, besides his old) | 3 yrs. | £ 21. 10. 0. |
| Philadelphia | Servant | 5 yrs., 5 mo. 13 days. | £ 12. 0. 0. |
| Philadelphia | Servant, have six months' night schooling.[1] | 5 yrs. | £ 21. 0. 0. |
| Lower Chichester, Chester co. | Servant | 5 yrs. | £ 21. 0. 0. |
| Salisbury twp., Bucks co. | Servant | 4 yrs. | £ 16. 0. 0. |
| Worcester twp., Phila. co. | Servant[3] | 6 yrs. | £ 30. 0. 0. |
| Philadelphia | Servant[1] | 4 yrs. | £ 22. 13. 8. |
| Philadelphia | Servant | 4 yrs. | £ 22. 13. 8. |
| Philadelphia | Servant[1] | 4 yrs. | £ 19. 18. 0. |
| Philadelphia | Servant[3] | 3 yrs., 6 mo. | £ 20. 16. 0. |
| Concord twp., Chester co. | Servant[3] | 2 yrs., 9 mo. | £ 19. 6. 6. |
| Faun twp., York co. | | 3 yrs., 6 mo. | £ 13. 0. 0. |
| Faun twp., York co. | Servant[1] | 3 yrs. | £ 7. 19. 0. |
| Philadelphia | Servant (note 1, and £ 3 in money) | 4 yrs., 6 mo. | £ 21. 0. 0. |
| Philadelphia | Servant[1] | 5 yrs. | £ 30. 0. 0. |
| Philadelphia | Servant (note 2, besides his old) | 2 yrs., 10 mo., 17 d. | £ 20. 0. 0. |
| Philadelphia | Servant (note 2, besides his old) | 3 yrs., 6 mo. | £ 20. 0. 0. |
| Wilmington | Apprentice | 12 yrs. | £ 12. 0. 0. |
| Philadelphia | Servant (note 3, and £ 10 Pa. currency). | 2 yrs., 6 mo. | £ 20. 17. 0. |
| Hereford, Berks co. | Servant[5] | 2 yrs., 6 mo. | £ 20. 17. 0. |
| | Apprentice, taught housewifery, sew, knit and spin, read and write well.[3] | 6 yrs. | |
| Lehigh twp., Northampton co. | Servant, taught to read in Bible, write a legible hand (note 6, or £ 10 Pa. currency). | 8 yrs., 6 mo. | £ 26. 0. 0. |
| Philadelphia | Apprentice, taught to read in Bible, write a legible hand, cypher through rule of 3, also the whitesmith trade.[3] | 8 yrs., 25 d. | |
| Philadelphia | Servant, taught to read and write[1]. | 6 yrs. | £ 30. 0. 0. |
| Philadelphia | Apprentice, taught house carpenter's trade.[6] | 5 yrs., 2 mo. 24 d. | |
| Northern Liberties | Servant[3] | 4 yrs., 6 mo. | £ 21. 2. 6. |
| Philadelphia | Servant[3] | 8 yrs. | £ 24. 0. 0. |
| Philadelphia | Servant[3] | 2 yrs., 6 mo. | £ 16. 11. 0. |
| Lancaster | Servant, taught the tanner's business.[3] | 4 yrs., 6 mo. | £ 21. 7. 6. |
| Lancaster | Servant[3] | 4 yrs. | £ 20. 19. 6. |
| Vincent twp., Chester co. | | 3 yrs., 6 mo. | £ 16. 0. 0. |
| Philadelphia | Apprentice, taught tailor's trade, have four quarters' evening schooling (note 3, of the value of £ 10 Pa. money). | 6 yrs., 5 mo. 20 d. | |
| Lower Millford twp., Bucks co. | Servant (note 2, besides his old) | 2 yrs. | £ 10. 0. 0. |
| Lower Millford twp., Bucks co. | Servant[3] | 6 yrs. | £ 30. 0. 0. |
| Lower Millford twp., Bucks co. | Servant[3] | 9 yrs. | £ 20. 0. 0. |

| Date. | Name. | From the Port of | To Whom Indentured. |
|---|---|---|---|
| 1772. | Schoulgas, Maudelena | Rotterdam | Michael Bishop and his assigns |
| | Wietzer, Solima | Rotterdam | Jacob Freese and his assigns |
| | Elgertin, Catherine Elizabeth | Rotterdam | John Wilcocks and his assigns |
| | Koentzin, Johan Martin | Rotterdam | Benedict Dorsey and his assigns |
| | Keylhauver, Martin | Rotterdam | Daniel Burkhard and his assigns |
| | Fritzinger, John | Rotterdam | Henry Funk and his assigns |
| | Fritzinger, John | | Jacob Miller and his assigns |
| | Thiess, Henry | Rotterdam | Andrew Forsyth and his assigns |
| | Thess, Christiana Wilhelmina | Rotterdam | Andrew Forsyth and his assigns |
| | Fritzenger, Ernst, and Mary Elizabeth, his wife. | Rotterdam | Benjamin Thule |
| Dec. 9th | McKee, John | | Hugh Torance and his assigns |
| | Hymen, Mary | Rotterdam | John Rub and his assigns |
| | Raser, Christian, and Elizabeth, his wife. | Rotterdam | Jacob Freese and his assigns |
| | Holtz, John | Rotterdam | John Williamson and his assigns |
| | Smith, John | | Ralph Moor and his assigns |
| | Meyer, John William | Rotterdam | Jacob Winey and his assigns |
| | Hartman, Henry | Rotterdam | Jacob Winey and his assigns |
| | Miller, Daniel | Ireland | John Rees and his assigns |
| | Weinnheimer, Henry | | Henry Kepple and his assigns |
| | Samolt, Lena | Rotterdam | Didimus Lewis and his assigns |
| | Miller, John | Rotterdam | John Vaulashe and his assigns |
| | Luger, Christopher | | Wandel Tarban and his assigns |
| | Rise, Daniel, and Catherena, his wife. | Rotterdam | Nicholas Burghart and his assigns |
| | Louks, Catherine | Rotterdam | Thomas Nedrow and his assigns |
| | Louks, Juliana | Rotterdam | Jacob Miller and his assigns |
| | Sonman, Anna Margaret | Rotterdam | Dr. Frederick Phite and his assigns |
| | Hyer, Jacob | Rotterdam | James Templin and his assigns |
| | Powell, Peter | Rotterdam | Richard Templin and his assigns |
| | Mulryan, Eleanor | | Levis Pennock and his assigns |
| | Rotenbergh, Peter | Rotterdam | Abbe Lippincott and his assigns |
| Dec. 10th | Smith, Philip William | Rotterdam | Frederic Deeds |
| | Pleifer, John George | Rotterdam | William Hodge and his assigns |
| | Poulsin, Catherine | Rotterdam | Jacob Franks and his assigns |
| | Sturgeon, John | | John Robertson |
| | Bull, John Jacob | Rotterdam | William Rogers and his assigns |
| | Huber, Paul; Joanna Teressa, his wife; Anthony, their son; and Johana Mira, their daughter. | Rotterdam | John Old and his assigns |
| | Dise, Jacob Ludwig | Rotterdam | George Shafer and his assigns |
| | Woollen, Thomas | | Stephen Phipps and his assigns |
| Dec. 10th | Skinner, William | | Jonathan Meredith |

## List of Indentures.

| Residence. | Occupation. | Term. | Amount. |
|---|---|---|---|
| Lower Millford twp., Bucks co. | Servant[3] | 10 yrs. | £10.17.6. |
| Upper Alloways Creek, Salem co., W. Jersey. | Servant[3] | 6 yrs., 6 mo. | £30.0.0. |
| Philadelphia | Servant[3] | 8 yrs. | £20.0.0. |
| Philadelphia | Servant, taught to read, write and cypher through rule of 3.[3] | 9 yrs., 6 mo. | £29.13.3. |
| Passyunck twp., Phila. co. | Servant (note 3, and £4 lawful money of Pa.). | 3 yrs., 3 mo. | £22.0.0. |
| Philadelphia | Servant (note 3, or £8 lawful money of Pa.). | 3 yrs., 6 mo. | £17.13.0. |
| Sadsbury twp., Lancaster co. | | 3 yrs., 6 mo. | £17.13.0. |
| Philadelphia | Servant, taught to read and write well.[3] | 12 yrs. | £20.0.0. |
| Philadelphia | Servant, learn to read and write[1]. | 7 yrs. | £30.0.0. |
| Malbro twp., Phila. co. | { Servant (note 1, or £10 in cash).. Servant[3] | 3 yrs., 6 mo. each. | £36.15.6. |
| Neils Settlement, Rowan co., N. C. | Servant, to have six months' schooling.[3] | 6 yrs., 6 mo. 1 w. | £16.0.0. |
| Philadelphia | Servant (note 3, and 10 shillings in cash). | 4 yrs., 6 mo. | £25.0.0. |
| Upper Alloways Creek, Salem co., W. Jersey. | Servants (note 2, besides their old, each). | 4 yrs. each. | £33.0.0. |
| Newter twp., Chester co. | Servant[3] | 4 yrs. | £23.2.6. |
| Philadelphia | Apprentice, taught the art and mystery of a mariner and navigation, read, write and cypher[3]. | 11 yrs., 4 mo. | |
| Philadelphia | Servant (note 1, or £10 in money) | 3 yrs., 3 mo. | £20.8.10. |
| Philadelphia | Servant[1] | 5 yrs. | £25.2.4. |
| Pencader Hundred, N. Castle co. on Delaware. | Servant[5] | 2 yrs., 5 mo. 17 d. | £13.0.0. |
| Philadelphia | Apprentice, taught to read and write the German and English language and cypher.[3] | 6 yrs., 10 mo. | £20.0.0. |
| New Town, Chester co. | Servant[1] | 5 yrs. | £20.15.2. |
| West Nantmill, Chester co. | Servant[3] | 4 yrs. | £21.17.2. |
| Philadelphia | Servant[5] | 1 yr., 6 mo. | £15.0.0. |
| Bristol twp., Phila. co. | Servant (note 3 (each), or £10 Pa. currency for the man's suit which he may choose). | 3 yrs. each. | £33.1.6. |
| Bristol twp., Phila. co. | Servant[3] | 4 yrs. | £24.0.0. |
| Cheltenham twp., Phila. co. | Servant[3] | 4 yrs. | £24.0.0. |
| Philadelphia | Servant[5] | 3 yrs., 6 mo. | £17.3.6. |
| E. Nantmill, Chester co. | Servant[3] | 11 yrs., 6 mo. | £16.8.6. |
| E. Caln twp., Chester co. | Servant[3] | 12 yrs. | £16.8.6. |
| W. Marlborough, Chester co. | | 4 yrs. | £14.0.0. |
| Eaveham twp., Burlington co., W. Jersey. | Servant (note 3, and £3 Penna. currency). | 4 yrs., 6 mo. | £20.9.8. |
| Philadelphia | Servant[1] | 4 yrs., 3 mo. | £22.19.6. |
| Philadelphia | Servant[3] | 4 yrs. | £21.5.10. |
| Philadelphia | Servant[3] | 8 yrs., 6 mo. | £25.0.0. |
| Southwark | Apprentice, taught art and mystery of a mariner and navigation.[6] | 7 yrs., 17 d. | |
| Evesham twp., Burlington co., W. N. Jersey. | Servant (note 3, and 12 Spanish dollars). | 4 yrs. | £20.2.4. |
| W. District, Berks co. | Servant[1] | 5 yrs. each. | £63.14.6. |
| Philadelphia | Servant (note 3, or £8 Pa. currency). | 5 yrs. | £30.0.0. |
| Philadelphia | Apprentice | 6 yrs., 7 mo. | £16.0.0. |
| Philadelphia | Apprentice, to learn the art and trade of tanner and currier, | 10 yrs., 3 mo. | |

| Date. | Name. | From the Port of | To Whom Indentured. |
|---|---|---|---|
| 1772. | | | |
| | Kershaw, Jacob Ludwick | Rotterdam.. | Philip Wager and his assigns....... |
| | Olivce, James | Ireland .... | James McDowall and his assigns.... |
| | Crossan, Neal | Ireland .... | James McDowall and his assigns.... |
| Dec. 11th... | Steinhaur, Frederick | Rotterdam.. | Mary Jenkins and her assigns....... |
| | Ruple, John George | Rotterdam.. | John Carman and his assigns........ |
| | Fink, Jacob | Rotterdam.. | Philip Mouse and his assigns....... |
| | Vandam, Catherine | Rotterdam.. | John Luken and his assigns.......... |
| | Maxfield, William | | Jonathan Jones and his assigns...... |
| | Graff, Johan Gottlib | Rotterdam.. | Samuel Howel and his assigns....... |
| | Discoll, Jeremiah | | Thos. Tisdell and his assigns........ |
| | McDonald, Hugh | | Michael Caner and his assigns...... |
| | Keller, Peter | Rotterdam.. | Dietrick Reese and his assigns....... |
| Dec. 12th... | Schnell, Johan Tyce | Rotterdam.. | Wm. Stradleman and his assigns..... |
| | Diamond, Jacob | Rotterdam.. | Godfrey Haga and his assigns....... |
| | House, John Peter | Rotterdam.. | Isaac Donsten and his assigns........ |
| | Roberts, John | | Peter January and his assigns....... |
| | Oalwain, Warnert | Rotterdam.. | Thomas Sinnickson and his assigns... |
| | Tamer, Johan Yost | Rotterdam.. | Allen Moone and his assigns........ |
| | Millerin, Maria Catherin | Rotterdam.. | Henry Haines and his assigns....... |
| Dec. 14th... | Lyell, John Ulrick | | John Nixon and his assigns.......... |
| | Levers, Mary | | James Glenn ...................... |
| | Yeager, John George | Rotterdam.. | Christian Hair and his assigns....... |
| | Yegerin, Anna Christiana | Rotterdam.. | John Breckbill and his assigns....... |
| | Yegerin, Magdelena | Rotterdam.. | Christian Forrer and his assigns...... |
| | Saneftian, Elizabeth | Rotterdam.. | Hugh Roberts and his assigns....... |
| | Cline, Theobald | | George Wert and his assigns........ |
| | Easmans, Elizabeth | Rotterdam.. | Charles West and his assigns....... |
| | Falconer, John | | Richard Collier and his assigns...... |
| | Broadley, Margery | | Robert Carson .................... |
| | Hubnerin, Frederica Regina. | Rotterdam.. | John William Hoffman and his assigns |
| | Martin, Mary | Ireland .... | William Weston and his assigns..... |
| Dec. 15th... | Sickfried, John | | Henry Cress and his assigns........ |

## List of Indentures.

| Residence. | Occupation. | Term. | Amount. |
|---|---|---|---|
| | three months' day and three months' evening schooling.[3] | | |
| Philadelphia | Servant[3] | 4 yrs. | £ 19. 7. 6. |
| Oxford twp., Chester co. | Servant[5] | 1 yr., 11 mo., 16 d. | £ 7. 10. 0. |
| Oxford twp., Chester co. | Servant[1] | 6 yrs., 11 mo., 16 d. | £ 16. 0. 10. |
| Philadelphia | Servant[3] | 4 yrs., 6 mo. | £ 19. 12. 6. |
| Northampton twp., Burlington co., W. N. Jersey. | Servant[3] | 5 yrs. | £ 25. 7. 6. |
| Philadelphia | Servant[3] | 4 yrs., 3 mo. | £ 24. 7. 6. |
| | Servant[3] | 4 yrs., 3 mo. | £ 22. 3. 6. |
| Philadelphia | Apprentice, taught the trade of a saddle tree maker, read in Bible, write a legible hand, cypher through rule of 3.[3] | 6 yrs., 6 mo. 13 d. | |
| Philadelphia | Servant[3] | 4 yrs. | £ 22. 14. 2. |
| Philadelphia | Servant, to be employed wholly at the ropemaking and flaxseed business.[6] | 3 yrs., 4 mo. 17 d. | £ 15. 0. 0. |
| Philadelphia | Apprentice | 2 yrs., 9 mo. 3 w., 4 d. | £ 5. 0. 0. |
| Philadelphia | Servant (note 3, or £ 8 Pa. currency). | 4 yrs., 6 mo. | £ 21. 3. 2. |
| Lower Merion twp., Phila. co. | Servant[3] | 4 yrs. | £ 22. 2. 4. |
| Philadelphia | Servant[3] | 5 yrs. | £ 19. 0. 0. |
| Rock Hill twp., Bucks co. | Servant, taught to read in Bible, write a legible hand.[3] | 13 yrs. | £ 12. 0. 0. |
| Philadelphia | Apprentice, to have meat, drink, washing, lodging and working apparel and taught the trade of a cordwainer and at expiration pay for one quarters' night schooling. | | |
| Salem, Salem co., in western division of New Jersey. | Servant, taught to read in Bible[3] | 8 yrs. | £ 30. 0. 0. |
| Philadelphia | Servant[3] | 6 yrs., 6 mo. | £ 30. 0. 0. |
| Philadelphia | Servant[3] | 4 yrs. | £ 18. 18. 0. |
| Philadelphia | Servant[1] | 7 yrs. | £ 24. 12. 0. |
| Philadelphia | Apprentice, taught housewifery, read well in Bible, write a good legible hand and sew.[6] | 10 yrs., 2 mo., 25 d. | |
| Lampeter twp., Lancaster co. | Servant, taught to read in Bible, write a legible hand.[1] | 13 yrs. | £ 9. 11. 10. |
| Strasburg twp., Lancaster co. | Servant[1] | 5 yrs. | £ 21. 0. 0. |
| Lampeter twp., Lancaster co. | Servant, taught to read in Bible[1] | 12 yrs. | £ 5. 0. 0. |
| Philadelphia | Servant[3] | 4 yrs. | £ 24. 15. 6. |
| Philadelphia | Servant, taught tailor's trade[3] | 4 yrs. | £ 16. 0. 0. |
| Northern Liberties | Servant (note 1, or £ 3 Penna. currency). | 5 yrs., 6 mo. | £ 21. 0. 0. |
| Philadelphia | Apprentice | 9 yrs., 11 mo. | £ 25. 0. 0. |
| Southwark | | See Nov. 7, last. | £ 13. 0. 0. |
| Philadelphia | Servant, (note 3, to serve the residue of her indenture and £ 8 in money, with lawful interest for the same). | 3 yrs., 6 mo. | £ 8. 10. 3. |
| Philadelphia | Servant[5] | 2 yrs. | £ 6. 0. 0. |
| Philadelphia | Apprentice, taught the cordwainer's trade, have two quarters' schooling (note 3, also a kit of tools). | 6 yrs. | |

| Date. | Name. | From the Port of | To Whom Indentured. |
|---|---|---|---|
| 1772. | Green, William | | John Hannah |
| | Whitestick, Henry | Rotterdam.. | John Breckbill and his assigns....... |
| | Tickin, Henretta | Rotterdam.. | George Goodwin and his assigns..... |
| | Willin, Catherina | | William Simpson and his assigns.... |
| | Babjohn, John | | Philip Sinclair |
| | Stevens, William | England | Ellis Newlin and his assigns |
| Dec. 16th... | Easy, Edmund | | Michael Dawson and his assigns |
| | Furniss, Catherine | | Adam Deshler |
| | Matzenbacher, John Adam | Rotterdam.. | Jacob Brown and his assigns |
| | Matzenbacher, John Adam | | Adam Carver and his assigns |
| | Maldrom, Margaret | | Michael Davenport and wife |
| | Garnet, George | | James Wharta and his assigns |
| | Able, Jacob | | William Stots |
| Dec. 17th... | Schaffer, Catherine | | George Myers |
| | Sheckell, Mary | | Stephen Carmeek |
| | Sleving, William | | Samuel Wright, mariner |
| Dec. 18th... | Hacket, Mary | | Presly Blackiston and his assigns |
| | Weiscop, Jacob | Rotterdam.. | John Stoner |
| | Duff, John | | Robert Morris and his assigns |
| | Bettsin, Margaret | Rotterdam.. | Johan Geo. Fishack and his assigns... |
| | Bettsin, Margaret | | Abraham Riske and his assigns |
| | Betts, Iohan Frederick | Rotterdam.. | John George Fishack and his assigns. |
| | Betts, Johan Frederick | | Abraham Rise and his assigns |
| Dec. 19th... | Bottenfeld, John Justice | Rotterdam.. | John George Fishack and his assigns.. |
| | Bottenfeld, John Justice | | Eronimus Hensilman and his assigns. |
| Dec. 21st... | Caldwell, Arthur | | Thomas Shields |
| | Peddle, George | | Joseph Master and his assigns |
| Dec. 22nd... | Knox, Thomas | Ireland | William Carson and his assigns |
| | Wells, William | | Robert Harper |
| | Cake, Philip | | Matthias Cake |
| | Hollen, James | | Benjamin Town and his assigns |

| RESIDENCE. | OCCUPATION. | TERM. | AMOUNT. |
|---|---|---|---|
| Philadelphia | Apprentice, taught the brush maker's trade, have three quarters' day schooling (note 3, and of broadcloth). | 5 yrs., 5 mo. | |
| Strasburg twp., Lancaster co. | Servant[3] | 5 yrs. | £25.0.0. |
| Philadelphia | Servant[3] | 4 yrs., 6 mo. | £25.15.0. |
| Peatang twp., Lancaster co. | | 5 yrs. | £1.10.0. |
| Philadelphia | Apprentice, to learn the tailor's art, taught to read well in Bible and write a good legible hand and cypher as far as rule of 3[3]. | 11 yrs., 11 mo. | |
| Christiana Hundred, N. Castle co. | Servant, taught to read and write a legible hand and cypher as far as rule of 3.[1] | 11 yrs. | £15.0.0. |
| Philadelphia | Apprentice, taught the art and mystery of a pilot in bay and river of Delaware, have nine months' schooling.[3] | 6 yrs., 4 mo. 15 d. | |
| Whitehall twp., Bucks co. | Apprentice, taught housewifery, to sew, knit and spin (note 2, besides his old). | 2 yrs., 10 mo. | |
| Philadelphia | Servant[3] | 3 yrs. | £19.12.0. |
| Heidelberge twp., Lancaster co. | Servant[5] | 3 yrs. | £19.12.0. |
| Southwark | Apprentice, taught housewifery and sew, read in Bible, have one quarter schooling, taught to write.[3] | 8 yrs., 8 mo. | |
| Philadelphia | Servant, employed at the rope making business. | 9 yrs. | £5.0.0. |
| Southwark | Apprentice, taught the tailor's trade, have five quarters' schooling.[3] | 6 yrs., 11 mo., 15 d. | |
| Reading, Berks co. | Servant | 6 yrs. | £0.5s. |
| Philadelphia | Apprentice, taught housewifery, read and write.[6] | 4 yrs., 4 mo. | |
| Philadelphia | Apprentice, to learn his art and taught the art of navigation.[3] | 5 yrs., 8 mo. | |
| Philadelphia | Servant | 4 yrs. | £6.0.0. |
| Union twp., Berks co. | Servant[1] | 6 yrs. | £27.0.0. |
| Philadelphia | Apprentice, taught the art of a mariner, found meat, drink, washing and lodging. | 6 yrs. | |
| Manheim twp., Lancaster co. | Servant[3] | 3 yrs., 6 mo. | £14.14.9. |
| Manheim twp., Lancaster co. | Servant | 3 yrs., 6 mo. | £14.14.9. |
| Manheim twp., Lancaster co. | Servant[3] | 3 yrs., 6 mo. | £24.14.9. |
| Manheim twp., Lancaster co. | Servant | 3 yrs., 6 mo. | £24.14.9. |
| Manheim twp., Lancaster co. | Servant[3] | 3 yrs., 6 mo. | £21.0.0 |
| Manheim twp., Lancaster co. | Servant | 3 yrs., 6 mo. | £21.0.0 |
| Philadelphia | Servant, to be found all necessaries and taught to read well in Bible. | 5 yrs. | |
| Philadelphia | Apprentice, taught the cooper's trade, have nine months' schooling.[1] | 4 yrs., 9 mo. | |
| Philadelphia | Servant (note 5, have £5 in money). | 2 yrs., 11 mo., 5 d. | £12.0.0. |
| Northern Liberties | Apprentice, have one year schooling.[3] | 6 yrs., 8 mo. 25 d. | |
| Philadelphia | Apprentice, taught the cooper's trade, have three winters' night schooling, the father paying for one (note 2, besides his old). | 4 yrs. | |
| Philadelphia | Apprentice, taught the trade of a copper smith, have one quarter schooling at night next winter, | 7 yrs., 11 mo., 13 d. | |

| Date. | Name. | From the Port of | To Whom Indentured. |
|---|---|---|---|
| 1772. | Carr, David | | Thomas Penrose and his assigns |
| | Smith, Benjamin | | William Hay and his assigns |
| | Seibele, Maria Elizabeth | Rotterdam | Richard Wister and his assigns |
| Dec. 23rd | Cramp, John, Jr. | | Michael Kamper and his assigns |
| | Harman, Michael | Rotterdam | William Will and his assigns |
| | Harman, Michael | | John Houts and his assigns |
| | Fowlo, Mary | Ireland | Robert McCurley and his assigns |
| | Scanlan, Ann | | John Frazier and his assigns |
| | Hatmanin, Elizabeth Margaret. | Rotterdam | Henry Kepple Sr., and his assigns |
| | Hatmanin, Elizabeth Margaret. | | Martin Lauman and his assigns |
| | Swaine, Edward | | Cornelius Cooper and his assigns |
| Dec. 24th | Folchin, Maria Elizabeth | Rotterdam | John Fritz and his assigns |
| | McCreary, Mary | | Robert Nelson and his assigns |
| | Tamer, Ludwig | | Nicholas Miller and his assigns |
| | Weighel, Johannes | Rotterdam | William Lawrence and his assigns |
| | Lambach, Conrad | Rotterdam | John Hunter and his assigns |
| | Thillen, Anna Catherina | Rotterdam | Thomas Pryer and his assigns |
| | Hefferin, Eave Catherina | Rotterdam | John Musser and his assigns |
| | Hefferin, Eave Catherina | | Christian Forry and his assigns |
| | Jongerblood, Clary | Rotterdam | William Forbes and his assigns |
| | Millerin, Anna Maria | Rotterdam | Thos. Prior and his assigns |
| | Albachin, Elizabeth, Margaret. | Rotterdam | Daniel Burkhart and his assigns |
| | Albachin, Catherine | Rotterdam | Rudolph Feel and his assigns |
| | Neichell, Barnard | Rotterdam | Nathan Garrett and his assigns |
| | Nametter, Jacob | Rotterdam | John Duncan and his assigns |
| Dec. 26th | Spider, John Jacob | Rotterdam | Nathan Levering and his assigns |
| | Stilling, Andrew | Rotterdam | Risstore Lippincott and his assigns |
| | Ulrich, John Peter | Rotterdam | Henry Kemmerer and his assigns |
| | Ulrich, John Peter | | Catherine Shitz and her assigns |
| | Pifer, John Jacob | Rotterdam | Job Whittell and his assigns |
| 1772. Dec. 26th | Reily, James | Rotterdam | Samuel Howell and his assigns |
| | Tinges, John William | Rotterdam | George Cooper and his assigns |
| | Tinges, John William | | Christian Petre and his assigns |
| | Tinges, John Peter | Rotterdam | Philip Cauble and his assigns |
| | Yerm, John Jacob | Rotterdam | Henry Haines and his assigns |
| | Ward, John | Ireland | Philip Price and his assigns |

[1] To be found all necessaries and at the expiration have freedom dues.
[2] To be found all necessaries and at the expiration have one new suit of apparel.
[3] To be found all necessaries and at the expiration have two complete suits of apparel, one whereof to be new.

## List of Indentures.

| Residence. | Occupation. | Term. | Amount. |
|---|---|---|---|
| | one other quarter the last year of his apprenticeship (note 2, besides his old). | | |
| Southwark | Apprentice [5] | 8 yrs., 10 mo. | £24.0.0 |
| Nottingham twp., Burlington co., W. N. Jersey. | Apprentice | | £12.10.0 |
| Philadelphia | Servant, to serve her time in the province of N. Jersey.[3] | 4 yrs. | £15.10.6 |
| Philadelphia | Apprentice, taught the cedar cooper's trade, have one year day and one year night schooling (note 1, or £10 in money, also £5 in money). | 9 yrs. | |
| Philadelphia | Servant, taught to read in Bible[3] | 5 yrs., 7 mo. | £25.5.0 |
| Other side Cunnowag Mash Criek Settlement, York co. | Servant | 5 yrs., 7 mo. | £23.5.0 |
| Hellum twp., York co. | Servant[1] | 4 yrs. | £14.0.0 |
| Philadelphia | Servant | 4 yrs. | £13.11.4 |
| Philadelphia | Servant[1] | 4 yrs. | £25.16 |
| Lancaster | Servant | 4 yrs. | £25.16 |
| Philadelphia | Servant | 5 yrs. | £14 |
| Southwark | Servant[1] | 5 yrs. | £27.3.0 |
| Fair Manor twp., Cumberland co. | Servant | 6 yrs. | £10.0.0 |
| Philadelphia | Apprentice, taught the tailor's trade, read in Bible write a legible hand and cypher through rule of 3.[3] | 13 yrs. | |
| Debtford twp., Gloster co., N. J. | Apprentice[3] | 3 yrs. | £24.0.0 |
| Coventry twp., Chester co. | Apprentice[1] | 5 yrs. | £28.2.0 |
| Philadelphia | Servant[1] | 6 yrs. | £32.17.0 |
| Lancaster | Servant[1] | 4 yrs. | £25.7.6 |
| Lampeter twp., Lancaster co. | Servant | 4 yrs. | £25.7.6 |
| Philadelphia | Servant[3] | 5 yrs. | £23.12.0 |
| Philadelphia | Servant[3] | 5 yrs. | £13.15.0 |
| Passyunk twp., Phila. co. | Servant[3] | 6 yrs. | £29.12.6 |
| Moyamensing twp., Phila. co. | Servant[3] | 6 yrs. | £30.7.6 |
| Upper Derby twp., Chester co. | Servant[3] | 3 yrs., 4 mo. | £21.19.0 |
| Philadelphia | Servant, taught to read and write English perfectly.[6] | 4 yrs., 6 mo. | £25.13.6 |
| Roxbury twp., Phila. co. | Servant[3] | 6 yrs. | £29.5.0 |
| Greenage twp., W. Jersey | Servant[3] | 5 yrs., 3 mo. | £23.2.0 |
| Philadelphia | Servant[3] | 3 yrs. | £29.16.0 |
| Lower Merion twp., Phila. co. | Servant | 3 yrs. | £29.16.0 |
| Debtford twp., Gloster co., W. N. Jersey. | Servant (note 1, or £10 which said servant may choose and £5 exclusive of the ten pounds, Penna. currency). | 5 yrs. | £31.14.6 |
| Philadelphia | Servant, employed to the business of a seaman and taught the art of a mariner.[3] | 3 yrs. | |
| Philadelphia | Servant, taught the stocking weaver's business.[1] | 7 yrs. | £21.7.0 |
| Lancaster | Servant | 7 yrs. | £21.7.0 |
| Overslferd twp., Phila. co. | Servant[3] | 6 yrs., 2 mo. | £30.0.0 |
| Philadelphia | Servant[1] | 6 yrs., 6 mo. | £25.0.0 |
| Kingsess twp., Phila. co. | Servant[1] | 3 yrs. | £10.0.0 |

[4] To be found all necessaries and at the expiration have two complete suits of apparel, one whereof to be new, and 40s. in money.

[5] At expiration have two complete suits of apparel, one whereof to be new.

| Date. | Name. | From the Port of | To Whom Indentured. |
|---|---|---|---|
| 1772. | Broadley, Margary | | William Laidley and his assigns |
| Dec. 26th | Prendergast, Thomas | Ireland | James Ross and his assigns |
| Dec. 28th | Herter, Charles | Rotterdam | Matthias Lendenbergher and his assigns. |
| | Kledi, Jacob | | Henry Oxbecher and his assigns |
| | Levy, Michael | | Joseph Gavin and his assigns |
| | Brian, Archibald | | Mary Sendray and her assigns |
| | Maxzeymour, Elizabeth | Rotterdam | John Vanderin and his assigns |
| | Junghin, Elizabeth | Rotterdam | John Vanderin and his assigns |
| | Hartranffts, Leonard | | Henry Hyman and his assigns |
| | Keynts, Henry, and Baltzai, his son. | Rotterdam | William Bryant and his assigns |
| | Germane, Catherine Elizabeth | Rotterdam | Christian Shade and his assigns |
| | Maxzeymour, John William | Rotterdam | Leonard Karg and his assigns |
| | Maxzeymour, John William | | Ludwick Lauman and his assigns |
| | Sewell, Philip | | Francis Springer and his assigns |
| | Pleiferin, Maria Elizabeth | Rotterdam | Jacob Hiltzheimer and his assigns |
| | Pleiferin, Christiana Elizabeth. | Rotterdam | Charles Lyan and his assigns |
| | Finger, Valentine | Rotterdam | Nathaniel Donald and his assigns |
| Dec. 29th | Scanlan, Ann | | John Brown and his assigns |
| | Hood, Thomas | | Samuel Simpson and his assigns |
| | Beckerin, Elizabeth | Rotterdam | John Peter and his assigns |
| | Willis, Pheebe | | John Burrough and his assigns |
| | Williams, Jane | Ireland | Thomas Hale and his assigns |
| | Sullivan, Honor | Ireland | John Willson and his assigns |
| | Newman, Richard | Galloway | Michael Robinson and his assigns |
| | Heits, John | Rotterdam | Henry Kuygen and his assigns |
| | Dingas, John Matthias | Rotterdam | Daniel Drinker and his assigns |
| | Swartz, George | Rotterdam | Peter Dick and his assigns |
| | Millen, Charles | | David Jones and his assigns |
| | Meyerin, Maria Elizabeth | Rotterdam | Benjamin Olden and his assigns |
| | Konckerlin, Anna Margaret | Rotterdam | Thomas Proctor and his assigns |
| Dec. 30th | Stoll, Adam | Rotterdam | Charles Chamberlain |
| | Dingasey, Anna Catherina | Rotterdam | Levy Hollingsworth and his assigns |
| | Dingasey, Anna Catherina | | Henry Weaver and his assigns |
| | Pister, Gotfrid | Rotterdam | Ludwig Kuhn and his assigns |
| | Pister, Godfrid | | Henry Shoemaker and his assigns |
| | Hall, Ann | | William Gra |
| | Kisler, George | Rotterdam | Ludwig Kuhn and his assigns |
| | Kisler, George | | Charles Shoemaker and his assigns |

## List of Indentures.

| RESIDENCE. | OCCUPATION. | TERM. | AMOUNT. |
|---|---|---|---|
| Philadelphia | Servant | 4 yrs. | £ 13. 14. 0. |
| Kingsess twp., Phila. | Servant[1] | 3 yrs. | £ 10. 0. 0. |
| Philadelphia | Servant[3] | 5 yrs. | £ 22. 15. 0. |
| Stow Creek twp., Cumberland co., W. N. Jersey. | Apprentice, taught the potter's trade, have six months' English schooling (note 5, have £ 10 in money in lieu of freedom). | 4 yrs. | |
| Philadelphia | Apprentice, taught the cordwainer's trade, have two quarters' schooling.[3] | 3 yrs., 11 mo., 14 d. | |
| Philadelphia | | 4 yrs. | £ 9. 0. 0. |
| Roxbury twp., Phila. co. | Servant[3] | 5 yrs., 6 mo. | £ 20. 0. 0. |
| Roxbury twp., Phila. co. | Servant[3] | 4 yrs. | £ 21. 17. 8. |
| Philadelphia | Apprentice, taught the tailor's trade, have one quarter schooling.[5] | 6 yrs., 10 mo., 9 d. | |
| Near Trenton, Burlington co., W. N. Jersey | Servant[3] | 4 yrs., 6 mo. | £ 30. 0. 0. |
| | Servant[5] | each. | |
| Marlborough twp., Phila. co. | Servant, taught to read in Bible, write a legible hand.[8] | 8 yrs. | £ 11. 0. 0. |
| Lancaster, Lancaster co. | Servant, taught to read in Bible, write a legible hand.[3] | 8 yrs. | £ 20. 0. 0. |
| Lancaster, Lancaster co. | Servant | 8 yrs. | £ 20. 0. 0. |
| Philadelphia | Apprentice, taught the cordwainer's trade, to read and write a legible hand.[3] | 13 yrs., 10 mo., 22 d. | |
| Philadelphia | Servant[3] | 6 yrs. | £ 31. 19. 0. |
| Philadelphia | Servant[3] | 8 yrs. | £ 20. 0. 0. |
| Philadelphia | Servant[3] | 5 yrs. | £ 22. 7. 6. |
| Willistown twp., Chester co. | Servant | 4 yrs. | £ 0. 5. 0. |
| Philadelphia | Apprentice, taught the cordwainer's trade, have four quarters' schooling.[3] | 8 yrs., 3 mo. | |
| Philadelphia | Servant[3] | 4 yrs., 6 mo. | £ 25. 0. 0. |
| Newtown twp., Glocester co. | Servant[5] | 1 yr. | £ 2. 10. 0. |
| Philadelphia | Servant (note 5, to be paid the usual allowance according to the custom of the country in the like kind). | 2 yrs., 11 mo. | £ 13. 10. 0. |
| Philadelphia | Servant[1] | 5 yrs., 11 mo. | £ 13. 0. 0. |
| Philadelphia | Servant[1] | 4 yrs. | £ 10. 0. 0. |
| Pitts Grove, Salem co., W. Jersey. | Servant, read in Bible well and write a legible hand.[1] | 10 yrs., 8 mo. | £ 12. 0. 0. |
| Philadelphia | Servant, taught to read in Bible, write a legible hand.[3] | 10 yrs. | £ 16. 19. 0. |
| Philadelphia | Servant, to be employed at the tailor's business only.[3] | 5 yrs. | £ 22. 17. 0. |
| Philadelphia | Apprentice | 13 yrs. | £ 13. 10. 0. |
| Philadelphia | Servant[3] | 4 yrs., 3 mo. | £ 27. 1. 0. |
| Philadelphia | Servant, to read and sew (note 3, and £ 5 in cash). | 8 yrs. | £ 30. 11. 0. |
| Philadelphia | Servant[1] | 5 yrs., 6 mo. | £ 21. 2. 8. |
| Philadelphia | Servant[1] | 6 yrs. | £ 30. 0. 0. |
| Strasburg twp., Lancaster co. | Servant (as per record above) | | |
| Philadelphia | Servant (note 3, or £ 10 currency) | 3 yrs., 3 mo. | £ 27. 3. 0. |
| Windsor twp., Berks co. | Servant[5] | 3 yrs., 3 mo. | £ 27. 3. 0. |
| Warwick twp., Bucks co. | Servant | 11 yrs. | £ 9. 0. 0. |
| Philadelphia | Servant (note 3, or £ 10 Penna. currency). | 2 yrs., 3 mo. | £ 27. 4. 10. |
| Windsor twp., Berks co. | Servant[5] | 2 yrs., 3 mo. | £ 27. 4. 10. |

| Date. | Name. | From the Port of | To Whom Indentured. |
|---|---|---|---|
| 1772. | Schenediffer, Hans Geo., and Dorothea, his wife. | Rotterdam.. | Samuel Howell and his assigns...... |
| | Schenediffer, Anna Maria.... | ............ | Samuel Howell and his assigns...... |
| | Schenediffer, Adam ......... | ............ | Samuel Howell and his assigns...... |
| | Shafer, Adam ............ | Rotterdam.. | Ludwig Kuhn and his assigns....... |
| | Shafer, Adam ............ | ............ | Henry Mullen and his assigns....... |
| | Frickaver, Simon ............ | ............ | Peter Schreiver (butcher) and his heirs. |
| | Downs, Michael ............ | Ireland .... | Thomas Badge and his assigns....... |
| | Shearer, Jacob ............ | Rotterdam.. | John Beatler and his assigns......... |
| | Helfrigen, Catherine Elizabeth. | Rotterdam.. | Charles Lyng and his assigns........ |
| | Helfrigen, Catherine Elizabeth. | ............ | George Musser and his assigns...... |
| Dec. 30th... | Grafmayer, John Godfred... | Rotterdam.. | William Lamburn and his assigns.... |
| | Bouyin, Anna Juliana ...... | Rotterdam.. | William Lamburn and his assigns.... |
| | Burk, John ............ | Ireland .... | John Suber and his assigns.......... |
| | Short, William ............ | Ireland .... | Lamb Talbot and his assigns....... |
| | Regan, Lott ............ | ............ | Zebulon Rudolph and his assigns..... |
| | Frederick, Fogle, and Catherin Barbara, his wife. | Rotterdam.. | Jacob Paum and his assigns........ |
| | Tiseman, Ludwig Henry..... | Rotterdam.. | Benamin Poultney and his assigns.... |
| | Tiseman, Ludwig Henry..... | ............ | Robert Park and his assigns......... |
| | Bess, Simon Jacob ......... | Rotterdam.. | Mary Jenkins and her assigns........ |
| | Piferin, Anna Elizabeth .... | Rotterdam.. | John Field and his assigns.......... |
| | Miffet, Johan Henry ........ | Rotterdam.. | Adam Foulke and his assigns....... |
| | Miffet, Johan Henry ........ | ............ | Adam Reigard and his assigns...... |
| Dec. 31st... | Tress, Jacob ............ | Rotterdam.. | James Sparks and his assigns........ |
| | Maxzusmour, Henry Adam.. | Rotterdam.. | Anthony Groff and his assigns...... |
| | Meyerin, Maria Catherine... | Rotterdam.. | Richard Bache and his assigns...... |
| | Burn, Mary ............ | ............ | Martin Zuges and his assigns........ |
| | Meyerin, Anna Margaret ... | Rotterdam.. | Jeremiah Warder and his assigns.... |
| | Lederigh, Nicholas ......... | Rotterdam.. | John Baldwin and his assigns....... |
| | Henrickson, Peter ............ | ............ | Frederica Burd .................... |
| | Orbel, John Frederic........ | Rotterdam.. | William Henry .................... |
| Jan. 1st.... | Moore, Hannah ............ | Ireland .... | Henry Starrett and his assigns....... |
| | Karr, James ............ | ............ | John Flinn and his assigns.......... |
| | Tamerin, Anna Margaret, Jr............ | ............ | George Smith and wife ............ |

## List of Indentures.

| RESIDENCE. | OCCUPATION. | TERM. | AMOUNT. |
|---|---|---|---|
| Philadelphia | Servant¹ | 5 yrs. | £ 30. 0. 0. |
| | Servant¹ | 18 yrs. | £ 2. 10. 0. |
| Philadelphia | Servant¹ | 19 yrs. | £ 2. 10. 0. |
| Philadelphia | Servant (note 3, or £ 10 Penna. currency, it is agreed by the parties if his friends can pay the consideration money and the expenses, this indenture to be void). | 3 yrs., 4 mo. | £ 30. 10. 0. |
| Windsor twp., Berks co. | Servant⁵ | 3 yrs., 4 mo. | £ 30. 10. 0. |
| Philadelphia | Apprentice, to learn his art and trade, have two winters' night schooling (note 3, and £ 7 in cash). | 5 yrs., 6 mo. | |
| Southwark | Servant, shall immediately give him a decent suit of clothes worth £ 5 to be worn only on Sundays. | 4 yrs. | £ 12. 0. 0. |
| Union twp., Berks co. | Servant³ | 5 yrs. | £ 20. 0. 0. |
| Philadelphia | Servant³ | 4 yrs., 6 mo. | £ 25. 10. 0. |
| Lancaster | Servant | 4 yrs., 6 mo. | £ 25. 10. 0. |
| Kennet twp., Chester co. | Servant³ | 5 yrs. | £ 25. 7. 0. |
| Kennet twp., Chester co. | Servant³ | 7 yrs. | £ 21. 10. 0. |
| Middle twp., Bucks co. | Servant¹ | 4 yrs. | £ 16. 0. 0. |
| Newtown twp., Bucks co. | Servant¹ | 4 yrs. | £ 12. 0. 0. |
| Maryland | | 3 yrs. | £ 15. 0. 0. |
| Northern Liberties | Servant³ | 3 yrs. each.. | £ 37. 7. 6. |
| Philadelphia | Servant¹ | 7 yrs. | £ 31. 10. 0. |
| Chester co. | Servant, according to the terms of the above indenture. | | |
| Philadelphia | Servant³ | 2 yrs. | £ 17. 15. 6. |
| Philadelphia | Servant³ | 7 yrs. | £ 22. 6. 0. |
| | Servant³ | 5 yrs. | £ 23. 18. 6. |
| Lancaster | Servant | 5 yrs. | £ 23. 18. 6. |
| Philadelphia | Servant, taught to read in Bible, write a legible hand.³ | 14 yrs. | £ 12. 11. 0. |
| Philadelphia | Servant³ | 4 yrs. | £ 27. 16. 6. |
| Philadelphia | Servant³ | 4 yrs., 6 mo. | £ 27. 12. 0. |
| Philadelphia | Servant | 4 yrs. | £ 12. 0. 0. |
| Philadelphia | Servant³ | 5 yrs. | £ 27. 12. 0. |
| Philadelphia | Servant³ | 14 yrs. | £ 13. 0. 0. |
| | | 1 yr., 9 mo.. | £ 8. 0. 0. |
| | Servant¹ | 4 yrs., 6 mo. | £ 28. 12. 0. |
| Philadelphia | Servant¹ | 2 yrs., 10 mo., 25 d. | £ 10. 0. 0. |
| Philadelphia | Apprentice, taught the cabinet maker's trade, read in Bible, write a legible hand and cypher through the rule of 3, found meat, drink, washing and lodging and working apparel, the mother to find Sunday apparel during the first two years and the master to find Sunday apparel the remaining part of the term. | 6 yrs., 5 mo. 21 d. | |
| Northern Liberties | Servant, taught housewifery, to sew, knit and spin, read in Bible, write a legible hand.³ | 12 yrs. | |

| Date. | Name. | From the Port of | To Whom Indentured. |
|---|---|---|---|
| 1773. Jan. 2nd | Winter, Frederick | Rotterdam | Jacob Coblance and his assigns |
| | Fingar, Valentine | Rotterdam | James Brinton and his assigns |
| | Cellier, Peter | | William Shippen |
| | Smith, George | | Peter Cress and his assigns |
| Jan. 4th | Martin, John | | John Raynolds and his assigns |
| | Maxfield, Mary | | Andrew Bunner and his assigns |
| | Reineck, John Christian | Rotterdam | Michael Immel and his assigns |
| | Woodward, James | | John Scattergood and his assigns |
| Jan. 5th | Spaunin, Susanna | Rotterdam | Rev. John Ewing and his assigns |
| | Fordysh, Barbara | Rotterdam | Francis Wade and his assigns |
| | Bartholomew, Edward | | George Wilson and his assigns |
| Jan. 6th | Karla, John | | Peter Cooper and his assigns |
| | Ford, James | | Jacob Maag and his assigns |
| Jan. 7th | Olonnor, Charles | | Thomas Moore and his assigns |
| | Taylor, George | | Amariah Fannsworth |
| Jan. 8th | Nevell, John | | John Handlyn and his assigns |
| 1773. Jan. 8th | Lyens, Bartholemew | | James Starr and his assigns |
| | Wiesmiller, Henry | Rotterdam | George Ross and his assigns |
| | Undersee, Conrad | Rotterdam | George Ross and his assigns |
| | Lincoln, Mary | | Mary Pugh and her assigns |
| | Lincoln, Mary | | Mary Pugh and her assigns |
| | Clark, John | | John Marshall and his assigns |
| Jan. 9th | Donald, Thomas M. | | William Richardson and his assigns |
| Jan. 11th | Nevell, John | | Thomas Nevell and his assigns |
| | Tucker, Charlotte | | Townsend White and his assigns |

## List of Indentures.

| Residence. | Occupation. | Term. | Amount. |
|---|---|---|---|
| Bristol twp., Phila. co. | Servant[3] | 3 yrs., 6 mo. | £21.6.6. |
| Pennsborough twp., Chester co. | Servant, taught to read in Bible, write a legible hand.[3] | 7 yrs. | £22.17.6. |
| Philadelphia | Apprentice, taught the cooper's trade.[3] | 2 yrs. | |
| Philadelphia | Apprentice, taught the trade of a coach harness maker.[5] | 1 yr., 23 d. | |
| Philadelphia | Servant[3] | 2 yrs. | £5.0.0. |
| Philadelphia | Apprentice, taught housewifery, to sew have six months schooling.[3] | 5 yrs., 6 mo. | |
| Philadelphia | Servant[3] | 3 yrs. | £14.11.6. |
| Northern Liberties | Apprentice, taught the tanner and currier's trade, allowed time to go to night schooling during the term his brother paying the expense.[5] | 5 yrs., 6 mo. | |
| Philadelphia | Servant[3] | 5 yrs. | £20.0.0. |
| Philadelphia | Servant[3] | 4 yrs., 6 mo. | £27.13.10. |
| Philadelphia | Apprentice, taught the art and mystery of a hatter, found meat, drink, washing, lodging, the master to provide shoes and hats and give him four quarters' night schooling at the master's expense and four quarters' night schooling at the mother's expense. | 7 yrs. | |
| Philadelphia | Apprentice, taught the cordwainers trade, have two quarters' evening schooling.[5] | 1 yr. | |
| Passyunk twp., Phila. co. | Apprentice, taught the trade of wheelwright, have five quarters' schooling, one quarter of which to be in the last year of his time (note 3, or £10 lawful money of Pa.). | 8 yrs., 9 mo. 24 d. | |
| Philadelphia | Servant | 2 yrs., 4 mo. | £6.10.0. |
| Burdentown, N. J. | Servant | 4 yrs. and 1 yr., 8 mo. | £13.0.0. |
| Philadelphia | Apprentice | 5 yrs., 2 mo. 27 d. | £1.5.0. |
| Philadelphia | Apprentice, taught the cordwainer's trade, have two quarters' night schooling (note 3, and a kit of tools). | 3 yrs., 4 mo. 21 d. | |
| Philadelphia | Servant[3] | 3 yrs., 9 mo. 12 d. | £27.0.0. |
| Philadelphia | Servant[3] | 4 yrs. | £27.0.0. |
| Upper Merion, Phila. co. | Servant | 12 yrs., 7 mo. | £5.15.0. |
| Upper Merion twp., Phila. co. | Apprentice, taught housewifery, sew, knit and spin, read in Bible, write a legible hand.[3] | 9 yrs., 10 mo., 23 d. | |
| Moyamensing, Phila. co. | Servant, found meat, drink, washing and lodging, two pair shoes, two pair hose, two shirts. | 1 yr. | £5.3.11. |
| Fawn twp., York co. | Servant (note 2, besides his old). | 2 yrs. | £2.0.0. |
| Philadelphia | Apprentice | 5 yrs., 2 mo. 27 d. | £1.5.0. |
| Philadelphia | Apprentice, taught housewifery and sew, read in Bible, write a legible hand.[3] | 10 yrs., 6 mo. | |

| Date. | Name. | From the Port of | To Whom Indentured. |
|---|---|---|---|
| 1773. Jan. 11th.... | Bro. Joseph | | Joseph Hudle and his assigns........ |
| | Reineck, Ludwick, and Maria Elizabeth, his wife. | Rotterdam.. | James Vaux and his assigns ........ |
| | Haus, John Christopher ..... | Rotterdam.. | Samuel Howell and his assigns...... |
| | Brunner, Paul Frederick .... | Rotterdam.. | John Rupp and his assigns.......... |
| | Stephens, William ................. | | Eleazor Levi and his assigns........ |
| Jan. 12th... | Albright, Salome ................. | | John Mayer and his assigns......... |
| | Hanson, John ..................... | | Andrew Moynipan and his assigns... |
| | Manly, James .................... | | Robert Hopkins, Jr., and his assigns.. |
| Jan. 13th... | Drinker, John .................... | | Bowyer Brooke and his assigns...... |
| | Wood, Isaac ..................... | | Bowyer Brooke and his assigns...... |
| | Taaffe, Patrick .................. | | James Lees and his assigns.......... |
| | Mitchell, John; Cleark, William; Peters, George; Flintham, John; Mills, John; Farley, William. | | William Montgomery ............... |
| Jan. 14th... | Farrel, Michael; Rogers, Owen. | | William Montgomery and his assigns. |
| | Auwor, Anthony, and Dorothea, his wife. | Rotterdam.. | Joseph Mitchell and his assigns...... |
| | McArthur, Duncan, Jr.......... | | James Fisher ...................... |
| | McDonald, James .......... | Ireland .... | John Scantlan and his assigns....... |
| Jan. 16th... | Connell, John .............. | Ireland .... | Robert Gray and his assigns......... |
| | Vicker, John ............... | St. Croix... | Robert Turner and his assigns....... |
| | Portia, Lewis .................... | | Samuel Penrose and his assigns...... |
| Jan. 18th... | Connell, George ................. | | John Pollard and his assigns........ |
| | Coupel, Anthoney ............... | | Matthew Potter and his executors.... |

## List of Indentures.

| Residence. | Occupation. | Term. | Amount. |
|---|---|---|---|
| Southwark | Apprentice, taught the cooper's trade, have six months' night schooling (note 1, or £8 in money). | 3 yrs. | |
| Providence twp., Phila. co. | Servant (note 2, besides their old). | 6 yrs. each.. | £50.0.0. |
| Philadelphia | Servant[3] | 9 yrs. | £13.0.0. |
| Philadelphia | Servant[3] | 3 yrs., 3 mo. | £22.0.0. |
| New York City, N. Y. | Servant | 11 yrs. | £15.0.0. |
| Northern Liberties, Phila. co. | Apprentice, taught to read in Bible, write a legible hand in English, housewifery, sew, knit and spin. | 7 yrs., 2 mo. 25 d. | |
| Philadelphia | Found meat, drink, washing and lodging, and have 20/ each and every month during the term.[3] | 1 yr. | 20 shillings per month. |
| Philadelphia | Servant | 8 yrs. | £15.0.0. |
| Philadelphia | Apprentice, taught the boat building trade, have two quarters' evening schooling, found meat, drink, washing, lodging and working apparel, and at expiration have one complete new suit of apparel. | 5 yrs., 5 mo. 16 d. | |
| Philadelphia | Apprentice, taught the boat builder's trade, have three quarters' evening schooling, found meat, drink, washing, lodging and working apparel, and at expiration have one complete new suit of apparel. | 5 yrs., 6 mo. 6 d. | |
| Philadelphia | Servant[3] | 2 yrs. | £15.0.0. |
| Augusta co., Va. | Servant[3] | 4 yrs. each.. | £12.0.0. for each of their uses. |
| Augusta co., Va. | Servant (note 2, besides his old).. | 2 yrs., 6 mo. | £8.0.0. |
| Tredyffrin, Chester co. | Servant[1] | 5 yrs., 3 mo. each. | £41.14.2. |
| Philadelphia | Apprentice, taught the business of shopkeeping, read, write and cypher through rule of 3.[2] | 3 yrs., 9 mo. | |
| Chester | Servant[1] | 3 yrs. | £13.0.0. |
| Philadelphia | Servant[3] | 4 yrs. | £14.0.0. |
| Philadelphia | Servant[3] | 3 yrs., 10 mo., 20 d. | £10.0.0. |
| Kingsess twp., Phila. co. | Servant (note 3, if he shall pay or cause to be paid to Samuel Penrose or assigns £9.10 on Sept. 10. 1774, this indenture shall be void and the said servant shall receive his freedom dues). | 3 yrs., 7 mo. 24 d. | £33.10.0. |
| Philadelphia | Apprentice, taught the trade of a house carver, to be found all necessaries except apparel, the two first years the master to give him two quarters' night schooling, one of which to be in the last year of his time.[6] | 5 yrs. | |
| Philadelphia | Apprentice, to serve either in Penna. or N. Jersey, taught the art of blacksmith.[3] | 3 yrs. | |

| Date. | Name. | From the Port of | To Whom Indentured. |
|---|---|---|---|
| 1773.<br>Jan. 18th... | Hurry, Arther | | John McCalla and his assigns |
| Jan. 19th... | Till, Elizabeth | | William Fisher and his assigns |
| | Mahony, Mary | | Charles White |
| | Wright, William | | Enoch Hughes and his assigns |
| | Meffert, John Conrad, Maria Dorothy, his wife, and Catherine, their daughter. | | Jacob Morgan, Jr., and his assigns |
| | Thorn, Samuel | | Joseph Marsh and his assigns |
| | Miffert, John Conrad, Mary Dorothy, his wife, and Anna Catherine, their daughter. | | Jacob Morgan, Esq., and his assigns |
| | Lutz, Jacob | | Jacob Rees and his assigns |
| | Zauch, Catherine | | John George Kemleaf and wife |
| Jan. 20th... | Dinges, Juliana | Rotterdam | David Bleid and his assigns |
| | Lepp, Michael | Rotterdam | Lawrence Lepp and his assigns |
| | Dorrington, William George | | Robert Parish and his assigns |
| Jan. 21st... | Feierabend, John | Rotterdam | Ludwig Kuhn and his assigns |
| Jan. 21st... | Coleman, Luke | | John Hiller and his assigns |
| | Job, John | | John White and his assigns |
| Jan. 22nd... | Scott, Christopher | | David Solomon and his assigns |

## List of Indentures.

| Residence. | Occupation. | Term. | Amount. |
|---|---|---|---|
| Philadelphia | Apprentice, taught the trade of a tailor, found meat, drink, lodging and washing. | 8 yrs., 9 mo. 12 d. | £25.0.0. paid to father or guardian an equal proportion to be paid yearly to find him in apparel. |
| Philadelphia | Apprentice, taught housewifery and sew, have six months' half day schooling.[3] | 4 yrs. | |
| Philadelphia | | 4 yrs. | £11.0.0. |
| Philadelphia | Apprentice, taught the painter's and glazier's business, have two quarters' night schooling.[3] | 5 yrs., 1 mo. 12 d. | |
| Philadelphia | Servant (note 1, and the man or his wife to have one two-year-old heifer, two sheep and four dollars). | 4 yrs. each | £40.9.9. |
| Southwark | Apprentice, taught the shipwright's trade, found meat, drink, washing and lodging and mending, and at expiration have the necessary working tools. | 5 yrs. | |
| Carnarven twp., Berks co. | | 7 yrs. | £40.9.9. |
| Philadelphia | Apprentice, taught the trade of a cedar cooper, have four quarters' night schooling, if the master should die the apprentice shall have liberty to choose himself a master.[3] | 7 yrs. | |
| Philadelphia | Apprentice, taught housewifery, sew, knit and spin, read and write (note 6, and £4 in cash). | 5 yrs., 11 mo., 15 d. | |
| | Servant[3] | 7 yrs. | £11.15.0. |
| Philadelphia | Servant[3] | 4 yrs. | £24.0.0. |
| Philadelphia | Apprentice, taught the trade of a wheat fan maker and plain maker, to be found all necessaries except washing, have four quarters' winter night schooling[6] | 8 yrs., 9 mo. 7 d. | |
| | Servant, if he causes to be paid during the term £21.0.9, the indenture to be void. | 4 yrs. | £21.0.9. |
| Philadelphia | Apprentice, to be taught the trade of a cooper, to be found all necessaries, his master to give him two quarters' night schooling. | 3 yrs. | |
| Passyunk, Phila. co. | Apprentice, taught the art of farming, read write and cypher as far as rule of 3 (note 3, or £10 in cash). | 17 yrs., 2 mo. | |
| Philadelphia | Apprentice, taught the cedar cooper's trade, read, write, and cypher through the rule of 3 (note 3, and a complete set of cooper's tools). | 4 yrs., 2 mo. 12 d. | |

| Date. | Name. | From the Port of | To Whom Indentured. |
|---|---|---|---|
| 1773. Jan. 22nd | Bell, Thomas | | George Claypoole and his assigns |
| | Mackzeinor, Eliza. Margt. | Rotterdam | William Bettle and his assigns |
| | Smith, Thomas | | Christel Bartling and his assigns |
| | Tracey, William | Rotterdam | John Kling and his assigns |
| | Mead, Jane | Ireland | Charles Risk and his assigns |
| | Mead, Jane (see record above). | | Robert Park and his assigns |
| | Hollman, George | | John Hollman and his assigns |
| | Sterch, Ludwig | | George Baker and his assigns |
| Jan. 23rd | Bakely, Daniel | | John Stall and his assigns |
| | Starch, Ludwig | | Henry Summers and his assigns |
| | Strawcutter, John | | Philip Worn |
| | Dawes, Elisha | | John Prish and his assigns |
| | Bendiker, James | | John Hide Coster and his assigns |
| Jan. 25th | Myers, John | | Richard Humphreys and his heirs |
| 1773. Jan. 26th | Hubnerin, Frederica Regina | | George Hidle and his assigns |
| | Catz, Jacob | | Martin Bisch and his assigns |
| | Sexin, Barbara | | John Wm. Hoffman and his assigns |
| | Ulrick, John Peter | | William Hoffman and his assigns |
| | Apps, John | | Richard Ham and his assigns |
| | Hudson, John | | William Singleton and wife |
| | Black, James | | Michael Brother and his assigns |
| Jan. 28th | Grub, Jacob | | Matthew Grimes and his assigns |
| | Bickerton, John | | Christian Rudolph and his assigns |
| | Armitage, Joseph | | Benjamin Armitage and his assigns |
| | Hall, Robert | | Robert Allison and his assigns |
| | Leech, Robert | | Robert Allison and his assigns |

## List of Indentures.

| RESIDENCE. | OCCUPATION. | TERM. | AMOUNT. |
|---|---|---|---|
| Philadelphia | Apprentice, taught the cabinet maker's trade, found meat, drink, washing, lodging and working apparel. | 5 yrs., 2 mo. 23 d. | |
| Northern Liberties | Servant, taught to read in the English Bible, allowed time to attend the minister for preparation to receive the sacrament.[3] | 7 yrs., 6 mo. | £13.2.3. |
| Philadelphia | Apprentice, taught the house carpenter's trade (note 1, to the value of £7). | 7 yrs., 11 d. | |
| Northern Liberties | Servant[1] | 5 yrs. | £21.15.0. |
| Philadelphia | Servant[3] | 3 yrs., 10 mo. | £15.0.0. |
| W. Caln twp., Chester co. | Servant | 3 yrs., 10 mo. | £15.0.0. |
| Plymouth twp., Phila. co. | Servant[5] | 2 yrs. | £6.12.0. |
| Norrington twp., Phila. co. | Servant[5] | 2 yrs., 6 mo. | £25.0.0. |
| Philadelphia | Apprentice, taught the art, trade and mystery of a coach harness maker and trimmer, have nine months' night schooling (note 1, to the value of £10, or £10 in money). | 4 yrs., 2 mo. 22 d. | |
| Northern Liberties, Phila. co. | Servant | 2 yrs., 6 mo. | £25.0.0. |
| Northern Liberties, Phila. co. | Apprentice, to learn blacksmith's art and trade, have four quarters' night schooling (note 1, or £10 in cash). | 6 yrs. | |
| Philadelphia | Apprentice | 6 yrs., 8 mo. 25 d. | £12. |
| Philadelphia | Apprentice, the master to give him six months' night schooling[3] | 4 yrs. | |
| Philadelphia | Apprentice, taught the trade of a silver smith, allowed time to go to evening school one month every winter the first three years, his friends paying the expense[3]. | 5 yrs., 5 mo. 25 d. | |
| Philadelphia | Servant | 3 yrs., 6 mo. | £9.2.3. |
| Philadelphia | Apprentice, taught the trade of a cordwainer, to read in the Dutch Bible, write a legible hand.[6] | 11 yrs., 2 mo., 6 d. | £6.0.0. |
| Philadelphia | | 3 yrs., 6 mo. | £21.8.0. |
| Durker Town, Lancaster co. | Servant[3] | 2 yrs., 11 mo. | £29.16.0. |
| Philadelphia | Apprentice, taught the art of a mariner.[3] | 3 yrs., 3 mo. 23 d. | |
| Southwark, Phila. co | Apprentice, taught the trade of a house carpenter, have one quarter night schooling every winter[3] | 3 yrs., 6 mo. | |
| Philadelphia | Apprentice, taught the silver smith's trade, read, write and cypher through rule of 3.[3] | 13 yrs., 8 mo., 21 d. | |
| Philadelphia | | 12 yrs., 11 mo. | £3.0.0. |
| Philadelphia | | 9 yrs., 1 mo. 3 w. | £3.0.0. |
| Bristol twp., Phila. co. | Apprentice | 4 yrs., 7 w. | £0.5. |
| Southwark | Apprentice, taught the house carpenter's trade, found meat, drink, washing and lodging only | 2 yrs. | |
| Southwark | Apprentice, taught the house carpenter's trade, time to go to evening school one quarter each | 5 yrs., 10 mo., 26 d. | |

| Date. | Name. | From the Port of | To Whom Indentured. |
|---|---|---|---|
| 1773. Jan. 29th | Neef, John David | Rotterdam | Casper Wister and his assigns |
| | Steel, Catherine | Rotterdam | Casper Wister and his assigns |
| | Chard, Rachel | | Thomas Bradford and his assigns |
| Jan. 30th | Grill, Charles Matthew | | John Musser and his assigns |
| Feb. 1st | Founder, Mary | | Andrew Summers and his assigns |
| | Knode, Jacob | | Godfrey Gebler and his assigns |
| Feb. 2nd | Chard, George | | Edward Wells and his assigns |
| | Mason, John | | Joseph Wood and his assigns |
| | Solcher, Stephen | | Christopher Ludwig and his assigns |
| | Mitchell, John | | John Lukins |
| | Hempbill, Christiana Frederica | Rotterdam | Samuel Rhoads, Jr., and his assigns |
| | Reinhold, Elizabeth | Rotterdam | Adam Hubley, Jr., and his assigns |
| | Reinhold, Elizabeth | | Henry Keppell and his assigns |
| | Humphreys, Gislin | | Thomas Redman and his heirs |
| Feb. 4th | Nusser, John Jacob | Rotterdam | William Frautwin and his assigns |
| | Inglebood, Anna Maria | Rotterdam | James Wallace and his assigns |
| | Inglebood, Anna Maria | | Daniel Clark and his assigns |
| | Braizer, Anthony Joseph | | Robert Hopkins, Jr., and his assigns |
| | Moser, Jacob, and Catherine, his wife. | Rotterdam | Jacob Dietrick and his assigns |
| | Hitz, Maria Barbara | Rotterdam | Christopher Dietrick and his assigns |
| | Hitz, Tobias | Rotterdam | Christopher Dietrick and his assigns |
| Feb. 5th | Rogers, Bridget | | Dr. Richard Farmer and his assigns |
| | Riddle, Richard | | John King |
| Feb. 6th | Izenminger, Nicholas | | John Reinhard and his assigns |
| | Scheller, George Frederick | | Lewis Brachl and his assigns |
| | Simmers, Joseph | | Peter Robison and his assigns |
| | Shibe, Casper | Rotterdam | George Kopper and his assigns |

## List of Indentures.

| RESIDENCE. | OCCUPATION. | TERM. | AMOUNT. |
|---|---|---|---|
| Kings co., New York | Servant (note 3, and provided he behaves himself faithfully in every respect, said master to give him $16.00). winter, and found meat, drink, washing, lodging and shoes only. | 5 yrs. | £24.15.6. |
| Kings co., New York | Servant (note 3, and provided she serves her time faithfully, the master to give her 3 half Johannes). | 6 yrs. | £27.0.0. |
| Philadelphia | Apprentice, taught housewifery, to sew, read in Bible, write a legible hand and cypher.[3] | 8 yrs., 1 mo. 10 d. | |
| Lancaster | | 3 yrs. | £15.0.0. |
| Philadelphia | Servant | 6 yrs. | £6.10.0. |
| Philadelphia | Apprentice, taught the blacksmith's trade, read in Bible, write a legible hand.[3] | 11 yrs., 6 mo. | |
| Philadelphia | Apprentice, taught the bricklayer's trade, read in Bible, write a legible hand and cypher through rule of 3.[3] | 13 yrs., 10 mo., 4 d. | |
| Philadelphia | Servant, found meat, drink, washing and lodging only. | 1 yr. | £1.5.0. |
| Philadelphia | Servant | 4 yrs., 6 mo. | £22.0.0. |
| Philadelphia | | 4 yrs. | £15.0.0. |
| Philadelphia | Servant, taught to read in Bible, write a legible hand.[3] | 9 yrs., 10 mo. | £12.0.0. |
| Philadelphia | Servant[3] | 4 yrs., 6 mo. | £30.0.0. |
| Philadelphia | Servant | 4 yrs., 6 mo. | £30.0.0. |
| Philadelphia | Apprentice, taught the trade of a tin plate worker, have seven quarters' night schooling.[3] | 10 yrs. | |
| Northern Liberties | Servant[3] | 4 yrs. | £24.19.6. |
| Philadelphia | Servant[3] | 5 yrs. | £22.0.0. |
| Maxfield, Bucks co. | Servant | 5 yrs. | £22.0.0. |
| Philadelphia | Apprentice | 5 yrs., 7 mo. | £10.0.0. |
| Waterford twp., Gloucester co., W. Jersey. | Servant[3] | 5 yrs. each. | £43.15.6. |
| Waterford twp., Gloucester co., W. Jersey. | Servant[3] | 3 yrs., 6 mo. | £12.0.0. |
| Waterford twp., Gloucester co., W. Jersey. | Servant, have six months' schooling.[3] | 13 yrs., 11 mo. | £13.0.0. |
| Philadelphia | Servant | 4 yrs. | £13.0.0. |
| Philadelphia | Apprentice, taught the house carpenter's trade and found meat, drink, washing and lodging, also to have two pair shoes, one pair of stockings every year. | 3 yrs. | |
| Southwark, Phila. co. | Apprentice, taught the trade of a house carpenter, have four quarters' night schooling.[3] | 3 yrs., 11 mo., 10 d. | |
| Philadelphia | Servant | 3 yrs., 6 mo. | £20.0.0. |
| Philadelphia | Apprentice, taught the cordwainer's trade, give him schooling to read and write a legible hand and cypher to the rule of 3, and three days every harvest, and a new suit of apparel and kit of tools in the last year.[5] | 11 yrs., 1 mo., 16 d. | |
| Philadelphia | Servant, have four quarters' night schooling (note 3, worth £10 money of Pa.). | 13 yrs. | £20.0.0. |

| Date. | Name. | From the Port of | To Whom Indentured. |
|---|---|---|---|
| 1773. Feb. 2nd | Moylan, Sarah | | Philip Worn and wife |
| Feb. 8th | Miller, Charles | Rotterdam | Matthias Meyer and his assigns |
| | Fritzin, Margaret Barbara | Rotterdam | Christian Derrick and his assigns |
| | Fritz, Johannes | Rotterdam | Christian Derrick and his assigns |
| | Larshin, Catherine | Rotterdam | Lawrence Upman and his assigns |
| | Larshin, Maria Elizabeth | Rotterdam | Lawrence Upman and his assigns |
| | May, John | | Samuel Read and his assigns |
| Feb. 9th | Downs, Michael | | Robert Magill and his assigns |
| | Kelly, Margaret | | Daniel King and his assigns |
| | Mageath, John | | John Hannah |
| | Fenn, Elinor | | Charles Mayn and his assigns |
| | Troy, Daniel | | Gamalion Garrison and his assigns |
| | Newman, Richard | | Stephen Shewell and his assigns |
| Feb. 11th | Harper, Jacob | | Christopher Bink and his assigns |
| | McClure, John | | William Green and his heirs |
| Feb. 12th | Kemp, Henry William | Rotterdam | John Williamson and his assigns |
| | Maglathery, James | | William Robinson and his assigns |
| | Meyeria, Anna Margt | Rotterdam | John Sowder and his assigns |
| | Krammer, Jacob | | Hugh Henry and his assigns |
| | Slour, John | | John Pyle and his assigns |
| Feb. 13th | Downs, Michael | | Foster McConnell and his assigns |
| | Finley, Mary | | George Beuner and his assigns |
| | Evans, Williams | | John Watkins and wife |
| | Weiargan, Patrick | | Philip Moore and his assigns |
| | McDonald, Marion | | Robert Lumsden and his assigns |
| | Gosshaw, Gabriel | | John Inglis and his assigns |
| Feb. 15th | Turner, Neil | | Leonard Tweid and his assigns |
| | Caldwell, Michael | | Thomas Bond, Jr., and his assigns |

[1] To be found all necessaries and at the expiration have freedom dues.
[2] To be found all necessaries and at the expiration have one new suit of apparel.
[3] To be found all necessaries and at the expiration have two complete suits of apparel, one whereof to be new.

## List of Indentures.

| Residence. | Occupation. | Term. | Amount. |
|---|---|---|---|
| Northern Liberties, Phila. co. | Apprentice, taught housewifery, sew, knit and spin, read in Bible, write a legible hand.[3] | 8 yrs., 8 mo. 20 d. | |
| Philadelphia | Servant[8] | 5 yrs., 10 mo., 20 d. | £ 38. 12. 9. |
| Moyamensing twp., Phila. co. | Servant, have one year's schooling[3] | 10 yrs. | £ 4. 0. 0. |
| Moyamensing twp., Phila. co. | Servant, taught to read in Bible, write a legible hand and cypher[3] | 17 yrs. | £ 3. 0. 0. |
| Northern Liberties, Phila. co. | Servant[3] | 5 yrs., 9 mo. | £ 29. 11. 8. |
| Northern Liberties | Servant[3] | 5 yrs., 9 mo. | £ 29. 11. 8. |
| Philadelphia | Apprentice, taught to pull and cut fur, color and finish hats, read, write and cypher.[3] | 7 yrs., 3 mo. 20 d. | |
| Philadelphia | Servant | 4 yrs. | £ 14. 0. 0. |
| Philadelphia | Servant[3] | 2 yrs., 10 mo., 23 d. | £ 11. 0. 0. |
| | Servant | 3 yrs., 5 mo. 18 d. | £ 8. 0. 0. |
| Philadelphia | Servant | 5 yrs. | £ 6. 0. 0. |
| Manaten Precinct, Salem co. | Servant | 4 yrs. | £ 16. 0. 0. |
| Philadelphia | Apprentice, taught the biscuit baking business, have four quarters' night schooling, to go to sea the last eighteen months of his time and taught navigation (note 2, besides his old). | 5 yrs., 6 mo. | £ 10. 0. 0. |
| Philadelphia | Apprentice taught the trade of a sadler, found meat, drink, lodging only during the first three years of his time and all necessaries during the last three years, to be allowed time to go to night school four quarters' in the term, he choosing his own time in the term. | 6 yrs. | |
| Philadelphia | Apprentice, taught the trade of a house carpenter, have two winters' night schooling.[5] | 5 yrs., 11 21 d. | |
| Burlington twp., Burlington co., W. Jersey. | Servant[3] | 4 yrs. | £ 26. |
| Philadelphia | Apprentice, taught the tailor's trade, have three months' evening schooling.[3] | 5 yrs., 10 mo., 15 d. | |
| Philadelphia | Servant[3] | 6 yrs. | £ 22. 10. 0. |
| Philadelphia | | 6 yrs., 3 mo. | £ 20. 0. 0. |
| Brandywine Hundred, N. Castle co. | Servant (note 2, besides his old) | 3 yrs. | £ 23. 0. 0. |
| Philadelphia | | 4 yrs. | £ 12. 0. 0. |
| Middle Town twp., Bucks co. | | 5 yrs., 9 mo. | £ 7. 0. 0. |
| Warminster twp., Bucks co. | Apprentice, taught the house carpenter's trade, have five months' day schooling (note 3, and a set of bench tools). | 3 yrs., 6 mo. 20 d. | |
| Philadelphia | Apprentice | 5 yrs., 6 mo. | £ 8. 0. 0. |
| Philadelphia | Servant | 4 yrs. | £ 6. 16. 0. |
| Philadelphia | Servant | 4 yrs. | £ 22. 0. 0. |
| Northern Liberties | Apprentice | 3 yrs. | £ 10. 0. 0. |
| Philadelphia | Servant, found meat, drink, washing, lodging and have 20/ per month during the term, 15 shil- | 1 yr. | £ 20. 0. 0. |

[4] To be found all necessaries and at the expiration have two complete suits of apparel, one whereof to be new, and 40s. in money.

[5] At expiration have two complete suits of apparel, one whereof to be new.

| Date. | Name. | From the Port of | To Whom Indentured. |
|---|---|---|---|
| 1773. Feb. 15th | Funks, Hannah | | Archibald McIllroy and his assigns.. |
| | Vanwrinckle, John | | Thos. Darrah |
| | Shrunk, George | | Christopher Zimmerman and his assigns. |
| | Kemble, Samuel, Jr. | | Tench Francis and Tench Tilghman. |
| Feb. 16th | Cooke, Philip | | Daniel Barnes and his assigns |
| | Campble Eleanor | | Arthur Campble |
| | Peacock, Jane | | William Bispham and his assigns |
| | Patterson, Mary | | John Burley and wife |
| Feb. 17th | Binder, Jacob | | George Hey and his assigns |
| | McDonald, Marion | | James Biddle and his assigns |
| Feb. 18th | Fitchet, Rebecca | | Edward Bonsall and his assigns |
| | Lawerswyler, Barnet, Jr. | | Jacob Schreiner and his assigns |
| | O'Conner, Charles | | James Starr and his assigns |
| Feb. 19th | Naglee, Joseph | | John Naglee and his assigns |
| | Myardie, Barbara | | John Ellet and his assigns |
| | Thomas, James | | John Moyer and wife |
| | Fitzgerald, Mary | | William Moore and his assigns |
| | Carins, John | | Thomas Thompson and his assigns |
| Feb. 20th | McKay, Margaret | | Jedediah Snowden and his assigns |
| | Downs, Michael | | Finley McDonnall and his assigns |
| Feb. 22nd | Gordon, Henry | | William Haslewood |
| | Treicle, Jonathan | Rotterdam | John Philips and his assigns |
| | Simeda, Anthony | | Anthony Pettan |
| Feb. 23rd | Reineck, Ludwig | | John Soltar and his assigns |
| | Bower, John | | Morris Freeman and his assigns |
| Feb. 24th | Kilpert, Christian | | Jacob Kilpert and his assigns |
| | Keen, Grace | | James Tompson |

## List of Indentures.

| Residence. | Occupation. | Term. | Amount. |
|---|---|---|---|
| | lings per month to be given in apparel. | | |
| Philadelphia | Apprentice | 5 yrs., 14 d. | £ 3. 18. 6. |
| Philadelphia | Apprentice, to learn the art of a sadler and harness maker, have three months' night schooling.[3] | 3 yrs., 5 mo. 19 d. | |
| Northern Liberties | Apprentice, taught the cordwainer's trade, read in Bible and write a legible hand (note 2, of the value of £ 10, or £ 10). | 5 yrs., 3 mo. | |
| Philadelphia | Apprentice, taught the art and mystery of a merchant and book-keeping, found meat, drink and lodging. | 2 yrs., 6 mo. | |
| Philadelphia | Servant, to be employed at and learn the bricklayer's trade.[3] | 3 yrs. | £ 9. 0. 0. |
| | | The residue of her indenture. | |
| Philadelphia | Apprentice | 12 yrs., 4 mo. | £ 10. 0. 0. |
| Upper Maxfield twp., Bucks co. | Apprentice, taught housewifery, to sew.[a] | 1 yr., 11 mo. | |
| Philadelphia | Apprentice, taught the skinners and breeches maker's business, have nine months' English night schooling.[3] | 5 yrs. | |
| Southwark | Servant (note 3, and £ 3 lawful money of Pa., besides freedom) | 3 yrs., 7 mo. 18 d. | £ 6. 16. 0. |
| Philadelphia | Apprentice, taught housewifery and to sew, have one quarter's schooling.[3] | 1 yr., 9 mo. | |
| Philadelphia | Apprentice, taught the trade of a leather dresser and found meat, drink, washing and lodging. | 3 yrs., 8 mo. 2 w. | |
| Philadelphia | | 2 yrs., 4 mo. | £ 4. 0. 0. |
| Philadelphia | Apprentice | 10 yrs., 4 mo., 14 d. | £ 5. 0. 0. |
| Philadelphia | | 7 yrs. | £ 30. 0. 0. |
| Northern Liberties | Apprentice, taught the joiner's trade, have four quarters' evening schooling.[3] | 5 yrs., 9 mo. | |
| Philadelphia | Servant | 4 yrs. | £ 10. 0. 0. |
| Southwark | Servant | 1 yr., 6 mo. | £ 10. 0. 0. |
| Philadelphia | Apprentice, taught housewifery and sew, to read in Bible and write a legible hand.[3] | 11 yrs., 6 mo. | |
| Southwark | Servant, have one decent suit of clothes to be worn only on Sundays.[3] | 3 yrs., 10 mo., 10 d. | £ 5. 0. 0. |
| Philadelphia | Apprentice, taught the comb maker's trade (note 1, to the value of £ 10). | 3 yrs., 2 mo. | |
| Philadelphia | Servant, have two quarters' schooling.[3] | 4 yrs., 9 mo. 1 d. | £ 12. 0. 0. |
| | Servant | 12 yrs. | £ 45. 0. 0. |
| Philadelphia | Servant[3] | 5 yrs., 10 mo., 15 d. | £ 28. 0. 0. |
| Philadelphia | Apprentice, taught the paper maker's business, read in Bible, write a legible hand, cypher through rule of 3.[3] | 9 yrs., 1 mo. 22 d. | |
| Germantown twp., Phila. co. | Servant | 3 yrs., 6 mo. | £ 25. 5. 3. |
| Oxford twp., Phila. co. | Apprentice[3] | 4 yrs., 6 mo. | |

| DATE. | NAME. | FROM THE PORT OF | TO WHOM INDENTURED. |
|---|---|---|---|
| 1773. Feb. 24th | Winters, James | | Robert Wickersham and wife |
| Feb. 27th | Clark, John | | Michael Schwarts and his assigns |
| | Simmerman, Henry | | Rudolph Huber and his assigns |
| | Bryan, Mary | | Joseph Richardson and his assigns |
| | Altimus, David | | Rudolph Neff and his assigns |
| Mar. 1st | Barry, Michael | | John Hall and his assigns |
| | Farrel, Michael | | John Smith and his assigns |
| | Robinson, John | | Joseph Moore and his assigns |
| | Cook, Philip | | John Buckingham and his assigns |
| | Wilson, Alexander | | George Falker |
| | Rowland, John | | John Parrish and his assigns |
| | Hamilton, John | | Henry Hill and his assigns |
| Mar. 3rd | Lutz, Leonard | | Henry Kurtz and his assigns |
| | Statebach Christopher | | Alexander Greenwood and his heirs |
| | Hall, James | | Levy Masks and his assigns |
| | Geary, John | | Francis Trumble and his assigns |
| | Bedly, Elizabeth | | John Philips and his assigns |
| Mar. 4th | Hall, Margaret | | Robert Thomas and his assigns |
| | Hallowell, Ann | | Peter Sutter and his assigns |
| | Lear, Adam | | John Creus |
| Mar. 5th | Frider, John | | Christian Fess and his assigns |
| | Hubneun, Frederica Regina | | Rosina Henizen and her assigns |
| | Trapple, Jacob | | Jacob Vansciver |

## List of Indentures.

| Residence. | Occupation. | Term. | Amount. |
|---|---|---|---|
| Blockley twp., Phila. co......... | Apprentice, taught the art of a farmer, have four quarters' schooling in the third and fourth years of his apprenticeship (note 3, and £17 lawful money of Pa.) | 6 yrs., 1 mo. 11 d. | |
| Plumstead, Bucks co............. | | 1 yr........ | £ 8.0.0. |
| Philadelphia ................... | | 4 yrs....... | £ 22.0.0. |
| Providence twp., Phila. co....... | | 4 yrs....... | £ 13.0.0. |
| Oxford twp., Phila. co.......... | Apprentice, taught the wheel wright's trade (note 2, besides his old). | 3 yrs., 4 mo. 1 d. | |
| Philadelphia ................... | | 4 yrs....... | £ 16.0.0. |
| Radnor twp., Chester co......... | | 2 yrs., 6 mo. | £ 10.0.0. |
| Philadelphia ................... | Apprentice, taught the cordwainer's trade (note 5, and have £ 5) | 4 yrs., 8 mo. | |
| Northern Liberties ............. | Servant[3] ....................... | 2 yrs., 11 15 d. | £ 9.0.0. |
| Philadelphia ................... | Apprentice, have six months' night schooling (note 3, and a kit of tools). | 3 yrs., 11 mo., 24 d. | |
| Philadelphia ................... | Apprentice, taught the bricklayer's trade, have one quarter's evening schooling.[3] | 3 yrs., 6 mo. | |
| Philadelphia ................... | Servant, found meat, drink and lodging. | 3 yrs....... | £ 24.0.0. paid him annually. |
| Philadelphia ................... | Apprentice, taught the tailor's trade, have two quarters' night schooling.[3] | 5 yrs., 4 mo. 27 d. | |
| Philadelphia ................... | Apprentice, taught the cordwainer's trade taught to read in Bible and write a legile hand.[3] | 8 yrs., 9 mo. | |
| Philadelphia ................... | Servant, to be employed in the tailor's business (note 3, and £ 3 in cash). | 15 mo. | |
| Southwark .................... | Servant[5] ....................... | 1 yr........ | £ 10.0.0. |
| Philadelphia ................... | Servant, have two quarters' schooling, and when free £ 4 in cash, a good sheep, a spinning wheel and legal freedom dues (note 1, and £ 4 in money). | 5 yrs., 10 mo. | £ 6.0.0. |
| Upper Hanover twp., Phila. co... | | 15 yrs. | |
| Philadelphia ................... | Apprentice, taught housewifery, to sew, read in Bible and write a legible hand, the master not to dispose of the apprentice out of the city without the consent of the mother.[3] | 11 yrs. | |
| Philadelphia ................... | Apprentice, taught the art of a blacksmith, have three quarters' day schooling (note 3, or £ 12 in cash). | 6 yrs., 9 mo. 23 d. | |
| Philadelphia ................... | Apprentice, taught the trade of a Dutch fan maker.[3] | 4 yrs. | |
| Northern Liberties, Phila. co.... | Servant[5] ....................... | 1 yr., 6 mo. | £ 9.2.3. |
| Northern Liberties ............. | Apprentice, taught cordwainer's trade, have one quarter's night schooling in the first year, one quarter in the fourth and two quarters' in the last year, and if the master shall want to dispose of said apprentice, he shall have the liberty to choose himself a master.[3] | | |

| Date. | Name. | From the Port of | To Whom Indentured. |
|---|---|---|---|
| 1773. | White, Jane | | Thomas Church and his assigns...... |
| Mar. 6th... | Castill, Frederic, Doyer, Francis; Treper, Zetman; Bildsteur, Francis. | Lisbon ..... | William Hasleton, Sr., and his assigns. |
| | Brindle, Barbary | | Conrad Weaver and his assigns...... |
| | Thomasin, Anna Margaret | | Adam Mulladore and his assigns.... |
| | Wilkinson, William | | Thomas Paul and wife.............. |
| | McAfee, Isaac | | James Armitage and his heirs....... |
| | Wagg, John | | Michael Brothers and his assigns.... |
| Mar. 8th... | Smith, William | | Samuel Richards and his assigns..... |
| | Tuncks, William | | Archibald McIlroy and his assigns... |
| Mar. 9th... | Creemer, John | Rotterdam.. | John Souder and his assigns......... |
| | Creemer, Maria Magdalena. | Rotterdam.. | John Souder and his assigns......... |
| Mar. 10th.. | Campbell, John | | Philip Jacobs and his assigns........ |
| Mar. 11th.. | Onongst, Elizabeth | | Martin Weis and his assigns........ |
| | Isherd, Abel | | Thomas Stroud .................... |
| Mar. 13th.. | Shoemaker, Robert | | Jonathan Delworth and his assigns... |
| | Murray, William | | Alexander Henderson and his assigns. |
| | McGlocklin, Edward | | John Cox and his assigns............ |
| | Connoly, Terrance | | Christopher Dietrick and his assigns.. |
| | Raine, Nathaniel | | Jacob Godshalk, his heirs and assigns. |

## List of Indentures.

| Residence. | Occupation. | Term. | Amount. |
|---|---|---|---|
| Limerick twp., Phila. co. | Servant | 3 yrs., 3 mo. | £13.0.0. |
| In the three lower counties on Delaware. | Servant[3] | 4 yrs. each. | £20.0.0. |
| Bristol twp., Phila. co. | Apprentice, taught housewifery, to read and write well (note 3, and £5 in cash). | 7 yrs., 11 mo., 18 d. | |
| Passyunk twp., Phila. co. | Servant | 4 yrs., 6 mo. | £25.0.0. |
| Lower Dublin twp., Phila. co. | Apprentice, taught the art of a farmer, read in Bible, write a legible hand and cypher as far as rule of 3, master not to take him out of Phila. co. without the consent of his mother.[3] | 14 yrs., 2 mo., 29 d. | |
| Southwark, Phila. co. | Apprentice, taught the trade of a house carpenter, found all necessaries except six pair shoes which his father is to send him. | 4 yrs. | |
| Philadelphia | Apprentice, taught the trade of a silver smith, have three quarters' night schooling (note 5, have £6 lawful money of Pa. in lieu of freedom dues). | 4 yrs., 2 mo. 24 d. | |
| Philadelphia | Apprentice, taught the cordwainer's trade.[3] | 3 yrs., 6 mo. | £15.0.0. |
| Philadelphia | Apprentice, taught the peruke maker and hair dresser's trade, read, write and cypher as far as rule of 3.[6] | 11 yrs., 7 mo., 26 d. | |
| Deerfield twp., Cumberland co., N. J. | Servant (note 3, worth £10, or £10 lawful money of Pa.). | 4 yrs. | £24.2.6. |
| Deerfield twp., Cumberland co., N. J. | Servant, taught to read well in Bible and write a legible hand[3]. | 12 yrs., 9 mo. | £8.5.3. |
| Racoon Creek, Jersey | Servant[5] | 3 mo. | £1.5.0. |
| Philadelphia | Apprentice, taught the trade of a leather breeches maker, have three month' English day schooling.[3] | 3 yrs. | |
| Brandywine Hundred, N. Castle co. | Apprentice, taught the business of a waterman (note 1, and £5 in cash). | 2 yrs. | 40/. |
| Philadelphia | Apprentice, taught the business of a house carpenter, found meat, drink, washing and lodging, shirts and stockings and when free a cloth coat, vest and breeches and a hat. | 4 yrs., 3 mo. | |
| Philadelphia | Apprentice, taught the art of a mariner and navigation, read in Bible, write a legible hand.[3] | 10 yrs. | |
| Philadelphia | Apprentice, taught the art of navigation, read in Bible, write a legible hand and cypher, and at expiration of the term give him freedom dues). | 5 yrs. | |
| Waterford twp., Glocester co., N. Jersey. | Servant, to be found meat, drink, washing, lodging, one shirt, one pair trousers, one pair shoes, one pair stockings. | 3 mo., 2 w. | 20 s. |
| Philadelphia | Apprentice, taught art of clock making, give him one month's night schooling every year, the father paying for the schooling | 4 yrs., 6 mo. 5 d. | |

| Date. | Name. | From the Port of | To Whom Indentured. |
|---|---|---|---|
| 1773. Mar. 15th | Cruise, Thomas | Ireland | Richard Porter and his assigns |
| | Magrath, John | | Cornelius Cooper and his assigns |
| Mar. 16th | Campbell, Margaret | | William Bonham and his assigns |
| | Nourse, Joseph | | Amas Shettde |
| Mar. 16th | Campbell, James | | Andrew Philler and his assigns |
| | Maag, Henry | | Thomas Search and his assigns |
| | McCanly, Elizabeth | | Thomas Leiper and his assigns |
| | Hymen, Mary | | Christian Detterer and his assigns |
| | Albright, John Frederick | | John Zeller |
| | Burman, Mary | | Rachel McCollough and her assigns |
| | Burman, Rachel | | Rachel McCollough |
| | Folckin, Maria Elizabeth | | John Sommers |
| | Ferguson, Margaret | | James Pyat and his assigns |
| Mar. 18th | McConnaghill, Neil | | John Marshall and his assigns |
| Mar. 19th | Everding, Catherine | Rotterdam | Jacob Dietrick and his assigns |
| Mar. 20th | Heysham, Wm. Postlethwait | | Capt. John Souder |
| | Pamlerine, Anna Maria | | Mathias Keen and his assigns |
| Mar. 22nd | Fitzgerald, Thomas | | Martin Noll and wife, Elizabeth |
| | Griffin, Joanna | | Archibald Gardner and his assigns |
| | Freile, Frederick | | William Murray and his assigns |
| Mar. 23rd | Land, Samuel | | Gunsring Bedford and his assigns |

## List of Indentures.

| Residence. | Occupation. | Term. | Amount. |
|---|---|---|---|
| | (note 5, a complete suit of common working apparel). | | |
| Philadelphia | Servant[5] | 1 yr., 8 mo., 19 d. | £ 7. 10. 0. |
| Philadelphia | Servant | 3 yrs., 5 mo. 18 d. | £ 11. 10. 0. |
| Philadelphia | Apprentice, taught housewifery and sew, read in Bible, write a legible hand.[3] | 8 yrs., 1 mo. | |
| Philadelphia | Apprentice, taught the trade of a merchant, found all necessaries, except clothing, and at end of sixteen months pay him £ 20 and at the end of the term the further sum of £ 20. | 2 yrs., 4 mo. | |
| Philadelphia | Apprentice, taught the cordwainer's trade, read in Bible, write a legible hand and cypher as far as rule of 3.[2] | 10 yrs., 6 mo., 20 d. | |
| Southwark | Apprentice, taught the wheelwright's trade, found meat, drink, washing, lodging, shoes, stockings and working shirts, and his step-father to find him his other apparel. | 10 mo., 13 d. | |
| Philadelphia | Apprentice, taught housewifery and sew, read in Bible (note 3, and 40/ in money). | 4 yrs., 7 mo. 15 d. | |
| Rock Hill twp., Bucks co. | Servant | 4 yrs., 6 mo. | £ 25. 12. 6. |
| | Servant, the said Zeller acquits and discharges said Albright from his indenture of servitude 21st April, 1772. Said servant now being in perfect health. | | £ 16. 0. 0. |
| Philadelphia | Apprentice, taught housewifery, sew, read in Bible, write a legible hand and cypher.[3] | 8 yrs., 5 mo. | |
| Philadelphia | Apprentice, taught housewifery sew, read in Bible, write a legible hand and cypher.[3] | 10 yrs., 10 mo., 18 d. | |
| Manor of Moorland, Phila. co. | | 5 yrs. | £ 28. 0. 0. |
| Derby twp., Chester co. | | 2 yrs., 11 mo., 20 d. | £ 8. 0. 0. |
| Moyamensing twp., Phila. co. | Servant, found meat, drink, washing, lodging and one jacket, one shirt, one pair trousers, one pair stockings and one pair shoes. | 4 mo. | £ 0. 15. 6. |
| Philadelphia | Servant[3] | 6 yrs. | £ 12. 0. 0. |
| Philadelphia | Apprentice, taught the art and mystery of a mariner and navigator, and found meat, drink, washing and lodging only. | 4 yrs. | |
| Oxford twp., Phila. co. | | 5 yrs., 3 mo. | £ 18. 10. 0. |
| Philadelphia | Apprentice, taught the baker's business, have two winters' evening schooling.[8] | 2 yrs., 11 mo., 9 d. | £ 10. 0. 0. |
| Philadelphia | | 4 yrs. | £ 10. 0. 0. |
| Caskaskey, in the Illinois | Servant | 4 yrs. | £ 12. 0. 0. |
| Philadelphia | Apprentice, taught house carpenter's trade and found meat, drink, washing and lodging, allowed time to go to school evenings each winter, the mother paying the expense of schooling, | 6 yrs., 2 mo. 28 d. | |

| Date. | Name. | From the Port of | To Whom Indentured. |
|---|---|---|---|
| 1773. Mar. 23rd.. | Bowers, William | | Daniel Evans |
| | Venall, James | | Francis Trumble and his assigns |
| | Habackin, Ann Elizabeth.... | | Michael Steetz |
| Mar. 24th.. | Coleman, Luke | | Casper Schnyder and his assigns |
| | Clarke, Joseph, Jr.. | | Jonathan Evans and his heirs |
| | Souder, John | | Matthias Gilbert and his assigns |
| Mar. 25th.. | Hamcher, John | Rotterdam.. | Sarah Davis and her assigns |
| | Hamcher, Mary Elizabeth... | Rotterdam.. | John Duffield |
| | Bartholomew, George | | John Hood and his assigns |
| | Lepp, Michael | | Frederick Frailey and his assigns |
| Mar. 26th.. | Gilbert, Nicholas | | Casper Muratt |
| Mar. 27th.. | Cline, Theobald | | William McIlvain and his assigns |
| | Bignal, John | | Jesses Williamson and his assigns |
| | Featherman, Charles Frederick. | Rotterdam.. | Valentine Standley and his assigns |
| Mar. 29th.. | Riggen, Charles | | Alexander Rutherford and his assigns. |
| | Thompson, George | | Philip Hayd and his assigns |
| | Buxton, Grace | | Joseph Coffer and his assigns |
| | Asfler, Godfrey | | Jacob Biduman and his assigns |
| | Reineck, Maria Elizabeth.... | | John Shea and his assigns |
| Mar. 30th.. | Fisher, Anna Spess | Rotterdam.. | George Frederick Boyer and his assigns. |
| | Thomas, Arthur | | Joseph Carr and his assigns |
| Mar. 31st.. | Miller, John | | John Bigler and his assigns |
| | Hyams, Emanuel | | John Henry and his assigns |
| April 1st... | Cotter, James | | Henry Weaver and his assigns |
| | Hempel, Charles Gotleib | | Martin Weis and his assigns |
| April 2nd... | Butler, John | | Anthony Fortune and his assigns |

## List of Indentures.

| RESIDENCE. | OCCUPATION. | TERM. | AMOUNT. |
|---|---|---|---|
| | and also allowed one week twice each year to go to see his mother | | |
| Philadelphia | Apprentice | 8 yrs. | £ 3. 10. 0. |
| Southwark | Apprentice, taught the trade of a windsor chair maker, have four quarters' evening schooling, serve the additional term above the age of 21 years on condition of being taught the above trade[1]. | 4 yrs. | £ 10. 0. 0. |
| Back Creek Hundred, Cecil co., Md. | | 4 yrs., 6 mo. | £ 17. 0. 0. |
| Philadelphia | | 3 yrs. | £ 3. 0. 0. |
| Philadelphia | Apprentice, taught the cooper's trade, have four quarters' night schooling.[2] | 5 yrs., 2 mo. | |
| Philadelphia | Apprentice, taught the potter's trade (note 3, worth £ 10 Pa. currency, or £ 10 in money). | 3 yrs., 6 mo. | |
| Slow Creek Precinct, Cumberland co., W. Jersey. | Servant, the mistress to find and provide meat, drink, washing, lodging and apparel for his son, Jacob Hamcher.[3] | 5 yrs. | £ 21. 1. 6. |
| Philadelphia | Servant[3] | 11 yrs., 6 mo. | £ 8. 0. 0. |
| Philadelphia | Apprentice, taught the trade of silk and stuff shoemaker, have four quarters' evening schooling[1] | 6 yrs., 6 mo. | |
| Philadelphia | | 4 yrs. | £ 24. 0. 0. |
| Philadelphia | Apprentice, taught the trade of a chaise maker, found meat, drink, washing, lodging and working apparel, have five months' evening schooling, and at expiration have £ 10 lawful money of Pa., allowed two weeks each year to go and see his parents. | 2 yrs., 10 mo. | |
| Philadelphia | Servant, taught the tailor's trade[1]. | 4 yrs. | £ 18. 0. 0. |
| Philadelphia | Servant, taught bookkeeping and merchant's accounts. | 9 yrs., 3 mo. 15 d. | |
| Philadelphia | Servant[3] | 4 yrs. | £ 22. 17. 0. |
| Philadelphia | | 6 yrs., 1 mo. | £ 2. 0. 0. |
| Philadelphia | Apprentice, taught the tailor's trade, read in Bible, write a legible hand and cypher through rule of 3.[3] | 8 yrs., 6 mo. | |
| Gloucester, Gloucester co., W. Jersey. | Apprentice, taught housewifery, sew, knit and spin, read in Bible, write a legible hand.[1] | 3 yrs., 6 mo. | |
| Northern Liberties | | 2 yrs. | £ 10. 0. 0. |
| Philadelphia | Servant[3] | 5 yrs., 9 mo. 13 d. | £ 24. 0. 0. |
| Philadelphia | Servant, have six months' schooling and freedom dues. | 11 yrs. | £ 8. 0. 0. |
| Philadelphia | | 7 yrs. | £ 10. 0. 0. |
| Philadelphia | | 4 yrs., 6 mo. | £ 18. 0. 0. |
| Philadelphia | Servant[5] | 1 yr. | £ 2. 0. 0. |
| Strasburg twp., Lancaster co. | Servant (note 1, and £ 30 current money of Pa.). | | £ 30. 0. 0. |
| Philadelphia | | 5 yrs., 6 mo. | £ 40. 0. 0. |
| Philadelphia | Servant, found meat, drink, washing and lodging, and paid 20/ each month during the term. | 6 mo. | £ 20. 0. 0. |

| Date. | Name. | From the Port of | To Whom Indentured. |
|---|---|---|---|
| 1773. April 2ᵈ... | Davis, William | | John Quick and his assigns |
| | Brown, Richard | | Richard Mason and his assigns |
| | Garret, Robert | | Benjamin Griffith and his assigns |
| | Quill, Thomas | | James Wilson |
| April 3ʳᵈ... | Collis, John | | David Ware and his assigns |
| | Hempel, Charles Godleib | | David Shaver and his assigns |
| | Sheppard, John | | Richard Inkson |
| April 5ᵗʰ... | Awalt, Jacob | | Frederick Walter |
| | Winey, Juliana | | William Moulder and his assigns |
| | West, James | | Thomas Hough and his assigns |
| | Arnell, William, Jr. | | John Piles and his heirs |
| | Rogers, Thomas | | Jacob Young and his assigns |
| | Reeburg, William | | Thomas Redman |
| | Roark, Henry | | Jnotham Adams and his assigns |
| | Schenediffer, Hans George, and Dorothy, his wife. | | Gilbert Rodman and his assigns |
| | Schenediffer, Adam | | Gilbert Rodman and his assigns |
| April 5ᵗʰ... | Schenediffer, Anna Maria | | Gilbert Rodman and his assigns |
| April 6ᵗʰ... | Albert, John, Jr. | | John Reidle and his assigns |
| April 7ᵗʰ... | Owen, Griffith | | Jacob Godshalk, his heirs and assigns. |

## List of Indentures.

| Residence. | Occupation. | Term. | Amount. |
|---|---|---|---|
| Oxford twp., Sussex co., W. Jersey. | Servant[5] | 6 mo. | 11/. |
| Northern Liberties | Apprentice, taught the trade of a cabinet maker, have two quarters' evening schooling, found meat, drink, washing, lodging and shoes, and at expiration freedom dues. Not to be assigned to any one but with consent of his father or himself. | 5 yrs., 7 mo. | |
| Southwark, Phila. co | Apprentice, taught the bricklayer's trade, a quarter's night schooling every winter.[3] | 5 yrs. | |
| Pequea, Lancaster co | | 4 yrs. | £ 10. 10. 0. |
| Philadelphia | Apprentice | 10 yrs. | £ 0. 5. 0. |
| Philadelphia | Servant | 5 yrs., 6 mo. | £ 40. 0. 0. |
| Philadelphia | Apprentice, taught the art and mystery of a mariner and navigation.[1] | 9 yrs. | |
| Philadelphia | Apprentice, taught the bricklayer's trade, have two quarters' evening schooling, said apprentice is not the Hodd (note 1, to value of £ 10 lawful money of Pa.). | 3 yrs. | |
| Philadelphia | | 11 yrs., 6 mo. | £ 15. 0. 0. |
| Philadelphia | Apprentice, taught the cooper's trade, found meat, drink, mending and washing and allowed time to go to evening school three winters, his guardian paying the expense of schooling, who is also to diet said apprentice on Sundays. | 5 yrs., 4 mo. 7 d. | |
| Philadelphia | Apprentice, taught the house carpenter's trade, found meat, drink, washing, lodging and working apparel, have six months' schooling and allowed two weeks each year to go and see his parents, also allowed time to go to evening school one year, his father paying the expense of the schooling, who is likewise to find him Sunday apparel. | 4 yrs., 7 mo. 1 w. | |
| Philadelphia | Apprentice, taught the weaver's trade, read in Bible, write a legible hand and cypher as far as rule of 3 (note 1, to the value or £ 10 lawful money of Pa.). | 13 yrs., 5 mo., 22 d. | |
| Philadelphia | Apprentice, taught the tin plater's trade, have two quarters' night schooling.[5] | 4 yrs. | |
| Philadelphia | Servant (note 2, or £ 7 lawful money of Pa.). | 2 yrs. | £ 4. 0. 0. |
| Bensalem twp., Bucks co | Servant | 5 yrs. | £ 27. 0. 0. |
| Bensalem twp., Bucks co | Servant | 19 yrs. | £ 1. 0. 0. |
| Bensalem twp., Bucks co | Servant | 14 yrs. | £ 2. 0. 0. |
| Philadelphia | Apprentice | 8 yrs., 27 d. | £ 15. 0. 0. |
| Philadelphia | Apprentice, taught the clock maker's trade, have one months' evening schooling each year.[2] | 7 yrs. | |

| Date. | Name. | From the Port of | To Whom Indentured. |
|---|---|---|---|
| 1773. | Sadleigh, Margaret | | William Lawrence and his assigns.. |
| April 8th... | Warner, Elizabeth | | Joseph Jenkins and his assigns...... |
| April 10th.. | Liz, Henry | | Adam Stone and his assigns........ |
| | Jones, Elizabeth | | John Joseph and Hannah, his wife, and their assigns. |
| April 12th... | Fetterman, Johann Frederick. | Rotterdam.. | Martin Kreider and his assigns..... |
| | McKay, John | | Hector McKay and his assigns...... |
| | Bristol, Dan | | Robert Warrill and his assigns...... |
| April 13th.. | Figely, Godlip | | Abraham Kinsey and his assigns..... |
| | Monney, Joseph | | Jacob Tryne and his assigns......... |
| | Feierabend, John | | Reverend Frederick Muhlenberg and his assigns. |
| | Sharick, Henry | | George Scaskoltz and his assigns.... |
| | Bryan, Alice | | John Murray and his assigns........ |
| | Moss, Samuel | | Charles Stow and his assigns........ |
| April 14th.. | Coxe, Amarias | | Henry Cary and his assigns.......... |
| | May, William | | John Reynolds and his assigns........ |
| | Milner, John, Jr. | | Samuel Barrow .................... |
| | Rowan, John | | Jacob Peters and his assigns......... |
| | Thillen, Anna Cath. | | Michael Croll and his assigns........ |
| | Bacon, Margaret | | Lawrence Fagan and his assigns..... |
| | Musgrove, William | | William Williams and his assigns.... |
| | Hartranffts, Leonard | | Godfrey Hagee and his assigns...... |
| | Kough, Dennis | | Conrad Alster and his assigns........ |
| | Harper, Edward | | Christopher Collis and his assigns.... |
| | McSparran, Archibald | | George Hyle and his assigns........ |
| | Edwards, John | | Henry Neal and his assigns.......... |
| | Davie, James | | Henry Neal and his assigns.......... |

## List of Indentures.

| RESIDENCE. | OCCUPATION. | TERM. | AMOUNT. |
|---|---|---|---|
| Deptford twp., Gloucester co., W. Jersey. | | 5 yrs. | £18.0.0. |
| Philadelphia | Apprentice, taught housewifery, sew and mark, read in Bible and write a legible hand.[3] | 6 yrs. | |
| Philadelphia | Apprentice, taught the butcher's trade (note 5, have £10 current money of Pa.). | 3 yrs. | |
| Philadelphia | Apprentice, Hannah Joseph to teach her the art and mystery of a staymaker, taught to read in Bible, write a legible hand, found meat, drink, washing and lodging, apparel.[6] | 14 yrs., 10 mo., 10 d. | |
| Philadelphia | Servant[3] | 5 yrs. | £24.0.0. |
| E. Nottingham, Chester co. | | 14 yrs., 6 mo. | £5.0.0. |
| Philadelphia | Apprentice, taught the cordwainer's trade, have three quarters' night and one quarter day schooling.[3] | 10 yrs. | |
| Philadelphia | Servant | 4 yrs., 3 mo. | £21.0.0. |
| Passyunk twp., Phila. co. | Servant[5] | 2 yrs. | £12.1.3. |
| Heidelberg twp., Lancaster co. | | 4 yrs. | £21.9.0. |
| Cowishaopper, Phila. co. | Servant, taught the potter's trade, have two months' schooling.[8] | 7 yrs., 6 mo. | £25.0.0. |
| Providence twp., Phila. co. | | | |
| Philadelphia | Apprentice, taught the tailor's trade, found apparel and at expiration have legal freedom dues, the father to find meat, drink, washing and lodging the first year and during the remainder to be found by his master. | 4 yrs., 6 yrs., 1 mo. 15 d. | £15.0.0. |
| Philadelphia | | 13 yrs., 3 mo. | £7.0.0. |
| Philadelphia | Servant[2] | 1 yr., 7 mo. | £6.8.0. |
| Philadelphia | Apprentice, taught the watch maker's trade, found meat and drink, allowed time to go three quarters to evening school, the father paying expense of schooling. | 3 yrs. | |
| Philadelphia | | 4 yrs., 6 d. | £15.0.0. |
| Upper Salford twp., Phila. co. | | 6 yrs. | £28.5.0. |
| Northern Liberties | Servant (note 3, and £5 in cash). | 2 yrs. | |
| Northern Liberties | Apprentice, taught the boat builder's trade, have four months' evening school each winter.[3] | 8 yrs., 10 mo., 24 d. | |
| Philadelphia | | 6 yrs., 10 mo., 9 d. | £6.0.0. |
| Philadelphia | Apprentice, taught the cordwainer's trade, read, write and cypher through the rule of 3.[3] | 8 yrs., 8 mo. 11 d. | |
| Philadelphia | | 4 yrs. | £15.0.0. |
| Philadelphia | Apprentice, taught the skinner and leather breeches maker's business, found all necessaries, have one months' evening schooling every winter. | 5 yrs., 8 mo. | |
| Philadelphia | | 4 yrs. | £16.0.0. |
| Philadelphia | | 7 yrs. | £17.0.0. |

| Date. | Name. | From the Port of | To Whom Indentured. |
|---|---|---|---|
| 1773. April 15th.. | Muffin, Maria Catherine..... | .......... | Jacob Waggner and his assigns...... |
| | Mulattoe, Betty ............. | .......... | Samuel McClure and his assigns..... |
| | Zinn, John .................... | .......... | George Wack and his assigns........ |
| | Carney, Owen, and Dodd, William. | .......... | William Montgomery and his assigns. |
| | Haley, Luke .................. | .......... | William Montgomery and his assigns. |
| | Burns, John ................... | .......... | Bernard Swung and his assigns...... |
| | Harrold, John ................. | .......... | Edward Cather and his assigns...... |
| April 16th.. | Brown, Thomas ............... | .......... | Edward Cather and his assigns...... |
| | Colford, Sarah ............... | .......... | John Menge and his assigns......... |
| | Duguid, Alexander ........... | .......... | Richard Armit and his assigns....... |
| | Marshall, Thomas ........... | .......... | William Montgomery and his assigns. |
| | Mayfield, Thomas, and Montgomery, Daniel. | .......... | Barnard Sweeny and his assigns...... |
| | Murphy, John ................. | .......... | Edward Cather and his assigns...... |
| | Aydelott, Joseph .............. | .......... | Peter January and his assigns........ |
| April 17th.. | Kitts, Michael ................. | .......... | George Cooper and his assigns...... |
| | Shoemaker, Gertrude ........ | Rotterdam.. | Edward Penington and his assigns... |
| | Murray, Martha; Moore, Francis; Nickols, Mary; Humphreys, Mary. | .......... | James Taylor and his assigns........ |
| April 19th.. | Frazier, Sarah; Conner, Judith. | .......... | James Taylor and his assigns........ |
| | Thompson, Sylannah.......... | .......... | James Taylor and his assigns........ |
| | Bankson, Benjamin............ | .......... | Samuel Burgs ...................... |
| | Quinn, Sophia ................ | .......... | James Nevil and his assigns......... |
| | Clark, Elizabeth .............. | .......... | Robert Bill and his assigns.......... |
| | Chambers, John ............... | .......... | Casper Souder ..................... |
| | Fox, Henry ................... | .......... | Jacob Brand and his assigns........ |

[1] To be found all necessaries and at the expiration have freedom dues.
[2] To be found all necessaries and at the expiration have one new suit of apparel.
[3] To be found all necessaries and at the expiration have two complete suits of apparel, one whereof to be new.

## List of Indentures. 213

| Residence. | Occupation. | Term. | Amount. |
|---|---|---|---|
| Philadelphia | Apprentice, taught housewifery and to sew, read in Bible (note 3, and £3 in money). | 6 yrs. | |
| Southwark | | 14 yrs. | |
| Philadelphia | Apprentice, taught the cordwainer's trade, read in bible, write a legible hand and cypher through rule of 3.[2] | 8 yrs., 4 mo. 4 d. | |
| Augusta co., Va. | Servant[1] | 4 yrs. each | £15.0.0. |
| Augusta co., Va. | Servant[3] | 2 yrs. | £8.0.0. |
| Augusta co., Va. | Servant[3] | 2 yrs. | £8.15.0. |
| Augusta co., Va. | Servant[3] | 2 yrs. | 20/ and clothes to the value of £5.0.0. |
| Augusta co., Va. | Servant[3] | 2 yrs. | £8.0.0. |
| Northern Liberties | Servant | 11 yrs., 9 mo. | £8.0.0. |
| Philadelphia | Apprentice, taught the trade of a house carpenter, found meat, drink, washing and lodging, and apparel during the last half of his apprenticeship.[6] | 3 yrs., 11 mo., 9 d. | |
| Augusta co., Va. | Servant[3] | 5 yrs. | £15.0.0. |
| Augusta co., Va. | Servant[1] | 4 yrs. each | £12.0.0. £11.0.0. |
| Augusta co., Va. | Servant[3] | 4 yrs. | £15.0.0. |
| Philadelphia | Apprentice, taught the cordwainer's trade, found meat, drink, washing, lodging and working apparel, have one quarter evening schooling in the last year. | 4 yrs., 10 mo., 11 d. | |
| Philadelphia | Apprentice, taught the skin dresser's trade, found meat, drink, washing and lodging and working apparel. | 1 yr., 8 mo. | |
| Philadelphia | Servant, at expiration have legal freedom dues. | 5 yrs. | £24.19.6. |
| Shippensburgh, Cumberland co. | Servant (note 3, or £5 in cash). | 3 yrs. each. | 50/. |
| Shippensburgh, Cumberland co. | Servant[1] | 4 yrs. each | £6.0.0. £5.0.0. |
| Shippensburgh, Cumberland co. | Servant[3] | 3 yrs. | 50/. |
| Philadelphia | Apprentice, taught the trade of a distiller, found meat, drink, lodging, washing and apparel, except Sunday clothes, and mending, shirts and stockings. | 5 yrs., 5 mo. | |
| Northern Liberties, Phila. co. | Apprentice, taught housewifery, sew and knit, read in Bible, write a legible hand.[5] | 12 yrs. | |
| Philadelphia | Servant (note 1, or £5 in money). | 3 yrs. | £2.10.0. |
| Northern Liberties, Phila. co. | Apprentice, taught the cordwainer's trade, have eighteen months' schooling.[1] | 11 yrs., 6 mo., 6 d. | |
| Philadelphia | Apprentice, taught the trade of a cedar cooper, read in Bible, | 8 yrs., 8 mo. 6 d. | |

[4] To be found all necessaries and at the expiration have two complete suits of apparel, one whereof to be new, and 40s. in money.

[5] At expiration have two complete suits of apparel, one whereof to be new.

| Date. | Name. | From the Port of | To Whom Indentured. |
|---|---|---|---|
| 1773.<br>April 19th | Bourgeois, Jeremiah | | Frederick Hitmer and his assigns |
| April 20th | Stacy, Richard | | Levy Marks and his executors |
| | Haley, Michael | | Hugh McCullock and his assigns |
| | Milward, Samuel | Ireland | William Pierson and his assigns |
| | McMichael, Daniel | | George Way and his assigns |
| | Cummings, Thomas | | Stephen Phipps |
| April 22nd | Creber, Henry | | George White and his assigns |
| | Lavers, James | | Edward Bonsell and his assigns |
| | Blanck, Catherine | Rotterdam | Joseph Pemberton and his assigns |
| | Harmanson, Levin | | Robert Loosely and his assigns |
| | Kemp, Mathias | | Jacob Sivevell and his assigns |
| | Weller, Peter | | George Way |
| | Coleman, Luke | | Chamless Allen and his assigns |
| | Mitchell, Mary | | Jonathan Newhouse and his wife |
| April 22nd | McIlroy, Mary | | Charles Prior and his assigns |
| April 23rd | Kegan, James | | John Wilcocks and his assigns |
| April 24th | Enoss, James | | John Martin |
| April 26th | Waggoner, Elizabeth | | Benjamin Davis and wife |
| | Canjumtach, Ann | | Thomas Bishop |
| | Owen, Hugh | Liverpool | Jonathan Meredith and his assigns |

## List of Indentures.

| Residence. | Occupation. | Term. | Amount. |
|---|---|---|---|
| | write a legible hand and cypher through rule of 3.[3] | | |
| Philadelphia | Apprentice, taught the tin plate worker's trade, have four quarters' night schooling.[3] | 8 yrs., 4 mo. 24 d. | |
| Philadelphia | Apprentice, taught the trade of a tailor, have three quarters' night schooling.[3] | 6 yrs. | |
| Philadelphia | Apprentice, taught the art and mystery of a mariner and navigation.[1] | 4 yrs. | |
| Northern Liberties, Phila. co | Apprentice[1] | 4 yrs. | £ 15. 0. 0. |
| Philadelphia | Apprentice, taught the art and mystery of a coach maker, six months' night scholing, at expiration of the term, give him freedom dues or £ 10. | 6 yrs., 6 mo. | |
| Philadelphia | Apprentice to learn the art of a tailor, to be found all necessaries except shoes, shirts, stockings and washing, to give him one quarter's day schooling and another at the expense of his father, and freedom dues. | 5 yrs., 7 mo. | |
| Philadelphia | Apprentice, taught the trade of a tailor, have two quarters' day and two quarters' night schooling (note 5, have £ 10 lawful current money of Pa.). | 9 yrs., 8 mo. 16 d. | |
| Philadelphia | Apprentice, taught the house carpenter's trade, have one quarter's night schooling at expense of his master and liberty to go at any time to night schooling at the expense of his friends.[5] | 6 yrs., 2 mo. 7 d. | |
| Philadelphia | Servant[1] | 4 yrs., 8 mo. | £ 23. 0. 0. |
| Philadelphia | Apprentice, taught the cordwainer's trade, have two quarters' night schooling (note 3, and a complete set of tools). | 6 yrs., 8 mo. 6 d. | |
| Philadelphia | Apprentice, taught the trade of a blacksmith, have twelve months' schooling.[3] | 7 yrs. | |
| Philadelphia | Apprentice, taught the coach maker's trade.[5] | 7 mo. | |
| Philadelphia | | 3 yrs. | £ 3. 10. 0. |
| New Britain twp., Bucks co | Apprentice, taught the tailoress and bonnet making business, two quarters' day schooling.[3] | 5 yrs., 6 mo. | |
| Philadelphia | Servant (note 3, worth £ 5, or £ 5 current money of Pa.). | 2 yrs., 21 d. | £ 10. 0. 0. |
| | | 4 yrs. | £ 16. 0. 0. |
| Philadelphia | Apprentice, taught the trade of a tailor, have six months' day schooling.[3] | 7 yrs., 8d. | |
| | Apprentice, taught housewifery, sew, knit and spin, read and write and when free to have freedom dues and £ 5 in cash. | 6 yrs., 3 mo. 8 d. | |
| | | 10 yrs. | £ 13. 0. 0. |
| Philadelphia | Apprentice, to be learned the art and trade of a currier (note 3, and £ 10 in cash. | 5 yrs. | £ 10. 0. 0. |

| Date. | Name. | From the Port of | To Whom Indentured. |
|---|---|---|---|
| 1773. | Mortimer, Robert | | Jonathan Meredith and his assigns |
| April 28th | Oquener, Ann | | Guy Johnson |
| | Hasleton, John | | Samuel Brusster and his assigns |
| | Yardley, Thomas | | Samuel Brusster and his assigns |
| | Bakely, Daniel | | George Furback and his assigns |
| | Cooper, Paul | | Uriah Woolman and his assigns |
| | Cowell, Robert | | Edennond Milose and his assigns |
| | Belfour, James | | Archibald Graham and his assigns |
| | Schnitzer, George | | Matthias Shereman |
| | Filliston, William | | Archibald Graham and his assigns |
| April 29th | Rifey, Adam | | Michael Graff and his assigns |
| | Horean, Elizabeth | | John Habyers and his assigns |
| | Becket, William | Liverpool | James Starr and his assigns |
| April 30th | Brandt, Christian | London | Joseph Potts and his assigns |
| | Cooper, Francis | | Robert Patterson and his assigns |
| | Gleckner, Charles | London | Israel Morris, Jr., and his assigns |
| | Gleckner, Charles | | Samuel Morris, Jr. |
| | Meyer, John Gerad | London | John Mitchell and his assigns |
| | Rintleman, John Fredk | | Dr. Adam Kuhn and his assigns |

## List of Indentures.

| Residence. | Occupation. | Term. | Amount. |
|---|---|---|---|
| Philadelphia | Apprentice, to learn the trade of a currier.³ | 6 yrs. | |
| Albany co., Province of N. Y. | | 7 yrs. | £ 20. 0. 0. |
| Northern Liberties | | 11 yrs. | 1/. |
| Northern Liberties | Apprentice, taught the art and mystery of a ship carpenter, one quarter's night schooling every winter, at the expiration of his term freedom dues or £ 10. | 5 yrs., 11 mo., 2 d. | |
| Northern Liberties, Phila. co. | Apprentice, taught the trade of a house carpenter, two quarters' night schooling.³ | 4 yrs. | |
| Philadelphia | Apprentice, taught the art of a mariner and navigation, found meat, drink, lodging and washing. | 1 yr., 8 mo. 13 d. | |
| Philadelphia | Servant⁵ | 8 mo. | £ 5. 14. 6. |
| Frederick co., Va. | Servant found all necessaries except clothing and when free £ 9 Penna. money. | 1 yr. | |
| Philadelphia | Apprentice, learn the trade of a cordwainer, have six months' English schooling.⁸ | 8 yrs., 11 mo., 24 d. | |
| Virginia | Servant³ | 3 yrs. | £ 7. 16. 0. |
| Northern Liberties | Apprentice, taught the trade of a tanner and currier, one quarter day and three quarters' night schooling (note 1, or £ 10 in cash). | 11 yrs. | |
| Philadelphia | Apprentice, taught the trade of a mantua and bonnet maker.³ | 3 yrs., 11 mo. | |
| Philadelphia | Servant⁵ | 2 yrs. | £ 13. 3. 0. |
| | Servant³ | 3 yrs. | £ 17. 4. 10. |
| Philadelphia | Apprentice, taught art of a mariner and navigation, read, write and cypher.³ | 6 yrs., 8 mo. 3 d. | |
| Philadelphia | Servant, to be found only during the term, six working shirts and three fine ones, and shoes. | 15 mo. | 9 guineas. |
| Philadelphia | Servant | 15 mo. | 9 guineas. |
| Philadelphia | Servant, in case any person shall pay within two years three guineas to the master for Christopher Rintteman then the said servant is to serve only three years and six months' at the expiration of which he is to have the same legal dues as if he had served four years.¹ | 4 yrs., 6 mo. | 9 guineas and 3 guineas in part of the passage of Christopher Rintleman for which he voluntarily undertakes to serve. |
| Philadelphia | Servant, it at any time within two years any person shall pay to the master the three guineas for the part pasage of Christopher Rintteman, the servant is to serve but three years and six months.⁶ | 4 yrs., 6 mo. | 9 guineas and 3 guineas in part of the passage of Christopher Rintleman for which he voluntarily undertakes to serve. |

| DATE. | NAME. | FROM THE PORT OF | TO WHOM INDENTURED. |
|---|---|---|---|
| 1773. April 30th.. | Miller John<br>Doyle, Peter | London | William Allison and his assigns<br>Philip Druckimiller |
| | Gibower, Godfrey | London | Robert Parrish and his assigns |
| | Fegan, Daniel | | Martin Jugis |
| | Fegan, Hugh | | William Martin and his assigns |
| May 1st | Frazier, Elizabeth | | William Hodge and his wife, Eleanor. |
| | Bosserman, Frederick<br>Wood, William<br>Connoly, William | London | Francis Hopkinson and his assigns<br>George Correy and his assigns<br>Patrick Farrel and his assigns |
| May 3rd | Alexander, Charles | | William Pierson and his assigns |
| | Woodrow, John | London | John Balderston, Jr., and his assigns.. |
| | Nick, William | | Philip Druckenmiller and his assigns. |
| | Meyland, Simon | London | James Poupaid and his assigns |
| | McQuillen, Edward<br>McGown, Meredith<br>Puriol, John<br>Koneg, Anthony<br>Riffet, Nathan | Ireland<br><br>London<br>London | Aaron Ashbrodge<br>James Baker and his assigns<br>Andrew Beckman and his assigns<br>William Logan and his assigns<br>William Tolbert |
| May 4th | Calaker, Catherine<br>Walker, Rachael<br>Murphy, Ann<br>Murray, Ann<br>Marlier, Henry | <br><br>Ireland<br><br>London | John Evans and his assigns<br>Walter Shea and his assigns<br>George Stanforth<br>James Logan and his assigns<br>Richard Bundhe and his assigns |
| | Low, Samuel | | James Lees and his assigns |
| | Biggart, Robert | Ireland | James Blaxton and his assigns |
| | McKivan, Margaret<br>McEvoy, Daniel<br>McEvoy, Daniel<br>Blair, Jane<br>Monypenny, Clemens<br>Honeyman, William | Ireland<br>Ireland<br><br>Ireland | Patrick Burn and his assigns<br>James Stewart and his assigns<br>William Pierson<br>Job Fallows<br>Job Fallows and his assigns<br>Robert Smith and his assigns |

## List of Indentures.

| RESIDENCE. | OCCUPATION. | TERM. | AMOUNT. |
|---|---|---|---|
| Philadelphia | Servant (note 2, besides his old). | 2 yrs. | £9.3.0. |
| Philadelphia | Apprentice, taught the trade of a tailor, have two quarters' day and two quarters' night schooling.[3] | 7 yrs. | |
| Philadelphia | Servant, found meat, drink, washing, lodging and apparel, at expiration of the term freedom dues. | 3 yrs. | £15.5.8. |
| Philadelphia | Apprentice, taught the trade of a cabinet maker, have nine months' night schooling (note 1, or £8 in cash). | 7 yrs., 11 mo., 23 d. | |
| Philadelphia | Apprentice, taught the trade of an upholder, have nine months' night schooling (note 1, or £8). | 10 yrs., 4 mo., 26 d. | |
| Philadelphia | Apprentice, taught housewifery, sew and knit, have six months' schooling.[3] | 5 yrs., 8 mo. | |
| Philadelphia | Servant[1] | 3 yrs. | £15.0.0. |
| New London twp., Chester co. | Servant | 4 yrs. | £17.0.0. |
| Philadelphia | Servant, taught the trade of a cooper, have two quarters' night schooling the last of his time.[3] | 4 yrs., 6 mo. | |
| Kensington, Phila. co. | Apprentice, taught the trade of a blacksmith, have nine months' night schooling.[3] | 7 yrs., 4 mo. 8 d. | |
| Solbury twp., Bucks co. | Apprentice, taught the trade of a farmer, read, write and cypher as far as rule of 3.[3] | 9 yrs., 2 mo. 13 d. | £7.14.0. |
| Philadelphia | Apprentice, taught the trade of a tailor, have six months' night schooling.[4] | 5 yrs., 10 mo., 15 d. | |
| Philadelphia | Servant, suit of broadcloth within a month.[3] | 3 yrs. | £16.17.6. |
| Goshen, Chester co. | | 2 yrs. | £12.0.0. |
| Uwchlan twp., Chester co. | Servant | 4 yrs. | £20.0.0. |
| Philadelphia | Servant[3] | 3 yrs. | £17.6.9. |
| Philadelphia | Servant (note 1, and £5 in cash). | 4 yrs. | £16.19.3. |
| Northern Liberties | Apprentice, taught the tailor's trade, have three months' schooling the first year, two months the second and one month each year following.[3] | 6 yrs. | |
| Philadelphia | Servant | 5 yrs. | £12.0.0. |
| Philadelphia | | 4 yrs. | £15.0.0. |
| Princeton, N. J. | Servant[1] | 4 yrs. | £15.0.0. |
| Philadelphia | | 4 yrs. | £16.0.0. |
| Philadelphia | Servant, taught to read and write[1]. | 11 yrs., 6 mo. | £14.12.1. |
| Philadelphia | Servant, to be found all necessaries except clothes and paid when free £20. | 1 yr. | £8.0.0. |
| Chester twp., Chester co. | Servant, found meat, drink, washing and lodging, two shirts, one pair shoes and one pair stockings | 14 mo. | £10.0.0. |
| Southwark | | 4 yrs. | £15.0.0. |
| Philadelphia | Servant[1] | 4 yrs. | £17.0.0. |
| Northern Liberties | Servant | 4 yrs. | £17.0.0. |
| Ashe Town, Chester co. | | 3 yrs., 6 mo. | £14.0.0. |
| Ashe Town, Chester co. | Servant[1] | 5 yrs. | £12.0.0. |
| Philadelphia | Apprentice, learn the trade of a hatter, found meat, drink, washing, mending and lodging, al- | 7 yrs., 30 d. | |

| Date. | Name. | From the Port of | To Whom Indentured. |
|---|---|---|---|
| 1773.<br>May 4th | Smart, Samuel | | Robert Kennedy and his assigns |
| May 5th | Undersee, Conrad<br>McConnell, Adam<br>Tagert, Patrick<br>Gable, John Peter | Ireland<br>London | George Kastner and his assigns<br>John Smith and his assigns<br>John Smith and his assigns<br>Reuben Hain and his assigns |
| | Gable, John Peter | | William McClay and his assigns |
| | Sweeney, John<br>Gondex, John Francis | London | Dennis Sweeney<br>Machael Lapp and his assigns |
| | McGee, Mary<br>Boger, Henry Conrad<br>Smart, Sarah<br>Hoober, Jacob | London | Benjamin Lightfoot and his assigns<br>Levis Tohur and his assigns<br>John Sheirman and his assigns<br>John Bouch and his assigns |
| May 6th | Riddle, Thomas<br>McCloud, Margaret<br>Hile, Patrick<br>McGillis, George<br>Clarke, David | London | William Cliffton and his assigns<br>George Ranhen and his assigns<br>James Fullton and his assigns<br>Selwood Griffin and his assigns<br>Francis Tremble and his assigns |
| | Loughlin, James<br>McIvers, John<br>Hutchinson, Mary<br>Donnan, Mary<br>Piles, Esther | Ireland<br>Ireland<br>Ireland<br>Ireland | William Alleson and his assigns<br>John Steel and his assigns<br>Samuel Shoemaker and his assigns<br>Jacob Miller and his assigns<br>Hannah Donaldson |
| May 6th | Doyle, John<br>Yourt, John | Ireland | William Dibly and his assigns<br>William Donnell and his assigns |
| | Menge, John | | Jacob Weaver and his assigns |
| May 7th | Keith, Patrick | | Benjamin Davis and his assigns |
| | Graham, John | | Isaac Coran |
| | Miller, John Henry | London | Thomas Penrose and his assigns |
| | Danderin, Christina Barbara<br>Rourke, Daniel<br>Hart, John | Rotterdam<br>Ireland | Thomas Penrose and his assigns<br>John Englis and his assigns<br>Charles Gibbs |
| | Durre, Cornelius<br>Kite, James<br>Merrifield, Jeremiah; Hartley, William; Waghorne, William; Bragg, John.<br>Davies, John | | William Blythe and his assigns<br>John Goodwin and his assigns<br>Abram Kinsing and his assigns |

## List of Indentures.

| RESIDENCE. | OCCUPATION. | TERM. | AMOUNT. |
|---|---|---|---|
| | lowed time to go five quarters' night schooling at expense of the father. | | |
| Philadelphia | Apprentice, taught copper plate printing, picture frame making, to gild and glaze.[a] | 5 yrs. | £16.0.0. |
| Whitpain twp., Phila. co. | Servant (note 3, or £10 in cash). | 3 yrs., 8 mo. | £27.0.0. |
| Lower Chichester, Chester co. | Servant[5] | 3 yrs. | £17.10. |
| Lower Chichester, Chester co. | Servant[5] | 4 yrs., 6 mo. | £17.10. |
| Philadelphia | Servant (note 5, two suits of clothes, or £9 in cash). | 2 yrs., 8 mo. | £15.0.0. |
| Sunbury, Northumberland co. | Servant (note 5, two suits of clothes, or £9 in cash). | 2 yrs., 8 mo. | £15.0.0. |
| Carlisle | | | 1 shilling. |
| East Whiteland twp., Chester co. | Servant (note 5, £10 in cash in lieu of freedom dues). | 5 yrs. | £15.10.9. |
| Reading, Berks co. | Servant (note 1, or £10 in cash). | 4 yrs. | £15.0.0. |
| Philadelphia | | 4 yrs. | £17.15.7. |
| Philadelphia | Servant[5] | 3 yrs. | £15.0.0. |
| Philadelphia | Apprentice, taught the trade of a skinner, have two quarters' night schooling (note 5, £10 in cash). | 4 yrs. | |
| Southwark | Servant (note 3, and £8 in cash). | 3 yrs. | £15.0.0. |
| Philadelphia | | 4 yrs. | £15.0.0. |
| Philadelphia | Servant[5] | 3 yrs., 3 mo. | £17.0.0. |
| Philadelphia | | 4 yrs. | £18.0.0. |
| Philadelphia | Apprentice, found all necessaries except clothing. | 3 yrs. | |
| Philadelphia | Servant[1] | 4 yrs. | £16.0.0. |
| North Carolina | Servant[3] | 3 yrs. | £15.0.0. |
| Philadelphia | Servant[5] | 4 yrs. | £15.0.0. |
| Northern Liberties | Servant[5] | 3 yrs., 6 mo. | £14.0.0. |
| Philadelphia | Apprentice, taught housewifery and sew, give her one quarter schooling in the two last years of her time.[3] | 4 yrs., 5 mo. 25 d. | |
| Philadelphia | | 7 yrs. | £18.0.0. |
| Philadelphia | Apprentice, taught the chocolate grinding business (note 1, and £3 in cash). | 4 yrs. | £17.0.0. |
| Northern Liberties | Apprentice, taught the trade of a tanner and currier, have three quarters' night schooling (note 3, or £12 in cash). | 4 yrs., 3 mo. 25 d. | |
| Philadelphia | Found all necessaries except clothing. | 1 yr. | £14.0.0. |
| Philadelphia | Apprentice, taught tavern keeping, taught to read and write.[6] | 7 yrs., 6 mo. | |
| Southwark | Apprentice, taught the mast making business, four quarters' night schooling and when free a set of working tools and £4 in cash or £6 without the tools. | 8 yrs. | 12 guineas. |
| Southwark | Apprentice, one quarter schooling[1]. | 5 yrs. | £30.0.0. |
| Philadelphia | Apprentice[6] | 4 yrs. | £16.0.0. |
| Maryland | Servant, found all necessaries except clothing. | 1 mo. | 12 shillings. |
| Philadelphia | Servant | 2 yrs. | £7.0.0. |
| Philadelphia | | 5 yrs. | £22.10.0. |
| Philadelphia | | 4 yrs. each.. | £20.0.0. for each. |
| | Servant[5] | 7 yrs. | £20.0.0. |

| Date. | Name. | From the Port of | To Whom Indentured. |
|---|---|---|---|
| 1773. May 8th | Warner, Charles | | Benjamin Hooton and his assigns |
| | Howard, Henry | | Joseph Warner and his assigns |
| | Manner, John | | John Fox and his assigns |
| | Orcle, Richard | Bristol | Joseph Lackett |
| | Simmes, William | Liverpool | Samuel Meridith and his assigns |
| | Powell, Robert | Liverpool | Edward Wells and his assigns |
| | McAnully, Daniel | | Jacob Richardson and his assigns |
| | Hobbs, Thomas | Bristol | John Brown and his assigns |
| | Porter, James | | John Hanna and his assigns |
| | Watson, Thomas | | John Britton and his assigns |
| | Blatchly, Peter | Bristol | James Sharswood and his assigns |
| May 10th | McCartney, Mabel | | John Hopkins |
| | Ponsler, John | | Henry Sheatz |
| | Johnston, Joshuah | | William Milner and his assigns |
| | Hansen, Isabella | | Elizabeth Hanun and her assigns |
| | Hopkins, William | | Benjamin Cathrall and his assigns |
| | Beer, James | | John Fuss |
| | Bell, John | | Stephen Watts |
| | Hind, William | | John Aikin |
| | Carr, James | | Richard Parmer and his assigns |
| | Coupal, Anthony | | Jacob Ritter and his assigns |
| | Jayne, Aaron | | Andrew Buckhard and his assigns |
| May 11th | Fitzgerald, Mary | | William Ellon and his assigns |
| | Ellis, Ann | | Michael Troy |
| | Fully, William | | William Brown |
| | Grames, Thomas | | George Rankin and his assigns |
| | Fitzgerald, Mary | | James Taylor |
| | Moser, Jacob, and Catherin, his wife. | | Adam Erbin and his assigns |
| | Allison, Margaret | | James Taylor and his assigns |
| | Watkins, John | | Jacob Derrick and his assigns |
| | Armstrong, Eleanor | | James Taylor and his assigns |
| | Sopp, Thomas | | Samuel Bringhurst and his assigns |
| | Russell, Richard | | Richard Johns and his assigns |
| | Kaise, Henry | London | Israel Morris, Jr., and his assigns |
| | Kaise, Henry | | Samuel Morris, Jr., and his assigns |
| | Wilson, Jane | | William Patterson and his assigns |
| | Byrne, Lawrence | | Michael Troy and his assigns |
| May 12th | Anster, Nathaniel | | Peter Robinson and his assigns |
| | Harlin, Thomas | | Aron Brown |

## List of Indentures.

| Residence. | Occupation. | Term. | Amount. |
|---|---|---|---|
| Philadelphia | Apprentice, taught the trade of a hatter, found all necessaries except apparel. | 7 yrs. | |
| Philadelphia | Apprentice, taught the trade of a boat builder, found all necessaries except apparel. | 6 yrs., 3 mo. 25 d. | |
| Gresham twp., Phila. co. | Apprentice, taught the trade of ———, read, write and cypher as far as rule of 3.[3] | 12 yrs., 8 mo., 22 d. | |
| Plights Town twp., Bucks co. | Apprentice[5] | 5 yrs. | £ 25. 0. 0. |
| Philadelphia | Apprentice[6] | 5 yrs. | £ 25. 0. 0. |
| Philadelphia | Apprentice[5] | 5 yrs. | £ 25. 0. 0. |
| Upper Merion twp., Phila. co. | Servant | 4 yrs. | £ 15. 0. 0. |
| Willis Town twp., Chester co. | Servant (note 3, and £ 5 lawful money of Pa.). | 3 yrs., 6 mo. | £ 14. 0. 0. |
| Philadelphia | Servant | 3 yrs., 6 mo. | £ 25. 0. 0. |
| Northern Liberties, Phila. co. | Servant | 4 yrs. | £ 25. 0. 0. |
| Philadelphia | Servant, employed at the business of a house carpenter (note 5, have £ 6 lawful money of Pa.). | 2 yrs. | £ 14. 0. 0. |
| Salisbury twp., Lancaster co. | Servant[5] | 4 yrs. | £ 14. 0. 0. |
| Whitemarsh twp., Phila. co. | Apprentice, taught the trade of a paper maker, read and write.[3] | 6 yrs., 6 mo. | |
| Philadelphia | | 11 yrs., 9 mo. | |
| Philadelphia | Apprentice, taught housewifery, (note 5, paid £ 6 in cash). | 2 yrs. | £ 8. 0. 0. |
| Newtown | Servant | 4 yrs. | £ 20. 0. 0. |
| Philadelphia | Apprentice, to be provided with meat and drink only. | 5 yrs. | |
| Philadelphia | Servants[5] | 6 yrs. | £ 25. 0. 0. |
| Pamader twp., Chester co. | | 4 yrs. | £ 20. 0. 0. |
| Philadelphia | Apprentice, learn the trade of a joiner and chair maker, found meat, drink, lodging, washing, mending and shoes, to go two quarters to school at expense of the father. | | |
| Philadelphia | | 3 yrs. | £ 15. 7. 6. |
| Philadelphia | Servant (note 5, give him £ 10 in cash in lieu of freedom dues). | 3 yrs. | £ 14. 0. 0. |
| Philadelphia | Servant | 4 yrs. | £ 3. 0. 0. |
| Paxton twp., Lancaster co. | | 3 yrs. | £ 14. 0. 0. |
| Philadelphia | | 6 yrs. | £ 25. 0. 0. |
| Philadelphia | Servant[5] | 6 yrs. | £ 15. 0. 0. |
| Shippensburg, Cumberland co. | | 4 yrs. | £ 5. 0. 0. |
| Philadelphia | | 5 yrs. | £ 43. 15. 6. |
| Shippensburg, Cumberland co. | Servant[1] | 4 yrs. | £ 4. 0. 0. |
| Waterford twp., Gloucester co., N. J. | Servant[1] | 4 yrs. | £ 12. 0. 0. |
| Shippensburg, Cumberland co. | Servant[3] | 3 yrs. | £ 3. 0. 0. |
| Germantown twp., Phila. co. | Servant[3] | 2 yrs., 6 mo. | £ 14. 0. 0. |
| Dedford twp., Gloster co., N. J. | Servant[5] | 6 yrs. | £ 25. 0. 0. |
| Philadelphia | Servant, found meat, drink, washing, lodging, six working shirts, three fine shirts and shoes. | 1 yr., 6 mo. | £ 8. 18. 0. |
| Philadelphia | | 1 yr., 6 mo. | £ 8. 18. 0. |
| Turbet twp., Northumberland co. | Servant | 4 yrs. | £ 13. 0. 0. |
| Sunbury twp., Northumberland co. | Servant | 4 yrs. | £ 13. 0. 0. |
| Philadelphia | | 1 yr., 9 mo. | £ 5. 0. 0. |
| Pittsgrove, Salem co., N. J. | Servant | 5 yrs. | £ 20. 0. 0. |

| Date. | Name. | From the Port of | To Whom Indentured. |
|---|---|---|---|
| 1773.<br>May 13th... | Daniel, Owen | | Anthony Billig |
| | Williams, John | | Thomas Shortell and his assigns |
| | Garwood, Joseph | | Bowyer Brooke and his assigns |
| | Fitzgerrald, Mary | | William Golden and his assigns |
| | Hall, John | Ireland | John Care and his assigns |
| May 13th... | Gray, Jean | | Fargust Purdon and his assigns |
| | Fortiner, Simeon | | Israel Hollowell |
| | Vernor, Philip | | John Crush |
| | Randles, Margaret | Ireland | John McCollogh and his assigns |
| | McCardles, Mary | | Peter Howard and his assigns |
| | Fitsgerrald, George | | John Bringhurst and his assigns |
| | Fitsgerrald, Ann | | Noel Todd |
| | Conner, James | Ireland | William Henry |
| | Smith, John | London | John Steinmetz and his assigns |
| | Black, George | Ireland | Samuel Blackwood and his assigns |
| May 14th... | Carr, Henry | | Samuel Jarvis and his assigns |
| | Trimby, Daniel | | Joseph White and his assigns |
| | Brooks, George | Bristol | John Merrick and his assigns |
| | Crawford, Margaret | | James Lukins and his assigns |
| | Outen, Abraham | | John Hamilton |
| | Raine, Thomas | | Simon Shirlock and his assigns |
| | Davis, Thomas | Bristol | Peter Biggs and his assigns |
| May 15th... | Hand, Nicholas | | John Hood |
| | Garrs, Joseph | London | Richard Gibbs and his assigns |
| | Kelly, Francis | | David Jones and his assigns |
| | Dougherty, Robert | | Martin Judges and his assigns |
| | Thomas, John | | Richard Collins and his assigns |
| | Meloy, John | Ireland | Harman Fritz and his assigns |
| | Gillis, Sarah | | John Hoskins and his assigns |
| | Kelly, William | London | Samuel Griscom and his assigns |
| | Davis, Robert | London | Jacob Waggoner and his assigns |
| May 17th... | Woster, Catherine | | Nicholas Brum and his assigns |

## List of Indentures.

| RESIDENCE. | OCCUPATION. | TERM. | AMOUNT. |
|---|---|---|---|
| Philadelphia | Apprentice, taught the trade of a cordwainer, have one quarter night schooling the last year.³ | 3 yrs., 5 mo. 5 d. | |
| Philadelphia | Apprentice, taught the trade of a cooper. | 5 yrs., 8 mo. | £ 4. 0. 0. |
| Philadelphia | Apprentice, taught the trade of a boat builder, have four quarters' night schooling.⁵ | 3 yrs., 7 mo. | |
| Philadelphia | Servant³ | 2 yrs., 11 mo., 16 d. | £ 8. 0. 0. |
| Philadelphia | Servant, taught the art of a saddle-tree maker and when free to have freedom dues. | 6 yrs. | £ 18. 0. 0. |
| Philadelphia | Servant | 2 yrs. | £ 8. 0. 0. |
| Philadelphia | Apprentice | 5 yrs., 10 mo. | £ 30. 0. 0. |
| —— twp., Lancaster co. | | 8 yrs. | £ 30. 0. 0. |
| Philadelphia | Servant⁵ | 4 yrs. | £ 15. 0. 0. |
| Philadelphia | Servant⁵ | 4 yrs. | £ 14. 0. 0. |
| Germantown | Servant¹ Discharged and set free this day by Noel Todd. | 4 yrs. | £ 20. 0. 0. |
| George Town, Md. | Servant¹ | 5 yrs., 2 mo. 3 d. | £ 18. 0. 0. |
| Philadelphia | Servant³ | 3 yrs. | £ 16. 2. 3. |
| Deptford twp., Gloster co., N. J. | | 4 yrs. | £ 14. 0. 0. |
| Philadelphia | Apprentice, taught the trade of a house carpenter, found meat, drink, washing and lodging, the making of all his clothes, found shirts and shoes, and four quarters' schooling. | 8 yrs., 5 mo. 13 d. | |
| Bristol twp., Bucks co. | | 7 yrs. | £ 25. 0. 0. |
| Frales twp., Bucks co. | | 6 yrs. | £ 25. 0. 0. |
| Philadelphia | | 4 yrs. | £ 0. 7. 6. |
| Philadelphia | Apprentice, taught the art of a mariner and navigation.⁵ | 3 yrs. | |
| Southwark | Apprentice | 7 yrs. | £ 15. 0. 0. |
| | Servant, allowed one shilling per week (note 3, or £ 10 lawful money of Pa.). | 3 yrs. | £ 14. 0. 0. |
| Philadelphia | Apprentice | 8 yrs., 6 mo. | £ 2. 0. 0. |
| Bensalem twp., Bucks co. | Servant, have four quarters' schooling.³ | 9 yrs., 10 mo. | £ 14. 0. 0. |
| Philadelphia | Servant | 4 yrs. | £ 17. 0. 0. |
| Philadelphia | Apprentice, taught the art of a carver and gilder, the father engaging to give him one suit of clothes during the term.³ | 6 yrs. | |
| Newtown twp., Gloster co., N. J. | | 4 yrs. | £ 20. 0. 0. |
| | Servant⁵ | 2 yrs., 2 mo. 15 d. | £ 10. 0. 0. |
| Burlington, N. J. | Servant³ | 4 yrs. | £ 15. 0. 0. |
| Philadelphia | Servant, found meat, drink, washing and lodging, employ him at house carpenter's business. | 1 yr. | £ 15. 16. 0. |
| Blockely twp., Phila. co. | Found meat, drink, washing and lodging. | 14 mo. | £ 14. 0. 0. |
| Northern Liberties | Apprentice, taught housewifery, sew knit and spin, taught to read in the Bible, found meat, drink, washing and lodging, apparel.⁶ | 9 yrs. | |

| Date. | Name. | From the Port of | To Whom Indentured. |
|---|---|---|---|
| 1773. | Seyfert, Conrad | | William Mentz and his assigns |
| May 18th | Graydon, Hannah | Bristol | Samuel Read and his assigns |
| | Turmuel, Maria | London | Jacob Groff and his assigns |
| | Smith, John Sebastian Cline | | Anthony Forten and his executors |
| | Culley, Timothy | | Thomas Norris and his assigns |
| | Pirry, John | Liverpool | Richard Tittemary and his assigns |
| | Stock, John | | Daniel Bender and his assigns |
| | Church, John | | Jacob Giles, Jr., and his assigns |
| | Clinesmith, Andrew | London | Michael Bishop and his assigns |
| May 19th | Giddons, Edward | | Thomas Wharton, Sr., and his assigns. |
| | Neilson, Sarah | | James Hinchman and his assigns |
| | Walsh, John; Morgan, Patrick. | | James Black and his assigns |
| | Mushell, Margaret | | Israel Hallowell and his assigns |
| | Heffernon, Hugh | | Simeon Shurlock and his assigns |
| | Reily, Thomas | | Robert Calender |
| | Crosby, Patrick | | Robert Calender |
| | Seyfert, Sybella | | Robert Bell and his assigns |
| | Smith, Nicholas | | Philip Flick and his assigns |
| | Kingshalle, John | | George Goodwine and his assigns |
| | Murphy, Thomas | | Joshua Bunting and his assigns |
| | Dunlap, Sarah | | Joseph Rhoads and his assigns |
| | Hope, John Misbell | | John Lefeavor and his assigns |
| | Dunn, William | | George Haywood |
| | Gray, William | Ireland | Robert Craig and his assigns |
| | Ferris, James | | John Supplee and his assigns |
| | Robinson, Thomas | | Thomas James and his assigns |
| | Murphy, Mary | | George Stevenson |
| | Dilany, Anne | | Thomas Cully and his assigns |
| May 20th | Ward, William | Bristol | James Brenton and his assigns |

## List of Indentures.

| Residence. | Occupation. | Term. | Amount. |
|---|---|---|---|
| Philadelphia | Apprentice, taught the trade of a bookbinder, given two years' day schooling successively, and two quarters' night schooling, taught tongue and write (note 1, or £ 10 in cash). | 14 yrs., 5 mo., 23 d. | |
| Philadelphia | Servant [1] | 4 yrs. | £ 16.0.0. |
| Philadelphia | Servant [3] | 3 yrs. | £ 17.11.6 |
| Philadelphia | Servant, found all necessaries except clothing, to receive at the end of six months £ 6 and at the end of 12 months £ 6 | 12 mo. | |
| Merion twp., Phila. co. | Servant | 4 yrs. | £ 16.0.0. |
| Southwark, Phila. co. | Apprentice, taught the trade of a rope maker, have one and a half quarters' night schooling every winter (note 3, or £ 10 lawful money of Pa.). | 6 yrs. | £ 16.0.0. |
| Philadelphia | Servant | 7 yrs. | £ 20.0.0. |
| St. Georges Parish, Baltimore co., Md. | Servant | 6 yrs. | £ 25.0.0. |
| Lower Millford twp., Bucks co. | Servant, found meat, drink, working apparel, washing and lodging and at expiration £ 8 Pa. currency. | 2 yrs. | £ 7.3.7. |
| Philadelphia | Servant | 4 yrs. | £ 20.0.0. |
| Woolwich twp., Gloster co., N. J. | Servant | 3 yrs. | £ 13.0.0. |
| Kent, Md. | Servant | 4 yrs. | £ 15.0.0. each. |
| Philadelphia | Apprentice, taught housewifery, sew, read in Bible, write a legible hand (note 3, and £ 5 lawful money of Pa.). | 4 yrs., 5 mo. 13 d. | |
| Southwark | Servant | 4 yrs. | £ 18.0.0. |
| Middletown twp., Cumberland co. | | 4 yrs. | £ 15.0.0. |
| | | 4 yrs. | £ 15.0.0. |
| Philadelphia | Apprentice, taught sewing and folding of books, read and write and housewifery, and not to assign her without giving the father the choice refusing two of the reputable persons (note 5, and £ 5 in cash). | 9 yrs., 10 mo., 15 d. | |
| Philadelphia | Servant | 4 yrs. | £ 15.0.0. |
| Philadelphia | Servant | 3 yrs. | £ 12.0.0. |
| N. Jersey | Servant | 4 yrs. | £ 17.0.0. |
| Southwark | | 5 yrs., 10 mo. | £ 5.0.0. |
| Worcester twp., Phila. co. | Apprentice, taught to read and write English and arithmetic, to understand the rule of 3, taught the cordwainer's trade (note 5, give him a set of shoemaker's tools and £ 5 in money). | 16 yrs., 4 mo., 9 d. | |
| Evesham, Burlington co., Jersey | Apprentice [5] | 6 yrs. | £ 18.0.0. |
| Donegal twp., Lancaster co. | Servant [5] | 3 yrs. | £ 14.15.0. |
| Blockly twp., Phila. co. | Servant [5] | 4 yrs. | £ 16.0.0. |
| | Servant, paid 25/ every year [3] | 3 yrs. | £ 12.0.0. |
| Carlisle, Cumberland co. | | 4 yrs. | £ 14.0.0. |
| Christiana Bridge, New Capel co. | Servant | 4 yrs. | £ 15.0.0. |
| Pensbury twp., Chester co. | Servant, found meat drink, washing and lodging, apparel, at expiration give him freedom dues. | 2 yrs., 6 mo. | £ 12.0.0. |

| Date. | Name. | From the Port of | To Whom Indentured. |
|---|---|---|---|
| 1773. May 20th | Beech, Rebecca | | Jacob Barge and his assigns |
| | Dell, Nicholas | | James Dalton |
| | Jobson, Samuel | | Samuel Noble and his assigns |
| | Leonard, Christopher; Jackson, Samuel; McHugh, Thomas; McQuinn, John; Smyth, James; Moore, Andrew; Stoys, Matthew; Cook, Alexander; Byrn, John; Mahoney, James; Burnett, John; Owen, Simon; Field, John; Phillips, Lawrence; Davis, James; Magrath, James; Bolton, John; Keating, Thomas. | Dublin | James Ray and his assigns |
| | Conyers, Robert | Dublin | James Ray and his assigns |
| | Carney, Mary; Kelly, Jane; Murphy, Esther. | Dublin | James Ray |
| | Jourdan, Christopher | | John Budenheimer and his assigns |
| | Ferdysh, Barbara | | Frederick Phile and his assigns |
| | Sharpe, William | | Joshua Cooper and his assigns |
| | Phillips, Lawrence | | James Ray and his assigns |
| | Hefferin, Bridget | Dublin | John Hannum and his assigns |
| | Moore, Andrew | | Robert Leverly and his assigns |
| | Fennell, Daniel | | William Dungan |
| | Nelson, Jane | | William Ruse and his assigns |
| May 21st | Kane, Francis; Gibson, James; Keating, Ignatius; Lount, Gabriel; Kelly, Margaret. | | David and Thomas Fulton and their assigns. |
| | Duffey, Rose; Godfrey, Sarah; Reily, Christopher; Wilkinson, John; Biggs, John; Ready, Nicholas; Gill, Mary. | | David and Thomas Fulton and their assigns. |
| | Magines, Patrick | Ireland | Peter Ott and his assigns |
| | McCallister, George | | Henry Graham and his assigns |
| | Thompson, Aaron | | Samuel Pancoast and his assigns |
| | Davis, William | | Samuel Harrold and his assigns |
| | Atkins, William | | Charles West and his assigns |
| May 22nd | Mercer, Eleanor | Dublin | John Davidson and his assigns |
| | Fitzgerrald, Mary | | Robert Mullen and his assigns |
| | Thompson, Michael | | John McCullough and his assigns |
| | Younger, Elizabeth | | Thomas Carpenter and his assigns |

[1] To be found all necessaries and at the expiration have freedom dues.
[2] To be found all necessaries and at the expiration have one new suit of apparel.
[3] To be found all necessaries and at the expiration have two complete suits of apparel, one whereof to be new.

| Residence. | Occupation. | Term. | Amount. |
|---|---|---|---|
| Philadelphia | Servant | 4 yrs. | £ 5. 0. 0. |
|  | This day discharged and set free from his indenture under the hand and seal of the said James Dalton. |  | £ 6. 0. 0. |
| Northern Liberties | Apprentice, taught the trade of a tanner and currier, have five quarters' schooling or learn to rule of 3.[3] | 11 yrs., 2 mo., 20 d. |  |
| Little Britain twp., Lancaster co. | Servants[5] | 4 yrs. each | £ 14. 0. 0. for each of their passages. |
| Little Britain twp., Lancaster co. |  | 3 yrs. | £ 14. 0. 0. |
| Little Britain twp., Lancaster co. | Servant[5] | 4 yrs. | £ 14. 0. 0. each. |
| Philadelphia | Servant[5] | 4 yrs. | £ 15. 0. 0. |
| Philadelphia |  | 4 yrs., 6 mo. | £ 26. 13. 10. |
|  | Servant | 4 yrs. | £ 18. 0. 0. |
| Little Britain, Lancaster co. | Servant | 4 yrs. | £ 14. 0. 0. |
|  | Servant[1] | 4 yrs. | £ 13. 0. 0. |
| Philadelphia | Apprentice, learn the trade of a woman shoemaker.[3] | 4 yrs., 6 mo. | £ 18. 0. 0. |
| New Britain twp., Bucks co. | Servant[1] | 4 yrs. | £ 16. 0. 0. |
| Newtown twp., Chester co. | Servant | 4 yrs. | £ 13. 10. 0. |
| Nottingham, Chester co. | Servants[1] | 4 yrs. each | £ 13. 0. 0. each. |
| Nottingham, Chester co. | Servants[1] |  | £ 13. 0. 0. each. |
| Blockley twp., Phila. co. | Servant[3] | 3 yrs. | £ 18. 0. 0. |
| Chester, Chester co. | Servant[5] | 4 yrs. | £ 15. 0. 0. |
| Philadelphia | Apprentice, taught the trade of a house carpenter, given nine months' evening schooling (note 5, £ 5 worth of clothes). | 6 yrs., 10 mo., 6 d. |  |
| Buckingham twp., Bucks co. | Servant[5] | 4 yrs. | £ 20. 0. 0. |
| Deptford, Gloster City, N. J. | Servant[5] | 4 yrs. | £ 20. 0. 0. |
| Philadelphia | Servant[5] | 3 yrs. | £ 10. 0. 0. |
| Philadelphia | Servant | 2 yrs., 11 mo., 16 d. | £ 8. 0. 0. |
| Philadelphia | Apprentice, taught the house carpenter's trade (note 5, except clothing, but provide him with shoes). | 4 yrs., 5 mo. 26 d. |  |
| Moyamensing twp. | Servant[1] | 3 yrs. | £ 8. 0. 0. |

[4] To be found all necessaries and at the expiration have two complete suits of apparel, one whereof to be new, and 40s. in money.

[5] At expiration have two complete suits of apparel, one whereof to be new.

| Date. | Name. | From the Port of | To Whom Indentured. |
|---|---|---|---|
| 1773. May 22nd... | Sterling, Letitia | | Henry Barr and wife, Elizabeth.... |
| | Bard, Elizabeth | | John Little and his assigns......... |
| May 24th... | Byrne, Michael | | Thomas Laycock and his assigns.... |
| | Fagan, Bridget | | Thomas Laycock and his assigns.... |
| | Mitchell, Samuel | | William Pusey and his assigns..... |
| | Bedwell, Henry | | James Old and his assigns......... |
| | Sutton, John Jacob | | James Old and his assigns......... |
| | Brangan, Christopher | | William Todd and his assigns....... |
| | Oharra, George | Dublin | William Todd and his assigns....... |
| | Hamen, Isabella | | John Palmer ...................... |
| | Halbon, Edmond | London | Lewis Grant and his assigns........ |
| | Palmer, Joseph | Ireland | Samuel Wigfall and his assigns..... |
| | Sharman, John | | William Cooper and his assigns..... |
| May 25th... | Kite, Charles | | Thomas Tyson and his assigns...... |
| | Breadhawr, Johan Casper | | Jacob Barge ...................... |
| | Kerknerin, Anna Elizabeth | | Andreas Kerknerin ................ |
| | McGinnis, Arthur | | John Knox and his assigns ........ |
| | Goir, Judith | Ireland | John Reynolds and his assigns...... |
| | Johnston, Margaret | | John Dunlap and his assigns........ |
| | Anquitel, John | | Joseph Liblune and John Christ Waggoner. |
| | Onessems, John | | William Golding and his assigns..... |
| | Kopfer, Jacob Henry | Rotterdam | Joseph Dean and his assigns........ |
| | Connell, James | Ireland | Hercules Courtney and his assigns... |
| May 26th... | Doyle, Matthew | | Aaron Hibbard and wife, Elizabeth.. |
| | Shea, Richard | | William Burn and his assigns....... |
| May 26th... | Doyle, John; Galliger, Michael. | | John Haskins ..................... |
| | Anster, Nathaniel | | Christopher Frederick and his assigns. |
| | Graham, Sarah | Ireland | James Lyon and his assigns......... |
| | Gavin, John | | Thomas Craig .................... |
| | Huddy, Elizabeth | | Chamless Allen ................... |
| | Deadman, John | London | George Edleman and his assigns..... |
| | Deal, Daniel | | George Smith and his assigns....... |

| Residence. | Occupation. | Term. | Amount. |
|---|---|---|---|
| Northampton twp., Burlington co. N. J. | Apprentice, taught housewifery, sew, knit and spin, read in Bible, write a legible hand.[3] | 11 yrs., 6 mo. | |
| Philadelphia | Apprentice, taught housewifery, sew, knit and spin, to read, write and arithmetic, to understand the rule of 3.[5] | 7 yrs., 9 mo. 27 d. | |
| Chichester twp., Chester co. | Servant | 4 yrs. | £14.0.0. |
| Chichester twp., Chester co. | Servant | 4 yrs. | £14.0.0. |
| Philadelphia | Servant[5] | 4 yrs. | £15.0.0. |
| E. Nantmill, Chester co. | Servant | 4 yrs. | £20.0.0. |
| E. Nantmill, Chester co. | Servant | 7 yrs. | £20.0.0. |
| Philadelphia | Servant | 4 yrs. | £18.0.0. |
| Philadelphia | Servant[1] | 4 yrs. | £18.0.0. |
| Northern Liberties | Apprentice | 2 yrs. | £7.0.0. |
| Philadelphia | Servant, shall be wholly employed in the business of a brass founder.[2] | 3 yrs. | £17.18.6. |
| Philadelphia | Apprentice, taught the trade of a cutler, have £5 Pa. currency in the fifth year, £6 in the sixth year and £7 in the seventh year.[3] | 7 yrs. | £15.0.0. |
| St. Georges Hundred, New Castle co. | Servant | 4 yrs. | £22.0.0. |
| Abbington twp., Phila. co. | Servant | 6 yrs. | £13.0.0. |
| Philadelphia | | 6 yrs., 7 mo. | £20.8.0. |
| | | 7 yrs. | £0.5.0. |
| Southwark | Apprentice, taught the art and mystery of a hatter, found meat, drink, washing and lodging and working apparel, to go every winter to night schooling, the brother paying the expense. | 6 yrs., 6 mo. | |
| Philadelphia | Servant | 4 yrs. | £16.0.0. |
| Philadelphia | Servant[6] | 3 yrs., 6 mo. | £15.0.0. |
| Philadelphia | Apprentice, taught the trade of a peruke maker and hair dresser, read and write well.[3] | 4 yrs. | £20.0.0. |
| Philadelphia | Servant[5] | 1 yr. | £6.0.0. |
| Philadelphia | Servant[3] | 5 yrs., 1 mo. | £16.11.0. |
| Philadelphia | Servant, employ and instruct him in the art of carving and gilding, and about no other business[3] | 6 yrs. | £15.0.0. |
| Blockley twp., Phila. co. | Apprentice, taught farming, read and write well, have two complete suits of clothes and 50 shillings in cash when free. | 10 yrs., 8 mo., 4 d. | |
| Philadelphia | Apprentice, taught the trade of a hair dresser.[3] | 6 yrs. | £14.0.0. |
| Philadelphia | Servant[5] | 4 yrs. each.. | £14.0.0. each. |
| Waterford twp., Gloster co., N. J. | Servant[3] | 3 yrs., 6 mo. | £12.0.0. |
| Norrington, Phila co | Servant[5] | 3 yrs. | £10.0.0. |
| Philadelphia | Servant[5] | 4 yrs. | |
| Philadelphia | Apprentice, taught the mantua making business, sew and knit, have six months' schooling, allowed a week every year to go to Salem to see her friends.[6] | 6 yrs. | |
| Allens twp., Northampton co. | Servant[3] | 3 yrs., 3 mo. | £18.0.0. |
| Philadelphia | Apprentice, taught the blacksmith's trade (note 1, or £8 in cash). | 4 yrs. | |

| Date. | Name. | From the Port of | To Whom Indentured. |
|---|---|---|---|
| 1773. | Smith, Jonathan | | Joshua Moore and his assigns |
| May 27th | Dasher, Peter | London | Abraham Kensing and his assigns |
| | Neil, Hugh | | Peter Sutor |
| | Norman, John | | Thomas Clifford, Jr., and his assigns |
| | Fordysh, Barbara | | John Whitmore and his assigns |
| | Norman, John | | James Old |
| | Pope, William | | James Old |
| May 28th | Higgons, Thomas | | Daniel King and his assigns |
| | Olof, Sears; Platfoot, John; Clarke, John; Neale, Nicholas; Lang, Alice, Vergin, John; Magus, Joshua; Eyers, Joseph; Thomas, Richard; Bedford, Robert. | Bristol | James Taylor and his assigns |
| | Mabbely, William; Light, William; Moore, William, Morgan, John. | Bristol | James Taylor and his assigns |
| | McKnown, William | Bristol | James Taylor and his assigns |
| | Clifford, John | Bristol | Robert Lewis and his assigns |
| | Wash, Margaret | | Abraham Peter |
| | Decker, Christopher | | Jacob Schreider and his assigns |
| | Jones, Samuel | Bristol | James Taylor and his assigns |
| | Lang, Alice | Bristol | Capt. William Gamble and his assigns. |
| | Wagenarin, Maria | Rotterdam | Anthony Grove and his assigns |
| | Sheredan, Thomas; Clark, Edward; Martin, Molly; Burk, John; Dunn, Edward; Gec, Ralp. | Dublin | James Taylor and his assigns |
| | Hines, Thomas | Bristol | Samuel Purviance, Sr., and his assigns. |
| | Richard, John | Bristol | John Stillie and his assigns |
| May 29th | Mason, Sibason | Bristol | John Dunlap and his assigns |
| | Johnston, Charles | | Samuel Jackson and his assigns |
| | Wall, John | Bristol | Thomas Tisdell and his assigns |
| | Marlier, Rose | London | Jonah Foster and his assigns |
| | Fitzgerrald, George | | Simon Murray and his assigns |
| | Dunn, Edward; Sheridan, Thomas. | | Joseph Taylor and his assigns |
| | Shedaker, David | | James Hunter and his assigns |
| | Haslet, James | Ireland | Robert Johnston and his assigns |
| May 31st | Towns, Thomas | London | John Flin and his assigns |

## List of Indentures.

| Residence. | Occupation. | Term. | Amount. |
|---|---|---|---|
| Philadelphia | Apprentice, taught the trade of a cabinet maker (note 5, a good suit of apparel). | 5 yrs., 3 mo. 20 d. | |
| Philadelphia | Servant[1] | 4 yrs. | £ 17. 9. 6. |
| | Apprentice | 7 yrs. | £ 15. 0. 0. |
| Philadelphia | Servant | 7 yrs. | £ 20. 0. 0. |
| Rapho twp., Lancaster co. | Servant | 4 yrs., 6 mo. | £ 20. 0. 0. |
| E. Nantmill twp., Chester co. | | 7 yrs. | £ 20. 0. 0. |
| E. Nantmill twp., Chester co. | Servant[5] | 4 yrs. | £ 15. 0. 0. |
| Philadelphia | Servant, taught the trade of a brass founder.[3] | 5 yrs. | £ 12. 0. 0. |
| Shippensburgh twp., Cumberland co. | Servant | 4 yrs. each | £ 16. 0. 0. each. |
| Shippensburgh twp., Cumberland co. | Servant | 5 yrs. each | £ 16. 0. 0. each. |
| Shippensburgh twp., Cumberland co. | Servant | 6 yrs. | £ 16. 0. 0. |
| Philadelphia | Servant | 4 yrs. | £ 16. 0. 0. |
| Philadelphia | Apprentice taught housewifery, read well in Bible, write a legible hand.[3] | 6 yrs., 11 mo. | |
| Northern Liberties | Apprentice, taught the trade of a painter and glazier, read and write (note 3, worth £ 8. 20. 0 in money). | 6 yrs., 2 mo. 13 d. | £ 20. 0. 0. |
| Shippensburgh, Cumberland co. | Servant[1] | 4 yrs. | £ 16. 0. 0. |
| Philadelphia | Servant | 4 yrs. | £ 16. 0. 0. |
| Philadelphia | Servant[3] | 3 yrs., 5 mo. | £ 23. 0. 0. |
| Shippensburgh, Cumberland co. | Servant[5] | 4 yrs. each | £ 16. 0. 0. each. |
| Pits Grove twp., Salem co., N. J. | Servant[5] | 7 yrs. | £ 16. 0. 0. |
| Philadelphia | Servant[5] | 4 yrs. | £ 18. 0. 0. |
| Philadelphia | Servant[5] | 4 yrs. | £ 16. 0. 0. |
| Philadelphia | Apprentice, taught the art of a mariner, allowed three months' time during the term to learn navigation, allowed £ 3 Pa. currency each year, found all necessaries except apparel. | 4 yrs. | |
| Philadelphia | Apprentice, taught the art and mystery of a rope maker.[3] | 7 yrs. | £ 16. 0. 0. |
| Eversham twp., Burlington co. | Servant, give her nine months' day schooling.[3] | 9 yrs., 8 mo. | £ 10. 0. 0. |
| Philadelphia | Servant[2] | 3 yrs. | £ 20. 8. 0. |
| Upper Freehold twp. Monmouth co., E. Jersey. | Servant | 4 yrs. each | £ 15. 0. 0. each. |
| Philadelphia | Apprentice, taught the art and mystery of a shopkeeper, found meat, drink, apparel, washing and lodging. | 6 yrs., 9 mo. | |
| New Landing twp., Chester co. | Servant, found meat, drink, washing, lodging and wearing apparel. | 3 yrs., 6 mo. | £ 15. 0. 0. |
| Philadelphia | Servant, employed at the cabinet maker's trade.[3] | 2 yrs., 11 mo., 2 d. | £ 23. 2. 5. |

| Date. | Name. | From the Port of | To Whom Indentured. |
|---|---|---|---|
| 1773.<br>May 31st | Manipenny, Catherine | | Benjamin Estteurn and his assigns |
| | Parkes, Isaac | London | Andrew, Boyd and William Pillars and their assigns. |
| | Weisman, Johannes | London | Joseph Ridgeway and his assigns |
| | Fye, Frederick | London | James McConaghy and his assigns |
| | Kreiger, Martin | London | Joseph Lamb and his assigns |
| | Phifer, Christian | London | John Brown and his assigns |
| | Bagel, Christopher | London | Michael Stofflet and his assigns |
| | McIlmoyal, Elizabeth | | Sarah Wilson |
| June 1st | Wrink, Marcus | | Cornelius Cooper and his assigns |
| | Frank, Andrew | London | Ballas Clymer and his assigns |
| | McDonald, Charles | | Thomas Leper and his assigns |
| | Burgaden, Anna Magdelene | Rotterdam | William Hembel and his assigns |
| | Folstick, Balser | London | John Butcher and his assigns |
| | Dady, Patrick | | Benjamin Mitchell and his assigns |
| | Smith, John | | Patrick Colvin and his assigns |
| | Hamilton, Richard | London | Joseph McKibbins and his assigns |
| June 2nd | Long, James | London | David Griffith |
| | Reincke, Christopher | London | Michael Schnuder and his assigns |
| | Ogden, Joseph | | Joseph Baker and his assigns |
| | Williams, Nicholas | Bristol | William Gamble and his assigns |
| | Williams, Nicholas | | Joseph Worral and his assigns |
| | Gabehard, Conrad | | Charles Barry and his assigns |
| | Lejeun, Jacob | London | Jacob Winey and his assigns |
| | Ferhager, Everhard | London | Joseph Brunlinger and his assigns |
| | Poor, John | | John Handlin and his assigns |
| | Patterson, James | | William McMullen and his assigns |
| | Horn, Michael | London | Paul Faker and his assigns |
| | Wright, John, Jr. | | Edward James |
| | Myover, Levy | | William Brown and his assigns |
| | Barts, Nicholas | London | John Ney and his assigns |

## List of Indentures.

| Residence. | Occupation. | Term. | Amount. |
|---|---|---|---|
| Kitochin Hundred, Frederick co., Md. | Servant[3] | | 5 shillings. |
| Hopewell twp., Cumberland co. | Servant, employed in the tanning and currying business.[5] | 2 yrs., 8 mo. | £10.10.0. |
| Springfield twp., Burlington co., N. J. | Servant[3] | 4 yrs. | £15.7.4. |
| West Nantmill twp., Chester co. | Servant, taught to make flower cask.[3] | 7 yrs. | £15.7.4. |
| Hanover twp., Burlington co., W. Jersey. | Servant[3] | 4 yrs. | £15.7.4. |
| Deptford twp., Gloster co., W. Jersey. | Servant (note 1, and £5 Pa. currency). | 3 yrs. | £15.7.4. |
| Colebrookdale twp., Berks co. | Servant[3] | 4 yrs. | £16.1.7. |
| Philadelphia | Apprentice, taught housewifery, read, write a legible hand, cypher, to understand the rule of 3 and to sew.[5] | 10 yrs. | |
| Philadelphia | Servant | 7 yrs., 6 mo. | £10.0.0. |
| Philadelphia | Servant[3] | 3 yrs., 6 mo. | £15.13.0. |
| Philadelphia | Apprentice, taught the trade of a tobacconist, read in Bible, write a legible hand.[3] | 8 yrs., 7 mo. | |
| Philadelphia | Servant[3] | 5 yrs., 6 mo. | £30.0.0. |
| Philadelphia | Servant, to be employed at the tailor's trade.[3] | 3 yrs., 9 mo. | £15.7.4. |
| Philadelphia | Apprentice, found meat, drink, washing and lodging and £30 at expiration of the first year, and £30 at the end of the term and have his shirts and stockings mended, and out of the last year's payment it is agreed to deduct the consideration money paid for his use. | 2 yrs. | £15.18.0 |
| | Servant[1] | 4 yrs. | £16.0.0. |
| Armagh twp., Cumberland co. | Servant[5] | 4 yrs. | £22.0.0. |
| Dincader Hundred, near Castle co. | | 4 yrs. | £20.10.0. |
| Northern Liberties | Servant (note 1, or £8 in cash, when free). | | £14.19.6. |
| Philadelphia | | 7 yrs. | £15.0.0. |
| Philadelphia | Servant[3] | 5 yrs. | £16.0.0. |
| Trenttown, N. J. | | 5 yrs. | £16.0.0. |
| Philadelphia | Apprentice, taught the trade of a painter and glazier, read and write in the English and Dutch, have three quarters' drawing schooling (note 1, or £12 current money of Pa.). | 2 yrs., 3 mo. 12 d. | |
| Philadelphia | Servant[3] | 3 yrs., 6 mo. | £15.17.4. |
| Douglas twp., Phila. co. | Servant (note 1, or 8 English guineas). | 3 yrs., 6 mo. | £15.7.4. |
| Philadelphia | Apprentice, to learn the turner's trade, have liberty to go to school every winter at his mother's expense.[3] | | |
| | Servant[5] | 2 yrs., 6 mo. | £21.11.8. |
| Elses twp., Berks co. | Servant, taught the trade of a paper maker.[3] | 4 yrs. | £18.11.9. |
| Southwark | | 8 yrs. | £10.0.0. |
| Northern Liberties | Apprentice, to be taught the trade of a shipwright, have one quarter night schooling every year (note 3, and common tools). | 5 yrs., 11 mo., 24 d. | |
| Antrim twp., Cumberland co. | Servant[3] | 3 yrs. | £16.1.7. |

| Date. | Name. | From the Port of | To Whom Indentured. |
|---|---|---|---|
| 1773. June 3rd.... | Campble, William | | Anthony McKendley and his assigns. |
| | Course, Henry | London | Thomas Moore and his assigns...... |
| | Hemlick, Andrew | | Wendale Hipshman and his assigns.. |
| | Milck, Jacob | London | Daniel Heister, Jr., and his assigns... |
| | Wigmore, John | | Peter Ridge ....................... |
| | Almen, John | London | Christian Schneider and his assigns.. |
| | McIlwrath, John | Ireland | James Roney ...................... |
| | Lerrue, Mary | | Philatitia Stretull and her assigns.... |
| | Tully, Patrick | | George Oakley and his assigns...... |
| June 4th.... | Leetchtin, Maria Barbara | | Jacob Charles ..................... |
| | Boger, Henry Conrad | | Jacob Latchshaver ................. |
| | McCleash, Ann | | Alex. Minnis and his wife, Margaret. |
| 1773. June 5th.... | Dugee, Samuel | London | Samuel Pleaseant and his assigns.... |
| | Harvey, John | London | Thomas Earl and his assigns........ |
| | Heyer, Nicholas | London | William Newbold and his assigns.... |
| | Ross, George | | Jacob Reindoller and his assigns..... |
| | Bohn, Philip | London | Sebastian Miller and his assigns..... |
| | Collins, Mary | | Henry Kreps and Catherine, his wife. |
| June 7th.... | Engel, John | London | Schlessir and Franks and their assigns. |
| | Davy, Mary | London | Zebulon Rudulph and his assigns.... |
| | Davy, Mary | | Philip Syng and his assigns......... |
| | Pfotzer, George | | Christopher Marshall, Jr., and his assigns. |
| | Jones, Evan | | Samuel Powell and his assigns....... |
| | Grube, Jacob | London | Thomas Wallace and his assigns .... |
| | Grube, Jacob | | Henry Kendrieth and his assigns.... |
| | Robinson, Edward | Ireland | Robert Johnson and his assigns...... |
| | Cannon, Jacob; Somervill, George. | | Robert Johnson and his assigns...... |
| | Capes, Peter | | Christian Golley and his assigns..... |
| | Iden, Mary | | Elijah Brown and Mary, his wife.... |

## List of Indentures.

| Residence. | Occupation. | Term. | Amount. |
|---|---|---|---|
| Baltimore, Md. | Servant[1] | 4 yrs. | £ 7. 6. 6. |
| Bethall twp., Northampton co. | Servant[3] | 3 yrs. | £ 15. 12. 4. |
| | Servant (note 5, £ 10 in cash). | 3 yrs. | £ 17. 10. 0. |
| Upper Solford twp., Phila. co. | Servant (note 3, or £ 8 Pa. currency). | 2 yrs., 6 mo. | £ 15. 12. 4. |
| Philadelphia | Apprentice, taught the ship rigger's trade, have five quarters' night schooling (note 2, besides his old). | 5 yrs. | |
| Derry twp., Lancaster co. | Servant (note 5, have £ 10 lawful money of Pa. in lieu of freedom dues). | 3 yrs. | £ 16. 5. 0. |
| Philadelphia | Servant[1] | 4 yrs. | £ 9. 0. 0. |
| Philadelphia | Servant[1] | 4 yrs. | £ 20. 0. 0. |
| Philadelphia | Apprentice, taught merchant's account and bookkeeping, found all necessaries and be paid £ 3 Jamaica currency each year and afterwards assigned to serve (with his consent) Thomas Oakely of Spanish Town in Jamaica. | | £ 15. 18. 1. |
| Harford twp., Chester co. | | 5 yrs. | £ 16. 0. 0. |
| Colebrook Dale, Bucks co. | | 4 yrs. | £ 27. 0. 0. |
| Northern Liberties | Apprentice, taught housewifery, read and write, knit and sew.[5] | 12 yrs., 6 mo., 20 d. | |
| Philadelphia | Servant, (note 5, £ 8 in lieu of freedom and two quarters' schooling during the term). | 4 yrs. | £ 17. 13. 3. |
| Springfield twp., Burlington co., N. Jersey. | Servant | 4 yrs. | £ 22. 0. 0. |
| Chesterfield twp., Burlington co., N. Jersey. | Servant[3] | 3 yrs., 3 mo. | 16. 8 pence. |
| Philadelphia | Apprentice, taught the trade of a tailor, have three months' day and three months' night schooling.[3] | 6 yrs., 4 mo. 15 d. | |
| Germantown, Phila. co. | Servant (note 3, and 27 shillings in cash). | 3 yrs. | £ 16. 1. 9. |
| Southwark | Apprentice, taught the mystery of a mantua maker, taught to read in Bible and write a legible hand.[3] | 8 yrs. | |
| Philadelphia | Servant[3] | 3 yrs., 3 mo. | £ 18. 2. 6. |
| Philadelphia | Servant[3] | 3 yrs., 6 mo. | £ 9. 16. 6. |
| Lower Merion twp., Phila. co. | Servant | 3 yrs., 6 mo. | £ 15. 18. |
| | Servant (note 5, have £ 10 in cash in lieu of freedom). | 3 yrs., 6 mo. | £ 15. 0. 0. |
| Philadelphia | Apprentice, taught the trade of a house carpenter, have one quarter's night schooling each winter.[3] | 7 yrs., 8 mo. 22 d. | |
| Newport, New Castle co. | Servant[3] | 4 yrs. | £ 18. 17. 8. |
| Mastic twp., Lancaster co. | Servant | 4 yrs. | £ 18. 17. 8. |
| New London twp., Chester co. | Servant[5] | 4 yrs. | £ 13. 0. 0. |
| New London twp., Chester co. | Servant[5] | 4 yrs. each. | £ 15. 0. 0. each. |
| Philadelphia | Servant, employed as a tabaces spinner.[1] | 4 yrs. | £ 16. 1. 7. |
| Philadelphia | Apprentice, taught housewifery, have one quarter's schooling, learn to sew and mark two quarters', learn writing and arithmetic (note 3, also give her | 7 yrs., 10 mo., 18 d. | |

| Date. | Name. | From the Port of | To Whom Indentured. |
|---|---|---|---|
| 1773.<br>June 7th | Stockerly, Peter | | John McCalla and his assigns |
| | Swain, James | | Jonathan Isyard and his assigns |
| | Swain, Nezer | | Jonathan Isyard and his assigns |
| | Reed, Mary | | Robert Armstrong and his assigns |
| | Robinson, Mary | | Robert Armstrong and his assigns |
| | Geraty, Daniel; Kelly Owen. | Dublin | Robert Armstrong and his assigns |
| | Pearstead, Joakin | London | Adam Weaver and his assigns |
| June 8th | Might, John | Dubland | Robert Armstrong and his assigns |
| | Sparing, Henry | | Richard Collier and his assigns |
| | Town, Joseph | | John Duchie and his assigns |
| | Sefton, William | | Thomas Hale and his assigns |
| | Reily, Catherine | London | Christopher Marshall, Jr., and his assigns. |
| | Jourdan, Thomas | | Edward Tabor and his assigns |
| | Walter, Mary | London | Lucy Leonard and her assigns |
| | Walter, Mary | | Mary Yard and her assigns |
| | Flyer, Michael | | Abraham Resar |
| | Brooks, Dickman | Bristol | Joseph Griffith and his assigns |
| | Squire, William | Bristol | Joseph Fox and his assigns |
| | Kyle, James | | Blair McClenneghan and Samuel Jackson. |
| June 9th | Younger, Elizabeth | | George Heisel and his assigns |
| | Farrel, Michael | | John Smith and his assigns |
| | Farrel, Michael | | Peter Robinson and his assigns |
| | Davis, John; Darling, Mary.. | | Dury Wake |
| | Norton, Edward | | Lewis Phraity and his assigns |
| | Law, Samuel | | James Lees and his assigns |

## List of Indentures.

| Residence. | Occupation. | Term. | Amount. |
|---|---|---|---|
| | board so long that she may learn the mantua making business). | | |
| Philadelphia | Apprentice, taught the tailor's trade, found all necessaries except clothing, to receive from his master £4 annually for the first six years and 20 shillings for the last until £25 are paid. | 7 yrs., 4 mo, 21 d. | |
| Philadelphia | Apprentice, have twelve months' night schooling.[3] | 6 yrs., 8 mo. 26 d. | |
| Philadelphia | Apprentice, give him six months' night schooling, three months of it to be in the last year of his time. If the master should want to part with the apprentice he is to give the first offer to his guardian.[1] | 4 yrs., 1 mo. 14 d. | |
| Augusta Parish, Augusta co., Va. | Servant (note 5, give her £3.10 shillings Virginia money). | 3 yrs | £3.0.0. |
| Augusta Parish, Augusta co., Va. | Servant (note 5, give her £3.10 shillings Virginia money). | 3 yrs | £3.0.0. |
| Augusta Parish, Augusta co., Va. | Servant | 4 yrs. each | £15.0.0. each. |
| Leacock twp., Lancaster co. | Servant (note 3, or £10 Pa currency). | 3 yrs | £15.7.4. |
| Augusta Parish, Augusta co., Va. | Servant | 4 yrs | £14.0.0. |
| Philadelphia | Servant, found all necessaries except apparel, kept at the trade of a cordwainer. If he pays his master the sum of 17.13.3 in six months the indenture to be void. | 2 yrs | £17.13.3. |
| Southwark | Apprentice, taught the business of a boat builder, have three quarters' night schooling (note 5, his working tools). | 6 yrs., 9 mo. 5 d. | |
| Philadelphia | Apprentice, taught the trade of a carpenter allowed time to go to night school one quarter each winter, his father paying the expense of schooling.[5] | 6 yrs., 8 mo. | |
| Philadelphia | Servant[3] | 3 yrs | £14.11.6. |
| | Apprentice, taught the trade of a tailor, have twelve months' night schooling.[3] | 8 yrs., 28 d. | |
| Philadelphia | Servant[3] | 3 yrs | £16.15.0. |
| Philadelphia | Servant | 3 yrs | £16.15. |
| Springfield twp., Bucks co. | Servant (note 5, and £7 in cash in lieu of freedom). | 3 yrs., 6 mo. | £15.7.4. |
| Edgemand twp., Chester co. | Servant[5] | 5 yrs | £20.0.0. |
| Philadelphia | Servant[5] | 3 yrs | £17.0.0. |
| Philadelphia | Apprentice, taught the art of a mariner. | 3 yrs. | |
| Passyunck twp., Phila. co. | Servant | 3 yrs | £6.0.0. |
| Merion twp., Phila. co. | Servant (note 2, besides his old) | 3 yrs., 6 mo. | £3.0.0. |
| Philadelphia | Servant | 3 yrs., 6 mo. | £15.0.0. |
| Burlington, N. J. | Servant[1] | 4 yrs. each. | £11.0.0. each. |
| Philadelphia | Servant, allowed six hours every week for himself, to be employed at the smith's business.[3] | 4 yrs | £17.13.10. |
| Philadelphia | Servant (note 5, and have one shilling every week during the term) | 2 yrs., 6 mo. | £26.0.0. |

| Date. | Name. | From the Port of | To Whom Indentured. |
|---|---|---|---|
| 1773. | Craft, Joseph | Bristol | Benjamin Fuller and his assigns |
| June 9th | Bayliss, William | | Andrew Banner and his assigns |
| | Venall, James | | Benjamin Fuller and his assigns |
| June 10th | Bryan, Mary | | David Cummings and his assigns |
| | Wayne, Benjamin | | John Galloway and his assigns |
| | Ellers, John | London | Aaron Ferman and his assigns |
| | Maneight, Elizabeth | Ireland | James Roney and his assigns |
| | Stock, John | Bristol | Matthias Landenburger and his assigns. |
| June 11th | Ross, Christopher | | John Gensell and his assigns |
| | Salmon, Patrick | Dublin | Cyrus Copper and his assigns |
| | Brown, Jane; Gordan, Mary; Purcell, Ann. | Dublin | Cyrus Copper and his assigns |
| | Melton, Thomas; Conner, Lawrence; Breriton, Thos.; Purcell, John. | Dublin | Cyrus Copper and his assigns |
| | Burk, John | Ireland | Cyrus Copper and his assigns |
| | Trested, Richard | London | John Nickilson and his assigns |
| | Borell, Mathew | | Henry Ayemich and his assigns |
| | Reinhart, Andrew | | John Geyer and his assigns |
| | Garche, Augustine | London | Adam Arth and his assigns |
| June 12th | Delany, Ann | | William Brooks and his assigns |
| | Gready, Michael | | Thomas Mason and his assigns |
| | Raverty, John | | Samuel Leppencot |
| | Ready, Nicholas | | John James and his assigns |
| | Hayes, James | | Joseph Drinker and his assigns |
| June 14th | Dewees, William | | Thomas Williams and his assigns |
| | Hopkins, William | | William Austin and his assigns |
| | Smith, Andrew | London | Isarel Morris, Jr., and his assigns |
| | Smith, Andrew | | Samuel Morris, Jr., and his assigns |
| | Barge, Boltis | | Peter Wagoner and his assigns |
| June 15th | Neil, Hannah | | Samuel Minshall |
| | Marble, Richard, and Elizabeth, his wife. | London | George Wood and his assigns |
| | Smith, John | Newry | Thomas Lancaster and his assigns |
| | Dickson, Robert | Ireland | John Tittermay and his assigns |
| | Butler, Anthony | | Thomas Mifflin |

| Residence. | Occupation. | Term. | Amount. |
|---|---|---|---|
| Philadelphia | | 5 yrs. | £19.0.0. |
| Philadelphia | | 5 yrs. | £19.0.0. |
| Philadelphia | Apprentice, taught the art and mystery of a mariner and when the ship arrives in port he is to have the privilege to go to school.[3] | 3 yrs., 9 mo. | £10.0.0. |
| Philadelphia | Servant | 4 yrs. | £12.0.0. |
| Philadelphia | Apprentice, taught the trade of a tailor.[1] | 4 yrs., 7 mo. 21 d. | |
| Kingwood twp., Hunterdon co., W. Jersey. | Servant[3] | 3 yrs. | £15.1.0. |
| Hanover twp., Lancaster co. | Servant[3] | 4 yrs. | £12.0.0. |
| Philadelphia | Servant (note 5, etc.) | 7 yrs. | £20.0.0. |
| Philadelphia | Apprentice, taught the art of a mariner and navigation.[6] | 2 yrs., 6 mo. 26 d. | |
| Alexandria, Va. | Servant | 3 yrs. | £16.0.0. |
| Alexandria, Va. | Servant | 4 yrs. each. | £14.0.0. each. |
| Alexandria, Va. | Servant | 4 yrs. each. | £16.0.0. each. |
| Alexandria, Va. | Servant[1] | 4 yrs. | £16.0.0. |
| Philadelphia | Servant, to be employed at the gunsmith business.[1] | 3 yrs. | £14.2.7. |
| Heycock twp., Bucks co. | (Note 5, and £10) | 3 yrs. | £15.7.4. |
| Philadelphia | Servant[3] | 3 yrs., 6 mo. | £19.2.8. |
| Lebanon twp., Lancaster co. | Servant (note 3, and tobacco for his use during the term). | 3 yrs., 3 mo. | £18.12.6. |
| Philadelphia | Apprentice, taught housewifery, sew, read in Bible and write a legible hand.[3] | 11 yrs., 7 mo., 11 d. | |
| Philadelphia | At sea or on shore[6] | 3 yrs., 6 mo. 26 d. | £12.0.0. |
| Northampton twp., Burlington co. | Servant | 3 yrs., 6 mo. | £18.0.0. |
| Philadelphia | Servant | 4 yrs. | £6.0.0. |
| Northern Liberties | Apprentice, taught the trade of a cooper, have three quarters' night schooling in the term.[3] | 10 yrs., 4 mo., 4 d. | |
| Philadelphia | Apprentice, taught the art and mystery of a cordwainer, taught to read and write.[3] | 9 yrs., 16 d. | |
| Philadelphia | Servant | 4 yrs. | £20.0.0. |
| Philadelphia | Servant, found meat, drink, washing and lodging, necessary working apparel and three fine shirts. | 2 yrs. | £12.0.0. |
| Philadelphia | Servant | 2 yrs. | £12.0.0. |
| Philadelphia | Apprentice, taught the art and mystery of a cordwainer, found meat, drink, washing and lodging, shoes and one shirt and one pair breeches. | 1 yr., 6 mo. | |
| Southwark | | 2 yrs., 3 mo. | £8.0.0. |
| Bedford, Bedford co. | Servant | 4 yrs. each. | £15.0.0. each. |
| Whitemarsh twp., Phila. | Servant | 2 yrs., 6 mo. | £15.0.0. |
| Moyamensing twp., Phila. co. | Apprentice, taught the art and mystery of a rope maker, to go every winter to night school.[3] | 5 yrs. | £16.0.0. |
| Philadelphia | Apprentice, to be instructed in the art of a merchant, found all necessaries during the term ex- | 6 yrs. | £150.0.0. |

| Date. | Name. | From the Port of | To Whom Indentured. |
|---|---|---|---|
| 1773. June 15th | Pady, Thomas | Newry | Hugh Commons and his assigns |
| | Harding, Lydia | | Mary Roberts, her executors or assigns |
| | Clyde, William | | William Moore and his assigns |
| | Groves, Thomas | Newry | William Key and his assigns |
| June 16th | Adams, Andrew | Ireland | John Stewart and his assigns |
| | Gahan, John | | Joshua Dungen and his assigns |
| | Gaynor, Edward | | Josuah Dungen and his assigns |
| | Hyde, Ann | | William Harrison |
| | McBoy, Sarah | Newry | John Fleming and his assigns |
| | Wahlen, Thomas | | Stephen Ford and his assigns |
| | Martea, Henry | London | David Dishler and his assigns |
| | Soloman, Margaret | | Henry Helmuth |
| | Matthews, James | Ireland | William Maris and his assigns |
| | Cames, Janet | Ireland | Thomas Campbell and his assigns |
| | Magginnis, John | Ireland | William Hunter and his assigns |
| | Magginnis, John | | Archable Montgomery, near the Gap Tavern, in Lancaster co., and his assigns. |
| June 17th | Martin, William | Ireland | John Hall and his assigns |
| | Black, William | Ireland | William Simple and his assigns |
| | Perry, William | Newry | Thomas Wright and his assigns |
| | Cameron, Angus | | John Smith and his assigns |
| | Evans, Lettiss | | Elinor McKnight and her assigns |
| | Evans, Lettiss | | John Shields and his assigns |
| | Donald, Mary | Ireland | David Jones and his assigns |
| | O'Neal, Phealix | Ireland | Peter Brown and his assigns |
| | Saunders, John | | Samuel Whalor and his assigns |
| | Brooks, George | | John Adams and his assigns |
| June 18th | Laverty, John | Ireland | William Kennedy and his assigns |
| | Adams, James | | Loodwick Liggets and his assigns |
| | Tame, John | | Frederick Wentz and his assigns |

| Residence. | Occupation. | Term. | Amount. |
|---|---|---|---|
| | cept clothing. In case of the death of the master during the apprenticeship a valuable part of the fee shall be returned in proportion to the time from such demise to end of term. | | |
| Northampton twp., Bucks co. | Servant[5] | 4 yrs., 6 mo. | £14.0.0. |
| Philadelphia | Apprentice, taught housewifery, sew, knit and mark, read in Bible, write a legible hand.[3] | 4 yrs., 1 mo. 11 d. | |
| Philadelphia | (Note 5, except clothing.) | 2 yrs. | £15.10.0. |
| Woolwich twp., Glocester co., N. J. | Servant, to go to the Jersey | 4 yrs. | £17.0.0. |
| Oxford twp., Chester co. | Servant, found meat, drink, washing, lodging and wearing apparel. | 2 yrs., 6 mo. | £7.10.0. |
| Warwick twp., Bucks co. | Servant[5] | 4 yrs. | £15.0.0. |
| Warwick twp., Bucks co. | Servant[5] | 4 yrs. | £15.0.0. |
| Gloscester twp., Glocester co., N. J. | Servant[5] | 2 yrs. | £7.10.0. |
| W. Caln twp., Chester co. | Servant | 3 yrs. | £15.0.0. |
| Philadelphia | Apprentice, taught the trade of a tailor, have nine months' schooling.[3] | 13 yrs., 1 mo., 8 d. | |
| Salborough twp., Northampton co. | Servant (note 1, or £9.10.0) | 2 yrs. | £15.8.0. |
| | Apprentice, taught housewifery (note 3, and £5 in cash). | 2 yrs., 11 mo. | |
| Philadelphia | Servant (note 3, or £5 Penna. currency). | 3 yrs., 6 mo. | £20.0.0. |
| New London twp., Chester co. | Servant, found meat, drink, washing and lodging, apparel and when free freedom dues. | 6 yrs. | £14.15.0. |
| W. Caln twp., Chester co. | Servant[5] | 3 yrs. | £16.0.0. |
| | Servant[5] | 3 yrs. | £16.0.0. |
| N. Susquehannah Hundred, Cecil co., Md. | Servant[5] | 2 yrs., 1 mo. | £10.5.0. |
| Philadelphia | Servant[3] | 4 yrs. | £14.10.0. |
| Plumstead twp., Bucks co. | Servant | 3 yrs. | £8.0.0. |
| Philadelphia | Servant[5] | 2 yrs. | £8.0.0. |
| Philadelphia | Apprentice, taught housewifery, three quarters' day schooling.[6] | 3 yrs., 11 mo. | |
| Philadelphia | Servant[5] | 3 yrs., 11 mo. | £5.0.0. |
| Philadelphia | Servant[3] | 4 yrs., 3 mo. | £14.0.0. |
| Northern Liberties | Apprentice, taught the art and mystery of a blacksmith.[3] | 5 yrs. | £16.0.0. |
| Philadelphia | Servant[5] | 3 yrs., 6 mo. | £14.0.0. |
| Southwark | Apprentice, taught the art and mystery of a cordwainer, taught to read in Bible, write a legible hand and cypher as far as and through rule of 3 (note 3, and a complete set of tools). | 17 yrs., 8 mo. | |
| Philadelphia | Servant, found meat, drink, washing, lodging, one coat, three shirts and two pair trousers in the term. | 1 yr., 6 mo. | £8.0.0. |
| East Town twp., Chester co. | | 2 yrs., 6 mo. | £8.0.0. |
| Philadelphia | Apprentice, taught the trade of a surgeon-barber and wigmaker, read in Bible, write a legible | | |

| Date. | Name. | From the Port of | To Whom Indentured. |
|---|---|---|---|
| 1773.<br>June 18th | Brown, Peter | Ireland | William Bonham and his assigns |
| | Burges, Edward | Ireland | Samuel Dell and his assigns |
| June 19th | McKinney, Catherine; Brown, Robert. | | David and Thomas Fulton and their assigns. |
| | McCarry, John | | David and Thomas Fulton and their assigns. |
| | Clarke, Edward | Ireland | Samuel Richard and his assigns |
| | Ross, John | Ireland | Robert Martin and his assigns |
| | Geely, Patrick; Shaw Elizabeth. | | David and Thomas Fulton and their assigns. |
| | Quinn, John | | David and Thomas Fulton and his assigns. |
| | Lockerd, Agnes | Newry | James Hunter and his assigns |
| | Hegen, John | Ireland | Thomas Reynolds and his assigns |
| | Wilson, John | | John Harry and his assigns |
| | McKenney, Catherine | | David Copeland and his assigns |
| | Carson, John | | John Hannah and his assigns |
| | Wilkison, John | | John Ross and his assigns |
| | Thompson, Thomas | | Andrew Hodge and his assigns |
| | Osbourn, William | | Abraham Furnace and his assigns |
| | Johnston, Jane | | John Shaunan and his assigns |
| | Mateer, John | | John Shannon and his assigns |
| | Shaw, Elizabeth | Ireland | Christian Grover and his assigns |
| | Stevenson, Elizabeth | Ireland | Thomas Keats and his assigns |
| June 21st | Neal, Agnes | | Edward Hanlon and his assigns |
| | Channon, Thomas | | Jonathen Meridith and his assigns |
| | Lear, Mary | | Peter Deal |
| | Morrell, Stephen | London | Richard Meredith and his assigns |
| | Rupendall, Jacob | London | Docr. John Kearsley and his assigns |
| | Sexin, Barbara | | Theodore Memminger and his assigns |
| | Sexin, Barbara | | Frederick Weis and his assigns |
| | Rhea, Robert | | Samuel Shearh and his assigns |
| June 22nd | Gardner, John | | Samuel Simpson and his assigns |
| | Gee, Ralph | Ireland | Thomas Little and his assigns |

[1] To be found all necessaries and at the expiration have freedom dues.
[2] To be found all necessaries and at the expiration have one new suit of apparel.
[3] To be found all necessaries and at the expiration have two complete suits of apparel, one whereof to be new.

## List of Indentures.

| Residence. | Occupation. | Term. | Amount. |
|---|---|---|---|
| | hand and cypher as far as the rule of 3.[3] | | |
| Philadelphia | Apprentice, taught the trade of a grocer, read in Bible, write a legible hand and cypher as far as the rule of 3. The apprentice shall not be disposed of without the consent of the mother out of Philadelphia, and he is to do any kind of work the master shall employ him about.[3] | 11 yrs., 9 mo., 29 d. | £ 2. 0. 0. |
| Berry twp., Lancaster co. | Servant, found meat drink, washing and lodging and working apparel. | 15 mo. | £ 8. 0. 0. |
| W. Nottingham, Chester co. | Servant | 3 yrs., 6 mo. each | £ 14. 0. 0. each. |
| W. Nottingham, Chester co. | Servant | 2 yrs., 6 mo. | £ 14. 0. 0. |
| Tredyffrin twp., Chester co. | Servant | 4 yrs. | £ 14. 0. 0. |
| Hanover twp., Lancaster co. | Servant[1] | 3 yrs. | £ 13. 0. 0. |
| W. Nottingham, Chester co. | Servant | 3 yrs. each | £ 14. 0. 0. |
| W. Nottingham, Chester co. | Servant | 6 yrs. | £ 14. 0. 0. |
| Newtown twp., Chester co. | Servant | 4 yrs. | £ 15. 0. 0. |
| New Hanover twp., Burlington co., W. J. | Servant[3] | 7 yrs. | £ 10. 0. 0. |
| Whitemarsh twp., Phila. co. | Servant[5] | 4 yrs. | £ 13. 0. 0. |
| Chester | Servant | 3 yrs., 6 mo. | £ 14. 10. 0. |
| Philadelphia | Servant | 3 yrs. | £ 15. 0. 0. |
| Philadelphia | Apprentice, taught the art of a mariner.[1] | 5 yrs. | |
| Philadelphia | Servant | 3 yrs., 6 mo. | £ 15. 0. 0. |
| Eaveham twp., Burlington co. | Apprentice, taught the art of a waterman, the master to give him six months' day schooling (note 1, or £ 10 Penna. currency) | 3 yrs. | |
| Norrington twp., Phila. co. | Servant[5] | 3 yrs., 6 mo. | £ 12. 0. 0. |
| Norrington twp., Phila. co. | Servant[5] | 2 yrs. | £ 12. 0. 0. |
| Passyunk twp., Phila. co. | Servant[3] | 4 yrs. | £ 14. 0. 0. |
| Philadelphia | Servant[3] | 4 yrs. | £ 14. 0. 0. |
| Philadelphia | Servant[5] | 3 yrs. | £ 12. 0. 0. |
| Philadelphia | Servant[5] | 4 yrs. | £ 20. 0. 0. |
| Philadelphia | Apprentice, taught housewifery, knit, sew and spin, read and write Dutch well.[3] | 7 yrs. | |
| Buckingham twp., Bucks co. | Servant[3] | 2 yrs. | £ 18. 0. 0. |
| Philadelphia | Servant[3] | 2 yrs., 9 mo. | £ 15. 2. 4. |
| Philadelphia | Servant | 3 yrs., 6 mo. | £ 21. 8. 0. |
| Philadelphia | Servant | 3 yrs., 6 mo. | £ 21. 12. 0. |
| Hanover twp., Lancaster co. | | 2 yrs., 6 mo. | £ 13. 0. 0. |
| Philadelphia | Apprentice, taught the art and mystery of a cordwainer, allowed time every Quakers' yearly meeting to go one day to meeting, and give him two quarters' night schooling, allowed to go to Quakers' meeting every Sunday.[6] | 5 yrs., 3 mo. 11 d. | |
| Nockemixin twp., Bucks co. | Servant[3] | 4 yrs. | £ 11. 0. 0. |

[4] To be found all necessaries and at the expiration have two complete suits of apparel, one whereof to be new, and 40s. in money.

[5] At expiration have two complete suits of apparel, one whereof to be new.

| Date. | Name. | From the Port of | To Whom Indentured. |
|---|---|---|---|
| 1773. June 22nd | Smith, Mary | Belfast | John Aiken and his assigns |
| | Smith, William | | James Martin and wife |
| | Coleburn, Francis | | Jacob Jones and his assigns |
| | Favel, William | | Frederick Fraley and his assigns |
| | Peters, Abijah | | John Fullarton and his assigns |
| June 23rd | Founder, Barbara | | Phillip Nue and his assigns |
| | O'Neal, Ester | | Alexander Rotherford and his assigns. |
| | Bahrat, Zackarias | London | John Fritz and his assigns |
| | Bahrat, Zackarias | | Peter Kershner and his assigns |
| June 24th | Maag, Sybilla | | Daniel Burkhart |
| | Maag, Barbara | | Daniel Burkhart |
| | Magg, Catherine | | Daniel Burkhart |
| | Norton, Edward | | Whitehead Humphreys |
| | Crowly, Mary | | James Campbell and his assigns |
| | Pouponnot, Peter Charles | London | Lewis Fohrer and his assigns |
| June 25th | Hammond, Charles | | Jeremiah Warder, Jr |
| | Egert, John George | London | Martin Kreider and his assigns |
| | Logan, John | Ireland | George Kelly and his assigns |
| June 26th | Melarty, Daniel | | Phillip Tanner and his assigns |
| | Olet, Shears | | John Reynolds and his assigns |
| June 28th | Dryburgh, James | | Elias Bohner and his assigns |
| | Richardson, Joseph | | Edward Pole |

## List of Indentures.

| Residence. | Occupation. | Term. | Amount. |
|---|---|---|---|
| —— twp., Chester co.......... | Servant ........................... | 4 yrs....... | £ 12. 0. 0. |
| Moyamensing twp., Phila. co.... | Apprentice, taught the art of a farmer, to read in Bible, write a legible hand and cypher as far as rule of 3 (note 3, or £ 6 lawful money of Pa. in lieu of the new suit). | 17 yrs., 1 mo. | |
| Southwark ................. | Apprentice, taught the art and mystery of an oak cooper, taught to read in Bible, write a legible hand and cypher as far as rule of 3.⁶ | 9 yrs., 6 mo. 5 d. | |
| Philadelphia .................. | Apprentice, taught the trade of a baker, read in Bible, write a legible hand and cypher as far as rule of 3.³ | 17 yrs., 3 mo. | |
| Philadelphia ................. | Apprentice, found £ 20 worth of clothes during the term.⁶ | 6 yrs., 6 mo. | |
| Frank Coney twp., Phila. co..... | Apprentice ........................... | ........... | £ 7. 0. 0. |
| Philadelphia ................. | Servant ........................... | 3 yrs....... | £ 14. 0. 0. |
| Philadelphia ................. | Servant (note 1, or £ 10 Pa. currency). | 3 yrs., 1 mo. | £ 22. 18. 7. |
| ........................... | Servant (note 1, or £ 10 Pa. currency). | 3 yrs., 1 mo. | |
| Passyunk twp., Phila. co........ | Apprentice, taught housewifery, read in Bible, write a legible hand (note 6, and a feather bed, or £ 6 Pa. currency). | 4 yrs., 10 mo., 17 d. | |
| Passyunk twp., Phila co........ | Apprentice, taught housewifery, read in Bible, write a legible hand (note 3, and a feather bed, or £ 6 Pa. currency). | 6 yrs., 4 mo. 19 d. | |
| Passyunk twp., Phila. co........ | Apprentice, taught housewifery, read in Bible, write a legible hand (note 6, and a feather bed, or £ 6 Pa. currency). | 9 yrs., 7 mo. 25 d. | |
| Philadelphia ................. | Servant¹ ........................... | 4 yrs....... | £ 18. 0. 0. |
| Plymouth twp., Phila co........ | ........................... | 4 yrs....... | £ 10. 0. 0. |
| Philadelphia ................. | Servant¹ ........................... | 3 yrs....... | £ 18. 8. 6. |
| | Apprentice, taught the art of a mariner and navigation, found meat, drink, sea clothes, washing and lodging. | 6 yrs. | |
| Philadelphia ................. | Servant (note 3, or £ 10 Pa. currency). | 2 yrs., 3 mo. | £ 17. 0. 0. |
| Philadelphia ................. | Servant, found meat, drink, washing and lodging and wearing apparel. | 2 yrs....... | £ 22. 0. 0. |
| E. Nottington twp., Chester co... | Apprentice, taught the business of a farmer, read and write and cypher as far as rule of 3.³ | 18 yrs. | |
| Allens Town, Monmouth co., E. Jersey. | Servant ........................... | 4 yrs....... | £ 16. 0. 0. |
| Philadelphia ................. | Apprentice, taught the trade of a saddler and harness maker, have two quarters' night schooling in the third and fourth years of his time and two quarters' in the 9th and 10th years of his time. The master shall not dispose of said apprentice without his father's consent.³ | 11 yrs., 2 mo., 9 d. | |
| Philadelphia ................. | Apprentice, taught to read and write (note 2, besides his old). | 6 yrs. | |

| DATE. | NAME. | FROM THE PORT OF | TO WHOM INDENTURED. |
|---|---|---|---|
| 1773. June 26th... | Spicer, John | London | Bryan Cuniffe and his assigns |
| | Murray, Mary | | John Rogers and his assigns |
| June 28th... | Means, William | | John Bayard |
| | Cook, James | London | Richard Reynolds and his assigns |
| | Pompey | | Joseph Whitell and his assigns |
| June 29th... | Clark, Elizabeth | | Edwark Hicks |
| | Gillmore, David | | George Kennedy and his assigns |
| | Batson, Richard | | Joseph Moulder |
| | Keeler, Abraham | | Peter Henderson and his assigns |
| | Spence, Jane | Ireland | Peter McKinley and his assigns |
| | Hill, John | Bristol | William Johnston and his assigns |
| | Kurtz, Michael | | George Higher and his assigns |
| June 30th... | Cutman, Nicholas | London | Andrew Bowers and his assigns |
| | McConnal, Hugh | Ireland | Jacob Rindollar and his assigns |
| | Wester, John | | Jasper Carpenter and his assigns |
| | Meyerin, Maria Elizabeth | | Benjamin Hooton and his assigns |
| | Singleton, Sarah | Ireland | John Ewing and his assigns |
| | McGown, Hercules | Ireland | Phillip Rodman and his assigns |
| | Horne, Elizabeth | | James Roney and his assigns |
| July 1st... | Barnes, Robert | | George Emlen and his assigns |
| | Mullan, Edward | Ireland | James Roney and his assigns |
| July 2nd... | Boyd, Jane | Ireland | James Roney and his assigns |
| | Green, Mary | | James Larman and his assigns |
| | Engel, Henry | | John Webb and his assigns |
| | Lehman, John Daniel | London | Phineas Bond and his assigns |
| | Day, Thomas | | Abraham Kensing and his assigns |
| | Demare, Lewis | London | Phillip Upp and his assigns |
| | Patterson, John | London | John Backhus and his assigns |
| | Farrel, Michael | | Andrew Richmond and his assigns |
| July 3rd... | Scinner, James | | John Wilson and wife, Elizabeth |
| | Campbell, John | | George Henry |

## List of Indentures.

| Residence. | Occupation. | Term. | Amount. |
|---|---|---|---|
| Philadelphia | Servant | 5 yrs. | £ 20. 0. 0. |
| Pikeland twp., Chester co. | Apprentice, taught to read in Bible, write a legible hand (note 3, and £ 3 in cash and a small spinning wheel). | 14 yrs. | |
| Philadelphia | Apprentice, taught the art of a merchant and bookkeeping, found meat, drink and lodging. | 5 yrs. | |
| Musmillion Hundred, Kent co., on Delaware. | Servant | 4 yrs. | £ 19. 0. 0. |
| Philadelphia | Servant[5] | 15 yrs., 2 mo. | £ 20. 0. 0. |
| Goshen twp., Chester co. | | 4 yrs. | £ 15. 0. 0. |
| Philadelphia | Servant | 2 yrs. | £ 5. 0. 0. |
| Philadelphia | Apprentice, taught the trade of a sail maker.[3] | 5 yrs., 3 mo. 29 d. | |
| Philadelphia | Servant, employed at the business of a turner.[3] | 3 yrs., 6 mo. | £ 21. 0. 0. |
| Philadelphia | Servant | 4 yrs. | £ 12. 0. 0. |
| Philadelphia | Servant | 4 yrs. | £ 20. 0. 0. |
| Northern Liberties, Phila. co. | Servant | 4 yrs., 1 mo. 3 w. | £ 0. 10. 0. |
| Northern Liberties, Phila. co. | Servant[3] | 4 yrs., 6 mo. | £ 16. 0. 0. |
| Philadelphia | Servant, the master to employ him at the tailor trade.[1] | 3 yrs. | £ 15. 0. 0. |
| Philadelphia | Apprentice, taught the joiner's trade, have four quarters' night schooling.[3] | 4 yrs., 8 mo. 12 d. | |
| Philadelphia | Servant[3] | 4 yrs. | £ 27. 0. 1. |
| Philadelphia | Servant, when free to have 20/ in cash. | 3 yrs. | £ 13. 0. 0. ? |
| Kinglass twp., Phila. co. | Servant | 1 yr. | £ 7. 0. 0. |
| Hanover twp., Lancaster co. | Servant[6] | 3 yrs., 6 mo. | £ 10. 0. 0. |
| Philadelphia | Apprentice, taught the art of a mariner and navigation (note 2, besides his old). | 3 yrs., 4 mo. 8 d. | |
| Lancaster | Servant | 21 mo. | £ 12. 0. 0. |
| Lancaster | Servant | 4 yrs., 6 mo. | £ 14. 0. 0. |
| Philadelphia | Servant (note 3, and £ 5 in cash). | 2 yrs. | £ 1. 10. 0. |
| Philadelphia | Apprentice, taught the trade of a cabinet and chair maker, taught to read and write and cypher as far as rule of 3.[3] | 12 yrs., 8 mo. | |
| Philadelphia | Servant[8] | 3 yrs., 4 mo. | £ 9. 9. 0. sterling. |
| Philadelphia | Servant | 2 yrs. | £ 7. 0. 0. |
| Greenwich twp., Sussex co., N. J. | Servant[3] | 3 yrs. | £ 24. 0. 0. |
| Philadelphia | Servant, found meat, drink, apparel, washing and lodging. | 3 yrs. | £ 20. 0. 0. |
| Woolwich twp., Gloster co., W. Jersey. | Servant[5] | 3 yrs., 6 mo. | £ 15. 0. 0. |
| Horsham twp., Phila. co. | Apprentice, taught the art and mystery of farmer, read and write well and cypher as far as rule of 3; agreed in case of death of the master and mistress, the mother of the apprentice shall have liberty of choosing a master for the apprentice (note 6, and 40 shillings, an ax and grubbing hoe). | 14 yrs., 6 mo., 27 d. | |
| Philadelphia | Apprentice, taught the art and mystery of a cordwainer, taught | 10 yrs., 7 mo., 12 d. | |

| Date. | Name. | From the Port of | To Whom Indentured. |
|---|---|---|---|
| 1773. July 3rd | Brooks, Thomas | | Joseph Ashston and his assigns |
| July 5th | Shell, George | | George David Sickell and his assigns. |
| | Riley, Benjamin | | John Young, Jr., and his assigns |
| | Cloudsdall, Andrew | | Samuel Fisher, Jr., and his assigns |
| | Koonin, Maria | | Henry Kain and his assigns |
| | Grindle, Jonathen | Ireland | John Titterman and his assigns |
| | Rowe, Thomas | Ireland | William Lavering and his assigns |
| | Franklin, Samuel | | Joseph Bullock and his assigns |
| | Bandell, Benjamin | Bristol | Thomas Clifford, Jr., and his assigns. |
| | Taylor, Robert | Ireland | Adam Kerr and his assigns |
| July 6th | Bryan, Patrick | Ireland | Michael McKannon and his assigns |
| | Magrath, James | Ireland | Thomas McWaters and his assigns |
| | Burkelow, William | | Ezekiel Letts and his assigns |
| | Barry, Mary | | John Clark and his assigns |
| | Bacon, Margaret | | Duncin Campbell and his assigns |
| | Lawrence, Mary | | John Lawrence and his assigns |
| | Martin, Robert | | Robert Bell |
| | Bready, Hugh; Condon, John; Thompson, Charles; Brenan, John; Quirk, Joseph. | | John Black and his assigns |
| | Roche, Catherine; Farrell, Mary; Cunningham, Mary. | | John Black and his assigns |
| | Mullowney, William | | John Black and his assigns |
| | Gready, Dennis | Ireland | Benjamin Loder and his assigns |
| | Callachan, Edward | Ireland | Abraham Boys and his assigns |
| | Goff, William | | Joseph Greenway and his assigns |
| | Clark, Jeane | Ireland | William Mansell and his assigns |
| | Aichin, John | Ireland | William Taylor and his assigns |
| | Aichin, John | | Thomas Mendinhall and his assigns |
| July 7th | Patterson, David | | Robert Hardie, William Dancie & Co., and their assigns. |

## List of Indentures.

| Residence. | Occupation. | Term. | Amount. |
|---|---|---|---|
| | to read and write and cypher as far as rule of 3." | | |
| Lower Dublin twp., Phila. co. | Servant[5] | 2 yrs. | £11.10.0. |
| Philadelphia | Apprentice, taught the art and mystery of a butcher (note 1, and £4 Pa. currency). | 4 yrs. | £6.0.0. |
| Philadelphia | Apprentice, taught the art and mystery of a saddler, have the privilege of going two winters to night school, his friend paying the expense, at the expiration of his term freedom dues. | 4 yrs., 10 mo. | |
| Philadelphia | Apprentice, taught the art of a mariner. | 4 yrs. | |
| New Holland twp., Lancaster co. | Servant | 7 yrs. | £5.0.0. |
| Moyamensing twp., Phila. co. | Servant (note 5, £3 Penna. currency). | 2 yrs. | £13.10.0. |
| Roxborough twp., Phila. | Servant[3] | 4 yrs. | £17.0.0. |
| Philadelphia | Servant[3] | 5 yrs., 10 mo., 2 d. | £20.0.0. |
| Philadelphia | Servant | 6 yrs. | £20.0.0. |
| Warwick, Bucks co. | Servant[5] | 2 yrs. | £7.10.0. |
| Philadelphia | Apprentice, taught the art and mystery of a plasterer; agreed in the winter when he can't work at the plastering business in sweeping of chimneys.[3] | 6 yrs. | £15.13.2. |
| Philadelphia | Servant[3] | 3 yrs. | £13.8.0. |
| Philadelphia | Apprentice, taught the trade of a tailor, have two quarters' night schooling in the two first years and three quarters' in the three last years.[3] | 9 yrs., 6 mo. 13 d. | |
| Bristol twp., Bucks co. | Servant[5] | 4 yrs. | £15.0.0. |
| Northern Liberties | Servant | 2 yrs. | £3.0.0. |
| Southwark | Apprentice[5] | 8 yrs., 2 mo. | £1.5.0. |
| Philadelphia | Apprentice, taught the trade of a printer, read in Bible, write a legible hand and cypher as far as rule of 3.[3] | 12 yrs., 8 mo., 11 d. | |
| Derry twp., Lancaster co. | Servant | 4 yrs. each. | £14.0.0. each. |
| Derry twp., Lancaster co. | Servant | 4 yrs. each. | £12.0.0. each. |
| Derry twp., Lancaster co. | Servant | 5 yrs. | £14.0.0. |
| Philadelphia | Servant, found meat, drink, apparel, washing and lodging. | 2 yrs., 6 mo. | £15.15.10. |
| New Cassell Hundred, New Castle co. | Servant[5] | 3 yrs. | £17.0.0. |
| Philadelphia | Apprentice, taught the art and mystery of a cooper, give him four quarters' night schooling, privilege of one quarter's night schooling the last year of the time, the father paying the expense (note 3, the cloth to be at 30 shillings per yard). | | |
| Philadelphia | Servant[5] | 18 mo. | £7.0.0. |
| Philadelphia | Servant[5] | 2 yrs. | £16.18.4. |
| Lancaster | Servant[5] | 2 yrs. | |
| Philadelphia | Apprentice, taught the art and mystery of navigation, found | 3 yrs., 6 mo. | |

| Date. | Name. | From the Port of | To Whom Indentured. |
|---|---|---|---|
| 1773. July 7th | Magee, Robert | Ireland | Joseph Mather and his assigns |
| | Mustard, Mary | Ireland | Edward Crucks and his assigns |
| | Mustard, James | Ireland | Edward Crooks and assigns |
| | Mustard, Elizabeth | Ireland | Edward Crooks and assigns |
| | Hassen, Arthur | Ireland | Jacob Wilson and his assigns |
| | Bready, Hugh | | Samuel Parr and his assigns |
| July 8th | Cummins, Timothy | | Isarel Hallowell |
| | Andrews, Daniel | Ireland | Andrew Steward and his assigns |
| | Andrews, Daniel | | William McFarland and his assigns |
| | Hastings, Morris | Ireland | Thomas Badge and his assigns |
| | Gallagher, Rose | | John Dealing and his assigns |
| | Karr, Darby | Ireland | John Holmes and his assigns |
| | McCabe, Mary | London Derry. | John Brown and his assigns |
| | Ellis, Elizabeth | Belfast | Jacob Reindollar and his assigns |
| | Fitzhenry, Thomas | | Hugh Lloyd and his assigns |
| July 9th | Kennedy, Margaret | Waterford | Peter January and his assigns |
| | Morrow, Mary | | George Bryan |
| | Currin, William | | John Bedle and his assigns |
| | O'Murray, Neal | | Samuel Parr and his assigns |
| | Hamill, Alexander | | Christopher Sickler and his assigns |
| | McFalls, James | | James McCollough and his assigns |
| July 9th | Roseburn, James | | John Back and his assigns |
| | Kinnan, Thomas | Ireland | John Hickson and his assigns |
| July 10th | Doyle, Luke | | Edward Tabor and his assigns |
| | Crawford, George | | Conrad Lambert and his assigns |

## List of Indentures.

| Residence. | Occupation. | Term. | Amount. |
|---|---|---|---|
|  | meat, drink, apparel, washing and lodging. |  |  |
| Germantown, Phila. co. | Servant[3] | 5 yrs. | £ 14. 10. 0. |
| London Grove twp., Chester co. | Servant, found meat, drink, washing and lodging. If the master find the servant any apparel during her servitude, at expiration of the term she is to pay him, the master to give her one pair new shoes. | 18 mo. | £ 6. 6. 8. |
| London Grove twp., Chester co. | Servant, found meat, drink, shoes, washing, lodging and a pair of trousers. | 1 yr., 6 mo. | £ 6. 6. 8. |
| London Grove twp., Chester co. | Servant, found meat, drink, washing and lodging. If the master find said servant any wearing, except one pair shoes, she is to pay him the expense at the expiration of the term. | 1 yr., 6 mo. | £ 6. 6. 8. |
| Londonderry twp., Chester co. | Servant, found meat drink, washing and lodging. | 14 mo. | £ 7. 10. 0. |
| Armstrong twp., Westmoreland co. | Servant[1] | 4 yrs. | £ 18. 0. 0. |
| Philadelphia | Apprentice, taught the trade of a house carpenter, found meat, drink, shoes, washing and lodging; to serve either in Phila., Northern Liberties or Southwark with and under the care of his master, allowed three weeks every year in December to go and see his parents, and time to go to night school every winter, his father paying the expense of schooling. | 4 yrs. |  |
| Philadelphia | Servant[1] | 3 yrs. | £ 12. 0. 0. |
| Philadelphia | Servant | 3 yrs. | £ 12. 0. 0. |
| Southwark | Servant, found meat drink, apparel, washing and lodging. | 2 yrs., 6 mo. | £ 10. 0. 0. |
| Philadelphia | Servant | 4 yrs. | £ 10. 0. 0. |
| Middle Prencinct, Cape May co., N. J. | Servant[5] | 2 yrs., 6 mo. | £ 9. 0. 0. |
| Northern Liberties | Servant | 4 yrs. | £ 15. 0. 0. |
| Philadelphia | Servant | 5 yrs. | £ 14. 10. 0. |
| Ridley twp., Chester co. | Servant[5] | 5 yrs. | £ 18. 0. 0. |
| Philadelphia | Servant | 7 yrs. | £ 15. 0. 0. |
| Southwark | Servant (note 5, have £ 3 in cash in lieu of freedom). | 3 yrs., 6 mo. | £ 10. 4. 0. |
| Philadelphia | Servant[3] | 2 yrs. | £ 12. 0. 0. |
| Armstrong twp., Westmoreland co. | Servant[5] | 1 yr., 6 mo. | £ 7. 11. 6. |
|  | Servant, taught to read in Bible, writes a good legible hand.[1] | 4 yrs. | £ 12. 10. 0. |
| New York | Servant | 4 yrs. | £ 15. 0. 0. |
| Philadelphia | Servant (to go to New York) | 3 yrs., 6 mo. | £ 13. 0. 0. |
| Philadelphia | Servant, found meat, drink, apparel, washing and lodging. | 2 yrs. | £ 10. 0. 0. |
|  | parel, washing and lodging. | 2 yrs., 2 mo. | £ 12. 15. 0. |
| Northern Liberties | Servant, agreed if he shall pay or cause to be paid the master £ 24 any time before the expiration of the term then the indenture to be void.[3] | 5 yrs. | £ 24. 0. 0. |

| Date. | Name. | From the Port of | To Whom Indentured. |
|---|---|---|---|
| 1773.<br>June 10th... | Bell, John | | Drewry and his assigns |
| | Reily, Charles | | Ralph Nailor |
| | Meleir, Sarah; Allen, Mary; Gefries, Michael; Ligget, Martha; Muffat, Margaret; Smith, Margaret. | | James Rhea and his assigns |
| | Dougherty, Edward | Ireland | James Rhea and his assigns |
| | Smith, Elizabeth | | James Rhea and his assigns |
| | Doyle, John | | Henry Baggs and his assigns |
| | Russell, James; English, Charles. | | James Rhea and his assigns |
| | Crowe, Elizabeth | | James Rhea and his assigns |
| | Colvin, Hugh | | James Rhea and his assigns |
| | Duffy, James | | Ralph Nailer and his assigns |
| | Clayton, Peter; Fallon, Stephen; Colkins, Patrick. | | James Rhea and his assigns |
| | McFall, James | Ireland (passage paid). | James McCollough and his assigns |
| | Evans, Anthony | | John McCelland and his assigns |
| | Mulloy, Martin | Ireland | James Rhea and his assigns |
| | Harris, Elizabeth | | James Martin and his assigns |
| July 12th... | Caldwell, David | Ireland | William Robinson and his assigns |
| | Clelan, Elizabeth | | Elizabeth Robinson and her assigns |
| | Jourden, Michael | Ireland | William Bedford and his assigns |
| | Neeley, Rebecca | | Lawrence Vance and his assigns |
| | Meyer, Rachael | | William Weaver and his assigns |
| | Wainwright, William | | Stephen Phipps and his assigns |
| | McGavren, Mary | | Samuel Bullus and his assigns |
| | Gilmore, Alles | Ireland | Jonathan Norton and his assigns |
| | Milligan, James | Ireland | Alexander Blain and his assigns |
| | Gallway, James; McCarthy, Honora. | | John Pinchback and his assigns |
| | McGee, Mary | | Arthur Lindon and his assigns |
| | Willson, James | | Leonar Kissler and his assigns |
| | McCardell, Mary | | Mathew McHugh and his assigns |
| | McGwire, James | Ireland | John Marchall and his assigns |
| | Hiss, John | | Michael Sentzer and wife |

# List of Indentures.

| Residence. | Occupation. | Term. | Amount. |
|---|---|---|---|
| .................................. | Servant, employed at the trades of ropemaking and flax dressing. | 3 yrs., 6 mo. | £ 14. 0. 0. |
| Carlisle ....................... | Servant[5] ....................... | 2 yrs., 7 mo. | £ 15. 0. 0. |
| Little Brittain twp., Lancaster co. | Servant[6] ....................... | 4 yrs. each. | £ 13. 0. 0. each. |
| Little Brittain twp., Lancaster co. | Servant[3] ....................... | 4 yrs., 6 mo. | £ 15. 0. 0. |
| Little Brittain twp., Lancaster co. | Servant ....................... | 4 yrs., 6 mo. | £ 13. 0. 0. |
| Philadelphia .................. | Servant ....................... | 4 yrs........ | £ 14. 0. 0. |
| Little Brittain twp., Lancaster co. | Servant ....................... | 3 yrs., 6 mo. | £ 13. 0. 0. each. |
| Little Brittain twp., Lancaster co. | Servant ....................... | 3 yrs........ | £ 13. 0. 0. |
| Little Brittain twp., Lancaster co. | Servant ....................... | 2 yrs........ | £ 13. 0. 0. |
| Carlisle ....................... | Servant[5] ....................... | 2 yrs., 6 mo. | £ 14. 0. 0. |
| Little Brittain twp., Lancaster co. | Servant ....................... | 4 yrs. each. | £ 13. 0. 0. |
| Philadelphia .................. | Servant[3] ....................... | 2 yrs., 10 mo., 8 d. | |
| Springhill twp., Westmoreland co. | Servant[5] ....................... | 3 yrs......... | £ 14. 10. 0. |
| Little Brittain twp., Lancaster co. | Servant[3] ....................... | 4 yrs........ | £ 13. 0. 0. |
| Moyamensing twp., Phila. co.... | Servant[3] ....................... | 4 yrs........ | £ 12. 14. 0 |
| Southwark .................. | Servant, found meat, drink, washing and lodging and 40 shillings worth of clothes during the term. | 14 mo...... | £ 8. 1. 6. |
| Philadelphia .................. | .................................. | 7 yrs........ | £ 15. 0. 0. |
| Philadelphia .................. | Servant, if the master find the said servant any wearing apparel he is to pay him the expense at the expiration of his term. If the said servant pay or cause to be paid £ 10. 13. 6 the indenture to be void, the said servant is to allow him for laying out of the money. | 1 yr........ | £ 10. 13. 6. |
| District of Southwark........... | Apprentice ....................... | 6 yrs., 10 mo. | £ 4. 10. |
| Philadelphia .................. | Apprentice, taught housewifery, sew, knit and spin, read in Bible, write a legible hand (note 3, a spinning wheel and £ 4. 10 in cash). | 6 yrs., 11 mo., 22 d.. | |
| Philadelphia .................. | Apprentice, taught the art and mystery of a tailor, found all necessaries except shoes, shirts, washing and stockings, which are to found by the father during the term, one quarter's day schooling and permit him to go another quarter at his father's expense.[6] | 5 yrs., 7 mo. 8 d. | |
| Gloster twp., Gloster co., W. J... | Servant (to go to Jersey)......... | 3 yrs........ | £ 8. 0. 0. |
| .................................. | Servant[5] ....................... | 2 yrs., 3 mo. | £ 10. 0. 0. |
| Carlisle ....................... | Servant[5] ....................... | 2 yrs........ | £ 8. 9. 6. |
| Lemmirie twp., Phila co......... | Servant[5] ....................... | 4 yrs. each. | { £ 18. 0. 0. <br> { £ 16. 0. 0. |
| Upper Merion twp., Phila. co.... | Servant[5] ....................... | 3 yrs., 6 mo. | £ 15. 0. 0. |
| Philadelphia .................. | Servant[5] ....................... | 4 yrs........ | £ 18. 0. 0. |
| Millers twp., Lancaster co....... | Servant ....................... | 4 yrs........ | £ 16. 0. 0. |
| Moyamensing twp., Phila. co.... | Servant, found meat, drink, apparel, washing and lodging. | 3 yrs........ | £ 15. 0. 0. |
| Northern Liberties, Phila........ | Apprentice, taught the tailor's trade, have one year's day | 10 yrs., 9 mo. | |

| Date. | Name. | From the Port of | To Whom Indentured. |
|---|---|---|---|
| 1773. July 12th | Kenny, Lawrence | | John McCutchon and his assigns |
| July 13th | Watkinson, Benjamin Stokely | | Samuel Richards and his assigns |
| | Crosman, Mary | | Joseph Engle and his assigns |
| | Fullerton, William | Ireland | William McIlvaine and his assigns |
| | Sweall, Esther | Newry | Dr. Francis Allison and his assigns |
| | McKigney, Catherin | | John Reynolds and his assigns |
| | Crooke, William (see Record Sept. 8, 1773). | | |
| | Mallon, Patrick | Ireland | Henry Rawlins and his assigns |
| July 14th | Magher, Mary; Cummings, James. | | John Clark and his assigns |
| | Doyle, Thomas | | Alexander Carlisle and his assigns |
| | Moore, Mary | | Isaac Morton |
| | Castels, John | Ireland | Peter January and his assigns |
| | Castels, John | | Jacob Wayne and his assigns |
| | Houser, Jacob | | Charles Chamberlin and his assigns |
| | Harrington, Timothy | Ireland | Joseph Alexander and his assigns |
| | Carson, Francis | Ireland | Dennis Milligan and his assigns |
| July 15th | Sullivan, Owin<br>Welsh, Robert<br>Garvey, Patrick<br>Buckley, Michael<br>Shea, John<br>Keasy, Peter<br>Loughlin, John<br>Reed, Joseph<br>Currin, John<br>Murphy, Milchol<br>Morrissy, Patrick<br>Coole, James<br>Reynolds, Thomas<br>White, Richard<br>Grimes, Susanna<br>Boyle, Mary<br>Parker, John | | David and Thomas Fulton and their assigns. |
| | McLean, James | Ireland | Edmond McDaniel and his assigns |
| | Wright, Abell | | Robert Hardie and William Duncan |
| | McCarty, Eleanor | Cork | Richard Wolley and his assigns |
| | Malone, Honora | | Edmond Milne and his assigns |
| | Hammon, Luke | London | John Peterkin and his assigns |
| | Hagons, Mary | Ireland | Charles Connor and his assigns |
| | Doyle, John | | Robert Loosely and his assigns |
| | Burk, Ann; Welsh, John; Ray, Mary; Hindley, Michael; Fowler, Timothy; Donely, Joseph; Fox, Honora; Mortal, James; | | John Hawkins and his assigns, and Jeremiah Dealy and his assigns. |

## List of Indentures.

| Residence. | Occupation. | Term. | Amount. |
|---|---|---|---|
|  | schooling, one winter's night schooling (note 3, worth £ 10, or £ 10 Pa. currency in cash). |  |  |
| Willis Town twp., Chester co... | Servant[3] | 3 yrs. | £ 18.0.0 |
| Philadelphia | Apprentice[1] | 11 yrs., 10 mo. | £ 15.0.0 |
| Northern Liberties | Apprentice, taught housewifery, read in Bible, write a legible hand and cypher, sew and knit[6]. | 9 yrs., 9 mo. |  |
| Philadelphia |  | 1 yr. | £ 10.10.0 |
| Philadelphia | Servant | 2 yrs., 6 mo. | £ 11.0.0 |
| Strawberry All, Phila | Servant | 2 yrs. | 7.1 a. |
| Springfield twp., Chester co | Servant[5] | 2 yrs. | £ 8.0.6 |
| Augusta twp., Northumberland co. | Servant[5] | 4 yrs. each. | £ 13 & £ 14 |
| Philadelphia | Servant | 4 yrs. | £ 15.0.0 |
| Philadelphia | Servant, in case of death of the master the servant to be free.[3] | 2 yrs. | £ 4.0.0 |
| Philadelphia | Servant[5] | 2 yrs. | £ 16.0.0 |
| —— twp., Chester co | Servant | 2 yrs. | £ 16.0.0 |
| Philadelphia | Apprentice, taught the art and mystery of a cordwainer, four quarters' night schooling, when free to have all his working tools, at expiration freedom dues or £ 8 Pa. currency. | 8 yrs. |  |
| Lurgan twp., Cumberland co... | Servant | 4 yrs. | £ 18.0.0 |
| Lebanon twp., Lancaster co | Servant, found meat, drink, washing and lodging, shirts, shoes, stockings and trousers, employed at the mason's trade. | 1 yr. | £ 8.1.6 |
| West Nottingham twp., Chester co | Servants[5] | 4 yrs. each. | £ 14.0.0 <br> £ 14.0.0 <br> £ 14.0.0 <br> £ 14.0.0 <br> £ 14.0.0 <br> £ 14.0.0 <br> £ 14.0.0 <br> £ 12.0.0 <br> £ 14.0.0 <br> £ 14.0.0 <br> £ 14.0.0 <br> £ 14.0.0 <br> £ 14.0.0 <br> £ 14.0.0 <br> £ 13.0.0 <br> £ 13.0.0 <br> £ 14.0.0 |
| Philadelphia | Servant[3] | 2 yrs., 6 mo. | £ 13.8.0 |
| Philadelphia | Apprentice, taught the art of navigation (note 3, sailor's apparel). | 3 yrs., 6 mo. |  |
| Philadelphia | Servant | 5 yrs. | £ 15.0.0 |
| Philadelphia | Servant | 4 yrs. | £ 16.0.0 |
| Philadelphia | Servant, employed at the tailor's trade. | 4 yrs. | £ 24.0.0 |
| Philadelphia | Servant[3] | 4 yrs. | £ 13.0.0 |
| Philadelphia | Servant | 3 yrs. | £ 15.0.0 |
| Philadelphia | Servants[5] | 4 yrs. each.. | £ 15.0.0 |

| Date. | Name. | From the Port of | To Whom Indentured. |
|---|---|---|---|
| 1773. July 15th... | Bryan, Honor; Donohue, Darby; Sullivan, Daniel. Spillane, Elizabeth | | John Hawkins and Jeremiah Dealy and their assigns. |
| | Rogers, Susannah | | John Hawkins and Jeremiah Dealy and their assigns. |
| | Keese, Mary | | John Hawkins and Jeremiah Dealy and their assigns. |
| | Sweing, Catherine; Burke, Catherine. | | Jeremiah Dealy and his assigns...... |
| | Murphy, Bartholomew | | James Forrest and his assigns........ |
| | Saxen, Barbara and infant... | | John William Hoffman and his assigns. |
| | Murphy, John | | Edward Jones and his assigns........ |
| | Veach, Henry | Ireland | Allen McLean and his assigns........ |
| July 16th... | Donnevan, Patrick | Ireland | William Hornbuy and his assigns.... |
| | Butler, Charles | | William Sheadaoze and his assigns... |
| | Watkeys, Edward | Ireland | William Shute and his assigns....... |
| | Allport, Mary | | Andrew McCormick and his assigns.. |
| | Harrison, James | | Joseph Ogden and his assigns........ |
| July 17th... | Nichoal, William | Ireland | William Little and his assigns........ |
| | McCready, James | | Frederick Watts and his assigns...... |
| | Torton, Charles | | John Farran and his assigns......... |
| | McDanald, Bridget | Ireland | George Taylor and his assigns....... |
| | Haughton, Hercules, and Jane, his wife. | | Henry Tinms and his assigns........ |
| | Scott, Catherine | Ireland | Francis Bourcheir and his assigns.... |
| July 17th... | Dunlap, Robert | Ireland | George Taylor and his assigns...... |
| July 19th... | Andrews, John | Ireland | George Taylor and his assigns...... |
| | Marshall, William | Ireland | George Taylor and his assigns...... |
| | Metier, John | Ireland | James Young and his assigns........ |
| | Mitchell, John | Ireland | William Hurry and his assigns...... |
| | Brian, Mary | Ireland | John Odenheimer and his assigns.... |
| | Ryan, John | | John Butcher and his assigns........ |
| | Beck, Ann | Ireland | William Bonham and his assigns.... |
| | Haninger, John Frederick | | John Jocaim and his assigns......... |

## List of Indentures.

| Residence. | Occupation. | Term. | Amount. |
|---|---|---|---|
| Philadelphia | Servant[5] | 7 yrs. | £15. 0. 0. |
|  | Servant[5] | 5 yrs. | £15. 0. 0. |
|  | Servant[5] | 4 yrs., 6 mo. | £15. 0. 0. |
| Philadelphia | Servant | 4 yrs. each. | £15. 0. 0. |
| Philadelphia | Servant | 4 yrs. | £16. 0. 0. |
| Philadelphia | Servant, the master to maintain the infant during the term of this indenture.[1] | 4 yrs. |  |
| Northern Liberties | Servant[3] | 7 yrs. | £15. 0. 0. |
| Philadelphia | Servant[1] | 2 yrs. | £8. 0. 0. |
| Philadelphia | Servant[3] | 4 yrs. | £20. 0. 0. |
| Philadelphia | Apprentice, taught the trade of a biscuit baker, have 6 months' night schooling.[3] |  | £9. 0. 0. |
| Philadelphia | Servant, found meat, drink, working apparel, washing and lodging and £5 Penna. currency at the expiration of his term. | 18 mo. | £7. 10. 0. |
| Philadelphia | Servant[5] | 4 yrs. | £12. 0. 0. |
| Philadelphia | Servant | 4 yrs. | £14. 0. 0. |
| Southwark | Apprentice, taught the art and mystery of a ship joiner (note 3, and one pair of shoes). | 4 yrs. | £7. 10. 0. |
| Rye twp., Cumberland co. | Apprentice[3] | 3 yrs. | £11. 0. 0. |
| Philadelphia | Apprentice, taught the trade of a ——, given 6 months' day and 2 quarters' night schooling, allowed 3 days at Christmas, 3 days at harvest, 2 days at Easter and 2 days at Whitsuntide, every year, to himself.[8] | 5 yrs., 21 d. |  |
| Derry twp., Lancaster co. | Servant[3] | 5 yrs. | £15. 0. 0. |
| W. Whiteland twp., Chester co. | Servant | 18 mo. | £16. 10. 0. |
|  | Servant, to have meat, drink, washing and lodging. In case he should want clothing he is to pay for them after the expiration of this indenture. | 2 yrs. |  |
| Southwark | Servant[5] | 3 yrs. | £12. 0. 0. |
| Derry twp., Lancaster co. | Servant[3] | 4 yrs. | £15. 0. 0. |
| Derry twp., Lancaster co. | Servant, employed 6 months each year at the brick layer's or mason's business.[6] | 2 yrs. | £12. 0. 0. |
| Derry twp., Lancaster co. | Servant[5] | 3 yrs. | £12. 0. 0. |
| Philadelphia |  | 8 yrs. | £14. 0. 0. |
| Southwark | Servant, found meat, drink, washing and lodging, 1 pair new shoes and to mend his clothes. | 1 yr. | £7. 10. 0. |
| Philadelphia | Servant[3] | 4 yrs. | £14. 0. 0. |
| Philadelphia | Servant | 4 yrs. | £16. 0. 0. |
| Philadelphia | Servant[3] | 4 yrs. | £15. 0. 0. |
| Philadelphia | Servant, found meat, drink, apparel, washing and lodging. In consideration of the master having given up 10 months of time, the servant is not to have freedom dues. | 2 yrs. | £20. 0. 0. |

| Date. | Name. | From the Port of | To Whom Indentured. |
|---|---|---|---|
| 1773. July 19th | Cearney, Esther | | Dr. William Plunket and his assigns. |
| | Lawrence, John | Ireland | Samuel Paul and his assigns |
| | Truman, William | | David Howell and his assigns |
| | Killpatrick, John; Kirkpatrick, George. | Ireland | William Curry and his assigns |
| | McGlone, Barney | Ireland | Thomas Simpson and his assigns |
| | Phegan, Mary | Ireland | William Patterson and his assigns |
| | Hughes, James | Ireland | Henry Funk and his assigns |
| | McGinnis, Patrick | Ireland | William Plunkett and his assigns |
| July 20th | McGinnis, Owen | | William Plunkett and his assigns |
| | McAnnelly, Ann | Ireland | William Salsbery and his assigns |
| | Ker, Mibsam | | Silas Engles and his heirs |
| | Davidson, John | Ireland | Phillip Clumbag and his assigns |
| | Fitzgerrald, John | | Andrew Woller |
| | Jarrard, Wilson | | Frederick Tucker |
| | Killpatrick, Rose | Ireland | Martin Bear and his assigns |
| July 21st | Burchell, Andrew | Ireland | Thomas Penrose and his assigns |
| | Whitehead, Lydia | | Mary Brown |
| | Dougherty, James, and Catherine, his wife. | | Thos. Edward Wallace and his assigns. |
| | Lenon, John; Smith, Patrick | Ireland | William Pearson and his assigns |
| | Hannon, John | Ireland | Presly Blackiston and his assigns |
| | McClory, Archibald | Ireland | John O'Brien and his assigns |
| | Bird, William | | Benjamin Gibbs and his assigns |
| | Darrough, James | Ireland | John Mertz and his assigns |
| | Goggin, John | Ireland | John James and his assigns |
| July 22nd | Mason, Jane | | Caleb Jonas and wife |

[1] To be found all necessaries and at the expiration have freedom dues.
[2] To be found all necessaries and at the expiration have one new suit of apparel.
[3] To be found all necessaries and at the expiration have two complete suits of apparel, one whereof to be new.

| Residence. | Occupation. | Term. | Amount. |
|---|---|---|---|
| Turbott twp., Northumberland co. | Servant | 4 yrs. | £ 15. 0. 0. |
| Greenage twp., Gloster co., N. J. | Servant (note 1, and £ 5 Penna. currency). | 2 yrs., 6 mo. | £ 10. 0. 0. |
| Tredyffrin twp., Chester co. | Servant | 3 yrs., 6 mo. | £ 14. 0. 0. |
| Paxtang twp., Lancaster co. | Servant | 2 yrs., 3 mo. each. | £ 18. 0. 0. each. |
| Paxtang twp., Lancaster co. | Servant | 2 yrs., 6 mo. | £ 13. 0. 0. |
| Turbert twp., Northumberland co. | Servant, found meat, drink, apparel, washing and lodging.[6] | 4 yrs., 6 mo. | £ 16. 0. 0. |
| Philadelphia | Servant[3] | 5 yrs. | £ 15. 0. 0. |
| Turbert twp., Northumberland co. | Servant, taught to read in Bible, write a legible hand and cypher through the five common rules.[3] | 6 yrs. | £ 13. 0. 0. |
| Turbert twp., Northumberland co. | Servant[5] | 3 yrs. | £ 12. 0. 0. |
| Philadelphia | Servant, found meat, drink, apparel, washing and lodging. | 2 yrs., 3 mo. | £ 10. 0. 0. |
| Southwark | Apprentice, taught the art and mystery of a house carpenter, the father to find the apprentice apparel 1 year from this date.[1] | 6 yrs., 2 mo. 28 d. | |
| Philadelphia | Servant[3] | 4 yrs. | £ 14. 11. 0. |
| | Apprentice, learn to read, write and cypher through rule of 3. To be taught ———.[3] | | |
| Philadelphia | | 4 yrs., 11 mo., 20 d. | |
| Mastic twp., Lancaster co. | Servant (note 2, besides his old) | 3 yrs., 6 mo. | £ 15. 10. 0. |
| Southwark | (Note 5, give him £ 7 in lieu of freedom). | 4 yrs. | £ 14. 0. 0. |
| Philadelphia | Apprentice, taught the trade of a bonnet, hat and cloak maker, not put to the trade till the two last years of her apprenticeship, the other part of the time to be employed about any kind of housework (note 5, have 2 complete suits). | 5 yrs., 8 mo. | |
| Southwark | Servant, agreed in case Catherine shall bear a child during her servitude, James shall after the expiration of his term pay the master £ 3 for the loss of time, etc., of his wife.[5] | 18 mo. each. | £ 11. 10. 0. |
| Kensington, Phila. co. | Servant | { 3 yrs.<br>{ 4 yrs. | £ 15. 0. 0. each. |
| Philadelphia | Servant[1] | 3 yrs., 6 mo. | £ 14. 0. 0. |
| Philadelphia | Apprentice, taught the art and mystery of a tailor.[5] | 2 yrs., 6 mo. | £ 7. 10. 0. |
| Philadelphia | Apprentice, taught the art and mystery of a mariner and taught navigation.[1] | 3 yrs. | |
| Pikeland twp., Chester co. | Servant[1] | 3 yrs. | £ 15. 0. 0. |
| | Servant, found meat, drink, washing, lodging and clothes to the value of £ 10 Pa. currency, employed at the business of a barber and hair dresser. | 2 yrs. | £ 10. 0. 0. |
| Philadelphia | Apprentice, taught housewifery, read in Bible, write a legible hand and cypher.[3] | 3 yrs., 8 mo. 8 d. | |

[4] To be found all necessaries and at the expiration have two complete suits of apparel, one whereof to be new, and 40s. in money.

[5] At expiration have two complete suits of apparel, one whereof to be new.

| Date. | Name. | From the Port of | To Whom Indentured. |
|---|---|---|---|
| 1773. July 23rd... | Murphy, George | Ireland | Robert Allison and his assigns |
| | Ridgeway, Edward | | Christian Fiss and his assigns |
| | O'Neil, Betty | Ireland | Thomas Kennedy and his assigns |
| | Trenor, Morris | Ireland | Charles French and his assigns |
| | Logan, William, and Wilkinson Logan, his wife. | Ireland | William Brown and his assigns |
| | Hart, John | | John Imrick and his assigns |
| July 23rd... | Ryan, James | Ireland | Thomas Gilpin and his assigns |
| | Miller, John | Ireland | Thomas Ramsay and his assigns |
| | Dawson, James | Ireland | John Whitehall and his assigns |
| July 24th... | McVicker, Archibald | | Isaac Morton and his assigns |
| | O'Neal, Henry | Ireland | Robert Robinson and his assigns |
| July 26th... | Walsh, Maurice | Ireland | Watson Welding and his assigns |
| | Turmuel, Maria | | Lewis Phrail and his assigns |
| | Townly, Richard | Ireland | Michael McGannon and his assigns |
| | Smith, John | Ireland | William Drewry and his assigns |
| | Bibery, Jacob | | Jacob Kintner and his assigns |
| | Scott, William | | Jeremiah Reily and his assigns |
| | Taylor, Anthony | | Rudolph Lear |
| | Crooke, William | | Thomas Proctor and his assigns |
| | Robinson, Benjamin | | Isaac Powell and his assigns |

## List of Indentures.

| RESIDENCE. | OCCUPATION. | TERM. | AMOUNT. |
|---|---|---|---|
| Uwchland twp., Chester co. | Servant, found meat, drink, apparel, washing and lodging. | 2 yrs., 9 mo. | £11.0.0. |
| Philadelphia | Servant, till he shall pay the sum to his master of £12. 1s. 10d., his master is to employ him at the business of a carpenter or fan maker at the rate of 16 shillings per week. | | £11.17.4. |
| Hanover twp., Lancaster co. | Servant | 3 yrs. | £14.0.0. |
| Philadelphia | Servant[5] | 1 yr., 6 mo. | £7.11.6. |
| Philadelphia | Servant (note 2, besides their old, each). | 2 yrs. | £13.0.0. |
| | Servant, William Logan to serve his master either at sea or on shore. | | |
| Philadelphia | Apprentice, taught the art and mystery of a baker, read in Bible, write a legible hand cypher as far as rule of 3.[6] | 7 yrs. | |
| Philadelphia | Servant | 4 yrs. | £14.0.0. |
| Tinicum twp., Bucks co. | Servant[3] | 3 yrs., 6 mo. | £12.13.0. |
| Philadelphia | Servant, found meat, drink, washing, lodging, 1 pair new shoes and 1 pair breeches. | 1 yr., 6 mo. | £8.11.6. |
| Philadelphia | Apprentice, taught the art and mystery of a biscuit baker.[6] | 4 yrs., 1 mo. | £10.10.0. |
| Brandywine Hundred, New Castle co. | Servant, found meat, drink, washing, lodging, 2 pair shoes, 2 pair stockings, 2 pair trousers, 1 pair leather breeches and a hat. | 1 yr., 3 mo. | £9.8.6. |
| Buckingham twp., Bucks co. | Servant (note 2, besides his old and £10 Pa. currency in cash). | 2 yrs. | £10.0.0. |
| Philadelphia | Servant | 3 yrs. | £17.11.0. |
| Philadelphia | Apprentice, taught the art and mystery of a plasterer, found meat, drink, apparel, lodging and washing, at expiration of his term freedom dues. | 4 yrs. | £10.0.0. |
| Southwark | Apprentice, taught the art and mystery of a rope maker, read in Bible, write a legible hand.[3] | 6 yrs. | £12.0.0. |
| Philadelphia | Apprentice, taught the art and mystery of a cordwainer, six months' night schooling, at the expiration of his term freedom dues or £8 Pa. currency and all his working tools. | 4 yrs. | |
| Southwark | Apprentice, taught the art and mystery of a cordwainer.[3] | 3 yrs., 3 mo. | |
| Philadelphia | Apprentice | 4 yrs., 8 mo. 6 d. | |
| Philadelphia | Apprentice, taught the art and mystery of a house carpenter, found meat, drink, washing and lodging, privilege of going to night school in the winter season, his friend paying the expense of night schooling. | 5 yrs. | |
| Philadelphia | Apprentice, taught the art and mystery of a cabinet and chair maker, to serve his time within the city and liberties of Philadelphia, his father to give him | 7 yrs., 8 mo. 3 w. | |

| Date. | Name. | From the Port of | To Whom Indentured. |
|---|---|---|---|
| 1773. | | | |
| July 27th | Henin, Maria Catherine | | Abraham Housewert |
| | Wilson, Thomas | | William Green and his assigns |
| | Porter, James | Ireland | David Cambers and his assigns |
| | January, William | | Esekiah Hilbert and his assigns |
| | Miller, John | | William Wilson and his assigns |
| | Muckelhetton, Michael | Ireland | William Wilson and his assigns |
| | Neale, William | Ireland | William Wilson and his assigns |
| | Barnoutt, Elizabeth | Ireland | John White and his assigns |
| | Barnoutt, Elizabeth | | Alexander Moor and his assigns |
| | Miller, David | Ireland | William Wilson and his assigns |
| | Morrow, James | Ireland | William Wilson and his assigns |
| | Wills, James | Ireland | William Wilson and his assigns |
| | Conway, Lawrence | Ireland | William Wilson and his assigns |
| | McGuire, William | | William Wilson and his assigns |
| | Mante, Jacob | | Robert Hardic and William Duncan and their assigns. |
| | Logan, Patrick | | William Wilson and his assigns |
| | Fritz, John Andreas | | Moses Bartram and his assigns |
| | Worrell, Morris | | George Inglis and his assigns |
| July 28th | Harrison, Joseph | Ireland | John Palmer and his assigns |
| | Mercer, Elizabeth | | Uriah Woolman and his assigns |
| | Coburn, Thomas | Ireland | Thomas Blackledge and his assigns |
| | Defrees, Joseph | | David Evans and his assigns |
| | Porter, James | | John Davison and his assigns |
| | Boyle, Lewis | | Owen Brooke and his assigns |

## List of Indentures.

| Residence. | Occupation. | Term. | Amount. |
|---|---|---|---|
| | the three first winters' night schooling, but in case of his father's death his master is to perform that part of schooling.[3] | | |
| New York | Servant, and with the servant's consent to go to New York. | 4 yrs. | £ 14. 0. 0. |
| Philadelphia | Apprentice, taught the art and mystery of a house carpenter, found meat, drink and lodging. | 2 yrs., 2 mo. | |
| Philadelphia | Servant (note 2, besides his old). | 3 yrs. | £ 15. 0. 0. |
| Philadelphia | Apprentice, found meat, drink, washing and lodging, shirts and stockings, taught the trade of a house carpenter. | 1 yr., 9 mo. | |
| New Castle Hundred, New Castle co. | Servant[3] | 4 yrs. | |
| New Castle Hundred, New Castle co. | Servant[1] | 3 yrs. | £ 12. 0. 0. |
| New Castle Hundred, New Castle co. | Servant | 2 yrs., 6 mo. | £ 16. 0. 0. |
| Philadelphia | Servant[5] | 3 yrs. | £ 15. 0. 0. |
| Cohansey, N. J. | Servant | 3 yrs. | £ 15. 0. 0. |
| New Castle Hundred, New Castle co. | Servant, found meat, drink, apparel, washing and lodging. | 2 yrs. | £ 10. 0. 0. |
| New Castle Hundred, New Castle co. | Servant | 3 yrs. | £ 16. 0. 0. |
| New Castle Hundred, New Castle co. | Servant[1] | 2 yrs., 6 mo. | £ 15. 0. 0. |
| New Castle Hundred, New Castle co. | Servant[1] | 3 yrs. | £ 16. 0. 0. |
| New Castle Hundred, New Castle co. | Servant[1] | 2 yrs. | |
| Philadelphia | Apprentice, taught the art and mystery of a mariner and navigation. In case the master wants to part with him he is to be disposed to a captain that sails from the port of Philadelphia.[3] | 5 yrs. | |
| New Castle Hundred, New Castle co. | Servant[1] | 1 yr., 6 mo. | |
| Philadelphia | Servant | 9 yrs. | £ 20. 0. 0. |
| Philadelphia | Apprentice, taught the art and mystery of a house carpenter, give him three months' night schooling every winter for three years, the remainder of his apprenticeship, the privilege of going every winter to night school, his mother or guardian paying the expense, at the expiration customary freedom dues. | 7 yrs., 3 mo. 27 d. | |
| Philadelphia | Servant[5] | 2 yrs. | £ 13. 5. 0. |
| Philadelphia | Servant | 3 yrs. | £ 13. 0. 0. |
| Rocksbury twp., Phila. co. | Servant[3] | 4 yrs. | £ 11. 10. 0. |
| Southwark | Apprentice, taught the art and mystery of a house carpenter, three quarters' night schooling[1]. | 3 yrs. | |
| Philadelphia | Apprentice, taught the art and mystery of a saddler, one quarter night schooling.[5] | 4 yrs., 9 mo. | £ 14. 0. 0. |
| Limerick twp., Phila. co. | Apprentice, taught the art and mystery of a cabinet maker, three months' night schooling every winter.[3] | 4 yrs., 5 mo. 19 d. | |

| Date. | Name. | From the Port of | To Whom Indentured. |
|---|---|---|---|
| 1773. July 28th | McMaghon, Rose | Ireland | John Cunningham and his assigns |
| | Neff, Isaac | | Joseph Heart and his heirs |
| July 29th | Duff, William | | George Watson and his assigns |
| | Veach, Henry | | James Ewing and his assigns |
| | Lemon, William | | Robert Ewing and his assigns |
| | Hammon, William | Ireland | John Milleman and his assigns |
| | Crutcher, James | | Nathaniel Lewis and his assigns |
| July 30th | Galler, John | | Francis Trumble and his assigns |
| | Flynn, John | Ireland | James Gallagher and his assigns |
| | Sheely, Dorothy | Ireland | Robert Fitzgerrald and his assigns |
| | Woods, James | Ireland | Matthias Brenner and his assigns |
| | Fogerty, Catherine | | Thomas Tisdall and his assigns |
| July 31st | Morphy, Patrick | Ireland | John Jack and his assigns |
| | Morphy, Margaret | Ireland | William McMichael and his assigns |
| | Morphy, William | Ireland | William McMichell and his assigns |
| | Till, George Adam | | Jacob Udree and his assigns |
| | Morphy, Mary | | Ann Loremar and her executors |
| | King, Barbara | Ireland | John Taylor and his assigns |
| | Lamb, Elizabeth | | John Taylor and his assigns |
| | Johnston, Ann | Ireland | John Taylor and his assigns |
| Aug. 2nd | Triggs, Susannah | | Patrick Rice and his assigns |
| | McEnery, John | | Robert Porter and his assigns |
| | O'Harra, James | | James Weldon Roberts, the said Roberts to bind the apprentice to a house carpenter for five years to learn the trade. |
| | Kins, George | | Conrad Lentner and his assigns |
| | Gervan, Henry | Ireland | John Trapnall and his assigns |
| | Queen, Eleanor | Ireland | James Watson and his assigns |
| | Moore, Andrew | | Christian Duy and his assigns |

| Residence. | Occupation. | Term. | Amount. |
|---|---|---|---|
| Philadelphia | Servant[1] | 3 yrs. | £14.0.0. |
| Norwister twp., Bucks co. | Apprentice, taught the art and mystery of a miller and flour cask cooper, read in Bible, write a legible hand.[3] | 13 yrs., 5 mo., 13 d. | |
| The Forks of Brandywine, New Castle co. | Servant | 4 yrs. | £13.10.0. |
| Upper Darby, Chester co. | Servant, found meat, drink, washing and lodging, 25 shillings during the term to purchase clothes and if any are supplied by the master they are to be paid for by the servant at expiration of the term. | 2 yrs. | £8.10.0. |
| | Apprentice, taught the art of a mariner. | 3 yrs. | £14.0.0. |
| Chester twp., Chester co. | Servant[5] | 2 yrs. | £7.11.6. |
| New Jersey, Chesterfield twp., Burlington co. | Apprentice, taught the trade of a cooper, read, write and cypher as far as rule of 3.[6] | 12 yrs., 2 mo., 5 d. | |
| Southwark | Apprentice, taught the art and mystery of a windsor and chair maker.[1] | 18 mo. | £8.0.0. |
| Philadelphia | Servant[3] | 3 yrs., 3 mo. | £10.0.0. |
| Philadelphia | Servant[3] | 4 yrs. | £14.0.0. |
| Philadelphia | Servant[3] | 4 yrs. | £13.0.0. |
| Philadelphia | Servant | 4 yrs. | £14.13.0. |
| Newtown twp., Cumberland co. | Servant[3] | 2 yrs., 6 mo. | £12.0.0. |
| Kensington, Phila. co. | Servant, taught to read well in Bible, sew and spin.[3] | 10 yrs. | £6.10.0. |
| Kensington, Phila. co. | Servant, read in Bible, write a legible hand and cypher as far as through rule of 3.[3] | 10 yrs. | |
| Philadelphia | Apprentice, taught the art and mystery of a potter, one quarter's night schooling.[1] | 4 yrs., 6 mo. | |
| Kensington, Phila. co. | Apprentice, taught housewifery, taught to read in Bible, write a legible hand, sew, knit and spin.[6] | 13 yrs. | |
| Philadelphia | Servant[5] | 3 yrs. | £15.0.0. |
| Philadelphia | Servant[5] | 3 yrs. | £16.0.0. |
| Philadelphia | Servant[5] | 3 yrs. | £15.0.0. |
| Philadelphia | Servant | 4 yrs. | £9.0.0. |
| Philadelphia | Apprentice, taught the trade of a saddler, one winter's night schooling.[3] | 7 yrs. | |
| Southwark | Aged seven years[3] | Until he attains 21 years, except 5 years from the 12th of his age. | |
| Southwark, Phila. co. | Apprentice, taught the trade of a surgeon barber, taught to read in Bible, write a legible hand, cypher as far as rule of 3.[3] | 8 yrs. | |
| Darby, Chester co. | Servant | 2 yrs., 6 mo. | £13.1.6. |
| W. Pensborough twp., Cumberland co. | Servant[5] | 3 yrs. | £12.0.0. |
| Germantown, Phila co. | Apprentice, taught the cordwainer's trade. | 4 yrs., 6 mo. | £20.0.0. |

| Date. | Name. | From the Port of | To Whom Indentured. |
|---|---|---|---|
| 1773. Aug. 2nd | Johns, Thomas | | Joseph North and John Waggoner and their assigns. |
| | May, John | Ireland | Joshua Gilbert and his assigns. |
| | Letterough, Mary | | Andrew Lepenback |
| | Groope, Henry | | John Weaver and his assigns. |
| Aug. 3rd | Magary, John | Ireland | James Hamilton and his assigns. |
| | Doyles, John | | Jonathan Coats and his assigns. |
| | Montgomery, Edward | Ireland | Asher Mott and his assigns. |
| | McCalvy, Daniel | Ireland | Asher Mott and his assigns. |
| | Mallon, Patrick | | John Hickson and his assigns. |
| | Rowe, Thomas | | William Cowan and his assigns. |
| | Cole, Richard | Ireland | John Smallman and his assigns. |
| | Lee, John | | Jacob Ritter and his assigns. |
| | Simmons, Charles Howell | | John James |
| | Callihan, Bridget | Ireland | James Roney |
| | McElwrath, John | | James Watson and his assigns. |
| Aug. 4th | Franklin, William | Ireland | Caleb Parry and his assigns. |
| | Franklin, William | | Obiah Park and his assigns. |
| | Green, James | | Matthew Strong and his assigns. |
| | Fullerton, Richard | | Thomas Shields and his assigns. |
| | Ward, John | Ireland | Thomas Shields and Mary Shields and their assigns. |
| | Whaler, Sarah | | William Garrigues and his assigns. |
| | Hamble, John | | Robt. Fulton and his executors. |
| | McRoddin, John | Ireland | Thomas Shields and his assigns. |
| | McRoddin, John | | James Shields and his assigns. |
| | Dougherty, Margaret | Ireland | John Page |
| | Steward, Mary | Ireland | David Rose and his assigns. |
| | McDonald, Archibald | | Robert McKim and his assigns. |
| | Carlisle, David | | John McKean and his assigns. |
| | Malone, John | Ireland | William Clifton and his assigns. |
| | Gilbert, Edward | Ireland | William Cliffton and his assigns. |
| Aug. 5th | Gravely, Mary | | John Riboun and his assigns. |

| Residence. | Occupation. | Term. | Amount. |
|---|---|---|---|
| Northern Liberties | Apprentice, taught the trade of a tanner and currier, found meat, drink, washing and lodging and working apparel, shoes and hats, have four quarters' night schooling, when free, freedom (clothes?) dues, or £10 Pa. currency in cash. | 3 yrs., 9 mo., 28 d. | |
| Buckingham twp., Bucks co. | Servant[5] | 3 yrs. | £14.10.0. |
| Philadelphia | Apprentice, taught housewifery, sew, read and write Dutch and English (note 3, and a spinning wheel). | 14 yrs. | |
| Philadelphia | Apprentice, taught the trade of a tailor, have three quarters' day schooling.[3] | 4 yrs., 6 mo. | |
| Paxtang twp., Lancaster co. | Servant[5] | 2 yrs., 4 mo. | £7.10.0. |
| Leacock twp., Lancaster co. | Servant | 7 yrs. | £15.10.0. |
| Byless Island, near Trent Town. | Servant[5] | 2 yrs. | £10.10.0. |
| Byless Island, near Trent Town. | Servant[5] | 3 yrs. | £16.0.0. |
| Philadelphia | Apprentice, taught the trade of a breeches maker (note 3, or £5 Penna. currency in cash). | 4 yrs. | £12.3.2. |
| Philadelphia | Apprentice, taught the trade of a saddler, read, write and cypher so as to keep his accounts.[3] | 7 yrs. | |
| Philadelphia | Servant[3] | 2 yrs. | £8.10.0. |
| Philadelphia | Servant[5] | 3 yrs. | £17.0.0. |
| Charles Town, S. C. | Apprentice, taught the mystery of a merchant.[5] | 1 yr., 5 mo. 8 d. | |
| Philadelphia | Servant[5] | 3 yrs. | £15.0.0. |
| W. Pensborough twp., Cumberland co. | Servant | 4 yrs. | £18.0.0. |
| Blockley twp., Phila. | Servant[3] | 5 yrs. | £16.0.0. |
| W. Caln twp., Chester co. | Servant | 5 yrs. | £16.0.0. |
| Philadelphia | Apprentice, taught the art of a pilot in the river and bay of Delaware, have three months' day schooling and 5 shillings for every vessel he shall pilot up and down the said river and | 4 yrs., 9 mo. | |
| Philadelphia | Apprentice, taught the art of a goldsmith, found meat, drink and lodging. | 4 yrs., 11 mo. | |
| Philadelphia | Apprentice[1] | 4 yrs. | £15.0.0. |
| Newlinton twp., Chester co. Philadelphia | Servant | 13 yrs., 6 mo. | £8.10.0. |
| Philadelphia | Apprentice, taught the trade of a tailor, read in Bible, write a legible hand and cypher as far as rule of 3.[3] | 6 yrs., 3 mo. 6 d. | |
| Philadelphia | Servant[3] | 3 yrs. | £15.0.0. |
| Newlington, Chester co. | Servant, as above | | £15.0.0. |
| Upper Pensneck, Salem co., N. J. | Servant | 4 yrs. | £15.0.0. |
| Northern Liberties, Phila. | Servant | 4 yrs. | £14.0.0. |
| Brandywine Hundred, New Castle co. | Servant | 4 yrs. | £15.0.0. |
| Philadelphia | Servant[1] | 4 yrs. | £16.0.0. |
| Philadelphia | Servant[1] | 2 yrs., 6 mo. | £10.0.0. |
| Philadelphia | Servant[1] | 7 yrs. | £16.0.0. |
| Philadelphia | Apprentice, taught the trade of a leather breeches maker, have two quarters' night schooling.[3] | 4 yrs., 10 mo. | |

| Date. | Name. | From the Port of | To Whom Indentured. |
|---|---|---|---|
| 1773. Aug. 5th.... | Craffly, Catherine | | Conrad Lentner and his assigns...... |
| | McAfee, Isaac | | William Collady and his assigns..... |
| | Porter, Ann | Ireland .... | William Crispin and his assigns..... |
| | Anderson, William | Ireland .... | Andrew Crawford and his assigns... |
| | Forbes, James | | Edward Dunlop .................... |
| | Adams, John | | Jacob Hauser ....................... |
| | Pentz, John | Rotterdam.. | Francis Casper Hassenclever and his assigns. |
| | McCay, Daniel | Ireland .... | John Graham and his assigns........ |
| | Grogan, Charles; Sands, Robert. | Ireland .... | James Hamilton and his assigns...... |
| | Girvan, Sarah | | Alexander Rutherford. |
| | Girvan, Sarah | | Alexander Russell ................. |
| | Wilson, John | Ireland .... | James Hamilton and his assigns..... |
| | Hanson, Thomas | Ireland .... | James Hamilton and his assigns..... |
| | McCullough, Mary | | William Wilson and his assigns..... |
| | Deady, Jeremiah | | William McEnery and his assigns.... |
| | Drew, Henry | Ireland .... | Arthur Thomas and his assigns...... |
| Aug. 6th.... | Crosgrove, Thomas | Ireland .... | James Hamilton and his assigns...... |
| | Cambell, Francis | | Dennis Whalen and his assigns...... |
| | Crampton, Jane | | William West and his assigns........ |
| | Flemming, Martha | | John Moyes and his assigns........ |
| | Askin, Sarah | Ireland .... | Timothy Berret and his assigns...... |
| Aug. 7th.... | Nelson, James | Ireland .... | William Allen and Joseph Turner and their assigns. |
| | Murphy, Daniel | Ireland .... | Andrew Watson and his assigns..... |
| | McLoud, Martha | Ireland .... | Alexander Chisolm and his assigns.. |
| | Humphreys, John | | George Connoly and his assigns..... |
| | Anderson, Abram | Ireland .... | James Given ....................... |
| | Anderson, Abram | | William Owen ...................... |
| | Smith, Ann | | John Shoub and his assigns.......... |
| | Martin, Baptist | Ireland .... | Alexander Kearns and his assigns... |
| | Steward, Archibald | Ireland .... | Henry Schreiber and his assigns..... |
| | Wallace, Isabella | Ireland .... | Adam Guier and his assign ......... |
| | Duffy, Ann | | John Grimlade ..................... |

## List of Indentures.

| Residence. | Occupation. | Term. | Amount. |
|---|---|---|---|
| Southwark, Phila. co............ | Apprentice, taught the trade of a mantua maker, read in Bible, write a legible hand.[3] | 6 yrs., 9 mo. 27 d. | |
| Philadelphia ................. | Apprentice, found meat, drink, working clothes, lodging and washing. | 3 yrs., 5 mo. | |
| Philadelphia ................. | Servant[1] ........................ | 4 yrs....... | £ 15. 0. 0. |
| Plymouth twp., Phila. co........ | Servant, found meat, drink, washing, lodging, 1 shirt, a pair trousers. In case the master shall supply the servant with any other clothes he is to pay for them at the expiration of the term. | 1 yr., 6 mo. | £ 9. 10. 0. |
| Allowes Creeks twp., Salem co., N. J. | Servant ........................ | 4 yrs....... | £ 14. 0. 0. |
| | | 11 yrs...... | £ 0. 1. 0. |
| Philadelphia .................. | Servant[1] ........................ | 3 yrs., 6 w.. | £ 23. 0. 0. |
| W. Nantmill twp., Chester co.... | Servant ........................ | 3 yrs....... | £ 14. 0. 0. |
| Paxtang twp., Lancaster co...... | Servant ........................ | { 2 yrs., 3 mo. 2 yrs., 6 mo. | £ 10. 10. 0. each. |
| Philadelphia .................. | Servant, given one quarter schooling at reading and one quarter at writing, terms of the above indenture.[1] | 6 yrs....... | £ 10. 0. 0. |
| Philadelphia .................. | Servant ........................ | | £ 10. 0. 0. |
| Paxtang twp., Lancaster co...... | Servant[1] ........................ | 7 yrs....... | £ 14. 10. 0. |
| Paxtang twp., Lancaster co...... | Servant, found meat, drink, washing and lodging, shoes, stockings and tobacco. | 1 yr., 2 mo. | £ 5. 10. 0. |
| Tinicum twp., Bucks co......... | Apprentice, taught housewifery, sew, knit and spin, read well in Bible, write a legible hand.[3] | 12 yrs., 10 mo. | |
| Philadelphia .................. | Apprentice, learn the trade of a house carpenter, found meat, drink, washing, lodging, shoes and stockings, given two winters' schooling and when free a complete suit of broadcloth clothes. | | |
| Northern Liberties, Phila........ | Apprentice, taught the trade of a leather breeches maker, have one week's day schooling each year[3]. | 5 yrs....... | £ 7. 11. 6. |
| | Servant[1] ........................ | 6 yrs....... | £ 17. 0. 0. |
| Uwchland twp., Chester co...... | Servant[1] ........................ | 6 yrs....... | £ 17. 0. 0. |
| Philadelphia .................. | Servant ........................ | 4 yrs....... | £ 15. 0. 0. |
| Philadelphia .................. | Servant, taught to read and write[1]. | 7 yrs....... | 4/. |
| Philadelphia .................. | Servant ........................ | 4 yrs....... | £ 16. 5. 0. |
| Lebanon twp., Hunderton co., N. J. | Servant ........................ | 2 yrs., 6 mo. | £ 15. 0. 0. |
| Halloways Creek, Salem co., N. J. | Servant, taught the trade of a weaver.[5] | 2 yrs., 6 mo. | £ 9. 0. 0. |
| Burlington, N. J............... | Servant[1] ........................ | 4 yrs....... | £ 12. 0. 0. |
| Philadelphia .................. | Servant[5] ........................ | 3 yrs....... | £ 12. 0. 0. |
| | Servant[1] ........................ | 5 yrs....... | £ 15. 0. 0. |
| Uwchland twp., Chester co...... | (Agreeable to the terms above)... | | £ 15. 0. 0. |
| Horsham twp., Phila. co......... | Apprentice, taught to read in Bible, write a legible hand, sew, knit and spin, and housewifery.[3] | 10 yrs., 6 mo. | |
| Springfield, Chester co.......... | Servant[5] ........................ | 2 yrs....... | £ 10. 11. 4. |
| Tinicum Island, Chester co...... | Servant[5]........................ | 1 yr., 3 mo. | £ 7.10. 0. |
| Kingsess twp., Phila. co......... | Servant ........................ | 4 yrs....... | £ 15. 0. 0. |
| Woolwich twp., Gloster co., N. J. | Servant ........................ | 4 yrs....... | £ 14. 0. 0. |

| Date. | Name. | From the Port of | To Whom Indentured. |
|---|---|---|---|
| | McDowall, Hugh | Ireland | Richard Swanwick and his assigns |
| | McDowall, Andrew | | James Roney |
| | Christy, James | Ireland | John Grinslaid and his assigns |
| | Lawson, Tellet | | Allen McLean and his assigns |
| | Bryan, Augustin | | Peter Woglam and his assigns |
| Aug. 9th | Loge, John | Ireland | Thomas Norris and Thomas Sinnickson and their assigns. |
| | Corry, Francis | Ireland | John McCutcheon and his assigns |
| | Rainey, Elizabeth | | Hugh Robinson and his assigns |
| | Taylor, James | | Richard Truman and his assigns |
| | Petterson, John | Ireland | John Wall and his assigns |
| | Boyd, Samuel | | James Huston and his assigns |
| | Pot, Matthias | | Peter Trace and his assigns |
| | Wattson, James | | James Wattson and his assigns |
| | Murry, Jane | | William Day and his assigns |
| | Wright, Robert | | John McCutcheon and his assigns |
| | Wallace, Richard | Ireland | John Tittermary and his assigns |
| | Quin, Arthur | | Peter Biggs and his assigns |
| | Kirke, Sarah | | Robert McGougen |
| | Salmond, James | | Patrick Brown and his assigns |
| | McNeil, Daniel | | Thomas Hewit and his assigns |
| | Collons, John | | Henry Sharpneck and his assigns |
| Aug. 10th | Ferrall, Michael | | Peter Robinson and his assigns |
| | McNarten, Dennis | | Thomas Trueman and his assigns |
| | Stagg, Benjamin | | James Glenn |
| | Stoop, Andrew | Ireland | Christian Minick and his assigns |
| | Harrison, James | | Henry Philler and his assigns |
| | Kirk, Agnes; Kirk, Rosanna | | James Roney and his assigns |
| | Spence, Agnes | Ireland | Henry Wilson and his assigns |
| | Euert, John | Ireland | John Black and his assigns |
| | Twaddle, Archibald | Ireland | John Black and his assigns |
| | Steen, Sarah | Ireland | William Benham and his assigns |
| | Beck, Ann | | Fergus McMenemy |
| Aug. 11th | McCormick, Jane | Ireland | William Bedford and his assigns |

| Residence. | Occupation. | Term. | Amount. |
| --- | --- | --- | --- |
| Philadelphia | Servant | 2 yrs., 6 mo. | £ 20.0.0. |
| Hanover twp., Lancaster co. | Servant[5] | 2 yrs. | £ 9.0.0. |
| Woolwich twp., Gloster co., N. J. | Servant[1] | 5 yrs. | £ 16.0.0. |
| Philadelphia | Servant[3] | 3 yrs. | £ 14.0.0. |
| Philadelphia | Apprentice | 4 yrs., 10 mo., 16 d. | £ 9.0.0. |
| Salem, Salem co., W. N. J. | Servant | 3 yrs. | £ 15.0.0. |
| Willis Town, Chester co. | Servant[3] | 4 yrs. | £ 16.0.0. |
| E. Nantmill twp., Chester co. | Servant[1] | 4 yrs. | £ 15.0.0. |
| Philadelphia | Servant[5] | 1 yr. | £ 8.0.0. |
| Philadelphia | Servant[1] | 7 yrs. | £ 15.0.0. |
| Philadelphia | Servant[5] | 1 yr., 3 mo. | £ 7.10.0. |
| Philadelphia | Apprentice, taught the trade of a leather dresser, have four quarters' night schooling, found all necessaries, except Sunday clothes.[6] | 4 yrs. | |
| Earl twp., Lancaster co. | Servant, found meat, drink, washing and lodging. | 2 yrs. | £ 8.0.0. |
| Philadelphia | Servant[3] | 9 yrs. | £ 8.10.0. |
| Willis co. | Servant[5] | 2 yrs. | £ 12.0.0. |
| Passyunk twp., Phila. co. | Servant, have three years winters' night schooling (note 5, £ 10 in cash). | 3 yrs. | £ 16.0.0. |
| Philadelphia | Servant, to be employed at the marble mason's trade (note 5, have £ 7 Pa. currency in cash). | 2 yrs. | £ 7.10.0 |
| Easttown, Chester co. | Servant | 3 yrs. | £ 13.0.0. |
| | Apprentice, taught the art of a mariner (note 2, or £ 8 in cash). | 4 yrs., 6 mo. 15 d. | |
| Greenwich, Gloster co., N. J. | Servant, kept at the trade of a tailor.[2] | 2 yrs. | £ 9.0.0. |
| Germantown, Phila. co. | Apprentice, taught the trade of a saddle tree maker, have three months' day schooling in the term and three months' night schooling in the last year.[3] | 6 yrs. | £ 15.0.0. |
| Philadelphia | | 3 yrs., 6 mo. | |
| Sadsbury, Chester co. | Servant, found meat, drink, washing and lodging. If the master shall pay anything for him except the £ 9 for necessaries, etc., the servant is to pay for them at the expiration of the term. | 1 yr., 3 mo. | £ 9.0.0. |
| Philadelphia | Apprentice, taught the trade of a brick layer, given three quarters' night schooling (note 1, worth £ 12, or so much in cash). | | |
| Bristol twp., Bucks co. | Servant[1] | 4 yrs. | £ 15.0.0. |
| Philadelphia | Apprentice, taught the cordwainer's trade, have six months' evening schooling.[3] | 4 yrs., 9 mo. 15 d. | |
| Hanover twp., Lancaster co. | Servant[5] | 3 yrs. | £ 13.0.0. for each. |
| Philadelphia | | 3 yrs., 6 mo. | £ 12.0.0. |
| Derry twp., Lancaster co. | Servant | 3 yrs., 6 mo. | £ 16.0.0. |
| Derry twp., Lancaster co. | Servant, found meat, drink, washing and lodging, trousers and one pair of shoes. | 1 yr., 6 mo. | £ 7.10.0. |
| Philadelphia | Servant[5] | 3 yrs. | £ 17.0.0. |
| | Servant[5] | 4 yrs. | £ 17.0.0. |
| Philadelphia | Servant[5] | 3 yrs. | £ 14.10.0. |

| Date. | Name. | From the Port of | To Whom Indentured. |
|---|---|---|---|
| 1773. Aug. 11th... | Steen, Margaret; Steen Elizabeth. | | Robert Wetherow and his assigns.... |
| | Stevenson, James | Ireland .... | William Carson and his assigns...... |
| | Coler, Margaret | | Theodore Meninger and his assigns.. |
| | Vellois, Martha | | Samuel Simpson and his assigns..... |
| | Donnely, Mary | Ireland .... | Fergus McMenemy and his assigns... |
| | Pollock, Ephraim | | Alexander Frazer and his assigns... |
| | Hugg, Joseph | | Esekiah Hibbert and his assigns..... |
| | Bones, Thomas; Bones, Peter; Bones, James; Bones, Jannet | Ireland .... | John Gray and George Dunlap and their assigns. |
| | McPeak, John | Ireland .... | John Hoffman and his assigns....... |
| | Williams, Jane | | Joseph Lounes ...................... |
| | McMullans, William | Ireland .... | Thomas McKean .................... |
| | Nutter, John | | William Downes .................... |
| | Ord, John | | Jacob Magargell and his assigns..... |
| Aug. 12th... | Douglas, Henry | Ireland .... | Hugh Crawford and his assigns..... |
| | Grier, James | | James Ramsay ...................... |
| | Stewart, Alexander | | Jacob Cook ........................ |
| | Graffy, Mary | | George Button and his assigns....... |
| 1773. Aug. 12th... | Kain, Francis | | Robert Allison and his assigns....... |
| | McGough, Sarah | Ireland .... | John Black and his assigns.......... |
| | McGines, Arthur | Ireland .... | John Black and his assigns.......... |
| | Nowls, Mary | | John Taylor ........................ |
| | Bradley, Marery | | James Taylor and his assigns........ |
| Aug. 13th... | Brown, Mathew | | John Duer and his assigns........... |
| | Cample, Ann | Ireland .... | John McCollegh and his assigns..... |
| | Brady, Barnard | Ireland .... | Joseph Fox and his assigns.......... |
| | Fielding, Hugh | | Elenezer Call and his assigns....... |
| | Boyd, Ann | Ireland .... | Dedrick Reese ...................... |
| | Boyd, Ann | | Thomas Turbert and his assigns..... |
| | Fearby, John | Ireland .... | Michael Graham and his assigns..... |
| | McPeak, James | Ireland .... | William Brisbin and his assigns..... |
| Aug. 14th... | Legate, James | | Alexander Rutherford and his assigns. |
| | Kaighn, Patrick | | Enoch Morgan and his assigns....... |
| | Conner, Ann | Ireland .... | John Hodgson and his assigns....... |
| | Dalton, George | | William Huston and his assigns..... |
| | Miller, Alexander | | James Thompson and his assigns..... |
| | Sheals, Toby | Ireland .... | James Pennell and his assigns....... |

## List of Indentures.

| Residence. | Occupation. | Term. | Amount. |
|---|---|---|---|
| W. Caln twp., Lancaster co. | Servant [5] | 2 yrs., 6 mo. each. | £7.10.0. each. |
| Philadelphia | Servant [5] | 2 yrs. | £10.0.0. |
| Philadelphia | Servant [3] | 3 yrs., 2 mo. 15 d. | £19.13.0. |
| Philadelphia | Apprentice, taught the art of a milliner.[5] | 2 yrs., 11 mo. | |
| Philadelphia | Servant [5] | 3 yrs. | £14.10.0. |
| Philadelphia | Apprentice, taught the trade of a cabinet and chair maker, have six months' evening schooling, the father paying the expense.[3] | 5 yrs., 7 mo. | |
| Philadelphia | Apprentice, taught the trade of a house carpenter, found meat, drink, shoes, shirts, lodging and washing, allowed time one quarter every winter to go to night school. | 4 yrs., 8 mo. 25 d. | |
| Philadelphia | | 7 yrs. | £7.10.0. |
| | | 7 yrs. | £7.10.0. |
| | | 12 yrs. | £7.10.0. |
| | | 10 yrs. | £7.10.0. |
| Pitts Grove twp., Salem co., N. J. | Servant [5] | 1 yr., 6 mo. | £7.10.0. |
| Passyunk, Phila. co. | | 2 yrs., 11 mo. | |
| Eastown twp., Chester co. | | 3 yrs. | £13.0.0. |
| Lewistown | Apprentice, taught the business of a pilot, given six months' day schooling (note 2, worth £10 besides his wearing apparel or £10 in cash). | | |
| Oxford twp., Phila. co. | Apprentice, taught the art of a farmer, read in Bible, write a legible hand and cypher as far as the rule of 3.[3] | 7 yrs. | |
| Roxborough twp., Phila. co. | Servant | 2 yrs., 6 mo. | £12.0.0. |
| Antrim twp., Cumberland co. | | 3 yrs. | £14.10.0. |
| Derry twp., Lancaster co. | | 3 yrs., 6 mo. | £15.9.6. |
| Philadelphia | Apprentice, taught housewifery and sewing.[3] | 5 yrs., 2 mo. | £10.0.0. |
| Southwark | Apprentice, taught the trade of a house carpenter, read in Bible, write a legible hand and cypher as far as rule of 3.[6] | 13 yrs., 1 mo., 26 d. | |
| Derry twp., Lancaster co. | Servant [5] | 3 yrs. | £11.0.0. |
| Derry twp., Lancaster co. | Servant [5] | | £17.10.0. |
| Ridley twp., Chester co. | | 3 yrs. | £14.0.0. |
| Conecocheague, Cumberland co. | Servant [3] | 3 yrs., 2 mo. 16 d. | £14.0.0. |
| Lower Maxfield twp., Bucks co. | Servant [3] | 4 yrs. | £17.0.0. |
| | Servant [3] | 4 yrs. | £17.10.0. |
| | Servant | 1 yr. | £17.10.0. |
| Philadelphia | Apprentice | 3 yrs., 6 mo. | £5.2.3. |
| Philadelphia | Servant | 3 yrs. | £10.0.0. |
| Upper Merion | (On conditions of the above indenture). | | |
| W. Nantmill, Chester co. | Servant [5] | 1 yr., 6 mo. | £8.10.0. |
| Solsbury twp., Lancaster co. | Servant | 1 yr. | £7.10.0. |
| Philadelphia | Servant [3] | 3 yrs. | £12.0.0. |
| Durham twp., Bucks co. | Servant [5] | 2 yrs. | £10.0.0. |
| Philadelphia | Servant [3] | 4 yrs. | £14.0.0. |
| Philadelphia | Servant [5] | 2 yrs., 6 mo. | £20.0.0. |
| Hackett Town, Sussex co., N. J. | Servant [3] | 2 yrs. | £12.16.6. |
| Middle Town, Chester co. | Servant [1] | 2 yrs. | £11.0.0. |

| Date. | Name. | From the Port of | To Whom Indentured. |
|---|---|---|---|
| 1773. | Thompson, John | Ireland | Alexander Woodburn and his assigns. |
| Aug. 14th | Jameson, Francis | Ireland | Alexander Woodburn and his assigns. |
| Aug. 16th | Beard, John | | David Uber and his assigns......... |
| | Robison, Sarah | | John Norris and his assigns......... |
| | Sneckberger, Francis | London | John Halberstadt and his assigns.... |
| | Driver, Hopkins | | Joseph Serrmon and his assigns...... |
| | Driver, Hopkins | | Joseph Holdstack and his assigns.... |
| | Bloss, Peter | | Jacob Parker and his assigns........ |
| | Major, Mary | Ireland | Robert Loosely and his assigns....... |
| | Anderson, Margaret | | William Hunter and his assigns...... |
| | Anderson, James | Ireland | William Hunter and his assigns...... |
| | Haughey, John | | Thomas Bullard and his assigns.... |
| Aug. 17th | Miller, Ann | | John Plankinhorne and his assigns... |
| | Moody, William | | James Kettary and his assigns....... |
| | McNamara, John | | Conrad Pigeon and his assigns........ |
| | Schnider, John | | Anthony Sechler and his assigns..... |
| | Brian, Archibald | | Abraham Franks and his assigns..... |
| | Daragh, George | Ireland | James Kirk and his assigns......... |
| | Wans, Samuel | Ireland | Thomas Hales and his assigns....... |
| | McGregor, Duncan | | Archibald Scott and his assigns...... |
| | Pearcy, John | | Andrew Todd and his assigns....... |
| | Anderson, Agness | | John Taylor and his assigns........ |
| | Anderson, Jane | | John Taylor and his assigns........ |
| Aug. 18th | Martin, John | Ireland | John Galloway and his assigns...... |
| | Lamb, Terence | Ireland | John Galloway and his assigns...... |
| | Bradley, Margery | | John Chandler and his assigns....... |
| | Fourder, Charles | | James Hood and his assigns......... |
| | McLean, Archibald | Ireland | Joseph Rhoads and his assigns....... |

[1] To be found all necessaries and at the expiration have freedom dues.
[2] To be found all necessaries and at the expiration have one new suit of apparel.
[3] To be found all necessaries and at the expiration have two complete suits of apparel, one whereof to be new.

## List of Indentures.

| Residence. | Occupation. | Term. | Amount. |
|---|---|---|---|
| Oxford twp., Chester co. | Servant[1] | 2 yrs. | £7.0.0. |
| Oxford twp., Chester co. | Servant[1] | 4 yrs. | £13.2.6. |
| Northern Liberties | Apprentice, taught the trade of a butcher, read well in Bible, write a legible hand, cypher as far as rule of 3.[2] | 13 yrs. | |
| Kensington | Servant[3] | 2 yrs., 6 mo. | £10.10.0. |
| Philadelphia | Servant, and is to make up any time he may lose by sickness not to exceed six months.[5] | 2 yrs. | £29.10.0. |
| Philadelphia | Servant | 3 yrs. | £7.10.0. |
| Philadelphia | Servant | 3 yrs. | £7.10.0. |
| Philadelphia | Apprentice, taught the trade of a cooper, taught to read in Bible, write a legible hand, cypher as far as rule of 3.[2] | 6 yrs., 5 mo. 3 d. | |
| Philadelphia | Servant[3] | 4 yrs. | £14.0.0. |
| East Town, Chester co. | Servant, taught to read in Bible and write a legible hand.[5] | 6 yrs. | £11.0.0. |
| East Town, Chester co. | Servant, taught to read in Bible, write a legible hand and cypher as far as rule of 3.[2] | 8 yrs. | £11.0.0. |
| Sadsbury twp., Lancaster co. | Servant[5] | 7 yrs. | £14.10.0. |
| Southwark | Apprentice, have two years' schooling, taught housewifery and sewing.[2] | 13 yrs., 7 mo. | £8.0.0. |
| Earl twp., Lancaster co. | Servant[5] | 3 yrs. | £16.0.0. |
| Southwark | Servant[5] | 6 yrs. | £20.0.0. |
| Northern Liberties | Apprentice, taught the art and mystery of a blacksmith, given one quarter's night schooling, one hammer and one sledge, at expiration, freedom dues or £10 Pa. currency. | 4 yrs. | |
| Philadelphia | Servant | 4 yrs. | £3.0.0. |
| Philadelphia | Servant, give him one quarter's day schooling.[1] | 6 yrs., 2 mo. | £17.10.0. |
| Philadelphia | Servant[5] | 1 yr. | £9.0.0. |
| Philadelphia | Servant, found meat, drink, washing, lodging, two shirts, two pair trousers and one pair shoes, and if any more clothes are supplied by the master the servant is to pay for them at expiration of the term. | | £7.10.0. |
| East Whiteland twp., Chester co. | Servant, found meat, drink, washing, lodging, two pair shoes, one pair trousers and a shirt. | 1 yr., 3 mo. | £9.0.0. |
| Philadelphia | Servant[5] | 3 yrs., 6 mo. | £12.0.0. |
| Philadelphia | Servant[5] | 3 yrs., 9 mo. | £12.0.0. |
| Welsh Tract, New Castle co. | Servant | 3 yrs. | Passage paid. |
| Welsh Tract, New Castle co. | Servant, found meat, drink, apparel, washing and lodging. | 3 yrs. | Passage paid. |
| Philadelphia | Servant | 3 yrs., 2 mo. 16 d. | £12.15.0. |
| Southwark | Apprentice, taught the art and mystery of a cooper (note 1, or £6 Pa. currency). | 5 yrs., 1 mo. 8 d. | |
| Southwark, Phila. co. | Servant[1] | 4 yrs. | £19.10.0. |

[4] To be found all necessaries and at the expiration have two complete suits of apparel, one whereof to be new, and 40s. in money.

[5] At expiration have two complete suits of apparel, one whereof to be new.

| Date. | Name. | From the Port of | To Whom Indentured. |
|---|---|---|---|
| 1773. Aug. 18th... | Darragh, George | Ireland | John Cooper and his assigns |
| | Keelan, John | | Judah Foulk and his assigns |
| | Kelly, Mary | | John Milns and his assigns |
| | Panslerine, Anna Maria | | George Knorr and his assigns |
| | Fraim, John | | John Wiggans and his assigns |
| Aug. 19th... | Brillighan, Thomas | | Robert Carson and his assigns |
| | Brillighan, Thomas | | Nicholas Dale and his assigns |
| | Campble, Ann | | Samuel Culey and his assigns |
| | Auld, James | | Richard Martin and his assigns |
| | Bayley, Mary | | Hugh Dunn and his assigns |
| | Jones, Ann | | Hugh Dunn and his assigns |
| | McCauseland, James | | Jacob Cline |
| | Crow, Timothy | Ireland | William Barnes and his assigns |
| | Shales, Francis | Ireland | Isaac Hibbert and his assigns |
| | McKnown, Hugh | | John Bryan and his assigns |
| | Welsh, James | Ireland | William Ross and his assigns |
| Aug. 20th... | McCullum, John | | Christopher Byerly and his assigns |
| | McCullum, James | | Nicholas Ripe and his assigns |
| Aug. 21st... | Johnston, James | | William Niles and his assigns |
| | McCoy, Ann | | Margaret Morris and her assigns |
| | Madden, Mary | | Bartholomew Bushiere and his assigns |
| | Powell, James | Ireland | Jacob Jones and his assigns |
| | McCafferty, Charles | Ireland | Archibald McIlroy and his assigns |
| | McCann, Michael | Ireland | Richard Collins and his assigns |
| | McGinly, John | | Thomas Livezey and his executors |
| | Gorel, Isabel | Ireland | James Claypool and his assigns |
| | Read, Mary | | Joseph Mathers and his assigns |
| | Read, Elizabeth | Ireland | Bartholomy Mathers and his assigns |
| | Read, Hugh | Ireland | Michael Simpson and his assigns |
| | Read, Hugh | | Thomas Meas and his assigns |
| | Dillman, John | | Valentine Hagoner and his assigns |
| | Gray, Ann | | James Pegnam and his assigns |
| | McCherry, Peter | Ireland | William Griffith and his assigns |
| Aug. 23rd... | McGregger, Alexander | Ireland | John Sweethen and his assigns |
| | Beaks, Mary | | David Diver and his assigns |

## List of Indentures.

| RESIDENCE. | OCCUPATION. | TERM. | AMOUNT. |
|---|---|---|---|
| Woodbury, Gloscester co., West Jersey. | Servant, found meat, drink, apparel, washing and lodging, one quarter's day schooling. | 6 yrs., 2 mo. | £ 7. 10. 0. |
| Philadelphia | Servant[5] | 4 yrs | £ 18. 0. 0. |
| E. Nottingham twp., Chester co. | Servant[1] | 4 yrs | £ 9. 0. 0. |
| Philadelphia | Servant[5] | 5 yrs., 3 mo. | £ 10. 0. 0. |
| Paxtang, Lancaster co. | Servant[1] | 5 yrs | £ 16. 0. 0. |
| Philadelphia | Servant (note 5, have £ 7, 10 shillings in cash). | 2 yrs | £ 7. 10. 0. |
| Tinicum, Chester co. | | The term above mentioned. | £ 15. 0. 0. |
| Paxton twp., Lancaster co. | Servant[1] | 4 yrs | £ 15. 10. 0. |
| | Servant, taught to read, write and cypher through the rule of 3.[3] | 8 yrs | £ 9. 0. 0. |
| Stow Crick twp., Western Division in Cumberland co., West New Jersey. | Servant (note 1, and £ 5 Pa. currency). | 3 yrs | 20 shillings. |
| Stow Crick twp., Western Division in Cumberland co., West New Jersey. | Servant (note 1, and £ 5 in cash Pa. currency). | 3 yrs | 20 shillings. |
| Philadelphia | Servant[5] | 2 yrs | £ 9. 0. 0. |
| Philadelphia | Servant[1] | 4 yrs | £ 13. 0. 0. |
| Derby twp., Chester co. | Servant[5] | 2 yrs | £ 12. 0. 0. |
| Redly twp., Chester co. | Servant[5] | 1 yr | £ 7. 10. 0. |
| Philadelphia | Servant[1] | 4 yrs | £ 14. 0. 0. |
| Philadelphia | Apprentice, taught the trade of a cooper, read in Bible, write a legible hand (note 3, or £ 10 Pa. currency in cash). | 5 yrs. | |
| Philadelphia | Apprentice, taught the art and mystery of a wheelright, read in the Bible, write a legible hand (note 3, or £ 10 Pa. currency). | 3 yrs., 6 mo. | |
| Philadelphia | Servant[5] | 7 yrs | £ 8. 0. 0. |
| Burlington, N. J. | Servant | 5 yrs | £ 8. 0. 0. |
| Southwark | Servant | 3 yrs | £ 14. 0. 0. |
| Southwark | Servant, found meat, drink, apparel, washing and lodging. | 1 yr | £ 7. 10. 0. |
| Philadelphia | Servant[3] | 3 yrs | £ 12. 0. 0. |
| New Jersey | Servant[5] | 3 yrs | £ 18. 0. 0. |
| ——— twp., Phila. co. | Servant, found all necessaries except apparel and if any clothes are supplied by the master, the servant is to pay for them at the expiration of the term. | 1 yr., 6 mo. | £ 9. 0. 0. |
| Philadelphia | Servant, found meat, drink, apparel, washing and lodging. | 2 yrs., 6 mo. | £ 7. 10. 0. |
| Germantown, Phila. co. | Servant[5] | 2 yrs | £ 9. 0. 0. |
| Chatnan twp., Phila. co. | Servant, found meat, drink, apparel, washing and lodging. | 2 yrs | £ 9. 0. 0. |
| Paxton twp., Lancaster co. | Servant[5] | 2 yrs | £ 9. 0. 0. |
| Paxton twp., Lancaster co. | Servant | 2 yrs | £ 9. 0. 0. |
| Philadelphia | Apprentice, taught the trade of a cedar cooper (note 3, give him a single set of tools for the trade) | 7 yrs., 6 mo. | |
| Philadelphia | Servant | 3 yrs | £ 0. 5. 0. |
| Aston twp., Chester co. | Servant[1] | 4 yrs | £ 13. 0. 0. |
| Maidenhead, N. J. | Servant, employed at the weaving business.[8] | 2 yrs., 3 mo. | £ 7. 0. 0. |
| Hunterdon co. | Apprentice, taught to sew, spin, read in Bible and write.[3] | 11 yrs., 9 mo. | |

| Date. | Name. | From the Port of | To Whom Indentured. |
|---|---|---|---|
| 1773.<br>Aug. 23rd... | Nick, Henry | | Rudolph Neil and his assigns |
| | Daugherdy, James | | William Robinson and his assigns |
| | Coats, Michael | | Samuel Loftis and his assigns |
| | Ewong, Elizabeth | Rotterdam | Peter Kurtz and his assigns |
| | Ehrlebachin, Catherine | Rotterdam | Christopher Sowers and his assigns |
| | Goedecke, Johannes | Rotterdam | John Christopher Wagganer and his assigns. |
| | Goedecke, Johannes | | Jeremiah Heinzellman and his assigns |
| | Fox, John Francis | Rotterdam | William Rush and his assigns |
| | Miller, John Jacob | Rotterdam | Conrad Weaver and his assigns |
| | Sherp, Anthony | Rotterdam | Phineas Lord and his assigns |
| | Branish, Anna Elizabeth | Rotterdam | John Pinkirhen and his assigns |
| | Couchman, Catherine | Rotterdam | James Varee and his assigns |
| | DeCranville, Joseph Alexander | Rotterdam | Zebulon Rudolph and his assigns |
| Aug. 24th... | Hooffman, Celia | Rotterdam | George Cooper and his assigns |
| | Davis, Elizabeth | Ireland | John Nicholson and his assigns |
| | Barham, Heins Henry | Rotterdam | Richard Handly |
| | Bosse, John Christopher | Rotterdam | Charles Robinson and his assigns |
| | Woolfe, George | Rotterdam | Jacob Keebler and his assigns |
| | Horning, Leonard | Rotterdam | Jacob Morgan |
| | Horning, Leonard | | John Lesher |
| | Marree, Daniel | Rotterdam | John Curts |
| | Nibble, Henry | Rotterdam | Amour Grubb and his assigns |
| | Patterson, Sarah | Ireland | Samuel Jones and his assigns |
| | Mingling, Arnst | Rotterdam | Isaac Grub and his assigns |
| | Brown, John | Rotterdam | Emanuel Grubb and his assigns |
| | Leitz, Casimer | Rotterdam | Jacob Wentz, Jr., and his assigns |
| | Keyzer, Philip | Rotterdam | Philip Wintz and his assigns |
| | Augustus, John | Rotterdam | John Garrett and his assigns |
| | Cribbs, Peter | | Joseph Fox and his assigns |
| | McCourt, John | Ireland | Isaac Wayne and his assigns |
| | Deney, Peter | Rotterdam | John Jessop and his assigns |
| | Pompey | | Thomas York and his assigns |
| | Folstick, Balser | | Samuel Opman and his assigns |
| | McClintock, Lidia | Ireland | Daniel Robinson and his assigns |
| | Patree, John | Rotterdam | Conrad Kerlinger and his assigns |
| | Hapus, John Henry | Rotterdam | John Groof and his assigns |
| | Crampton, Margaret | Ireland | Isaac Coran and his assigns |

## List of Indentures.

| RESIDENCE. | OCCUPATION. | TERM. | AMOUNT. |
|---|---|---|---|
| Philadelphia | Apprentice, learn the art and mystery of a surgeon barber (note 5, have £9 Pa. currency). | 4 yrs. | |
| Philadelphia | Apprentice, taught the art and mystery of a house carpenter, found meat, drink, apparel, washing and lodging, two quarters' night schooling. | 5 yrs. | |
| Philadelphia | Apprentice, taught the trade of a chaise maker, have four quarters' night schooling at the expense of the father (note 3, except shoes). | 5 yrs. | |
| Philadelphia | Servant[3] | 7 yrs. | £28.2.6. |
| Germantown, Phila. co. | Servant[3] | 5 yrs., 6 mo. | £35.9.0. |
| Philadelphia | Servant[3] | 4 yrs. | £28.10.0. |
| Manheim twp., Lancaster co. | Servant | 4 yrs. | £28.10.0. |
| Philadelphia | Servant[3] | 4 yrs., 6 mo. | £27.7.6. |
| Bristol twp., Phila. co. | Servant[3] | 4 yrs., 3 mo. | £30.16.8. |
| Deptford twp., Glocester co., N. J. | Servant[3] | 6 yrs., 6 mo. | £28.3.0. |
| Philadelphia | Servant[3] | 7 yrs. | £27.7.6. |
| Burlington, N. J. | Servant[3] | 4 yrs., 6 mo. | £31.0.0. |
| Philadelphia | Servant, taught to read in Bible, write a legible hand.[3] | 7 yrs., 6 mo. | £24.13.1. |
| Philadelphia | Servant[1] | 8 yrs., 6 mo. | £28.14.6. |
| Philadelphia | Servant | 4 yrs. | £10.0.0. |
| Brandywine Hundred, New Castle co. | Servant[3] | 5 yrs. | £26.18.3. |
| Brandywine Hundred, New Castle co. | Servant (note 3, and £3 Pa. currency). | 4 yrs., 6 mo. | £27.8.6. |
| Brandywine Hundred, New Castle co. | Servant[1] | 5 yrs. | £29.6.3. |
| Philadelphia | Servant[3] | 4 yrs. | £26.1.6. |
| Oley, Bucks co. | According to the terms above mentioned. | | |
| Brandywine Hundred, New Castle co. | Servant (note 1, or £6 in cash) | 3 yrs. | £26.10.6. |
| Brandywine Hundred, New Castle co. | Servant, have one quarter schooling.[3] | 6 yrs. | £31.12.3. |
| Tredyffrin twp., Chester co. | Servant[3] | 4 yrs. | £11.0.0. |
| Brandywine Hundred, New Castle co. | Servant (note 3, and £3 in money) | 5 yrs. | £26.9.6. |
| Brandywine Hundred, New Castle co. | Servant (note 3, and £3 Pa. currency). | 4 yrs., 6 mo. | £28.14.7. |
| Worcester twp., Phila. co. | Servant (note 3, or £10 Pa. currency in cash). | 4 yrs., 6 mo. | £29.10.6. |
| Worcester twp., Phila. co. | Servant[3] | 5 yrs. | £28.7.6. |
| Whitemarsh twp., Phila. co. | Servant[3] | 5 yrs., 3 mo. | £29.3.0. |
| Philadelphia | Apprentice, taught the trade of a blacksmith and farrier, two quarters' night schooling in the term.[3] | 5 yrs. | |
| East Town, Chester co. | Servant[5] | 3 yrs. | £13.0.0. |
| Debtford twp., Glocester co., W. Jersey. | Servant[3] | 4 yrs. | £29.5.3. |
| Philadelphia | Apprentice | 15 yrs., 2 mo. | £23.0.0. |
| Northern Liberties, Phila. co. | Servant[3] | 3 yrs., 6 mo. 5 d. | £19.0.0. |
| Philadelphia | Servant, one quarter schooling.[3] | 6 yrs. | £10.0.0. |
| Plymouth twp., Phila. co. | Servant[3] | | £27.12.6. |
| Plymouth twp., Phila. co. | Servant[3] | 7 yrs., 6 mo. | £31.14.0. |
| Philadelphia | | 7 yrs. | £11.0.0. |

| Date. | Name. | From the Port of | To Whom Indentured. |
|---|---|---|---|
| 1772.<br>Aug. 24th... | Hilliard, Henry | Rotterdam.. | Jacob Frees and his assigns |
| | Engle, Jacob | Rotterdam.. | Charles Syng and his assigns |
| | Engle, Jacob | | Geo. Rein and his assigns |
| Aug. 25th... | Cooley, Elizabeth | | Thomas Mushet and his assigns |
| | Bird, Christiana | | William Straker and wife |
| | Beale, William | | Seth Mattock and his assigns |
| | DeQuinville, Gerard Antoin. | Rotterdam.. | Christopher Marshall, Jr., and his assigns. |
| | Fawsell, John Christopher | Rotterdam.. | John Bratzman and his assigns |
| | Fawsell, John Christopher | | David Deshler and his assigns |
| | Gatter, Martin | | Michael Groce and his assigns |
| | Walter, Johan Peter | Rotterdam.. | John Salter and his assigns |
| | Shank, John George | Rotterdam.. | George Godfrid Welper and his assigns. |
| | Crimel, Godfried Warner | Rotterdam.. | Henry Kner and his assigns |
| | Merks, Johan Yudocus | Rotterdam.. | George Emerich and his assigns |
| | Dawman, John | Rotterdam.. | Jacob Miller and his assigns |
| | Pater, Ernst Augustus | Rotterdam.. | David Candler and his assigns |
| | Strietzell, John Godfried | Rotterdam.. | Philip Care and his assigns |
| | Fratcher, Johan Henry | Rotterdam.. | Jacob Liday and his assigns |
| | O'Harrow, Margaret | Ireland | Henry Hurper and his assigns |
| | Brillow, Ulius Bearnhart | Rotterdam.. | Joseph Morgan and his assigns |
| | January, Mary | | Williamson Talbott |
| | Boyd, John | | Robert Bethel |
| | Nestler, Johan Godfried | Rotterdam.. | Samuel Garrigues, Sr., and his assigns |
| Aug. 26th... | Spence, Agness | | William Atkinson and his assigns |
| | Morton, George | | Levy Hollingsworth and his assigns |
| | Boyle, John | | Levy Hollingsworth and his assigns |
| | Bittner, John Charles | Rotterdam.. | Charles Smith and his assigns |
| | Fronmoyer, Martin | Rotterdam.. | Jacob Shoemaker and his assigns |
| | Grant, George | | Joseph Haight and his assigns |
| Aug. 27th... | McLean, Daniel | | Joseph Simpson and his assigns |
| | Smith, Charles | | Vendel Zerben and his assigns |
| | Schildbach, Charles Enoch | Rotterdam.. | Ellis Lewis and his assigns |
| | Rosegrance, John Charles | Rotterdam.. | Ambrous Smedly and his assigns |
| | Adams, John | | James Hill and his assigns |

## List of Indentures.

| RESIDENCE. | OCCUPATION. | TERM. | AMOUNT. |
|---|---|---|---|
| Upperareis Creek twp., Salem co., W. Jersey. | Servant³ | 4 yrs., 6 mo. | £30.16.6. |
| Philadelphia | Servant (note 3, or £16 Pa. currency in cash). | 3 yrs. | £20.10.0. |
| Earl Town Lancaster co. | Servant, the terms above mentioned. | | £20.10.0. |
| Moyamensing twp., Phila. co. | Servant | 4 yrs. | £14.0.0. |
| Philadelphia | Apprentice, taught housewifery, sew and read, and if the master take her to the West Indies he shall cause her to be brought back again.³ | 2 yrs. | |
| Philadelphia | Apprentice, taught the trade of a cooper.³ | 4 yrs., 10 mo., 9 d. | |
| Philadelphia | Servant, taught to read and write³. | 9 yrs. | £24.0.6. |
| Salsburgh twp., Northampton co. | Servant³ | 4 yrs., 6 mo. | £29.16.6. |
| Salsburgh twp., Northampton co. | Servant⁵ | 4 yrs., 6 mo. | £29.16.6. |
| Northern Liberties | Apprentice, taught the trade of a cordwainer, one year schooling at Dutch, and six months' at English, after he arrives at the age of 12 years.³ | 16 yrs., 2 mo., 11 d. | |
| Northern Liberties, Phila. co. | Servant, employed at the baker's trade.³ | 5 yrs. | £30.0.0. |
| Philadelphia | Servant³ | 3 yrs., 6 mo. | £26.17.6. |
| Vincent twp., Chester co. | Servant³ | 4 yrs., 6 mo. | £28.1.6. |
| Pikeland twp., Chester co. | Servant¹ | 4 yrs., 3 mo. | £28.17.6. |
| Chelttenham twp., Phila. co. | Servant³ | 4 yrs., 9 mo. | £27.18.0. |
| York Town, York co. | Servant³ | 5 yrs. | £28.5.0. |
| Chestnut Hill, Phila. co. | Servant³ | 5 yrs. | £27.15.6. |
| Frankoney twp., Phila. co. | Servant³ | 6 yrs. | £29.11.6. |
| Philadelphia | Servant | 3 yrs. | £13.0.0. |
| Waterford twp., Glocester co. | Servant³ | 6 yrs. | £28.8.6. |
| Northern Liberties | Apprentice | 8 yrs., 7 mo. 19 d. | |
| | Apprentice, taught the trade of a mariner and the art of navigation and allowed while in the port of Philadelphia to sleep at his father's. | 4 yrs. | |
| Philadelphia | Servant³ | 5 yrs., 6 mo. | £28.7.6. |
| Philadelphia | Servant | 3 yrs., 6 mo. | £12.0.0. |
| Philadelphia | Apprentice, taught the art of a merchant.³ | 4 yrs., 3 mo., 3 d. | |
| Philadelphia | Servant | 5 yrs. | £16.0.0. |
| Eversham twp., Burlington. co., N. J. | Servant³ | 6 yrs. | £30.0.0. |
| | Servant¹ | 5 yrs. | £27.14.0. |
| Burlington | Servant | 3 yrs. | £13.10.0. |
| Philadelphia | Apprentice, taught the trade of a painter and glazier, have two quarters' night schooling.³ | 4 yrs. | £7.11.6. |
| Philadelphia | Servant, found meat, drink, washing and lodging, one pair shoes and one pair stockings, one check shirt. | 7 mo. | £10.0.0. |
| Philadelphia | Servant (note 1, or £10 Pa. currency). | 5 yrs. | £28.11.3. |
| Middletown twp., Chester co. | Servant (note 3, and £2 Pa. currency). | 5 yrs. | £27.19.9. |
| Philadelphia | Apprentice, taught the art and | 3 yrs. | |

| Date. | Name. | From the Port of | To Whom Indentured. |
|---|---|---|---|
| 1773. | | | |
| Aug. 27th | Losch, Peter | Rotterdam | Nathan Follwell and his assigns |
| | Remeller, Joseph | Rotterdam | George Douglass and his assigns |
| Aug. 28th | Shulser, John Christopher | Rotterdam | Adam Grubb and his assigns |
| | McCounan, Mary | | James Brown and his assigns |
| | Lighte, Christian | Rotterdam | Christopher Natts and his assigns |
| | Baker, John Jacob | Rotterdam | David Shafer and his assigns |
| | Bear, Margaret | Rotterdam | William Key and his assigns |
| | Dewees, Abraham | | Abraham Charlesworth and his assigns |
| | Temple, Johan Lawrence | Rotterdam | John Abbott and his assigns |
| | Alborst, William | Rotterdam | Thomas Dudley and his assigns |
| | Cuzens, Ann | | Benjamin Flower and his assigns |
| | Meyers, Anne | Rotterdam | Charles Ferguson and his assigns |
| | Steffee, John David | Rotterdam | Robert Paul and his assigns |
| Aug. 30th | Diveler, Frederick | Rotterdam | Conrad Shimer and his assigns |
| | McCarty, Eleanor | | Jeremiah Dealy and his assigns |
| | Mark, Johann Christian | Rotterdam | Daniel Bartolet and his assigns |
| | Scwhetcher, John Hendrick | Rotterdam | Francis Rood and his assigns |
| | Hubner, John Barnard | Rotterdam | Henry Rood and his assigns |
| | Nicholas, Eve | Rotterdam | James Jenkins and his assigns |
| | Schlokkirman, Christopher | Rotterdam | Peter Briell and his assigns |
| | Van Amerongen, Johanna | Rotterdam | Thomas Whitlock and his assigns |
| | Neimrich, Johan Godfried | Rotterdam | Andrew Burkhard and his assigns |
| Aug. 31st | Shultze, Henry Conrad Hyronimus. | Rotterdam | Edward Oxley and his assigns |
| | Higgons, William | Ireland | Daniel Harker and his assigns |
| | McCausland, Andrew | Ireland | James Caldwell and his assigns |
| | Peter, John William | Rotterdam | Thomas Perry and his assigns |
| | Woods, Ann | | Daniel Harker and his assigns |
| | Harkeson, Margaret | | Thomas Hale and his assigns |
| | Hisser, John Tobias | Rotterdam | Charles Chamberlin and his assigns |
| Sept. 1st | Manders, Sophia | | Alexander Fraser and his assigns |
| | Brachman, Johan Conrad | Rotterdam | John Fritz and his assigns |
| | Dryman, John Henry | Rotterdam | Dennis Whilon and his assigns |
| | Yons, Earls | Rotterdam | Fanton, Earl of, and his assigns |
| | Scales, Absalom | | Peter Wikoff and his assigns |
| | Higgens, Thomas | Ireland | Joshua Elder and his assigns |
| | Lelifield, Maria | Rotterdam | William Saldsbury and his assigns |
| | Fright, John | Rotterdam | Peter Sowder and his assigns |
| | Nicholas, James | | John Malnor and Thomas Hough and their assigns. |

## List of Indentures.

| Residence. | Occupation. | Term. | Amount. |
|---|---|---|---|
| | mystery of a wheelwright, have two quarters' night schooling.[6] | | |
| Springfield, Burlington co. | Servant (note 1, and £3 Pa. currency). | 5 yrs. | £27.13.9. |
| Philadelphia | Servant (note 1, and £3 Pa. currency). | 5 yrs. | £29.8.8. |
| Chester twp., Chester co. | Servant[3] | 4 yrs., 6 mo. | £28.14.6. |
| Philadelphia | Servant | 3 yrs., 11 mo., 25 d. | £7.10.0. |
| Lower Dublin twp., Phila. co. | Servant[3] | 5 yrs. | £28.19.6. |
| Philadelphia | Servant (note 3, and £2 Pa. currency). | 5 yrs., 6 mo. | £34.4.6. |
| Woolwich twp., Glocester co., W. N. Jersey. | Servant[3] | 7 yrs. | £33.11.6. |
| Upper Dublin twp., Phila. co. | Apprentice, taught the trade of a farmer, read in Bible, write a legible hand and cypher.[3] | 17 yrs. | |
| Nottingham twp., Burlington co. | Servant (note 3, and £4 Pa. currency in cash). | 5 yrs. | £30.8.6. |
| Evesham twp., Burlington co., W. Jersey. | Servant (note 3, and £5 Pa. currency in cash). | 7 yrs. | £29.9.3. |
| Philadelphia | Servant, taught housewifery, sew, read in Bible (note 3, and £5 Pa. currency in cash). | 10 yrs., 3 mo. | |
| Philadelphia | Servant[3] | 6 yrs., 6 mo. | £27.4.6. |
| Bensalem twp., Bucks co. | Servant[3] | 6 yrs. | £29.0.3. |
| Windsor twp., Chester co. | Servant[1] | 4 yrs. | £26.11.8. |
| Philadelphia | Servant | 5 yrs. | £15.0.0. |
| Oley twp., Berks co. | Servant (note 3, or £8 Pa. currency). | 5 yrs. | £28.12.3. |
| Cumru twp., Berks co. | Servant (note 3, or £7 Pa. currency). | 6 yrs. | £27.18.0. |
| Cumru twp., Berks co. | Servant (note 3, or £5 Pa. currency). | 6 yrs. | £29.9.3. |
| Philadelphia | Servant[3] | 6 yrs., 6 mo. | £26.14.6. |
| Oley twp., Berks co. | Servant (note 3, or £5 Pa. currency). | 4 yrs., 6 mo. | £28.6.3. |
| Philadelphia | Servant[3] | 6 yrs. | £25.9.6. |
| Philadelphia | Servant[3] | 4 yrs., 6 mo. | £28.17. |
| Philadelphia | Servant[3] | 4 yrs. | £27.3.6. |
| Hardwick, Sussex co., N. J. | Servant | 2 yrs. | £10.10.0. |
| Philadelphia | Servant | 5 yrs. | £16.0.0. |
| Union twp., Berks co. | Servant[3] | 6 yrs. | £27.8.6. |
| Hardwick, Sussex co., N. J. | Servant | 3 yrs., 6 mo. | £12.0.0. |
| Philadelphia | Servant | 3 yrs., 11 mo., 20 d. | £7.0.0. |
| Philadelphia | Servant[3] | 6 yrs. | £29.2.6. |
| Philadelphia | Servant (note 5, have her old clothes). | 2 yrs. | £3.0.0. |
| Douglass twp., Phila. co. | Servant (note 3, and £3 in cash). | 7 yrs. | £30.19.9. |
| Uwchland twp., Chester co. | Servant[1] | 5 yrs. | £28.2.0. |
| Springfield twp., Burlington co., W. N. Jersey. | Servant[3] | 6 yrs. | £26.2.6. |
| Philadelphia | Apprentice, taught the art of a mariner and navigation.[3] | 7 yrs. | |
| Paxton twp., Lancaster co. | Servant[3] | 3 yrs. | £10.0.0. |
| Philadelphia | Servant[3] | 7 yrs. | £27.7.6. |
| Hill twp., Berks co. | Servant[3] | 5 yrs. | £31.3.0. |
| Philadelphia | Apprentice, taught the trade of a cooper, have one quarter's night schooling and time for another, his father paying the expense.[5] | 7 yrs., 6 mo. 13 d. | |

| Date. | Name. | From the Port of | To Whom Indentured. |
|---|---|---|---|
| 1773. Sept. 1st.... | Hood, Mary | | Joshua Elder and his assigns |
| | Mutzler, Francis | Rotterdam | John Richard and his assigns |
| | Lirig, Valentine Christian | Rotterdam | Henry Spear and his assigns |
| | Herrington, Thomas | | Isaac Thomas and his assigns |
| | Waxmoth, John Daniel | Rotterdam | John Fegan and his assigns |
| | Waxmoth, John Daniel | | John Young and his assigns |
| | Bowen, Cornelius | Europe | James Budden and his assigns |
| | Ham, Mathias | Rotterdam | John Fegan and his assigns |
| | Ham, Mathias | | John Young and his assigns |
| | Kleyben, Johannes | Rotterdam | William Newbold and his assigns |
| | Cossinborgh, Willimy | Rotterdam | Caleb Newbold and his assigns |
| | Wagner, Andreas | Rotterdam | Caleb Newbold and his assigns |
| | Van Berg, George | Rotterdam | Caleb Newbold and his assigns |
| | Kleylen, Peter | Rotterdam | Caleb Newbold and his assigns |
| | Philebacker, Johan Henrich | Rotterdam | Caleb Newbold and his assigns |
| | Sims, Thomas | | George Craig and his assigns |
| | McKnown, Charles | Ireland | John Schritole and his assigns |
| Sept. 2nd.... | Parker, George | | Pressly Blackiston and his assigns |
| | Beck, Johan Frederick | Rotterdam | George Sturnfetts and his assigns |
| | Willson, Robert | London Derry | James Hunter and his assigns |
| | Willson, Catherine | | James Hunter and his assigns |
| | McKivan, Margaret | | George Moore and his assigns |
| | Herrington, Thomas | | Thomas Heneby and his assigns |
| | Piser, Henry | Rotterdam | Simon Litzenberger and his assigns |
| | Kimberger, John Valentine | Rotterdam | Davis Bevan and his assigns |
| | Fitz, Francis | Rotterdam | Leonard Neighbour and his assigns |
| | Potz, John Christopher | Rotterdam | George Albert and his assigns |

## List of Indentures.

| Residence. | Occupation. | Term. | Amount. |
|---|---|---|---|
| Paxtang twp., Lancaster co. | Servant [5] | 2 yrs., 6 mo. | £ 9. 0. 0. £ 2. 0. 0. paid for her use. |
| Whitemarsh twp., Phila. co. | Servant (note 3, and £ 3 Pa. currency). | 6 yrs. | £ 29. 4. 3. for her passage. |
| Bedford co. | Servant (note 3, or £ 6 Pa. currency). | 5 yrs., 6 mo. | £ 29. 10. 0. |
| Upper Merion twp., Phila. co. | Servant | 4 yrs. | £ 12. 0. 0. |
| Philadelphia | Servant [3] | 6 yrs. | £ 28. 17. 1. |
| French Creek Forge, Chester co. | Servant [5] | 4 yrs. | £ 28. 17. 1. |
| Philadelphia | Apprentice, taught the art of a mariner and navigation.[3] | 4 yrs. | |
| Philadelphia | Servant [3] | 6 yrs. | £ 27. 6. 6. |
| French Creek Forge, Chester co. | Servant | 6 yrs. | £ 27. 6. 6. |
| Chesterfield twp., Burlington co., W. N. Jersey. | Servant [3] | 7 yrs., 1 mo. | £ 28. 10. 3. |
| Springfield twp., W. Jersey | Servant [3] | 7 yrs. | £ 35. 0. 0. |
| Springfield twp., W. N. Jersey | Servant [3] | 6 yrs. | £ 28. 6. 6. |
| Springfield twp., W. Jersey | Servant [3] | 6 yrs. | £ 27. 10. 4. |
| Springfield twp., W. Jersey | Servant [3] | 12 yrs. | £ 27. 4. 6. |
| Springfield twp., W. N. Jersey | Servant [3] | 6 yrs. | £ 26. 16. 4. |
| Philadelphia | Apprentice, taught the trade of a cooper, have three quarters' night schooling.[3] | 4 yrs., 4 mo. | |
| Cumru twp., Berks co. | Servant, found meat, drink, apparel, washing and lodging. | 3 yrs. | £ 14. 0. 0. |
| Philadelphia | Apprentice, taught the trade of a cordwainer, have three months' night schooling (note 5, his own wearing apparel). | 3 yrs., 9 mo. 16 d. | |
| Philadelphia | Servant [3] | 6 yrs. | £ 29. 7. 0. |
| | Servant, found meat, drink, washing the lodging. In case he pay or cause to be paid to James Hunter or his assigns 18. 15. 0, on or before Nov. 15th, next, this indenture as well as another indenture of this date, signed by Catherine Willson to James Hunter, shall become void. | 2 yrs. | £ 18. 15. 0. for the passage of his wife Elizabeth, his son James, his daughter Catherine. |
| | Servant, found meat, drink, apparel, washing and lodging. | 11 yrs. | £ 18. 15. 0. for her passage and that of her mother, Elizabeth Willson, and her brother James. |
| Southwark | Servant | 4 yrs. | £ 12. 0. 0. |
| Philadelphia | Servant; if the servant pay to the master the sum of 12. 5. 0. before the expiration then the above to be void.[3] | 2 yrs., 4 mo. 5 d. | £ 12. 5. 0. |
| Harford twp., Chester co. | Servant (note 1, or £ 7 Pa. currency). | 5 yrs. | £ 27. 0. 6. |
| Philadelphia | Servant [1] | 6 yrs., 4 mo. | £ 29. 6. 6. |
| Roxberry twp., Morris co. | Servant (note 3, or £ 8 Pa. currency). | 5 yrs. | £ 26. 8. 0. |
| Finixberry twp., Hunterdon co. E. N. Jersey. | Servant (note 3, or £ 8 Pa. currency in cash). | 5 yrs. | £ 28. 18. 0. |

| Date. | Name. | From the Port of | To Whom Indentured. |
|---|---|---|---|
| 1773. Sept. 3rd | Umfougord, Adolf | Rotterdam | Thomas Clark and his assigns |
| | Sotting, Ann Maria | Rotterdam | Peter Streck and his assigns |
| | Arnold, Maria Margareta | Rotterdam | Samuel Burrough and his assigns |
| | Fogle, Godfrid | Rotterdam | Samuel Bourough and his assigns |
| Sept. 4th | Madole, Jane | | George Lesshur and his assigns |
| | Gray, William | | Michael Kaner and his assigns |
| | Smith, John Adam | Rotterdam | Henry Slissman and his assigns |
| | Johnson, John | London | Godfrey Twells and his assigns |
| | Keller, Peter | | Jacob Cauffman and his assigns |
| Sept. 4th | King, Francis | London | John Wood and his assigns |
| | Brady, Jane; Sampson, Martha; Cormick, Ann; Nicholson, Mary; McGee, Catherin; Rivan, Esther; Gallant, James; Conners, Daniel; Kenny, Daniel. | Ireland | James Ray and his assigns |
| | Newsam, Ambros; Carr, William; Reily, Mary; Horan, Edward; Finnegan, Christopher; Foy, Charles; Pursell, John; Johnston, Peter; Allen, Richard; Divyer, James; Carrin, John; Smith, Peter. | Ireland | James Ray and his assigns |
| | Kissner, John | Rotterdam | Rudolph Niff and his assigns |
| | Douglass, John; Reynolds, Joseph. | Ireland | James Ray and his assigns |
| | Thornton, George | London | Jonathan Meredy and his assigns |
| | Sibson, Joseph | London | John Baldwin and his assigns |
| | Kulman, Johan Henry | Rotterdam | Thomas Wilson and his assigns |
| | Koberick, Johann Peter | Rotterdam | Thomas Wilson and his assigns |
| | Reilly, John | Dublin | James Ray and his assigns |
| | Smales, Thomas | | Jonathan Meredith and his assigns |
| | Brian, Terrance | Ireland | James Ray and his assigns |
| | Yoner, Leanord | Rotterdam | Richard Collins and his assigns |
| | Van Keffle, Luna | Rotterdam | John Ridge and his assigns |
| Sept. 6th | Brixey, John | London | Daniel Dudley and his assigns |
| | Thornton, Joseph | | Bethanath Hodgkinson and his assigns |
| | Wittsen, Madelea Sophia | Rotterdam | Adam Sheffer and his assigns |
| | Crossman, William | | Peter Walters and his assigns |
| | Roedolff, Joham Harme | Rotterdam | Benjamin Holme and his assigns |
| | Farncorn, Andrew | Rotterdam | George Phillips and his assigns |
| | Thiale, John Henry | Rotterdam | John Reepe and his assigns |
| | Kensler, William | | Robert Stephenson and his assigns |
| | Kensler, William | | David Beverige and his assigns |

| Residence. | Occupation. | Term. | Amount. |
|---|---|---|---|
| Windsor twp., Middlesex co., E. Jersey. | Servant[3] | 6 yrs. | £28.6.3. |
| Philadelphia | Servant[3] | 4 yrs. | £25.0.0. |
| Waterford twp., Glocester co. | Servant[3] | 7 yrs., 6 mo. | £32.18.6. |
| Waterford twp., Glocester co. | Servant[3] | 7 yrs. | £31.6.0. |
| Passyunk twp., Phila. co. | Servant | 3 yrs. | £2.0.0. |
| Philadelphia | Servant | 4 yrs. | £25.0.0. |
| Philadelphia | Servant[3] | 6 yrs. | £28.1.6. |
| Philadelphia | Servant[3] | 4 yrs. | £9.3.6. |
| Eastwest twp., Chester co. | Servant | 4 yrs., 6 mo. | £22.0.0. |
| Philadelphia | Servant[5] | 1 yr., 9 mo. | £9.3.6. |
| Little Britain twp., Lancaster co. | Servant[5] | 4 yrs. each. | £13.10.0. each. |
| Little Britain twp., Lancaster co. | Servant[5] | 4 yrs. each. | £13.10.0. |
| Frankford twp., Phila. co. | Servant[3] | 6 yrs. | £28.17.6. |
| Little Britain twp., Lancaster co. | Servant | 5 yrs. | £13.10.0. each. |
| Philadelphia | Servant[5] | 4 yrs. | £25.0.0. |
| Concord twp., Chester co. | Servant | 5 yrs. | £18.0.0. |
| Christiana Hundred, New Castle co. | Servant[3] | 6 yrs. | £28.5.6. |
| Christiana Hundred, New Castle co. | Servant[3] | 5 yrs., 6 mo. | £26.18.6. |
| Little Britain twp., Lancaster co. | Servant[3] | 4 yrs. | £13.10.0. |
| Philadelphia | Servant, employed as a leather cutter and currier. | 4 yrs. | £25.0.0. |
| Little Britain twp., Lancaster co. | Servant[3] | 4 yrs. | £13.10.0. |
| New Town twp., Glocester co., W. Jersey. | Servant[3] | 4 yrs., 7 mo. | £27.17.2. |
| Philadelphia | Servant[3] | 8 yrs. | £23.14.6. |
| Evesham twp., Burlington co. | Servant | 4 yrs. | £18.0.0. |
| Philadelphia | Apprentice, taught the trade of a joiner, have two quarters' night schooling in the first three years and two quarters' in the last two years.[3] | 8 yrs., 8 mo. 10 d. | |
| Deerfield Precinct, Cumberland co., W. Jersey. | Servant[3] | 6 yrs. | £32.3.6. |
| Philadelphia | Apprentice, taught the art and mystery of a blacksmith, read in Bible, write a legible hand and cypher, at expiration of the term freedom dues. | 15 yrs., 6 mo., 14 d. | |
| Elsenborough twp., Salem, W. N. Jersey. | Servant (note 3, and £5 Pa. currency). | 5 yrs. | £29.14.7. |
| Rockhill twp., Bucks co. | Servant (note 3, or £8 Pa. currency in cash). | 4 yrs., 4 mo. | £29.4.0. |
| Philadelphia | Servant[1] | 6 yrs. | £27.16.3. |
| Philadelphia | Servant, taught the art and mystery of a mariner and navigation, read in Bible and write.[6] | 4 yrs. | |
| Philadelphia | Apprentice (on the condition as above). | | £0.5.0. |

| Date. | Name. | From the Port of | To Whom Indentured. |
|---|---|---|---|
| 1773. Sept. 6th.... | Schammer, John Gotlip | Rotterdam.. | Amos George and his assigns....... |
| | Sucher, Jacob | | Michael Shenneck and his assigns.... |
| | Lang, James | Ireland .... | Thomas Tittermery and his assigns.. |
| | Yescow, Georacle Daniel | Rotterdam.. | Daniel Trimble and his assigns...... |
| | Stelling, Anna Maria | Rotterdam.. | Enoch Storey, for account of James Christie, and his assigns. |
| | Scott, David | London .... | Thomas Palmer and his assigns...... |
| | Durand, Andrew | London .... | Thomas Hale and his assigns........ |
| | Walsh, Jane; Reilly, John; Donnavan, Nicholas; Coleman, William. | Ireland .... | Mark Pattin and his assigns.......... |
| | Gibbons, Edward; Criman, Cornelius. | London .... | Mark Pattin and his assigns.......... |
| | Rice, Philip | Ireland .... | Stephen Cronin and his assigns...... |
| | Lee, Edward | Ireland .... | Mark Pattin and his assigns......... |
| | Wallace, John | London .... | Matthew Taylor and his assigns..... |
| | Culley, Margaret | Ireland .... | Mark Pattin and his assigns......... |
| Sept. 7th.... | Ahrens, John Conrad | Rotterdam.. | John Cleary and his assigns......... |
| | Grubb, Jacob | | Isaac Fitzrandolph ................. |
| | Bones, Peter | | Joseph Wilson and his assigns....... |
| | Wilson, Robert | London .... | Hugh Lennox and his assigns........ |
| | Fortiscue, Joseph | | Joseph Gamble and his assigns...... |
| | Fordham, George | | Abraham Collings .................. |
| | Don Ouden, Cornelius John.. | London .... | John Fagan and his assigns......... |
| | Don Ouden, Cornelius John.. | London .... | John Young and his assigns......... |
| | Schnider, Frederick Reim | London .... | Thomas Affelick and his assigns..... |
| | Murray, Donald | Scotland ... | William Craig and his assigns...... |
| | McLeod, Angus | Scotland ... | William Craig and his assigns...... |
| | McLeod, Donnald | Scotland ... | Levy Hollingworth and his assigns.. |
| | McLeod, Donnald | | Levy Hollingworth and his assigns.. |
| | Graham, Donnald | Scotland ... | Samuel Lyon and his assigns........ |
| | Morrison, Allen | Scotland ... | Henry Neil and his assigns.......... |
| 1773. Sept. 7th.... | Smith, Donnald | Scotland ... | John Lyon and his assigns.......... |
| | McFarlan, John | Scotland ... | Richard Farmer and his assigns..... |
| | Dihauser, Dorothy | Rotterdam.. | George Douglass and his assigns.... |
| | Krabbe, Elizabeth | Rotterdam.. | Richard S. Smith and his assigns.... |
| | Smith, Ann | Scotland ... | William Hollingshead and his assigns |
| | McLennen, Catherine | Scotland ... | John Head and his assigns.......... |

## List of Indentures.

| Residence. | Occupation. | Term. | Amount. |
|---|---|---|---|
| Blockley twp., Phila. co. | Servant (note 3, and £ 3 Pa. currency). | 6 yrs. | £ 27. 12. 6. |
| Philadelphia | Apprentice, taught the art and mystery of a cordwainer, read in Bible, write a legible hand and cypher.[6] | 8 yrs., 6 mo. | |
| Moyamensing twp., Phila. co. | Servant, found meat, drink, working clothes, washing and lodging, at expiration of his term, £ 10 Pa. currency and one-sixth every week during his servitude. | 4 yrs. | £ 13. 16. 0. |
| Concord twp., Chester co. | Servant, taught to read in Bible, write a legible hand.[1] | 8 yrs. | £ 28. 3. 6. |
| | Servant[1] | 4 yrs. | £ 23. 0. 6. |
| Philadelphia | Servant[6] | 4 yrs. | £ 15. 6. 1. |
| Philadelphia | Servant[5] | 4 yrs. | £ 22. 10. 0. |
| W. Pensborough twp., Cumberland co. | Servant | 4 yrs. | £ 13. 10. 0. |
| W. Pensborough twp., Cumberland co. | Servant | { 5 yrs. <br> 6 yrs. } | £ 13. 10. 0. |
| Philadelphia | Servant, found meat, drink, apparel, washing and lodging, at expiration £ 6 Pa. currency. | 2 yrs., 6 mo. | £ 7. 10. 0. |
| Pensborough twp., Cumberland co. | Servant[1] | 4 yrs. | £ 13. 10. 0. |
| Philadelphia | Servant | 4 yrs. | £ 16. 0. 0. |
| Pensborough twp., Cumberland co. | Servant | 4 yrs. | £ 13. 0. 0. |
| Waterford twp., Gloster co. | Servant (note 3, or £ 10 in cash). | 5 yrs. | £ 28. 16. 0. |
| Philadelphia | Apprentice | 12 yrs., 11 mo. | £ 2. 0. 0. |
| | Servant[1] | 5 yrs. | £ 14. 0. 0. |
| Philadelphia | Servant, employed at the business of a store or counting house.[5] | 3 yrs. | £ 15. 2. 9. |
| Philadelphia | Apprentice, taught the art of a pilot in the river and bay of Delaware, have nine months' day schooling.[3] | 7 yrs., 5 mo. | |
| Northern Liberties | Apprentice, taught the trade of a sail maker, have five quarters' night schooling.[3] | 7 yrs., 9 mo. 23 d. | |
| Philadelphia | Servant[3] | 3 yrs. | £ 16. 12. 3. |
| Coventry twp., Chester co. | Servant | The term as above mentioned. | £ 16. 12. 3. |
| Philadelphia | Servant (note 3, worth £ 10 Pa. currency). | 3 yrs. | £ 18. 17. 5. |
| Philadelphia | Servant[6] | 5 yrs. | £ 16. 0. 0. |
| Philadelphia | Servant[6] | 4 yrs. | £ 16. 0. 0. |
| Philadelphia | Servant[1] | 8 yrs. | £ 16. 0. 0. |
| Head of Elk, Md. | Servant, with the servant's consent to go to Maryland.[5] | 8 yrs. | |
| Milford twp., Cumberland co. | Servant[3] | 4 yrs. | £ 18. 0. 0. |
| Philadelphia | Servant, taught the trade of a biscuit baker.[6] | 4 yrs. | £ 16. 0. 0. |
| Milford twp., Cumberland co. | Servant[3] | 4 yrs. | £ 18. 0. 0. |
| Philadelphia | Servant[3] | 5 yrs. | £ 15. 0. 0. |
| Philadelphia | Servant[3] | 6 yrs. | £ 27. 0. 0. |
| Philadelphia | Servant[3] | 6 yrs. | £ 29. 5. 0. |
| Philadelphia | Servant[3] | 7 yrs. | £ 15. 0. 0. |
| Philadelphia | Servant[3] | 5 yrs. | £ 14. 0. 0. |

| Date. | Name. | From the Port of | To Whom Indentured. |
|---|---|---|---|
| 1773. Sept. 7th | Campbell, John | Scotland | John Head and his assigns |
| | McLenan, Ann | Scotland | Peter Shiras and his assigns |
| | McDonald, Norman | Scotland | Edward Middleton and his assigns |
| | Murray, Ann | Scotland | Alexander Tod and his assigns |
| | Murray, Ann | | Margaret Hall and her assigns |
| | Dowling, Daniel | London | John Gromow and his assigns |
| | Dowling, Daniel | London | Josuah Evans and his assigns |
| | Creamer, Daniel | Dublin | William Fliningham and his assigns |
| | Bostian, Jacob | Rotterdam | Samuel Burgh and his assigns |
| | Schrewter, Jacob | Rotterdam | Thomas Mayberry and his assigns |
| | Bonhill, Tobias | Rotterdam | Thomas Mayberry and his assigns |
| | Wigmore, Francis | | William Dickenson and his assigns |
| Sept. 8th | Martain, Angus | Scotland | Benjamin Davids and his assigns |
| | Morrison, Nancy | Scotland | Alexr. Carlisle and his assigns |
| | Smith, Donnald | Scotland | Mary McBeane and his assigns |
| | McCauly, Catherine | Scotland | John McCalley and his assigns |
| | McCauly, Catherine | | William Hollins, Jr., and his assigns |
| | Smith, Donald | Scotland | Benjamin Poultney and his assigns |
| | Bennett, Sarah | London | Thomas Livesday and his assigns |
| | Straugham, George | Dublin | Joseph Kidd and his assigns |
| | McLeod, William | Scotland | Amos Strettell and his assigns |
| | McKinnee, Annaple | Scotland | William Wishart and his assigns |
| | McKinnee, Annaple | | Isaac Loyd and his assigns |
| | Gunn, Catherine, and McDonal, Norman. | Scotland | Henry Lisle and his assigns |
| | McDonald, Ann | Scotland | Phineas Massy and his assigns |
| | McDonald, Malcom | Scotland | Benjamin Mather and his assigns |
| | Dixon, Aston | London | John Leek and his assigns |
| | Gillis, Margaret | Scotland | Moses Coxe and his assigns |
| | Crooke, William | | Thomas Proctor and his assigns |
| | Wright, Nathaniel | | Robert Wilson |
| | Frazer, Allace | Dublin | Samuel Purvyance and his assigns |
| | Cuff, Patrick | Ireland | Samuel Corry and his assigns |
| | Cuff, Patrick | | Samuel Purvyance and his assigns |
| | Ceakel, Teauge | Ireland | James McGlocklin and his assigns |
| | McBride, Mary | Ireland | James McGlocklin and his assigns |

[1] To be found all necessaries and at the expiration have freedom dues.
[2] To be found all necessaries and at the expiration have one new suit of apparel.
[3] To be found all necessaries and at the expiration have two complete suits of apparel, one whereof to be new.

## List of Indentures.

| Residence. | Occupation. | Term. | Amount. |
|---|---|---|---|
| Philadelphia | Servant[3] | 5 yrs. | £16.0.0. |
| Mt. Holland, N. J. | Servant, taught to read[6] | 5 yrs., 6 mo. | £15.0.0. |
| Philadelphia | Servant, taught to read in Bible, write a legible hand.[6] | 10 yrs. | £13.0.0. |
| Philadelphia | Servant[3] | 4 yrs. | £15.0.0. |
| Alesinberry twp., Salem co., N. J. | Servant (the above term) | | £15.0.0. |
| Tredyffrin twp., Chester co. | Servant, found meat, drink, washing and lodging, shoes, stockings, trousers and four new shirts. | 2 yrs. | £14.15.0. |
| Willis Town, Chester co. | Servants, found meat, drink, washing, lodging, shoes, stockings, trousers and four new shirts. | 2 yrs. | £14.15.0. |
| New Town twp., Glocester co. | Servant (note 3, and £3 Penna. currency). | 4 yrs. | £13.12.0. |
| Philadelphia | Servant (note 3, £11. 5 s. in cash). | 5 yrs. | £31.6.0. |
| Mallborough twp., Phila co. | Servant[1] | 7 yrs. | £32.2.6. |
| Mallborough twp., Phila co. | Servant[1] | 6 yrs. | £29.16.3. |
| Philadelphia | Apprentice, taught to sew, mark, read in Bible, write a legible hand (note 3, and £5 Pa. currency). | 7 yrs. | |
| Philadelphia | Servant, have six months' night schooling.[3] | 8 yrs. | £16.0.0. |
| Philadelphia | Servant, taught to read in Bible well.[3] | 7 yrs. | £15.0.0. |
| Philadelphia | Servant, taught to read and write[5]. | 9 yrs. | £12.0.0. |
| Philadelphia | Servant[3] | 4 yrs. | £14.0.0. |
| Fairfield, Cumberland co. | Servant | | £14.0.0. |
| Philadelphia | Servant, taught to read in Bible[1]. | 9 yrs. | £16.0.0. |
| Roxberry twp., Phila. co. | Servant | 4 yrs. | £16.0.0. |
| Manington twp., Salem co., N. J. | Servant | 4 yrs. | £16.0.0. |
| Philadelphia | Servant[3] | 10 yrs. | £15.0.0. |
| Philadelphia | Servant[3] | 4 yrs. | £15.0.0. |
| Darby, Chester co. | (Term as above mentioned) | | £15.0.0. |
| Philadelphia | Servant[3] | 9 yrs. each | £14.0.0. / £16.0.0. |
| Willis Town twp., Chester co. | Servant[3] | 4 yrs. | £14.0.0. |
| Cheltenham twp., Chester co. | Servant[3] | 4 yrs. | £18.0.0. |
| Little Egg Harbour, Burlington co., W. N. Jersey. | Servant[3] | 4 yrs. | £14.0.0. |
| Philadelphia | Servant[1] | 4 yrs. | £15.0.0. |
| Philadelphia | Apprentice, taught the art and mystery of a house carpenter, found meat, drink, lodging and washing, have the privilege of going to night school in the winter season, his friend paying the expense of said schooling. | 5 yrs. | |
| Talbot co., Md. | Servant[3] | 2 yrs. | £1.10.0. |
| Pittsgrove, Salem co., N. J. | Servant, the servant's consent to go to the New Jerseys. | 4 yrs. | £12.10.0. |
| | Servant[3] | 4 yrs. | £13.12.0. |
| Pittsgrove, Salem co., N. J. | Servant, the term above mentioned and same consideration, the servant's consent to go to the New Jersey's. | | |
| Philadelphia | Servant | 6 yrs. | £15.0.0. |
| Philadelphia | Servant | 3 yrs., 6 mo. | £15.0.0. |

[4] To be found all necessaries and at the expiration have two complete suits of apparel, one whereof to be new, and 40s. in money.

[5] At expiration have two complete suits of apparel, one whereof to be new.

| Date. | Name. | From the Port of | To Whom Indentured. |
|---|---|---|---|
| 1773. Sept. 8th.... | Fallye, Mathias | Rotterdam.. | Benjamin Shoemaker and his assigns. |
| | McLeod, Forgell | Scotland ... | Alexr. Smith and his assigns........ |
| | McLeod, John | Scotland ... | Thomas Penrose, Hugh Low and their assigns. |
| | Deal, John Jeremiah | Rotterdam.. | Daniel Hister, Jr., and his assigns... |
| | Harter, Ludwig | Rotterdam.. | Peter Miller and his assigns......... |
| | Smith, Catherine | Scotland ... | Samuel Lad and his assigns......... |
| | Riggs, John | | Robert White and his assigns........ |
| | McLeod, Mary | Scotland ... | Samuel Herrold and his assigns...... |
| | McMaghon, Rose | | John Fagon and his assigns.......... |
| | McKinzie, Catherine | Scotland ... | Robert Parish and his assigns....... |
| | Wigmore, Margaret | | Meriam Haselton and her executors.. |
| Sept. 9th.... | Martin, Margaret | Scotland ... | Frederick Phile and his assigns...... |
| | Bremer, Hans Hendrius Christian. | Rotterdam.. | John McCleary and his assigns...... |
| | Clark, Jane | Ireland .... | William Lippincott and his assigns... |
| | McIver, Ann | Scotland ... | Thomas Norris and his assigns...... |
| | McCullum, John | | Mathew Taylor and his assigns...... |
| | Forrest, Thomas | | George Bartram ................... |
| | McDonald, Donald, and McLeod, Catherine. | Scotland ... | John Pearson and his assigns........ |
| | Smith, Angus | Scotland ... | Joseph Claypole and his assigns......, |
| | Gunn, John | Scotland ... | William Clayton and his assigns..... |
| | Brogan, Thomas | Ireland .... | Benjamin Loxley and his assigns..... |
| Sept. 10th... | Connoly, Catherine | Ireland .... | William Wilson and his assigns...... |
| | West, Isaac | | Frederick Kisselman ............... |
| | Morrison, John | Scotland .. | Stephen Carmack and his assigns.... |
| | McDonald, Catherine | Scotland ... | Benjamin Harbinson and his assigns.. |
| | Bones, Thomas | Ireland .... | Thomas West and his assigns....... |
| | Bones, James | Ireland .... | John Hart and his assigns........... |
| | Monteluis, Frederick Marcus. | Rotterdam.. | Samuel Garrigues and his assigns.... |
| | Webster, Nicholas | London .... | William Dibley and his assigns...... |
| | Hillebrand, Henricus | Rotterdam.. | Lewis Trimble and his assigns....... |
| | Henry, Philip | Ireland .... | John Johnson and his assigns........ |
| | Wilsnoch, John Yocim | Rotterdam.. | John Hoover and his assigns........ |
| | Smith, Mary | Scotland ... | John Warnock and his assigns...... |
| | Lyon, Benjamin | Ireland .... | William Taylor and his assigns...... |
| | Burrus, Margaret | | George Taylor and his assigns...... |
| | Harper, Tobias | | John Myer and his assigns.......... |
| Sept. 11th... | Bockinturf, John Jacob | Rotterdam.. | William Meredith and his assigns.... |
| | Botting, Henry | London .... | John Howard and his assigns....... |
| | McLeod, John | Scotland ... | Joseph Morris and his assigns....... |
| | Johnson, Catherine | | James Taylor and his assigns....... |
| | Farrell, Alice | Ireland .... | Samuel Purvyance and her assigns... |
| | Smith, Charles | Ireland .... | Robert Lewis and his assigns........ |
| | Turner, John | London .... | Alexander Bartram and his assigns... |
| | Martin, Margaret | Scotland ... | Thomas Newland and his assigns.... |
| | McCarron, John | Ireland .... | Alexander Neill and his assigns..... |

## List of Indentures.

| Residence. | Occupation. | Term. | Amount. |
|---|---|---|---|
| Philadelphia | Servant (note 3, and £10 Pa. currency). | 5 yrs. | £27. 3. 6. |
| Philadelphia | Apprentice, taught the art and mystery of a whitesmith.[1] | 5 yrs. | £16. 0. 0. |
| Southwark | Servant, taught the art and mystery of a mast maker, three quarters' night schooling.[3] | | £16. 0. 0. |
| Upper Saulford twp., Phila. co. | Servant[3] | 5 yrs., 6 mo. | £28. 16. 6. |
| Linton twp., Northampton co., N. J. | Servant (note 3, or £5 Pa. currency). | 7 yrs. | £25. 14. 9. |
| Deptford twp., Glocester co., N. J. | Servant[3] | 4 yrs. | £14. 0. 0. |
| Philadelphia | Servant | 4 yrs. | £6. 0. 0. |
| Buckingham twp., Bucks co. | Servant, taught to read in Bible[3] | 6 yrs. | £15. 0. 0. |
| Philadelphia | Servant | 3 yrs. | £10. 0. 0. |
| Philadelphia | Servant[3] | 4 yrs. | £15. 0. 0. |
| Philadelphia | Apprentice, taught housewifery, sew, have three quarters' schooling (note 3, and £5 Pa. currency in cash). | 5 yrs., 5 mo. 15 d. | |
| Philadelphia | Servant[3] | 4 yrs. | £14. 0. 0. |
| Waterford twp., Glocester co., W. N. J. | Servant[3] | 5 yrs. | £27. 19. 0. |
| Philadelphia | Servant[5] | 3 yrs., 6 mo. | £14. 5. 0. |
| Merion twp., Phila. co. | Servant[1] | 4 yrs. | £13. 2. 6. |
| Philadelphia | Apprentice, taught to read in Bible, write a legible hand, cypher as far as rule of 3, and the art and mystery of a miller[3]. | 14 yrs., 6 mo. | |
| Philadelphia | Apprentice (note 5, give him £20) | 3 yrs., 8 mo. | £17. 0. 0. |
| Darby twp., Chester co. | Servant[3] | 4 yrs. each. | £14. 0. 0. |
| Philadelphia | Servant[3] | 5 yrs. | £15. 0. 0. |
| Tredyffrin twp., Chester co. | Servant, when free, freedom dues. | 3 yrs. | £12. 0. 0. |
| Philadelphia | Servant[3] | 3 yrs. | £13. 12. 0. |
| Shippensburgh, Cumberland co. | Servant[1] | 3 yrs., 6 mo. | £13. 12. 0. |
| Philadelphia | Servant[3] | 3 yrs. | |
| Philadelphia | Servant[3] | 5 yrs. | £15. 0. 0. |
| Philadelphia | Servant[1] | 7 yrs. | £15. 0. 0. |
| Philadelphia | Servant[3] | 4 yrs., 6 mo. | £13. 0. 0. |
| Philadelphia | Servant, teach him to read in Bible and write a legible hand.[1] | 5 yrs. | £6. 0. 0. |
| Philadelphia | Servant[3] | 6 yrs., 6 mo. | £30. 0. 0. |
| Philadelphia | Servant[1] | 2 yrs., 1 mo. | £14. 19. 7. |
| Ridley twp., Chester co. | Servant[3] | 6 yrs. | £31. 7. 0. |
| Philadelphia | Servant[5] | 2 yrs. | £13. 0. 0. |
| Philadelphia | Servant[5] | 2 yrs. | £29. 6. 6. |
| Little Britain twp., Lancaster co. | Servant[3] | 4 yrs. | £14. 0. 0. |
| Philadelphia | Servant[6] | 3 yrs. | £13. 12. 0. |
| Hanover twp., Lancaster co. | Servant[3] | 4 yrs. | £3. 0. 0. |
| Northern Liberties, Phila. co. | Apprentice, taught the trade of a tanner and white leather dressing, read in Bible and write a legible hand.[3] | 12 yrs. | |
| Plumstead twp., Bucks co. | Servant[3] | 7 yrs. | £28. 19. 3. |
| Philadelphia | Servant | 4 yrs. | £20. 0. 0. |
| Philadelphia | Servant[3] | 4 yrs. | £18. 0. 0. |
| Hanover twp., Lancaster co. | Servant[8] | 3 yrs., 6 mo. | £4. 10. 0. |
| Pittsgrove twp., Salem co., N. J. | Servant | 4 yrs. | £13. 12. 0. |
| Philadelphia | Servant[3] | 4 yrs. | £13. 12. 0. |
| Philadelphia | Servant, to be employed as store keeper or clerk.[5] | 3 yrs. | £15. 2. 8. |
| Concord twp., Chester co. | Servant[3] | 4 yrs. | £15. 0. 0. |
| W. Pensborough twp., Cumberland co. | Servant[5] | | £17. 0. 0. |

| Date. | Name. | From the Port of | To Whom Indentured. |
|---|---|---|---|
| 1773. Sept. 11th... | McFarlan, Angus | Scotland | Robert Lumsden and his assigns |
| | Hambell, Barthia | | James Cockran and his executors |
| | O'Neil, Charles | Ireland | Presley Blackiston and his assigns |
| | Morrison, Mary | | Daniel McCarley |
| | Ordt, Mary | | Isaac Collins |
| | Morrison, Peggy | | David Beveridge and his assigns |
| | Smith, Peggy | Scotland | David Beveridge and his assigns |
| | Smith, Peggy | | Peter Lewis and his assigns |
| | Wainright, John | | George Taylor and his assigns |
| | Felton, Ann | | George Taylor and his assigns |
| | Mahen, Hugh | Ireland | William Wilson and his assigns |
| | McLeod, Mary | Scotland | Daniel Evans and his assigns |
| | Levon, Isaac | Rotterdam | William Boyes and his assigns |
| | McMaghan, Sarah | Ireland | John Knowles and his assigns |
| | Smith, Murdock; McLeod, Christiana. | Scotland | Robert White and his assigns |
| | Smith, Gormal | Scotland | Richard Eyres and his assigns |
| | Daker, Ann | Rotterdam | Jonathan Meredith and his assigns |
| | Hinkley, Mary | | Frederick DeShong and his assigns |
| | McLeod, John | Scotland | John Englis and his assigns |
| Sept. 13th... | Southard, Thomas | | David Thompson and his assigns |
| | Gunn, Malcom | Scotland | Geo. Bartram and his assigns |
| | Gunn, Malcom | | Captain James Wilson and his assigns |
| | Martin, Murdo | Scotland | William Carson and his assigns |
| | Campbell, Daniel | Scotland | David Jackson and his assigns |
| | Eybing, William | Rotterdam | Jacob Wilkins and his assigns |
| | Ritter, Anthony Henry | Rotterdam | Thomas Wilkins and his assigns |
| | Gunn, Donald | Scotland | James Gibson and his assigns |
| | Gunn, Donald | | John Abraham De Normandy and his assigns. |
| Sept. 14th... | McLeod, John | Scotland | William Hodge and his assigns |
| | Price, Lewis | | William Budden and his assigns |
| | Murrarty, Dennis | | Edward Wells and his assigns |
| | Clarke, Francis | Ireland | Lewis Phrall and his assigns |
| | McLeod, Elizabeth | Scotland | James Craig and his assigns |
| | Martin, Donald; McAskell, John; McKay, Neil; Gunn, John. | Scotland | Fergus McManhan and his assigns |

| RESIDENCE. | OCCUPATION. | TERM. | AMOUNT. |
| --- | --- | --- | --- |
| Philadelphia | Servant, at expiration give him legal freedom dues. | 4 yrs. | £18.0.0. |
| Philadelphia | Apprentice, taught to sew, knit and spin, read in Bible, write a legible hand and cypher as far as rule of 3.[3] | 8 yrs., 2 mo. | |
| Philadelphia | Servant[6] | 2 yrs., 6 mo. | £12.0.0. |
| Philadelphia | Apprentice, taught housewifery, sew, knit and spin, read and write.[3] | 9 yrs. | 5/. |
| Burlington | | 9 yrs. | £15.0.0. |
| Philadelphia | Apprentice, taught housewifery, read in Bible, write, sew, knit, and spin.[3] | 13 yrs., 3 mo. | |
| Philadelphia | Apprentice, taught housewifery, read in Bible, write, sew, knit and spin.[3] | 10 yrs. | 5 shillings. |
| Southwark | Apprentice, the terms as above mentioned. | | 5 shillings. |
| Hanover twp., Lancaster co. | Servant (note 1, and 40 shillings Pa. currency). | 4 yrs. | £3.13.6. |
| Hanover twp., Lancaster co. | Servant[3] | 4 yrs. | £3.7.6. |
| New Castle Hundred, New Castle co. | Servant[3] | 3 yrs. | £14.0.0. |
| W. Whiteland twp., Chester co. | Servant[3] | 4 yrs. | £14.0.0. |
| Uwchlan twp., Chester co. | Servant (note 1, or £7 in cash). | 7 yrs. | £27.13.0. |
| Ridley, Chester co. | Servant[6] | 3 yrs. | £11.0.0. |
| Philadelphia | Servant, taught to read in Bible and have freedom as above.[3] | { 4 yrs. <br> { 7 yrs. | £16.0.0. <br> £11.0.0. |
| Philadelphia | Servant, taught to read and write[3]. | 9 yrs. | £12.0.0. |
| Philadelphia | Servant[3] | 7 yrs. | £28.14.6. |
| Passyunck twp., Phila. co. | Apprentice, taught to read in the Dutch Bible and write a legible hand.[3] | 13 yrs., 7 mo., 3 d(?) | |
| Philadelphia | Servant[3] | 4 yrs. | £16.0.0. |
| Southwark | Apprentice, found meat, drink, lodging and washing, 20 shillings per month and at expiration £6 Pa. currency and his tools. | 2 yrs. | |
| Philadelphia | Servant, taught to read[3]. | 9 yrs. | £13.10.0. |
| Philadelphia | Servant (the term above mentioned). | | £13.10.0. |
| Glocester twp., Glocester co. | Servant[3] | 4 yrs. | £18.0.0. |
| Northern Liberties | Servant, taught to read and write[3]. | 9 yrs. | £12.0.0. |
| Evesham twp., Burlington co. | Servant[3] | 7 yrs. | £27.3.3. |
| Evesham twp., Burlington co. | Servant[3] | 6 yrs., 6 mo. | £28.12.9. |
| Philadelphia | Servant, taught to read and write[6]. | | £16.0.0. |
| Bristol twp., Bucks co. | Servant | 5 yrs. | £16.0.0. |
| Philadelphia | Servant, have six months' schooling.[3] | 10 yrs. | £12.0.0. |
| Philadelphia | Apprentice, have four months' day schooling, taught the art and mystery of a mariner and navigation (note 2, besides his old ones). | 4 yrs. | |
| Philadelphia | Servant | 6 yrs. | £17.0.0. |
| Philadelphia | Servant (note 3, or £10 Pa. currency). | 3 yrs. | £13.12.0. |
| Philadelphia | Servant[3] | 4 yrs. | £14.0.0. |
| Straban twp., York co. | Servant[3] | 4 yrs. | £14.0.0. each. |

| Date. | Name. | From the Port of | To Whom Indentured. |
|---|---|---|---|
| 1773. Sept. 14th... | Weidelegh, Frederick | London | Thomas Affleck and his assigns |
| | Weidelegh, Frederick | | Lewis Gordon and his assigns |
| | Hackett, Anne Elizabeth | London | Edward York and his assigns |
| | Hobart, Charles | London | Thomas Francis and his assigns |
| | DeBon, Petronella | Rotterdam | Arnold Billig and his assigns |
| | Grocius, George | | John Painter and his assigns |
| | McLeod, William, and Mary, his wife. | Scotland | Fergus McManemy and his assigns |
| | McLeod, William, and Margaret, his wife. | Scotland | Fergus McManemy and his assigns |
| | McLean, Catherine | Scotland | Josuah Ash and his assigns |
| | Rankin, Rosana | | John Framberger and his assigns |
| | Smith, Elizabeth | | George Taylor and his assigns |
| Sept. 15th... | McGillis, Catherine | Rotterdam | Joseph Duer and his assigns |
| | Buser, Christian Ludwig | Rotterdam | Kepple, Jr., and his assigns |
| | Clayton, Mary; Howard, Thomas; Jefferson, John Wood; Dorrington, William; Johnston, Margaret; Racey, Philip; Fassett, Robert; Colling, Jane; McLean, Jean; Davidson, William. | London | David and Thomas Fulton and their assigns. |
| | Croker, Ambrose | London | David and Thomas Fulton and their assigns. |
| | McMullen, James | Ireland | William Craig and his assigns |
| | Johnson, Lydia | London | Michael Horning and his assigns |
| | McLeod, Catherine | Scotland | Zebulon Rudolph and his assigns |
| | McLeod, Catherine | | James Patridge and his assigns |
| | Batting, James; Savage, Burnet; Ward, John; Burleigh, Francis; Low, John; Farrar, Francis; Heath, John; Cock, Thomas; Preston, Thomas; Bayley, John; Harvey, George; Racey, Luke; King, William. | | David and Thomas Fulton and their assigns. |
| | Chipperfield, Susanna | London | John Fegan and his assigns |
| | McArthur, John | Scotland | John Pierce and his assigns |
| | Gunn, Malcom | Scotland | John Righter and his assigns |
| | Toole, James | Ireland | William Drewry and his assigns |
| | Bryan, Edward | Ireland | William Drewry and his assigns |
| | Owens, Robert | Ireland | Isaac Snowden and his assigns |

## List of Indentures.

| Residence. | Occupation. | Term. | Amount. |
|---|---|---|---|
| Philadelphia | Servant[3] | 3 yrs., 6 mo. | £19.9.7. |
| Easton twp., Northampton co. | Servant (term above mentioned) | | £19.9.7. |
| Philadelphia | Servant | 5 yrs. | £18.0.0. |
| Philadelphia | Servant, found all necessaries except clothes, employed at the business of a leather dresser. | 3 yrs. | £14.19.7. |
| Albany twp., Berks co. | Servant[3] | 4 yrs. | £27.17.6. |
| Northern Liberties | Apprentice, taught the art and mystery of a cordwainer, the master to give him 12 months' Dutch and 6 months' English day schooling.[3] | 12 yrs., 6 mo., 21 d. | |
| Straban twp., York co. | Servants, they shall not be separated at a further distance than four miles, and shall have liberty to see each other once in every week.[3] | 4 yrs. each | £14.0.0. |
| Straban twp., York co. | Servants, they shall not be separated at a further distance than four miles, and shall have liberty to see each other once in every week.[5] | 2 yrs. each | £7.0.0. each. |
| Darby twp., Chester co. | Servant[3] | 4 yrs. | £14.10.0. |
| Philadelphia | Servant, taught housewifery, sew, knit and spin and read in Bible[6]. | 4 yrs. | £12.7.6. |
| Hanover twp., Cumberland co. | Servant[3] | 2 yrs. | £2.0.0. and 10/ for her workhouse fees. |
| Lower Maxfield twp., Bucks co. | Servant, taught to read in Bible[6]. | 6 yrs. | £13.0.0. |
| Philadelphia | Servant[3] | 4 yrs. | £29.0.0. |
| Nottingham twp., Chester co. | Servant | 4 yrs. each | £12.0.0. each. |
| Nottingham twp., Chester co. | Servant | 6 yrs. | £12.0.0. |
| Brandywine Hundred, New Castle co. | Servant, taught to read and write[3]. | 7 yrs. | £13.11.6. |
| Providence twp., Phila co. | Servant | 4 yrs. | £15.0.0. |
| Philadelphia | Servant, taught to read[3]. | 5 yrs. | £15.0.0. |
| New Castle co. | Servant (the term above) | | £15.0.0. |
| Nottingham twp., Chester co. | Servant[3] | 4 yrs. each | £12.0.0. each. |
| Philadelphia | Servant | 4 yrs. | £6.9.9. |
| Concord twp., Chester co. | Servant[3] | 4 yrs. | £17.15.0. |
| Lower Merion twp., Phila. co. | Servant, have one year's schooling, read and write English.[3] | 9 yrs. | £13.0.0. |
| Philadelphia | Servant[3] | 3 yrs. | £14.0.0. |
| Philadelphia | Servant | 5 yrs. | £18.0.0. |
| Philadelphia | Servant, taught the art and mystery of a currier.[6] | 3 yrs., 4 mo. | £15.0.0. |

| Date. | Name. | From the Port of | To Whom Indentured. |
|---|---|---|---|
| 1773. Sept. 15th | Graham, Ann | Scotland | Thomas Sinnickson and his assigns |
| | Nossamer, John Conrad | Rotterdam | Job Cose and his assign |
| Sept. 16th | Zeigler, Martin | Rotterdam | Joshua Lippencott and his assigns |
| | Gage, Lousia | | George Aston and his assigns |
| | Gage, Lousia | | Christopher Bridenheart and his assigns. |
| | Carrole, Ann; Mackey, Elizabeth; Bryne, William; Ledwith, Lawrence; Connor, Mary; Tabbott, John. | Ireland | James Jordan and William Musgrove and their assigns. |
| | Halfpenny, James | Ireland | William Ellison and his assigns |
| | Duff, William | | John Hannah and his assigns |
| | McLeod, John | Scotland | Captain William Grant and his assigns. |
| | McLeod, Malcom | Scotland | Dr. Charles Moor and his assigns |
| | Ward, John | | William Dewees, Jr., and his assigns. |
| | Barton, Isaac | Ireland | James Jordon and William Musgrove and their assigns. |
| | Reed, John; Farrell, James | Ireland | James Jordon and William Musgrove and their assigns. |
| | McDonald, Donald, and Isabel, his wife; Morrison, John. | Scotland | William Dewees, Jr., and his assigns. |
| | Brian, Mary | | Samuel Carson and his assigns, Thos. Barclay and his assigns, William Mitchell and his assigns. |
| | Graham, Angus | Ireland | William Dewees, Jr., and his assigns. |
| | Beaty, Peter | London | David Franks and his assigns |
| | Davis, Catherine | London | John Stilly and his assigns |
| | Mullen, Ann | London | William Stanley and his assigns |
| | Fendler, Josuah | London | Richard Wister and his assigns |
| | Candy, Dorothy | London | Edward Oxley and his assigns |
| | Jones, John | London | Isaac Zeans and his assigns |
| Sept. 17th | Beck, Henry | Rotterdam | William Meredith and his assigns |
| | Finnigan, John | Ireland | James Roney and his assigns |
| | Streper, John | | William Streper and his assigns |
| | Rock, John | | James Roney and his assigns |
| | McCaddon, George | Ireland | James Montgomery and his assigns |
| | Young, Ann | | Robert Duncan and wife |
| | McNeagh, James | Ireland | James Montgomery and his assigns |
| | Morrison, Catherine | Scotland | William Ottinger and his assigns |
| | Brown, Henry | London | John Caner and his assigns |
| | Rix, Susanna | London | Mary Brown and her assigns |
| Sept. 18th | Morrison, John; Morrison, Mary. | Scotland | John Greenslaid and his assigns |
| | Best, James | London | David Riddinhouse and his assigns |
| | McCloskey, James | Ireland | John Burnett and his assigns |
| | McDonald, Christian | Scotland | George Aston and his assigns |
| | McDonald, Christian | | William Nice and his assigns |
| | Shitz, Daniel | Rotterdam | Jacob Angna and his assigns |

| RESIDENCE. | OCCUPATION. | TERM. | AMOUNT. |
|---|---|---|---|
| Salem, Salem co., W. N. Jersey.. | Servant, have six months' schooling.[3] | 7 yrs. | £12.0.0. |
| Waterford twp., Glocester co., W. Jersey. | Servant[3] | 6 yrs. | £32.6.6. |
| Woolwick twp., Glocester co.... | Servant[3] | 7 yrs. | £27.18.3. |
| Philadelphia | Apprentice, taught housewifery, read in Bible and write.[6] | 10 yrs. | £8.0.0. |
| Lancaster, Lancaster co. | Servant | 10 yrs. | £8.0.0. |
| Middle Town twp., Cumberland co. | Servant | 4 yrs. each.. | £13.12.0. |
| | Servant | 4 yrs. | £15.0.0. |
| Philadelphia | Servant[3] | 4 yrs. | £10.0.0. |
| | Servant[3] | 6 yrs. | £15.0.0. |
| Philadelphia | Servant, taught to read and write a legible hand.[3] | 9 yrs., 6 mo. | £13.0.0. |
| Upper Merion twp., Phila. co.... | Servant | 4 yrs. | £18.0.0. |
| Middletown twp., Cumberland co. | Servant | 4 yrs. | £13.12.0. |
| Middletown twp., Cumberland co. | Servant | 5 yrs. each.. | £13.12.0. each. |
| Upper Merion twp., Phila. co.... | Servant[3] | 4 yrs. each.. | £26.0.0. for Donald and wife. £18.0.0. |
| | Servant | 4 yrs. | £14.0.0. |
| Upper Merion twp., Phila. co. | Servant[3] | 5 yrs. | £16.0.0. and 1 guinea paid his father. |
| Philadelphia | Servant | 4 yrs. | £16.0.0. |
| Philadelphia | Servant | 4 yrs. | £20.0.0. |
| Philadelphia | Servant | 4 yrs. | £16.0.0. |
| Philadelphia | Servant[3] | 4 yrs. | £16.3.7. |
| Philadelphia | Servant | 6 yrs. | £18.0.0. |
| Frederic co., Va. | Servant | 4 yrs. | £35.0.0. |
| Plumstead twp., Bucks co. | Servant[3] | 7 yrs. | £32.5.6. |
| Hanover twp., Lancaster co. | Servant | 2 yrs., 6 mo. | £12.0.0. |
| Germantown twp., Phila. co.... | Apprentice | 3 yrs., 5 mo. 2 w. | £0.5.0. |
| Hanover twp., Lancaster co. | Servant | 4 yrs. | £10.0.0. |
| Philadelphia | Apprentice, taught the art of a mariner and navigation.[3] | 4 yrs., 6 mo. | |
| | Apprentice, taught housewifery, read and write a legible hand.[6] | 6 yrs., 11 mo. | |
| Philadelphia | Servant | 7 yrs. | £0.5.0. |
| Springfield twp., Phila. co. | Servant, have one year schooling, read and write and when free, legal freedom dues. | 8 yrs. | £13.10.0. |
| Philadelphia | Servant | 4 yrs. | £17.0.0. |
| Philadelphia | Servant | 4 yrs. | £16.0.0. |
| Woolwich twp., Glocester co. | Servant[3] | 4 yrs. each | £16.0.0. £14.0.0. |
| Philadelphia | Servant[5] | 3 yrs. | £15.0.0. |
| Concord twp., Chester co. | Servant[1] | 1 yr., 11 mo. | £8.10.0. |
| Philadelphia | Servant[3] | 2 yrs. | £7.0.0. |
| Springfield, Chester co. | Servant, terms in above record.... | 3 yrs. | £7.0.0. |
| Bedminster twp., Bucks co. | Servant[3] | | £19.16.0. |

| Date. | Name. | From the Port of | To Whom Indentured. |
|---|---|---|---|
| 1773.<br>Sept. 18th... | Overteer, Philip | Rotterdam.. | Michael Ferston and his assigns |
| | Hink, John Mathias | Rotterdam.. | Thomas Lewis and his assigns |
| | Amich, Johan, Conrad | Rotterdam.. | George Delph and his assigns |
| | Murrey, William | Scotland ... | Thomas Earl and his assigns |
| | McKinsey, Angus, and Christiana, his wife. | Scotland ... | Robert Emley and his assigns |
| | McDonald, Malcom | Scotland ... | Samuel Shoemaker and his assigns |
| | Motts, Paul | Rotterdam.. | Samuel Noble and his assigns |
| | Mingott, Arthur | Rotterdam.. | John Hollandsed and his assigns |
| | Young, Michael | Rotterdam.. | Owen Stoufer and his assigns |
| | Tagen, Jacob | Rotterdam.. | Henry Mag and his assigns |
| | Mullin, Elizabeth | Ireland .... | John Room and his assigns |
| | Wincell, John Charles | Rotterdam.. | George Knorr and his assigns |
| | Dagen, Catherine, Elizabeth.. | Rotterdam.. | Lawrence Sentman and his assigns |
| | Wrightnower, Nicholas | Rotterdam.. | Schlosser and Franks and their assigns |
| | Nigh, Jacob | Rotterdam.. | Thomas Greswold and his assigns |
| Sept. 20th... | New, Christopher | Rotterdam.. | Matthias Martin and his assigns |
| | Freer, Martin | Rotterdam.. | John Everly and his assigns |
| | Ellick, George Melchor | Rotterdam.. | Catherin Greeanleaf and her assigns. |
| | McIlkenny, William | Ireland .... | Paul Fooks and his assigns |
| | McMurtrie, William | | John Carnan and his executors |
| | Weaver, John Barnet | Rotterdam.. | John Frederick Mealfelt and his assigns. |
| | Hershiltin, Mary Christiana.. | Rotterdam.. | William Davis and his assigns |
| | Brown, Mathias | Rotterdam.. | Abell Lippencott and his assigns |
| | Weiss, Adam | Rotterdam.. | Joseph Funks and his assigns |
| | Frick, Jacob | | Elenezar Rogers and his assigns |
| | McDonald, Donald | Scotland ... | James Roney and his assigns |
| Sept. 20th... | Weaver, Anthony; Bastian; John Nicholas. | Rotterdam.. | Thomas Gilpin and his assigns |
| | Tippen, Margaret | Ireland .... | Samuel Hunter |
| | Saters, Getruck | Rotterdam.. | Abell Lippencott and his assigns |
| | Delpig, Ann | Rotterdam.. | John Brown and his assigns |
| | Weneren, Margaret | Rotterdam.. | Jacob Sink and his assigns |
| | Chester, Martha Ta | Rotterdam.. | John Patterson and his assigns |
| | Young, Johan Henry | Rotterdam.. | William Sitgreaves and his assigns |
| | Daugherty, George | | John Wilson and his assigns |
| | Hughton, John | Ireland .... | Alexander Powell and his assigns |
| | Schott, Jacob | Rotterdam.. | John Fasey and his assigns |
| | Erbst, Henry | Rotterdam.. | Jacob Overholt and his assigns |
| | Schitz, Christian | Rotterdam.. | Christian Krepps and his assigns |
| | Young, Elizabeth | Rotterdam.. | William West and his assigns |
| | Squibb, William | Ireland .... | Edmund Milne and his assigns |
| | Kelly, Peggy | Ireland .... | Joseph Smith and his assigns |
| | Kerchbaun, John Michael | Rotterdam.. | Sharp Delany and his assigns |
| | McDonnald, John | Scotland ... | Robert Johnson and his assigns |
| | Shenell, Adam | Rotterdam.. | John Schnider and his assigns |
| | McLenon, Roderick | Scotland ... | Joseph Shoemaker and his assigns |
| | Smith, Francis | Rotterdam.. | Boshan Waggoner and his assigns |
| | McKinsey, Kenneth | | James Roney and his assigns |

## List of Indentures.

| Residence. | Occupation. | Term. | Amount. |
|---|---|---|---|
| Rockhill twp., Bucks co. | Servant[3] | 2 yrs., 6 mo. | £17.18.0. |
| Springfield twp., Chester co. | Servant[3] | 6 yrs., 6 mo. | £26.19.8. |
| Frankoney twp., Phila. co. | Servant[3] | 4 yrs. | £27.11.0. |
| Springfield twp., Burlington co., W. N. J. | Servant[1] | 4 yrs. | £15.0.0. |
| Chesterfield twp., Burlington co., W. N. J. | Servant[3] | 4 yrs. each.. | £20.0.0. |
| Philadelphia | Servant[1] | 5 yrs. | £16.0.0. |
| Northern Liberties | Servant[3] | 5 yrs. | £21.5.0. |
| Chester twp., Burlington co. | Servant (note 3, and 34 shillings in cash). | 4 yrs. | £27.13.0. |
| Bedminster twp., Bucks co. | Servant[3] | 3 yrs., 5 mo. | £20.19.0. |
| Passyunk twp., Phila. co. | Servant[1] | 5 yrs. | £21.9.0. |
| Deptford twp., Phila. co. | Servant[3] | 5 yrs. | £15.10.0. |
| Philadelphia | Servant[1] | 3 yrs., 6 mo. | £21.9.0. |
| Moorland twp., Phila co. | Servant[3] | 5 yrs., 6 mo. | £28.6.0. |
| Philadelphia | Servant[3] | 5 yrs. | £19.15.0. |
| Northern Liberties | Servant[3] | 4 yrs., 6 mo. | £20.3.0. |
| Upper Dublin twp., Phila. co. | Servant[1] | 4 yrs., 6 mo. | £20.3.0. |
| Passyunk twp., Phila. co. | Servant[3] | 4 yrs. | £23.9.0. |
| Philadelphia | Servant[1] | 5 yrs. | £20.7.0. |
| Philadelphia | Servant[1] | 6 yrs., 2 mo. | £16.0.0. |
| Philadelphia | Apprentice (note 5, except apparel) | 4 yrs., 9 mo. 14 d. | |
| Passyunk twp., Phila. co. | Servant (note 1, or £7 Pa. currency). | 4 yrs. | £26.9.0. |
| Philadelphia | Servant[3] | 4 yrs. | £17.18.0. |
| Evesham twp., Burlington co. | Servant[3] | 6 yrs. | £27.12.0. |
| Northern Liberties | Servant[3] | 2 yrs. | £9.18.0. |
| Marthas Vineyard, New England. | Servant, taught to read and write[6]. | 3 yrs., 7 mo. 11 d. | £15.0.0. |
| Philadelphia | Servant, employed at the shoe making business and dismiss him with lawful freedoms. | 5 yrs. | £16.0.0. |
| Philadelphia | Servant[3] / Servant[5] | 6 yrs. / 2 yrs. | £22.0.0. / £18.0.0. |
| Augusta twp., Northumberland co. | Servant | 4 yrs. | £15.0.0. |
| Evesham twp., Burlington co. | Servant[8] | 7 yrs. | £33.6.6. |
| Philadelphia | Servant[3] | 7 yrs. | £20.7.0. |
| Passyunk twp., Phila. co. | Servant[8] | 5 yrs. | £20.7.0. |
| Philadelphia | Servant | 3 yrs. | £5.10.0. |
| Philadelphia | Servant[3] | 9 yrs. | £25.0.0. |
| Tredyffrin twp., Chester co. | Servant | 4 yrs. | £14.10.0. |
| | Servant | 1 yr., 6 mo. | £9.0.0. |
| Philadelphia | Servant, cause him to read and write a legible hand.[6] | 10 yrs. | £21.0.0. |
| Bedminster twp., Bucks co. | Servant[1] | 3 yrs. | £18.11.0. |
| Northern Liberties | Servant[3] | 3 yrs. | £19.9.0. |
| Philadelphia | Servant, at the expiration of the term customary freedom dues. | 7 yrs. | £17.18.0. |
| Philadelphia | Servant, employed at the business of a silversmith.[5] | 2 yrs. | £13.12.0. |
| Mannington twp., Salem co., W. N. J. | Servant[3] | 3 yrs. | £13.0.0. |
| Philadelphia | Servant[1] | 5 yrs. | £22.1.0. |
| Salem co., N. J. | Servant[3] | 4 yrs. | £17.15.0. |
| Pikeland twp., Chester co. | Servant[1] | 3 yrs., 6 mo. | £18.3.0. |
| Germantown twp., Phila. co. | Servant, give him one year's schooling.[3] | 7 yrs. | £14.0.0. |
| Charlestown, Chester co. | Servant[3] | 3 yrs., 6 mo. | £21.13.0. |
| Philadelphia | Apprentice, taught to read in Bible and write a legible hand | 16 yrs. | |

| Date. | Name. | From the Port of | To Whom Indentured. |
|---|---|---|---|
| 1773. Sept. 20th | Cross, John Henry | Rotterdam | John Rowland and his assigns |
| | Cross, John Henry | | Samuel Rowland and his assigns |
| | Higgins, Edward | | Nicholas Night and his assigns |
| | Linck, John George | Rotterdam | Isaac Roush and his assigns |
| | Hawes, Peter | Rotterdam | Joseph Johnson and his assigns |
| | Netcher, Conrad | Rotterdam | Samuel Pleasants and his assigns |
| | Black, Margaret | | James Taylor and his assigns |
| | Cake, Henry | Rotterdam | Mathias Landinburgher and his assigns. |
| | Gerlinger, Ludwig | Rotterdam | Adam Baker and his assigns |
| | Nelson, Thomas | Ireland | George McLaughlin and his assigns |
| | Miller, George | Rotterdam | Lawrence Uppman and his assigns |
| | Miller, George | | John Rock and his assigns |
| | Buhze, Traugoll Leberecht | Rotterdam | Theodore Meminger and his assigns |
| | Drichayser, Ann | Rotterdam | Abraham Matlack and his assigns |
| | Morrow, John | Ireland | James Benson, Jr., and his assigns |
| Sept. 21st | Harrison, Humphrey | | Jacob Kimberlin |
| | Antonymass, Charles | Rotterdam | Philip Maser and his assigns |
| | McLean, Patrick | Ireland | John Hall and his assigns |
| | Link, John Simon; Keaner, Andrew; Kendall, George; Link, John Philip. | Rotterdam | Jacob Winey and his assigns |
| | Hoes, John George | Rotterdam | Francis Wade and his assigns |
| | Flowers, John | | Peter Trace |
| | Funk, Michael | Rotterdam | John Ferree and his assigns |
| | Haas, Michael; Krimp, Johan | Rotterdam | Balser Barkman and his assigns |
| | Agle, Peter | Rotterdam | George Way and his assigns |
| | Lenard, Catherine | | Christiana Malaby and her assigns |
| | Graham, Angus | Scotland | George Bartram and his assigns |
| | While, John George | Rotterdam | Andreas Kichline and his assigns |
| | Carson, Samuel | | John Ross and his assigns |
| | Reinhard, Hans Tergan | Rotterdam | John Bern and his assigns |
| | Wanner, John George | Rotterdam | Joshua Dudley and his assigns |
| | McKenzie, Mary | Scotland | Samuel Cooper and his assigns |

## List of Indentures.

| Residence. | Occupation. | Term. | Amount. |
|---|---|---|---|
| | and cypher as far as rule of 3, taught the cordwainer's trade.[6] | | |
| N. Orburth Hundred, Sussex co. | Servant[3] | 5 yrs. | £27.1.0. |
| N. Orburth Hundred, Sussex co. | Servant, the term above mentioned. | | £27.1.0. |
| Whitemarsh twp., Phila. co. | Servant[1] | 3 yrs. | £17.0.0. |
| Philadelphia | Servant (note 3, or £10) | 3 yrs., 9 mo. | £22.2.0. |
| Germantown twp., Phila. co. | Servant (note 3, or £10 Pa. currency). | 3 yrs., 6 mo. | £18.3.0. |
| Philadelphia | Servant (note 3, or £8 Pa. currency). | 5 yrs. | £26.9.0. |
| Hanover twp., Lancaster co. | Servant[1] | 3 yrs. | £4.10.0. and 20 shillings for her workhouse fees. |
| Philadelphia | Servant[3] | 3 yrs., 9 mo. | £17.17.6. |
| Bristol twp., Bucks co. | Servant (note 3, or £7 Pa. currency in cash). | 3 yrs. | £24.7.0. |
| Martic twp., Lancaster co. | Servant[5] | 2 yrs. | £8.5.0. |
| Northern Liberties | Servant, it is agreed if the servant's friends pay £23.17.0. and the expense occurring thereon in one month from this date, this indenture to be void (note 3, or £10 in cash). | 3 yrs., 6 mo. | £23.17.0. |
| New Cusha, Upper Phila. | Servant | 3 yrs., 6 mo. | £23.17.0. |
| | Servant, the master to allow him 1 shilling per week (note 3, and £12 in cash). | 3 yrs. | £6.8.0. |
| Evesham twp., Burlington co. | Servant[3] | 7 yrs. | £27.5.6. |
| Uwchland twp., Chester co. | Servant[5] | 1 yr., 9 mo. | £10.0.0. |
| Frederick co., Md., Antietam Settlement. | Servant (note 1, or £7 in cash) | 4 yrs., 6 mo. | £7.10.0. |
| Philadelphia | Servant (note 1, or £9 in cash) | 5 yrs. | £22.0.0. |
| Philadelphia | Servant[1] | 7 yrs. | £16.0.0. |
| Philadelphia | Servant[3] | 3 yrs. each. | £22.2.0. £17.8.0. £17.18.0 £22.2.0. |
| Philadelphia | Servant[1] | 4 yrs. | £24.0.0. |
| | Apprentice, taught the art and mystery of a skinner and breeches maker, have nine months' night schooling.[3] | | |
| Strasburgh twp., Lancaster co. | Servant[1] | 4 yrs. | £19.3.0. |
| Strasburgh twp., Lancaster co. | Servant[3] | 4 yrs. each | £21.15.0. £19.11.0. |
| Philadelphia | Servant (note 1, or £10 Pa. currency). | 4 yrs. | £29.10.0. |
| Southwark | Apprentice, taught housewifery, sew, read in Bible, write a legible hand.[3] | 11 yrs. | |
| Philadelphia | Servant, taught to read and write a legible hand.[3] | 9 yrs. | £12.0.0. |
| Rockhill twp., Bucks co. | Servant (note 3, and £3 Pa. currency). | 4 yrs. | £21.4.0. |
| Oxford twp., Chester co. | Servant[5] | 2 yrs., 3 mo. | £8.0.0. |
| Douglass twp., Phila. co. | Servant[3] | 8 yrs., 6 mo. | £18.2.0. |
| Evesham twp., Burlington, W. J. | Servant (note 1, and £6 Pa. currency). | 8 yrs. | £26.17/. |
| Newtown twp., Gloster co., W. N. J. | Servant, taught to read and write well.[3] | 10 yrs. | £12.0.0. |

| Date. | Name. | From the Port of | To Whom Indentured. |
|---|---|---|---|
| 1773. Sept. 21st | McCleod, Ann | | Elizabeth Mitchell and her assigns |
| | Meyer, Henry Andrew | Rotterdam | Chrisley Bartley and his assigns |
| | Statlebaur, John George | Rotterdam | John Torr and his assigns |
| | McKenzie, Roderick | Scotland | William Dewees, Jr., and his assigns |
| | Panigh, John Peter | Rotterdam | Richard Wister and his assigns |
| | Madden, Daniel | Ireland | John Dougan |
| | King, Christian | London | George West and his assigns |
| | Marting, James | Ireland | John Reiner and his assigns |
| | Hobach, Michael; Power, George. | Holland | George Streeper |
| | Hobach, Michael | | Baltzar Smith |
| | Moore, George | Ireland | Francis Lea and his assigns |
| | Scollen, Ann | Ireland | Jonathan Hoopes and his assigns |
| | Rinehartin, Solomea | Rotterdam | John Hoover and his assigns |
| | Young, Daniel | Rotterdam | Joseph Ferree and his assigns |
| | Young, Daniel | | John Wither and his assigns |
| | Shutt, Peter | Rotterdam | Joseph Ferrees and his assigns |
| | Shutt, Peter | | John Wither and his assigns |
| Sept. 22nd | Beckers, Margaret | Rotterdam | Thomas Wharton and his assigns |
| | Walker, John | | Lewis Trucenmiller and his assigns |
| | Gunn, Mary | Scotland | John Lockton and his assigns |
| | Fenlan, Henry | | John Patton and his assigns |
| | Baker, Frederick | Rotterdam | George Honey, Jr., and his assigns |
| | Baker, Frederick | | Philip Gardener and his assigns |
| | Shelock, Albartus | Rotterdam | Abraham Lerew and his assigns |
| | Fitzharries, Arthur; Fitzharries, Mary. | Ireland | William Tod and his assigns |
| | Fralichin, Ann Catherine | Rotterdam | John Poole and his assigns |
| | Fralichin, Ann Catherine | | Abraham Eewling and his assigns |
| | Shootts, Lawrence | Rotterdam | Nathaniel Sweaker and his assigns |
| | Shumannah, Catherine | | Peter Tick Taylor and his assigns |
| | Field, John | London | Joseph Knight and his assigns |
| | McKinzie, Ann | | Hugh Barclay and his assigns |
| | Rose, Godfrey Charles | Rotterdam | John Groves and his assigns |
| | Rose, Godfrey Charles | | Owen Use and his assigns |
| | Henderson, James | | John Morton and his assigns |

| Residence. | Occupation. | Term. | Amount. |
|---|---|---|---|
| Philadelphia | Apprentice, taught to sew, knit and spin, give her twelve months' schooling.[6] | 9 yrs. | |
| Philadelphia | Servant (note 5, £10 in lieu of freedoms). | 2 yrs., 9 mo. | £15.14.1. |
| Evesham twp., Burlington co. | Servant[1] | 4 yrs. | £21.9.9. |
| Upper Merion twp., Phila. co. | Servant[3] | 4 yrs. | £14.0.0. |
| Philadelphia | Servant[3] | 6 yrs. | £27.0.0. |
| Easttown twp., Chester co. | Servant[5] | 1 yr., 9 mo. | £10.10.0. |
| Philadelphia | Servant[3] | 2 yrs., 6 mo. | £16.18.0. |
| W. Caln, Chester co. | Servant, found all necessaries except apparel. | 1 yr. | £7.10.0. |
| Philadelphia | Servant[6] | 2 yrs., 9 mo. | £17.0.0. for each. |
| Macungie, Berks co. | For the same term and consideration mentioned in his indenture above. | | |
| Philadelphia | Servant, teach him to read and write and cypher as far as rule of 3.[3] | 11 yrs. | £8.0.0. |
| E. Caln twp., Chester co. | Servant[1] | 3 yrs., 6 mo. | £15.0.0. |
| Hempfield twp., Lancaster co. | Servant[1] | 5 yrs., 6 mo. | £29.6.0. |
| Strasburgh twp., Lancaster co. | Servant[1] | 4 yrs. | £19.3.0. |
| Strasburgh twp., Lancaster co. | Servant | 4 yrs. | £19.3.0. |
| Strasburgh twp., Lancaster co. | Servant[1] | 5 yrs., 6 mo. | £26.17.0. |
| Strasburgh twp., Lancaster co. | Servant | 5 yrs., 6 mo. | £26.17.0. |
| Philadelphia | Servant[1] | 6 yrs. | £22.3.0. |
| Philadelphia | Apprentice | 8 yrs., 1 mo. | |
| Philadelphia | Servant, have one year's schooling.[6] | 7 yrs. | £12.0.0. |
| Philadelphia | Apprentice, taught the art and mystery of a store keeper.[3] | 4 yrs. | |
| Philadelphia | Servant[3] | 4 yrs., 3 mo. | £27.7.0. |
| ———, York co. | Servant | 4 yrs., 3 mo. | £27.7.0. |
| Bensalem twp., Bucks co. | Servant (note 3, and 40 shillings Pa. currency in cash). | 3 yrs., 6 mo. | £17.16.6. |
| Philadelphia | Servants (note 6, the master obliges himself, heirs and assigns that Arthur and his wife shall not be sold or assigned or obliged to live in any other place than the city aforesaid without their consent). | 3 yrs. 4 yrs. | 8 guineas each. |
| Burlington twp., Burlington co., W. J. | Servant[3] | 3 yrs., 6 mo. | £18.0.0. |
| Burlington twp., Burlington co., W. J. | Servant | 3 yrs., 6 mo. | £18.0.0. |
| Heidelburg twp., Lancaster co. | Servant[3] | 3 yrs. | £18.3.0. |
| Philadelphia | Apprentice, taught housewifery and sew, have two quarters' schooling (note 6, and £5 Pa. currency in cash). | 5 yrs. | £1.10.0. |
| Northern Liberties | Servant, nine months' schooling (note 1, and £5). | 4 yrs., 6 mo. | £14.14.10. |
| Warrington, Bucks co. | Apprentice, taught housewifery, sew, knit and spin, have 18 months' schooling (note 6, and at expiration a good cow and calf, or £9 Pa. currency). | 10 yrs. | |
| Plymouth twp., Phila. co. | Servant[3] | 6 yrs., 9 mo. | £29.0.0. |
| Middle Creek twp., Berks co. | Servant | 6 yrs., 9 mo. | £29.0.0. |
| Philadelphia | Apprentice, taught the art and mystery of a miller.[3] | 5 yrs. | |

| DATE. | NAME. | FROM THE PORT OF | TO WHOM INDENTURED. |
|---|---|---|---|
| 1773. Sept. 22nd... | Henderson, James | | Joseph Tatnall and his assigns....... |
| | Wilkin, James | Ireland | Alexander Russell and his assigns.... |
| | Morrison, Donald | Scotland | John Terratt and his assigns........ |
| | Gunn, Margaret | Scotland | Anthony Williams, Jr., and his assigns. |
| | Smith, John | Scotland | John Englis and his assigns......... |
| | Kunkle, Philip, and Barbara Bunakle, his wife. | Rotterdam.. | William Smith and his assigns....... |
| | Rewle, Margaret | | Robert Fleming and his assigns...... |
| Sept. 23rd... | Morrison, John | Scotland | William Hinklin and his assigns..... |
| | Campbell, Murdoch | Scotland | John Reynolds and his assigns....... |
| | Hancy, James | Ireland | Robert Clenneghan and his assigns... |
| | Hancy, James | | John Reynolds and his assigns...... |
| | Bryan, Honar | | Jeremiah Dailey and his assigns..... |
| | Malone, Honora | Rotterdam.. | Gunner Rambo and his assigns...... |
| | Young, John Charles | | Philip Truckenmiller and his assigns. |
| | Kershaw, Jacob Ludwick | | Stephen and Joseph Sewell and their assigns. |
| | Schneider, Matthias | | Stephen and Joseph Sewell and their assigns. |
| | Young, Anthony | Rotterdam.. | John Cauffman and his assigns...... |
| | Meyer, Gotleib | Rotterdam.. | William Redman and his assigns..... |
| Sept. 23rd... | Reinhard, Jacob | Rotterdam.. | James Hockley and his assigns...... |
| | Cline, John | Rotterdam.. | John Browbaker and his assigns..... |
| | Cooper, William | | Andrew Waid and his assigns....... |
| | McLeod, John | | William Hartley and his assigns.... |
| | Munro, George | Scotland | James Craig and his assigns........ |
| | Sutherland, Andrew | Scotland | Samuel Ingliss and his assigns...... |
| | Pratt, Cornelius | Ireland | Josuah Gilbert and his assigns...... |
| | Dougherty, James | Ireland | William Shippen, Jr., and his assigns. |
| | Taylor, Mary | | Thomas Clifford, Jr., and his assigns. |
| | Taylor, Elizabeth | | Susannah Harrison ................ |
| | Ropp, John Henry | Rotterdam.. | John Mease and his assigns......... |
| | Istrickin, Sophia Leonora | Rotterdam.. | Matthias Aspen and his assigns...... |
| | Fisher, Michael | Rotterdam.. | Christian Allberryer and his assigns.. |
| | Wanner, Jacob, and Ann Mariah, his wife. | Rotterdam.. | John Hall and his assigns.......... |
| Sept. 24th... | Sweatman, Joseph | London | Jacob Ritter and his assigns........ |
| | Gunn, John | Scotland | Thomas Middleton and his assigns... |
| | Mertz, Johan Philip; Vybinger, Jacob; Shonfler, Jacob. | Rotterdam.. | Richard Wister and his assigns...... |
| | Douglas, Charles | Ireland | Robert Ritchie and his assigns...... |

## List of Indentures.

| Residence. | Occupation. | Term. | Amount. |
|---|---|---|---|
| Brandywine Hundred, New Castle co. | Apprentice | 5 yrs. | £0.5.0. |
| Philadelphia | Servant[1] | 3 yrs. | £11.0.0. |
| Upper Dublin twp., Phila. co. | Servant, one year's schooling[6] | 9 yrs. | £13.0.0. |
| Cheltenham twp., Phila. co. | Servant, have one year's schooling[5] | 9 yrs. | £12.0.0. |
| Philadelphia | Servant, taught to read in Bible and write a legible hand.[8] | 6 yrs. | £16.0.0. |
| Manington twp., Salem co. | Servant[6] | 4 yrs., 6 mo. each. | £48.0.0. |
| Philadelphia | Apprentice, taught to read in Bible and write a legible hand, the last year to learn the mantua making business (note 3, and £10 Pa. currency in cash). | 9 yrs. | |
| Brandywine Hundred, New Castle co. | Servant[3] | 4 yrs. | £14.0.0. |
| Frederick co., Va., within 6 miles of Winchester. | Servant[3] | 4 yrs. | £14.0.0. |
| Frederick co., Va. | Servant[5] | 2 yrs. | £8.15.0. |
| Frederick co., Va. | Servant | 2 yrs. | £8.15.0. |
| Philadelphia | Servant | 4 yrs. | £15.10.0. |
| Limerick twp., Phila. co. | Servant | 4 yrs. | £15.10.0. |
| Philadelphia | Servant[3] | 4 yrs. | £17.18.0. |
| Philadelphia | Servant | 4 yrs. | £20.0.0. |
| Philadelphia | Servant | 6 yrs. | £20.0.0. |
| Maiden Creek, Berks co. | Servant[3] | 10 yrs. | £20.6.0. |
| Bensalem, Bucks co. | Servant[3] | 4 yrs. | £20.4.0. |
| Douglass twp., Phila co. | Servant[1] | 11 yrs. | £24.0.0. |
| Earl twp., Lancaster co. | Servant[1] | 1 yr., 9 mo. | £10.16.6. |
| Philadelphia | Apprentice, taught the art and mystery of a mariner and navigation.[6] | 3 yrs. | |
| Mt. Hollow Bridge twp., Burlington co., W. N. J. | Servant, taught the art and mystery of a waterman, read in Bible, write a legible hand and cypher as far as rule of 3 (note 6, and £10 Pa. currency in cash) | 13 yrs., 6 mo. | £6.0.0. |
| Philadelphia | Servant[3] | 5 yrs. | £16.0.0. |
| Virginia | Servant[1] | 5 yrs. | £16.0.0. |
| Bibery twp., Phila. co. | Servant | 4 yrs. | £16.0.0. |
| Philadelphia | Servant (note 3, and £5 Pa. currency in cash). | 5 yrs. | £16.0.0. |
| Philadelphia | Apprentice, taught to read and write a legible hand and sew.[9] | 4 yrs., 8 mo. 23 d. | |
| Philadelphia | Apprentice, taught housewifery, sew, read in Bible and write a legible hand.[3] | 7 yrs. | |
| Philadelphia | Servant, have one quarter's evening schooling.[8] | 5 yrs. | £22.17.0. |
| Philadelphia | Servant[3] | 5 yrs. | £23.11.0. |
| Northern Liberties | Servant[3] | 4 yrs., 6 mo. | £23.0.0. |
| South Siscaanah Hundred, Scyell co. | Servant[3] | 5 yrs. each.. | £35.16.0. |
| Philadelphia | Servant (note 5, have £6 Pa. currency in cash). | 2 yrs., 6 mo. | £15.15.6. |
| Philadelphia | Servant, taught to read in Bible[3] | 4 yrs. | £17.0.0. |
| Philadelphia | Servant (note 3, and £3.8 shillings Pa. currency in cash). | 8 yrs., 6 mo. | £22.0.0. |
| | | | £26.18.0. |
| | | 4 yrs. | £18.0.0. |
| | | 4 yrs. | |
| Philadelphia | Servant[3] | 4 yrs. | £15.10.0. |

| Date. | Name. | From the Port of | To Whom Indentured. |
|---|---|---|---|
| 1773. Sept. 24th | Douglas, Charles | | Joseph Nickolson and his assigns.... |
| | Kirk, Mary | Ireland | John Honore Mursiguct and his assigns. |
| | McLeod, Catherine | | William Barber and his assigns...... |
| | Newhouse, Hannah | Rotterdam | Samuel Huees and his assigns........ |
| | Gillies, Ann | Scotland | Elias Botner and his assigns......... |
| | Young, Nicholas Adam | Rotterdam | John Weaver and his assigns........ |
| | Phleger, John Philip | Rotterdam | William Pusey and his assigns...... |
| | Tinkart, Sophia | | Rachael Ralfe ..................... |
| Sept. 25th | Seizer, Elizabeth | | John Witmore, Jr., and his assigns... |
| | Buckley, Philip | | Cawalder Dickenson and his assigns.. |
| | Groffenberger, Ignatius | Rotterdam | Samuel Silver and his assigns........ |
| | Van Pauke, Francis | Rotterdam | John Ridgeway and his assigns...... |
| | Leidich, Christian, and Ann Margaret, his wife. | Rotterdam | Joshua Shreve and his assigns...... |
| | Roofe, Michael | Rotterdam | William Curless and his assigns..... |
| | Shaferin, Margaret | Rotterdam | Isaac Wharton and his assigns...... |
| | Shaferin, Margaret | | Samuel Wharton and his assigns.... |
| | Eberhart, Martin | Rotterdam | Peter Shepard and his assigns....... |
| | Long, Alexander | Ireland | Amos Hoops and his assigns........ |
| | Bennet, Sarah | London | Captain Stephen Jones and his assigns. |
| | Delwissh, Cassamer | London | Matthias Slow and his assigns....... |
| | Kertsgaw, John; Tripple, Conrad. | London | Abel James and his assigns.......... |
| | Richards, Joseph; Hamilton, Gustavus. | Europe | John Wood and his assigns......... |
| | Sharp, John | Scotland | John Hollansshead and his assigns... |
| | Hassack, Hugh | Scotland | Samuel Kearsley and his assigns..... |
| | Reid, Alexander | Scotland | Samuel Kearsley and his assigns..... |
| | Breamer, William | Scotland | John Hollansshead and his assigns... |
| | Neil, Ann | | Samuel Kearsley and his assigns..... |
| | McLeod, Ann | Scotland | Daniel Evans and his assigns........ |
| | Gunn, John, and Margaret, his wife. | Scotland | Daniel Evans and his assigns........ |
| | Rolff, Marcus | Rotterdam | William Silver and his assigns...... |
| | Barends, Engetye | Rotterdam | Isaac Key and his assigns........... |
| | Everhart, John | Rotterdam | Martin Garricker and his assigns.... |
| | Bowman, Thomas | Rotterdam | Jacob Beery and his assigns......... |
| | Dowling, Samuel | London | Joseph Fox and his assigns.......... |
| Sept. 27th | Logan, Mary | Ireland | Eleonor Lordan and her assigns..... |
| | Holsman, Hans Christian | Rotterdam | James Gibbons and his assigns....... |
| | Hood, James | Ireland | David King and his assigns......... |

## List of Indentures.

| Residence. | Occupation. | Term. | Amount. |
|---|---|---|---|
| Maryland | Servant, the term above mentioned. | | £15.10.0. |
| Philadelphia | Servant | 4 yrs. | £10.0.0. |
| Philadelphia | Apprentice, have one year's schooling.[3] | 11 yrs. | 40s. |
| Woolwich twp., Glocester co. | Servant[3] | 7 yrs. | £32.0.6. |
| Philadelphia | Servant, taught to read and sew[3]. | 9 yrs. | £12.0.0. |
| Philadelphia | Servant[1] | 4 yrs. | £20.0.0. |
| Philadelphia | Servant (note 3, or £10 Pa. currency). | 4 yrs., 6 mo. | £25.0.0. |
| Philadelphia | Apprentice, taught housewifery, sew, read in Bible, write a legible hand (note 3, and £3 Pa. currency). | 9 yrs. | |
| Lampeter twp., Lancaster co. | Servant | 6 yrs. | £12.0.0. |
| Philadelphia | Apprentice, have three quarters' night schooling in the last six years, and leave to go three quarters more during the term, his mother paying the expense.[3] | 9 yrs. | |
| Pittsgrove twp., Salem co., W. N. J. | Servant[3] | 6 yrs. | £28.6.3. |
| Springfield twp., Burlington co., N. J. | Servant[1] | 5 yrs. | £28.7.6. |
| Springfield twp., Burlington co., N. J. | Servant (note 3, and £10 in cash to the husband). | 5 yrs. each. | £43.0.0. |
| Springfield twp., Burlington co., N. J. | Servant (note 3, and £8 Pa. currency in cash). | 5 yrs. | £25.16.0. |
| Philadelphia | Servant[3] | 4 yrs., 6 mo. | £23.0.0. |
| | Servant, the term above mentioned. | | £23.0.0. |
| Rockhill twp. | Servant (note 3, and £7 in cash). | 3 yrs. | £14.14.10. |
| Westtown, Chester co. | Servant | 4 yrs. | £15.18.0. |
| Philadelphia | Servant | 4 yrs. | £16.0.0. |
| Lancaster, Lancaster co. | Servant (note 3, and 2 Spanish pistoles in cash). | 3 yrs. | £14.0.0. |
| Philadelphia | Servant (note 3, and £10 Pa. currency in cash). | 3 yrs. | £15.16.3. |
| | Servant (note 3, and 1 guinea in cash). | 3 yrs. | £14.14.10. |
| Philadelphia | Apprentice, taught the art and mystery of a mariner and navigation (each to read, write and cypher as far as rule of 3).[3] | 3 yrs. each. | |
| Chester twp., Burlington co., W. N. J. | Servant[5] | 1 yr. | £6.0.0. |
| Carlisle twp., Cumberland co. | Servant[3] | 4 yrs. | £15.0.0. |
| Carlisle twp., Cumberland co. | Servant[3] | 2 yrs. | £15.0.0. |
| Chester twp., Burlington co., W. N. J. | Servant[5] | 1 yr. | £6.0.0. |
| Carlisle twp., Cumberland co. | Servant | 4 yrs. | £8.0.0. |
| West Whiteland twp., Chester co. | Servant, have one year's schooling[3] | 9 yrs. | £7.0.0. |
| West Whiteland twp., Chester co. | Servant[3] | 4 yrs. each. | £24.0.0. |
| Pittsgrove twp., Salem co., W. N. J. | Servant[3] | 6 yrs., 6 mo. | £29.1.6. |
| Waterford twp., Glocester co. | Servant[3] | 8 yrs. | £31.14.2. |
| Windsor twp., Berks co. | Servant, taught to read and write[6]. | 6 yrs. | £25.0.0. |
| Hartford twp., Chester co. | Servant[4] | 4 yrs. | £22.8.0. |
| Philadelphia | Servant (note 5, have £5 Pa. currency in cash). | 2 yrs., 6 mo. | £18.12.0. |
| Philadelphia | Servant[5] | 2 yrs. | £7.10.0. |
| Lampeter twp., Lancaster co. | Servant[3] | 4 yrs. | £22.19.6. |
| New Garden twp., Chester co. | Servant | 5 yrs. | £15.0.0. |

| Date. | Name. | From the Port of | To Whom Indentured. |
|---|---|---|---|
| 1773. Sept. 27th... | Porter, John | | John Gallerway and his assigns..... |
| | McMullan, Izal | Ireland .... | Sebastian Miller and his assigns..... |
| | McMullan, Mary | Ireland .... | Thomas Livesay and his assigns..... |
| | McLeod, Ann | Scotland ... | William Barber and his assigns...... |
| | McLeod, Ann | | Joy Castle and his assigns......... |
| | Granger, Judah | | John Chaise and his assigns........ |
| | Pullan, Peter | | William Illhenny and his assigns.... |
| Sept. 28th... | Batz, Johannes | Rotterdam.. | Joseph Farree and his assigns........ |
| | Batz, Johannes | | Baltzafun Kennan and his assigns... |
| | Schreer, George | Rotterdam.. | Jacob Morgan and his assigns....... |
| | Schreer, George | | John Leisshure and his assigns...... |
| | Strope, John | | George Easterly and his assigns..... |
| | Swing, John Godfrey | London .... | John Caner and his assigns......... |
| | Sternfields, George | Rotterdam.. | George Sternfields and his assigns.... |
| | Neibell, Metcher | Rotterdam.. | Christian Congell and his assigns.... |
| | McClelland, Ann | Scotland ... | James Fulton and his assigns......... |
| | Dawson, Nathan | | Davenport Marot .................. |
| | Coster, Nicholas Peter | London .... | Thomas Tilbury and his assigns..... |
| | Telb, George Conrad | Rotterdam.. | Daniel Reiff and his assigns......... |
| | Fitzgerrald, George | | John Bruce and his assigns.......... |
| | Jagerin, Elizabeth | Rotterdam.. | Philip Dick and his assigns.......... |
| | Monrow, William | | David Thompson and his assigns..... |
| | Wilds, Philip Frederick | London .... | Samuel Powell and his assigns....... |
| | Graham, Molcom | Scotland ... | Vincett Bonsell and his assigns...... |
| | Seagalin, Ann Margaret | Rotterdam.. | Lewis Farmer and his assigns........ |
| | Beterman, Maria Catherine | Rotterdam.. | Moses Brinton and his assigns....... |
| | Reninger, Adam | Rotterdam.. | William Englefield and his assigns... |
| | McEntyre, Donald | London .... | James Webb, Jr., and his assigns.... |
| | Campbell, Alexander | | John Appowen and his assigns....... |
| | Branner, Eva Maria | Rotterdam.. | Samuel Allinson and his assigns..... |

| Residence. | Occupation. | Term. | Amount. |
|---|---|---|---|
| Philadelphia | Servant | 2 yrs., 6 mo. | £ 8. 0. 0. |
| Germantown twp., Phila. co. | Servant[3] | 5 yrs. | £ 14. 0. 0. |
| Roxburgh twp., Phila. co. | Servant[3] | 5 yrs. | £ 14. 0. 0. |
| Philadelphia | Servant[3] | 6 yrs. | £ 13. 0. 0. |
| Philadelphia | Servant | 6 yrs. | £ 13. 0. 0. |
| Philadelphia | Servant | 4 yrs. | £ 5. 0. 0. |
| Philadelphia | Apprentice, taught the art and mystery of a tailor, have three quarters' night schooling (note 6, found all necessaries except washing and mending). | 6 yrs., 1 mo. 5 d. | |
| Strasburgh twp., Lancaster co. | Servant[3] | 3 yrs., 6 mo. | £ 21. 15. 0. |
| Earl twp., Lancaster co. | Servant | 3 yrs., 6 mo. | £ 21. 15. 0. |
| Philadelphia | Servant[3] | 4 yrs. | £ 23. 1. 0. |
| Oley twp., Berks co. | Servant | 4 yrs. | £ 23. 1. 0. |
| Philadelphia | Apprentice, taught the art and mystery of a blacksmith, have two quarters' night schooling.[3] | 4 yrs., 2 w. | |
| Philadelphia | Servant[3] | 4 yrs. | £ 21. 10. 0. |
| Philadelphia | Servant, taught the baking business, when free give him legal feedom dues. | 8 yrs. | £ 21. 6. 0. |
| Philadelphia | Servant, three months' English schooling.[1] | 8 yrs. | £ 20. 16. 6. |
| Philadelphia | Servant, one year's schooling[1] | 12 yrs. | £ 12. 0. 0. paid for her parents' passage from Scotland. |
| Philadelphia | Apprentice, taught the trade of a spinning wheel and chair maker, have three quarters' day schooling.[1] | 6 yrs., 4 mo. 1 d. | |
| Philadelphia | Servant[3] | 3 yrs. | £ 14. 15. 6. |
| Oley twp., Berks co. | Servant, the master to allow him time to go to the minister to receive the Sacrament; taught to read in Bible and write a legible hand, at expiration customary freedom dues. | 7 yrs. | £ 22. 5. 0. |
| Philadelphia | When free give him £ 10 in cash or freedom dues, allow the wife of said servant to live in the house. | 18 mo. | £ 20. 0. 0. |
| Philadelphia | Servant, at expiration give her customary freedom dues. | 5 yrs., 6 mo. | £ 18. 16. 4. |
| Southwark | Apprentice, taught the art and mystery of a ship carpenter, have one quarter's evening schooling each year (note 5, and £ 7 in cash in lieu of freedom dues and his working tools). | 5 yrs. | |
| Philadelphia | Servant (note 5, have £ 10 Pa. currency in lieu of freedom dues) | 3 yrs., 6 mo. | £ 18. 3. 4. |
| Wilmington twp., New Castle co. | Servant[3] | 4 yrs. | £ 17. 0. 0. |
| Philadelphia | Servant[1] | 4 yrs. | £ 22. 4. 0. |
| Leacock twp., Lancaster co. | Servant[3] | 5 yrs. | £ 28. 15. 0. |
| Philadelphia | Servant[3] | 3 yrs., 3 mo. | £ 21. 13. 0. |
| Lancaster twp., Lancaster co. | Servant[3] | 4 yrs. | £ 15. 0. 0. |
| Philadelphia | Apprentice, taught the trade of a sail maker, have three quarters' night schooling.[3] | 5 yrs., 6 mo. | |
| Burlington | Servant[3] | 4 yrs., 6 mo. | £ 26. 17. 0. |

| Date. | Name. | From the Port of | To Whom Indentured. |
|---|---|---|---|
| 1773. | Harbst, John Henry | Rotterdam | Philip Ottenhimer and his assigns |
| | Precher, John | Rotterdam | Frederick Haner and his assigns |
| | Queen, Catherine | | John Cumings and his assigns |
| | Schlotterin, Ann Mary | Rotterdam | John Lukins and his assigns |
| | Shefer, John | Rotterdam | Philip Reiff and his assigns |
| | Steer, Nicholas | Rotterdam | Philip Oler and his assigns |
| | Seely, Adam | Rotterdam | Philip Oler and his assigns |
| | Steer, Nicholas | | William Wendall and his assigns |
| | Seely, Adam | | Christian Rists and his assigns |
| | Smidten, Anna Catherine | Rotterdam | Joseph Low and his assigns |
| | McKever, Margaret | | Thomard Ball and his assigns |
| | Poor, William | London | James Webb, Jr., and his assigns |
| | Smidt, Philip Andreas | Rotterdam | Detrick Reese and his assigns |
| | Smidt, Philip Andreas | | Martin Gross and his assigns |
| | Perry, Robert | | John Erwin and his assigns |
| | Fiffenback, John Philip | Rotterdam | Peter Horning and his assigns |
| | Schuman, John Nicholas | Rotterdam | Matthias Slough and his assigns |
| | Kraushaar, Valentine | Rotterdam | John Gross and his assigns |
| Sept. 28th | Leanord, John Yost | Rotterdam | Abel James and his assigns |
| | Meyerin, Maria Catherine | | Samuel Becket and his assigns |
| | Meyerin, Maria Catherine | | Peter Becket and his assigns |
| | Horner, Jacob | Rotterdam | Jacob Kirk and his assigns |
| | Lenhardt, George | Rotterdam | Jonathan Tyson and his assigns |
| | Ahrens, John Conrad; Hamper, Andreas. | Rotterdam | John Fulton and his assigns |
| | Bush, William | Rotterdam | Isaac Whetstone and his assigns |
| | Vant, John Frederick | | Adam Whitmore and his assigns |
| | Zimmerman, Johannes | Rotterdam | George Schmidt and his assigns |
| | Kieffer, Johannes | Rotterdam | John Waggoner and his assigns |
| | Bell, Charles | London | George Napper and his assigns |
| | Millen, Eve Mary | Rotterdam | Frederick Houseman and his assigns |
| | Waggonhurst, Susannah | | Jacob Winey and his assigns |
| | Baumen, Margaret Grich | Rotterdam | Michael Ley and his assigns |
| | Millern, Anna Maria | Rotterdam | Thomas Bausler and his assigns |
| | Horn, Michael | Rotterdam | Simon Bausly and his assigns |
| | Tromheller, Henrich; Smidt, John Peter. | Rotterdam | Joseph Griswald |
| | Gotz, Charles Jacob | Rotterdam | John Lukins and his assigns |
| | Fry, Verinoca | | John Lukins and his assigns |
| | Robscher, John George | Rotterdam | Reinhard Lawbauch and his assigns |
| | Herstone, John | Rotterdam | Lazerus Widenor and his assigns |
| | Brown, George Frederick | Rotterdam | Matthias Probst and his assigns |
| | Bell, Buldthaser | Rotterdam | Daniel Smith and his assigns |
| | Basinger, Carolina | Rotterdam | Matthias Probst and his assigns |
| | Van Nievenhouser, Bart. | Rotterdam | Lorance Bachman and his assigns |
| Sept. 29th | Ludecker, Jost | Rotterdam | Jacob Shartin and his assigns |
| | Sheffengton, Henry | Ireland | William Sherrett and his assigns |
| | Griger, James | Scotland | Joseph Penrose and his assigns |
| | Soare, William | London | Samuel Eseley and his assigns |
| | Fisher, Andrew | Rotterdam | Joseph Fry and his assigns |

## List of Indentures.

| Residence. | Occupation. | Term. | Amount. |
|---|---|---|---|
| Philadelphia | Servant[1] | 3 yrs. | £18.0.0. |
| Philadelphia | Servant[3] | 5 yrs. | £24.0.0. |
| Philadelphia | Apprentice, taught housewifery and sew, read in Bible.[3] | 11 yrs. | |
| Moyamensing twp., Phila. co. | Servant[1] | 4 yrs., 6 mo. | £21.15.0. |
| Oley twp., Berks co. | Servant[3] | 2 yrs., 9 mo. | £18.2.0. |
| Philadelphia | Servant (note 3, or £10 in cash) | 3 yrs., 6 mo. | £22.18.2. |
| Philadelphia | Servant[3] | 3 yrs., 6 mo. | £21.18.2. |
| Manheim twp., Lancaster co. | Servant | 3 yrs., 6 mo. | £22.18.2. |
| Manheim twp., Lancaster co. | Servant | 3 yrs., 6 mo. | £21.18.2. |
| Deptford twp., Gloster co., N. J. | Servant[1] | 4 yrs. | £20.17.6. |
| Sunbury twp., Northumberland co. | Servant | 4 yrs. | £12.10.0. |
| Lancaster twp., Lancaster co. | Servant[1] | 4 yrs. | £15.0.0. |
| Philadelphia | Servant[8] | 4 yrs. | £21.10.6. |
| Lancaster | Servant, the term as above | | £21.10.6. |
| Antrim twp., Cumberland co. | Servant[3] | 2 yrs., 6 mo. | £11.5.0. |
| New Providence twp., Phila. co. | Servant (note 5, have £8.6s.8d. in lieu of freedom dues). | 3 yrs. | £18.0.0. |
| Lancaster | Servant[1] | 3 yrs. | £20.7.0. |
| Maxatawney twp., Berks co. | Servant[3] | 4 yrs. | £19.2.0. |
| Philadelphia | Servant (note 1, and £5 Pa. currency). | 3 yrs. | £23.15.0. |
| Woolwich twp., Glocester co., Jersey. | Servant[3] | 4 yrs., 6 mo. | £20.0.0. |
| Woolwich twp., Glocester co., N. J. | The term as above mentioned | | £20.0.0. |
| Abbington twp., Phila. co. | Servant[3] | 4 yrs., 6 w. | £22.14.0. |
| Upper Dublin twp., Phila. co. | Servant (note 3, and 3 dollars) | 3 yrs., 9 mo. | £19.5.0. |
| E. Nottingham, Chester co. | Servant[3] | 6 yrs., 6 mo. | £28.16.6. |
| | Servant (note 6, or £10 in cash). | 6 yrs. | £28.16.6 |
| Northern Liberties | Servant[3] | 3 yrs., 6 mo. | £21.17.0. |
| Reading, Berks co. | Servant | 3 yrs. | £8.0.0. |
| Heidelburgh twp., Lancaster co. | Servant[1] | 3 yrs., 3 mo. | £21.17.0. |
| W. Caln twp., Chester co. | Servant[3] | 3 yrs., 3 mo. | £21.17.0. |
| Philadelphia | Servant (note 5, have 50 shillings in cash). | 2 yrs., 6 mo. | £16.13.3. |
| Maxatawney, Berks co. | Servant[3] | 4 yrs., 6 mo. | £20.3.0. |
| Philadelphia | Servant | 5 yrs., 6 mo. | £24.0.0. |
| Heidelburg twp., Lancaster co. | Servant[6] | 4 yrs. | £19.2.0. |
| Heidelburg twp., Lancaster co. | Servant[3] | 4 yrs. | £19.18.4. |
| Heidelburg twp., Lancaster co. | Servant (note 1, or £8 Pa. currency). | 3 yrs., 6 mo. | £23.7.4. |
| New York | Servant[3] | 3 yrs., 6 mo. / 3 yrs., 1 mo. | £20.15.0. / £21.7.6. |
| Philadelphia | Servant[8] | 7 yrs. | £22.10.0. |
| Philadelphia | Apprentice, taught to read and write English, housewifery and sew.[6] | 9 yrs. | |
| Lower Saucon twp., Northampton co. | Servant (note 1, or £10 Pa. currency). | 5 yrs., 6 mo. | £28.7.0. |
| Oley twp., Berks co. | Servant[3] | 4 yrs. | £19.13.8. |
| Lynn twp., Northampton co. | Servant (note 3 (worth £10), and 2 dollars in cash). | 3 yrs., 8 mo. | £21.15.0. |
| Albany twp., Berks co. | Servant[6] | 3 yrs. | £20.10.0. |
| Lynn twp., Northampton co. | Servant[8] | 7 yrs. | £31.9.6. |
| Lynn twp., Berks co. | Servant[8] | 5 yrs. | £25.17.0. |
| Maxatawney twp., Berks co. | Servant[3] | 3 yrs., 6 mo. | £19.11.0. |
| Hopewell twp., Cumberland co. | Servant[3] | 2 yrs. | £7.11.6. |
| Philadelphia | Servant[3] | 2 yrs. | £7.10.0. |
| Greenwich twp., Glocester co., W. N. Jersey. | Servant[3] | 4 yrs. | £16.0.0. |
| Lower Saucon twp., Northampton co. | Servant[3] | 3 yrs., 6 mo. | £20.5.0. |

| Date. | Name. | From the Port of | To Whom Indentured. |
|---|---|---|---|
| 1773. Sept. 29th | Fisher, Andrew | | Anthony Lark and his assigns |
| | Cockoo, John Frederick | Rotterdam | Mordacai Lee and his assigns |
| | Cockoo, John Frederick | Rotterdam | John Starr and his assigns |
| | Bean Christopher | Rotterdam | George Ellick and his assigns |
| | Mink, Philip; Fockin, Barbara | Rotterdam | Jacob Kieslaw and his assigns |
| | Reinhard, John George | Rotterdam | Jacob Cline and his assigns |
| | Flatshern, Emericka | Rotterdam | Peter Miller and his assigns |
| | Watthern, Ann Margaret | Rotterdam | George Rhode and his assigns |
| | Egell, John | Rotterdam | Jacob Miller and his assigns |
| | Egell, George | Rotterdam | David Levy and his assigns |
| | Egell, Jacob | Rotterdam | Nicholas Miller and his assigns |
| | Backer, Nicholas | Rotterdam | Michael Ohl and his assigns |
| | Harms, John Nicholas | Rotterdam | James Hutton and his assigns |
| | Fricken, Elizabeth | Rotterdam | Abraham Borton and his assigns |
| | Bertsch, Nicholas; Gysen, Maria; Stockers, Elizabeth. | Rotterdam | William Peters and his assigns |
| | Gysen, Maria | | William Peters, Jr., and his assigns |
| | Leib, Andrew | Rotterdam | William Peters, Jr., and his assigns |
| | Derr, Michael | | George Cooper and his assigns |
| | Spies, John William | Rotterdam | Henry Strauk and his assigns |
| | Spice, John | Rotterdam | George Smith and his assigns |
| | Spies, Harman | Rotterdam | Adam Hoffman and his assigns |
| | Hamen, Balthaser | Rotterdam | Andrew Mattern and his assigns |
| | Schnyder, Matthias | Rotterdam | Jacob Wagganer and his assigns |
| | Lowershegerin, Eave Mary | Rotterdam | Boltis Weach and his assigns |
| | Cain, William | | William Appleby and his executors |
| Sept. 30th | Boyer, Michael | | John Stilly and his assigns |
| | Malone, Honora | | John Dealy and his assigns |
| | Reden, Barbara | Rotterdam | Philip Moser and his assigns |
| | Reden, Barbara | | William Bausman and his assigns |
| | Segelin, Ann Margeret | | Peter Huffinagle and his assigns |
| | Croener, Jacob | | Jacob Kentner and his assigns |
| | Cline, George | Rotterdam | Adam Phote and his assigns |
| | Connely, Thomas | | George Henry and his assigns |

## List of Indentures.

| Residence. | Occupation. | Term. | Amount. |
|---|---|---|---|
| Lower Saucon twp., Northampton co. | Servant | 3 yrs., 6 mo. | £ 20. 5. 0. |
| Maiden Creek twp., Berks co. | Servant [1] | 6 yrs., 6 mo. | £ 28. 13. 6. |
| Maiden Creek twp., Berks co. | Servant | 6 yrs., 6 mo. | £ 28. 13. 6. |
| Cocalico twp., Lancaster co. | Servant wear his own clothes he now has (note 3, or £ 10 in lieu of freedoms). | 3 yrs. | £ 21. 16. 0. |
| Guywit twp., Phila. co. | Servant [3] | 3 yrs., 7 mo. | £ 19. 3. 6. |
|  |  | 3 yrs., 6 mo. | £ 19. 9. 0. |
| Philadelphia | Servant [3] | 5 yrs. | £ 23. 0. 0. |
| Widemarsh twp., Phila. co. | Servant [3] | 4 yrs. | £ 19. 13. 0. |
| Maltberd twp., Phila. co. | Servant (note 3, or £ 5 Pa. currency in cash). | 4 yrs. | £ 19. 2. 0. |
| Upper Hanover twp., Phila. co. | Servant [3] | 3 yrs., 6 mo. | £ 20. 15. 0. |
| Upper Hanover twp., Phila. co. | Servant [3] | 3 yrs., 9 mo. | £ 21. 8. 0. |
| Upper Hanover twp., Phila. co. | Servant, when free give him besides freedom dues an axe, a grubbing hoe, a pair of iron wedges and rings for a maul. | 4 yrs. | £ 20. 15. 0. |
| Heidelburgh twp., Northampton co. | Servant [3] | 3 yrs., 4 mo. | £ 19. 1. 0. |
| Maiden Creek twp., Berks co. | Servant (note 5, and freedom dues) | 6 yrs. | £ 29. 6. 0. |
| Evesham twp., Burlington co., N. J. | Servant (note 1, and 2 dollars) | 4 yrs. | £ 18. 3. 0. |
| Aston twp., Chester co. | Servant [3] | 6 yrs. | £ 28. 13. 6. |
|  |  | 7 yrs. | £ 27. 12. 6. |
|  |  | 7 yrs. | £ 28. 12. 6. |
| Aston twp., Chester co. |  | 7 yrs. | £ 27. 12. 6. |
| Aston twp., Chester co. | Servant, taught the trade of a tanner and currier.[6] | 5 yrs. | £ 27. 14. 0. |
| Philadelphia | Apprentice, taught the art and mystery of a skindresser, two quarters' night schooling [3]. | 5 yrs. |  |
| Heidelburgh twp., Lancaster co. | Servant [1] | 3 yrs., 6 mo. | £ 20. 12. 0. |
| Heidelburgh twp., Lancaster co. | Servant [1] | 3 yrs., 6 mo. | £ 20. 12. 0. |
| Heidelburgh twp., Lancaster co. | Servant [3] | 3 yrs., 6 mo. | £ 20. 12. 0. |
| Northern Liberties | Servant, taught the trade of a potter (note 6, or £ 10 Pa. currency in cash). | 3 yrs., 8 mo. | £ 9. 18. 0. |
| Blockley twp., Phila. co. | Servant (note 3, or £ 10 Pa. currency in cash). | 4 yrs. | £ 19. 13. 0. |
| North Wales | Servant [1] | 4 yrs. | £ 19. 12. 0. |
| Philadelphia | Servant, found all necessaries except apparel; if he pays or cause to be paid 40 shillings per month till the sum of £ 11. 10. 0. and other expense occurring this indenture to be void. | 2 yrs. | £ 11. 10. 0. |
| Philadelphia | Apprentice, taught the art and mystery of a tailor, three months' night schooling.[1] | 8 yrs., 2 mo. 28 d. |  |
| Philadelphia | Servant | 4 yrs. | £ 6. 0. 0. |
| Philadelphia | Servant [1] | 4 yrs. | £ 13. 15. 0. |
| Lancaster | Servant | 4 yrs. | £ 23. 15. 0. |
| Lancaster | Servant | 4 yrs. | £ 22. 4. 0. |
| Philadelphia | Apprentice, taught the art and mystery of a cordwainer, one quarter's English night schooling and time to go to the minister to take the sacrament (note 6, or £ 10 Pa. currency in cash). | 4 yrs. |  |
| Philadelphia | Servant (note 3, or £ 5, in cash) | 5 yrs., 6 mo. | £ 21. 11. 0. |
| Philadelphia | Apprentice, taught the art and | 8 yrs., 7 mo. |  |

| Date. | Name. | From the Port of | To Whom Indentured. |
|---|---|---|---|
| 1773.<br>Sept. 30th | Baniger, Charlotte Margaret | Rotterdam | James Gibbons and his assigns |
| | Morrison, Christiana | | John Townsend and his assigns |
| | Keysonck, Jacob Fogle | Rotterdam | Samuel Jenney and his assigns |
| | Maxfield, James | | Daniel Topham and his assigns |
| | Swincell, Andrew Frederick | Rotterdam | John Dihoff and his assigns |
| | Fritz, Johannes | Rotterdam | George Rine and his assigns |
| | Gatz, Christian | Rotterdam | Henry Weaver and his assigns |
| | Erich, John Leonard, and Margaret, his wife. | Rotterdam | Henry Weaver and his assigns |
| Oct. 1st | Hamen, John | Rotterdam | Robert Fisher and his assigns |
| | Fielding, Harman | Rotterdam | John Lamborn and his assigns |
| | Newton, John | | Daniel Murphey and wife |
| | Hanson, John | | Samuel Burkelo and his assigns |
| | Shauk, Joseph | Rotterdam | Richard Wister and his assigns |
| | Bourne, Margaret | Ireland | George Clements and his assigns |
| | Vocht, John George | Rotterdam | William Rex and his assigns |
| | Fritz, Martin | Rotterdam | Peter Rae and his assigns |
| | Lanbinnin, Maria Catherine | Rotterdam | Andrew Oyl and his assigns |
| | Parker, John | | Jacob Souder |
| | Etherlow, Casper | | Adam Gilbert |
| | Dunns, Peter | Ireland | Robert Curry and his assigns |
| | Rixroth, Zakeria, and Ann Margaret, his wife | Rotterdam | Barnet Robb and his assigns |
| | Schutz, John Conrad | Rotterdam | Anthony Williams, Jr., and his assigns. |
| | Shaffier, John Adam | Rotterdam | Daniel Beery and his assigns |
| | Cleamens, Adam | Rotterdam | John Himmose and his assigns |
| | Gormer, John | Rotterdam | Daniel Lintner and his assigns |
| | Robscher, John Peter | Rotterdam | Isaac Kirk and his assigns |
| | Able, Melechis | Rotterdam | David Ridgeway and his assigns |
| | Nagle, Arthur | | Samuel Ridley and his assigns |
| | Geissin, Maria Elizabeth | Rotterdam | Mordecai Evans and his assigns |
| | Gruber, Philip | Rotterdam | Jacob Leech and his assigns |
| | Gearheart, Conrad | Rotterdam | Henry Magg and his assigns |
| | Good, John Christopher | Rotterdam | William Lowman and his assigns |
| | Robscher, John Leonard; Muhlheiser, John. | Rotterdam | Abraham Kensing and his assigns |
| | Schlater, Jacob | Rotterdam | Antony Wette and his assigns |
| | Dorn, Johan Henry | Rotterdam | Antony Wette and his assigns |
| Oct. 1st | Dorn, Johan Henry | | Philip Clise and his assigns |

## List of Indentures.

| Residence. | Occupation. | Term. | Amount. |
|---|---|---|---|
|  | mystery of a cordwainer, twelve months' schooling.[2] | 26 d. |  |
| Lampeter twp., Lancaster co. | Servant, taught to read[3] | 10 yrs., 2 mo. | £20.0.0. |
| Ben Salem twp., Bucks co. | Apprentice, taught housewifery, 18 months' day schooling.[3] | 12 yrs. | £3.0.0. |
| Lowden co., Va., near Cattockton Mountains. | Servant (note 3, or £8 Pa. currency). | 4 yrs. | £27.9.0. |
| Philadelphia | Apprentice, taught the trade of a potter, read and write and cypher as far as rule of 3.[3] | 8 yrs., 11 mo. |  |
| Lancaster | Servant (note 1, or £10 Pa. currency). | 3 yrs., 6 mo. | £21.0.0. |
| Earl twp., Lancaster co. | Servant[3] | 3 yrs. | £18.12.0. |
| Carnarvan twp., Lancaster co. | Servant[1] | 3 yrs. | £17.15.0. |
| Carnarvan twp., Lancaster co. | Servant[3] | 2 yrs., 1 mo. each. | £21.19.0. |
| Pensbrough twp., Chester co. | Servant[3] | 3 yrs., 3 mo. | £20.17.0. |
| Kennett twp., Chester co. | Servant[3] | 6 yrs. | £21.19.2. |
| Philadelphia | Apprentice, taught the art and mystery of a pilot in the river and bay of Delaware, have six months' schooling and be allowed time to go three months more at the expense of the father.[3] | 5 yrs., 10 mo., 16 d. |  |
| Philadelphia |  | 1 yr. | £3.0.0. |
| Philadelphia | Servant (note 1, and £22 Pa. currency in cash). | 5 yrs., 6 mo. | £25.0.0. |
| Providence twp., Phila. co. | Servant | 6 yrs. | £11.10.0. |
| Heidleberg twp., Northampton co. | Servant (note 1, or £10 Pa. currency). | 4 yrs. | £20.16.6. |
| Heidleberg twp., Northampton co. | Servant[3] | 4 yrs. | £18.12.0. |
| Malbrough twp., Phila. co. | Servant (note 3, and a spinning wheel). | 3 yrs., 9 mo. | £19.9.0. |
| Philadelphia | Apprentice, taught the art and mystery of a bricklayer, have two quarter's night schooling.[5] | 2 yrs., 1 mo. |  |
| Douglas twp., Phila. co. | Apprentice (note 1, or £8 Pa. currency). | 6 yrs. |  |
| Norrington twp., Phila. co. | Servant | 2 yrs. | £10.0.0. |
| Whitemarsh twp., Phila. co. | Servant[3] | 4 yrs. each. | £42.14.4. |
| Cheltenham twp., Phila. co. | Servant (note 3, and 2 dollars) | 6 yrs. | £17.12.3. |
| Coventry twp., Chester co. | Servant[1] | 3 yrs. | £19.11.0. |
| Coventry twp., Chester co. | Servant (note 1, or £9 Pa. currency). | 4 yrs. | £21.17.0. |
| Strasburgh twp., Lancaster co. | Servant[3] | 5 yrs. | £24.19.0. |
| Upper Dublin twp., Phila. co. | Servant[3] | 8 yrs. | £20.5.0. |
| Springfield twp., Burlington co. | Servant[3] | 6 yrs., 6 mo. | £30.0.0. |
| Philadelphia | Apprentice, taught the art and mystery of a painter and glazier.[3] | 2 yrs. |  |
| Limerick twp., Phila. co. | Servant[3] | 6 yrs. | £26.5.0. |
| Cheltenham twp., Phila. co. | Servant[1] | 5 yrs., 9 mo. | £28.16.0. |
| Passyunk twp., Phila. co. | Servant[3] | 3 yrs., 1 mo. | £19.16.0. |
| Passyunk twp., Phila. co. | Servant[1] | 6 yrs. | £25.13.8. |
| Philadelphia | Servants, each to have freedom dues and £5 in cash, Robscher to be taught to read and write. | 8 yrs. / 5 yrs. | £20.0.0. / £21.7.0. |
| Lancaster | Servant[3] | 3 yrs., 9 mo. | £21.13.6. |
| Lancaster | Servant[3] | 3 yrs., 9 mo. | £22.10.4. |
| Lancaster | Servant, the term as above. |  | £22.10.4. |

| Date. | Name. | From the Port of | To Whom Indentured. |
|---|---|---|---|
| 1773.<br>Oct. 1st.... | Auldhouse, Yost | Rotterdam.. | Francis Rode and his assigns........ |
| Oct. 2nd.... | Gretel, John Adam | Rotterdam.. | Peter Heist and his assigns......... |
| | Shutz, Johan Philip | Rotterdam.. | Job Thomas and his assigns......... |
| | Storger, Henry | Rotterdam.. | Isaac Clutz and his assigns......... |
| | Storger, Henry | | Stopel Stedler and his assigns........ |
| | Jones, Thomas | London .... | Jonathan Gostleow and his assigns... |
| | Boddin, Ann Mary | Rotterdam.. | John Wister and his assigns......... |
| | Graham, Henaritta | Scotland ... | Thomas Tompson and his assigns.... |
| | McLeod, Murdoch | Scotland ... | William Fisher and his assigns...... |
| | Beck, Christian | Rotterdam.. | Samuel Funk and his assigns........ |
| | McConegall, Elizabeth | Ireland .... | George Aston and his assigns........ |
| | McConegall, Elizabeth | | James Stirling and his assigns....... |
| | Schiglin, Margaret | Rotterdam.. | Joseph Marsh and his assigns....... |
| | Sigler, John | Rotterdam.. | Joshua Ballinger and his assigns..... |
| | Toarmenin, Magdelin | Rotterdam.. | Mathias Shefely and his assigns..... |
| | Mickelfretz, John | Rotterdam.. | John Shultz and his assigns.......... |
| | Yeagerin, Anna Maria | Rotterdam.. | William Ekart and his assigns....... |
| | Weaverin, Mary Catherine | Rotterdam.. | Henry Funk and his assigns......... |
| | Weaverin, Mary Catherine | | Jacob Hinkle and his assigns........ |
| | Doineus, John Philip | Rotterdam.. | Godfrey Haga and his assigns...... |
| | Thinguss, Mary | | Godfrey Haga and his assigns,..... |
| | Hartman, John | Rotterdam.. | John Hartman and his assigns....... |
| | Sausman, Johan Frederick | Rotterdam.. | Philip Dirst and his assigns......... |
| | Sausman, Johan Frederick | | Henry Dirst and his assigns......... |
| | Mathis, John Charles | Rotterdam.. | Philip Dirst and his assigns......... |
| Oct. 4th.... | Beaton, John | Ireland .... | Arthur Dondaldson and his assigns... |
| | Hess, John | Rotterdam.. | George Whike and his assigns...... |
| | Weaver, Conrad | | Christian Shaffer and his assigns..... |
| Oct. 4th.... | Bush, John Hoyes | Rotterdam.. | Michal Syburt and his assigns....... |
| | Meyer, Henry | Rotterdam.. | Henry Kreider and his assigns...... |
| | Krickeson, Andrew | Rotterdam.. | William Elder, Jr., and his assigns... |
| | Team, Lawrence | Rotterdam.. | George Wither and his assigns...... |
| | Kunkle, Michael | Rotterdam.. | George Hamey and his assigns...... |
| | Dunako, Humphrey | | Benjamin Freeman ................ |
| | Bear, John | | Matthias Foltz .................... |
| | Stayenbring, Henry | Rotterdam.. | John Rhrine and his assigns......... |
| | Eberhardin, Martin Adolph | Rotterdam.. | Richard Wistar and his assigns...... |
| | Righart, Adam | Rotterdam.. | Jacob Winey and his assigns........ |
| | Garter, Jacob | Rotterdam.. | Jacob Winey and his assigns........ |

## List of Indentures.

| Residence. | Occupation. | Term. | Amount. |
|---|---|---|---|
| Saltzberg twp., Northampton co. | Servant (note 3, one axe, and one grubbing hoe). | 3 yrs., 6 mo. | £ 25. 7. 4. |
| Mulberry twp., Phila. co. | Servant [3] | 5 yrs., 9 mo. | £ 20. 0. 0. |
| Hilltown twp., Bucks co. | Servant, taught to read and write [1]. | 8 yrs. | £ 19. 0. 0. |
| Macungie twp., Northampton co. | Servant (note 6, and 20 shillings in cash) | 3 yrs., 6 mo. | £ 19. 2. 0. |
| Macungie | Servant, the term above mentioned. | | £ 19. 2. 0. |
| Philadelphia | Servant | 4 yrs. | £ 13. 10. 0. |
| Philadelphia | Servant, at expiration freedom dues and 30 shillings. | 4 yrs., 6 mo. | £ 22. 12. 0. |
| Southwark, Phila. co. | Servant [1] | 5 yrs. | £ 15. 0. 0. |
| Philadelphia | Servant [1] | 5 yrs. | £ 15. 0. 0. |
| Rockhill twp., Bucks co. | Servant, at expiration freedom or £ 10. | 3 yrs., 3 mo. | £ 21. 0. 0. |
| Philadelphia | Servant [1] | 4 yrs. | £ 15. 0. 0. |
| Burlington | Servant | 4 yrs. | £ 15. 0. 0. |
| Southwark | Servant [1] | 5 yrs. | £ 30. 0. 0. |
| Evesham twp., Burlington co., West Jersey. | Servant (note 1, and 1 Spanish dollar). | 4 yrs. | £ 21. 5. 0. |
| Mallbrough twp., Phila. co. | Servant [3] | 4 yrs., 3 mo. | £ 23. 17. 0. |
| Douglas twp., Phila. co. | Servant [1] | 6 yrs. | £ 19. 2. 0. |
| Philadelphia | Servant [1] | 5 yrs., 3 mo. | £ 30. 0. 2. |
| Philadelphia | Servant [3] | 5 yrs. | £ 27. 18. 0. |
| The Sign of the Spread Eagle on the Lancaster Road. | Servant | 5 yrs. | £ 27. 18. 0. |
| Philadelphia | Servant [3] | 3 yrs. | £ 21. 3. 0. |
| Philadelphia | Apprentice, taught housewifery, sew, knit and spin, have six months' schooling (note 6, and £ 3 Pa. currency in cash). | 10 yrs. | 40 shillings. |
| Exeter twp., Berks co. | Servant [1] | 4 yrs. | £ 28. 11. 0. |
| Exeter twp., Berks co. | Servant [3] | 3 yrs. | £ 18. 16. 0. |
| Exeter twp., Berks co. | Servant, the term as above. | | £ 18. 16. 0. |
| Exeter twp., Berks co. | Servant [3] | 6 yrs. | £ 25. 6. 10. |
| Philadelphia | Servant | 4 yrs. | £ 13. 0. 0. |
| Salisbury twp., Lancaster co. | Servant [1] | 4 yrs., 6 mo. | £ 25. 17. 4. |
| Philadelphia | Apprentice, have two quarters' night schooling, one this year and the other the year of his freedom, taught the art and mystery of a carpenter.[6] | 5 yrs., 3 mo. | |
| Greenwich twp., Sussex co., N. J. | Servant [3] | 3 yrs., 2 mo. | £ 21. 10. 0. |
| Lancaster twp., Lancaster co. | Servant [3] | 3 yrs. | £ 23. 2. 8. |
| Frederick co., Md. | Servant [3] | 6 yrs. | £ 26. 0. 0. |
| Heidelburg twp., Lancaster co. | Servant [3] | 3 yrs., 6 mo. | £ 19. 11. 0. |
| Haycock twp., Bucks co. | Servant [1] | 4 yrs., 6 mo. | £ 21. 0. 0. |
| Philadelphia | Apprentice, taught the art and mystery of a chair maker, have one quarter's schooling.[3] | 4 yrs. | |
| Lower Merion twp., Phila. co. | Apprentice, taught the art and mystery of a farmer, to read and write.[6] | 10 yrs., 10 mo. | |
| Heidelburg twp., Lancaster co. | Servant [6] | 3 yrs., 6 mo. | £ 23. 12. 0. |
| Philadelphia | Servant [1] | 8 yrs. | £ 20. 18. 0. |
| Philadelphia | Servant, employed at the milling business; in case he (Adam Righart) does not understand the business he is to have the privilege to pay the master the sum of 21. 17. 0. and expenses occurring, this indenture to be void.[3] | 3 yrs. | £ 21. 17. 0. |
| Philadelphia | Servant, kept at the business of a miner if he understands it.[3] | 3 yrs. | £ 21. 17. 0. |

| Date. | Name. | From the Port of | To Whom Indentured. |
|---|---|---|---|
| 1773. Oct. 4th | Otto, John | Rotterdam | Jacob Winey and his assigns |
| | Rossmeissel, Adam | Rotterdam | Jacob Winey and his assigns |
| | Kruss, Valentine | Rotterdam | John Smith and his assigns |
| | Stewart, John | | Jacob Levering and his assigns |
| | Brought, John Yost | Rotterdam | Jacob Bunn and his assigns |
| | France, John Ludwig | Rotterdam | Peter Cool and his assigns |
| | Reyney, Christie | Ireland | James Martin and his assigns |
| | Ernfred, John George, and Catherine Barbara, his wife | Rotterdam | Jacob Morgan and his assigns |
| | Ernfred, John George, and Catherine Barbara, his wife | | John Leshre and his assigns |
| | Brick, Frederick | Rotterdam | William Hambel and his assigns |
| | Dochman, Stephen | Rotterdam | John Lyndall and his assigns |
| | Clemens, John Nicholas | Rotterdam | Thealix Pinkley and his assigns |
| | Schnider, Joseph | Rotterdam | Adam Disseback and his assigns |
| | Raw, Johan Leonard | Rotterdam | Rynear Lukins and his assigns |
| | Metzger, Yost Hendrich | Rotterdam | Abraham Satler and his assigns |
| | Miller, Peter; Bushin, Susannah. | Rotterdam | John Stouffer and his assigns |
| | Hamerly Faban | London | Henry Epley and his assigns |
| | Stadleberger, Catherine | Rotterdam | Henry Bookwalder and his assigns |
| | Mechlinger, Melchoir | Rotterdam | Felix Pinkley and his assigns |
| | Flaugh, Matthias | Rotterdam | John Peter and his assigns |
| | Coarse, John | Rotterdam | William Sharp and his assigns |
| | Flennay, John Jacob | Rotterdam | William Hallaywell and his assigns |
| | Wexell, Matthias | Rotterdam | Rinear Hallowell and his assigns |
| | Bauman, Michael | Rotterdam | Anthony Williams and his assigns |
| | Hess, John | Rotterdam | Henry Kirson and his assigns |
| | Philgil, Craft | Rotterdam | Adam Aldstadt and his assigns |
| | Roebscher, Margaretta Elizabeth. | Rotterdam | Rynear Tyson and his assigns |
| | Wolfe, John Adam | Rotterdam | Abraham Kendrick and his assigns |
| | Conrad, Jonathen | Rotterdam | Dietrick Reise and his assigns |
| | Reinmar, John | Rotterdam | Conrad Camp and his assigns |
| Oct. 5th | Barge, Jacob | Rotterdam | Jacob Barge and his assigns |

## List of Indentures.

| Residence. | Occupation. | Term. | Amount. |
|---|---|---|---|
| Philadelphia | Servant, kept at the employment of a mining business if he understands it.³ | 3 yrs | £20.7.0. |
| Philadelphia | Servant, employed at the mining business if he understands it.³ | 3 yrs | £20.13.0. |
| Heidelburg twp., Lancaster co. | Servant, taught to read in Bible and write a legible hand.⁶ | 7 yrs | £22.1.0. |
| Roxberry twp., Phila. co. | Apprentice, taught the trade of a carpenter and joiner, have six months' night schooling.³ | 4 yrs. | |
| Alexandria twp., Hunderton co., W. Jersey. | Servant¹ | 5 yrs., 6 mo. | £30.0.0. |
| Heidelburg twp., Berks co. | Servant, taught to read and write⁶. | 7 yrs | £23.17.6. |
| Moyamensing twp., Phila. co. | Servant¹ | 4 yrs., 6 mo. | £14.10.0. |
| Philadelphia | Servant (note 3, and take with them the goods they have now with them). | 4 yrs | £36.16.0. |
| Oley twp., Berks co. | Servant, the term above mentioned. | | £36.16.0. |
| Philadelphia | Servant, the master to employ the servant at the tailor's trade.⁶ | 6 yrs | £29.16.6. |
| Oxford twp., Phila. co. | Servant, taught to read and write English; if the servant's friends come in 14 days and pay the sum and expense occurring thereon, then this indenture to be void.⁶ | 6 yrs | £30.0.0. |
| Lampeter twp., Lancaster co. | Servant, if the servant pay or cause to be paid £9 Pa. currency in six months' from this date the master is to deduct one year of his time.¹ | 4 yrs., 3 mo. | £32.13.6. |
| Lampeter twp., Lancaster co. | Servant³ | 3 yrs., 6 mo. | £20.0.0. |
| Upper Dublin twp., Phila. co. | Servant³ | 6 yrs | £30.0.0. |
| Perkiomen twp., Phila. co. | Servant³ | 4 yrs | £28.12.0. |
| Lampeter twp., Lancaster co. | Servant, taught to read and write³. | { 5 yrs.... 4 yrs.... | £20.18.0. and £22 for Bushin. |
| Philadelphia | Servant, found meat, drink, apparel, washing and lodging. | 2 yrs., 6 mo. | £24.13.0. |
| Lampeter twp., Lancaster co. | Servant, teach her to read and write (note 6, and £5 Pa. currency in cash). | 5 yrs., 3 mo. | £11.0.0. |
| Lampeter twp., Lancaster co. | Servant, at the expiration customary freedom dues. | 5 yrs | £30.10.0. |
| Philadelphia | Servant⁶ | 3 yrs., 3 mo. | £20.0.0. |
| Roeham co. Forth Creek Settlement, N. C. | Servant (note 3, or £6 Pa. currency in cash). | 5 yrs., 6 mo. | £24.15.4. |
| Abington twp., Phila. co. | Servant, taught to read and write, at expiration legal freedom dues. | 9 yrs | £30.0.0. |
| Abington twp., Phila. co. | Servant, cause him to read³. | 7 yrs | £21.6.0. |
| Bristol twp., Phila. co. | Servant⁶ | 6 yrs | £30.0.0. |
| Oley twp., Berks co. | Servant, taught to read in Bible and write a legible hand.³ | 7 yrs., 2 mo. | £31.15.0. |
| Exeter twp., Berks co. | Servant (note 6, or £9 Pa. currency in cash). | 3 yrs., 6 mo. | £22.12.0. |
| Abington twp., Phila. co. | Servant¹ | 6 yrs | £24.15.0. |
| Conestoga twp., Lancaster co. | Servant³ | 3 yrs., 5 mo. | £20.17.0. |
| Philadelphia | Servant (note 3, or £8 in cash).. | 6 yrs | £25.0.0. |
| Abington twp., Phila. co. | Apprentice, taught the art of a farmer, read and write.⁶ | 18 yrs | £0.7.6. |
| Philadelphia | Servant (note 3, or £8 Pa. currency). | 7 yrs., 2 mo. | £18.19.6. |

| Date. | Name. | From the Port of | To Whom Indentured. |
|---|---|---|---|
| 1773. | Barge, Jacob .................. | ............ | Staphey Mottell and his assigns...... |
| Oct. 5th..... | McCloud, Donnald, and Christian, his wife. | Scotland ... | Anthony Sykes and his assigns....... |
| | O'Bell, John ................ | ............ | James Roney and his assigns........ |
| | Young, Andrew ........... | Rotterdam.. | John Bick and his asigns............ |
| | Pyefrey, Maria, Elizabeth ... | Rotterdam.. | John Pelts and his assigns.......... |
| | Wall, Matthias; Sigle, John.. | Rotterdam.. | Benjamin Wilson and his assigns.... |
| | Wall, Matthias; Sigle, John.. | ............ | Joseph Tatnall and his assigns...... |
| | Conery, Nicholas .............. | ............ | William Nolan and his assigns...... |
| | Ferffler, John George ....... | Rotterdam.. | Hugh Low and Thomas Penrose and their assigns. |
| | Felchin, Catherine; Felckel, Frederich. | Rotterdam.. | Adam Austot and his assigns........ |

| Residence. | Occupation. | Term. | Amount. |
| --- | --- | --- | --- |
| Lancaster | Servant, term above mentioned | | £ 18. 19. 6. |
| Chesterfield twp., Burlington co., N. J. | Servant[3] | 4 yrs. each | £ 20. 0. 0. |
| Hanover twp., Lancaster co. | Servant | 6 yrs. | £ 11. 0. 0. |
| Philadelphia | Servant[3] | 6 yrs. | £ 33. 0. 0. |
| Persying twp., Phila. co. | Servant[3] | 4 yrs. | £ 19. 2. 0. |
| Wilmington, New Castle co. | Servant[3] | 4 yrs., 6 mo. / 6 yrs., 6 mo. | £ 26. 13. 10. / £ 30. 0. 0. |
| Wilmington, New Castle co. | Servant, term as above mentioned. | | £ 26. 13. 10. / £ 30. 0. 0. |
| Frankfort twp., Phila. co. | Apprentice, taught the art and mystery of a cordwainer.[3] | 5 yrs. | |
| Southwark, Phila. co. | Servant (note 1, or £ 6 Pa. currency and his working tools or 40 shillings in cash). | 4 yrs. | £ 32. 2. 0. |
| Exeter twp., Berks co. | Servant[3] | 8 yrs. / 7 yrs. | £ 30. 0. 0. for each. |

www.ingramcontent.com/pod-product-compliance
Lightning Source LLC
Chambersburg PA
CBHW082035230426
43670CB00016B/2659